2004

THE ESSENTIAL WRITINGS OF
Jawaharlal Nehru

THE ESSENTIAL WRITINGS OF
Jawaharlal Nehru

VOLUME II

Edited by

S. GOPAL
UMA IYENGAR

OXFORD
UNIVERSITY PRESS

OXFORD
UNIVERSITY PRESS

YMCA Library Building, Jai Singh Road, New Delhi 110 001

Oxford University Press is a department of the University of Oxford. It furthers the
University's objective of excellence in research, scholarship, and education
by publishing worldwide in

Oxford   New York

Auckland   Bangkok   Buenos Aires   Cape Town   Chennai
Dar es Salaam   Delhi   Hong Kong   Istanbul   Karachi   Kolkata
Kuala Lumpur   Madrid   Melbourne   Mexico City   Mumbai   Nairobi
São Paulo   Shanghai Taipei   Tokyo   Toronto

Oxford is a registered trade mark of Oxford University Press
in the UK and in certain other countries

Published in India
By Oxford University Press, New Delhi

ISBN   0 19 565324 6

Typeset by Guru Typograph Technology, Dwarka, New Delhi 110045
Printed at Rajshree Photolithographers, New Delhi 110032
Published by Manzar Khan, Oxford University Press
YMCA Library Building, Jai Singh Road, New Delhi 110 001

Contents

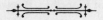

VOLUME I

(Plates between pages 344–5)

Preface • xvii

Jawaharlal Nehru: A Chronology • xxi

I. THE COUNTRY • 1

1. The Panorama of India's Past 3 • 2. Bharat Mata 7 • 3. Kisans 10 •
4. The Idea Behind India 13 • 5. India's Sickness: Famine 15 •
6. The Division of India 18 • 7. A Myth and An Idea, A Dream
and A Vision 22 • 8. Before India is Reborn 24 • 9. The Unity of
India 32 • 10. Aiming at A Democratic India 43 • 11. The Will of
the Nation 47 • 12. A Day of Rededication 50 • 13. The Innumerable
Faces of India 51 • 14. An Indian Worldview 54 • 15. Synthesis is Our
Tradition 60 • 16. India—Old and New 65

II. CULTURE AND CIVILIZATION • 69

1. The Lesson of History 71 • 2. The Quest of Man 73 •
3. Fascination of History 75 • 4. The Past and the Present 81 •
5. Hindu and Muslim Cultures 86 • 6. History and Tradition 89 •
7. Materialism 92 • 8. An Integrated Vision of Life 95 • 9. Out of
Tune with the Elements 101 • 10. March of Humanity 105 •
11. Cultural and Moral Values 107 • 12. Culture and Wisdom 109 •
13. Age of Contradictions 115 • 14. Museums and Culture 118 •
15. The Mind and Spirit of Man 121 • 16. Crisis of the Spirit 127 •
17. History in Perspective 132

III. RELIGION, TOLERANCE AND COMMUNALISM • 133

1. What is Religion? 135 • 2. Intolerance 138 • 3. Politics
and Religion 140 • 4. Sanatanists 142 • 5. Congress and
Communalism 145 • 6. Communal Disturbances 148 •

7. Bihar Disturbances 150 • 8. Do not Kill Your Neighbour 151 •
9. Bengal and Bihar Situation 154 • 10. Politics and Communalism
in Punjab 157 • 11. Cow Slaughter 159 • 12. Partition Riots 161 •
13. Muslim Population in India 164 • 14. Fascism—The New
Wave 167 • 15. Aftermath of Gandhi's Assassination 168 •
16. Pakistan and the Indian States 171 • 17. Separate Provinces for
Sikhs 176 • 18. The Akali Demand 179 • 19. Sealing of Muslim
Shops 182 • 20. The Communal Disease 184 • 21. A Hindu
Rashtra 186 • 22. Question of Minority Groups 187 •
23. New Phase of An Old Problem 190 • 24. Communalism and
Casteism 192 • 25. A Secular State 194 • 26. Emotional Integration 196 •
27. Communal Harmony 198

IV. TOWARD INDEPENDENCE • 199

1. Home Rule 201 • 2. The Rai Bareli Tragedy 203 •
3. Noncooperation 206 • 4. First Arrest 212 • 5. Statement at
Trial 214 • 6. Imperialism 218 • 7. Resolution on Independence 221 •
8. They Have Dared 223 • 9. Lahore Congress 225 •
10. The Dandi March 230 • 11. To the Youth of Bengal 231 •
12. Ballyhoo 233 • 13. Whither India? 236 • 14. Earthquakes—
Natural and Political 245 • 15. Faizpur Congress 249 •
16. The Choice Before Us 256 • 17. Congress Resolution on India and
the War 260 • 18. War Aims and Peace Aims 265 • 19. A Popular War
Must Have Popular Support 272 • 20. The Answer 274 •
21. Freedom is in Peril 277 • 22. The Art of Adaptation 279 •
23. Which Way? What Means? 280 • 24. Prudence or Courage? 283 •
25. Khadi 285 • 26. Individual Satyagraha 286 • 27. The Meaningless
Release of Prisoners 290 • 28. Insatiable Appetite for Freedom 293 •
29. A Vote of No-Confidence 295 • 30. The Shape of Things
to Come 298 • 31. Fear Complex 300 • 32. Fateful Years 303 •
33. Jai Hind 304 • 34. British Policy and India 307 • 35. On the
Cabinet Mission Statement 312 • 36. Finding A Solution 316 •
37. Appeal to Caesar 319 • 38. The Call of Destiny 321 •
39. Interim Government 322 • 40. Retention of British Troops 325 •
41. Aims and Objectives of the Constituent Assembly 328 •
42. The Many Forms of Struggle 332 • 43. On Transference of
Power 335 • 44. On the Constitutional Proposals 337 •

45. The Unavoidability of Partition 339 • 46. Resolution on the
National Flag 342 • 47. A Tryst with Destiny 346 •
48. The Appointed Day 348

V. THE PARTY • 351

1. The Congress Becomes Democratic 353 • 2. An Agrarian
Programme for the Congress 358 • 3. Defining Congress
Attitude 361 • 4. Message to the Nation 365 • 5. Election
Manifesto 367 • 6. The Evolution of the Congress 372 •
7. Office Acceptance 375 • 8. Congress and Civil Liberties 378 •
9. The A.I.C.C. and After 383 • 10. India and the War 388 •
11. Resolution on the War 390 • 12. The Price of Freedom 394 •
13. Quit India Resolution 395 • 14. Central Assembly
Elections 397 • 15. Party Work 401 • 16. Congress Objectives 403 •
17. Strengthening the Party 405 • 18. Aiming at A Welfare
State 407 • 19. Setting the Standards 411 • 20. Weakening the
Congress 417 • 21. Choice of Candidates 419 • 22. An Objective
Appraisal 422 • 23. Threat of War 426 • 24. Basic Congress
Policy 428 • 25. Disruptive Tendencies 430 • 26. Report to the
All India Congress Committee 432 • 27. Congress and Socialism 436 •
28. Fighting Elections 438

VI. BAPU • 441

1. And Then Gandhi Came . . . 443 • 2. Aftermath of Madras
Congress 446 • 3. Disagreement 451 • 4. On Gandhi's
Leadership 453 • 5. Negotiating in Britain 454 • 6. The Great
Peasant 455 • 7. Gandhi, Nehru and Religion 458 •
8. Spiritual Isolation 462 • 9. Impasse 466 • 10. Gandhi and
Nonviolence 469 • 11. Merging with the Masses 472 •
12. Concept of Satyagraha 474 • 13. Fast 482 •
14. Hindu–Muslim Riot 486 • 15. The Light has Gone Out 488 •
16. On the Death of Gandhi 490 • 17. A Glory that is
No More 492 • 18. The Perfect Artist 496 • 19. The Final
Pilgrimage 498 • 20. Two Weeks of Sorrow and Searching 500 •
21. Bapu's Message 503 • 22. The Legend 505 •
23. Gandhian Method 508

VII. INDIA AND BRITAIN • 511

1. The Psychology of Indian Nationalism 513 • 2. Quetta 524 •
3. Britain and India 529 • 4. Twenty Years 541 • 5. Reply to an
Open Letter 543 • 6. Hostility Towards Britain 559 •
7. Different Worlds 566 • 8. The Indian Situation 570 •
9. Note on Conversations with Gandhi 576 • 10. Two Backgrounds 579 •
11. Foreign Rule 583

VIII. PERSONALITIES • 587

1. The Buddha 589 • 2. Lenin 591 • 3. Mohammad Iqbal 595 •
4. The Aga Khan 596 • 5. Motilal Nehru 600 • 6. Ernst Toller 602 •
7. Maulana Azad 605 • 8. Adolf Hitler 607 • 9. C. Rajagopalachari 608 •
10. Khan Abdul Ghaffar Khan 610 • 11. Rabindranath Tagore 612 •
12. Madan Mohan Malaviya 614 • 13. Srinivasa Ramanujam 616 •
14. Aruna Asaf Ali 617 • 15. Aung San 619 • 16. Sarojini Naidu 620 •
17. Ramakrishna Parmahamsa 621 • 18. Vallabhbhai Patel 623 •
19. Joseph Stalin 625 • 20. John Fitzgerald Kennedy 627

IX. GENERAL • 629

1. Vicarious Charity 631 • 2. Victory Over the Air 633 •
3. Politicians 636 • 4. The Proscription and Censorship of
Books 639 • 5. Strikes 642 • 6. Cooperatives 645 • 7. Where do the
Riches Go? 646 • 8. Two Mosques 647 • 9. Providence and
Human • Failing 652 • 10. Prison Humours 654 • 11. Morale and
Nerve 656 • 12. Shirshasana 658 • 13. Indian Marriage 659 •
14. Examinations 660 • 15. Trade Unions 661 • 16. Temples 662 •
17. The Functions of a Municipality 663 • 18. Back Home 665 •
19. Prison Reforms 668 • 20. In the Surma Valley 669 •
21. Bharat Mata 670 • 22. Federation 671 • 23. The Monsoon
Comes to Bombay 674 • 24. Flying During the Monsoon 676 •
25. The Big Machine 679 • 26. Famine 681 • 27. Freedom of
the Press 683 • 28. Ganga 686 • 29. Writers and the War 688 •
30. A Sense of Values 690 • 31. Death 691 • 32. Birth 692 •
33. On Coming out of Jail 693 • 34. Note on Defence 695 •
35. Time in Prison 698 • 36. English Clubs 700 • 37. The INA 702 •
38. Civil Marriages 704 • 39. The National Anthem 706 •

40. The Conquest of the Air 708 • 41. The Message of the
Buddha 709 • 42. Time and World are Ever in Flight 711 •
43. Tribals 713 • 44. Journalism 715 • 45. Ostentation and Taste 720 •
46. The Ascent of Everest 722 • 47. The Employment of
Communists 724 • 48. Floods 725 • 49. Planning for Delhi 728 •
50. All India Police Sports Meet 730 • 51. The Equation of
Defence 732 • 52. Wildlife 733 • 53. Tribal Affairs 735 •
54. Indian Women 737 • 55. Brooms 739

VOLUME II

(Plates between pages 354–5)

I. POLITY AND GOVERNANCE • 1

1. Social Fabric of a Nation 5 • 2. The Basis of Society 8 •
3. Famine Relief 11 • 4. Zamindars and Taluqdars 14 • 5. Reality
and Myth 16 • 6. The Role of Women 21 • 7. A Socialized
Society 23 • 8. Scientific Socialism 25 • 9. Forces that Shape
Events 27 • 10. Significance of A Constituent Assembly 32 •
11. Planning for the Future 35 • 12. The Content of Social
Welfare 37 • 13. Can Indians Get Together? 40 • 14. Linguistic
Provinces 45 • 15. Economic Policy 46 • 16. The Role of the
Prime Minister 53 • 17. A National State 56 • 18. Abducted Men and
Women 60 • 19. Industrial Policy 63 • 20. The Hirakud Dam 66 •
21. Message on Independence Day 68 • 22. The Socialist Party 71 •
23. Objectives Resolution and the Draft Constitution 73 •
24. Development of River Valleys 78 • 25. Relief and
Rehabilitation 82 • 26. Formation of New Provinces 84 •
27. Horse Breeding 88 • 28. Reservations for Backward Groups 91 •
29. "Time and World are Ever in Flight" 95 • 30. Planning 97 •
31. Pernicious Influence of Technology 100 • 32. Planning for
the Future 102 • 33. Police and Students 107 • 34. Evacuee
Property 109 • 35. Hindu Code Bill 111 • 36. The Press Bill 114 •
37. Moulding Our Destiny 116 • 38. State Visits 123 •
39. Democratic Planning 125 • 40. Measuring Backwardness 129 •
41. Welfare State 131 • 42. Lessening Flagrant Inequalities 134 •
43. Inter-caste Marriage 140 • 44. Special Marriage Bill 141 •
45. Divorce 143 • 46. Essence of A Democratic State 145 •

47. Building India 147 • 48. The Avadi Resolution 149 •
49. Women's Education 151 • 50. Basic Education 152 •
51. The Socialistic Pattern of Society 155 • 52. Goa 158 •
53. Prohibition Policy 159 • 54. Foreign Tours 160 •
55. Mob Violence 161 • 56. The Concept of Panchsheel 163 •
57. Changing the Static Society 165 • 58. States Reorganization 167 •
59. Hindu Succession Act 169 • 60. The Public Sector and the
Private Sector 170 • 61. Public Health 172 • 62. The Dead have
No Problems 174 • 63. A World of Ghosts and Spectres 176 •
64. Cooperative Farming 178 • 65. The Basic Approach 180 •
66. Fundamentals of Social Behaviour 185 • 67. Family Planning 187 •
68. Town Planning 188

II. INDIA AND BEYOND • 189

1. A Foreign Policy for India 191 • 2. The Fascination of Russia 196 •
3. International Contacts 198 • 4. The Imperialist Danger 202 •
5. India and the World 205 • 6. World Events 211 • 7. Spain 215 •
8. A World Federation 216 • 9. A Real Commonwealth 218 •
10. Quatorze Juillet 220 • 11. Colonialism Must Go 222 •
12. Policy Towards Burma 225 • 13. A United Asia 229 •
14. Sympathy for Jews 233 • 15. Basic Principles 236 •
16. Note on Foreign Policy 241 • 17. The Occident and the
Orient 245 • 18. An Independent Foreign Policy 247 •
19. The Problem of Burma 249 • 20. Cooperation in the
Commonwealth 256 • 21. Relations with the Soviet Union 258 •
22. Commonwealth Prime Minister's Conference 260 •
23. A Voyage of Discovery 262 • 24. Exclusion of Some
Countries from the UN 265 • 25. World Affairs 267 •
26. Annexation of Tibet 271 • 27. World Today 274 •
28. Japanese Peace Treaty 276 • 29. The Nonviolent Struggle
in South Africa 280 • 30. An Overburdened World 282 •
31. South African Situation 284 • 32. The Great Adventure
of Man 288 • 33. Bulganin, Khrushchev Visit 292 •
34. Saudi Arabia 294 • 35. A World of Unreality 297 •
36. Suez Crisis 299 • 37. Non-aggression and Non-interference 301 •
38. Racial Discrimination 304 • 39. The Chinese Aggression 306 •
40. The Proclamation of Emergency 310 • 41. A Popular
Upsurge 313

III. INDIA, PAKISTAN AND KASHMIR • 315

1. Kashmir 317 • 2. The Trial of Sheikh Abdullah 320 •
3. The Kashmir Crisis 322 • 4. Broadcast on Kashmir 326 •
5. Frontier Province 330 • 6. Kashmir Plebiscite 332 • 7. Kashmir
and the United States 335 • 8. Arbitration on Kashmir Issue 338 •
9. Plight of Minorities 341 • 10. At the Edge of a Precipice 347 •
11. The Basis for Conflict 352 • 12. Military Confrontation 355 •
13. Indo-Pak Situation 358 • 14. Keeping Vigilant 363 •
15. The Question of Plebiscite 370 • 16. The Kashmir Policy 372 •
17. Kashmir and Indo-Pak Relations 375 • 18. The Good of
Kashmiris 378 • 19. Collective Aggression 380 • 20. The Question
of Kashmir 381

IV. WAR, PEACE AND DISARMAMENT • 385

1. The Danger of War 387 • 2. The Betrayal of Czechoslovakia 389 •
3. The Hoax 392 • 4. The New Europe 395 • 5. World Politics 397 •
6. Destiny 399 • 7. Treachery and Betrayal 400 • 8. A Crumbling
World 401 • 9. Nonviolence and the State 404 • 10. India's Day
of Reckoning 408 • 11. The Death Dealer 417 • 12. An Age of
Crises 419 • 13. The Role of the United Nations 421 • 14. Ends and
Means 425 • 15. India's Policy 431 • 16. Need for a Temper of
Peace 432 • 17. World Power Equilibrium 435 • 18. The New
Spirit of Asia 439 • 19. Formosa 442 • 20. World Peace and
Cooperation 444 • 21. War, Peace and Cooperation 452 •
22. The International Scene 462 • 23. The Abolition of
War 465 • 24. A Creeping Sickness 472 • 25. Weapons
of Destruction 475 • 26. Disarmament 477 • 27. Solving World
Problems 480

V. LANGUAGE • 487

1. On Translation 489 • 2. Lingua Franca of India 493 •
3. The Question of Language 495 • 4. Power of Words 498 •
5. A Poetic Testament 499 • 6. The Language Controversy 500 •
7. The Function of Language 502 • 8. The National Language 505 •
9. Translation of the Constitution 511 • 10. Linguistic Provinces 513 •
11. The Place of English 516

VI. SCIENCE AND TECHNOLOGY • 519

1. The Spirit of the Age 521 • 2. Science and the Community 522 •
3. Atomic Energy 526 • 4. The Responsibility of Scientists 528 •
5. The Spirit of Science 533 • 6. Technology and Man 536 •
7. Nuclear Energy 538 • 8. Temper of Science 540 •
9. The Creator and the Destroyer 542

VII. YOUTH AND EDUCATION • 545

1. Awakening in the Youth 547 • 2. On the Mission of Youth 548 •
3. Breaking Shibboleths 550 • 4. Students and Politics 557 •
5. Halls of Learning 560 • 6. Another Casualty 564 •
7. Nationalism and Internationalism 566 • 8. The Time for
Hard Labour 569 • 9. The World Around Us 576 •
10. The Need for Discipline 579 • 11. The Strength of the
Unafraid 581 • 12. The Purpose of Education 583 •
13. Universities 585

VIII. PERSONAL • 589

1. Cambridge 593 • 2. Finer Side of Life 595 • 3. Imprisonment 596 •
4. Lathi Charges 599 • 5. Human Endeavour 603 •
6. Bapu's Arrest 605 • 7. Reaction to Gandhi's Fast 607 •
8. Aims and Objectives of Life 610 • 9. Musings 612 •
10. The Death of Motilal Nehru 613 • 11. Back in Prison 615 •
12. Kamala 618 • 13. Introspection 620 • 14. Family Ties 624 •
15. A Solitary Traveller 627 • 16. A Hundred Pictures 630 •
17. The True Perspective 635 • 18. The Call of India 636 •
19. Dreams and Reality 637 • 20. A Private Person 638 •
21. A Bundle of Tempers 639 • 22. Human Personality 640 •
23. Restraining Feelings 642 • 24. Rashtrapati 643 •
25. Psychoanalyzing Oneself 647 • 26. Relationships 649 •
27. A Report on His Own Tour 651 • 28. Confining Barriers 654 •
29. Creeping Age 656 • 30. Writing from Prison 657 •
31. On Personal Style 660 • 32. Time 661 • 33. Voyage of
Discovery 662 • 34. Taking Decisions 664 • 35. Perceptions 669 •
36. Mountains and Rivers 671 • 37. Family as A Unit 673 •
38. Stray Notes 676 • 39. Effects of Jail Life 679 •
40. Cause and Effect 681 • 41. Bengal Famine 683 •
42. Philosophy and Life 685 • 43. Children 688 •

44. The Moon 690 • 45. Mental Perturbation 691 •
46. Beginning of Life 693 • 47. Philosophy of Life 694 •
48. Memories and Fancies 703 • 49. Uncertainties 705 •
50. Decisions and Responsibilities 706 • 51. Life 707 •
52. In Conversation with Norman Cousins 709 • 53. Kashmir and
the Constituent Assembly 726 • 54. Sense of Ineffectiveness 728 •
55. Controlling Emotions 730 • 56. Touring in India 733 •
57. Mountains 735 • 58. Laying down Office 736 •
59. Human Relations 738 • 60. Will and Testament 740

VOL. II

I
Polity and Governance

1. Social Fabric of a Nation   5
2. The Basis of Society   8
3. Famine Relief   11
4. Zamindars and Taluqdars   14
5. Reality and Myth   16
6. The Role of Women   21
7. A Socialized Society   23
8. Scientific Socialism   25
9. Forces that Shape Events   27
10. Significance of A Constituent Assembly   32
11. Planning for the Future   35
12. The Content of Social Welfare   37
13. Can Indians Get Together?   40
14. Linguistic Provinces   45
15. Economic Policy   46
16. The Role of the Prime Minister   53
17. A National State   56
18. Abducted Men and Women   60
19. Industrial Policy   63
20. The Hirakud Dam   66

21. Message on Independence Day   68

22. The Socialist Party   71

23. Objectives Resolution and the Draft Constitution   73

24. Development of River Valleys   78

25. Relief and Rehabilitation   82

26. Formation of New Provinces   84

27. Horse Breeding   88

28. Reservations for Backward Groups   91

29. "Time and World are Ever in Flight"   95

30. Planning   97

31. Pernicious Influence of Technology   100

32. Planning for the Future   102

33. Police and Students   107

34. Evacuee Property   109

35. Hindu Code Bill   111

36. The Press Bill   114

37. Moulding Our Destiny   116

38. State Visits   123

39. Democratic Planning   125

40. Measuring Backwardness   129

41. Welfare State   131

42. Lessening Flagrant Inequalities   134

43. Inter-caste Marriage   140

44. Special Marriage Bill   141

45. Divorce   143

46. Essence of A Democratic State   145

47. Building India   147

48. The Avadi Resolution   149

49. Women's Education   151

50. Basic Education   152

51. The Socialistic Pattern of Society   155

52. Goa 158
53. Prohibition Policy 159
54. Foreign Tours 160
55. Mob Violence 161
56. The Concept of Panchsheel 163
57. Changing the Static Society 165
58. States Reorganization 167
59. Hindu Succession Act 169
60. The Public Sector and the Private Sector 170
61. Public Health 172
62. The Dead have No Problems 174
63. A World of Ghosts and Spectres 176
64. Cooperative Farming 178
65. The Basic Approach 180
66. Fundamentals of Social Behaviour 185
67. Family Planning 187
68. Town Planning 188

1

Social Fabric of a Nation[1]

India is rapidly approaching the crossroads of its destiny, and we shall have to make a vital choice.

. . . Right action can only follow dispassionate thinking and some knowledge of the forces that are shaping the modern world. We have today a great number of people prescribing remedies for the diseases that afflict India. Nearly all lay stress on mass organization and many talk of unity among the various political groups. But there is seldom a consideration of principle, of ultimate ideals, of the place of India in the world. What are we aiming at? What manner of country should we like India to be?

Before we answer these questions, it is worthwhile taking a larger view of world events. We all know the great changes which have followed the Industrial Revolution, although they have not affected India as much as other countries. Industrialism has resulted in the concentration of wealth in a few countries and a few individuals, in a struggle for raw material and markets, and it has brought into existence the imperialism of the last century. It has caused wars and has laid the seed of future wars. Latterly, it has taken the shape of an economic imperialism, which without the possession of territory is as potent in exploiting other countries as any colonial empire of yesterday.

All this is known, but what perhaps is not sufficiently realized is the international character of industrialism. It has broken down national boundaries and has made each nation dependent on others. The idea of nationalism is almost as strong today as it was in the past, and in its holy name wars are still fought and millions slaughtered. But it is a myth which is not in keeping with reality. The world has become internationalized. Production is international, markets are international and transport is international. Only men's ideas continue to be governed by a dogma which has no real meaning.

Many of us, regardless of what is happening all around us, still live in the ancient past. Some want the Vedic age, others a reproduction of the early days of Islam. We forget that our ancient civilizations were meant for different conditions. Many of our traditions, habits and customs, our social laws, our class

[1] Article in *The New Leader*, 11 August 1928. Jawaharlal Nehru Collection, Nehru Memorial Museum and Library (henceforth JN Collection, NMML).

system, the position we give to women, and the dogmas which religion has imposed on us, are the relics of a past utterly out of joint with modern conditions. India will only progress, as Turkey and Russia have progressed, when she discards the myths and dogmas of yesterday in favour of the reality of today.

Many of us who denounce British imperialism in India do not realize that it is not a phenomenon peculiar to the British race or to India, or that it is the consequence of industrial development on capitalist lines. Capitalism necessarily leads to exploitation of one man by another, one group by another, and one country by another. If, therefore, we are opposed to this imperialism and exploitation, we must also be opposed to capitalism. The only alternative that is offered to us is some form of socialism.

As a necessary result of this decision, we must fight British dominion in India, not only on nationalistic grounds, but also on social and international grounds. Britain may well permit us to have a large measure of political liberty, but this will be worth little if she holds economic dominion over us. Another consequence of the socialistic view is that we must change all customs which are based on privilege of birth and caste. We must cast out all parasites and drones, so that the many who lack the good things of life may share in them. Poverty and want are not economic necessities. The world and our country produce enough (or can produce enough) for the masses to attain a high standard of well-being, but unhappily the good things are cornered by a few and the millions live in want. In India, the classic land of famine, famines are not caused by want of food, but by the want among the masses of the money to buy food. We may demand freedom for our country on many grounds, but ultimately it is the economic one that matters.

Our educated classes have so far taken the lead in the fight for swaraj, but in doing so they have seldom paid heed to the needs of the masses. And so the demand has taken the form of the 'Indianization of the services', of higher posts being thrown open to Indians. Whenever vital questions affecting the masses have arisen, they have been postponed till swaraj has been attained. But what shall it profit the masses of India—the peasantry, the landless labourers, the workers, the shopkeepers, the artisans—if every one of the offices held by Englishmen in India today is held by an Indian? It may benefit them a little, because they will be able bring more pressure to bear on an Indian than on an alien government but fundamentally their conditions cannot improve until the social fabric is changed.

Even from a narrow point of view it is now recognized that no effective pressure can be brought to bear on the British Government without mass support but there is fear of the masses and little is done. Mass support cannot come from vague ideals of swaraj. It is essential that we must clearly lay down an economic programme for the masses, with socialism as its ideal. We must cultivate a revolutionary outlook. Everything that goes towards creating a revolutionary atmosphere helps; everything that lessens it, hinders. I use the word 'revolutionary' without any necessary connection with violence. Indeed violence may be the very reverse of revolution. Acts of terrorism often have a counter-revolutionary effect and are injurious to the national cause.

2

The Basis of Society[1]

The basis of society is some measure of security and stability. Without security and stability there could be no society or social life, but how many today in our present-day society have this security and stability? You know that the millions have it not; they have hardly enough to keep body and soul together. And it is a mockery to speak to them of security. So long as the masses do not share in this security, you can have no stable society. And so you see in the history of the world, revolution after revolution, not because any group or person is a lover of bloodshed, anarchy and disorder, but because of this desire for greater security for larger number of persons. We shall have real security and stability in this world only when it has come to signify the well-being of the vast majority of the people, if not all, and not of small groups only. That time may not be near, but society is continually, sometimes it may even be a little blindly, struggling towards it. And the greater the struggle, the greater the urge to that end, the healthier and more vital the society. If this urge is wholly absent, society becomes static and lifeless and gradually withers away.

So long therefore as the world is not perfect, a healthy society must have the seeds of revolt in it. It must alternate between revolution and consolidation. It is the function of youth to supply this dynamic element in society; to be the standard-bearers of revolt against all that is evil and to prevent older people from suppressing all social progress and movement by the mere weight of their inertia. . . .

What do we find in this world of ours today? Utter misery is the lot of vast numbers of people and while a few live in luxury, the many lack even bread and clothing and have no opportunity for development. Wars and conflicts ravage the world and the energy that should go to build up a better order of society is spent largely in mutual competition and destruction. If that is the condition of the world at large, what of our own unhappy country? Foreign rule has reduced her to utmost poverty and misery and a rigid adherence to outworn customs and ideas has sapped the life out of her.

There is obviously something radically wrong with the world and one is led to doubt if there is any ultimate purpose behind this chaos and unhappiness.

[1] Presidential address, Bombay Presidency Youth Conference, Poona, 12 December 1928. JN Collection, NMML. Excerpts.

Two thousand and five hundred years ago the prince Siddhartha, who later became the Great Buddha, saw this misery and in agony of spirit put to himself the same question:

> How can it be that Brahma
> Would make a world and keep it miserable?
> Since if all powerful He leaves it so,
> He is not good, and if not powerful,
> He is not God!

But whether there is any ultimate purpose or not, the immediate purpose of every human being should be to reduce this misery and to help in building up a better society, and a better society must necessarily aim at the elimination of all domination of one nation over another or of man over man. It must replace competition by cooperation. . . .

Before we approach our ideal, we have to combat two sets of opponents—political and social. We have to overcome our alien rulers as well as the social reactionaries of India. In the past we have seen the curious phenomenon in India of the political extremist sometimes being a reactionary in social matters, and not unoften the political moderate has been socially more advanced. But it is impossible to separate the political life of the country from its social and economic life and you cannot cure the social organism by treating one part of it only. The infection from one affected part continually spreads to other parts and the disease takes firmer root. Your political and social philosophy must, therefore, be a complete whole and your programme must comprise every department of national activity. . . .

Religion has in the past often been used as an opiate to dull men's desire for freedom. Kings and emperors have exploited it for their own benefit and led people to believe in their divine right to rule. Priests and other privileged classes have claimed a divine sanction for their privileges. And with the aid of religion the masses have been told that their miseries are due to *kismat* or the sins of a former age. Women have been and are still kept down and in the name of religion in many places are made to submit to that barbarous relic of an earlier age—the purdah system. The depressed or the suppressed classes cry out to the world how infamously religion has been exploited to keep them down and prevent them from rising. Religion has been the fountainhead of authoritarianism and meek submission and it is because our rulers realize this and because their own rule is based on this ideology of authoritarianism that they seek to bolster up its cruder manifestations in India. If the spirit of intellectual revolt spreads to ancient custom and tradition, then the very basis of authoritarianism crumbles and takes with it the foundation of British rule. . . .

The freedom of India is dear to all of us here. But there may be many here who have the ordinary conveniences of life and are not hard put to it to find their daily bread. Our desire for freedom is a thing more of the mind than of the body, although even our bodies often suffer for the lack of freedom. But to the vast masses of our fellow-countrymen present conditions spell hunger and deepest poverty, an empty stomach and a bare back. For them freedom is a vital bodily necessity, and it is primarily to give them food and clothing and the ordinary amenities of life that we should strive for freedom. The most amazing and terrible thing about India is her poverty. It is not a dispensation from Providence or an inevitable condition of society. India has enough or can have enough for all her children if an alien government and some of her own sons did not corner the good things and so deprive the masses of their dues. "Poverty", said Ruskin,[2] "is not due to natural inferiority of the poor or the inscrutable laws of God, or drink, but because others have picked their pockets." And the control of wealth by the few not only means the unhappiness of many, but it exercises a power over men's minds so that they do not wish for freedom. It is this mental outlook which paralyses the poor and the oppressed and it is this mentality of defeatism that you will have to fight.

[2] John Ruskin (1819–1900); English writer and art critic.

3

Famine Relief[1]

26 June 1929

Sir,

Conditions in the district of Gonda and in its neighbouring district of Bahraich are terrible enough. Indeed many other districts in the province are little better. You say in your letter that the Government has done its part in relieving this distress and it is for private persons and organizations to do their share. In the face of an appalling catastrophe, as in the case of a critical illness, immediate relief measures have necessarily to be undertaken. But you will no doubt appreciate that such measures have a temporary significance only. They neither cure the disease of the social group, nor of the individual. To find the remedy you have to search for the causes of the distemper and to remove them.

Is it not a strange and disconcerting fact that such terrible famines should occur with more and more frequency, and even in the intervals, scarcity, own brother to famine, should prevail? And is it at all surprising that continued starvation should result in the "resistance of the people" being "seriously weakened" as the recent communiqué of the U.P. Government puts it? Surely there must be something very seriously wrong somewhere in the machinery of the state or the structure of society or both.

The days when we could cast the blame on the gods for all our ills are past. Modern science claims to have curbed to a large extent the tyranny and the vagaries of nature, to have increased production and to have introduced swifter

[1] To B.J.K. Hallowes. AICC File No. F-16/1928, pp. 17–23, NMML. Excerpts.

B.J.K. Hallowes, Deputy Commissioner, Allahabad, and President of the Famine Relief Fund of Gonda made an urgent appeal to the Congress committees for help. He had written: "If you commute the sentence on European clothes from burning to banishment, I guarantee that they will never return. You will not, I think, wish any longer to burn clothes, when you realize that there are thousands of your countrymen wearing rags which are too scanty even for decency. You have promised £1000 to the League Against Imperialism. Will you not give as much to the League Against Starvation? Prominent members of the Congress are collecting funds to save from prison 31 alleged communists at Meerut. Will you not do the same to save from famine five lakhs of hungry men at Gonda?"

methods of transportation and communication. And yet in spite of all this progress India faces almost continually famine and scarcity and her condition becomes steadily worse.

Your relief works must bring some solace, however temporary, to many. They are certainly to be appreciated. But do you not think that all this charitable relief does not touch even the fringe of the problem of Indian poverty? For the problem is one of poverty, not of failure of rains or other natural calamity. You do not ask me to send you food, but money. There is enough food in the country and enough of trains and conveyances to carry it to every famine area. But there is no money to buy it. How and why this state has arisen and how it can be remedied are vital questions which we must answer. Probably your method of tackling these questions is different from ours. But it is certain that the charity of the wealthy does not put down poverty and famine relief measures do not put an end to conditions which cause famines.

The whole raison d'etre of the National Congress is to put an end to such terrible conditions by removing the root causes. The Congress is convinced that only by changing the whole system of government and the structure of society can poverty be conquered and a measure of social well-being introduced. The Congress therefore fights for this change and in so doing faces a considerable measure of risk and suffering. And it is for this reason that the Congress associates itself with other organizations, like the League Against Imperialism, which also attack the root cause of poverty and inequality.

If the government at present functioning in India were really desirous of attacking and eradicating poverty they would do something much more and vastly different from the petty relief they give in times of acute distress. They would feel that in a country where there is such terrible poverty it is a tragic absurdity to have an expensive and top-heavy system of administration. They would feel that the whole political and economic system they have built up in the country, and the social structure they have bolstered up, have impoverished the country with great efficiency and rapidity, and this process continues. They would realize that the responsibility for this poverty is theirs and therefore the speediest way of ending it is to remove themselves from the scene of action, liquidate their government and make room for others who can tackle the problem with greater disinterestedness and competence than they have shown.

I cannot believe that anyone who has given some thought to this question can fail to arrive at this conclusion. Your sympathy for the poverty-stricken will not end by giving them temporary relief. You will want a surer remedy giving more permanent results than the quack's nostrum. I trust that you will appreciate this sure remedy lies in the complete replacement of the present system of government and a change in the social structure. Believing this to be the only right way which promises a measure of comfort and happiness to our suffering countrymen, the National Congress has determined to follow this path. Your cooperation, moral and material, as well as the cooperation of all others who object to the exploitation of a country or a people or a class by another, will be welcome.

Yours sincerely,
Jawaharlal Nehru

4

Zamindars and Taluqdars[1]

Allahabad, 5 November 1931

My Dear Raja Saheb,

The Congress stands for the removal of the hardships of the masses and the masses being chiefly the peasantry, the Congress has to stand for their interests. The Congress is not against the zamindars as such but where there is a conflict between the two interests the interest of the masses must prevail. That is, so far as I have been able to understand, the Congress viewpoint. My personal viewpoint is the same but in addition I am convinced that the zamindari system is a system which is injurious to society. This opinion has nothing to do with good zamindars or bad zamindars and taluqdars. It is based on purely economic reasons. Further I am convinced that this system is utterly divorced from modern conditions and is bound to topple over because of its inherent instability. All the world over one can see this process going on. It is the part of the wise man whether he is a zamindar or a tenant or a mere politician like myself to try to understand what is happening in the world, what economic and other forces are at play and to profit by the experience of others. It would be foolish for any of us to base general conclusions in regard to an economic system on the strength of goodness or badness of certain individuals who are parts of that system. As you know I have very many good friends among taluqdars and zamindars of this province. My contacts have been far greater with them than with the tenantry. How can I wish ill to those whom I have learned to respect in their individual capacities. But I cannot allow the personal question to blind me to the facts and these facts tell me that the existing economic system in India and specially in our province in regard to the land is out of date and it brings terrible misery to vast numbers. I do not believe in allowing fate and other unseen powers to do what they like without any effort on my part. I believe that human beings can control their destiny and so can society at large. If we have an economic depression today which has brought so much trouble to zamindars and kisans alike whose fault is it? Are these economic crises due to an act of god or mismanagement by incompetents who have unfortunately the fate of man

---

[1] To Rampal Singh. AICC File No. G-140/1931 (Pt. I), NMML. Excerpts.

in their hands? I have not a shadow of doubt that if existing conditions are allowed to continue both the zamindars and kisans will go to the wall.

I want therefore that the problem should be placed in its proper setting and perspective by everybody so that we might, by putting our heads together, evolve a satisfactory solution. If, however, some of us, ostrich-like, refuse to face facts they do so at their peril because facts do not disappear into thin air simply because someone does not recognize them.

I do not want to accelerate a class war between the zamindars and the tenants. But I am quite sure that unless a solution is found to the existing problems nothing in the world can avert such an unfortunate struggle.

I trust I have made my position clear. I owe it to you to do so because I do not wish to sail under any false colours or to give any wrong impression about myself to anyone. My views are slightly in advance of those held by the Congress as a whole but as a soldier of the Congress I act strictly within the limitations imposed by the Congress. I have the right, however, to try to convert both the Congress and the public at large to my viewpoint and I live in the hope of being able to convert not only the public at large and Congress but even our taluqdar friends to my viewpoint. For it is obvious that what is good for a part of it, and what is good for India must be good for the taluqdars.

Yours sincerely,
Jawaharlal Nehru

5

Reality and Myth[1]

The suggestion made by me that both political and communal problems in India should be solved by means of a constituent assembly has met with considerable favour. Gandhiji has commended it and so have many others. Others again have misunderstood it or not taken the trouble to understand it.

Politically and nationally, if it is granted, as it must be, that the people of India are to be the sole arbiters of India's fate and must therefore have full freedom to draw up their constitution, it follows that this can only be done by means of a constituent assembly elected on the widest franchise. Those who believe in independence have no other choice. Even those who talk vaguely in terms of a nebulous Dominion Status must agree that the decision has to be made by the Indian people. How then is this decision to be made? Not by a group of so-called leaders or individuals. Not by these self-constituted bodies called All Parties Conference which represent, if any body at all, small interested groups and leave out the vast majority of the population. Not even, let us admit, by the National Congress, powerful and largely representative as it is. It is of course open to the Congress to influence and largely control the constituent assembly if it can carry the people with it. But the ultimate political decision must be with the people of India acting through a popularly elected constituent assembly.

This assembly of course can have nothing in common with the sham and lifeless councils and assemblies imposed on us by an alien authority. It must derive its sanction from the people themselves without any outside interference. I have suggested that it should be elected under adult or near-adult franchise. What the method of election should be can be considered and decided later. Personally I favour the introduction, as far as possible, of the functional system of election as this is far more representative of real interests. The geographical system often covers up and confuses these interests. But I am prepared to agree to either or to a combination of both. I see no difficulty, except one, and that is an important one, in the way of such a constituent assembly

[1] Statement to the press, Allahabad, 5 January 1934. *The Tribune*, 8 January 1934. Reprinted in *Recent Essays and Writings,* (Allahabad, 1934) pp. 72–81. Selected Works of Jawaharlal Nehru (henceforth SWJN), Vol. 4, pp. 180–4. Excerpts.

being elected and functioning. This functioning will be limited to drawing up of a constitution and then fresh elections will have to be held on the basis of the new constitution.

The one difficulty I referred to is the presence and dominance of an outside authority, that is the British Government. It is clear that so long as this dominance continues no real constituent assembly can meet or function. So thus an essential preliminary is the development of sufficient strength in the nation to be able to enforce the will of the Indian people. Two opposing wills cannot prevail at the same time; there must be conflict between them and a struggle for dominance, such as we see today in India. Essentially, this struggle is for the preservation of British vested interests in India and the White Paper effort is an attempt to perpetuate them. No constituent assembly can be bound down by these chains, and so long as the nation has not developed strength enough to break these chains, such an assembly cannot function.

This assembly would also deal with the communal problem, and I have suggested that, in order to remove all suspicion from the minds of a minority, it may even, if it so chooses, have its representatives elected by separate electorates. These separate electorates would only be for the constituent assembly. The future method of election, as well as all other matters connected with the constitution, would be settled by the assembly itself.

I have further added that if the Muslim elected representatives for this constituent assembly adhere to certain communal demands I shall press for their acceptance. Much as I dislike communalism I realize that it does not disappear by suppression but by a removal of the feeling of fear, or by a diversion of interest. We should therefore remove this fear complex and make the Muslim masses realize that they can have any protection that they really desire. I feel that this realization will go a long way in toning down the feeling of communalism.

But I am convinced that the real remedy lies in a diversion of interest from the myths that have been fostered and have grown up round the communal question to the realities of today. The bulwark of communalism today is political reaction and so we find that communal leaders inevitably tend to become reactionaries in political and economic matters. Groups of upper class people try to cover up their own class interests by making it appear that they stand for the communal demands of religious minorities or majorities. A critical examination of the various communal demands put forward on behalf of Hindus, Muslims or others reveals that they have nothing to do with the masses. At the most they deal with some jobs for a few of the unemployed intellectuals but it is obvious that the problem even of the unemployed middle class intellectuals cannot be solved by a redistribution of state jobs. There are far too many unemployed persons of the middle class to be absorbed in state or other services and their number is growing at a rapid pace. So far as the masses are concerned there is absolutely no reference to them or to their wants in the numerous demands put forward by communal organizations. Apparently the communalists do not consider them as worthy of attention. What is there, in the various communal formulae, in regard to the distress of the agriculturists, their rent or revenue or the staggering burden of debt that crushes them? Or in regard to the factory or railway or other workers who have to face continuous cuts in wages and a vanishing standard of living? Or the lower middle classes who, for want of employment and work, are sinking in the slough of despair? Heated arguments take place about seats in councils and separate and joint electorates and the separation of provinces which can affect or interest only a few. Is the starving peasant likely to be interested in this when hunger gnaws his stomach? But our communal friends take good care to avoid these real issues, for a solution of them might affect their own interests, and they try to divert people's attention to entirely unreal and, from the mass point of view, trivial matters.

Communalism is essentially a hunt for favours from a third party—the ruling power. The communalist can only think in terms of a continuation of foreign domination and he tries to make the best of it for his own particular group. Delete the foreign power and the communal arguments and demands fall to the ground. Both the foreign power and the communalists, as representing some upper class groups, want no essential change of the political and economic structure, both are interested in the preservation and augmentation of their vested interests. Because of this, both cannot tackle the real economic problems which confront the country for a solution of these would upset the present social structure and devest the vested interests. For both, this ostrich-like policy of ignoring real issues is bound to end in disaster. Facts and economic forces are more powerful than governments and empires and can only be ignored at peril.

Communalism thus becomes another name for political and social reaction and the British Government, being the citadel of this reaction in India, naturally throws its sheltering wings over a useful ally. Many a false trail is drawn to confuse the issue; we are told of Islamic culture and Hindu culture, of religion and old custom, of ancient glories and the like. But behind all this lies political and social reaction, and communalism must therefore be fought on all fronts and given no quarter. Because the inward nature of communalism has not been sufficiently realized, it has often sailed under false colours and taken in many an unwary person. It is an undoubted fact that many a Congressman has almost unconsciously partly succumbed to it and tried to reconcile his nationalism with this narrow and reactionary creed. A real appreciation of its true nature would demonstrate that there can be no common ground between the two. They belong to different species. It is time that Congressmen and others who have flirted with Hindu or Muslim or Sikh or any other communalism should understand this position and make their choice. No one can have it both ways, and the choice lies between political and social progress and stark reaction. An association with any form of communalism means the strengthening of the forces of reaction and of British imperialism in India; it means opposition to social and economic change and a toleration of the present terrible distress of our people; it means a blind ignoring of world forces and events.

What are communal organizations? They are not religious, although they confine themselves to religious groups and exploit the name of religion. They are not cultural and have done nothing for culture, although they talk bravely of a past culture. They are not ethical or moral groups, for their teachings are singularly devoid of all ethics and morality. They are certainly not economic groupings, for there is no economic link binding their members and they have no shadow of an economic programme. Some of them claim not to be political even. What then are they?

As a matter of fact they function politically and their demands are political, but calling themselves non-political, they avoid the real issues and only succeed in obstructing the path of others. . . .

Even more important than the political objective is the economic objective. It is notorious that the era of politics has passed away and we live in an age when economics dominate national and international affairs. What have the communal organizations to say in regard to these economic matters? Or are they blissfully ignorant of the hunger and unemployment that darken the horizon of the masses as well as of the lower middle classes? If they claim to represent the masses they must know that the all-absorbing problem before these unfortunate and unhappy millions is the problem of hunger, and they should have some answer, some theoretical solution at least for this problem. What do they propose should be done in industry and in agriculture? How do they solve the distress of the worker and the peasant; what lands laws do they suggest? What is to happen to the debt of the agricultural classes; is it to be liquidated or merely toned down, or is it to remain? What of unemployment? Do they believe in the present capitalist order of society or do they think in terms of a new order? These are a few odd questions that arise and an answer to them, as well as to other similar questions, will enlighten us as to the true inwardness of the claims and demands of the communalists. Even more so, I think, will the masses be enlightened if the answers manage to reach them. The Muslim masses are probably even poorer than the Hindu masses but the 'fourteen points' say nothing about these poverty-stricken Muslims. The Hindu communalists also lay all their stress on the preservation of their own vested interests and ignore their own masses.

I am afraid I am not likely to get clear or perhaps any answers to my questions, partly because the questions are inconvenient, partly because communal leaders know little about economic facts and have never thought in terms of the masses. They are experts only in percentages and their battle ground is the conference room, not the field or factory or market place. But whether they like them or not the questions will force themselves to the front and those who cannot answer them effectively will find little place for themselves in public affairs. The answer of many of us can be given in one comprehensive word—socialism—and in the socialist structure of society.

But whether socialism or communism is the right answer or some other, one thing is certain—that the answer must be in terms of economics and not merely politics. For India and the world are oppressed by economic problems and there is no escaping them. So long as the fullest economic freedom does not come to us there can be no freedom whatever the political structure may be. Economic freedom must of course include political freedom. That is the reality today; all else is myth and delusion, and there is no greater myth than the communal myth.

6

The Role of Women[1]

If our nation is to rise, how can it do so if half the nation, if our womankind, lag behind and remain ignorant and uneducated? How can our children grow up into self-reliant and efficient citizens of India if their mothers are not themselves self-reliant and efficient? Our history tells us of many wise women and many that were true and brave even unto death. We treasure their examples and are inspired by them, and yet we know that the lot of women in India and elsewhere has been an unhappy one. Our civilization, our customs, our laws, have all been made by man and he has taken good care to keep himself in a superior position and to treat the woman as a chattel and a plaything to be exploited for his own advantage and amusement. Under this continuous pressure the woman has been unable to grow and to develop her capacities to her fullest, and then man has blamed her for her backwardness.

Gradually, in some of the countries of the West, women have succeeded in getting a measure of freedom, but in India we are still backward, although the urge to progress has come here too. We have to fight many social evils; we have to break many an inherited custom that enchains us and drags us down. Men and women, like plants and flowers, can only grow in the sunlight and fresh air of freedom; they wilt and stunt themselves in the dark shadow and suffocating atmosphere of alien domination.

For all of us, therefore, the first problem that presents itself is how to free India and remove the many burdens of the Indian masses. But the women of India have an additional task and that is to free themselves from the tyranny of man-made customs and laws. They will have to carry on this second struggle by themselves, for man is not likely to help them.

Many of the girls and young women present at the convocation will have finished their courses, taken their degrees, and prepared themselves for activities in a larger sphere. What ideals will they carry with them to this wide world, what inner urge will fashion them and govern their actions? Many of them, I am afraid, will relapse into the humdrum day-to-day activities of the household and seldom think of ideals or other obligations; many will think only

[1] Address at the Prayag Mahila Vidyapitha, Allahabad, 20 January 1934. JN Papers, NMML. Excerpts.

of earning a livelihood. Both these are no doubt necessary, but if this is all that the Mahila Vidyapitha has taught its students, it has failed in its purpose. For a university that wishes to justify itself must train and send out into the world knight-errants in the cause of truth and freedom and justice, who will battle fearlessly against oppression and evil. I hope there are some such amongst you, some who prefer to climb the mountains, facing risk and danger, to remaining in the misty and unhealthy valleys below.

But our universities do not encourage the climbing of mountains; they prefer the safety of the lowlands and valleys. They do not encourage initiative and freedom; like true children of our foreign rulers, they prefer the rule of authority and a discipline imposed from above. Is it any wonder that their products are disappointing and ineffective and stunted, and misfits in this changing world of ours?

. . . What will you do, graduates and others of the Vidyapitha, when you go out? Will you just drift and accept things as they are, however bad they may be? Will you be content with pious and ineffective expressions of sympathy for what is good and desirable and do nothing more? Or will you justify your education and prove your mettle by hurling defiance at the evils that encompass you? The purdah, that evil relic of a barbarous age, which imprisons the body and mind of so many of our sisters—will you not tear it to bits and burn the fragments? Untouchability and caste, which degrade humanity and help in the exploitation of one class by another—will you not fight them and end them and thus help in bringing a measure of equality in this country? Our marriage laws and many of our out-of-date customs which hold us back and especially crush our womenfolk—will you not combat them and bring them in line with modern conditions? Will you not also fight with energy and determination for the physical improvement of our women by games in the open air and athletics and sane living so that India may be full of strong and healthy and beautiful women and happy children? And, above all, will you not play a gallant part in the struggle for national and social freedom that is convulsing our country today?

7

A Socialized Society[1]

In considering a method for changing the existing order we have to weigh the costs of it in material as well as spiritual terms. We cannot afford to be too short-sighted. We have to see how far it helps ultimately in the development of human happiness and human progress, material and spiritual. But we have always to bear in mind the terrible costs of not changing the existing order, of carrying on as we do today with our enormous burden of frustrated and distorted lives, starvation and misery, and spiritual and moral degradation. Like an ever-re-curring flood this present economic system is continually overwhelming and carrying away to destruction vast numbers of human beings. We cannot check the flood or save these people by some of us carrying water away in a bucket. Embankments have to be built and canals, and the destructive power of the waters has to be converted and used for human betterment.

It is obvious that the vast changes that socialism envisages cannot be brought about by the sudden passing of a few laws. But the basic laws and power are necessary to give the direction of advance and to lay the foundation of the structure. If the great building-up of a socialized society is to proceed, it cannot be left to chance nor can it be done in fits and starts with intervals of destruction of what has been built. The major obstructions have thus to be removed. The object is not to deprive, but to provide; to change the present scarcity to future abundance. But in doing so the path must necessarily be cleared of impediments and selfish interests which want to hold society back. And the path we take is not merely a question of what we like or dislike or even of abstract justice, but what is economically sound, capable of progress and adaptation to changing conditions, and likely to do good to the largest number of human beings.

A clash of interests seems inevitable. There is no middle path. Each one of us will have to choose our side. Before we can choose, we must know and understand. The emotional appeal of socialism is not enough. This must be supplemented by an intellectual and reasoned appeal based on facts and arguments and detailed criticism. In the West a great deal of this kind of literature exists, but in India there is a tremendous lack of it, and many good books are not

[1] From *An Autobiography*, pp. 588–9.

allowed entry here. But to read books from other countries is not enough. If socialism is to be built up in India it will have to grow out of Indian conditions, and the closest study of these conditions is essential. We want experts in the job who study and prepare detailed plans. Unfortunately our experts are mostly in government service or in the semi-official universities, and they dare not go far in this direction.

An intellectual background is not enough to bring socialism. Other forces are necessary. But I do feel that without that background we can never have a grip of the subject or create a powerful movement.

8

Scientific Socialism[1]

For twenty years or more I have been closely associated with the Congress and have worked for it to the best of my ability, till I have come to consider myself almost as having merged into it. I have given the best part of my life to it because I believed that it was working for the ideals that I had in my heart. Inevitably, therefore, the Congress occupies a great part of my being and the ties that bind me to it are as hard as steel. I have also progressively accepted the ideology of a scientific socialism and I may claim to be now a socialist in the full sense of the term. Any organization that claims to represent these two ideas and ways must therefore have my goodwill, quite apart even from the detailed programme it might advance. I find further that many of my old colleagues whose opinions I have valued are now in the ranks of the Congress Socialist Party.

I have mentioned the two ways that have moved me, and I take it that they move also, in varying degrees, many of my countrymen. These are: nationalism and political freedom as represented by the Congress, and social freedom as represented by socialism. Socialism, it is obvious, includes political freedom, for without that there can be no social and economic freedom. But India being unhappily still politically a subject country, nationalism is the dominant urge of most of her politically-minded classes. That is a factor of primary importance and any socialist who ignores it does so at his peril. But no socialist need be reminded that nationalism by itself offers no solution to the vast problems that confront our country and the world; it ignores indeed the world and fails to realize that in doing so it makes an understanding of even the national position impossible. For the Indian problem is but a part of the world problem of imperialism, the two are indissolubly linked together, and that world problem is essentially an economic problem, though it has many changing faces.

To continue these two outlooks and make them an organic whole is the problem of the Indian socialist. Scientific socialism itself teaches us not to follow slavishly any dogma or any other country's example, which may have resulted from entirely different circumstances. Armed with a philosophy which

[1] A Message to the All-India Congress Socialist Conference, Meerut, 13 January 1936. JN Papers, NMML.

reveals the inner workings of history and human relations, and with the scientific outlook to guide him, the socialist tries to solve the problems of each country in relation to its varied background and stage of economic development, and also in relation to the world. It is a hard task. But then there is no easy way.

Ideas are the essential basis for action. But behind ideas there must be the men to carry them out and the character and discipline to translate them into results. No socialist can be true to his creed or mission if he seeks satisfaction merely in brave ideas and in criticism of others who do not agree with him. That is the way of facile intellectual opportunism. He has to remember that he is no armchair politician but one working for an object—for achievement. And achievement requires character and discipline and united action and the readiness to sacrifice the individual self for the larger cause. That discipline and character have been sadly lacking in India in recent months, and the brave memory of united and effective action is almost a dream that has faded. It is for us to make that dream real again, and real in an even more fundamental sense than it was in the past, for in the future it must be built upon a clear and well-understood ideology.

9

Forces that Shape Events[1]

Sixteen years ago, under the inspiration of our leader, we took a new and long step converting this Congress from an ineffective body, feebly functioning amongst the upper classes, into a powerful democratic organization with its roots in the Indian soil and the vast masses who live on it. A handful of our old friends, representing an age and a class which had its day, left us, fearful of this democratic upsurge and preferring the shelter and protection of British imperialism to joining hands with the new vital forces which convulsed the country and struggled for freedom. Historically they lapsed into the past. But we heard the rumbling of those forces and, for the moment, lined up with them and played a not unworthy part in current history. We sensed the new spirit of mass release, of psychological escape from the cramping effects of long subjection; we gloried in the breaking of the mental bonds that encompassed us. And because our minds became free we felt that political freedom could not be far, for it is often harder to break the bonds of the spirit than physical bonds and chains of iron and steel. We represented the spirit of the age and were marching step by step with countless others in our country and outside. The exhilaration of being in tune with the masses and with world forces came upon us, and the feeling that we were the agents of historic destiny.

We were engrossed in our national struggle, and the turn it took bore the powerful impress of our great leader and of our national genius. We were hardly conscious then of what was happening outside. And yet our struggle was but part of a far wider struggle for freedom, and the forces that moved us were moving millions of people all over the world and driving them into action. All Asia was astir from the Mediterranean to the Far East, from the Islamic West to the Buddhist East; Africa responded to the new spirit; Europe, broken up by the war, was struggling to find a new equilibrium. And right across a vast area in Europe and Asia, in the Soviet territories, a new conception of human freedom and social equality fought desperately against a host of enemies. There were great differences in the many aspects of this freedom struggle all over the

[1] Presidential address, Indian National Congress, Lucknow, 12 April 1936. JN Collection, NMML. Excerpts.

world and we were misled by them and did not see the common background. Yet if we are to understand these varied phenomena, and derive a lesson from them for our own national struggle, we must try to see and understand the whole picture. And if we do so we cannot fail to observe an organic connection between them which endures through changing situations. If once we grasp this organic bond, the world situation becomes easier to understand and our own national problems take their proper place in the wider picture. We realize then that we cannot isolate India or the Indian problem from that of the rest of the world. To do so is to ignore the real forces that are shaping events and to cut ourselves adrift from the vital energy that flows from them. To do so, again, is to fail to understand the significance of our own problems, and if we do not understand this how can we solve them? We are apt to lose ourselves, as we have indeed done, in petty conflicts and minor questions, like the communal problem, and forget the major issues; we are apt to waste our energy (like our moderate friends do) in interminable discussions over legal quibbles and constitutional questions. . . .

Meanwhile the decay of British imperialism in India becomes ever more apparent. It cannot, by its very nature, solve our economic problems and rid us of our terrible poverty which it has largely itself created. It subsists on a normal fare of the fiercest repression and a denial of civil and even personal liberty. It surrounds us with a wide network of spies and, among the pillars of its administration, is the tribe of informers and agent provocateurs and the like. Its services try to seek comfort for their obvious deterioration and incompetence by perpetually singing songs of mutual adulation. Argument gives place to the policeman's baton and the soldier's bayonet and prison and detention camp, and even our extraordinary finances are justified by the methods of the bully. It is astonishing to find to what depths of vulgarity our rulers have descended in their ardent desire to hold on to what they have got, and it is depressing, though perhaps inevitable, that some of our countrymen, more interested in British imperialism than the British themselves, should excel at this deplorable game. So wanting in mental equilibrium are they, so obsessed by fear of the Congress and the national movement it represents, that their wishes become thoughts, their thoughts inferences and their inferences facts, solemnly stated in official publications, and on which the majesty of the British Government rests in India, and people are kept in prison and detention camps without charge or trial. Being interested in psychology, I have watched this process of moral and intellectual decay and realized, even more than I did previously, how autocratic power corrupts and degrades and vulgarizes. All criticism hurts the sensitive skin of the government, and its reactions are quick and far-reaching. The more incompetent it grows the less it likes being told so. But this does not prevent it from indulging in reckless allegations about others.

This psychological aspect interests me even more than the more aggressive

manifestations of British authority in India, for it throws light on much that
has happened. It shows us how a clear and definite fascist mentality has developed among our rulers and how closely allied is imperialism to fascism. How
this fascist mentality has functioned in the recent past and is functioning today,
I shall not go into now. You know well the horror of these years and of the
nightmare that we all have experienced. We shall not easily forget it and if there
are some who have been cowed down by it, there are others who have steeled
themselves to a greater resolve to end this infamy in India.

But of one thing I must say a few words, for to me it is one of the most vital
things that I value. That is the tremendous deprivation of civil liberties in India.
A government that has to rely on the Criminal Law Amendment Act and similar
laws, that suppresses the press and literature, that bans hundreds of organizations, that keeps people in prison without trial, and that does so many other
things that are happening in India today, is a government that has ceased to have
even a shadow of a justification for its existence. I can never adjust myself to
these conditions; I find them intolerable. And yet I find many of my own countrymen complacent about them, some even supporting them, some who have
made the practice of sitting on a fence into a fine art, being neutral when such
questions are discussed. And I have wondered what there was in common
between them and me and those who think as I do. We in Congress welcome
all cooperation in the struggle for Indian freedom; our doors are ever open to
all who stand for that freedom and are against imperialism. But they are not
open to the allies of imperialism and the supporters of repression and those who
stand by the British Government in its suppression of civil liberty. We belong
to opposite camps. . . .

The real problem for us is how, in our struggle for independence, we can
join together all the anti-imperialist forces in the country, how we can make a
broad front of our mass elements with the great majority of the middle classes
which stands for independence. There has been some talk of a joint front but,
so far as I can gather, this refers to some alliance among the upper classes, probably at the expense of the masses. That surely can never be the idea of the
Congress, and if it favours it, it betrays the interests it has claimed to represent,
and loses the very reason for its existence. The essence of a joint popular front
must be uncompromising opposition to imperialism, and the strength of it
must inevitably come from the active participation of the peasantry and
workers.

I am convinced that the only right way of looking at our own problems is
to see them in their proper place in a world-setting. I am convinced that there
is an intimate connection between world events, and our national problem is
but a part of the world problem of capitalist imperialism. To look at each event
apart from the others and without understanding the connection between them
must lead to the formation of erratic and erroneous views. Look at the vast

panorama of world change today, where mighty forces are at grips with each other and dreadful war darkens the horizon: subject peoples struggling for freedom and imperialism crushing them down; exploited classes facing their exploiters and seeking freedom and equality; Italian imperialism bombing and killing the brave Ethiopians; Japanese imperialism continuing its aggression in north China and Mongolia; British imperialism piously objecting to other countries misbehaving, yet carrying on in much the same way in India and the Frontier; and behind it all a decaying economic order which intensifies all these conflicts. Can we not see an organic connection in all these various phenomena? Let us try to develop the historic sense so that we can view current events in proper perspective and understand their real significance. Only then can we appreciate the march of history and keep in step with it. . . .

I am convinced that the only key to the solution of the world's problems and of India's problems lies in socialism, and when I use this word I do not in a vague humanitarian way but in the scientific, economic sense. Socialism is, however, something even more than an economic doctrine; it is a philosophy of life and as such also it appeals to me. I see no way of ending the poverty, the vast unemployment, the degradation and the subjection of the Indian people except through socialism. That involves vast and revolutionary changes in our political and social structure, the ending of vested interests in land and industry, as well as the feudal and autocratic Indian States system. That means the ending of private property, except in a restricted sense, and the replacement of the present profit system by a higher ideal of cooperative service. It means ultimately a change in our instincts and habits and desires. In short, it means a new civilization, radically different from the present capitalist order. Some glimpse we can have of this new civilization in the territories of the USSR. Much has happened there which has pained me greatly and with which I disagree, but I look upon that great and fascinating unfolding of a new order and a new civilization as the most promising feature of our dismal age. If the future is full of hope it is largely because of Soviet Russia and what it has done, and I am convinced that, if some world catastrophe does not intervene, this new civilization will spread to other lands and put an end to the wars and conflicts which capitalism feeds on.

I do not know how or when this new order will come to India. I imagine that every country will fashion it after its own way and fit it in with its national genius. But the essential basis of that order must remain and be a link in the world order that will emerge out of the present chaos.

Socialism is thus for me not merely an economic doctrine which I favour; it is a vital creed which I hold with all my head and heart. I work for Indian independence because the nationalist in me cannot tolerate alien domination; I work for it even more because for me it is the inevitable step to social and economic change. I should like the Congress to become a socialist organization and to join hands with the other forces in the world which are working for the new civilization. But I realize that the majority in the Congress, as it is constituted today, may not be prepared to go thus far. We are a nationalist organization and we think and work on the nationalist plane. It is evident enough now that this is too narrow even for the limited objective of political independence, and so we talk of the masses and their economic needs. But still most of us hesitate, because of our nationalist background, to take a step which might frighten away some vested interests. Most of those interests are already ranged against us and we can expect little from them except opposition even in the political struggle.

Much as I wish for the advancement of socialism in this country, I have no desire to force the issue in the Congress and thereby create difficulties in the way of our struggle for independence. I shall cooperate gladly and with all the strength in me with all those who work for independence even though they do not agree with the socialist solution. But I shall do so stating my position frankly and hoping in course of time to covert the Congress and the country to it, for only thus can I see it achieving independence. It should surely be possible for all of us who believe in independence to join our ranks together even though we might differ on the social issue. The Congress has been in the past a broad front representing various opinions joined together by that common bond. It must continue as such even though the difference of those opinions becomes more marked.

How does socialism fit in with the present ideology of the Congress? I do not think it does. I believe in the rapid industrialization of the country and only thus, I think, will the standards of the people rise substantially and poverty be combated. Yet I have cooperated whole-heartedly in the past with the khadi programme and I hope to do so in the future because I believe that khadi and village industries have a definite place in our present economy. They have a social, a political, and an economic value which is difficult to measure but which is apparent enough to those who have studied their effects. But I look upon them more as temporary expedients of a transition stage rather than as solutions of our vital problems. That transition stage might be a long one, and in a country like India, village industries might well play an important, though subsidiary, role even after the development of industrialism. But though I cooperate in the village industries programme my ideological approach to it differs considerably from that of many others in the Congress who are opposed to industrialization and socialism.

The problem of untouchability and the Harijans again can be approached in different ways. For a socialist it presents no difficulty, for under socialism there can be no such differentiation or victimization. Economically speaking, the Harijans have constituted the landless proletariat, and an economic solution removes the social barriers that custom and tradition have raised.

10

Significance of
A Constituent Assembly[1]

This question of a constituent assembly has become one of the most vital questions of our day in India. It represents our demand for independence and full self-determination, and therefore it is desirable that every aspect of it should be fully considered by the public and its significance realized. . . .

It is right that we should have some knowledge of the history of the idea of the constituent assembly and how it has worked in different countries. And yet it is far more important that we should understand the dynamic significance of this idea and to appreciate what this demand really means for us in India. A constituent assembly may be any assembly which draws up the constitution of a country. And yet this is a poor enough definition of it. The real conception of such an assembly is a dynamic one. It does not mean a body of people, or a gathering of able lawyers, who are intent on drawing up a constitution. It means a nation on the move, throwing away the shell of its past political and possibly social structure, and fashioning for itself a new garment of its own making. It means the masses of a country in action through their elected representatives. It has thus a definite revolutionary significance. At any time this would be so, much more so at present when all the world is in the throes of a change and a rebirth. Therefore, to consider a constituent assembly divorced from this revolutionary background of masses in action and vital change is to miss entirely its significance.

It is because of this that the Congress has laid stress on the recognition by the British Government of Indian independence and of the right of a constituent assembly to frame India's constitution without any external interference. It is also because of this that adult suffrage is postulated, for that brings in the masses in its fold. A recognition of all this does not necessarily lead to revolutionary conditions. But it does create a psychological revolution in men's minds and gives freedom of action to that assembly. Obviously such an assembly can only function satisfactorily as a sovereign body for the particular object

[1] Foreword to Constituent Assembly and Indian Federation by Y.G. Krishnamurthy, Wardha, 18 April 1940. SWJN, Vol. 11, pp. 18-21. Excerpts.

for which it is elected, and giving place to a sovereign legislature of its own creation.

Ordinarily, such sovereign assemblies come into existence after a successful revolution in a country. But it is certainly a possibility, if not a probability, that the shadow of coming events and world changes might lead to an agreement that such an assembly should be elected and should function as formulated. The demand for such an assembly is ultimately a declaration of what we intend to do whenever we have the power to do so. That power may conceivably come to us by agreement without a conflict, or it may come after a conflict. Like the demand for independence, this is not the request for a gift from a dominating authority, but a declaration of our objective and will, which may be realized in a variety of ways. Whatever these ways might be, they represent ultimately a recognition of the power of the Indian nation. In the case of a successful revolution, there is a clean slate to write upon. In the event of an agreement, howsoever specific that might be, the slate is not so clean and all manner of difficulties might arise. Those difficulties have to be faced. It must be remembered that the acceptance of the premises of a real constituent assembly itself adds to the strength of the nation. The election and constitution of such an assembly adds still further to that strength and makes it difficult for external and internal disruptive forces to come in the way of its work.

The ideal of the Indian National Congress is the creation of an independent democratic state and so far we have thought in terms of some kind of parliamentary democracy. If this is the objective, then the only fully democratic method is the method of the constituent assembly elected by the mass of the people. The alternatives to this are no democracy or the Soviet form of democracy. The absence of democracy means either a continuation of foreign rule or individual or group dictatorship. Those who criticize the proposal for a constituent assembly should be clear in their own minds as to which of these alternatives they prefer. It is not good enough to adopt an attitude of mere negation. So far there has only been this negation from some of the critics. It is legitimate for us to know whether the opponents to this proposal do not like democracy, or they do not like independence for India and a break-away from British imperialism. I take it that few of them will agree to go a step further and advocate the Soviet form of government.

Behind our many problems, and ultimately behind the demand for independence itself, lie vast social and economic problems which insistently demand solution. Any constitution that fails to solve them will have a short life. Similar problems in other parts of the world have brought about the present war in Europe where rival imperialisms fight for mastery. Even if one of these imperialisms triumphs in the end, it will have to face these very problems in an accentuated form. It is well recognized today that if peace and freedom are to exist in the world, the imperialist structure must vanish and a new world order must be established. Such a world order will have to be largely based on socialistic principles.

For us in India also this aspect of the problem is important and cannot be ignored. We seek political freedom, but this freedom must lead rapidly to vital social and economic changes which will facilitate a solution of our many problems. The content of political freedom is therefore important. It may be arguable that these basic economic problems cannot ultimately be solved within the structure of a parliamentary state on the old model. And yet it need not necessarily be so. But it is quite clear that there is no chance of a solution if the content of political freedom is such that power rests in the hands of small groups at the top. The giving of the vote for the constituent assembly to the adult masses does not give them real power. But it does mean something and they can influence events and developments. To limit this franchise can only indicate a deliberate desire to keep out the masses and to avoid any vital economic change.

From the point of view of minority interests, a constituent assembly procedure is far the best. The Congress has laid down definite provisions further to safeguard these interests, for instance, declaration of fundamental rights, election by separate electorates where desired, decision of special minority problems, where this is not possible, by arbitration. It passes the wit of man to devise any further safeguards for a minority in India. But if any new suggestion is made which can be incorporated without offending the basic concept of Indian freedom, unity and democracy, that can also be considered.

Despite all this, if the idea of a constituent assembly is opposed, one must regretfully come to the conclusion that the idea of Indian freedom itself is opposed.

Recently proposals have been put forward for a partition of India. It is doubtful if these proposals are seriously meant, for they are fantastic in the extreme and they exhibit a strange ignorance of Indian history and of India's culture, as well as of present conditions in India and the world. All over the world today there is a demand for a removal of national barriers and for a closer union among nations. In India, however, to our misfortune, there are some elements who still think in medieval terms and on whom the lessons of history and even the tragedies of the present day have been completely lost.

11

Planning for the Future[1]

To some it may appear that this is a most unsuitable time for planning, which is essentially a labour of peaceful cooperation. It may be argued that we should wait for better times and more stable conditions, for who knows what the outcome of the present conflict will be? On what foundation shall we build, when no man can foretell what that foundation will be? And yet though we are so uncertain of the future, this we know well that the future will be very different from the past or even from this changing present. Already we see vast political and economic changes taking shape in the womb of the future. Can we plan in India with all this doubt and uncertainty?

These considerations fill our minds, as they should, and we must give careful thought to them. And yet these very considerations lead us to a contrary conclusion. For it is this very time of change and uncertainty that demands mental activity and a vision of the future that we desire. If we are mere onlookers now, and passive and helpless agents of circumstances or the will of others, we barter away our claim to that future. Instead of preparing for it, we hand the reins to others. Every conflict ends sometime or other, every war is followed by a peace, temporary or more enduring, every work of destruction has to be followed by construction. That construction will be chaotic and wasteful unless previous thought has been given to it. A period of war and dynamic change therefore demands, even more than the static times of peace, the planned activity of the mind, so that, when time and opportunity come, this may be translated with all speed into the planned activity of the nation.

For, thinking and planning for the future is essential if that future is not to end in misdirected energy and chaos. It is foolish to imagine that when the present crisis at long last ends, a new or better arrangement of world affairs or our national affairs will automatically emerge out of it. It is equally unwise to allow matters to drift, protesting occasionally perhaps, but otherwise looking on helplessly, for fear that what we may do might involve a risk or be taken unfair advantage of by our opponents. The world is full of risks and dangers today.

[1] Note to the Members of the National Planning Committee, 1 May 1940. JN Papers, NMML. Excerpts.

We cannot escape them. The greatest risk and danger is to drift and not give thought and energy to finding a way out. It is manifest that the old order has had its day and is dissolving, whether we like this or not. It has led to wars and upheavals and continuing conflicts which involve not only passion and hatred and an enormous waste of energy and resources, but also prevent us from achieving what is otherwise easily attainable. We have to understand the conflicts of forces that dominate the world today and seek to resolve these conflicts. It is certainly a possibility that the world may inevitably be led to social dissolution. We have to avoid that, if we can, but we cannot do so by shutting our eyes to the fact that the existing order is incapable of preventing this catastrophe. Something else, more in keeping with modern conditions, has to be evolved. Politics, in our country as elsewhere, dominates the scene and occupies men's minds. But the real changes that are shaping the world are deeper than politics. If we plan, we must consider them and have clear minds about them.

We shall thus have to consider, at this stage or later, the basic and fundamental policies that must govern our planning. Without a definite and clearcut objective in view, and an understanding of the path we must pursue, we shall plan ineffectively or perhaps even in vain.

Already the NPC has given some thought to this matter and we have come to some general but fundamental decisions. It is well to recapitulate some of them. We are aiming at a free and democratic state, which has full political and economic freedom. In this state the fundamental rights of the individual and the group—political, economic, social, and cultural—will be guaranteed, and the corresponding duties and obligations laid down. The state will be progressive and will utilize all scientific and other knowledge for the advancement of the people as a whole, and for the promotion of their happiness and material as well as cultural and spiritual well-being. The state will not permit the exploitation of the community by individuals or groups to the disadvantage of the former and to the injury of the nation as a whole. To realize the social objectives, the state has to plan through its representatives for the nation (whenever possible, in cooperation with other nations) and to coordinate the various activities of the nation so as to avoid waste and conflict and attain the maximum results. This planning will deal with production, distribution, consumption, investment, trade, income, social services, and the many other forms of national activity which act and react on each other. Briefly put, planning aims at the raising of the material and cultural standard of living of the people as a whole. In India our standards are so terribly low and poverty is so appalling that this question of raising standards is of the most vital importance. The NPC has suggested that national wealth should be increased between two and three times within the next ten years, and this should be so planned as to raise the general standard at least in a like measure.

12

The Content of Social Welfare[1]

What exactly is social welfare? The well-being of society, I take it. If so, it includes almost everything that one can think of—spiritual, cultural, political, economic and social. It covers thus the entire field of human activity and relationships. And yet, this wide and all-embracing sense is seldom applied to it, and we use the words in a far more restricted sense. The social worker, often enough, considers himself or herself as working in a field which is strictly separated from political action or economic theory. He or she will try to bring relief to suffering humanity, will fight disease and slum conditions, deal with unemployment, prostitution and the like. He may also seek to bring about some changes in the law in order to remedy present-day injustice. But he will seldom go down to the roots of the problem, for he accepts the general structure of society as it is and seeks only to tone down its glaring injustices.

The lady who visits the slums occasionally to relieve her conscience by the performance of good and charitable deeds is a type we need not consider. The less we have of this patronizing and condescending approach to the problem the better. But there are large numbers of earnest men and women who devote themselves to the service of their fellow creatures in the somewhat narrow way conceived above. They do good work, and to whatever extent they may benefit others, they certainly benefit themselves by the discipline and training that this service gives them.

Yet, it seems to me, that all this good work is largely wasted, because it deals with the surface of the problem only. Social evils have a history and a background, roots in our past, and intimate connections with the economic structure under which we live. Many of them are indeed the direct products of that economic system, just as many others are of religious superstition and harmful custom. Any scientific consideration of the problem of social welfare must, therefore, inevitably go down to these roots and seek out the causes. It must have the courage to look deep down into the well of truth and to proclaim fearlessly what it finds there. If it avoids politics and economics, and all that goes by the name of religion, for fear of treading on dangerous ground, then it moves

[1] *The Hindustan Times,* 20 October 1940. SWJN, Vol. 11, pp. 316–18.

on the surface only and can neither command much respect, nor achieve results.

For nearly two years now I have been associated with the National Planning Committee, and the conviction has grown upon me that it is not possible to solve any major problem separately by itself; they all hang together and they depend greatly on the economic structure. To social problems, in the limited sense, this applies with equal force. Recently, the Planning Committee considered the report of their Sub-Committee on Women's Role in Planned Economy. This sub-committee, more than any other, had to deal with social problems and it tackled them in all earnestness and with great ability. In doing so it was all the time coming up against political conditions and even more so economic aspects and religious injunctions, or just prejudices with the force of custom.

It is not easy to say which is more difficult to deal with—economic vested interests or religious vested interests. Both these series of vested interests want to maintain the status quo and are opponents of change. The path of the real reformer is thus a difficult one.

Before we seek any particular reform, we must be clear what our general objective is and what kind of society we are aiming at. It is obvious that if we have a social structure which assures work and security to all adults, proper education for the young, a widespread distribution of the necessities and amenities of life, and a measure of individual freedom for self-development, this, in itself, will solve many of our social problems. Crime will decrease rapidly and the criminal type will become an extreme rarity, prostitution will be infinitely less and there will be far better adjustments of human relations. If this background and basis are not provided, then the roots of evil remain.

The problem, therefore, has to be attacked on all fronts and possibly the greatest difficulty will be along the so-called religious front. Religion as such need not be touched, but there are so many rules and regulations which are presumed to have religious sanctions that any attempt to vary them is likely to meet with the solid and passionate opposition of the votaries of organized religion. Inheritance, marriage, divorce are all supposed to be parts of the personal law of various communities and this personal law is supposed to be part of religion. It is obvious that no change can be imposed from the top. It will thus become the duty of the government of the day to try to educate public opinion so as to make it accept the changes proposed. It should be clearly laid down, in order to avoid suspicion, that any change of this type will only apply to a community when that community itself accepts it. This will give rise to difficulties and a lack of uniformity but any other course will lead to greater difficulty and ill will, and laws passed may become dead letters so far as their application is concerned.

It seems to me that a uniform civil code for the whole of India is essential. Yet I realize that this cannot be imposed on unwilling people. It should, therefore, be made optional to begin with, and individuals and groups may voluntarily accept it and come within its scope. The state should meanwhile carry on propaganda in its favour.

One urgent need is the extension of the Civil Marriage Act to cover marriages between any two persons, to whatever religion they may belong, without any renunciation of religion, as at present. This will of necessity be optional.

Another desirable step is to have records kept of all marriages. This will be useful in many ways and it will gradually make people think in terms of civil marriages. The sacramental forms of marriage should certainly continue for all who want them, but it will be desirable later to have a civil registration also which the state will recognize.

Divorce laws, especially for the Hindus, are a crying need, and so indeed are so many other changes. We want changes which apply to both men and women, we want changes also especially applicable to women, who have suffered for ages past under a double burden. Let us accept the democratic principle of equal rights and equal obligations as between man and man, and man and woman, and frame our laws and social structure accordingly.

13

Can Indians Get Together?[1]

'Can Indians get together?' It is an odd title yet a significant one, for it tells us much in four words. It gives us an intimate and revealing glimpse into the minds of those who framed it. It reveals to us the premises and assumptions on which they base their consideration of the Indian problem. It displays that patronizing superiority of outlook which we have come to associate with westerners when they deal with eastern nations. It has something of the white man's burden about it. Because of all this I was disinclined to write on the subject, for there is little room for argument or reasoning when premises differ. Our minds function in set grooves, and if even the impact of a World War with its attendant revolutionary changes does not pull them out from those deep hollows, how much can we expect from an appeal to reason?

This war is stupendous military spectacle, and all over the world armies, navies and air forces clash with each other and seek to gain the mastery. . . .[2] These mighty conflicts already have changed the shape of the world and will undoubtedly still further change the shape of things to come. And yet greater changes are happening in the minds of men, possibly none so great as those invisible things that are affecting Asia and gradually but surely putting an end to the relations between Asia and Europe that subsisted for two hundred years. However this War may develop, whatever the end may be, no matter what the peace is going to be, it is certain that the western world can no longer dominate over Asia. If this is not realized and if the attempt is made to continue the old relationship in any form, this means the end of peace and another disastrous conflict.

Yet this is not realized by those who shape the policies of western nations, least of all by Britain. The France of Vichy, grovelling before Germany, still talks of the French Empire,[3] the Netherlands, having lost already many of her

---

[1] Article printed in *The New York Times Magazine*, 19 July 1942. SWJN, Vol. 12, pp. 518–23.

[2] As in the original.

[3] On 17 February 1941, an Imperial Committee was formed by the Vichy Government whose purpose was 'to make known to all Frenchmen the grandeur of the Empire.' In 1942 the Vichy Government from time to time claimed its Empire. In March 1942, it assured the Americans that the fate of Madagascar would not be the same as that of Indo-China.

vast possessions, still speaks the offensive language of Empire[4] and endeavours to cling to what is left. The nineteenth century is dead and gone but the minds of Britain's rulers still think in terms of that past. That way lies no hope for the war or for the peace that must inevitably come some time or the other. Unless London and Washington begin to think in terms of today and of a free and equal Asia they will never reach a solution of the problems that confront them.

That solution lies in accepting the fact of full and equal freedom for all the countries of Asia, of giving up the doctrine of racial superiority, which is no monopoly of the Nazis and which we in India have known in its most intense form for many generations. It lies in the recognition of Indian independence, which will not only release the suppressed and pent-up energies of a great nation but will be symbolic of a new freedom all over the world.

What a mess the nations of Europe made of this world with their perpetual conflicts, their eternal hates, their grabbing violence and cut-throat opportunism, with the misery they brought to their colonial territories, with two World Wars in the course of a single generation!

Not being able to look after their own houses, they presume to dominate over others and pose as their mentors. But no one values them at their achievements in science, literature or the application of science. Behind all this there is a lack of something which brings their achievements periodically to nought. Asia has looked at this changing scene with the strength of ages behind her, and the past 200 years, with all their suffering and mortification, are but a brief interlude in her long history.

That interlude is over. A new chapter must begin. Asia is learning rapidly what the West has to teach of science and its applications and is trying to harmonize them with her old-time genius. She has little to learn, much to teach about the philosophy of life and the art of living.

Can the Indians get together? Yes, certainly, if impediments in their way created by foreign authority are removed, if they can face their problems without external interference. Every problem finally will be solved either by peaceful means or by conflict, though this may give rise to new problems. Independent India will solve her problems or cease to be. The past history of India shows us how she has successfully tackled her problems and out of every conflict of opposing forces has produced a new synthesis. Synthesis is a dominant trait of India's civilization and history.

Except for China, there is no great country in the world which has shown such powerful unity throughout the ages as India. That unity took political shape only recently as it could not be stabilized until relatively recent developments in transport and communications made this easy. If these developments

[4] The exiled Netherlands Government in London appointed, on 21 May 1942, Dr. H.J. Van Hook as Minister of Colonies.

had not taken place it is possible that the United States of America might not have been a single nation.

Britain's rule over India led to political unity and also was a means to bring the Industrial Revolution to India. Development of that revolution was however, hindered by the British, who encouraged feudal elements and prevented industrial growth. The continuing process of synthesis also was stopped by this rule and disruptive forces were encouraged.

For the first time in India's history, here was the rule of a foreign people who had their political, financial, industrial and cultural roots elsewhere and who could only remain as foreigners exploiting the country for their own advantage. There could be no synthesis with them, and perpetual conflict was inevitable. Yet out of this very conflict rose the powerful all-India nationalist movement, which became and is the symbol of political unity.

Independence, democracy and unity were the pillars of this movement. In accordance with old Indian traditions toleration, fullest protection and autonomy were promised to all minorities, subject only to the essential unity of the country and to the democratic basis of its constitution. Independence meant severance from the British Empire, but in the new world it was realized that isolated national existence was not possible or desirable. So India was prepared to join any international federation on an equal basis. But that could come only after recognition of her independence and through her free will. There could be no compulsion. In particular, India wanted to associate herself closely with China.

There is now a demand on the part of some Muslims, represented by the Muslim League, for partition of India, and it must be remembered that this demand is a very recent one, hardly four years old. It must also be remembered that there is a large section of Muslims in India who oppose it. Few people take it seriously, as it has no political or economic background. Americans who fought the Civil War to keep their Union together can appreciate how a proposal to divide the country is resented by vast numbers of the Indian people.

Thirty years ago the British Government introduced the principle of separate religious electorates in India, a fatal thing which has come in the way of development of political parties. Now they have tried to introduce the idea of partitioning India, not only into two but possibly many separate parts. This was one of the reasons which led to bitter resentment of the Cripps proposals. The All India Congress could not agree to this, yet it went far and said if any territorial unit clearly declared its desire to break away, the Congress could not think in terms of compelling it to stay in the Union.

So far as minorities are concerned, it is accepted and common ground that they should be given fullest constitutional protection, religious, cultural, linguistic and in every other way. Backward minorities or classes should in addition be given special educational and other privileges to bring them rapidly to the general level.

The real problem so often referred to is that of the Muslims. They are hardly a minority, as they number about 90,000,000, and it is difficult to see how even a majority can oppress them. As it happens, they are largely concentrated in particular provinces. It is proposed to give full provincial autonomy to every province, reserving only certain all-India subjects for the central government, and this will give every opportunity for self-development in each cultural area. Indeed, there may even be smaller autonomous cultural areas within the province.

It is possible to devise many ways to give satisfaction to every conceivable minority claim. The Congress has said this must be done by agreement, not by a majority vote. If agreement is not possible on any point, then impartial arbitration should be accepted. Finally, if any territorial unit insists on breaking away after the experience of working in the Union, there is going to be no compulsion to force it to stay, provided such severance is geographically possible.

· It must be remembered that the problem of Indian minorities is entirely different from nationalities with entirely different racial, cultural and linguistic backgrounds. This is no so in India where, except for a small handful of persons, there is no difference between Hindu and Muslim in race, culture or language. The vast majority of Muslims belong to the same stock as the Hindus and were converted to Islam.

Few problems in the world today are basically so simple of solution as the Indian minority problem. For various reasons it is important today and comes in the way of progress, yet it is essentially a superficial problem without deep roots. The real problems of India are economic, the poverty and low standards. As soon as these are tackled aggressively, as they should be, and modern industry grows, bringing higher standards in its train, the minority problem fades away. It has been a product of unemployment of the middle classes who had few avenues of work open to them and looked for employment to the state. As state jobs were limited, demand rose for reservation of these for particular communities.

Every attempt to solve the problem thus far has failed because there was always a third party—the British Government. If that government fades away, the whole background of this problem changes when Indians have to look to themselves. Compulsion of events forces them to face reality and to come to agreement. The only alternative is conflict, which everyone is anxious to avoid, over a relatively trivial issue. But even if there is conflict, that is preferable to the present stalemate, and it will produce a solution.

The All India Congress proposal has been that this and other problems should be considered and finally decided by a constituent assembly elected by adult franchise. The widest franchise is considered necessary, for the consideration of these question should rest on those vast numbers of people who are far more interested in economic problems and who do not look for state employment.

Such economic problems cut across religious boundaries and are common to the Hindu, Muslim, Christian and Buddhist. If such an assembly could not come to an agreement on any particular minority matters they could be referred to international arbitration. We are perfectly prepared to abide by the decision of such an international tribunal in such matters. But the question of arbitration does not arise over the question of independence. That and the allied questions of self-determination must be recognized and accepted before there is a possibility of arbitration over minor matters. On independence we cannot compromise.

Can the Indians get together? I have no doubt that they can and they will. Even today there is an amazing unity of outlook among them and whatever their internal differences might be they stand for independence. The real obstacle in the way of real unity and progress is foreign domination. From every point of view it has become an urgent and immediate necessity that Britain should relinquish her hold in India and recognize Indian independence. There is no other way and it is certain, whether Britain likes it or not, that India must be given complete independence.

The approach of war to India has made this an even more vital question. Independent India would treat America and Britain as allies in a common enterprise to release her vast energy and resources against every aggressor who invaded her territory. But Indians can no longer function as slaves and underlings in their own country or outside or tolerate being treated as chattels by dominant foreign authority. Submission to this is for them the worst kind of spiritual degradation.

The East will put up with it no longer. Asia will come back to her own through whatever travail and suffering fate may have in store for her. China has poured out her heart's blood in defence of her freedom. India would do likewise if the opportunity came to her to fight for her freedom. She seeks no dominion over others, but she will put up with no dominion over herself. Only independence will release her from long bondage and allow her to play her part fittingly in the terrible drama of the world today.

14

Linguistic Provinces[1]

The Government is fully aware of the demand in some parts of the country for new provinces to be formed primarily on a linguistic and cultural basis. Many years ago this demand was recognized by the Congress and Government accepted the principle underlying that demand.[2] In giving effect to that principle, however, many other considerations have to be borne in mind. Apart from linguistic and cultural aspects sometimes also there is no clear demarcation and cultural and linguistic areas overlap. Hence a very careful enquiry is necessary before a decision can be arrived at. Government are anxious not to delay the enquiry or the decision. But, as the House is fully aware, the country has had to face, ever since the new order started functioning, a very critical situation resulting from partition. A living entity had a part severed from it and this unnatural operation resulted in all manner of distempers which have naturally affected the political, social and economic structure of the country. Reactionary forces took advantage of this situation to consolidate themselves and to raise separatist cries. The old equilibrium having been shaken up, disruptionist tendencies came to the fore. To a large extent we have faced this crisis and overcome it. But many dangers still surround us. There are numerous urgent demands in the economic and other spheres. When there are a multitude of such demands a certain priority has to be observed, otherwise there would be dispersion of effort and ineffectiveness. First things must come first and the first thing is the security and stability of India. Before we can undertake any major schemes we must have a strong state and a smoothly running governmental machinery. The first essential therefore is for India as a whole to be strong and firmly established, confident in her capacity to meet all possible dangers and face and solve all problems. If India lives, all parts of India also will live and prosper. If India is enfeebled, all her component elements grow weak.

[1] Reply to N.G. Ranga's question on Government's policy regarding the creation of new provinces on a linguistic basis, 27 November 1947. *Constituent Assembly of India (Legislative) Debates, Official Report*, Vol. I, 1947, pp. 793–5.

[2] In 1928 the report of the All Parties Committee (Nehru Report) recommended the formation of provinces on a linguistic basis. The election manifesto of December 1947 stipulated that the provinces should as far as possible, be constituted on linguistic and cultural basis.

15

Economic Policy[1]

Partition has had the most powerful effect on the economy of India, using the word 'India' in its larger sense including the present Dominion of India and the Dominion of Pakistan. India as a whole might well have been considered, and was, a fairly self-sufficient unit which could develop as such; in which planning could take place so that one part of it could fulfil the wants of the other part. Now, this partition has created all manner of difficulties in our economy—the more industrialized parts of India are in the Dominion of India and the more agricultural and less industrialized parts in Pakistan.

Some major industries have been peculiarly affected a great deal—the jute industry. We have jute cultivation very largely in Pakistan and the whole processing of jute in India. While we have the large bulk of the cotton textile factories in India, a good deal of the raw cotton comes from Pakistan. So also many other things. All this has created difficulties enough for each part of this divided India, formerly a more or less balanced unit. The divided parts are facing difficulties because they are not balanced units. And while ultimately they may become so in time probably the difficulties in the way of Pakistan are greater than the difficulties in the way of India.

Then again our economic life has been upset by many other factors due to partition. Our communications have been affected and many other things. I need not go into it all or into the other consequences of partition resulting in the major disaster in the Punjab and round about the Punjab causing such a tremendous strain upon us—a drain on our resources, diverting our resources to the relief and rehabilitation of vast numbers of human beings uprooted from their homes, diverting our transport system to the removal of the evacuees and the refugees from one part of the country to the other—with the result that most of our normal activities have been either suspended or delayed. You know what a vast undertaking this business has been; this exchange of populations which has run, I believe, to between seven and eight millions and on the whole it must be said that the organizations that were responsible for this exchange have done

[1] Address to the Associated Chambers of Commerce, Calcutta, 15 December 1947. Text excerpted from the proceedings of the annual general meeting of the Associated Chambers of Commerce, maintained by the ASSOCHAM. SWJN, Vol. 4 (II Series), pp. 557–70.

an extraordinary good piece of work. The railway administration, the military organization and other organizations—I can say so because I know every step of the process—they have done a very fine piece of work in bringing a vast number of uprooted human beings from one part of the Punjab to the other—from the East to the West and the West to the East. All these have been tremendously upsetting factors but I think we have got over the major difficulties. I think that, psychologically speaking and that is of greater importance at the present moment than any other aspect of the problem, we have gone a good distance towards the healing process, if I may say so, although much remains to be done. I do not know how long it will take for us to get over the results of this uprooting, but I believe that the process may also be not so long as I previously imagined. We have come to a number of agreements with the Dominion of Pakistan in regard to a large number of very controversial matters. That perhaps shows that there is a desire on both sides to come to a settlement so that we may both go ahead. There are still many difficult hurdles to surmount but the spirit to overcome those difficulties is there and I hope that, gradually or rapidly, we will be able to overcome most of them. . . . But the one thing that I should say is this: that the very consequences that have faced us, have shown even more than the theoretical considerations which we had before us then—how inherently unnatural partition is. We have to do many unnatural things by stress of circumstances and I have little doubt that it will require in the future many readjustments to make it less unnatural. It is obvious to me that the two countries constituted as the Dominion of India and the Dominion of Pakistan, not only geographically close to each other but historically, culturally, economically and in many other ways dependent on each other, cannot remain indifferent to each other. They have either to live as close friends or else they will drift further apart. There is no middle way. I hope and believe—I am certain—that somehow or other the only possible solution is to live as close friends, and have many things in common; naturally that is a development which can only be brought about by friendship, amity and goodwill. It is going to be an inevitable development; whether it takes place soon or a little later depends on the wisdom and statesmanship of the various people concerned.

. . . We thought till recently that the very first thing was political independence, and therefore our energies were diverted to that end. That having been achieved, obviously we have now to face the economic problem as a whole. How is one to face it? It is not an easy matter for anyone, for a person like me, layman, to say; and in dealing with these questions before this very distinguished and expert gathering, a layman like me might well quail. But a feeling I sometimes have is that great experts have a way of seeing things lopsided, and of thinking only of their particular aspect of the problem, knowing it thoroughly no doubt, but perhaps not attaching sufficient importance to the various other problems of this complicated life of ours. Now, a politician has many failings and may be superficial, as he often is. But he would cease to be a success-ful politician if he did not have the capacity to take into consideration and remember a thousand things at one and the same time; and that gives him a certain wideness of outlook, a certain balance and a certain poise. . . .

Democracy is presumably a means to an end. What is that end? The well-being and progress of the community. I am strongly in favour of democracy and of individual freedom because I think the individual cannot progress if he is regimented too much, unless he can grow to his proper stature. But, then there may be many kinds of regimentation and many kinds of pressure which curb and suppress individual growth. What opportunity for growth is there today for vast numbers of Indians whether they work in the field or elsewhere?

. . . Now, the system that has been applied—call it what you like—the political and the economic system which has led to this degradation of scores and scores of millions of Indian community—whatever 'ism' it may be—has been a failure because it has produced this degradation of Indian humanity. That, I think, is the first thing to understand and realize. Any system which produces misery and poverty in a country has failed somewhere. We may differ as to the cause of that failure but the fact of failure—the fact of poverty, the fact of unemployment—stares us in the face. Now, if this is so, we have to find out the remedy for that. We have to find out what objectives to aim at, apart from any 'isms', socialism or capitalism or anything. It may be thought that an imme-diate variation of the present capitalistic structure might meet our demand and help us to get rid of the poverty of the Indian people. If so, let us experiment with it. If not, then inevitably and all the more logically, scrap it and try something else because the essential thing before us is how effectively and fairly rapidly to solve this problem of poverty.

. . . Well, the war is over and in India our struggle for political independ-ence is also over; but another struggle and an equally important and perhaps much more important struggle, namely the economic well-being of the masses, is far from being over. In fact it is being pushed ahead with vigour. The only way to look upon it is in terms of war, that is to say, in terms of doing and encouraging the absolute necessity from the point of view of winning that struggle for the masses. All this leads us to think, to a large extent, in terms of a war outlook, a war not of violence but in terms of working hard and winning this struggle for the economic betterment of the people. What is the first priority in regard to that and how can that be done by any government unless there is careful thought and planning to that end and unless the vagaries of private enterprise are limited, unless the dominant motive of the country is not the motive of private profit but some other profit which leads to the betterment of the masses. The motive of profit may be left, private enterprise may well be left, but both become limited in scope because something which is more domi-nant comes into the picture. As a matter of fact, it is not merely a question of what I may say about it or you may think about it; it is a question of what—in a democratic government and country—what vast masses of people think about it, because their pressure does force government to certain actions and if that government is slow in taking them, then that action comes not in a proper and regulated way but in an unregulated and improper way which is worse for all concerned and is harmful to the country's interest. Even looking at it from the purely economic point of view—and not being an economist I speak with deference to those who are experts—it seems to me that conditions in India today, as in many other parts of the world, are conditions of such rapid change that old ideas and methods cannot possibly be applied without their being changed also. The logical and reasonable one would say that in a changing world, in order to keep pace with it, the social structure should also keep pace with the changing conditions.

. . . First things first. The first thing is the good of the Indian masses and everything should be judged by that standard. If there is any obstruction in the way of the good of the Indian masses, that obstruction must go. How do the millions of India benefit or prosper?—that is the real test of any policy, economic, political or otherwise, that we may put forward. I should have personally thought, apart from the immediate problems that face us, that one of our urgent needs was to develop and encourage, to put into operation, these various big schemes and projects in India which would give us greater power, electrical power, more land under irrigation and more power generally for industry etc. . . . These schemes are investments and we must find money for them. If necessary, we must borrow money in India or abroad and we must get them through. For unless we do that we cannot increase the productive capacity of India very greatly. That I would give first place; and for the rest, at the present moment I believe that the increase of production in every field of activity is most important. On that there is general agreement. . . .

We have talked such a lot about our 'Grow More Food Campaigns' but I confess it with shame that these campaigns have not resulted in any major development anywhere in regard to the production of more food. Of course, somewhere, in some back garden, we have produced a few vegetables and the like; but on a big scale I do not think anything much has been done. Why is that so? It troubles me. There is something wrong in the approach to this problem. There was previously the political difficulty—you could not somehow harness the energy of the nation in these campaigns. Well, we ought to be able to harness it today.

Then there is the labour difficulty to which you have referred in your address[2]. I agree with you that there has been a great deal of indiscipline among labour. A number of destructive tendencies have been at work which have

<hr>

[2] H.D. Cumberbath, President of ASSOCHAM.

interfered with production and the rest. At the same time it is rather an easy way of explaining this phenomenon by casting the blame on labour or on a number of agitators who inflame labour or on the Industrial Disputes Act[3] or certain adjudications which gave awards possibly not liked by certain employers. I think that is a very simple way of looking at the problem. There may be many other causes. But undoubtedly, at the present moment and for some time past, there has been a kind of psychological deadlock between the employer and the employee. That may have been encouraged and increased by those people who are called agitators but this business of making the agitator responsible for the evils of society is not, I think, very helpful. For my part I have long been an agitator myself and I feel a kind of fellow-feeling and sympathy for them. Agitators, like all other human beings, are both good and bad. Undoubtedly the field of labour offers an opportunity to encourage certain tendencies but the fact remains that this labour trouble is much deeper than something which has been created by the agitators and the rest.

After all it is not something in India only. We see in countries of Europe, in America and elsewhere the same phenomenon happening. There must be something behind it. We see also that we have got into this vicious circle of rising prices and we cannot get out of it. Apart from that there is a deep distrust among the workers in India of the employers. I entirely agree with you that employers are not ogres—they are both good and bad. But there is this deep distrust and I put it to you that during these war years the behaviour of at least some big business was such as to make people distrustful of its bona fides—all this business on a large scale of black-marketing and the rest which I have never been able to explain to myself—how and why in spite of this very heavy rate of taxation, vast fortunes were made.

Now, the result is that labour, apart from its great difficulties, is very distrustful and at the same time labour has gradually become more organized, more alert and more resentful of any steps taken against it. This is a natural phenomenon. We may regret, as I do regret, this indiscipline. It is a disruptive force and totally unnecessary strikes, often lightning strikes, whatever harm they may do to production, ultimately harm labour much more than anybody else. Nevertheless, the whole history of the development of industry for the last hundred years or more has involved this development of trade unions fighting for their rights and, these rights being denied to them, getting to a stage of deadlock through the favour the employer class gets from the government of the day. But in the process the labour was gradually growing in strength. . . .

In India we have to develop, we have to consider, many things and one is the balance between rural and urban economy. It is fair to say—and I think you

[3] The Industrial Disputes Act, which came into force from March 1947, provided for setting up of tribunals for the prevention and settlement of disputes. It made conciliation mandatory in disputes in public utility services and optional in other cases.

were right to say it, although you stressed a different aspect of the question—
that we have been thinking primarily in terms of urban economy and forgotten
the rural aspect of our national economy. Now we have to find a balance
between the two and you know there has always been trouble in every country
between the village and the town—whether that country is a capitalistic
country or trying to be socialistic. We have to find also a certain balance, an
equilibrium, between various parts of India.

. . . I have not a shadow of doubt that large-scale industry has to be encouraged in India. At the same time I am quite convinced that we have to encourage small-scale industry and cottage industry also. But what I wish to put
before you now is that, in the present context, when we wish to increase our
production, we have paid insufficient attention to the development of small-
scale industry producing common articles. Both large-scale industry and small-
scale industry are important from the point of view of finance, employment for
people and adding to the production of India.

Production by itself will not solve the problem, distribution is essential.
Obviously, if by introducing new methods of production, we increase our production and at the same time add to our unemployment problem, that will be
no solution of our difficulties. So we have to take all these things together, and
in getting rid of this unemployment problem immediately, we can take to
small-scale production in addition to large-scale production. I just do not see
any real conflict between the two and indeed, I think, today both are essential. . . .

I have not said anything about bigger economic policy because I do not
think it would be proper for me to commit the Government in any way but I
think I have indicated sufficiently that our approach to the problem will not
be a theoretical approach based on this 'ism' or the other, but is a practical
approach with the objective of achieving good results as rapidly as possible.
Nevertheless, I have little doubt that that approach will involve a large measure
of socialization in regard to certain industries. This does not mean that we are
going to do away with private enterprise. Private enterprise is going to continue
and I think ought to be encouraged, but in regard to certain basic, certain key
industries, I have little doubt that the tendency will be for them to be state-
owned or at any rate to be state-controlled. Probably we shall proceed on the
basis of having to control our public corporation. So basic key industries and
public utility concerns would normally be state-owned, whether the state is the
Central Government or a Provincial Government or a municipal corporation.
At the same time, if we have any kind of real planning, it is inevitable that a measure of state direction and state control should apply to other industries also.
But a large field will necessarily still be left to private enterprise. We want to
develop and industrialize our country rapidly and in order to do so undoubtedly it would help us greatly to have foreign assistance, foreign capital and

foreign technical assistance. We are not going to stop that. In fact we would welcome it. At the same time, you will realize that we are anxious to preserve our economic independence. We do not want to encourage foreign capital to come in at the cost of bartering away any part of that independence. We should like foreign capital to come on favourable terms. It will be a business transaction; we shall take technical assistance on advantageous terms. Obviously, for the Government of India the aim will be the good of India. Foreign creditors will of course consider their own aspect of the question, but I do think there is a large field in India, specially during the next many years when India is going to develop rapidly, if there is cooperation between other countries and India in this process of development. I think, therefore, that such British and other foreign interests as exist in India will have and should have this large field open to them; whether they will function exactly on the old lines, I cannot say, but inevitably such changes that have taken place in the economy will affect them, just as they will affect equally any other Indian business. You cannot have any special privileges for foreign interests in India.

16

The Role of the Prime Minister[1]

The Prime Minister's role is, and should be, an important role. He is not only a figurehead but a person who should be more responsible than anyone else for the general trend of policy and for the coordination of the work of various Government departments. The final authority necessarily is the Cabinet itself. But in the type of democratic set-up we have adopted, the Prime Minister is supposed to play an outstanding role. This, I think, is important (again quite apart from personal factors), as otherwise there will be no cohesion in the Cabinet and the Government and disruptive tendencies will be at work.

Speaking for myself, I have at present two functions to perform in Government. As Minister of External Affairs, I function like any other minister and my ministry is like any other ministry. As Prime Minister, however, I have a special function to perform which covers all the ministries and departments and indeed every aspect of governmental authority. This function cannot be easily defined and the proper discharge of it depends a great deal on the spirit of cooperation animating all the parties concerned. Inevitably, in discharging this function of Prime Minister I have to deal with every ministry not as head of one particular ministry, but as a coordinator and a kind of supervisor. Naturally, this can only be done effectively with tact and goodwill and without in any way diminishing the prestige of other ministers. Other ministers must not normally be interfered with and should have freedom to carry out their work without unnecessary interference.[2]

If this position is recognized, then no present difficulty arises, and if at any time a difficulty does arise, it can be resolved by personal contact and discussion between the parties concerned. Because of this I have endeavoured in almost every matter of importance to confer with Sardar Patel.

[1] Note to Mahatma Gandhi, 6 January 1948. *Sardar Patel's Correspondence 1945–50*, Vol. 6, pp. 17–21. SWJN, Vol. 5 (II Series), pp. 471–5. Excerpts.

[2] In his note of 12 January 1948, Patel questioned Nehru's interpretation of the Prime Minister's role as inconsistent with a democratic system of government, for it would raise him "to the positions of a virtual dictator". The Prime Minister was no doubt "first among equals," but he had no overriding powers over his colleagues "as responsibility for implementing policy decisions rested with the ministry concerned and on the minister in charge."

The immediate issue arose out of my sending Iengar to Ajmer.[3] I think that my sending him was not only completely within my competence but also it was an eminently desirable thing to do in the circumstances and that undoubtedly it did some good. This opinion of mine has been strengthened by my visit to Ajmer. Iengar had nothing to do with holding any kind of inquiry or sitting in judgement in any way on the officials in Ajmer.[4] He was sent as the eyes and ears of the Prime Minister and to convey the Prime Minister's regret for his having had to cancel his visit to Ajmer previously. In Ajmer and elsewhere, we have to deal with psychological problems and mental states. The approach to the people direct is always important when dealing with such problems. The importance of Ajmer had induced me to pay a visit there even at inconvenience. I could not go then because of a death in the family. My not going was variously interpreted in Ajmer and gave rise to all manner of suspicions and rumours. Iengar's going helped to lessen these suspicions somewhat among the people by making them realize that the Government was greatly interested in their peace and welfare. My subsequent visit, of course, did much more good. It did not, as it was not meant to, affect the position of the Chief Commissioner, whom indeed I praised publicly for his ability and impartiality. But apart from these facts the question remains: Is the Prime Minister entitled to take such a step and who is to be the judge of this? If the Prime Minister cannot even take this step and is not himself to be the judge of what is proper and what is not in such matters, then he cannot function properly or fulfil his functions.[5] Indeed, he does not function at all as the Prime Minister should. The mere fact that he is Prime Minister presumably leads to the conclusion that he is capable of judging aright and carrying out the policy laid down. If he is not capable of this, then he should cease to be Prime Minister. Indeed, this means abdication of his functions and he cannot in future function with any effectiveness. There will be no proper coordination of governmental authority and, in such circumstances, the administrative machinery weakens and there are rival pulls.

If this view is correct, then the Prime Minister should have full freedom to act when and how he chooses, though of course such action must not be an undue interference with local authorities who are immediately responsible. The Prime Minister obviously is as much interested as anyone else in having the loyalty and cooperation of the services.

[3] Patel said that the immediate issue was not H.V.R. Iengar's visit to Ajmer but Gopalaswami Ayyangar's direct correspondence with the East Punjab Government.

[4] Patel reiterated that "Iengar went to Ajmer, inspected various places, received deputations . . . the public mind is bound to associate it with an inquisition. The Chief Commissioner took it in that light and stated that the public also felt it as such."

[5] Patel felt "the question is not whether the Prime Minister was entitled to take this step or not or whether he is not to be the judge of the propriety of the action, but whether I, as a Minister, was wrong in pointing out to him the inadvisability of the course he had taken and the probable consequences it entailed."

In the event of the Prime Minister not functioning in this way, then he can hardly carry on as a mere figurehead and much harm may be done to the services as well as to the public at large by the enunciation of contradictory policies by ministers.

This is the background. But whatever the theory may be, practical difficulties continually arise. Normally speaking, the best way out of these difficulties would be for some rearrangement in the Cabinet to be made which would cast the responsibility on one person more than anyone else. In the present set-up this means that either I should go out or that Sardar Patel should go out. For my part, I would greatly prefer my going out.[6] Of course, this going out of either of us need not and should not mean any kind of subsequent opposition. Whether we are in or out of government we remain, I hope, not only loyal Congressmen but loyal colleagues, and we will still try to pull together in our respective spheres of activity.

Nevertheless, there can be little doubt that if either of us goes out at the present juncture it would create a sensation both nationally and internationally, and the consequences may not be good. At any time this position would have to be faced; but at the present juncture, with the Kashmir issue and the great problem of rehabilitation facing us, not to mention the states and the growth of communal organizations in India, any such parting of ways may well have very serious consequences affecting the good of India. None of us wants to do anything which may be at all injurious to the national good, even though our views of the national good may differ somewhat. After having given very serious thought to this matter during the last fortnight I have come to the conclusion that as far as possible we must avoid, at this particular juncture, any parting of ways in Government. We are too much in the transitional stage and a serious shake-up of Government may well lead to an upsetting of the apple-cart. I think that we should carry on for some months more till the Kashmir issue is more clarified and other problems have also been tackled to some extent. The way to do this must be the fullest consultation about every important matter. At the same time I do feel that the Prime Minister's function, as defined above, must be appreciated. . . .

[6] Patel replied: ". . . if anybody has to go, it should be myself. I have long passed the age of active service. The Prime Minister is the acknowledged leader of the country and is comparatively young; he has established an international position of pre-eminence for himself."

17

A National State[1]

For every sensitive human being in India the last six months have brought pain and sorrow, and what is worst of all, a humiliation of the spirit. It has been bad enough for those who are old in years and experienced, but I often wonder how the young feel who, at the threshold of their lives, have seen and experienced catastrophe and disaster. They will, no doubt, survive it, for youth is resilient; but it may well be that they will carry the mark of it for the rest of their days. Perhaps if we are wise and strong enough to think and act rightly even now, we may succeed in erasing that mark.

For my part I wish to say that, in spite of everything, I have a firm faith in India's future. Indeed, if I did not have it, it would not have been possible for me to work effectively. Although many of my old dreams have been shattered by recent events, yet the basic objective still holds and I see no reason to change it. That objective is to build a free India of high ideals and noble endeavour where there is equality of opportunity for all and where many variegated streams of thought and culture meet together to form a mighty river of progress and advancement for her people.

I am proud of India, not only because of her ancient, magnificent heritage, but also because of her remarkable capacity to add to it by keeping the doors and windows of her mind and spirit open to fresh and invigorating winds from distant lands. India's strength has been twofold; her own innate culture which flowered through the ages, and her capacity to draw from other sources and thus add to her own. She was far too strong to be submerged by outside streams, and she was too wise to isolate herself from them, and so there is a continuing synthesis in India's real history and the many political changes which have taken place have had little effect on the growth of this variegated and yet essential unified culture.

I have said that I am proud of our inheritance and our ancestors who gave an intellectual and cultural pre-eminence to India. How do you feel about this past? Do you feel that you are also sharers in it and inheritors of it and, therefore proud of something that belongs to you as much as to me? Or do you feel alien to it and pass it by without understanding it or feeling that strange thrill which

[1] Address, Aligarh Muslim University, 24 January 1948. JN Papers, NMML. Excerpts.

comes from the realization that we are the trustees and inheritors of this vast treasure? I ask you these questions, because in recent years many forces have been at play diverting people's minds into wrong channels and trying to pervert the course of history. You are Muslims and I am a Hindu. We may adhere to different religious faiths or even to none; but that does not take away from that cultural inheritance that is yours as well as mine. The past holds us together; why should the present or the future divide us in spirit?

Political changes produce certain results, but the essential changes are in the spirit and outlook of a nation. What has troubled me very greatly during these past months and years is not the political changes, but rather the creeping sense of a change of spirit which has created enormous barriers between us. The attempt to change the spirit of India was a reversal of the historical process through which we had been passing for long ages past and it is because we tried to reverse the current of history that disaster overwhelmed us. We cannot easily play about with geography or with the powerful trends which make history. And it is infinitely worse if we make hatred and violence the springs of action.

Pakistan has come into being, rather unnaturally I think. Nevertheless, it represents the urges of a large number of persons. I believe that this development has been a throw-back we accepted in good faith. I want you to understand clearly what our present view is. We have been charged with desiring to strangle and crush Pakistan and to force it into a reunion with India. That charge, as many others, is based on fear and a complete misunderstanding of our attitude. I believe that, for a variety of reasons, it is inevitable that India and Pakistan should draw closer to each other, or else they will come into conflict. There is no middle way, for we have known each other too long to be indifferent neighbours. I believe indeed that in the present context of the world India must develop a closer union with many other neighbouring countries. But all this does not mean any desire to strangle or compel Pakistan. Compulsion there can never be, and an attempt to disrupt Pakistan would recoil to India's disadvantage. If we had wanted to break Pakistan, why did we agree to the partition? It was easier to prevent it then than to try to do so now after all that has happened. There is no going back in history. As a matter of fact it is to India's advantage that Pakistan should be a secure and prosperous state with which we can develop close and friendly relations. If today by any chance I were offered the reunion of India and Pakistan, I would decline it for obvious reasons. I do not want to carry the burden of Pakistan's great problems. I have enough of my own. Any closer association must come out of a normal process and in a friendly way which does not end Pakistan as a state, but makes it an equal part of a larger union in which several countries might be associated.

I have spoken of Pakistan because that subject must be in your minds and you would like to know what our attitude towards it is. Your minds are probably in a fluid state at present, not knowing which way to look and what to do.

All of us have to be clear about our basic allegiance to certain ideas. Do we believe in a national state which includes people of all religions and shades of opinion and is essentially secular as a state, or do we believe in the religious, theocratic conception of a state which regards people of other faiths as somebody beyond the pale? That is an odd question to ask, for the idea of a religious or theocratic state was given up by the world some centuries ago and has no place in the mind of the modern man. And yet the question has to be put in India today, for many of us have tried to jump back to a past age. I have no doubt that whatever our individual answers may be, it is not possible for us to go back to a conception that the world has outlived and that is completely out of tune with modern conceptions. As far as India is concerned, I can speak with some certainty. We shall proceed on secular and national lines in keeping with the powerful trends towards internationalism. Whatever confusion the present may contain, in the future, India will be a land, as in the past, of many faiths equally honoured and respected, but of one national outlook, not, I hope, a narrow nationalism living in its own shell, but rather the tolerant creative nationalism which, believing in itself and the genius of its people, takes full part in the establishment of an international order. The only ultimate aim we can have is that of one world. That seems a far cry today with warring groups and preparations for and shouting of world war three. Yet, despite all this shouting, that is the only aim that we can keep in view, for the alternative to world cooperation is world disaster.

We must cultivate this broad outlook and not be led away by the narrowness of others into becoming narrow in spirit and outlook ourselves. We have had enough of what has been called communalism in this country and we have tasted of its bitter and poisonous fruit. It is time that we put an end to it. For my part I do not like the intrusion of this communal spirit anywhere, and least of all in educational institutions. Education is meant to free the spirit of man and not to imprison it in set frames. I do not like this university being called the Muslim University just as I do not like the Benares University to be called the Hindu University. This does not mean that a university should not specialize in particular cultural subjects and studies. I think it is right that this university should lay special stress on certain aspects of Islamic thought and culture.

I want you to think about these problems and come to your conclusions. These conclusions cannot be forced upon you except to some extent, of course, by the compulsion of events which none of us can ignore. Do not think that you are outsiders here, for you are as much flesh and blood of India as anyone else, and you have every right to share in what India has to offer. But those who seek rights must share in the obligations also. Indeed, if the duties and obligations are accepted, then rights follow by themselves. I invite you as free citizens of free India to play your role in the building of this great country and to be sharers, in common with others, in the triumphs and setbacks alike that may come our way. The present with all its unhappiness and misery will pass. It is the future that counts, more especially to the young, and it is that future that beckons to you. How will you answer that call?

18

Abducted Men and Women[1]

May I say one thing rather personal, if I may say it? It has been a terrible time
for those who have to shoulder any responsibility. It has been, no doubt, a
terrible time for any sensitive human being who lives in India. The name of
India—and when I say 'India' I am not referring to the Dominion of India but
this country of India which will remain India, whatever political divisions
may take place—became mud because of what many Indians had done—and
Indians still live in Pakistan and they continue to be Indians, whether they call
themselves so or as Pakistanis. The curious position arose that those of our
detractors and enemies who live abroad and who often have to manufacture all
manner of stories and tales against us did not have to manufacture anything.
All that they had to do was to quote one person against another. All that they
had to say was what certain persons in Pakistan wrote about India and what
certain persons in India wrote about Pakistan. Now, we need not balance that.
I am merely saying that, what appeared in foreign countries, just quotations
from what Indians said against each other. Now, it may be, and I believe it is,
that when such things occur, there is a measure of right on one side, more right
and perhaps a measure of less evil, and more evil on the other. I need not tell
the House what my opinion on this subject is, as to where more right lies or
more evil. But the point is that so far as the outside world is concerned, it is
there—this mud-slinging, these acts, these horrible acts. What could they think
of India then? We may have been interested in clearing our honour as against
Pakistan and the Pakistan people no doubt wanted to show that they were not
evil-doers, but the fact remained that whatever the right or wrong, the reputation of the whole of India suffered and it became a dreadfully difficult thing
to clear that reputation. Blood has flown and many millions of people have shed
tears in this country. It was not easy to wipe ourselves clear of that blood till at

[1] Speech at the end of a discussion on a motion of relief and rehabilitation of refugees,
moved by K.C. Neogy, Minister for Relief and Rehabilitation, 29 November 1947. SWJN,
Vol. 4 (II Series), pp. 192–9. Excerpts.

last we approached the question, not in the way we had been approaching it, but in a spirit of healing, and not in a spirit of revengeful retaliation or of recrimination, although recrimination may have been justified. Retaliation does not help. That is the first point which I venture to place before the House regarding the spirit in which we should deal with this problem.

The second point—and it is also related to the first one—is that in those days when we lived fevered lives—speaking personally—I do not think I could have carried this burden at all but for one fact, and that fact was the magic presence of our great leader, Mahatma Gandhi. I have not a shadow of doubt in my mind that just as he performed a miracle in Bengal, so also he performed his miracle here. The obvious miracle may not have occurred here, but nonetheless there was the miracle of his presence which affected the situation tremendously. I would beg of you, therefore, to consider this problem in this context in regard to the future of India.

Now, coming to the problem directly, I would mention two essential facts of it which I consider most important. We have to look after the refugees, do this and that for millions of people, but whenever there is a huge problem, one inevitably has to give certain priorities. Talking about everything, trying to do everything, means sometimes that you do nothing at all. What are the obvious priorities in this problem? I say the obvious priority is that the youth, the students, young boys and girls should be saved, because after all the future of India depends upon them. All honour and respect to the older generation who are suffering, but the first priority must go to the youth who should be saved not only from the point of view of life, but saved from the point of view of broader things. They must be educated, they must be looked after and they must be made proper citizens of India. I think, (if I may), even as a Member of the Government criticize our own government, that we have not paid sufficient attention to this aspect of the problem. . . .

The second, though it is not second really, it is at least as important, is the saving of our womenfolk who have been abducted, and when I say that, let me repeat again, this is not a one-sided problem. Women have been abducted in both the Punjabs and elsewhere. Women have been abducted by the thousands, not just a few cases. Nobody knows the exact figures, but if you know the estimated figures, both for West Punjab and East Punjab, you will be staggered at the number. Therefore, one of the highest priorities should be given for the relief of these women. Of course, attempts have been made and thousands have been rescued, but tens of thousands still remain. Now this work cannot be done easily without the full cooperation of the two governments in the Punjab. It cannot be done otherwise. You can take an army and march in, and you may conquer and defeat the enemy, but you do not rescue anybody thereby. Therefore, we have to approach this problem from the point of view of cooperating with each other and, naturally, all parties are concerned in that cooperation, and in a certain measure we have achieved that cooperation, but not enough yet. I hope that within the next few days a more efficient organization will grow up in cooperation with both governments for the rescue of these abducted women. These two aspects I place specially before the House for consideration.

19

Industrial Policy[1]

I have myself been concerned with the theoretical aspects of planning for a fairly considerable time. I realize that there is a great deal of difference between the theory of it and the practice of it; as in almost everything in life the theory is full of poetry, but when we come down to applying that poetry all manner of difficulties crop up. Normally, there would be those difficulties but, as we are situated today, with the peculiar situation of India after all that has happened in the course of the last seven or eight months, one has to be very careful of what step one might take which might not injure the existing structure too much. There has been destruction and injury enough, and certainly I confess to this House that I am not brave and gallant enough to go about destroying much more. I think there is room for destruction in India still of many things—they will no doubt have to be removed; nevertheless, there is a way of approach.

. . . It seems to me that in the state of affairs in the world today and in India, any attempt to have what might be called a clean slate, that is to say a sweeping away of all that we have got, would certainly not bring progress nearer but might delay it tremendously, which far from bringing economic progress may put us politically so far back that the economic aspect itself may be delayed tremendously. We cannot separate these two things. We have gone through big political upheavals and cataclysms and if in our attempt to get something that we liked, to go forward one step in one direction, we lose a few steps in another, then in the balance we have lost, not gained. Therefore, the alternative to that clean slate is to try to rub out here and there and to write on it, gradually to replace the writing on the whole slate—not very gradually, I hope, but nevertheless not with a great measure of destruction and strain. . . .

There are going to be greater burdens on industry because the state itself is burdened so much with its social problems; it has to solve them or cease to be a social state, and if it just becomes a police state then it ceases to be and some other state takes it place. It has to face its problems, and if it is to do that it must necessarily get the wherewithal to face those problems, and the burden on

[1] Speech in the Constituent Assembly (Legislative), on a motion regarding the industrial policy of the Government, 7 April 1948. *Constituent Assembly of India (Legislative) Debates, Official Report*, Vol. V, 1948, pp. 3417–22. Excerpts.

industry or the like becomes greater and greater. In fact, not because you think or I think or anybody thinks, but inevitably the trend of events is to make the state more and more the organizer of constructive industry, etc., and not the private capitalist or any other person. That is just quite inevitable so far as I can see objectively. I do not rule out entirely the profit motives; I do not know how long it will last in a smaller sense, but in the larger sense of the term it will come more and more into conflict with the new sense of the social state. That conflict will go on and one must survive, and it is clear that the state will survive, not that group which represents in its pure essence the profit motive in industry. That is an inevitable development. How are you to face that development? Are you then again to try to accelerate it as many of us would like to do, because quite apart from the economic aspect, the expert aspect, we have arrived at another stage which I trust every sensitive man feels somewhat, a psychological view of looking at things. That is that sensitive people cannot put up easily today with the vast gap between human beings, the distance between them, the difference between them, the lack of opportunities on the one side and the waste on the other.

It seems so vulgar, and vulgarity is the worst thing that a country or individual should support. We are arriving at a stage which cannot tolerate it. It was not, if I may say so, vulgar fifty or a hundred years ago. Although the profit motive was functioning very strongly and although there was probably greater suffering then, nevertheless the approach was different. Perhaps the sense of social values was different. But, in the context of the world today, it is becoming increasingly not only a wrong thing from the economic point of view, but a vulgar thing, from any sensitive point of view. So, those changes are bound to come.

How then are you going to bring about those changes? As I said, I would much rather bring them about without deliberate destruction and obstruction, because the destruction and obstruction, whatever the future may bring after them, undoubtedly lead to stoppage of growth at present. They stop production. They stop wealth-producing activities. One has the satisfaction of being able to do something afterwards more rapidly, no doubt, but it is not such a certain thing that afterwards you will be able to do so rapidly. One has, therefore, to compromise much. Although I hate the word compromise in this context or in any context, one has simply to do it, if one does not stick to with some kind of a notion in one's head without thinking about it.

That brings us to a transitional stage of economy. Call it what you like—'mixed economy' or anything else. It brings us to doing things in such a way as to continually add to the wealth of the country and to add not only to the wealth of the country as a whole but to the distribution of that wealth in the country and gradually arrive at a stage when the centre of gravity of the whole economy has shifted the other way. Now, I rather doubt myself whether it is possible, without a conflict or without repeated conflicts, to bring about these changes quite peacefully, because the people who are used to possessing certain vested interests or certain ideas do not easily accept new ideas and nobody likes to give up what he has got; at least no group likes it; individuals sometimes do. The conflicts are continually arising, but the point is that even those conflicts are rather foolish conflicts, if I may say so, because those conflicts cannot stop the trend of events. They may delay, and in delaying, the result is probably that those who hold on to those vested interests get an even worse deal at the end.

20

The Hirakud Dam[1]

New Delhi, 15 April 1948

My dear Premier,

The Hirakud Dam is part of the great Mahanadi scheme of river valley development. The entire scheme is a mighty one and when it is fully realized, it ought to change the whole face of the province. The disastrous floods that have periodically overwhelmed Orissa will be a thing of the past. Large fresh areas will be brought under cultivation. The erosion of the soil will be stopped and more than two million kilowatts of electric power will be available for industry or other purposes. It is proposed also to have a deep water canal to the sea for inland navigation. All this is a fascinating vision of the future which fills one with enthusiasm. As I threw in some concrete, which was to form the base of the great Hirakud Dam, a sense of adventure seized me and I forgot for a while the many troubles that beset us. I felt that these troubles will pass, but that the great dam and all that follow from it will endure for ages to come. This is the first of our great schemes on which work has actually started. I hope that the Damodar Valley scheme will also be inaugurated soon and the many others about which we have been thinking so long. Unfortunately most of these schemes and projects have taken many long years in process of incubation, sometimes as long as thirty or forty years. The Mahanadi project is an exception as it was thought of first only three or four years ago and a great deal of work has been put in since then.

The laying of the foundation-stone of the capital city of Bhubaneswar turned out to be more exciting than I had thought. The site is an ideal one, undulating ground and a cool breeze coming from the sea. The past is represented by ancient temples, some of them famous for their architecture and artistry. Otherwise there is a clean slate to write upon. The architect[2] and the Chief Engineer have thought of this future city in terms not of a few palatial buildings but of a happy community. The capital is planned to help the people

[1] To Premiers of Provinces. File No. 25(6)-47-8-PMS. SWJN, Vol. 6 (II Series), pp. 251–6.

[2] Otto H. Koenigsberger.

who have to live and work and play there. It will be, I hope, a pleasant city with attractive buildings. First attention has been paid to the health, safety and education of the children and their schools and playgrounds have been specially laid out with this object in view. The new town will be grouped in self-contained neighbourhood units, each comprising about 850 families. This will enable the town to grow without losing its community and neighbourly character. In each area residential houses will surround the schools and shopping centres and will be near to open fields and recreation grounds. In the centre of the town will be a group of public buildings with a Gandhi memorial pillar symbolizing the life and teachings of Gandhiji. The new city is fortunate in having an architect of vision and engineers of both vision and capacity and its growth will be watched with great interest.

Yours sincerely,
Jawaharlal Nehru

21

Message on Independence Day[1]

Fellow countrymen, comrades and friends,

A year ago on this very day and at this very hour, I broadcasted to you from this place. Free India is one year old today, but what trials and tribulations she has passed through during this infancy of her freedom. She has survived in spite of all the peril and disaster that might well have overwhelmed a more mature and well-established nation. We have reason to be thankful for this achievement and for the many other achievements that stand to the credit of our people.

Let us not belittle our record or forget the courage, the hard work and the sacrifice with which our people have faced and overcome many of these perils, during this fateful year. But let us also not forget where we have failed or where we have erred, for our failure and errors have been many, some of these are obvious enough, but the real failure has been a failure of the spirit and a falling away from the high standards set by the Father of our Nation, under whose wise guidance we had struggled and marched for over a quarter of a century. He had taught us, that worthy ends can only be achieved through worthy means, that ideals and objectives can never be divorced from the methods adopted to realize them. He had told us to cast out fear, for fear is not only ignoble, but is also the parent of hatred and violence.

Many of us forgot this lesson and fear gripped us. Fear, not of some distant adversary, but fear of one another, and evil deeds followed in its train. The master who guided us and inspired us is no more. We have to shoulder the burden ourselves, and now the first question that we have to put to ourselves is this: do we stand by this teaching and message or do we stray into new paths? I want to tell you that this year of hard trials has convinced me, more than ever, that if India is to prosper and grow in stature, as she must and will, it will be through adherence to that message and teaching.

I know I am feeble and have often proved unworthy of India to whose service I have pledged myself so often. But, however unworthy we may be of India, we have still something of the strength that the master gave us. That

[1] Broadcast from Delhi, 15 August 1948. AIR tapes, NMML.

strength comes not only from him but from his message, and so, today, I pledge myself anew to the service of the motherland and of the ideals that Gandhiji placed before us!

All of us talk of India and all of us demand many benefits from India. What do we give to her in return? We can take nothing from her beyond what we give her. India will ultimately give us what we give her out of love and service and productive and creative work. India will be what we are. Our thoughts and actions will shape her. Born of her fruitful womb, we are children of hers, little bits of the India of today, and yet we are also the parents of the India of tomorrow. If we are big so will India be, and if we grow little-minded and narrow in outlook so also will India be. Our troubles during the past year were largely the result of this narrowness in outlook and pettiness in action, which is so foreign to India's great cultural inheritance.

Communalism threatened to crush the free spirit of us; the communalism of the Muslim, of the Hindu and of the Sikh. Provincialism came in the way of that larger unity which is so essential to India's greatness and progress. The spirit of faction spread and made us forget the big things that we have stood for.

We have to find ourselves again and go back to the free India of our dreams. We have to rediscover the old values and place them in the new setting of a free India. For freedom brings responsibility and can only be sustained by self-discipline, hard work, and the spirit of a free people.

So let us be rid of everything that limits us and degrades us. Let us cast out fear and communalism and provincialism. Let us build up a free and democratic India, where the interest of the masses of our people has always the first place, to which all other interests must submit. Freedom has no meaning unless it brings relief to these masses from their many burdens.

Democracy means tolerance. Tolerance not merely of those who agree with us but of those who do not agree with us. With the coming of freedom, our patterns of behaviour must change also so as to fit in with this freedom. There is conflict and there are rumours of greater conflict in India and all over the world. We have to be ready for every emergency and contingency. When the nation is in peril, the first duty of every citizen is to give his or her service to the nation without fear or expectation of reward.

But today I do not wish to speak of conflicts and wars but rather of peace and cooperation. I want to say to all the nations of the world, including our neighbouring countries, that we stand for peace and friendship with them. The only war that we want to fight with all our might is the war against poverty and all its unhappy brood.

All the world suffers from the after-effects of the World War and inflation, and rising prices, and unemployment oppresses the people. In India, we have all these and, in addition, the care of vast numbers of our brothers and sisters, who have suffered untold hardship and have been driven away from their homes to seek a new life elsewhere. It is this war we have to fight, the war against economic crisis, and to rehabilitate the disinherited. In this war there is no hatred or violence, but only service of our country and our people. In this war, every Indian can be a soldier.

This is no time for individuals or groups to think of a narrow self-interest, forgetting the larger good. This is no time for wrangling or the spirit of faction, and so I appeal to all my countrymen and countrywomen, who have the love of India in their hearts and the passion to raise her masses, to cast aside the barriers that separate them and to join together in this historic and magnificent task worthy of a great people.

To all those in our services, civil and military, I would appeal for a single-minded devotion to the cause of India and for integrity, hard work, efficiency and impartiality. He who fails at this critical hour, fails in his duty to India and her people.

To the youth of the country, I would make a special appeal, for they are the leaders of tomorrow and on them will be cast the burden of upholding India's honour and freedom. My generation is a passing one, and soon we shall hand over the bright torch of India, which embodies her great and eternal spirit to younger hands and stronger arms. May they hold it aloft, undimmed and untarnished, so that its light reaches every home and brings faith and courage and well-being to our masses. *Jai Hind.*

22

The Socialist Party[1]

New Delhi, August 19, 1948

My dear Jayaprakash,

I am greatly distressed at many things in India. But perhaps what distresses me most is the wide gap which is ever growing between many of us and the Socialist Party. That, I think, is not good either for us or the Socialist Party, and certainly not good for the country. It may be that we are largely responsible for this. But I certainly think that the Socialist Party is at least as responsible. Responsibility apart, it seems to me patent that the Socialist Party is making itself rather ineffective at least for some time to come. Long-distance programmes may be followed, but when big crises occur in the near future, then long-distance programmes are of little use and indeed they are put out of joint by previous happenings. If I may remind you, the Socialist Party's attitude to the Constituent Assembly[2] was most unfortunate.

I had hoped that the going out of the Socialist Party from the Congress would reduce the internal tension. As a matter of fact it has had the opposite result and the gulf grows. Whatever the merits of the Socialist Party's programme may be, I do not see how, standing by itself, it can hope to be in a position to give effect to it for a considerable time to come. The result will naturally be that it will try to ally itself with various groups which, generally speaking, are undesirable and which will bring no credit to the Socialist Party. Indeed I have received reports of such attempts at alliance. I do hope they are not true. For it will be a bad day for the Socialist Party if it gets associated with small factions which are never likely to face responsibility, or even with reactionary groups which may indulge in tall talk but which are essentially reactionary.

[1] To Jayaprakash Narayan. S. Vijayalakshmi (ed.), *Sri Jayaprakash Narayan—Sixtyfirst Birthday Celebration: Commemoration Volume*, (Madras, 1962), p. 151. Excerpts.

[2] At the AICC meeting of 6 July 1946 the Socialists had opposed the Working Committee decision to accept the long-term proposals of the Cabinet Mission. Jayaprakash Narayan had said the Constituent Assembly would not bring independence for it was a creation of the British and could not work freely as long as British power remained. Later, on 24 November 1946 he said that the members of the AICC and not the Congress members of the Constituent Assembly should decide the shape of swaraj.

I know that you can and do criticize the present Government strongly. You may be right, and certainly I have no particular objection to your criticism, except it is usually rather negative criticism which does not help much. If the Socialist Party thinks in terms of controlling governmental policy, it must think also and act as if it was on the point of becoming a government and not merely negatively, and in any event it does not pay thus to run down individuals or groups who represent something that has strength in the country.

I think the next few months or years are going to be rather critical for our country and it will be a great pity if the gulf between the Socialist Party and the Congress is not bridged to some extent at least, and tends to grow. There will be a sense of frustration and ineffectiveness. I should like therefore to help in every way to reduce that gulf and I hope you will try to do the same.

. . . We have terrible problems in India and big things to accomplish. We cannot fulfil our destiny if we think too much in terms of a group or a party, however good that might be, and even in terms of that group or party an isolationist attitude can seldom help.

I write to you rather briefly, but even these few lines will convey to you something I have in my mind. I cannot, by sheer force of circumstance, do everything that I would like to do. We are all of us in some measure prisoners of fate and circumstances. But I am as keen as ever to go in a particular direction and carry the country with me and I do hope that in doing so I would have some help from you. I need not tell you that we are living at a very critical time and dangers threaten us in many directions. It may be that we are not strong enough or wise enough to face these problems, but for the moment I do not see any other group that can do so more successfully. You will remember at the least what the recent history of Europe has taught us, that an attempt at premature leftism may well lead to reaction or disruption.

Yours affectionately,
Jawaharlal Nehru

23

Objectives Resolution and the Draft Constitution[1]

Sir, we are on the last lap of our long journey. Nearly two years ago, we met in this hall and on that solemn occasion it was my high privilege to move a resolution which has come to be known as the Objectives Resolution.[2] That is rather a prosaic description of that resolution because it embodied something more than mere objectives, although objectives are big things in the life of a nation. It tried to embody, in so far as it is possible in cold print to embody, the spirit that lay behind the Indian people at the time.

. . . A constitution if it is out of touch with the people's life, aims and aspirations, becomes rather empty; if it falls behind those aims, it drags the people down. It should be something ahead to keep people's eyes and minds up to a certain high mark. I think that the Objectives Resolution did that. Inevitably since then in the course of numerous discussions, passions were roused about. What I would beg to say are relatively unimportant matters in this larger context of giving shape to a nation's aspirations and will. Not that they were unimportant, because each thing in a nation's life is important, but still there is a question of priority, there is a question of relative importance, there is a question also of what comes first and what comes second. After all there may be many truths, but it is important to know what is the first truth. It is important to know what in a particular context of events is the first thing to be done, to be thought of and to be put down, and it is the test of a nation and a people to be able to distinguish between the first things and the second things. If we put the second things first, then inevitably the first and the most important things suffer a certain eclipse.

Now I have ventured with your permission, Sir, to take part in this initial debate on this Draft Constitution,[3] but it is not my intention to deal with any particular part of it, either in commendation of it or in criticism, because a great deal has already been said and will no doubt be said. But in view of that perhaps

[1] Speech in the Constituent Assembly, 8 November 1948. *Constituent Assembly of India Debates, Official Report*, Vol. VIII, 4 November 1948 to 8 January 1949, pp. 317–23.

[2] See Vol. I, pp. 403–4.

[3] On 4 November B.R. Ambedkar, Chairman of the Drafting Committee, introduced the Draft Constitution.

I could make some useful contribution to this debate by drawing attention to certain fundamental factors again. . . .

We who have lived through this period of transition with all its triumphs and glories and sorrows and bitterness, we are affected by all these changes; we are changing ourselves; we do not notice ourselves changing or the country changing so much and it is a little helpful to be out of this turmoil for a while and to look at it from a distance and to look at it also to some extent with the eyes of other people. I have had that opportunity given to me. I am glad of that opportunity, because for the moment I was rid of the tremendous burden of responsibility which all of us carried and which in a measure some of us who have to shoulder the burden of government have to carry more. For a moment I was rid of those immediate responsibilities and with a mind somewhat free I could look at that picture and I saw from that distance the rising star of India far above the horizon and casting its soothing light, in spite of all that has happened, over many countries of the world, who looked up to it with hope, who considered that out of this new free India would come various forces which would help Asia, which would help the world somewhat to right itself, which would cooperate with other similar forces elsewhere, because the world is in a bad way, because this great continent of Asia or Europe and the rest of the world are in a bad way and are faced with problems which might almost appear to be insurmountable. And sometimes one has the feeling as if we were all actors in some terrible Greek tragedy which was moving on to its inevitable climax of disaster. Yet when I looked at this picture again from afar and from here, I had a feeling of hope and optimism not merely because of India, but because also of other things that I saw that the tragedy which seemed inevitable was not necessarily inevitable, that there were many other forces at work, that there were innumerable men and women of goodwill in the world who wanted to avoid this disaster and tragedy, and there was certainly a possibility that they will succeed in avoiding it.

But to come back to India, we have, ever since I moved this Objectives Resolution before this House—a year and eleven months ago, almost exactly—passed through strange transitions and changes. We function here far more independently than we did at that time. We function as a sovereign independent nation, but we have also gone through a great deal of sorrow and bitter grief during this period and all of us have been powerfully affected by it. The country for which we were going to frame this Constitution was partitioned and split into two. And what happened afterwards is fresh in our minds and will remain fresh with all its horrors for a very long time to come. And yet, in spite of all this, India has grown in strength and in freedom, and undoubtedly this growth of India, this emergence of India as a free country, is one of the significant facts of this generation, significant for us and for the vast numbers of our brothers and sisters who live in this country, significant for Asia, and significant for the world. . . .

Therefore, I would beg of this House to consider these great responsibilities that have been thrust upon India, and because we represent India in this as in many other spheres, on us in this House, and to work together in the framing of the Constitution or otherwise, always keeping that in view, because the eyes of the world are upon us and the hope and aspirations of a great part of the world are also upon us. We dare not belittle: if we do so, we do an ill-service to this country of ours and to those hopes and aspirations that surround us from other countries. It is in this way that I would like this House to consider this Constitution: first of all to keep the Objectives Resolution before us and to see how far we are going to act up to it, how far we are going to build up as we said in that Resolution, "an Independent Sovereign Republic, wherein all power and authority of the Sovereign Independent India, its constituent parts and organs of Government, are derived from the people, and wherein shall be guaranteed and secured to all of the people of India justice, social, economic and political; equality of status, of opportunity, and before the law; freedom of thought and expression, belief, faith, worship, vocation, association and action, subject to law and public morality; and this ancient land attains its rightful and honoured place in the world and makes its full and willing contribution to the promotion of world peace and the welfare of mankind."

I read that last clause in particular because that brings to our mind India's duty to the world. I should like this House when it considers the various controversies—there are bound to be controversies and there should be controversies because we are a living and vital nation, and it is right that people should think differently and it is also right that, thinking differently when they come to decisions, they should act unitedly in furtherance of those decisions. There are various problems, some very important problems, on which there is very little controversy and we pass them—they are of the greatest importance—with a certain unanimity. There are other problems, important no doubt, possibly of a lesser importance, on which we spend a great deal of time and energy and passion also, and do not arrive at agreements in that spirit with which we should arrive at agreements. In the country today, reference has been made—I will mention one or two matters—to linguistic provinces and to the question of language in this Assembly and for the country. I do not propose to say much about these questions, except to say that it seems to me and it has long seemed to me inevitable that in India some kind of reorganization should take place of provinces, etc., to fit in more with the cultural, geographical and economic condition of the people and with their desires. We have long been committed to this. I do not think it is good enough just to say linguistic provinces; that is a major factor to be considered, no doubt. But there are more important factors to be considered, and you have therefore to consider the whole picture before you proceed to break up what we have got and refashion it into something new. What I would like to place before the House is that, important from the point of view of our future life and governance as this question is, I would not have thought that this was a question of that primary importance, which must be settled here and now today. It is eminently a question which should be settled in an atmosphere of good-will and calm and on a rather scholarly discussion of the various factors of the case. . . .

The same argument, if I may say so, applies to this question of language. Now, it is an obvious thing and a vital thing that any country, much more so a free and independent country, must function in its own language. Unfortunately, the mere fact that I am speaking to this House in a foreign language and so many of our colleagues here have to address the House in a foreign language itself shows that something is lacking. It is lacking, let us recognize it, we shall get rid of that lacuna undoubtedly. But, if in trying to press for a change, an immediate change, we get wrapped up in numerous controversies and possibly even delay the whole Constitution, I submit to this House it is not a very wise step to take. Language is and has been a vital factor in an individual's and a nation's life and because it is vital, we have to give it every thought and consideration. Because it is vital, it is also an urgent matter; and because it is vital, it is also a matter in which urgency may ill serve our purpose. There is a slight contradiction. Because, if we proceed in an urgent matter to impose something, may be by a majority, on an unwilling minority in parts of the country or even in this House, we do not really succeed in what we have started to achieve. . . .

The House will remember that when I brought that motion of the Objectives Resolution before this House, I referred to the fact that we were asking for or rather we were laying down that our Constitution should be framed for an Independent Sovereign Republic. I stated at that time and I have stated subsequently this business of our being a Republic is entirely a matter for us to determine of course. It has nothing or little to do with what relations we should have with other countries, notably the United Kingdom or the Commonwealth that used to be called the British Commonwealth of Nations. That was a question which had to be determined again by this House and by none else, independently of what our Constitution was going to be. . . . We pass that Constitution for an Independent Sovereign Democratic India, for a Republic as we choose, and the second question is to be considered separately at whatever time it suits this House. It does not in any sense fetter this Constitution of ours or limit it because this Constitution coming from the people of India through their representatives represents their free will with regard to the future governance of India.

Now, may I beg again to repeat what I said earlier and that is this: that destiny has cast a certain role on this country. Whether anyone of us present here can be called men or women of destiny or not I do not know. That is a big word which does not apply to average human beings, but whether we are men or women of destiny or not, India is a country of destiny, and so far as we represent this great country with a great destiny stretching out in front of her, we also have to function as men and women of destiny, viewing all our problems in that long perspective of destiny and of the World and of Asia, never forgetting the great responsibility that freedom, that this great destiny of our country has cast upon us, not losing ourselves in petty controversies and debates which may be useful but which will in this context be either out of place or out of tune. Vast numbers of minds and eyes look in this direction. We have to remember them. Hundred of millions of our own people look to us and hundreds of millions of others also look to us; and remember this, that while we want this Constitution to be as solid and as permanent a structure as we can make it, nevertheless there is no permanence in Constitutions. There should be a certain flexibility. If you make anything rigid and permanent, you stop a nation's growth, the growth of a living vital organic people. Therefore, it has to be flexible. . . .

May I say one word again about certain tendencies in the country which still think in terms of separatist existence or separate privileges and the like? This very Objectives Resolution set out adequate safeguards to be provided for minorities, for tribal areas, depressed and other backward classes. Of course that must be done, and it is the duty and responsibility of the majority to see that this is done and to see that they win over all minorities which may have suspicions against them, which may suffer from fear. It is right and important that we should raise the level of the backward groups in India and bring them up to the level of the rest. But it is not right that in trying to do this we create further barriers, or even keep on existing barriers, because the ultimate objective is not separatism but building up an organic nation, not necessarily a uniform nation because we have a varied culture, and in this country ways of living differ in various parts of the country, habits differ and cultural traditions differ. I have no grievance against that. Ultimately in the modern world there is a strong tendency for the prevailing culture to influence others. That may be a natural influence. But I think the glory of India has been the way in which it has managed to keep two things going at the same time: that is, its infinite variety and at the same time its unity in that variety. Both have to be kept, because if we have only variety, then that means separatism and going to pieces. If we seek to impose some kind of regimented unity, that makes a living organism rather lifeless. Therefore, while it is our bounden duty to do everything we can to give full opportunity to every minority or group and to raise every backward group or class, I do not think it will be a right thing to go the way this country has gone in the past by creating barriers and by calling for protection. As a matter fact nothing can protect such a minority or a group less than a barrier which separates it from the majority. It makes it a permanently isolated group and it prevents it from any kind of tendency to bring it closer to the other groups in the country.

24

Development of River Valleys[1]

Life itself is a rather intricate and complicated affair for the individual and for the nation and it is sometimes difficult to say which of any two things is more important, for each depends upon the other. Nevertheless it is true that the development of river valleys in India is of the most basic and fundamental importance. For a number of years past I have been very greatly interested in this matter not as an engineer, because I am not an engineer, but in its wider public aspect of being, in a sense, the foundation of very large-scale planning in India. I have been interested in planning because it seems such an extraordinary and such an unfortunate fact that with all the potential resources available in India, and in a way it applies to the whole world, that all these enormous resources have not been utilized to raise the standard of living of our people and our nation.

There was a time in the past—in the long past—when it might have been said with some correctness that the world's resources were not really enough to raise the standard of living of the population of the world to the extent desired. Now I suppose it must be clear to the meanest intelligence that with the proper utilization of the present resources of the world, or of India if you like, we can raise the standard very greatly. That can be shown with a pencil and paper. Nevertheless the fact remains that not only did we not utilize them to the best advantage but we wasted these resources in destructive activities. That is the tragedy of the present generation, even more so than it has been of past generations.

As always found in history, we find to an acute degree today this conflict between the forces of constructive effort and of destruction. We find this conflict in the attitude of nations to one another, in groups and ultimately perhaps in the spirit of man himself. Now no man can be prophet enough to say what is going to happen. Nevertheless any man can work effectively, with the faith in him that the forces of constructive and creative effort shall win. I have no doubt that they will win but I do not know what damage the other forces might

[1] Address to the nineteenth annual meeting of the Central Board of Irrigation, New Delhi, 5 December 1948. File No. 17 (107)/48-PMS. Excerpts.

bring about by delaying the process of planning and of raising the standard of humanity.

Well, we have to convert this vast potential into actuality. Look at the map of Asia and of India. It stares me in my room and in my office and whenever I look at it, all kinds of pictures come into my mind; pictures of the long past of our history, of the gradual development of man from the earliest stages, of great caravan routes, of the early beginning of culture, civilization and agriculture, and of the early days when perhaps the first canals and irrigation works were made and all that flows from them. Then I think of the future. My attention is concentrated on that huge block of massive mountains called the Himalayas which guard our northern frontier. Look at them. Think of them. Can you think of any other part of the world similar to it in extent, which is as great a reservoir of power, of potential strength and power? I know no other place in the world which has as much tremendous power locked up as in the Himalayas and the water which comes to the rivers from them. How are we to utilize it? There are many ways. Essentially it is the job of the engineers to tap this tremendous reserve of power for the benefit of the people. It falls to the lot of you engineers to play a very effective and vitally important role in this work. Looked at from that point of view the profession and work of an engineer in India is of the highest importance and significance.

You can judge the growth of a nation by finding out which class of that nation, in a particular period of history, is held in honour and repute more than the others. At one time you may find that the landholder, the proprietor of the land is a noble man and he is held in greatest esteem. From that you can judge the nature of the society of that period. So you will find various occupations occupying the forefront at different periods and you can come to some conclusion as to the nature of the social background of the society of the time: whether it is static, whether it is creative or whether its growth is dynamically constructive.

. . . The world as it is constituted today is tremendously dynamic. That is right of course and that is inevitable even if somehow we have been failing in that because the world as it is constituted today is in a stage of revolutionary change of the kind that you just cannot help except to try but change yourself, otherwise, you get into trouble. Apart from that, coming back to India, we passed through a period—a fairly long one though it was very short in terms of India's long history—a period which though changing undoubtedly, was, nevertheless in another sense unchanging—this British period in our history. Changes work consciously and unconsciously but when the superior outside power dominates a certain situation, the various forces that are working inside the country are curbed by that power and they cannot easily find balance and adjustment between themselves. That finding of balance is achieved by the evolutionary process or by a revolutionary process or by peaceful or violent means. Always in any human society there is an attempt to find a balance and so long as it does not succeed, there is trouble. Now when some outside agency prevents that balance the result for the moment may be even good if you like, but the result is that problems accumulate—problems which history solves in its own way, sometimes peacefully sometimes in a bloody way. If you do not solve it, you solve the problems by killing it. So also with nations and communities, but when this extraordinary agency prevents that solution, problems accumulate. So in India problems accumulated. The problem of the Indian States has no doubt been solved. Our agrarian problems which ought to have been solved long ago dragged on and on till we had to face them and to solve them in a hurry when these should have been solved gradually and in a much better way. Now because problems have accumulated we have today to face not one problem but a multitude of problems and it is very difficult to say that you set aside all those problems or take up one or two first. We just cannot, because if we slacken our attempt to solve problems and merely concentrate on one or another, the other problems tend to overwhelm us. Let us take the problem of refugees—millions of them. It is not a fundamental problem as problems go. It is a temporary problem but it is of exceeding importance. It is important because a large number of human beings and their lives are involved and where human lives in large numbers are involved it is of vital significance to the nation. We cannot allow that human material to deteriorate and to simply go to pieces but apart from that, apart from the human aspect of it, if we try to ignore it, the problem becomes worse and comes in the way of other problems.

These accumulated problems have to be faced to some extent together. One has to proceed on various fronts and one has to see that progress is more or less coordinated on each front or else you go ahead in one front and there is a bottleneck and you have to stop. That is where planning comes in, planning becomes essential.

We have talked about planning for a considerable time in India. I myself have been associated with the planning schemes and the like. I must confess to a feeling of exceeding disappointment that all our effort has not yielded better results as I expected and as results should have been. When you know what has happened in the past and our difficulties and our failings in the matter it is well, if I may say so, for each one of us whether he happens to occupy a very responsible position as a Prime Minister or other minister or any other important officer of the state, it is well always to think in terms of any problem that we are entrusted with, not as if failure was somebody else's fault but that we are our-selves responsible for any failure that may occur. There is too much of a ten-dency for each one of us and again I say—I include the Prime Minister and other ministers in this category—always to think in terms of somebody else having failed. If each person thought of his own job and that he has failed in it we would get

on better with the problem. The fact is that each major job requires the cooperation and the good work of a large number of persons from the top to the bottom
and if that cooperation is lacking, this spirit of working together is lacking—
then that job is not done properly or is delayed and then it does not serve much
useful purpose for us to go on finding fault with each other though sometimes
that may be necessary. We have various jobs to do in this country in every field.
Somebody said once that we have been born in a period of world history which
is both changing and revolutionary and many inconceivable things are happening. Now it is no good complaining of those inconceivable happenings. Since
we are born we have to face them. We cannot escape. Not being able to escape
we have to face them like men and conquer these difficulties. I am afraid in our
generation—I do not know about succeed-ing generations—there is going to
be little rest or real peace. There are going to be no dividends of leisure and
repose brought about for our generation. The prospect before us is work, hard
labour. This generation is sentenced to hard labour. That hard labour can be
of the type of constructive activity which, however hard, is something that
raises the community and the nation, or it may be in fruitless ways, or even in
evil ways, but hard labour you cannot escape. Therefore let us divert that hard
labour into constructive and creative channels so that at least it may be said of
this generation that we helped to build up our country to the extent possible
so that the next generation and succeeding gene-rations may have leisure—
greater leisure, though I am not myself keen on too much leisure for any
individual but some leisure there ought to be.

25

Relief and Rehabilitation[1]

New Delhi, 6 March 1949

My dear Mohanlal,

I am greatly worried about the relief and rehabilitation situation. The immediate cause is the hunger-strike in Kingsway Camp.[2] But that is just a temporary cause. My real worry is that I have a feeling that there is very little human touch about our relief or rehabilitation schemes. All government or other activities require human understanding and human appeal. But in regard to relief and rehabilitation, this human appeal and understanding is of the most vital significance. I have an idea that vague schemes are put forward, very good in themselves, and usually left in the air with nobody to work for; that the Relief Ministry functions very strictly as a government department with no life in it and no human approach to the people concerned; that the ministry does not produce an impression of coordinated working or of carrying things to an end; policies are laid down and changed, and the people concerned are left in doubt as to where they are.

The scheme of converting relief camps into work centres was obviously a good one. Indeed it is the only way to proceed. And yet I do not know of any attempt really to work it out in practice and it was apparently expected that an automatic change would take place. There are some ideal work centres like Nilokheri, etc. But apart from these fine examples, things are left much to themselves. More especially in regard to the state, instructions are issued that relief camps should be turned into work centres and that the rations should either be stopped or reduced from a certain date. Having issued these instructions, no doubt the Relief Ministry thinks that it has done its duty. But the

[1] To Mohanlal Saksena, JN Papers, NMML. Excerpts.

[2] Eight refugees at Kingsway Camp went on hunger-strike for three days to protest against the proposed discontinuation of the "refugee allowance" and the generally unsympathetic attitude of the authorities towards the refugee problem. The demands put forward by the Camp Association included grant of individual loans, continuation of their rations and allowances till they were properly rehabilitated and allotted residential and business accommodation in Delhi.

persons concerned at the other end have no conception of how to convert a relief camp into a work centre. Indeed this requires very special training and only a trained person can bring about this change.

Therefore, it becomes necessary that a trained organization should be built up for the purpose of converting camps into work centres. This organization should have a team of workers, which would contain some technical men also and organizers and persons knowing social work. This is not the business of a government officer sitting in an office issuing orders. So far as I know, this approach has not been made. We have talked recently about training social workers and something is being done. But something much more has got to be done, if really we are going to have work centres and this must be done centrally and cannot be left to local authorities. It is not fair to pass an order, make no other arrangements and then suddenly stop rations. I can very well understand the resentment caused to people who are frustrated and spiritless. . . .

What worries me, I repeat, is the wooden way of dealing with this problem which seems to ignore human psychology. I wish you would impress upon all your officers that such an approach is completely ineffective. Indeed I should like to meet all your officers and address them myself. The Relief Ministry cannot function as a normal government department, but as a social welfare centre. Indeed I am beginning to think that the whole work should be organized from the social welfare point of view.

Yours sincerely
Jawaharlal Nehru

26

Formation of New Provinces[1]

In June 1948 the President of the Constituent Assembly of India appointed a Commission to examine and report on the formation of the new provinces of Andhra, Karnataka, Kerala and Maharashtra. The Chairman of this Commission was Shri S.K. Dar. This Commission presented its report on the eve of the Jaipur Congress.[2] The Congress thereupon appointed the Committee of which we are members, to consider the question of linguistic province and "to review the position and to examine the question in the light of the decisions taken by the Congress in the past and the requirements of the existing situation, (i) in view of the report of the Linguistic Provinces Commission, appointed by the President of the Constituent Assembly, and (ii) the new problems that have arisen out of the achievement of independence."

. . . The Congress had thus given the seal of its approval to the general principle of linguistic provinces. It was not faced with the practical application of this principle and hence it had not considered all the implications and consequences that arose from this practical application. There had, however, been a persistent demand and agitation for the formation of Andhra and the Karnataka Province. The Congress approval of this principle was partly due to the artificial manner in which existing provinces had been created by the British power in India. It was chiefly due to a desire to have, as far as possible, homogeneous cultural units which would presumably advance more rapidly because of this homogeneity.

It is clear that in giving effect to this principle a great many difficulties of a far-reaching character have to be faced. Whatever the origin of these provinces, and however artificial they may have been, a century or so of political, administrative and to some extent economic unity in each of the existing provincial areas had produced a certain stability and a certain tradition, and any change in this would naturally have considerable upsetting effect. It would have

[1] Draft prepared by Jawaharlal Nehru on 26 March 1949 and accepted by the Linguistic Provinces Committee appointed at the Jaipur Congress. President's Secretariat File No. 205–66/47. Excerpts.

[2] 55th Session of the Indian National Congress was held at Jaipur from 14–20 December 1948.

certain far-reaching consequences, political, economic, financial and administrative. These reasons of course were not necessarily enough for us to go back on, what had long been considered, a basic principle of the Congress. But these reasons could not be ignored, just as the course of history with all that had resulted from it could not be ignored. In the consideration of this problem, all these factors had to be kept in mind and balanced with each other.

But what we have to consider even more are, as the Congress resolution says, the new problems that have arisen since the achievement of independence. That independence was accompanied by a partition of the country and tremendous upheavals which shook the entire fabric of the state. Anti-social forces grew and assumed serious proportions just at a time when the closest unity was essential. A narrow provincialism became a menace to the progress and development of our great country. The Indian States underwent a tremendous sea-change into something new. Many of them were merged and lost their identity, though their internal structure underwent a change. The whole map of India was transformed. All these processes have already proceeded far and made a great difference to India. They are still continuing and the final picture has not wholly emerged yet.

Thus ever since the achievement of independence, we have been passing through an exceedingly dynamic stage of our country's existence; we have faced perils and dangers such as few countries have experienced in the initial stages of their freedom; we have tackled problems of great magnitude; and we have struggled against narrow-mindedness and faction as well as the more serious anti-social elements of society. Whether the result of our labours has been satisfactory or not, the future historian will have to decide. It is, however indispensable that if these changes have to be fully exploited in the country's interests, we must consolidate the gains and this must be done as quickly as possible. Nor can there be any doubt that these new problems that have arisen since August 1947 have made a vast difference to India. We have to adjust all our thinking and our activity to the new state of India and the problems of today. There can be no greater error than to think of today in terms of yesterday, or to seek to solve today's problem in terms of yesterday's.

It becomes incumbent upon us, therefore, to view the problem of linguistic provinces in the context of today. That context demands, above everything, the consolidation of India and her freedom, the progressive solution of her economic problems in terms of the masses of her people, the promotion of unity in India and of the close cooperation among the various provinces and states in most spheres of activity. It demands further stern discouragement of communalism, provincialism, and all other separatist disruptive tendencies. The achievement of political freedom for India and the integration that has come about do not mean the end of our labours or the toning down of that vivid patriotic sentiment which gave life and strength to our struggle for freedom.

Apart from the fact that freedom, in its political context, is not broad enough and has to be enlarged in the economic domain and can only then be called true freedom for the people, the preservation of even this political freedom is an urgent and ever-present necessity. If we cease to be vigilant and allow our minds to drift to other channels, we shall not only do an ill service to India, but might also imperil the very freedom which the past and the present generations have achieved after tremendous sacrifices.

This is the fundamental basis for the consideration of every problem in India and we can only consider the problem of linguistic provinces on this basis. All else, however, important and however desirable, have a lesser priority.

The partition of India, resulting in the formation of Pakistan, did grievous injury to this country. That injury was obvious enough in many ways and it upset the whole structure of the state and of our economy in a hundred ways. Both in India and in Pakistan these grievous consequences followed and it is only slowly that we are recovering from these deep wounds to the body, mind and spirit of India. This partition has led us to become wary of anything that tends to separate and divide. It is true there can be no real comparison between this partition and the linguistic regrouping of India. But it is also true that in the existing fluid state of India, even small things in themselves may lead to evil consequences and let loose forces which do injury to the unity of India. . . .

We have such, during the past year or more, passionate demands not only for new linguistic provinces to be formed, but also for a readjustment of boundaries between the existing provinces. These demands may often be justified on the merits, but the manner in which they have been presented and the passion that lay behind this presentation, has been a warning to all of us about the inherent danger of changing the existing structure. At the present moment of our history, when some of the smaller states have been merged into a province, a neighbouring province has objected with such violence and language that one would have almost thought that two countries were on the verge of war. These are evil symptoms and we have to be very careful lest we do anything to encourage them.

However definite such an area might be, it flows into another linguistic area and where the two may meet, is a mixed bilingual area. Inevitably if a linguistic division is made, there will be trouble about this middle area and it will not be easy to decide where it should go. Immediately conflict will arise and passions will be aroused. People's attention will be diverted from the urgent problems of the day, which are essentially economic, to this totally unnecessary conflict which can do good to no one. It is possible that when conditions are more static and the state of people's minds calmer, the adjustment of these boundaries or the creation of new provinces can be handled with relative ease and with advantage to all concerned. Such conditions do not prevail today in India and we are, therefore, entirely averse to recommending changes, unless vital considerations make such changes inescapable. While a language is a binding force, it is also a separating one. We have to balance all these considerations as well as many others in arriving at any decision. . . .

We feel that the conditions that have emerged in India since the achievement of independence are such as to make us view the problem of linguistic provinces in a new light. The first consideration must be the security, unity and economic prosperity of India and every separatist disruptive tendency should be rigorously discouraged. Therefore, the old Congress policy of having linguistic provinces can only be applied after careful thought being given to each separate case, and without creating serious administrative dislocation or mutual conflicts which would jeopardize the political and economic stability of the country. We would prefer to postpone the formation of new provinces for a few years so that we might concentrate during this period on other matters of vital importance and not allow ourselves to be distracted by this question. However, if public sentiment is insistent and overwhelming, we, as democrats, have to submit to it, but subject to certain limitations in regard to the good of India as a whole and certain conditions which we have specified above. Public sentiment must clearly realize the consequences of any further division so that it may fully appreciate what will flow from their demand. We feel that the case of Andhra Province should be taken up first and the question of its implementation examined before we can think of considering the question of any other province.

We are clearly of opinion that no question on rectification of boundaries in the provinces of northern India should be raised at the present moment, whatever the merit of such a proposal might be.

27

Horse Breeding[1]

New Delhi, 19 June 1949

My dear Premier,

From the facts that have been brought to my notice, the policy adopted by the Bombay Government in the late thirties was remarkably successful in promoting horse-breeding in India and keeping out import of foreign horses. Further it helped greatly in minimizing a great deal of illegal betting by having totalizators at the races. In other words, that policy was a marked success from both these points of view. A policy that has succeeded and that is showing results should not be easily abandoned at any time, more specially, at a time when we have to face very difficult problems in other spheres of national life. The attempted change means an upsetting of some things and a diversion of national energy and time and money to relatively unimportant matters when far more important matters demand that time, energy and money.

There is a certain practical aspect of this question which can be considered objectively and dispassionately from the point of view of the practical gains or losses consequent on any policy being adopted. There is also another aspect which I think is worthy of consideration. That is an aspect of the state making inroads into the personal liberty of the individual.

So far as the practical aspect is concerned, it seems to me clear that the immediate effect of any upsetting of the existing policy would certainly lead to a discouragement of horse-breeding, whatever the long-distance consequences might be. National Horse-Breeding and Show Society of India has shown good results in this respect during the fairly short period of its existence. It would be affected by any change and may have seriously to curtail its activities. It may be that the army or the civil government might undertake horse-breeding but that obviously would be a costly business, casting an additional burden on the nation's finances. Even so the incentive for improving the breed which comes from horse-racing would not be there. In recent years it has been shown with remarkable success that India can breed the best type of horses. This fact was not admitted previously. Undoubtedly if racing becomes a third-rate affair in

[1] To B.G. Kher. File No. 40(211).51–PMS. SWJN, Vol. II (II Series), pp. 21–3. Excerpts.

India or ceases, then certain inducements to produce the first quality of thoroughbreds would be lacking and the quality would go down. I think it is true that racing depends a good deal at the present moment on betting being associated with it. If betting goes, then racing also suffers greatly. The betting can of course be regulated in a variety of ways to prevent this mischief spreading.

. . . There is weight in the argument that an evil should not be encouraged even though it might be revenue-producing for the government. That may be perfectly true. But human frailties are not usually got rid of by legislation. The modern approach is somewhat different. What happens often enough is that when a direct attempt is made by legislation to put down what is considered an evil, this takes more serious and dangerous forms and thus the final result is even worse.

Then there is the wholly different approach to the question of what might be called moral legislation by the government. There is a view, strongly held, that a government should avoid as far as possible this type of legislation unless it is considered absolutely necessary. Opinions differ about what is moral and what is not even among the best of us. If a government starts interfering in this way by law, it is entering a dangerous field. One government may have one standard or measure of morals, another government another standard. Between various governments the unhappy citizen will not know where he stands and what he can do and what he cannot. Fundamentally moral standards can only be improved by the educational and like processes aided now and then by the law. A puritanical approach to human problems is bad enough when indulged in by individuals. It is indefinitely worse when a government begins to function in that way.

We have today to contend against very grave evils. To mention some of them, there is blackmarketing, there is anti-social activity of industrial groups, the evasion of taxes, the making of illegal profits; also anti-social activities of people like the communists and the like. We try to face these evils with very moderate success. We have the evil of poverty and unemployment and we tackle it bravely again with very, very moderate success. Is betting on the race course a greater evil than blackmarketing? I do not think so. It is far more important for us to tackle these major evils than to waste our energy on minor and rather personal failings of individuals. A social evil affecting the community is a more important thing than a personal failing affecting an individual.

I have mentioned to you in another context a growing apprehension among some people about what appears to be the desire of the Bombay Government to improve private morals by legislation.[2] These attempts have not succeeded in other countries in the past and there is little reason to hope that

[2] The Bombay Prevention of Gambling Act of 1887 was amended with a view to limiting the circulation of literature on horse races to control betting. Prohibition was introduced in the Bombay Province from 15 June 1949.

they will succeed here. Meanwhile they irritate and annoy large numbers of people and make government disliked. There is also the argument, which has some weight, about the interference in the personal liberty of the individual. That is a precious inheritance and we are too apt today in this and other fields to interfere with it.

28

Reservations for Backward Groups[1]

Sir, there has been such an abundance of goodwill shown towards this motion that it is hardly necessary for me to intervene in support of it. But I have felt the urge to do so because I wish to associate myself with this historic turn in our destiny for indeed it is a historic motion that my colleague, the Deputy Prime Minister, has put before this House.[2] It is a motion which means not only discarding something that was evil, but turning back upon it and determining with all our strength that we shall pursue a path which we consider fundamentally good for every part of the nation.

Now, all of us here, I believe, are convinced that this business of separatism, whether it took the shape of separate electorates or other shapes, has done a tremendous amount of evil to our country and to our people. We came to the conclusion some time back that we must get rid of separate electorates. That was the major evil. Reluctantly we agreed to carry on with some measure of reservation. Reluctantly we did so for two reasons. Reason number one was that we felt that we could not remove that without the goodwill of the minorities concerned. It was for them to take the lead or to say that they did not want it. For a majority to force that down their throats would not be fair to the various assurances that we had given in the past, and otherwise too, it did not look the right thing to do. Secondly, because in our heart of hearts we were not sure about ourselves nor about our own people as to how they would function when all these reservations were removed. We agreed to that reservation, but always there was this doubt in our minds, namely, whether we had not shown weakness in dealing with a thing that was wrong. So, when this matter came up in another

[1] Speech in the Constituent Assembly, 26 May 1949. *Constituent Assembly of India Debates, Official Report*, Vol. VIII, 16 May to 16 June 1949, pp. 329–32.

[2] Vallabhbhai Patel, while initiating the debate on the Report of the Advisory Committee on Minorities, etc., stated on 25 May 1949 that "notwithstanding any decisions already taken by the Constituent Assembly in this behalf . . . the Draft Constitution be so amended as to give effect to the recommendations contained in the said report" and proposed that "the following classes in East Punjab, namely, Mazhabis, Ramdasis, Kabirpanthis and Sikligars be included in the list of Scheduled Castes for the province so that they would be entitled to the benefit of representation in the Legislatures given to the Scheduled Castes."

context, and it was proposed that we do away with all reservations except in the case of the Scheduled Castes, for my part I accepted that with alacrity and with a feeling of great relief, because I had been fighting in my own mind and heart against this business of keeping up some measure of separatism in our political domain; and the more I thought of it the more I felt that it was the right thing to do not only from the point of view of pure nationalism, which it is, but also from the separate and individual viewpoint of each group, if you like, majority or minority.

We call ourselves nationalists, but perhaps in the mind of each the colour, the texture of nationalism that is present is somewhat different from what it is in the mind of the other. We call ourselves nationalists—and rightly so—and yet few of us are free from those separatist tendencies, whether they are communal, whether they are provincial or other. Yet, because we have those tendencies, it does not necessarily follow that we should surrender to them all the time. It does follow that we should not take the cloak of nationalism to cover those bad tendencies.

So I thought about this matter and I came to the conclusion that if at this stage of our nation's history, when we are formulating this Constitution, which may not be a very permanent one because the world changes, nevertheless which we wish to be a fairly solid and lasting one, if at this stage we put things into it which are obviously wrong, and which obviously make people look the wrong way, then it is an evil thing that we are doing to the nation. We decided some time ago in another connection that we should have no truck with communalism or separatism. It was rightly pointed out to us then that if that is so, why do you keep these reservations because this itself will make people think in terms of separate compartments in the political domain.

I would like you to consider this business, whether it is reservation or any other kind of safeguard for the minority, objectively. There is some point in having a safeguard of this type or any other type where there is autocratic rule or foreign rule. As soon as you get something that can be called political democracy, then this kind of reservation, instead of helping the party to be safeguarded and aided, is likely actually to turn against it. But where there is a third party, or where there is an autocratic monarch, or some other ruler, it is possible that these safeguards may be good. Perhaps the monarch may play one off against the other, or the foreign rule. But where you are up against a full-blooded democracy, if you seek to give safeguard to a minority, and a relatively small minority, you isolate it. Maybe you protect it to a slight extent, but at what cost? At the cost of isolating it and keeping it away from the main current in which the majority is going, I am talking on the political plane of course—at the cost of forfeiting that inner sympathy and fellow-feeling with the majority. Now, of course, if it is a democracy, in the long run or in the short run, it is the will of the majority that will prevail. Even if you are limited by various Articles in the Constitution to protect the individual or the group, nevertheless, in the very nature of things, in a democracy the will of the majority will ultimately prevail. It is a bad thing for any small group or minority to make it appear to the world and to the majority that "we wish to keep apart from you, that we do not trust you, that we look to ourselves and that therefore we want safeguards and other things." The result is that they may get one anna in the rupee of protection at the cost of the remaining fifteen annas. That is not good enough, looked at from the point of view of the majority either. It is all very well for the majority to feel that they are strong in numbers and in other ways and therefore they can afford to ride roughshod over the wishes of the minority. If the majority feels that way, it is not only exceedingly mistaken, but it has not learnt any lesson from history, because, however big the majority, if injustice is done to minorities, it rankles and it is a running sore and the majority ultimately suffers from it. So, ultimately the only way to proceed about it, whether from the point of view of the minority or from the point of view of the majority, is to remove every barrier which separates them in the political domain so that they may develop and we may all work together. That does not mean, of course, any kind of regimented working. They may have many ways of thinking: they may form groups; they may form parties; not on the majority or minority or religious or social plane, but on other planes which will be mixed planes, thus developing the habit of looking at things in mixed groups and not in separate groups. At any time that is obviously a desirable thing to do. In a democracy it becomes an essential thing to do, because if you do not do it, then trouble follows—trouble both for the minority and for the majority, but far more for the minority.

In the present state of affairs, whether you take India or whether you take a larger world group, the one thing we have to develop is to think as much as possible in larger terms; otherwise we get cut off from reality. If we do not appreciate what is happening, the vast and enormous changes happening elsewhere which really are changing the shape of things, and cut off our future almost completely from the past as we found it, if we stick to certain ideas and suspicions of the past, we shall never understand the present, much less the future that is taking shape. Many of our discussions here are inevitably derived from the past. We cannot get rid of them. None of us can, because we are part of the past. But we ought to try to get ourselves disconnected from the past if we are to mould the future gradually. Therefore from every point of view, whether it is theoretical or ideological or national or whether it is in the interests of the minority or of the majority or whether it is in order to come to grips with the realities of today and of tomorrow which is so different from yesterday, I welcome this proposal.

Frankly I would like this proposal to go further and put an end to such reservations as there still remain. But again, speaking frankly, I realize that in the present state of affairs in India that would not be a desirable thing to do, that is to say, in regard to the Scheduled Castes. I try to look upon the problem not in the sense of a religious minority, but rather in the sense of helping backward groups in the country. I do not look at it from the religious point of view or the caste point of view, but from the point of view that a backward group ought to be helped and I am glad that this reservation will be limited to ten years. . . .

So, now, let me take this decision—a major decision—of this honourable House which is going to affect our future greatly. Let us be clear in our own minds over this question that in order to proceed further we have—each one of us, whether we belong to the majority or to a minority—to try to function in a way to gain the goodwill of the other group or individual. It is a trite saying, still I would like to say it because this conviction has grown in my mind that whether any individual belongs to this or that group, whether in national or international dealings, ultimately the thing that counts is the generosity, the goodwill and the affection with which you approach the other party. If that is lacking, then your advice becomes hollow. If that is there, then it is bound to produce a like reaction on the other side. If there were something of that today in the international field, probably even the great international problems of today would be much easier of solution. If we in India approach our problems in that spirit, I am sure they will be far easier of solution. All of us have a blend of good and evil in us and it is so extremely easy for us to point to the evil in the other party. It is easy to do that, but it is not easy to pick out the evil in ourselves. Why not try this method of the great people, the great ones of the earth, who have always tried to lay emphasis on the good of the other and thereby draw it out? How did the Father of the Nation function? How did he draw unto himself every type, every group and every individual, and got the best from him? He always laid stress on the good of the man, knowing perhaps the evil too. He laid stress on the good of the individual or group and· made them function to the best of his ability. That I think is the only way to behave. I am quite convinced that ultimately this will be to our good. Nevertheless, as I said on another occasion, I would remind the House that this is an act of faith, an act of faith for all of us, an act of faith, above all, for the majority community because they will have to show after this that they can behave with others in a generous, fair and just way. Let us live up to that faith.

29

"Time and World are Ever in Flight"[1]

New Delhi, 2 September 1949

My dear Premier,

"Time and the world are ever in flight"[2] and we try vainly to keep up with them. Events follow each other relentlessly and problem piles upon problem. Sometimes one feels a little dispirited at being the slave, to a large extent, of events and external occurrences which should easily be controlled; at other times one has a certain feeling of excitement and exhilaration at having to wrestle with difficulties and in trying to overcome them with more or less success. Much depends upon the temperament of the individual or the mood of the moment. Great difficulties and perils often draw out an individual and a nation and the very hour of peril becomes the moment of victory. Smaller difficulties and obstructions usually embarrass much more and even produce occasionally a sense of frustration. It is not perhaps the problem or the difficulty that counts so much as the mental approach to it. There are occasions when a whole nation rises to heights of endeavour and performs miracles. There are also occasions when a spirit of lassitude creeps over one and paralyses mental and physical activity. We have had a long history and uncounted centuries lie behind us, having shaped us for what we are. During this vast period we have had experience of all these various moods of elation and depression, of high and brave endeavour and of static passivity or something even worse. Even during our lifetime we have experienced all this. When perils have confronted us, we have faced them with courage and then we have relapsed and allowed events to take their course, often a wrong course. What fate and determinism may have to do with human destiny is a matter for philosophers to argue. But men and women who have ideals and objectives before them and the urge to achieve them, do not wait for the turn of fortune's wheel. Nor do they seek anchorage in some kind of security which eludes them, as in a rapidly changing world it must. They try to be, to the best of their ability, moulders of destiny and not the pitiful object of an unkind fate.

---

[1] To Chief Ministers, File No. 25(6)–49/PMS. SWJN, Vol. 13 (II Series), pp. 187–8.
[2] From 'Into the Twilight', a poem by W.B. Yeats.

I am driven to these observations as I sit down to write this fortnightly letter to you and survey both the Indian scene and the world scene. What a mess the world is in, and India, and yet everywhere one seeks bright points of light, men and women of integrity and purpose and strength of will who are out to achieve some great purpose. To a casual onlooker the widespread dark patches might seem overwhelming, and yet it is those spots of light that count and each one of us can add to the gloom or to the light. Unhappily most of us spend our time and our energy in looking at others and criticizing them, instead of tending our own little light. It is so easy to emphasize the evil that surrounds us, but in the very act of doing so we add to it. We cannot and must not ignore it, for that would be folly. But while recognizing it, we have to feel strong enough to over-come it. That can only be so, if we hold to some basic ideals and objectives and have faith in them. Any task that is big enough takes a lot of doing; anything that is worthwhile must be achieved by great effort, otherwise it is trivial and of little moment.

Yours sincerely,
Jawaharlal Nehru

30

Planning[1]

New Delhi, 29 September 1949

My dear Matthai,

I do feel that at every stage, and more especially in our present difficulties, an attempt at a planned approach is essential. This does not mean our spending more money than we can afford. It does mean a clearer vision of the objectives from the economic, social and political points of view and some definite notion of the way we have to go in order to achieve those objectives. No planning can be dealt with as permanent. Day-to-day developments and circumstances must necessarily vary it. But without that clear objective and the means to achieve it, and without an attempt at a scientific approach to the problem, only confusion can result and haphazard methods of work involving frequent change as we try to catch up with changing events.

I have long been convinced of this and for years past I have thought on these lines. This is apart from the actual policy to be adopted, whatever that might be. The years I spent in the National Planning Committee influenced my mind greatly in this direction. Even before that, the Congress had talked about planning. Recently, that is some months ago, it reiterated this demand and asked us to go ahead with it.[2] Even since I have come into this Government, I have thought of it, but overriding causes and events have prevented us from doing much in that direction. Now that we have to face vital issues affecting our future, I feel that we can no longer delay this. The more I think of it, and I have given a great deal of thought during the past few months especially, the less I understand myself what we are aiming at. If I do not understand this clearly, how much less can we expect the intelligent or unintelligent public to understand it. And if they do not understand it, what support, not to speak of enthusiastic response, can we expect from them in regard to any policy that we pursue.

[1] To John Matthai. File No. 49-GG/49, President's Secretariat. Extracts.

[2] In a resolution adopted on 5 April 1949, the Congress Working Committee decided to form a National Planning Committee comprising the Congress President, the Prime Minister, the Minister of Industry and Supply, J.C. Ghosh, Ambalal Sarabhai and K.T. Shah to draw up a scheme to continue planning.

That support can only be on the basis of faith in personalities. That helps, but it is a weak plank and public life cannot be built up for long on that basis. Other groups and other parties can always take advantage of this position. It is true that they talk irresponsibly and sometimes even foolishly, because they do not shoulder the burden of government. Nevertheless, a country or a party cannot merely have a negative policy, more especially when that negative policy has brought no success at all. The negative policy of course may be necessary and even essential. But it is to be supplemented with something positive also.

The world today exhibits many conflicts of ideas and methods of approach in the political and economic plane. Able and intelligent people of integrity differ, because the situation is an exceedingly complicated one and no sensitive person can be complacent about it. Personally, as I have grown in years, I have had less and less liking for any dogmatic approach to an intricate and changing situation. I think that each country has its own problems, its own background, and its own genius. It is folly for any country to try to imitate any other, ignoring its own special features. Nevertheless, there are many common features in the world situation today and we can learn from them and adapt ourselves to them. We may make mistakes and pay for them, but surely the greatest mistake is not to view the whole scheme of things in its entirety, realistically and objectively, and to decide on clear objectives and plans. If once this is done, the next step of complete coordination follows much more easily and only by coordinated effort can real results be achieved.

One thing that is obvious to me is the failure all over the world of the present policies, whether political or economic, that are being followed. We drift towards some almost inevitable disaster and seem to be powerless to avert it. And yet I do not believe in the inevitability of this disaster in the world and I think that it is possible to prevent it. In any event it is man's job to try to do so. A continuation of present policies all over the world means that we cannot even profit by past errors. The old order has been in the process of cracking up in many ways for the last 35 years. I think it is quite incapable of solving the world's problems, if it continues in its old framework. The greater part of our lives have been spent in crisis after crisis. What changes must be introduced is not easy to determine, but changes there must be. Even to consider the problem, one must go to basic causes and seek basic remedies, or else the poison spreads. It is this consideration, therefore, of any major problem in all its aspects and with the national implications and its international consequences, that has to be considered as scientifically and objectively as possible. We must be courageous enough to look at it and to deal with it in the manner we think best.

You will forgive me for writing all this rather platitudinous stuff. But as I am going away very soon, I wanted to unburden myself. Keenly as I feel the necessity for the setting up of a planning authority in India, I feel also that we cannot do it just at present. We cannot take such a step in a hurry. This will have to wait till my return from America and fuller consideration. At the same time delay also appears to me to be dangerous and perhaps even fatal. I hope, in any event, that we shall take this subject up when I return.

In the meantime, it was my desire to prepare the ground for this planning authority in some way or other. Even that idea I am now giving up to some extent, as I do not wish to rush my colleagues without their having the fullest opportunity for consideration and discussion.

While we are postponing this matter for the present, something can still be done quietly and without any fuss.

Yours sincerely,
Jawaharlal Nehru

31

Pernicious Influence of Technology[1]

Mr. President,[2] Excellencies, Ladies and Gentlemen,

You will permit me to say something which I ought not to do, and that is to confess that in the course of the last few years we have not been able to be clear as to where we are going. That is to say, in the immediate present, we might have been clear about any step and in the broader aspects of distant policy we might also have been clear, vaguely clear. Nevertheless, there is an enormous field between the two, about which in these changing circumstances there is a great deal of difference of opinion in the country and among those who have given thought to it.

In India or any other country, vast and new social forces are at work, generated because of various causes and reasons but certainly and principally because of tremendous technological changes that go on taking place, generated by political changes, say, in our country, in Asia, by political urges, social urges generated as a result of those political changes by a new consciousness coming to vast numbers of people and a new desire not to submit to much that they have submitted to in the past. So, you see all these social forces at play and social conflicts taking place, sometimes resulting or rather leading to international conflicts on a major scale. . . .

To say that we want greater wealth, higher standards of living, greater production, that is, I take it, common ground. How to achieve it and how to achieve it not merely in some mechanical sense but in a social sense also. It is really absurd to talk of high standards in India where sometimes the lowest are lacking. We must have those basic standards, basic necessaries and then we may think of higher standards.

Nevertheless, there is such a thing—the social condition of the organism or the individual or the group. Frankly speaking, when I see some very highly developed nations of the world, I admire them. I want to copy many of their methods and yet a fear steals into my mind lest I grow like them because there are things there which I think are not good for the individual or the group,

[1] Speech at the twenty–fourth annual session of the Federation of Indian Chambers of Commerce and Industry, New Delhi, 31 March 1951. JN Papers, NMML. Excerpts.

[2] Tulsidas Kilachand, the outgoing President.

because this very thing that has brought wealth and prosperity to the entire world, that is, the growth of technology, industrialization and the rest—and may I say, in passing, that I am all in favour of industrialization of India: I am not speaking in any other terms—yet the growth of this has brought about the gradual and progressive turning of the human being into a machine, and I think that that is a very dangerous thing. You get the machine in man's normal functions and avocations; you even get the machine mind which cannot think except in the narrow grooves laid out for it; you get large groups thinking along certain ways.

That is helped by a variety of processes including to some extent the functioning of modern methods of propaganda and all that, so that in the ultimate analysis while you make great progress on certain planes—and that progress is necessary and desirable and must be achieved—you lose something which, I think, perhaps is very valuable and very precious. Now, must one pay the price of progress by losing that something or can we retain it and have both? . . .

I think personally that most of our world's ills today leading us to the verge of a terrible war are in the final analysis due to this growth of technology in a peculiarly narrow way. In the old days people were backward compared to today, but one had a sense of an integrated human life, a sense of balance. Today one has a sense of complete lack of balance in the individual, the group or the nations.

Of course, wise men apart—there are always wise men everywhere—we get highly qualified men in their special domains, very efficient and delivering the goods in their special domains, but taken out of their particular groove, almost completely ignorant of life and its ways, not even knowing the most elementary facts of life, as perhaps some simple persons might know them. So that while this excessive specialization and technological development does obviously lead to the larger good of humanity in many ways, a doubt creeps into my mind whether they are not undermining humanity and also at the same time and lowering the quality of the mind and the spirit and engendering tendencies of self-destruction and hara-kiri.

32

Planning for the Future[1]

It is essential that we make progress, or else we go down and for this purpose we must have the wherewithal for progress and a complete picture of what we are aiming at in the near future. It seems to me that both for the Government and the Congress, and indeed for all other parties and the people generally, the only right approach is through a consideration of the Planning Commission's report. . . .

I should like to say that I have been very deeply conscious of the lack of success in many matters, and more especially in these basic economic matters. I feel that, as Prime Minister, I must shoulder the responsibility for all that has happened, both the successes and the failures of Government, and I should like to be judged by that standard. . . .

Although nearly four years have elapsed since independence came to us, neither we nor the world have gone back to any degree of normality. We live in a precarious and dangerous age and this requires constant vigilance. The distance between freedom and the lack of it is not great and it is a possibility not to be forgotten that wrong policies might lead to a breakdown of some of the essentials of freedom. We have faced the spectre of famine and we hope that we have prevented it from materializing. Yet the situation requires constant and unremitting care. Disruptive and anti-social forces are at work in the country and the law and order situation also requires vigilance. We have not yet developed sufficiently a sense of loyalty to the nation, overshadowing the overriding regional and sectional loyalties. Or perhaps most of our people feel that freedom having been attained, any danger to the nation is past and, therefore, they can indulge in these narrow and sectional activities.

In spite of apparent differences and strong condemnation of each other, I believe that there is a very large measure of unanimity in the country about our basic objectives. If we are to succeed, presumably there should be also an equal measure of agreement in working for those objectives. I see no harm in differences in methods of approach or emphasis, provided there is a wide measure of

[1] Report of the All India Congress Committee, New Delhi, 6 July 1951. JN Papers, NMML. Excerpts.

agreement. Any national plan must necessarily have that large measure of agreement. There must also be adequate power to give effect to it and an administrative set-up suitable for it. It is necessary to have a strong Central government which can work out this national plan throughout the country in cooperation with the state governments. There has been sometimes a lack of this cooperation between the Centre and the states. Nothing would be more injurious to the nation's progress at this stage in history than to have weak and unstable governments which cannot adopt any firm policy or give effect to it.

There are risks and dangers in adopting any plan of democratic progress, but the greatest risk of all today is in remaining static. At the same time we must necessarily minimize risks and not indulge in adventurist policies, which may well lead to reaction, as they have done in some other countries. Broadly speaking, we aim at democracy with the essential features of socialism. Thus we would realize the purpose embodied in our Constitution and the objective of a cooperative commonwealth that the Congress has laid down.[2] To move slowly is dangerous, because events might overwhelm us. To move too fast might well lead to bitter conflicts and weaken the country and involve a heavier price in the end. Whether it is possible to find the middle path, I do not know. But we have to try our utmost to find that way, for any other path is likely to prove harmful. We have to function within the limits of the Constitution which has been drawn up with exceeding care. But that does not mean that, if urgent necessity arises, or experience points that way, we cannot amend or vary it.

Political and economic theories and doctrines are important as they are presumably based on knowledge and experience. But if they are to be worthwhile, they have to satisfy basic human needs. It is patent that these basic human needs are not satisfied in India and in many other countries for a vast number of people today. The existing economic structure has failed to that extent and to seek to maintain it unchanged is, therefore, to ignore reality and invite defeat. We must find some way out. Communism's appeal to the many has been based on its promise to satisfy certain essential human needs and to provide security. But we have seen that it brings in its train conflict and violence and authoritarianism and the suppression of the individual. Can we provide economic security and progress without sacrificing democratic liberties? There is no reason why this should not be possible though the path may be difficult. This will involve social vision and a social purpose in all our activities. This will mean our deliberately aiming at a new type of society whose chief purpose is the welfare of the people, not only in material living standards, but also in the things of the spirit. That is the welfare state, which may be far from us now, but which we can progressively realize if we set our minds and hearts to this great task. If

[2] The Congress manifesto advocated the modernization of industry and agriculture and social control of all sources of wealth, methods of production and distribution so that India may grow into a cooperative commonwealth.

we have to avoid authoritarianism, as we must, we have also to avoid unregulated private enterprise. We have to try to replace the acquisitive instinct with the spirit of cooperative effort in a common cause.

The world is full today of the spirit of conflict, and behind that lie fear and hatred. The destructive forces are at work and armaments pile up. Every man knows that even victory in a vast world of conflict means nothing to humanity, which will have to face a wilderness of destruction, and the growth of centuries of civilized effort will be shattered. Yet vast elemental forces push humanity to the brink and blind men's eyes. Violence and conflict cannot always be avoided, internationally or nationally, but their outcome seldom leads to human progress. At any rate we have arrived at a stage when the very survival of man and of all human values is threatened by unrestrained violence. From this world scene we can learn some lessons for our national problems. Those national problems, which are essentially human, have to be solved or else there is progressive degradation and perhaps disaster. If we try to solve them by large-scale conflict, we not only fail but possibly bring untold human suffering and go back for a generation or more. For us also it is a question of survival. The middle way is the democratic way, provided that such democracy is a vital force, with something of the revolutionary ardour about it.

India is a secular state. That is very basis of our Constitution and we must understand it with all its implications. That, of course, is the only modern and civilized approach. That approach is in keeping with the whole growth of our national movement. It is not only in consonance with our ideology but also with practical considerations. Any other approach is fraught with disaster and would be a negation of all that we have stood for. I am laying stress on this because there has been some flabbiness in this matter even in Congress circles. I feel that on this subject there can be no compromise of any kind. Unfortunately there are some communal groups in the country which challenge this secular aspect of the state and which nourish narrow and reactionary ideas. It is necessary for us, therefore, to be perfectly clear on this issue and to be prepared to stand or fall by it. As a consequence we have to give special care to all our minorities, such as Muslims, Sikhs, Christians and others. This fact has always to be remembered and in the forthcoming elections this should, more especially, be borne in mind.

Our objective in ensuring justice, social, economic and political, to all may take some time before we realize it fully. But it involves special attention being paid to the backward and unprivileged classes, including those living in the tribal areas, so that they might raise themselves educationally and economically.

I would certainly not call our women backward. In our national struggle for freedom they have played a splendid part and they have distinguished themselves in many fields. But it is true that they labour under great social disabilities and even in the political field they have not yet been given the position that they deserve. I think that a nation's progress depends far more, than many men think, on its women and on the care that is bestowed upon them. For some years past a legislative measure which sought to remove certain disabilities on Hindu women has been before the legislature.[3] I hope that it may be possible to pass the Hindu Code Bill before long.

We have been criticized for our economic policy and some of the criticisms are, as I have mentioned above, justified. But I feel that the criticisms would have had more weight if they had been based more on facts. Inevitably, our policy has been that of what is called a mixed economy with a public and a private sector. A policy of pure *laissez-faire* is not feasible and must therefore be rejected. The only alternative to a mixed economy is something in which the private sector hardly plays any important part. But this cannot be brought about merely by legislation unless we have the resources and the training for it. We have felt that there is still an honourable place for private enterprise. But, if we have any national plan, as we must, then the private sector must accept the objectives of that plan and fit into it. Indeed, both the public and private sectors must function, more or less as a single whole, in the interests of that plan and serve the same social ends. The only test of any system that we apply is that it gives the desired result. It is the objective that counts and not the method. To what extent there should be a public sector or a private sector must therefore be judged by the results achieved. Any plan will involve certain controls, certain priorities, and the adjustment of conflicting claims. It involves also a balance between present benefits and future progress. If we are to go towards the achievement of the purposes we aim at, then we must lay the foundations for more rapid economic growth in the future. We have to enlarge our resources and to some extent, sacrifice present good. Inevitably, this involves a certain degree of austerity, not as a virtue, but as a political and social necessity so as to secure the essentials of life for those who lack them and to ensure future progress. I am sure that this would be accepted by a great majority of our people, provided that the entire picture is before them, and provided that they realize that the burden is evenly borne. . . .

Because of our urgent need for economic development, which will add to our resources, many of our important plans for education and health have unfortunately suffered. Ultimately progress in these will depend upon our resources and these resources can only come from higher production and

[3] On 17 September 1951, Parliament resumed consideration of the Hindu Code Bill. The Hindu Succession Bill was introduced in the Rajya Sabha on 22 December 1951 and became law in June 1956. Its aim was to evolve a uniform system of law with regard to intestate succession among Hindus and for determining the rightful heirs to their property. The Bill for the first time gave a share of the property to the daughter and gave women absolute right to self-acquired property.

greater national wealth. Apart from formal education, I should like to lay stress on other forms of cultural progress which brighten the lives of our people and raise their standards of appreciation of beauty. I think the state should encourage art, drama and literature, music and song and dance.

There has been a great deal of criticism of the administrative machinery of the government. We have carried on with the old machinery and added to it. That has its advantages and disadvantages. I have no doubt that the advantages were greater than the disadvantages and that progressively the disadvantages will grow less. As a machine, it was as efficient as any in the world, but it is true that it was nurtured under a different tradition and it was not easy to change that tradition or the habits that grew out of it. There is no doubt that in the large number of persons that constitute the administrative machine, there are all kinds of persons, good, bad and indifferent. There are persons whose integrity is not beyond dispute and there are persons who are communal-minded. But I think that the strong criticism made is, by and large, not justified. We have had able and devoted service from a large number of the old civil servants and I am sure that none of them ever worked quite so hard as they have done in recent years. I think, however, that this whole question of the administrative machinery has to be considered afresh from the point of view of the general plan that the country may adopt. The administration must serve the purposes of that plan. The present rules governing government servants make it difficult to distinguish much between the efficient and the inefficient, the good worker and the bad, the man of integrity and the man whose integrity is in doubt. It is difficult to measure efficiency in terms of government rules; it is still more difficult to get proof of lack of integrity. These rules must be changed so that even the reputation for a lack of integrity should be enough to prevent an officer from holding any position of responsibility or influence. At the same time it is due to our officers to protect them from unfair attacks. In a democratic regime, the services are not usually criticized. It is the minister who is held responsible. We must endeavour to maintain moral standards in our public work and do so in a manner that the public understands and appreciates. Public confidence is essential. Where a charge of misconduct is made by a responsible person or there is a *prima facie* case for it, there should be an inquiry, however highly placed the person concerned might be.

Unhappily during the War and afterwards various types of corruption have grown. Controls have added to them and general standards have fallen, both in government servants and in the public. Blackmarketing in India is not merely an individual offence, but a social evil. There can be no two opinions that adequate measures should be taken to check and ends this degradation of our public life.

33

Police and Students[1]

New Delhi, 11 September 1951

My dear Rajaji,

A few days ago I received a letter from Asaf Ali enclosing a copy of a letter dated 28th August, 1951, from him to you. This related to a circular which had been issued from the Intelligence Bureau section of our Home Ministry and dealt with students and how to keep them in order.[2]

On receiving this letter I sent for the circular in question. This has now reached me.

I confess to a feeling of shock on reading this circular. The whole approach appears to me so entirely misconceived as to amount almost to a crime. Any student with a spark of life in him would react violently against the methods suggested in the circular. In fact, these methods are more likely to produce indiscipline and make students go to communism than any appeal from the Communist Party.

I have tried to think of what the reaction on me would have been when I was a student. People have changed since then no doubt, but still the normal urges and passions remain the same. So, I suppose that a present-day student would not be very different in this respect from the students of my generation. What amazes me still more is the complete lack of intelligence shown in issuing such a circular. Policemen are excellent in their proper place, but they are completely out of place in other places. After reading this circular, the first idea that struck me was that if policemen have to meddle with these affairs, they should be given a course of instruction in political, economic and like matters.

---

[1] To C. Rajagopalachari. File No. 7/18/51–Poll., M.H.A. SWJN, Vol. 16 (II Series), pp. 469–70.

[2] In a circular dated 7 October 1950, sent to all Chief Secretaries, the Home Ministry, without the knowledge of the Home Minister, had drawn attention to certain suggestions, emanating from a conference of Central and State intelligence officials held in April 1950, for countering subversion in schools and colleges. Seeing the suggestions, some of which related to spying on parents and guardians, Asaf Ali, Governor of Orissa, asked both C. Rajagopalachari and Jawaharlal Nehru: "Was the Intelligence Bureau going to decide education polices?"

That, I suppose, is difficult. Perhaps if they had that course of instruction, they might cease to be good policemen.

For our Intelligence service to issue circulars about guardians of students being asked to give undertakings to the effect that their wards should not take part in political activities appears to me to extraordinary as to be almost past belief. This is an insult to the guardian as well as to the student and it can only result in either driving the student to wrong courses or to his moral subservience and degradation. I would object to this even if it emanated from an educational authority. Coming from the police or the C.I.D. it is infinitely worse.

The advice given by policemen that lectures should be imparted to students advising them to keep away from communism is interesting. Have we come to this that policemen are in charge of our education and how to influence young people's minds?

C.I.Ds are asked to keep a careful watch over teachers and management of schools.[3] I do not know of any country outside the Communist fold, or perhaps Franco's Spain, where any such thing is suggested or done. The more I see of the police outlook in matters outside the strict scope of the police, the more I am frightened at its utter lack of intelligence and at the dangerous results which it might produce.

I see that the Home Secretary sent a copy of this secret circular to various Chief Secretaries and asked for their views on it. In the covering letter some doubt was thrown on the desirability of the suggestions made in the circular. The curious fact is mentioned that the circular had emanated as a result of consultations among senior police officers without the knowledge of the Government of India. Are police officers free to issue circulars of this or any kind relating to students or educational institutions? What business have they to interfere with education about which they know little or nothing?[4]

Yours,
Jawaharlal

---

[3] One of the measures suggested was that the C.I.Ds should keep a careful watch over teachers and management of schools for any adverse activities and report them to Government for action.

[4] Rajagopalachari replied that he entirely disapproved of the circular but added that there was "nothing wrong in the Government being informed of what the Intelligence officials had proposed, whatever we may think of the suggestions themselves."

34

Evacuee Property[1]

New Delhi, 22 September 1951

My dear Ajit Prasad,[2]

I quite realize the difficulties you are facing in regard to evacuee property cases. These difficulties are inherent in the situation and they have to be faced. Personally I am not at all affected by the kind of agitation that has been raised against the Cabinet decisions in the three cases you mention. I am quite clear that those decisions were right and I am prepared to defend them in public, if necessary. I have no sympathy at all for this kind of agitation or the motive that lies behind it. We have to act justly and I am sure that this will produce the right results in the end. In acting justly, of course, we should not act rashly. All this business of refugees looking at Muslim property in India as potentially theirs is pernicious nonsense and the sooner this is made clear, the better. This is against all domestic or international law and much more so against equity. I do not know how we have got into this tangle and why we are submitting to this kind of approach.

The fact of the matter is that, in spite of all our efforts, Muslims in India generally have a strong feeling of insecurity. We complain a great deal about the insecurity of the Hindus in East Pakistan. But we shut our eyes to the same conditions, though on a similar scale, in regard to Muslims in India. I had been horrified by the accounts of what has happened in Hyderabad State and elsewhere. The fact that 18 months ago a very large number of Muslims left their homes and lands in the U.P. and Rajasthan and went to Pakistan was not only significant but a painful reminder of the conditions in which Muslims live in parts of India. We can find excuses for all this and give reasons, but the fact remains that they felt insecure and had to go. Today, probably hundreds of Muslims are leaving almost daily for Pakistan across the Rajasthan border. They are doing so without any help and in spite of all kinds of difficulties. In our self-complacency we do not seem to appreciate the significance of all this. But the world sees it and judges us accordingly.

---

[1] To Ajit Prasad Jain. JN Collection, NMML. Excerpts.
[2] He was Minister for Relief and Rehabilitation at this time.

It is not governmental action that causes this, though sometimes it encourages it. This is, no doubt, due to a multitude of factors which go to make the Muslim feel unhappy and insecure in India. He is frustrated and down and out to a large extent. Public feeling is against him and treats him as a potential enemy, whatever his previous record of service. It has been a matter of the greatest pain to me that many Muslims who played a brave part in our national struggle and throughout their lives opposed the Muslim League, cannot find help or relief from us and are hounded out by communal persons, who have never done a day's service in the cause of the country or of freedom. I do not see why I should put up with it, whether the public likes it or not.

It is clear to me that the present hierarchy of the custodian, etc., not only functions, as government departments function, mechanically and without any human touch, but is also basically anti-Muslim in its outlook. That is not surprising, because they reflect the public mind. Sometimes they go much beyond it. If we see this kind of thing even in the Congress, how much more is it likely to be found in other quarters.

I have mentioned the Congress and I have constant complaints, as you know, that a majority in some places has squeezed out the minority. Applying that to this larger question the majority, inflamed with communal passion and greed of property, wants to squeeze out the minority. The administrative apparatus and tribunals that we have provided try generally to function in terms of the law. But their sympathy and urges all pull in one direction, whether they are refugees or not. There may be individual exceptions.

If this is so, then, both in the interests of justice and in the larger interests of the nation, it becomes essential that we should provide some means of bringing the personal and the human touch to the problem. That touch does not help much in the end and if it helps it helps only a few cases. But, nevertheless, it makes a difference for it makes people feel that they are treated like human beings and not like robots or as impersonal pieces of property. It is because of this that I meet many of them, whether they are Hindu refugees or Muslims in trouble, and try at least to give that human touch. I am a little ashamed that I cannot help them much. But I think that the few words that I say to them as gently as I can, does help a little.

We have, therefore, to find and to encourage this human touch, apart from the official machinery. We have to make the persons feel that we are interested in their individual welfare apart from our general impersonal approach. Obviously this cannot be done on a large scale. Still it is worthwhile doing it on a small scale.

Yours sincerely,
Jawaharlal Nehru

35

Hindu Code Bill[1]

New Delhi, 15 September 1951

My dear Mr. President,

I have received today your letter of the 15th September, and with it your note on the Hindu Code Bill. I have read this note with care.[2] As desired by you, I shall place it before the Cabinet.[3] The legal and constitutional questions you raise are important. In the last paragraph of your note you have mentioned that it may be necessary for you to inform Parliament of your viewpoint. You also refer to your right to examine the Bill on its merits when it is passed by Parliament before giving your assent to it.[4]

These are serious matters of great constitutional importance. They might involve a conflict between the President on the one side and the Government and Parliament on the other. They would inevitably raise the question of the President's authority and powers to challenge the decision of Government and of Parliament. The consequence would obviously be serious.

I do not wish to say much on this subject except that, in our view, the President has no power or authority to go against the will of Parliament in regard to a Bill that has been well considered by it and passed. The whole conception of constitutional government is against any exercise by the President of any such authority.

You have been good enough to mention to me, on several occasions, your disapproval of the Hindu Code Bill. I pointed out on each occasion that the

[1] To Rajendra Prasad. File No. 48(4)(a)/48–PMS.

[2] Rajendra Prasad's note to Nehru expressing a desire to act solely on his own judgement, independently of the Council of Ministers, when giving assent to Bills to Parliament for reconsideration. He maintained that the Provisional Parliament did not have the authority to enact such major legislation as the Hindu Code Bill because it was indirectly elected and its members lacked the public 'mandate' of a general election. He desired to use the power of his office either to force the Provisional Parliament to shelve the measure or, failing that, to veto it even against the advice of his Cabinet.

[3] Prasad had written: "I feel I owe it to you and to the Cabinet to put you in possession of my view so that you and the Cabinet may not be taken by surprise."

[4] Rajendra Prasad had also written: "But if I find that any action of mine at a later stage is likely to cause embarrassment to the Government, I may take such appropriate action as I may feel called upon to avoid such embarrassment consistent with the dictates of my own conscience."

Government had given the most earnest consideration to the principles underlying this Bill and were fully committed to them. This Bill is not a new measure and it has been before the country for a number of years. There has been a very great deal of discussion and argument about it outside and within Parliament. It is after the fullest consideration of all the factors that Government came to the conclusion to press this Bill forward in Parliament. It has already been discussed, in the earlier stages, at great length. There have been many informal committees, and noted public men, representing various viewpoints, have been consulted. As a result of such consultations, major changes have been made in the Bill. The object aimed at was to reduce controversy to a large extent and to gain as large a measure of approval of the Bill as possible.

The question of the competence of the present Parliament to enact such a measure was raised in Parliament itself, and after much discussion, the Speaker gave a ruling on the the subject. The various grounds mentioned in paragraph 1 of your note[5] were considered by Parliament and a decision taken thereon. It is hardly open to anyone, even the President, to challenge that decision. Otherwise, the question would arise as to whether Parliament is the supreme legislative authority in this country or not.

You refer to the revolutionary changes contemplated by the Bill. The Bill is now, in the opinion of many, a very moderate measure of social reform with very little, if any, of revolution about it. Indeed, it is very largely a codification of the existing law. In this codification even custom has often been accepted as a guidng factor. It was felt strongly by large numbers of people, of varying opinions, that some such codification was necessary to bring some certainty and uniformity in the law.

Certain changes have been introduced, but they can hardly be called far-reaching. Indeed, many of those persons who stood strongly in favour of this Bill are severely disappointed at it because of its very moderate character. The changes suggested are generally recognized by thinking people the world over as desirable and as being in consonance with modern conditions and the spirit of the times. Indeed, as you have pointed out yourself,[6] some of these changes have already been introduced in various states.[7] No one, to my knowledge, has

[5] He found it inconceivable for any Government or Parliament to undertake legislation of such a fundamental character without obtaining an express mandate from the electorate at a general election where the question was specially raised.

[6] Rajendra Prasad wrote: "It has been said that in some states polygamy has been prohibited by law while in others it still continues and it is considered necessary to enact the law to remove this anomaly."

[7] Monogamy had become a part of the law, in states like Madras, Bombay and Saurashtra and divorce was practised by a large number of people governed by the customary law, and it was statutorily recognized in Baroda.

called them revolutionary changes there, nor has there been any marked reactions against them.

It is true that when any social or economic changes are proposed in an existing structure of society, there are always some elements which are strongly in favour of them and some opposed to them very strongly. No reform can take place if this opposition is considered to be an adequate bar to change. The mere fact of long-established static conditions can hardly be considered an argument for no change, even though facts otherwise warrant it.

I hardly think that it is correct to say that public opinion is overwhelmingly against the proposed measure. Parliament is supposed to represent public opinion in this and other matters, and even apart from this there has been a very widespread expression of opinion in the country in favour of the Bill.

Yours sincerely,
Jawaharlal Nehru

36

The Press Bill[1]

My dear Premier,

As I write this letter, the Press Bill is being hotly argued in Parliament.[2] There has been a fierce attack upon it in the press and much misrepresentation has been indulged in.[3] It is stated that the Prime Minister and the Home Minister have broken the assurances they gave.[4] This is completely untrue. Many of us, and I am of that number, are most reluctant to pass legislation limiting the freedom of the press or of expression. But it seems clear to me, and indeed it is generally recognized, that something should be done to clarify the present position in regard to the press. This present position is chaotic. It is also generally admitted that some sections of the press are being used for purposes which are most injurious from various points of view. They preach rank communalism and inflame people's minds and passions. Their moral standards are terribly low and often the purpose of some of these disreputable journals is just pure blackmail. Something has to be done about this.

The chief objection to the press laws in the past was that they armed the executive with excessive powers and that executive was an irresponsible one then. Today the executives are popular and responsible; even so, the Press Bill does not give the executive any final power to take action. The decision has to be by judicial process. This itself is a tremendous change from the old press

[1] To Chief Ministers. JN Papers, NMML. Excerpts.

[2] The Press Bill introduced in Parliament on 31 August 1951 was passed on 7 October and received the President's assent on 23 October.

[3] On 24 June 1951, the All-India Newspapers Editors' Conference resolved to suspend the publication of newspapers on 12 July as a protest. It urged the electorate to demand from every candidate standing for election to Parliament and state Legislatures a pledge to work for the repeal of the amendment. Certain sections of the press and some members of Parliament charged that the Press Bill restricted the freedom of the press and feared that the clause defining objectionable matter would be utilized to punish innocent people.

[4] On 3 October 1951, several members of the opposition in Parliament charged that the Home Minister and the Prime Minister had gone back on the assurance given during the discussion on the Constitution Amendment Bill that all clauses in the Press Emergency Act which were criticized in the newspapers would be removed from the new Bill.

laws. The question in debate, therefore, should be a very limited one as to how far we should go in defining what should not be done. I think you will find that these definitions have been strictly limited and it is not fair to say that the government wants to interfere with the freedom of the press or with any kind of legitimate criticism. There is always a risk of a wrong step being taken, however good the law. There is also a more obvious risk of our public life being poisoned by a certain section of depraved journalism. Anyone can bring out a newspaper; any monied person can use the press for his own personal advantage.

It must be remembered that the press today is something different from what it was even a generation ago. Mechanical devices have made it easy to produce newspapers and periodicals on a large scale. Only money is required. There is no other standard of capacity or moral behaviour. No one suggests that the more dangerous weapons of war should be given freely to anybody who wants them or who can even pay for them. A press which is allowed to sink below a certain standard of behaviour might be more dangerous than any weapon of war, even the atom bomb, in degrading society and indeed in pulling down the standards of even the higher newspapers. Having said this, I should also like to say that when we try to control the press, we enter upon dangerous ground and great care has to be taken not to misuse any power that might be given.

Yours sincerely,
Jawaharlal Nehru

37

Moulding Our Destiny[1]

We have met here not to have academic debates about theoretical propositions but to face reality and to chalk out a programme of action. The world today is grim and cruel and the voice of calm and dispassionate reason has sunk to a whisper and is often drowned by strident and passionate cries. The proud culture and civilization, built up through ages of human effort, still endure in their outer semblance, but somehow they lose the inner content. The values and standards fade away. The quest for truth and beauty and goodness gives place to a race for unabashed power. The tenderness and graciousness, the sanctity and dignity of human life are replaced by callousness, vulgarity and naked force. Hate is propagated as a doctrine and politics and economics have assumed the form of dogmatic religion with all its fanaticism, which tolerates no heresies and persecutes those who differ from it.

This was the phase of fascism and authoritarianism as we knew them. A world war was fought against this degradation of the spirit of man. The war was won but the disease continued.

Communism, for all its triumphs in many fields, crushes the free spirit of man. Democracy itself gradually succumbs to the new cult of force and violence.

What then are we to do? The problem before us has to be viewed as an integrated whole, whether we think of the Congress, of our country or of the world. We cannot, to any large extent, affect the course of events in the world. We can mould our own destiny in some measure and thereby have some slight effect on world affairs. I want you to think of our problems in this perspective and on this broad canvas. We shall soon have general elections in this country on a colossal scale and already the fever of elections is raising the temperature of men's minds. These elections have an importance, but they are of little significance unless we see them in this larger perspective. What do we aim at and whither do we go? These are difficult questions to answer, but of one thing I am sure, that we shall not function rightly if we lose our own freedom of spirit

[1] Presidential Address, 57th Session of India National Congress, New Delhi, 18 October 1951. JN Papers, NMML. Excerpts.

and the springs of action that come out of it. Those of my generation can never forget the breath of freedom that came to us when our great leader, Mahatma Gandhi, came into our ken. That was something more than political freedom, which came much later. It was a freedom of the spirit that came to us, a fearlessness and a faith in our cause and in our country. Politically freedom has come to us and we are an independent country today, but I miss that fearlessness and that freedom of spirit. I miss these not only in our own country but elsewhere in the world. Indeed the predominant sensation in most countries, including the greatest, is that of fear, and fear is a bad companion and inevitably drives one to wrong action. Our Master taught us the ancient lesson of India, the lesson of *abhaya* and ahimsa, and even we, small men cast in a lesser mould, increased in status thereby.

He taught us also the importance of means and that means should not be subordinated to ends. Yet today nations encourage hatred and violence and prepare for the most terrible of wars. The lesson of history is forgotten, that these great wars have a way of following their own unpredictable courses and leading to results which were not desired or aimed at; that in fact wars do not solve any major problem.

We live in an age of science and that is supposed to be the moving spirit of the modern age. It is opposed to dogmatic religion. But, in spite of it, dogmas rule the world today, though they are not called religions. Science, which was a liberating force and which has brought untold benefits to humanity, threatens to destroy everything that it has built, including the mind of man.

Is this the ultimate result of the Industrial Revolution which began two hundred years ago or so and which has arrived at a stage when even the free mind and the spirit of man are becoming affected by the machine and are progressively incapable of that quest for truth and human happiness, which has distinguished humanity through millennia of painful effort?

I venture to place before you some of these ideas which trouble me and many others because I feel that we must find some answer to these questions before we can define our own objectives with clarity. Unless we have that answer, life becomes inactive and without meaning. The problem is a worldwide one. Culture and civilization are not the monopoly of any one or more nations and the hope of peace in the world is not just a pious aspiration but a vital necessity if civilized existence is to endure. We have a great deal to learn from other countries, but he have also to unlearn something and, in any event, I am convinced that if we lose our identity and the ideals that have inspired us in the past, then we cease to have any significance. We have served India not just because she is a geographical entity and the land of our birth, but because we thought that she represented certain ideals and objectives, the material and spiritual growth of man, and the unity of mankind. We have no desire to impose our ideas on others, but we were firmly convinced also that we would not allow any imposition on ourselves. If those ideals go and the service of India does not represent them, then our pride in India goes also and the urge to serve fades away.

We may be told that all this is impractical idealism, far removed from the cruel reality of today. It is this impractical idealism that brought success to us and it is the so-called reality that people talk about, that has brought great wars and might bring another and a greater one. This realism ignores the rise of great new historical forces which form the dynamics of revolution in the world today. Unless these forces are understood, there will be no correct appreciation of the situation. Gandhiji understood and represented in his own person these historical forces in the Indian context. That was why he was great and that was why he evoked a tremendous response from the millions of India. He understood also what India had stood for, her strength and weakness. His life was, therefore, devoted not only to the political freedom of India but also to the emancipation of suffering and downtrodden masses of people. He was a liberating force for these masses and for our womenfolk. But this mighty force for social justice and racial and economic equality was used without hatred and violence. It was his ambition to wipe every tear from every eye. It appears to be the ambition of many great men today to produce an ocean of tears and blood and in that way to try to solve the world's problems.

Our policies, domestic or foreign, flow from each other or affect each other and have to be integrated to some extent. They cannot be viewed separatelty. It is not our desire to play an important role in the world or even in Asia. Some people vainly imagine that India aspires to leadership elsewhere. This is a completely wrong assumption. But, as the world is constituted today, international cooperation has become essential and there can be no isolated existence for a nation. Either there is international cooperation or international conflict. Therefore, we are driven to cooperation and to have our say when circumstances require it. We would greatly prefer not to interfere in any way in the problems of other countries, just as we would like no interference from outside in our own problems. But we would welcome cooperation and help and, where possible, we would like to give our help in the solution of any problem.

The United Nations Organization and the great Charter, which was its basis, attracted us because it represented an ideal for world cooperation which had always been our own aim. Indeed we believe that some time or other, if this world is to survive, the idea of One World must take shape. We have given our allegiance to the United Nations even when some of its decisions have surprised and pained us. We still believe that it contains, within itself, the germs of that world order, which is the hope of mankind. But it has seemed to us that the UNO has somewhat drifted away from what it was meant to be and the intentions of its great founders have not been realized. It was meant to be a universal organization; it is something less now. This is a serious development and, in considering this, it is immaterial whose fault has led to this change. If the UNO ceases to have that universal background and appeal, then it begins to represent only a part of the world, however big and important that part might be. Instead of a mighty instrument for peace, it would tend to develop into something different. It is, therefore, becoming necessary to reconsider this problem afresh and perhaps to reorganize the UNO on a new basis, keeping to the old moorings, reiterating the Charter, but giving it a wider appeal and making it more in touch with reality.

Perhaps the danger of a world war is somewhat less now than it was previously. Yet fear of that war consumes and paralyses nations and much of their strength and energy is devoted to rearmament. A hungry and impoverished world cries for food and development, but the world's resources are directed not so much to development but to the production of weapons of destruction, and the mind of man is also turned away from constructive and cooperative effort. It is strange indeed that this should be so when the people of every country desire peace and everyone knows the terrible danger of war. Has something gone wrong with our thinking, and have we lost touch with the simple facts of life? Surely, it should be possible for the statesmen of the world to put a stop to this mighty race for rearmament and to divert this energy into more fruitful channels. The alternative is too dreadful to contemplate. Even if that final disaster is somehow avoided or delayed, this continuing process starves and degrades the world. Standards of life are lowered, frustration sets in, and the light of faith in the future, which has carried humanity through ages of suffering, grows dim. What shall we do when that light goes out?

There is aggression and fear of aggression and each feeds the other. Is it not possible to stop all aggression and interference by one country, so that each country can live according to its lights? We may not approve of the ways of another country and our ways might not be approved by others. But we are not likely to bring conviction by force and coercion. The only practical way is to accept that the world is various and diverse and that the people have different faiths and different ways of living. No doubt they will gradually approximate to each other because of modern conditions. To try to impose our system or our way of life on another is to provoke fierce resistance which defeats the very ends in view. There is plenty of evil in the world and evil has to be combated, but this will not be done by methods that are themselves evil, nor will it be achieved through hatred and violence.

If this is a correct approach, then India's foreign policy must be fashioned to this end. It has to adapt itself to changing conditions, but basically it must hold to these objectives. Indeed, throughout our struggle for freedom, we held to this viewpoint and it is natural that we should continue to adhere to it. To say that India is neutral or passive is completely incorrect. We are humble enough to know that we cannot do much to change the world, but we have a definite and positive approach to world problems and we would be untrue to ourselves if we discard it. We are convinced that any control imposed by one country over another, by whatever name this might be called, is bad and is a danger to peace. We are convinced also that the propagation and practice of racial inequality is an evil and is opposed to the basic principles of democracy. Large parts of the world today are underdeveloped and lack the primary necessities of human existence. This unbalance has to be rectified, for otherwise it will continually lead to conflict.

The First World War ended the world of the nineteenth century and upset the balance of power which had existed for a long time. The Second World War brought further upsets and a new set of political, economic and financial conditions were produced. It has been difficult for countries to adjust themselves to these new conditions, to the fact that Asia is a changed continent, where there is a mental ferment in vast masses of people and revolutionary changes are taking place. There is a passion for social and economic change in the hope of betterment. The land problem is the primary one for most people in Asia, but there are others also almost as important. These problems are not going to be solved by wars and large-scale destruction. Nor can they be held up by vested interests, either domestic or foreign. Liberating forces are at work everywhere and if they are not given a chance for proper development, they go in wrong directions. These forces represent the powerful urges of millions of people. Any attempt, therefore, to influence a situation must be such as to keep these liberating forces in view and direct them into right channels. To suppress them or to support some out-of-date system or reactionary force, which opposes them, is to fight against the current of history.

In India, as elsewhere, we have these conflicts between reactionary and static elements and dynamic and progressive forces. Essentially it is on the economic plane, but it touches the social life of the people in many ways. Thus, the Hindu Code Bill, which has given rise to so much argument, became a symbol of the conflict between progress and reaction in the social domain. I do not refer to any particular clause in that Bill, which might or might not be changed, but rather to the spirit underlying that Bill. This was a spirit of liberation and of freeing our people, and more especially, our womenfolk, from outworn customs and shackles that bound them. We cannot progress along one front and remain tied up on other fronts. We have, therefore, to keep in view this idea of integrated progress on all fronts, political, economic and social. That progress cannot be based on a rejection of our past, out of which we have grown, nor can it be a mere copying of what others do; it must be based on our own genius and cultural inheritance. But it has to reject many of the evils that have prevented social growth and it must take advantage of all that is good in the world.

. . . Communalism is a narrow and disrupting creed. It is completely out of place in the modern world. There can be no progress in India if we put up communal barriers amongst ourselves. This is not merely a question of Hindu and Muslim but of other religious and sectarian and caste groups also. Once this dangerous tendency spreads, we do not know where it will end and any dreams that we may have of rapid progress in this country will have to be given up.

We have seen communalism at work both in Pakistan and India in its different forms. It is based on hatred and violence and the narrowest bigotry. It attracts to its fold reactionary and anti-social elements who try to prevent social progress under cover of religion or some form of extreme nationalism, which really can only be applied to one community. Therefore it is not merely communalism that we have to deal with, but social reaction in every form. It is because of this that I have laid great stress upon the danger or vague thinking on this vital issue. There are not many who openly profess unabashed communalism, but there are a large number who unconsciously adopt its modes of thought and action. Some organizations proclaim that they are not communal and yet, they have functioned in the narrowest and most dangerous communal way.

Communalism bears a striking resemblance to the various forms of fascism that we have seen in other countries. It is in fact the Indian version of fascism. We know the evils that have flowed from fascism. In India we have known also the evils and disasters that have resulted from communal conflict. A combination of these two is thus something that can only bring grave perils and disasters in its train. It is degrading and vulgarizing; it plays upon the basest instincts of man. If India were to listen to this pernicious cry, then indeed India would not only have continuous trouble within her own borders, but would be isolated from the rest of the world, which would look down upon her.

Therefore it is a matter of vital importance today that we must curb and check and put an end to both conscious and unconscious communal thought in India. There can be no compromise with that and no quarter can be given. Only then can we realize true freedom and make progress. Only then can we live up to the old traditions of our country and to the heritage of our great movement for freedom.

In a much lesser degree, we have to face the disrupting nature of provincialism. India is a vast country which has a varied culture. All of us have a rich and common inheritance. We have also, in different parts of the country, variations in that common culture. While unity is essential, an enforced uniformity is not only not necessary but, I think, is undesirable. Why should we not keep this great variety which enriches our lives in addition to our basic unity? Most people, living in their particular corner of India, think of India as if it was a mere extension of that corner, and, therefore, want to impose their way on others. But India is much bigger than that part and much richer and deeper. It would be doing great harm to our concept of India, if we tried to confine it in a straitjacket of a particular point of view or some special customs or ways of life to which some of us are accustomed. There is a vast difference between the people in the southern tip of India and the people living across the Himalayas in Ladakh. Yet they both belong to the infinite pattern of India. Are we going to try to regiment them and make them all of one pattern? We cannot do so, because geography, climate and cultural inheritance prevent this regimentation.

There is also the cry of having what is called one culture for India, whatever that might be. India has a basic cultural outlook of her own, but it has been enriched in the distant past by numerous streams coming from various parts of Asia, and in later years, from the western world. All these are intimate parts of India now and have been woven into her rich and intricate pattern. It is this composite culture which is our proud heritage and which we have to preserve and develop. If we try to deprive ourselves of something that has grown with us and is part of us, we grow the poorer for it and we start a process of disruption which is bad for us politically, culturally, and in the domain of the spirit.

38

State Visits[1]

Camp: Munirabad, 28 September 1952

My dear Ramakrishna Rao,

I am very grateful to you and all the Ministers and officers who have taken so much trouble over my tour. I realize that this kind of touring takes a lot of organizing, and this is no easy matter.

While I greatly appreciate what all of you have done, you will permit me to offer some criticism and even some advice.

I have a strong impression that the arrangements almost everywhere were overdone. If this is what happens when I come, presumably, when the President comes, there is even more of this. I am sure the President would not like it even as I do not like it.

First of all, there is the question of expense. . . . Now, with all our repeated wish to economize and with so much of our work suffering for lack of money, any extravagance in reception of guests has to be avoided. I realize that some arrangements have to be made and they should be on a dignified scale. But dignity does not come through extravagance. In Hyderabad, traditions are those of great extravagance in this respect. You should reorganize this and check every unnecessary item of expenditure.

I think that there are far too many servants about, some of them apparently specially engaged. There is far too much food, far too many courses. All this does not fit in with the severe directions we issue from time to time about limitation of courses, etc. Indeed, in Delhi this would be an offence against the regulations. Good food does not mean a great variety of courses.

I have also found, to my surprise, that large quantities of furniture and other equipment have been sent ahead of me to the various places I have visited. This, in addition to a complete staff. I really do not understand why chairs and tables, etc., should be carted about in this way. Nobody wants these extra chairs or tables and the normal furniture of a place should be considered adequate. If any staff has to be sent, it should be the minimum required and certainly not nearly as many people as appear to have been sent.

[1] To B. Ramakrishna Rao. JN Collection, NMML. Extracts.

I am greatly distressed by the way traffic is held up for long periods in streets when I am supposed to pass. Presumably, this is under instructions from the Home Ministry. I agree that traffic has to be stopped on occasions, but this can be done a little more intelligently. Sometimes, when I was delayed, traffic was held up for hours on end, and this must cause great inconvenience to large numbers of people, to business, to students going to their schools or colleges and to others. . . . Surely, this kind of hold-up is very improper and some way should be devised to avoid this. I shall be writing to the Home Ministry about it also.

As I repeatedly wrote to you from Delhi, I think that anything in the way of feasting during such visits, or for the matter of that at other times, is undesirable and unbecoming. If it is necessary to meet a considerable number, they should be invited to some kind of a party where drinks only are provided, apart from nuts, etc. We should follow the rules we lay down for others and make no exception in our own cases. Indeed, we should make a point of adhering to these rules when a VIP comes. He has to set standards to others and not disregard the rules he helps in making.

Personally, there are very few things which exhaust and upset me more than banquets or an abundance of food. I am not used to it. In Delhi I have given up completely going out to meals or even parties at other places, except when some official function takes place at Rashtrapati Bhavan.

I am writing this to you because I think these matters have a certain importance and produce reactions in the public. Also if I think that my visit to Hyderabad is a burden to the state, and a nuisance to the public, I would hesitate to come there.

There is one other matter. There are far too many cars moving me about. These long processions do not look nice at all and there is no reason why so many people should go about with me.

Yours sincerely,
Jawaharlal Nehru

39

Democratic Planning[1]

Friends and Comrades,

Within a few hours, this year will come to an end and we shall all step into the New Year. I should like to wish all of you who listen to me tonight, as well as others, happiness, for the New Year, and work for the building up of our country. Happiness and work are really together for there can be no true happiness without a feeling of doing something worthwhile. What can be more worthwhile for any of us in this great land of India, than to participate in the building up of a new, ancient and ever-young country.

Three days ago, I was in the southern-most state of India, Travancore-Cochin, amidst some of the loveliest scenery that India possesses. In this state live a gifted people with educational standards higher than in any other part of the country. It is a progressive state, and I was happy to perform two important functions there. One was to start the construction of a new railway link joining the north and the south of the state and the other was to inaugurate a factory for processing monazite. I spent two unusual days in seclusion in a game sanctuary where wild animals live, protected from civilized man.

From the southern tip of India my mind pictured this great country spread out before me right up to the Himalayas in the north, and thought of its long and chequered story. What a wonderful inheritance is ours and how shall we maintain it, how shall we serve our country, which has given so much to us, and make her great and strong in spirit, and in the material things of the world, and make her people happy and prosperous.

We look at the world around us, and there is much to give us hope, but there is also a great deal to fill us with dismay for there is fear, hatred, violence and talk of war, just when it would seem that the prize that the world has so long sought was almost within its grasp. We look at our own country and find both good and evil, powerful forces at work to build her, and also disruptive forces, which would disrupt, and disintegrate her. We cannot do much, to affect the destiny of this world as a whole, but surely we can make a brave attempt to mould the destiny of our 360 million people. What then are we to do? What

[1] Broadcast to the Nation on New Year's eve, 31 December 1952. AIR tapes, NMML. Excerpts.

should we aim at? And by what road should we travel? It is of the first importance, that we should not lose ourselves in the passion and the prejudice of the moment. If we are to aim high, we must keep to our moorings and adhere to the high principles which have always formed the background of Indian thought, from the days of the Buddha, to our own day when Gandhiji showed us the path to right action.

Greatness comes from vision, from the spirit of tolerance, compassion, and an even temper, which is not ruffled by ill fortune or good fortune. Not through hatred and violence or internal discord can we make real progress. As in the world today, so also in our own country, the philosophy of force can no longer pay dividends, and our progress must be based on peaceful cooperation, and tolerance of each other. In India, the first essential is the maintenance of the unity of the country, not merely a political unity, but a unity of mind and heart, which discards the narrow urges, which separate and disunite, and which breaks down the barriers, which are raised in the name of religion or between state and state, or in any other form. Our economy and social structure have outlived their day and it has become a matter of urgent necessity that we should refashion them, so that they might promote the happiness of all our people both in the material things of the world, and in the domain of culture and the spirit.

We have to aim deliberately at a social philosophy, which seeks a fundamental transformation of the structure, a society which is not dominated by the urge of private profit, and individual greed, and where there is a distribution of political and economic power. We must aim at a classless society, based on cooperative effort, where there is opportunity for all. To realize this, we have to pursue peaceful methods in a democratic way. . . .

I want to tell you about the Five-Year Plan which after two-and-a-half year's labour, and much consultation, our Planning Commission has produced. Parliament has put its seal on it and now the time has come to implement it with all our strength all over India. That Plan endeavours to embody the social philosophy to which I have made reference. Democratic planning means the utilization of all our available resources, and in particular, the maximum quantity of labour, which is willingly given and rightly directed for the good of the community and the individual. I cannot tell you much about this Plan, within a few minutes and I should like you to study it or at least the summaries that have been available, because it affects each one of you, and in a democratic society everyone should understand and help in fulfilling the task ahead.

The Plan embraces the entire country, and deals also separately with each part of it, the states, as well as the smaller local areas. It offers also opportunities for voluntary organizations and voluntary workers to fulfil a vital and increasing role in national development. It has a public sector and a private sector, though even the latter has necessarily to have a measure of control so as to fit into the Plan. It endeavours to integrate various activities, i.e., agriculture, industry and social services. Agriculture is bound to continue to be our principal activity. Therefore, the greatest stress is laid upon this, as it is only on the basis of prosperous agriculture that we can make industrial progress. But agriculture has to be fitted into the larger economy of the nation.

The growth of industry, both big and small, is essential for any modern nation. Indeed, without industrial development, there can be no higher standards for our people, no strength in the nation and perhaps not even our freedom can be preserved. For the progress of agriculture, as indeed, for any kind of national progress, a proper land policy is basic. We have gone some way towards this, by putting an end, in many states to the zamindari and jagirdari systems. We must complete this task, and eliminate all intermediaries in land, and put a ceiling on the holding of land.

We hope that the next step will be cooperative farming, which will take advantage of the latest techniques in agriculture. Greater production is essential, both through agriculture and industry, if we are to fight poverty and raise standards, as we must. We want to develop therefore, as far as possible, self-sufficiency in our country, and balanced economy in various parts of it. We want to work more particularly for the expansion of the home market, so that standards may go up.

In this development of self-sufficiency, and in providing work and employment, village and cottage industries have a supreme importance. I shall mention a few of the targets that we have laid down. First and foremost, there is food. We must become self-sufficient in food so as not to have to go to other countries for our most essential requirement. The Plan raises food production, by nearly eight million tons. It is intended to provide new irrigation, through major works, to more than eight million acres, and through minor works to eleven million acres. Further, it is proposed to reclaim and develop more than seven million acres of land. You know about our great river valley schemes which, in addition to irrigation, will supply over a million kilowatts of power for industry. Power is the essential foundation of all development today. We have attached great importance to minor works of irrigation as they yield quicker and more widespread results all over the country. Cotton production will be raised by over twelve lakh bales, and jute by twenty lakh bales. It is proposed to increase handloom production from 800 to 1700 million yards. In steel and cement, there will be substantial increase in production. At Sindri, we have already a great fertilizer factory, and at Chittaranjan, a locomotive factory. We are setting up a new steel plant, a machine tool factory, and a plant for the manufacture of heavy electrical equipment. Air transport is being nationalized and modern ship-building industry developed.

You know about the many community centres, that have been started, all over the country. We attach great importance to these, for here an attempt is made to train our men and women in rural areas, in co-operative effort, for the good of the community. Here, even more than elsewhere, there is room for voluntary effort.

We have high ideals, great objectives, and compared to them, the Five-Year Plan appears to be a modest beginning. But, let us remember, that it is the first great effort of this kind, and that it is based not on our wishes, but on the realities of today. It has to be related to our present resources or else, it will be unreal. It is meant to be the foundation of bigger and better planning and progress in the future. Let us lay these foundations well, and that future will inevitably follow.

The Plan is not based on any dogmatic or doctrinaire approach to our problems, nor is it something rigid and inflexible. There is scope in it for advance and variation along any lines and at any time where such are considered necessary, and as we learn from experience, we shall improve.

It is a dynamic Plan for a dynamic nation determined to go ahead and stand on its own feet and to bring about a new social order free from exploitation and poverty, unemployment and social injustice. It is a step towards the establishment of a society, which gives security and employment to the individual, and scope and encouragement for creative activity and adventure. Properly appreciated and acted upon it will be a great liberating force for the energies of the nation. The Plan is a big one, embracing innumerable activities all over the country, but bigger than this is the vision which draws us forward, a vision inspired by courage and hope, and a reasoned optimism. Let us have faith in our country and ourselves. The Plan is essentially a programme of work. Let us work therefore, and abandon for a while empty and destructive criticism. I invite all of you to become partners in this great enterprise of building a new India. May the New Year take us along the road to achievement. *Jai Hind.*

40

Measuring Backwardness[1]

Rashtrapatiji, Kaka Saheb,[2] brothers and sisters,

First of all, I would like to say that I do not like the name of this Commission itself—the Backward Classes Commission.[3] It is as if we are first branding them and then, from our superior position, we shall try to uplift them. The whole approach seems fundamentally wrong to me, even if in fact they are backward. There is no necessity to publicize the fact. But I often doubt whether it is after all a fact and how far we are indeed superior, those of us who claim to do them good. It is obvious that there are certain differences. Perhaps there are differences in our lifestyle, our clothes may be better, all these things may be there.

But ultimately what is the yardstick to measure a man's culture? There can be many methods but ultimately I think it cannot be measured in terms of the dress people wear, or the houses they live in. There are other factors in the lives of the people and when I consider them, I doubt as to who is superior and who is inferior. Yes, some people are superior, even at first sight. But I am not talking of individuals but of classes. Therefore, if we were to go to any people in this huge country with the feeling that they are inferior or downtrodden and that we are going to uplift them, I think we would have messed up the job right at the beginning, instead of doing any good, because the method is all wrong.

If anyone were to come to me with the intention of uplifting me, I will not like it though there are many weaknesses in me. If anybody looks at me patronizingly, I will emotionally feel hostile to him, whoever he may be.

We must think a little, because I myself feel that we are not quite honest in our thinking. We are so irrevocably bound by the view that our way of life is superior to the others and that we are qualified to teach others. This is a wrong step right from the start. For one thing, this view is in itself wrong and it has a bad effect.

I often wonder why our brethren call themselves backward classes or

[1] Address to the Backward Classes Commission, 18 March 1953. AIR tapes, NMML. Excerpts

[2] D.B. Kalelkar was Chairman of the Backward Classes Commission.

[3] On 29 January 1953, a Backward Classes Commission was appointed to investigate the conditions of the socially and educationally backward classes and to make recommendations to the Centre and the States to remove their difficulties.

depressed classes. They must make an effort not to associate themselves with such names. After all, superiority or inferiority of an individual depends on his mind and heart. It is not a matter of dress or lifestyle. This is specially true of India and does not have to be spelt out because India is a country where the greatest man of our time did not live in a palace or wear beautiful clothes. So I shall with due respect warn the members of the Commission[4] advising anyone. They should understand and learn a little and then try to help by a process of mutual cooperation. A nation ultimately has to stand on its own feet. Others can help a rule, but if there is no strength within ourselves, we cannot rise. Therefore, whatever approach is adopted it should enable them to stand on their own feet. We must give them all possible help, educational, economic, etc.

It is my feeling that you will not find any group of people more eager and enthusiastic to learn and be educated than the tribal and backward classes. They are eager to go ahead by their own efforts. They merely need a little help and the opportunity to progress. There is no need to push them. Let them grow according to their own capacity. You do not have to stamp their progress with your views and ways of doing things. I want the Commission to think about these methods.

What are these backward classes? Is there an economic yardstick to measure backwardness? If that is so, perhaps 90 per cent of India's population will qualify as backward classes. Perhaps the number may be more. Where do you draw the line? Economically the majority of Indians are not well off. Most of them are very poor. The really well off people are a mere handful. Then whom are we going to uplift? The conclusion to be drawn is that we must find a way by which the whole country progresses, and not a few or a hundred or a thousand. These are difficult questions and the Commission can help us in finding a solution which I hope they will.

But ultimately the solution does not lie in legal remedies but in somehow trying to reach out to them emotionally, by doing service to them—no, even service is the wrong word, and I do not like it. We must cooperate with them and work as equals because even the idea of serving denotes superiority. Therefore I do not like the word though it is a nice word. I prefer cooperation and working together as equals. We are all equals. We must be prepared to live with them as equals and to teach and to learn from them, as two brothers would teach each other. This is how we must reach out to them so that they may recognize us as their brethren and that we do not consider ourselves superior to them but treat them as equals. Only by cooperating in big tasks, can we reach out to them.

[4] Bheekha Bhai, N.S. Kajrolkar, Shivdayal Singh Chaurasia, Rajeshwar Patel, Abdul Qayum Ansari, Lala Jagan Nath, T. Mariappa, Atma Singh Namdhari and N.R.M. Swamy were the members of the Commission.

41

Welfare State[1]

Camp: Srinagar, 24 May 1953

My dear Chief Minister,

I have visited, from time to time, various areas of scarcity where semi-famine conditions prevailed in Assam, in Bihar, in the U.P., in Rayalaseema, in Madras and lately in Maharashtra. There are, of course, others also and notably in certain parts of Rajasthan. Whenever I go to these areas, a sense of urgency fills me when I see human beings not getting their due from life. More particularly, I am distressed to see bright young children of India lacking food or clothing or shelter, not to mention education and health. Each such case produces a sense of failure in me, though I know that it is not possible to change the Indian scene by some magic and to produce plenty out of poverty. It is not possible to solve the 360 million problems of India within any reasonable compass of time. But are we moving fast enough in that direction? If this generation is condemned to large-scale poverty and low standards, must the next generation also suffer in this way?

Immediately, of course, the problem of relief arises where distress is most obvious. There is a great difference in our dealing with this problem now from the way the old British Government dealt with it. Without meaning any ill to that government, it must be recognized that its outlook in social and economic affairs was a very limited one. It took things as they were for granted and if famine occurred, it functioned in a routine way and set the old famine code in motion and gave some relief. We can never forget the death by starvation of thirty-five lakhs of persons in the Bengal famine ten years ago.

What a difference there is now! We have had to face calamities and earthquakes and floods in an abnormal measure during the last six years. We have not been able to give all the relief that we should, but we have at least saved people from dying of starvation. We have given them food and work and at least prevented that type of major catastrophe which used to occur previously. That is some achievement, I think, and it indicates the new social conscience of the

[1] To Chief Ministers. SWJN, Vol. 22 (II series), pp. 550–8. Excerpts.

nation. Where such need arises, we must help to the utmost of our capacity and in this matter we have to think of India as a whole each part helping the other.

This we have followed no doubt, but is the pace sufficient? Is it enough just to keep people from dying from starvation? Surely not. A welfare state, about which we talk so bravely, expects much more to be done. How then are we to do it? There is the Five-Year Plan which, I am convinced, is a magnificent achievement and which must lay the foundation of all our future Plans. And yet, while the Five-Year Plan gradually works itself out human beings in large numbers, including helpless little children, drag on their miserable lives with little hope in the near future. Everywhere I have gone, they ask for work and there is a positive dislike to the dole. That is a healthy sentiment which I have admired, for it is through work alone that they can go ahead and the nation will prosper. Work has been provided to the utmost capacity of the states concerned. Yet a large field remains uncovered and there are no resources left to deal with it in the present or in the near future.

Even the Five-Year Plan shows us that our estimated resources do not cover the expenditure we have to incur. There is a big gap which, we hope, will be covered by foreign loans or some internal effort, or both. There is no reason why we should not accept the foreign loans if there are no conditions attached. But for every benefit received, there is some moral obligation and living on benefits from outside tends to develop a sense of dependence on others, which is not a good thing. We have to strike a balance. It is clear that we must fulfil the Five-Year Plan and, if possible, go further, whether foreign help comes adequately or not. If our present methods do not yield the resources needed, we shall have to think of other methods. If our present social and economic structure comes in the way of finding these additional resources internally, then we shall have to think seriously of changing that structure.

The mass of unemployment in India rather terrifies me. What share have these unemployed in the welfare state that we are building up? And how can they have a sense of partnership in it? There is no lack of people willing and able to work and to produce if only we give them the opportunity to do so. The enthusiasm shown in many states in doing voluntary work has been surprising and most heartening. But voluntary labour, good as it is and to be encouraged, does not provide the purchasing power which those people need. It is only greater purchasing power leading to greater consumption which will ultimately help production. The problem then is how we can marry the unemployed to productive and preferably developmental work. . . .

It is often a good thing to try to see ourselves as others see us. We get so used ourselves to our environment that we do not notice any peculiarity in it. How far is it true then that our governments, Central or state, are influenced much by what might be called the conservative or vested interests in our society? We talk of the people. What are the people? The vast mass of peasants and industrial workers and landless labour appear somewhere in the background while special interests come to the front and make themselves heard. It would be a tragedy if we forgot the principal urge of the national movement that we are supposed to represent. That urge was always in favour of this vast mass of the common people and we have repeatedly declared that no private or vested interest should come in the way of the progress of these people. Do we act up to that declaration and assurance? Or are we gradually slipping away from it and forgetting our main task? It is a painful thought that foreigners should think that our governments resist the reforms advocated by the Congress. Our governments exist because of the Congress and are therefore called Congress governments. Governments have to be more realistic then popular organizations. But if they slide away from our basic platform and pledges, they will lose their influence and be accused of a betrayal of those pledges. The old cry of swadeshi is hardly heard now, although it supplied not only an economic, but a psychological need. So also old slogans fade away. It is for this reason that I asked for your special attention to the resolution on social and economic policy recently passed by the Congress Working Committee. That resolution is rather general and perhaps rather inadequate. But it does point to a certain direction and we must never forget to look in that direction. There is a tendency to look upon industrial labour as something rather hostile to the state and to be guarded against. It is true that sometimes organized labour is troublesome. But if we cannot carry organized labour with us and give it a sense of partnership in all our undertakings, we shall not go far. That would be so in any democratic state, but much more so in our state with our background.

Yours sincerely,
Jawaharlal Nehru

42

Lessening Flagrant Inequalities[1]

New Delhi, 10 September 1953

Dear friend,

I am venturing to address you on a subject which has been troubling me for a long time. Indeed, about a year ago, I drafted a letter on this very subject, but refrained from sending it then.[2]

Over six years ago, nearly all the old Indian States acceded to the then Dominion of India and various Covenants and Agreements were arrived at between the Government of India and the Rulers of those States. Those accessions, at that vital period of transition in India's history, demonstrated the wisdom of the parties concerned and the change-over was brought about peacefully and cooperatively. Few events that occurred in those memorable years struck the imagination of the world so much as this peaceful, and cooperative solution of a very difficult problem. This demonstrated afresh the genius and ability of India to solve its problems peacefully. Credit for that solution of the old Indian States problem was certainly due to the lessons we had learnt from Mahatma Gandhi and the general policy that we had pursued. It was indeed that policy which brought about that other remarkable change, a peaceful settlement between England and India resulting in the independence of India. But, undoubtedly, the Rulers of the Indian States deserve credit also for that solution.

It may be said that some such solution was inevitable because of the factual

[1] To the Rulers of Indian States. File No. 134/53. President's Secretariat. Copies of the letter were sent to 102 Princes who received a privy purse of rupees one lakh and above each. Sadar-i-Riyasat of Jammu and Kashmir was not addressed in this letter. On 20 August 1953, copies of a draft of this letter were sent to the President, Vice-President, Abdul Kalam Azad and K.N. Katju for their views. Rajendra Prasad writing back on 2 September said that the constitutional sanction should "be received if possible" but only with the princes' consent and "not in any way explicitly or implicitly repudiating the agreements made. Therefore, I consider your approach, if I may say so, to be quite correct, and I hope it will have the desired response."

[2] Jawaharlal Nehru had prepared a note for the Rajpramukhs and former Rulers of States on 25 August 1952 while in Camp Sonamarg, Kashmir. This letter is an expanded version of that note.

situation that existed in India then as well as the temper of the age. That may be so, but the fact remains that even obvious courses of action are objected to and resented. It was, therefore, a triumph of the Indian spirit which led all of us to tackle successfully this problem at that critical moment.

Over six years have passed since then and many changes have taken place in our country during this period. India has become a Republic and a new Constitution of the Republic was adopted and given effect to. In accordance with that Constitution, general elections were held early in 1952 and these elections demonstrated again the peaceful and democratic character of the Indian people. The political revolution in India was thus completed. But that did not mean that we had entered a static phase. Immediately we had to face economic problems and the vital and urgent necessity of increasing the well-being of the people of India. Indeed, these problems had been before us even earlier. They had been somewhat overshadowed by the political struggle for independence. The Constitution itself laid down certain basic principles of social justice and directive principles of policy.

The Constitution merely stated in dignified and emphatic language what all sensitive men and women the world over thought. Everywhere there was this urge for social change. In some places there had been violent revolutions and complete upsets of the existing social order. Crisis after crisis had arisen in various countries because of the impact of these social and economic forces. . . .

We have not only to meet the crisis of the moment, but also to lay firm foundations for preventing such crises occurring in our country. We have, in fact, to produce greater wealth and to see that it is properly distributed among our people. Both greater production and a more equitable distribution are essential. At the same time, we have to meet the problem of ever-increasing population which demands the necessaries of life. This increasing population leads to growing unemployment.

With our meagre resources it is difficult to produce the surplus which is necessary for future progress. It is only by large-scale investment in schemes of national development that we can advance. That advance, therefore, depends upon the surplus available for investment. This is the problem which the Planning Commission has to face continuously, and the consequences that force themselves upon their attention are not pleasing. We cannot expect miracles to happen or great progress to be attained suddenly. But the pace cannot be too slow either, for then events might well overwhelm us.

All this leads to serious thinking about the economic structure in which we function. Are there any impediments in that structure which come in the way of progress or our resources being tied up or not being used to full advantage? Can we move faster by removing those impediments or by changing that economic structure in some places? We have, of course, to proceed on democratic lines not only because of our Constitution, but because we value the essential features and bases of democracy and have full faith in them. How can we within that democratic structure achieve the best and quickest results in regard to social and economic progress? . . .

Apart from the actual economic and social changes that might be brought about, there is the psychological aspect of these problems which cannot be ignored. If we aim at social justice and equality of opportunity for all, as we do and as we have solemnly declared so often, then we must aim at the removal or a lessening of flagrant inequalities. That applies to every phase of our national life. Such flagrant inequalities are a constant irritant to the people and therefore tend to produce discontent and sometimes even conflict.

You have, no doubt, followed with sympathy and interest the progress of the Bhoodan movement in India initiated by Acharya Vinoba Bhave.[3] This has certainly caught the imagination of many people, and has even excited interest in other countries. Probably, no other country would have thought of starting such a movement. It is peculiar to the genius of India to try to settle a problem bristling with conflict and to unsettle deep-rooted vested interests by this peaceful method of appeal and persuasion. Nobody says that the entire land problem of India will be solved by the Bhoodan movement. It would be improper for any government to cast aside its own responsibility in regard to agrarian reform by relying only on the Bhoodan movement. But the fact remains that significant progress even on the practical side has been made by this movement. On the psychological side, the effect is even greater. It removes many a barrier and tones down much of the opposition of vested interests and thus makes it easier for the state to tackle this problem by legislation.

Can we apply this method, which is so much in consonance with the spirit of India and which produces results without the unfortunate trail of consequences that follow conflict, to other matters also? There are many economic problems which face us and which require this cooperative approach, if we are not to repeat the history of conflict in Europe and Asia. Vested interests, more especially in property and privilege, are not easy to dislodge. Past convention and even the authority of religion have been invoked in their favour. Any attempt to remove them often excites passion and anger, and yet the course of history, as you are doubtless aware, demonstrates to us a progressive change in the idea of property and in the conception of privilege. In ancient times, human beings were property, which could be treated like any other chattel by the owner. The autocrat ruler was supposed to own as property his country and the people there and do what he chose with them, subject always to the fear of rebellion. After bitter conflicts, slavery was abolished and this form of property ceased to exist. Probably there is no man today in the world who can justify the

---

[3] Acharya Vinoba Bhave (1895–1982) started the Bhoodan movement to collect land through donation for distribution to the landless; he toured practically the entire country on foot covering 40,000 miles.

institution of slavery. Other forms of property also underwent a progressive change. The serfs on land were given certain rights which could not be taken away. The old privileges gradually faded away, to a greater or lesser extent, in various countries. In fact, a test of the advancement of the country was how far it had got rid of inherited privileges and vested interests. Property ceased to be sacrosanct and social thinking gave the first place to the human being and the social groups. It was considered the right of every human being to have equality of opportunity with others. Property is a product of law, and by changes in law, constitutionally affected, we can alter the whole structure of property, inclusive of ownership, inheritance and maximum limits. Each one of us receives a great deal from society or from the nation. What do we give in return for that? If we take more than we give then we deprive others without justice. We must at least give as much as we receive. Indeed, we must give more so that the social group might progress.

I have stated this larger background because it is only when we keep this in view that we get the right perspective to consider any particular problem by itself. One of the problems before us is the present position and the future of the old Princes and Rulers in our country. As I have said above, it was an act of wisdom and statesmanship on their part to help by accession to produce an integrated and unified India. They deserve credit for that. The Government of India entered into certain covenants[4] with them and any such agreement arrived at by the Government must not be lightly reviewed. Whether I like that agreement or not, I would hesitate to go behind it, but at the same time, we cannot ignore the rapid pace of events in the country and in the world and the urgent demands of the present situation. There is no doubt that there is growing criticism all over the country about the terms agreed in many of these covenants. Reference has been made to them and resolutions moved in meetings of the Congress party and the All India Congress Committee. We have generally been able to restrain the members of the Congress, but others have expressed their criticism of the present arrangements more openly and in stronger language.

The fixation of very large sums of money as privy purses is totally out of keeping with the Directive Principles of our Constitution and the temper of the age. So also is the provision to have Rajpramukhs for life. We have Governors in our Part A States and they perform an important function. Rajpramukhs take the place of Governors in Part B States. As a matter of fact the functions they perform are, on the whole, less than those of the Governors in Part A States.

[4] In 1949, the Government of India introduced four Articles in the Constitution, namely, Article No. 291, 362, 366(22) and 363, which were directly continued with the assurances given to the Rulers about their privy purses and privileges. Foremost among them was Article 291 which provided: (a) such sums shall be charged on and paid out of the Consolidated Fund of India; and (b) the sums so paid to any Ruler shall be exempt from taxes on income.

Governors function for a fixed period; Rajpramukhs for life. Some principle of perpetuity is followed, though that principle has been given up elsewhere in our Constitution and in our political structure.

How long can we continue these anachronisms? How long can we justify to our people the payment of large sums of money from the public funds to the Princes, many of whom discharge no functions at all? We discuss frequently the problem of unemployment. Apart from the human misery involved in it and the bad economic consequences, in that the unemployed are an unproductive burden to the state, it is bad for any of them to be functionless. The unemployed at the other end of the social scale, that is, those who have no function and who give little or nothing to society by way of productive effort, and live on the earnings of others, are equally a burden to the state, and, as a group, socially undesirable. Moral, political and social theory does not justify the continuation of any functionless group, and more particularly, the payment of large sums of money to that group. In the context of India today, with famine and scarcity and the country struggling hard to overcome them, this anachronism becomes all the more glaring. Apart from theory, in a democratic state, where the masses of the people are politically and otherwise growing in awareness, no one can expect that this can continue for long. Ultimately the power rests with the people and the people will grow increasingly critical, and a time will come when they will exercise that power to put an end to anything that they consider unjust and a barrier to their own well-being. Should we wait till then when force of circumstances brings about a change or should we rather look at the present picture of our country and of Asia, with all its ferment and urge for progress, and bring about changes by cooperative and peaceful methods? Political wisdom consists in anticipating events and guiding them.

It is right that the old Rulers should live in dignity. We want our President, the Head of our Republic, to live and function with the dignity that is appropriate for the Head of our State. We have provided for that. Can it be said that others in India want to maintain some higher standard of dignity than even the President of India?

Many of our Princes have, apart from their privy purses, considerable private fortunes invested in India or abroad. There has been an unfortunate tendency to invest abroad. This is not in keeping with the service that India demands from each one of us, for India requires all her resources for her own development. Some of the Princes have left their ancestral homes and live elsewhere, cut off from their people. Some go to foreign countries almost every year and waste their time and substance there. I need hardly point out to you the impropriety of this behaviour and its reactions on the people. Whatever their private fortunes may be, certain arrangements in the past entitle the Princes to privy purses. But, is it right or proper from any point of view for those privy purses to be out of all proportion to standards in India?

I should like the Princes to give consideration to what I have said,[5] because events move fast in this world of ours and we ought to keep pace with those events. What might have been good yesterday may be wholly out of place today and tomorrow might compel a change. I am not making any positive suggestion in the matter at the present moment. I should like the Princes themselves to consider what I have written and themselves suggest how best we can deal with this situation.[6] Their own old States call loudly for development which suffer for lack of money. A part of the privy purse might well be set aside for the development of their own people. Private properties, many of which are now a burden to the owner, might be used for purposes of social welfare and public advantage. But, apart from the monetary aspect, I should like the Princes to line up with their people in other ways also and thus help in the great tasks which demand all our strength and energy.

Yours sincerely,
Jawaharlal Nehru

[5] On 27 November 1953, while replying to a question by Hukam Singh, Akali Member, in the House of the People, Jawaharlal Nehru said that no official communication had been sent to the former Princely Rulers by the Government of India about the possibility of scaling down the privy purses. Instead, he had written a personal letter to a number of Princes. Most of the replies received by him were in the nature of provisional replies, stating that the matter was being considered more fully. He further added that "it will not be desirable to give any further particulars about these replies at this stage." When Hukam Singh asked whether any of the Princes had conveyed to Nehru their refusal to reduce privy purses, the Speaker overruled him.

[6] While this letter evoked a lukewarm response, yet another appeal by Jawaharlal Nehru to the Princes in 1954, to agree to a voluntary contribution to the public revenues of ten to fifteen per cent of their privy purses, went unheeded. Subsequently, by the Presidential Order on 6 September 1970 derecognizing the rulers, the privy purses were also abolished. However, since the Order was declared *ultra vires* by the Supreme Court it became inoperative. Finally, by the passing of the Rulers of Indian States (Abolition of Privileges) Act in 1972, which removed the exemptions and immunities provided in respect of Rulers consequent on their derecognition by the Presidential Order of 1970, the privy purses and privileges were abolished.

43

Inter-caste Marriage[1]

27 May 1954

My dear Charan Singh,

You know that I attach the greatest importance to the ending of the caste system. I think this is certainly the biggest weakening factor in our society. I also agree with you that finally caste will not go till inter-caste marriages are not unusual and are looked upon as something which is quite normal. I would go further and say that there will be no real unity in the country till our prejudice against marriages between people of different religions also does not go.

But to say, as you do, that we should try to compel people by constitutional provisions and rules to marry outside their castes seems to me to offend against the basic principle of individual freedom. Marriage is very much a personal affair and we are trying to make it more and more a personal affair and to take it out of the old ruts of conventions and customs. What you suggest is definitely a retrograde step from that point of view, although it is meant to encourage a desirable tendency.

We have to create conditions otherwise. The Special Marriage Bill is one such step. Other steps should also follow. Ultimately people marry those who more or less fit in with their way of thinking and living. Indeed any other marriage is a misfit and any imposition from above is likely to lead to disaster in so far as the married couple are concerned. I cannot bring myself to think of the choice of marriage being controlled by legislation or by inducements offered.

Yours sincerely,
Jawaharlal Nehru

---

[1] 27 May 1954. To Charan Singh. JN Collection, NMML. Excerpts.

44

Special Marriage Bill[1]

Something rather curious had happened to Hindu society in this country, in the course of the last two or three hundred years. Hindu law was not an unchanging thing. In previous times, it was capable of change, and it did change—either they called it custom or whatever but it did change. With the coming of the British, it became much more rigid, oddly enough. They codified it, and did away with the customs or the changing character of it, and they consulted learned pandits, and learned maulvis in regard to the Islamic law, who naturally gave them what was written down in books many thousands of years ago. Although that has been changed by custom in many places, still it assumed a certain rigidity, which can be got rid of now only by legislation. And so we have come up to legislate—and that is right of course. But we have to remember that the rigidity that we have seen in the last many generations is not an original feature of Hindu society; it is a later development.

I do submit that this extreme reverence shown to what is called personal new law seems to me completely misplaced, whether it is the Hindu personal law or the Muslim personal law or any other. In fact, it means that you are extending the sphere of religion to all kinds of minor and temporary and changing situations in society. There may be certain basic concepts in a religion, which you accept. Now, if you go on adding all kinds of non-basic concepts to it, you are likely to weaken the basic concepts. The second thing is that if you admit that society changes—and I do not see how anybody can deny that society changes or that a social organization changes—to tend to bind it down with a certain organization which might have been exceedingly good at a certain time under certain circumstances, but which does not fit in with the later age, is itself not wise, for certainly it comes in the way of any advance or progress. And ultimately you put this alternative before the people governed by that society, that if you do not allow them to grow into something different, the only way out for them is to break away from it, to break away into some other society or into some other religion. It is a bad thing to give this alternative

[1] Lok Sabha Debates, on Special Marriage Bill. 14 September 1954, Vol. VII, Part II. JN Collection, NMML. Excerpts.

to any social organization. It should develop according to its own genius. It would be wrong, of course, to compel it or to force it to develop in any other way. And my own reading of our history is that in the past, there was that capacity for adaptation, for change, and that gave a certain stability to Hindu society.

45

Divorce[1]

We are often told that divorce is something against the basic conventions and ideas of Hindu society. It seems to me that almost anything can be described that way because Hindu society is so wide, so broad-based and so various that you can say anything about it either historically or as it actually exists today. While we talk about Hindu society, are we talking about a few high-caste people or are we talking and thinking in terms of the 250 or 300 million Hidus in this country? When we want to impress other people with numbers, we shout we are 270 million Hindus. But when we come to brass tacks, as when we talk about reforms, we think of a certain small group at the top. We cannot have it both ways.

Apart from that, what is Hindu society? In order to get the right conception, I say with all deference that you should not read some rigid enactments, like the commandments of Manu. You should rather look into the social life as evolved in our country in the past ages. A better way, probably, is to have some glimpses of the social life as found in our older books. Take one of our old plays, the *Mrichchaakatika*. Read it if you have not read it. See the tender humanity that is found in the play. There is in it no rigid puritanism but a human approach to the different problems of life. *Mrichchaakatika* was probably written in the fifth century AD, that is, about 1400 years ago or more. I need not describe the play. The point is that the man who wrote it reflected the life of his day. If you read it, you see a society which is highly cultured. The individual is highly developed. The test of an individual is how he treats his wife, his son or his neighbour. How he behaves towards another, how he functions in social relationship—that is the test of the individual. If this test is applied, our people in those days appear to have been amazingly advanced and tolerant and generous in outlook.

. . . In the national sphere, we try to settle problems peacefully. In the same way, in the domestic sphere, in the husband-and-wife sphere, cultured society avoids the rod of the policeman, that is, of the law coming down and punishing. It is a sign of the culture of a society or a nation to do away with the use of

[1] Speech in the Lok Sabha, 16 September 1954. JN Papers, NMML.

violence. If that is so in other spheres, much more so is it in this intimate, domestic sphere of the family. Whether it is husband and wife or father and child, the rod is not a good way of dealing with the situation. I use the word rod here for any law which oppresses, which constrains, which restricts, which punishes. Our laws, our customs—for the moment I am speaking of the upper strata—fall heavily on the womenfolk. That is why we are introducing this and other pieces of legislation. . . .

Divorce must not be looked upon as something which makes the custom of marriage fragile. I do not accept that. If that is so, I say that marriage itself has become a cloak. It is not a real marriage of the minds or bodies. If you compel and force people in this way, it will just be an enforced thing which has no value left in ethics and morality. Certainly stop them from acting rashly. Give them time. Make attempts to bring about a reconciliation. If all that fails, don't permit a state of affairs which, I think, is the essence of evil, which is bad for them, which is bad for the children, bad for everybody. I would particularly beg the House to take the view that this clause about divorce by mutual consent, subject to time, subject to reconciliation, subject to all such approaches, so that nothing may be done in a hurry, is a right and proper clause. It will produce a happier adjustment and a better relationship between the parties than would be produced if one party thinks that he can misbehave as much as he likes and nothing will happen.

The House knows that customs have grown up under which different standards of morality are applied to men and women. You will find women standing up for this right of divorce though some men may challenge it because men happen to be in a dominant position.

. . . Some people say that if we have divorce by mutual consent, the husband will exploit the wife, will kick her out and force her to give consent. It is a possibility; it may happen as many worse things often happen. I do not think it will happen if you give time. If the husband does want to behave in that way, the sooner the wife is rid of him the better.

46

Essence of A Democratic State[1]

For some time past, I have been deeply concerned at the growing tendency to indulge in some kind of violent activity in our public life. The very essence of a democratic state is its functioning in an atmosphere of peace. Problems, however difficult, are solved by peaceful methods, by discussion, negotiation, conciliation and persuasion. A decision once taken is accepted even by those who may not agree with it, who maintain the right to get the decision changed by peaceful methods. Till it is changed, they accept it. If this basic conception of democracy is not accepted, then democracy itself cannot function.

I recognize the right of any group to agitate for a cause, provided that agitation is completely peaceful. I can even conceive of peaceful satyagraha, although the occasions for this should be rare in a democratic society. But in no event should violent action be conceived or encouraged.

If we were against violence when we were carrying on our struggle for freedom, how much more so must we be now when we have attained that freedom and have the normal democratic apparatus for solving our problems. And yet, violence takes place over domestic problems. In the name of satyagraha, activities are indulged in which almost invariably lead to violent demonstrations. There have been many instances of this kind of thing happening among students as well as others.

I am not discussing any special incident or apportioning any blame. I am merely pointing out this tendency to try to attain some objective, however petty it might be, or to bring about a change through methods which are either violent in themselves or which inevitably lead to violence. I think that this is a very dangerous tendency. It is the business of every citizen to discourage it. It is more especially the business of Congressmen to do so.

What has troubled me very much have been occasional communal conflicts and violence. Some recent incidents, as at Aligarh, Pilibhit and Nizamabad, have been very painful. Again, I am not analysing any particular incident or apportioning blame. But certain factors stand out. Some rumour is spread or

[1] To Pradesh Congress Presidents, 18 September 1954. AICC Papers, Box No. 3, Youth Department, 1955–62, NMML.

some petty incident takes place which has no importance. This leads to excitement and conflict. Take the Nizamabad case. Some miscreant put up a Pakistani flag on a statue of Mahatma Gandhi at night. No one knew who had done it. It might have been an Indian or a foreigner, a Hindu, a Muslim or a Christian. Whoever he was, he was a mischief-maker, and the matter should have been dealt with on that level. But people get excited or are encouraged to become excited and arson and conflict follow.

This means that we are at the mercy of any mischief-maker who wants to create trouble. This is a very dangerous state of affairs. A foreign spy can excite our people and create trouble, or some goonda or other may do so, hoping to profit by the upset caused.

I want you and others to appreciate how ridiculous all this is, apart from its being rather shameful, and how it is discrediting us. In an organized state, people do not function in this way. If somebody misbehaves, the state deals with this matter and not the public.

I am writing to you briefly on this subject, but I feel strongly about it because this is bringing disgrace to our country and encouraging disruptive forces, whether Hindu or Muslim or any other. In the modern world, people do not quarrel because they belong to different religions. Unfortunately, they quarrel about other matters and even go to war, but they do not do so on the basis of religion. To do so is a sign of backwardness and exhibits a lack of that toleration of spirit for which India has prided herself.

I should like you to give consideration to this matter and to make all Congressmen feel that it is their duty to fight this tendency.

47

Building India[1]

Once I was asked, 'What is your principal problem? How many problems have you got?' I said, 'We have got 360 million problems in India.' Now that answer amused people, but it has an essential truth in it: that all our problems have to be viewed from the point of view of the 360 million individuals, not some statistical mass which you see drawn in curves and graphs on paper. Graphs are very useful to understand, but we must think in terms of individuals, individual happiness and individual misery.

We are starting planning for the 360 million human beings in India. We may sit down and argue about the theoretical approaches. We may argue about, let us say, whether we should have a socialistic approach or a private enterprise approach or a communistic approach or a Gandhian approach. We may go on listing any number of approaches; and it is interesting to argue and to clarify our minds, because thinking is helped by the sharp exchange of ideas. But, unfortunately, all these words which at one time had some precise meaning have gradually tended to become debased and to lose their meaning by association with hosts of new ideas, new conflicts, new passions.

Words are tricky things always. In the final analysis the word is the biggest thing in the world. All the knowledge we have, everything we possess, is a collection of words which represent ideas of course. A simple word like table or chair, if it is simply that, the matter ends there; but as soon as we get out of that category of tables and chairs and get to concepts which have emotional significance attached to them, they become very tricky. When we think of such words we get roused up; a certain emotion fills us. An emotion may fill us with enthusiasm but we cease to think straight. And when two persons meet whose emotions have been roused up in different ways by the same word, then it becomes quite impossible for them to have any reasonable discussion. In the international sphere today, there is so much emotion, passion and anger roused by words, and what the words are supposed to connote, that it is becoming very difficult to have consistent or reasonable discussion. Words are thrown at each

[1] Speech at a Meeting of the Coordination Board of Ministers for River Valley Projects, New Delhi, 13 October 1954. JN Papers, NMML. Excerpts.

other just as a bomb might be thrown at a person. Therefore, I say: Beware of words, great as they are. What do we want? Not words, even though words may signify much.

What do the 360 million people want? It is fairly easy to begin making a list—later there may be differences of opinion—but it is obvious enough that they want food; it is obvious enough that they want clothing, that they want shelter, that they want health. They want such things, regardless of the social or economic policies we may have in mind. I suggest that the only policy that we should have in mind is that we have to work for the 360 million people; not for a few, not for a group but the whole lot, and to bring them up on an equal basis. . . .

We are now at a stage when we can go forward in our journey with greater assurance. We have to utilize the experience we have gained, pool our resources and prevent wastage. . . . We cannot allow the nation's resources to be wasted. Democracy has many virtues, but one of its concomitants is wastage of time and energy. Nevertheless, for many reasons, we prefer democracy to other methods of government. That does not mean that we cannot avoid waste. We cannot afford waste, because the basic thing is that we should go ahead. The devil is at our heels, or as they say, '*Shaitan peechhe ata hai, to bhagte hain*'. I should like you to have this kind of feeling. To hell with the man who cannot walk fast. It serves him right if he gets out of the ranks and falls out. We want no sluggards. We want no slow people who always complain about their service conditions and their transfers and so on. I am fed up with such complaints. Service conditions and salary and status may be important. But I want work and work and work. I want achievement. I want men who work as crusaders. I want men who are going to fight for what they think is right and not submit humbly to wrong. I want you to do big things. I want you to build India. Can you conceive of a bigger thing than to build this immense country of ours? That is the spirit in which you have to undertake this job. And let the weak and the slow and lazy go to the wall. There should be no pity for them.

48

The Avadi Resolution[1]

We have said that we want a welfare state. Good, but remember that although a welfare state is in itself not a socialistic pattern, it is an essential part of a socialistic pattern. You may have a welfare state without a socialistic pattern but you cannot have a socialistic pattern without a welfare state. We want both for a variety of reasons. Now, do not think that we are going to achieve this quickly or rapidly. It is a very big thing. The point is that we must be set on the right path. We must look at that ideal and everything we might do should be governed by that ideal and that pattern. Therefore, it is necessary for the Congress now to state clearly that our Planning in future should be in terms of a socialistic pattern of society and that we should aim for that end from now on. The word 'socialism' has come to us from the West and sometimes it is a little unfortunate that it is a word with a history, and the past history of the word comes also.

Now the word 'socialism' in Europe has a past history and connotation. It is entangled with a great deal of struggle of the European Proletariat and others during the last 150 years or more and it is connected together with the struggles in regard to the last war, and in many other struggles. . . .

When I use the world 'socialism', I do not use it in the historical sense in which it has grown in Europe. Certainly, I adopt the principles because they are common to all but we shall have our own society. Our own way is to develop these things through peaceful methods and not through violence and certainly we should avoid what is much too common in peoples—'adventurism'—we are not going to get socialism by revolution or by a decree or by saying suddenly that there is socialism in the country. We can only get it by hard work, by increasing our production and by distributing it equally. And so this resolution points to this end, and I shall read it out to you in English now:

> In order to realize the object of the Congress as laid down in Article 1 of the Congress Constitution and to further the objective stated in the preamble and directive principles of state policy of the Constitution of India that it should

[1] Address at the Open Session of Indian National Congress, presenting the resolution. Avadi, 21 January 1955. JN Collection, NMML. Excerpts.

take place with a view to the establishment of a socialistic pattern of society where the principal means of production are progressively speeded up and there is equitable distribution of the national wealth.

I put this Resolution before you because I think it represents the wish, the hope and the aspirations of the people. I put it before you not merely for an aspiration but something with much more than that, as a pledge which you and I take, as a challenge to the future which we are determined to conquer.

49

Women's Education[1]

Truly no argument is required in defence of women's education. For my part, I have always been strongly of the opinion that while it may be possible to neglect men's education it is not possible or desirable to neglect women's education. The reasons are obvious. If you educate the women, probably men will also be affected thereby, and in any event children will be affected. For every educationist knows that the formative years of a person's life are the first seven or eight years. We talk about schools, and colleges which are no doubt important, but a person is more or less made in the first ten years of his or her life. Obviously, in that period, it is the mother who counts most of all. Therefore, the mother who has been well trained in various ways becomes essential to education. Most mothers, trained otherwise, I regret to say, are not good mothers. They are too soft. They stuff their children with all kinds of eatables, put too many clothes on them, wrap their necks and heads and ears with all kinds of woollen apparel and make the boy or girl almost an imbecile before he or she grows up. Therefore, it is necessary for women to be educated, if not for themselves, at any rate for their children. . . .

The idea that women should be kept away from most occupations no longer finds favour. It might be that certain occupations are not suited for women, but that is a different matter. There are plenty of occupations which they could engage in and which they do engage in. If we analyse the matter carefully, we shall find that the average women in India works in the field. In fact both men and women work in the field. It is only when one gets to the middle class that the question of distinction arises. The great majority of our women have to work because economic circumstances compel them to work. Unfortunately, the idea has been prevailing—I am glad to see that it is rapidly fading—that the less work one does the higher is one's status in society. Thus the person who never works at all has the highest status.

. . . A time is going to come when people will not tolerate a person who does no work. Therefore, apart from the intrinsic desirability of education, people should have education in sheer self-defence, whether it be defence as a nation against other nations of the world or within the nation itself.

[1] Speech in Madras, 22 January 1955. JN Papers, NMML. Excerpts.

50

Basic Education[1]

Friends and Comrades,

Looked at purely from the educational point of view, any modern educationist I think is bound to accept this method—called the basic method of education—and yet unfortunately, and to my great surprise, some educationists in our country have criticized it and have said that this is a throw-back to some primitive stage of education. I can only say that they have not taken the trouble to understand what basic education is. Further, they have not quite understood what India is aiming at today. The old style of education, it is well known, was originally started by the British and 150 years ago with the particular purpose of getting a number of Indians trained to help them in the administration of the country, in the lower grades. It is true that since then our education has progressed and it is also true that even under the old style of education India has produced some very fine specimens of humanity; very finely educated, cultured, trained great men and women have been produced by India. That is not an argument that that is a perfect type of education. For my part, I think that, given opportunities, India ought to produce a vast number of very high class persons, men and women.

I tell you nothing saddens me so much when I go abroad and when I see more especially little children who are denied education or proper education, sometimes denied even food or clothing. But if our children today are denied that, what is our India of tomorrow going to be?

It is the duty of the state to provide good education for every child in the country. That is true. And I would add that it is the duty of the state to provide free education to every child in the country, make proper provision for it. That is true. But unfortunately, we cannot do all these things quickly and suddenly because of our lack of resources, lack of finances, lack of trained personnel, lack of teachers, lack of many things. But we have to get going because after all whatever pattern of society we are looking forward to must contain trained human beings, not people who have just learned to read and write, but trained

[1] Address at the Avadi Session of the 60th Indian National Congress, 23 January 1955. AIR tape T.S. No, 12320 NM-181-Jawaharlal Nehru's Speeches. NMML. Excerpts.

human beings whose character has been developed, whose minds have some elements of culture about it and whose hands can do something.

Unfortunately in our country there has been a tradition that manual labour is something bad and degrading and meant for the lower class people. I doubt if anything has done more harm to India than this peculiar and fantastic notion that manual labour is meant for some lower class people and that the high class person should not move his hand but should only do what is called mental, intellectual work. That idea still persists. I can only describe it not only as a wrong idea but as a pernicious idea. I do not think that any nation that thinks that way can really progress. Apart from everything else from the point of view even of physical development, manual work is essential. . . .

This type of education which presumes to concern itself only with the reading of books, is, from any point of view incomplete. It is conceivable that you may become a high class mathematician or a high class something else as an individual but you will find you will be an even better mathematician if your body functions adequately and properly. Therefore it has become necessary in our country to lay the greatest stress on physical fitness. I do not like a person going about with a bent back. I want them to walk erect, ramrod straight. I want them to be quick in their walking, not loiter about, sauntering as many of us do. So it has become of extreme importance—this stress on two things, on physical culture, physical fitness, and the ability of their hands to do things. You can take it from me that if your hands can do things your minds will work more satisfactorily. I have no doubt about it. . . .

We say that we require "an education for the purpose of achieving the national aims and social objectives of free India and in particular to train the right type of personnel for the speedy execution of developmental plans." After all, you want to educate a person for something. What for? Well, perhaps previously it was to get a post or a job in government service. Well, government service is an honourable calling, there is nothing wrong about it, in free India certainly. . . .

There are hundreds of thousands and millions of ways of working. I do not confine you to this or that but you must, in some field of activity or other be a producer.

If that is our objective then our whole training must be aimed at that, ideological, intellectual as well as physical training. The whole concept of basic education is, as I understand it, that for a period of seven years everybody in India, boy and girl, between the ages of say 7 to 14 years, must go through this course of basic training and that training must give that person an adequate background to do something. He may at the later stage go to higher studies. Higher studies do not necessarily mean a degree like a B.A. or M.A. It will probably mean some kind of scientific or technical institute where he can specialize. But the first seven years of basic training will be common for all. That should give him I hope some cultural attainments, character, some capacity to work, that is fitness to carry on manual activity, and intellectual ability. Before that what I consider very very essential is pre-basic training, that is training of the child, from the moment almost of birth or at any rate, say after the child is a year or two old. Simple training but which is of the highest importance, more important than almost any training you may give afterwards, because the child's character is largely formed in the first five or ten years.

51

The Socialistic Pattern of Society[1]

The ideal of a socialistic pattern of society is not the ideal of any single party or group but of India as a whole. The words "socialistic pattern of Society" have not been used as a slogan or a vote-catching device.[2] The words have not been used in any rigid way but nevertheless they have been used in a definite and clear way to point out the direction in which the country is going. We are committed to it and we shall go that way. Let there be no mistake about it, not because I think that way—I have been talking about it for 40 years—but because the nation thinks that way and will go that way.

I want you to lift yourselves out of the old dogmas and think of the enormous opportunities before us, the enormous dangers before us, and make use of the opportunities we have of building us this great country, building it up peacefully and democratically, and building it up with as little conflict as possible, serving 360 million people and serving the world too. Attaining the socialistic pattern of society is not a question of legislation or something else. No doubt, the Finance Minister will gradually go that way, as he should. But ultimately it is all a question of our activity and the Planning Commission mentally looking that way and moving that way.

There is a talk in this connection of the private and public sectors and the conflicts between the two. To my mind there is no conflict between them at all. Some people, no doubt, feel that private enterprise should be given full and unrestricted scope. There can be no such unrestricted private enterprise and the state or rather planning has to come into the picture, and in a big way. With our limited resources we cannot allow people to go in all sorts of directions. There has to be planning whether for the public or the private sector. The private sector should be given a great deal of room but, broadly speaking, it must fit in with the plan. Planning will be no planning if it does not cover all our activities, public or private. The public sector will necessarily be more precise and definite.

Agriculture will necessarily be in the private sector. In that field our objective is to have small, peasant proprietors, though I am sorry to say that in that

[1] 13 April 1955. Newsletter No. 7. JN Papers, NMML. Excerpts.

[2] See ante p. 9, item no. 49. Refers to the resolution presented at the Avadi session of the Indian National Congress on 21 January 1955.

direction things are moving more slowly than they ought to. There will also have to be cooperative farming and all that. All manner of small enterprises should essentially be in the private sector. Small-scale and cottage industries should also essentially be in private sector, and not in any unregulated way.

So, apart from the vast fields I have indicated, I would welcome the private sector in others too and utilize all their experience and enterprise. But gradually what we should really aim at, whatever label we attach in our various sectors and aspects of national activity, is what is good from the people's point of view, what is good for the people as a whole and not a particular individual or group. If that is the test then gradually the public and private sectors will merge with each other. It has been the effort of myself and the Government to convince everybody in India and carry everybody with us. That does not mean everyone should think alike. That is uniform or regimented thinking. But there is such a thing called common ideal or objective, and I would certainly like a great deal of uniform thinking in regard to the objective or ideal. Just as during our struggle for independence, I certainly desired a certain uniform thinking that there should be independence in India, so also I feel there should now be in the country a certain uniformity of approach as to where we are going.

I do not want to use technical words as these always rouse passion by raising up in people's minds old arguments and suspicions whether it is capitalism, communism or socialism. The Constitution has definitely laid down some objectives in the sense of social justice and all that. First of all we should remember that whatever we desire it is for the 360 million people of the country and not for any small group or individuals. It does not mean that everyone will get everything but absolutely equal opportunities should be given to all the 360 million people. This cannot be achieved suddenly by magic or law. It will take time. But nevertheless we must move in that direction and must move fast. We can lay down targets. Everyone in the country should have the primary things of life, like food, clothing, housing, education, sanitation, medical health, employment and work. Once these things are put down, then the approach will be found to be very much simpler, whether it be capitalism, socialism or communism. The arguments will become much simpler. If we argue in this way, as I no doubt hope the Planning Commission will, without getting lost in theoretical arguments, the area of disagreement will be lessened considerably.

In India today there is a feeling of self-fulfilment, a certain hope and feeling that we are making progress and a certain satisfaction. I do not want that feeling in the slightest degree to be complacent. But there is that feeling in the country. And if you go outside the country, I think they are beginning to realize that something important has happened and is happening in India and that the vast masses of this country are on the move. That is a tremendous thing and something bigger than all your statistics about industrial production and the rest, though these statistics are themselves evidence, to some extent, of our being on the move. You might produce statistics of production much greater than today and yet there may be a feeling of conflict and despair in the country. If that feeling is there it will wreck all your work and check you.

So far as industrial production is concerned I should like that feeling in the country. It is not based on mere airy thinking or listening to some good speeches. I have great admiration for, and faith in, the judgement and good sense of the Indian people. They are not so easily swayed, though they may be temporarily, by religious passions or other slogans. We are all in the same boat with the people of the country and will either swim or sink with them. I am not going to jump out of the boat and seek safety somewhere else.

So when one looks around one will see the feeling of progress, hope and expectancy of something done and about to be done. What is that feeling due to? First, it is due to the improvements on the food front and, secondly, to the improvements in industrial output. The success of our community schemes, though they are not dramatic, have also contributed to this feeling in the country. While no doubt the community projects increase production, and bring in new roads, houses, etc., ultimately their main function is to build men and women and make a great number of people realize that we are building up India and are partners in this enormous enterprise. All this contributes to the feeling of achievement, self-fulfilment, and hope, and these are tremendous gains, greater than mere production here and there.

52

Goa[1]

A treaty has to be seen in terms of the historical developments that have since taken place. . . . So far as independent India is concerned, we are in no way bound by any old or modern treaty between other countries to which we have not subscribed, so that in no event are we concerned with the treaty between Portugal and England or other countries. . . .

I submit that in the existing conditions—I place my case quite clearly—the Portuguese retention of Goa is a continuing interference with the political system established in India today. I shall go a step further and say that any interference by any other power would also be an interference with the political system of India today. That need not be called a particular doctrine; it is just a statement of the present policy. It may be that we are weak and we cannot prevent that interference. But the fact is that any attempt by a foreign power to interfere in any way with India is a thing which India cannot tolerate, and which, subject to her strength, she will oppose. That is the broad doctrine I lay down. That applies in the existing conditions to the Portuguese retention of Goa.[2] Therefore, for a variety of reasons like national unity, national security and others I need not go into, we cannot possibly accept such interference or such foothold. When a foreign power has that foothold, it means that it is a foothold not of that country, but a group of countries with a large number of alliances, and therefore all kinds of possible dangers and entanglements might arise.

I do submit that the case of India in regard to Goa is as clear as any case that I can think of and it should not require really any great arguments to justify it.

. . . From any point of view, there can be only one decision of this question and that is, merger with the Indian Union.

[1] Reply to a Debate on Goa in the Lok Sabha, 26 July 1955. JN Papers, NMML. Excerpts.
[2] Alfonso de Albuquerque captured Goa for the Portuguese in 1510 and established Portuguese rule. In June 1946 Satyagraha Campaign for the liberation of Goa was started by the Goans. On 16 December 1961 Goa was liberated after 451 years of colonial rule.

53

Prohibition Policy[1]

New Delhi, 30 July 1955

My dear Gulzarilal,

One may rule out, if necessary, the financial aspect. I do not want mere finances to come in the way of any important social reform.[2] But the really important feature is how far prohibition, as applied in some places in India, has led to large-scale illicit making of liquor and law breaking. How can this be prevented? Merely to say that we should have stronger forces to prevent law breaking is not adequate because this very machinery tends to break down and becomes corrupted. This breaking down of the official machinery and the growth of law breaking leads to dangerous social consequences.

It is this basic question that has to be considered. I am anxious that prohibition should succeed, but I am by no means clear in my mind that it will do so by mere repetition of our desire or by even stronger legislation and police measures. I have had quite a number of cases pointed out to me where the police and our officials themselves go to pieces and are corrupted.

Again, there is rather a casual reference in the summary report to the North East Frontier Agency and the tribal areas in the North East. It is said that somebody from there came and told the Committee that they would like prohibition and therefore the Committee feels that prohibition should be extended there. I have no idea of what type of enquiry was made and how far it went. But I am rather alarmed at the casual way this very difficult question in the North East has been treated. We are dealing today there with a rebellious movement which is non-cooperating with every aspect of Government. In fact Government only functions in a small way in some of the areas, say in the Naga Hills. For us to imagine that we are going to impose prohibition there in these circumstances seems to me rather optimistic. This may well become a strong weapon in the hands of the rebellious elements.

I am just pointing out one or two aspects which have struck me on reading this brief report. I hope that the fuller report will answer some of my questions.

Yours sincerely,
Jawaharlal Nehru

[1] To Gulzarilal Nanda, JN Collection, NMML. Excerpts.
[2] Jawaharlal Nehru was responding to a summary of the Report of the Prohibition Committee appointed by Gulzarilal Nanda sent to him by the Planning Commission.

54

Foreign Tours[1]

New Delhi, 11 August 1955

My dear Ajit,

I must confess to a feeling of frustration when I see almost daily a new delegation packing up and going abroad. I suppose this is some kind of a penalty which big countries have to face. But surely there must be some restraint about this matter. An idea is grown in the Government of India that our work chiefly consists in our officers wandering about the world in deputations. No doubt they learn something, and I would be the last person to suggest that India should put up an iron curtain around it. But, after all, work has to be done in India and not in touring abroad. Therefore, tours must be strictly limited and should be avoided where not considered wholly necessary.

We seem to be very anxious to have the latest in everything, and yet in many cases we do not even take advantage of the elementary techniques that everyone knows. I have no doubt that if somebody goes abroad from here, he will come back and recommend some complicated and highly expensive machinery, because that is what he has seen abroad. Surely there is enough knowledge about dairying which every normal expert should know. What is the good of an expert if he does not know his job and if he is to rush about in foreign countries when he ought to be doing a good job of work here?

The fact that we are at last waking up to the importance of dairies in India should lead us to start work here. Indeed even the Indian Dairy Research Institute with its sub-institutes seems to me comparable to our having postgraduate courses without having primary and secondary schools. The best way to learn is to do something. If we have not got an expert, we should get one from abroad. But this wandering about seems to me very much overdone.

Yours sincerely,
Jawaharlal Nehru

---

[1] To Ajit Prasad Jain. JN Collection, NMML. Excerpts.

55

Mob Violence[1]

We see suddenly outbursts of mob fury and frenzy in Patna and Bihar, and, subsequently, the misbehaviour of mobs and unruly crowds in Bombay, Calcutta and even anger at certain events, but nothing can excuse this collapse of the people's discipline and their turning suddenly to violence and mischief.[2] Our complacency received a rude shock. Where was our policy of peace and goodwill; where was all the discipline that we thought that we had built up in our country? Was India, in spite of her achievements, doomed to fail? If so, then everything else had no substance and we would topple down at any rude impact.

This is a serious situation, almost too serious for us to talk about it much. I have referred to it briefly on one or two occasions, but I have said little of what I had in mind. My faith in India has essentially been based on faith in the soundness of the Indian people. So long as that held, other things would follow. But if that foundation itself was shaken, then the rest would collapse.

I have no doubt that you must also have given a good deal of thought to these occurrences and what they indicate. It may be that political parties or mischievous groups, taking advantage of the situation, have deliberately incited the people. Even so, why should the people respond in the way they did, forgetting all discipline and decency and all that they had been supposed to learn during the last thirty or forty years? Why should our students behave in the way they did? Most amazing of all, why do people not condemn wrong behaviour in students? I have heard few voices doing this. Indeed, at the height of this misbehaviour, everyone seemed to be praising students in Bihar, just when they were acting in a disgraceful way. All this stands quite apart from what the police did. Let us assume that the police were quite wrong. That does not justify students and citizens insulting the flag, insulting the Governor who was the Head of the State, doing public damage, causing grievous injury to

[1] To Chief Ministers, 26 August 1955. JN Papers, NMML. Excerpts.

[2] A minor altercation between the students of the BN College, Patna and the Rajya Transport Employees on 12 August 1955 led to police firing. Independence Day celebrations were disrupted by desecration of the national flag, leading to student-police clashes and black flag demonstrations.

hundreds of persons, attacking completely innocent passengers in railway trains and other places and generally creating violent anarchy. In Goa, tragedy occurred and India was shocked beyond measure. But it was a strange way to express sorrow by breaking other people's heads and demonstrating to the world how undisciplined and unruly we were. We, who talk of nonviolence and peace and coexistence, put up this show for the world to see. It was a painful thought. The only good it has done is to pull us up and make us realize the dangers of complacency. We shall have to work hard, and we shall have to work fearlessly if we are to meet this situation. There can be no compromise with this particular type of evil. Some people think that we may lose an election if we irritate the students or others. Perhaps so, but we are in the process of losing our souls and our integrity if we submit to this kind of thing.

56

The Concept of Panchsheel[1]

What are these five principles (Panchsheel)? They are very simple. The first one is: the recognition by countries of their independence and each other's independence, sovereignty and territorial integrity. The second one is non-aggression: the third is non-interference with each other; and the fourth is mutual respect and equality; and the fifth is coexistence.

I think we may take some credit for spreading this conception of a peaceful settlement, and above all, of non-interference. That each country should carve out its own destiny without interfering with others is an important conception, though there is nothing new about it. No great truths may be new. But it is true that an idea like non-interference requires emphasis because there has been in the past a tendency for great countries to interfere with others, to bring pressure to bear upon them, and to want these others to line up with them. I suppose that is a natural result of bigness. It has taken place throughout history.

This stress on non-interference of any kind—political, economic or ideological—is an important factor in the world situation today. The fact that it will not be wholly acted upon here and there is really of little relevance. You make a law, and the law gradually influences the whole structure of life in a country, even though some people may not obey it. Even those who do not believe in it gradually come within its scope.

The concept of Panchsheel means that there may be different ways of progress, possibly different outlooks, but that, broadly, the ultimate objectives may be the same. If I may use another type of analogy, truth is not confined to one country or one people; it has far too many aspects for anyone to presume that he knows all, and each country and each people, if they are true to themselves, have to find out their path themselves, through trial and error, through suffering and experience. Only then do they grow. If they merely copy others, the result is likely to be that they will not grow. And even though the copy may be completely good, perfectly good, it is something imposed upon them or something undertaken by them without that normal growth of the mind which really makes it an organic part of themselves.

[1] Speech in the Lok Sabha, 17 September 1955. JN Collection, NMML. Excerpts.

Our development in the past thirty years or so has been under Mahatma Gandhi. Apart from what he did for us or did not do, the development of this country under his leadership was organic. It was something which fitted in with the spirit and thinking of India. Yet it was not isolated from the modern world, and we fitted in with the modern world. This process of adaptation will go on. It is something which grows out of the mind and spirit of India, though it is effected by learning many things from outside, as it must be, because, if we are isolated, as we were for hundreds of years, we fall back. If we are submerged by others, then we have no roots left. Likewise, this idea of Panchsheel lays down the very important truth that each people must ultimately fend for themselves. I am not thinking in terms of military fending, but in terms of striving intellectually, morally, spiritually, and in terms of opening out all our windows to ideas from others, and learning from the experience of others. Each country should look upon such an endeavour on the part of the other with sympathy and friendly understanding and without any interference or imposition.

This is the role India has played. However little has been this role, during these past few years the general policy which we have sought to follow to the best of our ability has been progressively recognized in other countries. It may not have been accepted by all, certainly, not; some have disagreed with some parts of it or even the whole of it. But progressively there has been a belief in the integrity of the policy of India. There has been recognition that it is a sincere policy based essentially on goodwill and fellowship with other countries, with no ill will for any country.

57

Changing the Static Society[1]

I often refer in various contexts to the atomic bomb, to the hydrogen bomb, because quite apart from the terrible destruction that it might bring, the atomic bomb is the symbol to me of many things. It is a symbol, apart from destruction, of enormous forces coming into the world and ushering in the atomic age. It is a symbol of something not quantitatively different, but qualitatively different. It is not a question that if you use an atom bomb, more damage is done. Of course, much more damage is done. But it is something much more qualitative that has come about. In the same way, just as in the domain of warfare something qualitatively different has come because of the atom bomb and the hydrogen bomb, in the domain of politics and economics also qualitative changes are taking place, not merely quantitative. Something revolutionary is happening. The rapidity of technological advance is bringing this about and therefore it has become exceedingly difficult for most of us to keep pace in our thinking with the facts of life.

Now, there are broadly two types of thinking. One is what you might call more or less static, that is, following old grooves of thought which we know. The other is what you might call—if you like, I do not like to use these words—"dynamic" or "revolutionary", but you might for the moment use them, that is the type of thinking which is constantly thinking of change. Obviously, both are necessary. You cannot uproot something without having to pay a heavy price or having to build the whole thing afresh. At the same time, you cannot in a changing world stick to something when the world itself is changing. Now, the difficulty of those who think too much in static terms and of static societies, is obviously very great; when the world changes and is constantly changing, they are left behind. On the other hand, there is the grave danger to those who consider themselves high revolutionaries, of their living in a region of some dogmatic approach to an essentially changing phenomenon. The static person may be very reactionary; some persons who call themselves revolutionaries, may be equally reactionaries, in the sense that they get wedded to a fixed dogma and forget that the world changes.

[1] Speech at the FICCI Annual Session, 4 March 1956. JN Papers, NMML. Excerpts.

Now, take capitalism, socialism, communism and all that. I am not going to discuss these complicated things. But, broadly speaking, take capitalism. The capitalism of today in the highly developed capitalistic countries is very different from what it was fifty years ago or more. It is quite different. It has changed completely. Many of the theories that were formed then about it, both by the pro-capitalists and by the 'antis' have been proved to be not true. Some may be true. The capacity of growth, of production and all that, many things which seemed to be quite obvious fifty years ago are not so obvious today. It has changed its structure. It has shown much more life than many people imagine.

Take the other side, socialism and communism. The first thing is that even the most confirmed capitalist systems have tended, in spite of what they say, towards far greater socialist forms. It is inevitable in modern society, in a complicated modern society; one cannot help it. Even they have moved towards it, although they have maintained their capitalist structure. On the other hand, the socialist and communist approach has been followed in various ways, with various degrees of success or sometimes lack of success. Gradually, even that approach became very dogmatic and the great changes of the last thirty, forty or fifty years were rather ignored, with the result that whatever success it might have achieved became rather divorced from reality, or at any rate, divorced from reality in many parts of the world, because it was absurd to say that an identical approach should be made in every part of the world. That would be throwing overboard the scientific approach to the problem. Because the consideration of such a problem entails a consideration of the conditions, the objective conditions of a particular country. It is not something in the air. If the objective conditions of a certain part of Africa or of Asia are different, well, you have to think accordingly and find your solution, not by some magic formula whether capitalist, socialist or communist, but by applying certain basic principles to these objective conditions.

58

States Reorganization[1]

New Delhi, 10 May 1956

My dear Chief Minister,

There is no lack of drama in this changing world of ours and, even in India, we live in an exciting age. I have always considered it a great privilege for people of this generation to live during this period of India's long history and to take some little part in the shaping of that story. I have believed that there is nothing more exciting in the wide world today than to work in India. That very thought fills me with vitality and a desire to get the most out of this passing show in our fleeting lives.

But perhaps there can be too much excitement or the excitement can be of the wrong kind. As you know, our minds have been unhappily occupied during these past six or seven months with the question of the reorganization of the states.[2] It was not a question of high political or economic or social policy which usually stir people's minds. And yet it was a question which moved people powerfully and excited their passions. Those passions were not against an external enemy or some internal evil. They were against each other and the whole fabric that millions had built up by their labour through generations of effort seemed to crack up. Was this some temporary phase, an aberration of the moment, or was there something deeper to it, I do not know. I have tried to believe that this was a relic of the narrow regionalism and parochialism which had been our failing in the past and which were having a final spurt before this ghost was laid.

For the moment the ghost is there and we live a somewhat haunted existence. We may well blame each other, but that brings little solace or solution, for, in the context of India, we are all to blame and we have all to suffer the consequences. I have tried to search my mind and heart to find out where I have

[1] To Chief Ministers, JN Papers, NMML. Excerpts.

[2] The government of India appointed the States Reorganization Commission on 29 December 1953. The Report published on 10 October 1955 recommended the formation of 16 new states in India including Kashmir from the 27 states with three centrally administered territories of Delhi, Manipur and Andaman and Nicobar.

erred. What should I have done that I have not done and what should I have avoided doing that I have done? It is easy to be wise after the event. But the basic fact remains that we have yet to develop a unified nation. We distrust each other and sometimes even dislike each other. Under stress of some calamity or external danger, we may well unite. When that immediate urge is removed, we fall back into our respective shells and lose the sense of the whole. Painfully, we try to get out of these shells and build the unity of India. Step by step we advance and then something happens which lays bare our inner urges and failings. Whether it is caste or provincialism, we still live in a tribal age. Religion was exploited to break up our unity and now language, which should be a binding and ennobling factor, works in the same way. Meanwhile, caste remains to separate us and encourage narrow groupings.

I suppose we shall get over this distemper. But, for the moment, it results in a high temperature. The fever will go and we shall settle down to something more worthwhile. What tremendous tasks we have undertaken demanding all the strength and energies, and yet we fritter them and waste our substance.

Even this would not matter so much if we could face our problems peacefully and democratically, but we seem to live on the verge of violence, often crossing that borderline, and threats and coercive methods become the fashion. The very basis of democracy is threatened and our dreams of rapid progress become increasingly unsubstantial. Whatever our differences, there should be common ground about our broad methods, if we are to function democratically. These methods must be peaceful and we must recognize the worth of even those who oppose us, for we have to win them over. We have to learn how to accept decisions which are against us and which we do not like.

Yours sincerely,
Jawaharlal Nehru

59

Hindu Succession Act[1]

10 May 1956

Dear Chief Minister,

One piece of good news, which has heartened me, is the passage in the Rajya Sabha and the Lok Sabha of the Hindu Succession Act.[2] This will have to go back to the Rajya Sabha, as the Lok Sabha has made some amendments. But I think we can be fairly certain now that within a few days this Bill will become the law of India. It has had a long and difficulty journey and it has changed shape several times. At last we appear to be reaching the end of the journey. This Bill and the Hindu Marriage Act have a peculiar significance, not only because of the changes they bring about but chiefly because they have pulled out Hindu law from the ruts in which it had got stuck and given it a new dynamism. In that sense, the passage of this legislation marks an epoch in India. It indicates that we have not only striven for and achieved a political revolution, not only are we striving hard for an economic revolution but that we are equally intent on social revolution; only by way of advance on these three separate lines and their integration into one great whole, will the people of India progress.

Yours sincerely,
Jawaharlal Nehru

[1] To Chief Ministers. JN Papers, NMML. Excerpts.
[2] See fn. on p. 105.

60

The Public Sector and the
Private Sector[1]

We have said that our objective is a socialistic pattern of society. I do not propose to define precisely what socialism means in this context because we wish to avoid any rigid or doctrinaire thinking. Even in my life I have seen the world change so much that I do not want to confine my mind to any rigid dogma. But broadly speaking, what do we mean when we say 'socialist pattern of life'? We mean a society in which there is equality of opportunity and the possibility for everyone to live a good life. Obviously, this cannot be attained unless we produce the wherewithal to have the standards that a good life implies. We have, therefore, to lay great stress on equality, on the removal of disparities, and it has to be remembered always that socialism is not the spreading out of poverty. The essential thing is that there must be wealth and production.

There is a good deal of talk about ceilings, and one naturally tends to agree with it because one wants to remove disparities. But one has always to remember that the primary function of a growing society is to produce more wealth; otherwise it will not grow, and one will have nothing to distribute. If in the process of fixation of ceilings or in any other method of producing some kind of equality, you stop this process of wealth accumulation, then you fail in your objective. Therefore, whether it is in industry or agriculture, the one and primary test is whether you are adding to the wealth of the country by increasing the production of the country. If not, you become stagnant in that field. In order to reach equality, as I hope we shall, sometime or other, we need not follow the road of some artificial fixation of ceilings but a hundred paths which gradually take us there. An artificial attempt may indeed prevent us from reaching it. . . .

May I say here that while I am for the public sector growing, I do not understand or appreciate the condemnation of the private sector? The whole philosophy underlying this plan is to take advantage of every possible way of growth and not to do something which suits some doctrinaire theory or

[1] Speech in the Lok Sabha, 23 May 1956. JN Papers, NMML. Excerpts.

imagine we have grown because we have satisfied some textbook maxim of a hundred years ago. We talk about nationalization as if nationalization were some kind of a magic remedy for every ill. I believe that ultimately all the principal means of production will be owned by the nation, but I just do not see why I should do something today which limits our progress simply to satisfy some theoretical urge. I have no doubt that at the present stage in India the private sector has a very important task to fulfil, provided always that it works within the confines laid down and provided always that it does not lead to the creation of monopolies and other evils that the accumulation of wealth gives rise to.

. . . While the public sector must obviously grow—and even now it has grown, both absolutely and relatively—the private sector is not something unimportant. It will play an important role; though gradually and ultimately it will fade away. But the public sector will control and should control the strategic points in our economy. The private sector, as we have stated in the Industrial Policy Resolution, will be given a fairly wide field, subject to the limitations that are laid down. It is for us to decide, from time to time, how to deal with that sector. The point is that since we are an underdeveloped country, the scope for industrialization and advance is very vast. . . .

The way a government functions is not exactly the way that business houses and enterprises normally function. A government rightly has all kinds of checks, as it deals with public money. Usually it has time to apply these checks. But when one deals with a plant and an enterprise where quick decisions are necessary, which may make a difference between success and failure, the way a government functions is not sometimes suitable. I have no doubt that the normal governmental procedure applied to a public enterprise of this kind will lead to the failure of that public enterprise. Therefore, we have to evolve a system for working public enterprises where, on the one hand, there are adequate checks and protections, and, on the other, enough freedom for the enterprise to work quickly and without delay. Ultimately it has to be judged by the results, though one cannot judge a government by financial results alone. In judging a big enterprise, one has to judge by the final results.

61

Public Health[1]

The pursuit of health or the raising of the health standards of the nation does not mean merely the curing of disease, but much more so the prevention of it. Thus, while hospitals and the like are necessary, what counts most is the public health approach as well as health education. Health today does not consist merely in the avoidance of bodily ailments, but comprises in its scope health of the mind, which has a direct effect on the body, just as bodily ill health often affects the mind.

I am sure that the very first consideration in raising the standards of health of the nation is to supply adequate food, properly balanced. Poverty and health do not go together. Therefore, it is really more important for the health of the individual as well as of the community that there should be adequate nutrition. To this, I should like to add that food habits should be encouraged which would ensure a balanced diet. Unfortunately, we in India suffer most of all from inadequate nutrition, and even those who can afford to have what food they like, have seldom a balanced diet. Then, there is the necessity of a pure water supply, which is still lacking in a great part of our rural areas, though some progress has been made.

A war on disease and ill health is, therefore, essentially a war on poverty and all its evil brood. In effect, it is the raising of the standards of the nation in every way, and we come back to our Five-Year Plans whose aim it is to do this.

But, while this is being done some special attention has necessarily to be paid to the curative aspect as well as to the elimination of various painful diseases which affect large numbers of our people and either kill them or disable them. Malaria, I suppose, is the biggest scourge of all. Then, there is tuberculosis, venereal diseases, leprosy, etc. . . .

While our cities and towns require to be looked after much better than they are at present, it is really the village that has been terribly neglected and cries loudly for succour. Public health must, therefore, go to the village, and the village should not be compelled to come to the town in search of it. Our community development movement will, I am sure, play a very important part in

[1] Foreword to *Health in Independent India* by G. Borkar (1957).

this extension of public health services to our rural areas. I think that mobile vans should be increasingly used for this purpose.

I have no doubt that we should aim at a national health service which would supply free treatment and advice to all those who require it. But that is still a distant prospect, though we should keep it in view and endeavour to approach that objective.

One very important subject which affects the future of our country, is that of population and the control of population by family planning. I believe that our government is one of the very few governments in the world which have undertaken family planning in a scientific way. The progress made thus far may not be great, but it is commendable, and a basis for this has been laid.

... For us in India, it is of the utmost importance for the future of our country and our people that we should make this movement for population control by family planning a widespread and successful one. . . .

There is much controversy often about the place of the Ayurvedic and Yunani systems. There can be no doubt that both these ancient systems of India have an honourable history and that they had a great reputation. Most people know also that even now they have some very effective remedies. It would be wrong and absurd for us to ignore this accumulation of past knowledge and experience. We should profit by them and not consider them as something outside the scope of modern knowledge. They are a part of modern knowledge. But, in many directions, modern science, as applied to both medicine and surgery, has made wonderful discoveries and, because of this, health standards in advanced countries have improved tremendously. We cannot expect to improve our standards unless we take full advantage of science and modern scientific methods. There is no reason why we should not bring about an alliance of old experience and knowledge, as exemplified in the Ayurvedic and Yunani systems, with the new knowledge that modern science has given us. It is necessary, however, that every approach to this problem should be made on the basis of the scientific method, and persons who are Ayurvedic and Yunani physicians should have also a full knowledge of modern methods. This means that there should be a basic training in scientific methods for all, including those who wish to practise Ayurvedic or Yunani systems. Having got that basic training, a person may practise either of these systems or homoeopathy.

The question is thus not of a conflict between various systems but of sound education in knowledge as it is today and then the freedom to apply it according to any system. It is the scientific approach that is important.

62

The Dead have No Problems[1]

Parliamentary democracy demands many virtues. It demands, of course, ability. It demands a certain devotion to work. But it demands also a large measure of cooperation, of self-discipline, of restraint. It is obvious that a House like this cannot perform any functions without a spirit of cooperation, without a large measure of restraint and self-discipline in each group. Parliamentary democracy is not something which can be created in a country by some magic wand. We know very well that there are not many countries in the world where it functions successfully. I think it may be said without any partiality that it has functioned with a very large measure of success in this country. Why? Not so much because we, the members of this House, are exemplars of wisdom, but, I think, because of the background in our country, and because our people have the spirit of democracy in them.

We have to remember what parliamentary democracy means, more so in this time of change and ferment than in ordinary times. Even when the old order is good it has to yield place to a new one, lest one good custom should corrupt the world. Change there must be, change there has to be, particularly in a country like India which was more or less changeless for a long time, changeless not only because the dynamic aspect of the country was limited, restricted and confined by foreign domination but also because we had fallen into ruts of our own making, in our minds, in our social framework and the rest. So we had to take our souls out both from the ruts and from the disabilities and restrictions caused by alien rule. We had to make rapid changes in order to catch up.

But, while change is necessary there is another that is also necessary—a measure of continuity. There has always to be a balancing of change and continuity. Not one day is like another. We grow older each day. Yet, there is continuity in us, unbroken continuity in the life of a nation. It is in the measure that these processes of change and continuity are balanced that a country grows on solid foundations. If there is no change and only continuity, that means uprooting, and no country and no people can survive for long if they are uprooted from the soil which has given them birth and nurtured them.

[1] Speech in the Lok Sabha, 28 March 1957. JN Papers, NMML. Excerpts.

The system of parliamentary democracy embodies these principles of change and continuity. And it is up to those who function in this system, members of the House and the numerous others who are part of this system, to increase the pace of change, to make it as fast as they like, subject to the principle of continuity. If continuity is broken we become rootless and the system of parliamentary democracy breaks down. Parliamentary democracy is a delicate plant and it is a measure of our own success that this plant has become sturdier during these last few years. We have faced difficult and grave problems, and solved many of them; but many remain to be solved. If there are no problems, that is a sign of death. Only the dead have no problems; the living have problems and they grow by fighting with problems and overcoming them. It is a sign of the growth of this nation that not only do we solve problems but we create new problems to solve.

63

A World of Ghosts and Spectres[1]

We seem to be living in a world of ghosts and spectres. Over a hundred years ago a manifesto was issued by Marx in Europe which became rather famous in subsequent years. In this manifesto was the phrase "the spectres haunting Europe, spectres of revolution". This was the communist manifesto issued by Marx and Engels over a hundred years ago. Well, today, the spectre of war and apart from that spectre, there are so many ghosts that fill our minds today, there are the ghosts of old time which keep us tied to a state of affairs which no longer exists, ghosts of the past preventing us from thinking in the present or in the future, ghosts of Adam Smith thinking, making us, tying us up to some kind of economic thinking which has no application today, ghosts of Karl Marx also limiting our minds and making us think of something that he said a 100 years ago about conditions that existed one hundred and thirty years ago.

All these ghosts and spectres prevent us from realizing that we live in a terrifically dynamic and changing world, and what may well have been clear thinking some time back is out-of-date today in view of these new developments in science, in technology and the like. How are we to get rid of these ghosts and spectres that haunt us? It is very difficult, we in India have also to carry the burden which is both good value and bad, a burden, I do not know, of how many thousands of years of history and experience. Those thousands of years of the experience of our race certainly give us a certain balance, I hope a certain maturity which a race with this long experience has developed. But it also puts us into ruts of thought to some extent. And so we live in this world, this most dangerous world and yet it is so full of unreality, unreality in our thinking, in our actions, and yet there is the major reality of the hydrogen bomb hanging over us. . . . In recent years another phrase has been exploited and is bandied about "cold war". I do not know if previous to the last decade or so, people used these words. Maybe I don't remember it, cold war meaning all the apparatus of war and the psychology of war and the hatred and the propaganda of war, without shooting, actual shooting and killing. Personally, I should have thought that bad as the shooting and killing is, it is better than this continuous

[1] Address at a Meeting of the All–India Manufacturers' Organization, New Delhi, 13 April 1957. JN Papers, NMML. Excerpts.

propagation of hatred which eats into one's vitals and ultimately prevents us from either thinking or clear action. And if you look at this business of cold war in the context of these terrific powers exemplified by nuclear warfare, then you see the tremendous dangers that the world faces.

Cooperative Farming[1]

Nothing can be more important than the vital work of building Indian humanity. It is the peasant who has borne the burden of India for ages past. It is on the growth and betterment of our peasantry that the future of India must necessarily depend.

Today we are laying the greatest stress on two lines of advance—greater food production and more cottage and small-scale industries. Food has become the cornerstone of our planning and this means more intensive growth. We have made many appeals in the past for this purpose and they have brought results. The time has now come not merely for general appeals but for a specific and planned approach to each village and almost to each family, so that targets may be laid down and we may work up to them.

What is the future of our peasantry? A great number of them have barely one or two acres of land to cultivate. It is possible and necessary to increase the yield of this little patch of land and thus to better somewhat the condition of the peasant. But there is a limit to this—the limit laid down by the smallness of that holding.

There are too many people in India subsisting on land. This means that many people must take to other activities and occupations. Some of these can be whole-time activities and some part-time allied to agriculture. Herein is the importance of our cottage and small industries programme. No doubt, as large industries grow, many people from the rural areas will be attracted to them. But however speedy the growth of large industries, the major problem of unemployment and other occupations will not be solved by them. It can only be progressively solved by the development of cottage and small-scale industries.

Even so, how will the peasant function with his small patch of land? It is not possible for him to take advantage of modern techniques or the facilities offered by new methods unless he works in cooperation with others of his kind. Cooperation is the key to his future growth and the cooperative movement thus must spread all over the country and comprise all the villages and peasants of this vast land.

[1] Message to the fifth anniversary issue of *Kurukshetra*, 2 October 1957. *National Herald*, 3 October 1967. Excerpts.

What kind of cooperation? There are the so-called service cooperatives, there are those which deal with credit. We have in the past laid stress mostly on credit cooperatives and they are no doubt helpful, but they are not enough. We must cover a much larger field through our cooperative movement. Indeed, the co-operative movement should enter into the life of the peasant in as many ways as possible and, together with the panchayat, must be the main bulwark of our rural structure.

The next stage of cooperation is joint farming and there has been some argument about this. I have no doubt that joint farming, wherever possible and agreed to, will be good, but it must be clearly understood that this can be no imposition and can only be brought in by the agreement of the parties. To begin with, there must be the service cooperatives and as these succeed, the next step may well be some joint farms. Where new land is brought into cultivation, it may be possible to have the joint cultivation to begin with.

I would prefer relatively small cooperatives comprising one or two or three villages. It seems essential to me that a cooperative should not be controlled from above, not too officialized, but should represent the spirit of self-growth of the people. Also there should be an intimacy about its members, otherwise it becomes impersonal and difficult for the villagers to consider as something of their own.

This whole movement, as our entire political and economic structure in India, must be conditioned by the democratic process.

The community development programmes have undertaken a mighty task and they are gradually building up a trained and peaceful army of young men and women. If they are trained properly and work well, they will be the salt of the Indian earth.

65

The Basic Approach[1]

Nothing is so remarkable as the progressive conquest or understanding of the physical world by the mind of man today, and this process is continuing at a terrific pace. Man need no longer be a victim of external circumstances, at any rate, to a very large extent. While there has been this conquest of external conditions, there is at the same time the strange spectacle of a lack of moral fibre and of self-control in man as a whole. Conquering the physical world, he fails to conquer himself.

That is the tragic paradox of this atomic and sputnik age. The fact that nuclear tests continue, even though it is well recognized that they are very harmful in the present and in the future; the fact that all kinds of weapons of mass destruction are being produced and piled up, even though it is universally recognized that their use may well exterminate the human race, brings out this paradox with startling clarity. Science is advancing far beyond the comprehension of a very great part of the human race, and posing problems which most of us are incapable of understanding, much less of solving. Hence, the inner conflict and tumult of our times. On the one side, there is this great and overpowering progress in science and technology and of their manifold consequences, on the other, a certain mental exhaustion of civilization itself.

Religion comes into conflict with rationalism. The disciplines of religion and social usage fade away without giving place to other disciplines, moral or spiritual. Religion, as practised, either deals with matters rather unrelated to our normal lives and thus adopts an ivory tower attitude, or is allied to certain social usages which do not fit in with the present age. Rationalism, on the other hand, with all its virtues, somehow appears to deal with the surface of things, without uncovering the inner core. Science itself has arrived at a stage when vast new possibilities and mysteries loom ahead. Matter and energy and spirit seem to overlap.

In the ancient days, life was simpler and more in contact with nature. Now it becomes more and more complex and more and more hurried, without time for reflection or even questioning. Scientific developments have produced an

[1] *The AICC Economic Review*, Vol. X, Nos. 8–9, 15 August 1958.

enormous surplus of power and energy which are often used for wrong purposes.

The old question still faces us, as it has faced humanity for ages past: what is the meaning of life? The old days of faith do not appear to be adequate, unless they can answer the questions of today. In a changing world, living should be a continuous adjustment to these changes and happenings. It is the lack of this adjustment that creates conflicts.

The old civilizations with the many virtues that they possess, have obviously proved inadequate. The new western civilization, with all its triumphs and achievements and also with its atomic bombs, also appears inadequate and, therefore, the feeling grows that there is something wrong with our civilization. Indeed, essentially our problems are those of civilization itself. Religion gave a certain moral and spiritual discipline; it also tried to perpetuate superstition and social usages. Indeed, those superstitions and social usages enmeshed and overwhelmed the real spirit of religion. Disillusionment followed. Communism comes in the wake of this disillusionment and offers some kind of faith and some kind of discipline. To some extent it fills a vacuum. It succeeds in some measure by giving a content to man's life. But in spite of its apparent success, it fails, partly because of its rigidity, but, even more so, because it ignores certain essential needs of human nature. There is much talk in communism of the contradictions of capitalist society and there is truth in that analysis. But we see the growing contradictions within the rigid framework of communism itself. Its suppression of individual freedom brings about powerful reactions. Its contempt for what might be called the moral and spiritual side of life not only ignores something that is basic in man, but also deprives human behaviour of standards and values. Its unfortunate association with violence encourages a certain evil tendency in human beings.

I have the greatest admiration for many of the achievements of the Soviet Union. Among these great achievements is the value attached to the child and the common man. Their systems of education and health are probably the best in the world. But it is said, and rightly, that there is suppression of individual freedom there. And yet the spread of education in all is itself a tremendous liberating force which ultimately will not tolerate that supression of freedom. This again is another contradiction. Unfortunately, communism became too closely associated with the necessity for violence and thus the idea which it placed before the world became a tainted one. Means distorted ends. We see here the powerful influence of wrong means and methods.

Communism charges the capitalist structure of society with being based on violence and class conflict. I think this is essentially correct, though that capitalist structure itself has undergone and is continually undergoing a change because of democratic and other struggles and inequality. The question is how to get rid of this and have a classless society with equal opportunities for all. Can this be achieved through methods of violence, or is it possible to bring about those changes through peaceful methods? Communism has definitely allied itself to the approach of violence. Even if it does not indulge normally in physical violence, its language is of violence, its thought is violent and it does not seek to change by persuasion or peaceful democratic pressures, but by coercion and indeed by destruction and extermination. Fascism has all these evil aspects of violence and extermination in their grossest forms and, at the same time, has no acceptable ideal.

This is completely opposed to the peaceful approach which Gandhiji taught us. Communists as well as anti-communists, both seem to imagine that a principle can only be stoutly defended by the language of violence, and by condemning those who do not accept it. For both of them there are no shades, there is only black and white. That is the old approach of the bigoted aspects of some religions. It is not the approach of tolerance of feeling that perhaps others might have some share of the truth also. Speaking for myself, I find this approach wholly unscientific, unreasonable and uncivilized, whether it is applied in the realm of religion or economic theory or anything else. I prefer the old pagan approach of tolerance, apart from its religious aspects. But, whatever we may think about it, we have arrived at a stage in the modern world when an attempt at forcible imposition of ideas on any large section of people is bound ultimately to fail. In the present circumstances this will lead to war and tremendous destruction. There will be no victory, only defeat for everyone. Even then, we have seen, in the last year or two, that it is not easy for even great powers to reintroduce colonial control over territories which have recently become independent. This was exemplified by the Suez incident in 1956.[2] Also what happened in Hungary demonstrated that the desire for national freedom is even stronger than any ideology and cannot ultimately be suppressed. What happened in Hungary was not essentially a conflict between communism and anti-communism. It represented nationalism striving for freedom from foreign control.

Thus, violence cannot possibly lead today to a solution of any major problem because violence has become much too terrible and destructive. The moral approach to this question has now been powerfully reinforced by the practical aspect.

If the society we aim at cannot be brought about by big-scale violence, will small-scale violence help? Surely not, partly because that itself may lead to the big-scale violence and partly because it produces an atmosphere of conflict and of disruption. It is absurd to imagine that out of conflict the social progressive forces are bound to win. In Germany both the Communist Party and the Social Democratic Party were swept away by Hitler. This may well happen in other

[2] See Chapter 2, p. 300, also pp. 303–4.

countries too. In India any appeal to violence is particularly dangerous because of its inherent disruptive character. We have too many fissiparous tendencies for us to take risks. But all these are relatively minor considerations. The basic thing, I believe, is that wrong means will not lead to right results and that is no longer merely an ethical doctrine but a practical proposition.

Some of us have been discussing this general background and, more especially, conditions in India. It is often said that there is a sense of frustration and depression in India and the old buoyancy of spirit is not to be found at a time when enthusiasm and hard work are most needed. This is not merely in evidence in our country. It is in a sense a world phenomenon. An old and valued colleague said that this is due to our not having a philosophy of life and indeed the world is also suffering from this lack of a philosophical approach. In our efforts to ensure the material prosperity of the country, we have not paid any attention to the spiritual element in human nature. Therefore, in order to give the individual and the nation a sense of purpose, something to live for and, if necessary, to die for, we have to revive some philosophy of life and give, in the wider sense of the word, a spiritual background to our thinking. We talk of a welfare state and of democracy and socialism. They are good concepts but they hardly convey a clear and unambiguous meaning. This was the argument and then the question arose as to what our ultimate objective should be. Democracy and socialism are means to an end, not the end itself. We talk of the good of society. Is this something apart from and transcending the good of the individuals composing it? If the individual is ignored and sacrificed for what is considered the good of the society, is that the right objective to have?

It was agreed that the individual should not be so sacrificed and indeed that real social progress will come only when opportunity is given to the individual to develop, provided the individual is not a selected group, but comprises the whole community. The touchstone, therefore, should be how far any political or social theory enables the individual to rise above his petty self and thus think in terms of the good of all. The law of life should not be competition or acquisitiveness but cooperation, the good of each contributing to the good of all. In such a society the emphasis will be on duties, not on rights, the rights will follow the performance of the duties. We have to give a new direction to education and evolve a new type of humanity.

This argument led to the old Vedantic conception that everything, whether sentient or insentient, finds a place in the organic whole; that everything has a spark of what might be called the divine impulse or the basic energy or life force which pervades the universe. This leads to metaphysical regions which tend to take us away from the problems of life which face us. I suppose that any line of thought, sufficiently pursued, leads us in some measure to metaphysics. Even science today is almost on the verge of all manner of imponderables. I do not propose to discuss these metaphysical aspects, but this very argument indicates how the mind searches for something basic underlying the physical world.

If we really believed in this all-pervading concept of the principle of life, it might help us to get rid of some of our narrowness of race, caste or class and make us more tolerant and understanding in our approaches to life's problems.

But obviously it does not solve any of these problems and, in a sense, we remain where we were.

66

Fundamentals of Social Behaviour[1]

1. In spite of political differences, everyone should unite for the defence and well-being of the country and cooperate with others to implement programmes for the common good.
2. The unity and good of the nation should be given first importance and people should, therefore, rise above differences of caste, creed, language and province, and think more of the country as a whole.
3. Violence of any kind must be shunned and avoided. Violence creates hatred and is disruptive.
4. Religion is meant to raise an individual and to make him tolerant of others. Narrow prejudices and intolerance do not create respect for one's own religion in the eyes of others. We should honour not only our own religion but the religion of others also.
5. We should aim at equality of treatment and avoid feelings of high and low and touchable and untouchable.
6. We should aim at becoming good citizens, subordinating self-interest and aiming at the common good.
7. Women should be treated with respect and as comrades. They should not be kept in purdah or seclusion, but given opportunities to participate in national activities.
8. Children should be treated with affection and gentleness and not beaten or scolded.
9. Liquor and all other intoxicants should be avoided.
10. Village and cottage industries should be encouraged, and as far as possible khadi should be used.
11. Adulteration of foodstuffs and other articles must be prevented.
12. The giving or accepting of bribes is bad, both for the giver and the taker, and must be vigorously dealt with.
13. The house, street and village or town should be kept neat and clean.

[1] An Appeal to the People of India, 1959. JN Papers, NMML.

14. We should try to understand the great development work that is going on in the country, such as the Five-Year Plan, the community development schemes, etc., and cooperate in furthering and implementing it.

15. Manual labour should be respected and everyone should endeavour to engage himself in some form of manual labour for constructive work.

67

Family Planning[1]

Dear Dhanvanthi Rama Rau,

I am wholly in favour of family planning. Certainly one of its principal objects is to lessen the rate of population increase. This is very important. But there are other aspects also: to give a fuller life to the family and more particularly to the mother and the children. The standard of living, education, etc., in a large family is likely to be lower than that in a somewhat smaller family.

Any marked success in this movement will depend on two factors: (1) a widespread approach to our rural population, and (2) simple and cheap methods. We have heard much of oral contraceptives. Undoubtedly, if these are effective, they would go a long way to provide a suitable method.

If we have to approach the rural population, this means (1) a fairly widespread propaganda to create a background of acceptance, and (2) large numbers of clinics or centres where such information can be given. It would hardly be feasible to have separate family planning centres all over the country. This work will have to be coordinated, therefore, with other centres for maternity, child and various types of medical and health services.

In everything that we do in India, it must be remembered that the organizational structure should not be top-heavy and expensive. Otherwise it is limited in scope.

Yours sincerely,
Jawaharlal Nehru

---

[1] To Dhanvanthi Rama Rau, 18 October 1959. JN Papers, NMML. Excerpts.

68

Town Planning[1]

You know how attached I am to the concept of planning. What is planning? Planning is the application of your intellect to a logical, reasonable and better way of doing things. It passes my understanding how any person with a grain of intelligence can object to planning, because such an objection amounts to objecting to an intelligent approach to things. Whether it is in economics or politics, or anything else, planning is essential.

In the India of today, the growth of cities, big and small ones, is quite anarchic. It is ugly, it is horrible, in fact, it is painful to see it. I am surprised how it is tolerated by great corporations and city municipalities. The same thing applies, in a smaller sense, to the small towns and the larger villages, etc. You go to any of these big cities, even the good ones. You find their outskirts growing as if there were nobody to govern them. The corporation is busy dealing with the heart of the town, and not with what happens on its outskirts. No road should be built on the edge of a town which is not wide enough to contain all the traffic in the next 50, 60, 100 years, if you like. Sufficient room should be left for a widening of the road on either side. Nobody should be allowed to build there.

This is a very minor instance that I have placed before you. Town planning is becoming more and more important in India, not only planning of great cities like Delhi or Calcutta, which is very important, but smaller cities and smaller towns. Planning now means not only producing something more liveable but possibly doing away with many of the difficulties and dangers that may come later. You must think of that. You must build for the future. Build for the present, by all means, but build also for the future with schools and hospitals and playgrounds, markets and roads. All these things do not cost much except a little extra labour and thought. I am afraid the habit of thought is not particularly obvious among our municipal councillors. They are so busy with their day-to-day difficulties that they seldom think of the future.

[1] Speech at a Meeting of the Central Council of Local Self-governments, New Delhi, 6 September 1963. JN Papers, NMML. Excerpts.

VOL. II

II
India and Beyond

1.	A Foreign Policy for India	191
2.	The Fascination of Russia	196
3.	International Contacts	198
4.	The Imperialist Danger	202
5.	India and the World	205
6.	World Events	211
7.	Spain	215
8.	A World Federation	216
9.	A Real Commonwealth	218
10.	*Quatorze Juillet*	220
11.	Colonialism Must Go	222
12.	Policy Towards Burma	225
13.	A United Asia	229
14.	Sympathy for Jews	233
15.	Basic Principles	236
16.	Note on Foreign Policy	241
17.	The Occident and the Orient	245
18.	An Independent Foreign Policy	247
19.	The Problem of Burma	249
20.	Cooperation in the Commonwealth	256

21. Relations with the Soviet Union   258

22. Commonwealth Prime Minister's Conference   260

23. A Voyage of Discovery   262

24. Exclusion of Some Countries from the UN   265

25. World Affairs   267

26. Annexation of Tibet   271

27. World Today   274

28. Japanese Peace Treaty   276

29. The Nonviolent Struggle in South Africa   280

30. An Overburdened World   282

31. South African Situation   284

32. The Great Adventure of Man   288

33. Bulganin, Khrushchev Visit   292

34. Saudi Arabia   294

35. A World of Unreality   297

36. Suez Crisis   299

37. Non-aggression and Non-interference   301

38. Racial Discrimination   304

39. The Chinese Aggression   306

40. The Proclamation of Emergency   310

41. A Popular Upsurge   313

1

A Foreign Policy for India[1]

To some of us in India it may appear a foolish waste of time to indulge in fancies about a foreign policy for India. Our national movement is at an ebb and the country appears to be rent into many factions—religious, economic and political. Efforts are being made to bridge the gulf between the Hindu and the Muslim and to bring the various political groups under one banner. Laudable as these efforts are they seldom appear to take into consideration the fundamental causes of disunion or lay much stress on the underlying principles which only can form the basis of effective political action. Unity is good and worth striving for with all our might, but only if it is based on principles which matter and which are believed in. A patched-up unity at the cost of principles can only be followed by disruption at the moment of crisis and consequent disaster. It is bad ethics and worse policy. It is no waste of time, therefore, for us to consider some of these principles and the wider aspects of the India problem. . . .

What are these problems? There are many but the four principal ones appear to be: the question of minorities, our future economic structure, our social problem, and our foreign relations.

A consideration of the minorities problem will include the Hindu-Muslim question, the Brahmana and the non-Brahmana, the Sikhs and the smaller minorities. We shall have to see how far the existing friction is due to economic causes and to what extent merely to religious intolerance and bigotry. The latter will involve a comparison with other countries and would lead us to the regrettable conclusion that our country, with its age-long reputation for religious tolerance, is today the worst example of intolerance and bigotry. It will be for us to consider whether this narrow outlook and religiosity can be eradicated by cautious compromises between rival superstitions or by a frontal attack on all superstition and bigotry, wherever it may be.

Our second problem—the future economic structure of our country—raises the vital issue which is convulsing Europe today. Are we to aim at a continuation of the capitalist regime in India, or some form of socialism, or something else which is different from either of these? This will largely influence our constitution and our methods of government. It will also necessitate

[1] Article written in Montana, Switzerland, 13 September 1927. AICC. File No. 8, 1927, pp. 1–27. NMML. Excerpts.

a consideration of the causes of Indian poverty, of the terrible over-pressure on land, of land tenure and land revenue. We are apt to imagine that with the withdrawal of British political control the 'drain' of India's wealth will cease. We forget that the amount that India pays in the shape of salaries and pensions and the bank charges and the like is only a small part of her tribute, and it is quite conceivable that even self-government may not stop the exploitation of the country, unless it is followed by a change in our economic structure.

The third problem deals with our social evils and raises vital issues which must be faced and boldly tackled. Katherine Mayo's notorious book, *Mother India*,[2] has broadcast the most amazing generalizations and calumnies about our country. It would be easy enough for anyone so minded to write a similar book about France or England or America, and by picking out the most disgusting facts from the records of the police courts and the files of Sunday journals to point to the conclusion that it was a loathsome country, past all redemption. And yet everyone knows that this would be a false caricature and a calumny, and that France and England and America have a great deal that is admirable and noble and worth acquiring. It is difficult for an Indian to read Katherine Mayo's book without anger and resentment. No person, Indian or foreigner, who has any knowledge of India, can read the vile charges brought against our people as a whole, without knowing from his personal experience that they are false. The book is a particularly mean and disgraceful effort at propaganda, and yet I should like as many Indians as possible to read it. We have our plague spots. Let us face them squarely and root them all out.

The fourth and the last problem for us to consider is that of foreign policy. I propose only to deal with this here and not with the other three, although it is difficult to separate questions which are so intimately connected. Our foreign relations will include our relations with England and her empire, now called the British Commonwealth of Nations.

Many attempts have been made in recent years to induce the Congress to take up foreign propaganda, and although some resolutions favouring it have been adopted, little has been done. It has been rightly felt that our energy and money can be better employed at home. But the question we have now to consider is not one of propaganda to gain the sympathy of others but one of ending the isolation in which India has lived for generations and of developing contacts with other parts of the world. Whether we wish it or not India cannot remain, now or hereafter, cut off from the rest of the world. No country can do so. The modern world is too closely knit together to permit of such isolation. . . .

India cannot keep apart from this tangled web, and her refusing to take heed of it may indeed lead her to disaster. We must understand world movements and politics and fashion our own movement accordingly. This cannot

---

[2] Katherine Mayo was an American author who sought to show that India was socially backward and therefore unfit for freedom. Her book was written with the active assistance of British officials in London and India.

mean that we have to subordinate our interests or our methods of work to those of any other country or organization. Nor does it mean that we should expect any help from outside or slacken our efforts at home. It simply means that we must educate ourselves in problems of world polity so that we may be able to serve our country better. It means that whenever possible we may take part in international joint action when this is to our advantage. It means also that we should gradually train a body of men and women who can be relied upon to serve Indian interests abroad when the power for doing this comes into our hands. Let us remember that there are many countries and many peoples who suffer as India does today. They have to face the same problems as ours and it must be to the advantage of both of us to know more of each other and to cooperate where possible. . . .

What is the position of the Indian in foreign countries today? Apart from a few students and others, he has gone either as a coolie or as a mercenary soldier on behalf of England. As a coolie he is looked down upon with contempt and as a hireling of the exploiters he is hated. Indian soldiers and the police have been used by the British Government to further its own interests in China, Egypt, Abyssinia, Mesopotamia, the Persian Gulf, Arabia, Tibet, Syria, Afghanistan and Burma, and wherever they have gone they have made the name of India hated. In Burma one can understand the grievance of some people against their exploitation by the British and Indians and their desire to separate from India. In Mesopotamia our coutnrymen hold the country for the British and also join in the process of exploitation. Even in Annam, I am told by friends, the Indian community always sides with the French Government against the Annamese and, in the elections for a deputy for the French Chamber, cast their votes for the official nominee. In Shanghai the most hated are the Indian police who are made to do the dirty work of their imperial masters. It is not surprising, regrettable as it may be, that the Indian is not loved in those very countries which suffer a common fate with us and which should be our friends and allies. It is for the Congress to develop these contacts and to strive unceasingly for the withdrawal of all Indian armies and police from foreign countries. On the occasion of the despatch of Indian forces to Shanghai, the Viceroy declared that they were being sent to protect Indian interests in China. We have no interests there or anywhere which require the protection of armed force and even if we had such interests it is better for them to suffer than to be protected at the point of the bayonet. The only interests we wish to develop in any country are such as are acceptable to the people of that country. . . .

In developing our foreign policy we shall naturally first cultivate friendly relations with the countries of the East which have so much in common with us. Nepal will be our neighbour and friend; with China and Japan, Indonesia, Annam, and Central Asia we shall have the closest contact. So also with Afghanistan, Persia, Turkey and Egypt. Some people, living in a world of their own creation, imagine that there is a pan-Islamic block which may threaten India.

This is pure fancy. Every one of the Islamic countries is developing on intensely national lines and there is absolutely no room in them for an external policy based on religion. Indeed even their domestic policy has little to do with religious dogmas. The interests of these countries are and will continue to be our interests. With the European nations we are bound to develop further contacts. We have much to learn from them and closer intercourse will be to the advantage of both.

Russia offers a peculiar problem which requires special consideration. She has adopted an economic policy with the rigid faith of a new religion and she is continually trying to spread it to other countries. That policy even in Russia has undergone some change during the last few years and it is possible that it may further change. Whether a variant of that policy or some other form of socialism should be our aim is one of the problems which we have to solve. But even if we are wholly opposed to that policy we can have friendly relations with Russia. . . .

India will also have to keep watch on the many Indians who are abroad and lay down a policy for their guidance. They should be free to go where they like for purposes of labour or business but only to countries where they are welcome and are treated honourably. We cannot thrust them down in other lands and win for them a privileged position by force as the imperialist powers have so often done with their nationals. An Indian who goes to other countries must cooperate with the people of that country and win for himself a position by friendship and service. . . .

Many of these questions will only arise after we are free. We can hardly develop a foreign policy so long as we are dependent on a foreign government. We can do little now. But we can at least lay down the general lines of our future policy and try to keep in touch with movements in other countries. The League Against Imperialism offers us one way of doing so of which we should take full advantage. But we should not limit ourselves to it. There are many other ways also of our developing these contacts and it would be desirable for the Congress to open a foreign department to do so.

There is one vital issue, however, which we must face immediately. What will India do in case of a war in which England is involved? Thirteen years ago we were swept in before we knew what had happened and our manpower and resources were fully utilized for the benefit of England. Are we going to allow ourselves to be similarly exploited again? The danger of war coming in the near future is serious enough. All nations of Europe are making frenzied preparations for it, while their representatives spend pleasant days in Geneva discussing disarmament.[3] Russia is continually discussing the coming war. The whole of English policy seems to be based on it. And when nations prepare for war and

[3] Between 1919 and 1939, a series of bilateral and multilateral disarmament conferences were held under the aegis of the League of Nations.

expect it, it has a way of coming even though no country wants it. If war comes the East is sure to be involved and England is consequently strengthening her position in the Pacific and in India. The Singapore Base can be a challenge only to Japan and China. In India it is proposed to transfer the control of the army to the British War Office and to station a large part of the British Expeditionary Force within easy reach of the North-West Frontier. All this means a preparation for war with Russia. India has no quarrel with Russia; she has considerable sympathy for her, and there is much in her that she admires. Why then should we be dragged into a war against Russia for the benefit of British imperialism? But there is no doubt that we shall be dragged in if we patiently wait on and do nothing. The British dominions have established their right to join England in a war or not to do so as they choose, though it is difficult to imagine where the British Commonwealth will be if one part of it is at war and another at peace. India should also declare unequivocally that she will be no party to any war without her express consent, and if she is bullied or hustled into such a war, she will not help in any way. We must have this declaration made and repeatedly made and it should be made known to the people as widely as possible by press and platform. We have nothing to gain by being parties to such a conflict and we have a great deal to lose.

The Fascination of Russia[1]

Since my return from Europe I have frequently been asked about Russia. . . .
All the world is watching her, some with fear and hatred, and others with passionate hope and the longing to follow in her path.

It is difficult to feel indifferent towards Russia, and it is still more difficult to judge of her achievements and her failures impartially. She is today too much of a live wire to be touched without a violent reaction, and those who write about her can seldom avoid superlatives of praise or denunciation. Much depends on the angle of vision and the philosophy of life of the observer; much also on the prejudices and preconceived notions which he brings to his task. But whichever view may be right no one can deny the fascination of this strange Eurasian country of the hammer and sickle, where workers and peasants sit on the thrones of the mighty and upset the best-laid schemes of mice and men.

For us in India the fascination is even greater, and even our self-interest compels us to understand the vast forces which have upset the old order of things and brought a new world into existence, where values have changed utterly and old standards have given place to new. We are a conservative people, not over-fond of change, always trying to forget our present misery and degradation in vague fancies of our glorious past and an immortal civilization. But the past is dead and gone and our immortal civilization does not help us greatly in solving the problems of today. If we desire to find a solution for these problems we shall have to venture forth along new avenues of thought and search for new methods. The world changes and the truths of yesterday and the day before may be singularly inapplicable today. We have to follow the line of life in its ever-varying curves and an attempt to adhere rigidly to an outworn creed may take us off at a tangent from this curve of life and lead us to disaster.

Russia thus interests us because it may help us to find some solution for the great problems which face the world today. It interests us specially because conditions there have not been, and are not even now, very dissimilar to conditions in India. Both are vast agricultural countries with only the beginnings

[1] First published as an article in *The Hindu*, 3 April 1928. SWJN. Vol. 2, pp. 381–4. Excerpts.

of industrialization, and both have to face poverty and illiteracy. If Russia finds a satisfactory solution for these, our work in India is made easier.

Russia again cannot be ignored by us, because she is our neighbour, a powerful neighbour, which may be friendly to us and cooperate with us, or may be a thorn in our side. In either event we have to know her and understand her and shape our policy accordingly. The bogey of war with Russia is ever with us. In the days of the Tsar we were told that Russian imperialism wanted an outlet to the sea; now that the Tsar has gone we are warned against the insidious attempts of communists to subvert a peaceful and well-ordered world. The old political rivalry between England and Russia continues, whoever may occupy the seats of power in Whitehall or in Moscow or Petrograd. How far must India inherit this rivalry or be made to suffer from it? There are rumours and alarms of war and the problem is an urgent one for us.

It is right therefore that India should be eager to learn more about Russia.

3

International Contacts[1]

After a long period of not very splendid isolation India is again beginning to look to the outside world and to take interest in other countries. It is realized that the modern world is closely knit together and no part of it can ignore the rest. Science and industry and new methods of transportation have made each country dependent in a large measure on the others, and though the myth of nationalism flourishes and holds men's minds, it is an outworn creed and internationalism approximates more and more to reality. Wars can seldom be localized, nor can peace endure in a country when the rest of the world is at war. Idealists tell us that the only war to put an end to the ceaseless conflict between nations and to inaugurate an era of world peace is to create a super-state to which all nations will owe allegiance or to have a cooperative world commonwealth.

It is difficult for us in India to think of the larger issue, of world problems and world peace, when the problem that confronts us always is how to free ourselves from our present subjection. And yet our problem is but part of the larger one, and it may be that we shall also have helped greatly in establishing world peace. If imperialism is the real cause of most of the exploitation and troubles in the world today, the classical and typical example of imperialism is the British Empire of India, and the freedom of India becomes an essential condition for world freedom.

Many of our friends in India and outside are therefore continually laying stress on the necessity for us to develop contacts with other countries so that we may appreciate the forces that are moulding the world today and be able to coordinate our activities to them; some of them tell us that we should cooperate with all other anti-imperialist forces to combat imperialism; others favour an Asiatic federation; while a third group are sanguine enough to want us to utilize the machinery of the League of Nations for our benefit. But all these agree that international contacts are necessary for us. Some who are of a contrary opinion fear that too much of internationalism may make us forget the real work at

[1] Written on 13 May 1928 and published in *The New Era*, a quarterly published in Madras. Excerpts.

home and make us imagine that we can achieve our freedom with the help of outsiders. The fear is a real one but perhaps it is a little exaggerated. No one who has come up against the hard realities of the struggle is likely to forget that there is little of charity in international dealings and no country can make good except through its own efforts.

The advantages of international contacts from a purely political view point are evident enough. But there is another aspect of the question on which perhaps enough stress has not been laid.

Foreign rule and exploitation of a country have many sins to answer for. Some of the tragedies they bring in their train are obvious and frequent reference is made to them. But one unhappy, and yet unavoidable, consequence to which little attention is usually paid, is the concentration of nearly all activities in the struggle for freedom. The rich and many-coloured life of a nation loses its variety and its diversity and only one hue is visible, brilliant enough at times, but usually a drab grey covering the uniform misery of the people. The creative spirit can find little expression and the strength and energy of the chosen in the land are diverted to the long fight for freedom. There are brilliant episodes in this fight when the soul of a whole people is exalted and for the sake of an ideal even men of common clay do heroic deeds. But this work is one of destruction in the main and destruction and creation seldom go together. Ireland offers us a sad and yet a noble example of such a struggle for freedom. For seven hundred years or more she carried on her fight for independence. Her history is full of heroism and sacrifice but the rich and noble culture that was hers has almost passed away. India is another sorry example of stagnation and cultural death brought on by long years of foreign rule.

And yet the struggle for political freedom brings with it an intense desire for one's own culture and traditions. The hatred of foreign rule extends to the foreigner's ways and institutions, and an escape is sought from them in dreams of the past when the foreigner was not there. We think of the golden age of past times, of *Rama Raj*. And this very looking back makes us still more stagnant and rigid and incapable of creative work. We do not try to enrich the present with our thought and action. We merely worship the past and what we worship we make lifeless.

The culture of a people must have its roots in the national genius. It must smell of the soil and draw its inspiration from its past history. But it cannot live for ever on the earnings of its forefathers or on an old bank account to which nothing is added. It must be a live and growing thing responsive to new conditions and flexible enough to adapt itself to them. In India the moment we tried to make our culture rigid in order to protect it from foreign incursions, we stopped its natural growth, and slow paralysis crept in and brought it near to death. We talk vaingloriously of our immortal civilization, but what does it consist of today so far as the common people are concerned? Our religion is one of the kitchen, of what to touch and what not to touch, of baths and top-knots, of all manner of marks and fasts, and ceremonies that have lost all meaning; our very gods are manufactured in the factories of England or Japan; our music chiefly consists of painful noises which accompany processions and ceremonials and make the day or night almost unbearable, and usually result in broken heads, or the terrible din whereby our Muslim friends mourn an ancient tragedy that took place in Arabia twelve-and-a-half centuries ago; our artistic cravings are satisfied with hideous prints from Germany; our literature largely consists of sentimental and soppy effusions; in our thought there is little that is new, we merely repeat and paraphrase and expound ad nauseam what was said ages ago, or else we denounce it equally irrationally. The few brilliant exceptions that we have produced in recent times only serve to heighten the surrounding gloom.

We had everything in the past that made for a rich and varied culture and a progressive civilization. And yet we have landed ourselves in a stagnant quagmire from which escape is not easy. We can effectively escape from it only when the struggle for political independence is ended in our favour, and our energy can be diverted to more creative channels. But success in that struggle depends in some measure on our social and cultural progress. It is a vicious circle and we have to attack the enemy on all fronts, though necessarily the political and economic fronts will claim most attention.

Thus whether we consider our problems from the standpoint of politics or economics or of culture and civilization in their widest meanings, we are driven to the conclusion that we must end the isolation of India and try to understand world currents and world happenings. We must in addition to our nationalism develop an internationalism which is prepared to profit by the good things of other countries, and to cooperate with the progressive forces of the world. So far practically our sole contact with the outside world has been through England and the English language. This has been unfortunate for we have seen the world through English eyes and with English prejudices. And even with England our relations could not be healthy. Between the rulers and the ruled there can be no wholesome cooperation.

Our international contacts must now therefore be largely with countries other than England. Only thus can we gradually get out of the curious mentality of subservience to England, of the inevitability of the British connection, and see the world in proper perspective. Many of us imagine that because we are under British rule, England is the dominating force in the world today and we feel powerless before this colossus. A wider knowledge of the world situation will convince us that England is no longer what she was and the days of British dominion are numbered. But whatever the future of England may be the world is bigger than England and we cannot understand or profit by the varied cultures of different countries through England only. . . .

Some among us feel that contact with the West is dangerous for our culture, it may not be able to survive the impact. If our culture is such a feeble thing the sooner it dies a natural death the better. But if there is any life left in it, it will derive fresh vigour from the healthy impact of other forces and will survive, changed it may be and more suited to the conditions of today, but still based fundamentally on the genius of the race. But the surest way of killing this culture of ours is to isolate it and keep it away from fresh air and make it die of suffocation. . . .

"To understand all is to forgive all", says the French proverb, and to understand another people and another nation is to like them and appreciate their good points. International contacts promote mutual comprehension and the spirit of goodwill and are thus the surest guarantees of an enduring peace.

4

The Imperialist Danger[1]

I have had the privilege of being associated with the League since its formation at the Congress held in Brussels in February 1927. I welcomed its formation because I felt that it supplied a common platform for the two great movements of revolt against the existing conditions which we have in the world today, the struggle of labour against the entrenched citadel of capital and the nationalist movements in countries under alien domination. What is there in common between these two except indeed the common factor of exploitation? Labour looks beyond national boundaries and seeks to create a cooperative world commonwealth. A narrow patriotism is not enough for it. Nationalism, on the other hand, is necessarily limited in its outlook; it is based on an intimate patriotism and territorial boundaries are sacred to it. How then can the two be reconciled and brought to march together?

And yet there is, or ought to be much in common between the two, and unless the two are harmonized and made to work together for the common good, there can be no permanent solution of the problems of the day. Can there be a world commonwealth with half the world in chains? What kind of socialism will it be, if it is based on the exploitation of other countries? Indeed can the world of labour in western countries better its lot even in the smaller field of wages and hours of work and standards of living, so long as imperialism continues and capital has full freedom to exploit the weak and unorganized labour of colonial countries and pit it against the worker at home? The independence of colonial countries is very necessary to the inhabitants of those

[1] Foreword to P.J. Schmidt's *The Imperialist Danger*. Excerpts.

It was carried in *The Tribune*, 24 July 1929, with the following note by Jawaharlal Nehru: "The following foreword was written by me at the request of Mr. P.J. Schmidt, editor of *Recht en Vrijheid* of Amsterdam for a little book he had written called *The Imperialist Danger*. It was written more than a year ago, in May 1928. I do not know if the book has been published or not. The League Against Imperialism is attracting a great deal of attention now on account of the determined attacks being made on it by the British Government. Within a week the Second World Congress of the League meets at Frankfurt in Germany. This foreword, though written more than fourteen months ago, may not be wholly out of date and may interest some people."

countries, but it is clear today that it is equally necessary from the point of view of the European worker. And so both from the viewpoint of high idealism and the narrower and mundane one of self-interest, it has become the duty of the working class to combat imperialism and to help the nationalist movement of oppressed countries.

It is possible that the nationalist movement in a country under foreign domination may succeed in gaining independence without the support of labour. That may happen, as it has happened in the past, but it will result in creating a new capitalist state, nominally independent, but with little freedom for the worker. That will not bring peace any nearer or solve any of our problems.

The League Against Imperialism, for the first time, saw the common factors in the two movements and wisely sought to bring them together. It tried to bring home to the European worker the need for national independence of all countries; and it placed a new vision of social equality and freedom before the somewhat narrow nationalist movements of various countries. To all, it proclaimed that imperialism was the common enemy to be fought ceaselessly and rooted out before a better order could be established.

If the League had not done any other work, it would still have justified its formation. But during the year of its existence it has already brought nearer together the various peoples of Asia and Africa struggling for freedom, and it has made them realize in some measure that there is a bond between them and the worker of the West. And gradually even national movements like the Indian National Congress, conservative in their social outlook, are beginning to look towards the socialist ideal of society.

Such is the record of the League, and yet it is an amazing thing that those who call themselves socialists should attack it and seek to injure it, and that it should be necessary for Mr. Schmidt to refute their arguments. We in India have not concerned ourselves with the rivalries and conflicts between the Second and the Third Internationals. But even a casual acquaintance with facts is enough to show us the attitude of the two towards the nationalist movements of the East. Russia has not merely given pious expression to her sympathy but has acted up to it in China, in Persia and elsewhere. What the Second International has done, or rather not done, has been well shown by Mr. Schmidt. And specially we are interested in the doings of those pillars of the Second International—the British Labour Party. They have shown us the measure of their socialism and of their belief in the oft-repeated slogan of self-determination. They have proved to us that the possession of empire injures those who profit by it as much as those who suffer under it. In their deeds they have acted as full-blooded imperialists indistinguishable from the more blatant variety belonging to the Tory Party. Mr. Ramsay MacDonald's term of office as Prime Minister of England was signalized by the Bengal Ordinance under which hundreds of

Indians were kept in jail without trial or charge. And now he and his party have wholeheartedly agreed and cooperated with the Simon Commission appointed by the Tory Government against the declared will of all parties and groups in India. And because there was indignant protest in India Mr. MacDonald had lost his temper and has sent us hectoring and offensive messages after the manner of the choicest imperialists of the Tory School. Labour journals in England have supported him and joined in denunciation of Indian nationalists and its leaders. Is it any wonder that Indian public opinion of all shades has seen and fully realized that under the thin veneer of an academic socialism Mr. MacDonald and his party are as much imperialists and supporters of the present capitalist system as the Baldwins and Birkenheads. Indeed we prefer the frank brutality of the latter to Mr. MacDonald's imperious and hypocritical message of goodwill.

As I write we have had yet another demonstration of the British Labour Party's attitude towards imperialism. British warships have coerced the Egyptian Parliament and people in postponing a measure entirely dealing with internal order and these men of war have carried with them the goodwill of the Labour Party. Sir Austen Chamberlain tells us that British interests as stand today will be protected "for ever", and Mr. MacDonald has acquiesced in this monstrous assertion.

I wish well to the League against Imperialism, and wishing well to it, I am glad that Messrs MacDonald and Co. are not of it but are against it. I hope this League will never give shelter to men who talk glibly of the future socialist order and of the evils of imperialism and yet who belie their words by every action and betray their principles at every crisis.

The League is said to be a "Communist manoeuvre" and so it must be cursed with bell, book and candle. One of the organizations associated with the League is the Indian National Congress and even the leaders of the Second International should know that the Indian Congress is not a communist body, is not even as a whole socialist in its outlook, though it contains many socialists. But the Congress is not afraid as the Second International is afraid of cooperating with all forces that are anti-imperialist whether they are communist or non-communist. The Congress has no desire to have any dealings with those who merely talk and always fail at the moment of action.

For the best part of my adult years I have been associated with the Indian National Congress and I have desired the freedom of India passionately. But I believe in the socialist order of society and I trust and hope that India will evolve such an order. The League Against Imperialism offers a platform for both these ideals—national independence and social equality—and all such as believe in them should surely welcome the League and help it in its great task.

5

India and the World[1]

Faced by repeated crises and engrossed in their domestic troubles, it is not surprising that the people of the West should pay little attention to India. A few may feel drawn to the rich past of India and admire her ancient culture, some may feel an instinctive sympathy with a people struggling for freedom, others may have the humanitarian urge to condemn the exploitation and brutal suppression of a great people by an imperialist power. They have troubles of their own; why add to them?

And yet every intelligent dabbler in public affairs knows that the problems of the modern world cannot be kept in watertight compartments; they cannot be dealt with successfully separately and without regard to the others; they run into each other and, in the final analysis, form one single world problem with many different facets. Events in the deserts and waste lands of East Africa echo in distant chancelleries and cast their heavy shadow over Europe; a shot fired in eastern Siberia may set the world on fire. Many difficult problems trouble Europe today, and yet it may well be that the future historian, with a truer perspective, will consider China and India as the most significant problems of today, and as having a greater influence on the future shaping of world events. For, essentially, India and China are world problems, and to ignore them, or to minimize their significance, is to betray a woeful ignorance of the trend of world affairs and to fail to understand completely the basic disease from which all of us suffer.

The problem of India is thus of the present, of today. To admire or condemn her past does not help us much, except in so far as an understanding of the past helps us to understand the present. We have to realize that any big thing that will happen there will affect the larger world to a great extent, and none of us, wherever we may live and whatever national or other allegiance might claim us, can be unaffected by it. It is, therefore, from this wider point of view that we must consider it, as a part of the more immediate problems that confront us.

It is well known that the possession of India has for more than a century and a half vitally affected British foreign and domestic policy; the wealth and

[1] Badenweiler, First published in *Vendredi*, 6 January 1936. Paris, 1936. Reprinted in *India and the World* (London, 1936), pp. 200–9.

exploitation of India gave England the needed capital to develop her great industries in the early days of the Industrial Revolution and then provided her
with markets for her manufactured goods; India was ever in the background in
the Napoleonic wars as well as in the Crimean war,[2] and the desire to safeguard
the routes to India led England to interfere with Egypt and the countries of the
Middle East. That governing policy has continued in the post-War world, and
England still clings tenaciously to these routes. Soon after the Great War there
even came a grandiose vision to British statesmen of founding a great Middle
Eastern empire stretching from Constantinople to India. But that vision faded
chiefly because of Soviet Russia and Kemal Pasha, and the rise of Reza Shah[3]
in Persia, and Amanullah in Afghanistan, and the establishment of the French
mandate in Syria.[4] The great idea did not materialize, but, even so, England
managed to keep a fair measure of control over the land route to India and,
because of this, came into conflict with Turkey over Mosul.[5] It is that governing
policy which has induced England suddenly to become a champion of the
League of Nations in Ethiopia. Her moral instincts were not so much roused
when the League was flouted in Manchuria.[6]

The world problem is ultimately one of imperialism—finance-imperialism
of the present day. In Europe and elsewhere the rise of fascism is one very important aspect of the problem, as well as the rise and growing strength of Soviet
Russia, as representing a new order fundamentally opposed to that of imperialism.
The lining-up of Europe in mutually hostile and anti-fascist groups represents
the conflict of that imperialism with the new forces that threaten it. In the
colonial and subject countries the same conflict takes the shape of nationalist movements struggling for freedom, with an ever-developing social issue
colouring and influencing nationalism. Imperialism functions increasingly in
a fascist way in its colonial dependencies. Thus England, proudly laying stress
on its democratic constitution at home, acts after the fascist fashion in India.

It is clear that any breach in the imperialist front anywhere has its repercussions all over the world. A victory of fascism in Europe or elsewhere strengthens
imperialism and reacts everywhere, a setback to it weakens imperialism. Similarly, the triumph of a freedom movement in a colonial or subject country is

[2] Fought between Russia on the one hand and Britain, France and Turkey on the other
from 1854 to 1856.

[3] (1877–1944); Shah of Iran, 1925–41. He carried out reforms largely on the model of
Kemal Ataturk in Turkey.

[4] The French mandate in Syria, which gave France virtual control of internal affairs, was
established on 25 April 1920 and approved by the League of Nations on 24 July 1922.

[5] The inclusion of Mosul in Iraq had been disputed by Turkey for many years after World
War I.

[6] When Japan invaded Manchuria the major powers at the League took no action apart
from condemning Japan. But in 1935 England took the lead in imposing sanctions against
Italy.

a blow to imperialism and fascism, and it is therefore easy to understand why the Nazi leaders frown on Indian nationalism, and express their approval of the continuation of British domination in India.[7] The problem, considered in its basic aspects, is simple enough, and yet, in the intricate play of various world forces, it sometimes becomes very complicated, as when two imperialisms confront one another and each tries to exploit the nationalist or anti-fascist tendencies in the subject countries of the other. The only way to get over these complications is to consider the fundamental aspects and not to be led away by opportunist motives of gaining a temporary advantage. Else the temporary advantage is apt to prove a grave disadvantage and a burden later on.

India, both historically and by virtue of its importance, has been and is the classic land of modern imperialism. Any disturbance of the imperialist hold on India is bound to have far-reaching consequences in world affairs—it will make a tremendous difference to the world position of Great Britain, and it will give a great impetus to the freedom movements of other colonial countries and thus shake up other imperialisms. A free India would inevitably play a growing part in international affairs, and that part is likely to be on the side of world peace and against imperialism and its offshoots.

Some people imagine that India may develop into a free dominion of the British group of nations like Canada or Australia. This seems to be a fantastic idea. Even the existing dominions, in spite of their numerous links with Great Britain, are gradually drifting apart as their economic interests conflict. The drift is greatest in the case of Ireland, partly for historical reasons, and South Africa.[8] There are few natural links between India and England, and there is a historical and evergrowing hostility between them. In many parts of the empire there is racial ill-treatment and a policy of exclusion of Indians. But more important still, there is a conflict of economic interests. So long as India is controlled by the British Government this conflict is resolved in favour of Britain, but the moment India becomes a real dominion the two will pull different ways and a break would become inevitable, if the present capitalist order survives till then. There is another interesting aspect to this question. India, by virtue of her size, population, and potential wealth, is by far the most important member of the British Empire. So long as the rest of the empire exploits her, she remains on the imperial fringe. But a free India in the British group of

[7] Hitler wrote in *Mein Kampf* that "England will lose India only when the English administrative machinery in India will be composed of both the races . . . or when the sword of a powerful enemy will compel her to do so. Indian revolutionaries will never be able to do this . . . I would always wish to see India under English domination rather than under any other."

[8] In southern Ireland Eamon de Valera's ministry formed in 1932 demanded the removal of the oath of allegiance to the Crown and abolition of the Governor-Generalship. In South Africa the Minister of Defence warned on 5 February 1935 that attempts to "rashly commit South Africa in overseas war" would lead to civil war.

nations would inevitably tend to become the centre of gravity of that group, Delhi might challenge London as the nerve-centre of the empire. That position would become intolerable for England as well as the white dominions. They would prefer to have India outside their group, an independent but friendly country, rather than to be boss of their own household.

It seems likely, therefore, that there will be no real half-way house to Indian freedom. When India is strong enough, or when world events force the pace, she will emerge as a completely free country. What form that freedom will take and how far political freedom will be accompanied, or followed soon after, by social freedom and a new economic order, it is difficult to say, for this depends on so many factors. Inevitably world crises will affect her and hasten or delay that freedom and shape the social content of it. It is probable that the longer political freedom is delayed the more will the social question dominate the situation; even now it is in the forefront of Indian affairs. Economic conditions are forcing this issue forward, as well as the successful example of Soviet Russia.

When will Indian freedom come? It is dangerous to prophesy. But the world is moving rapidly and crisis succeeds crisis, and the weakening of the whole of British imperialism may be nearer than many people imagine. Within India the national movement has grown tremendously during the last sixteen years, ever since Mahatma Gandhi took its lead and inspired the millions to united effort and sacrifice. During these sixteen years it has continued without a break, though with ups and downs, and three times—in 1920-22, 1930-31, 1932-34—it has functioned through powerful movements of noncooperation and civil disobedience which shook the fabric of British rule in India. The strength of these movements can be judged from the British reaction to them. This took the shape of fierce repression of the typical fascist kind, with sup-pression of civil liberties, of press, speech, and meeting, of confiscation of funds, lands, and buildings; of the proscription of hundreds of organizations, including schools, universities, hospitals, children's societies, social work clubs, and of course political and labour organizations; of the sending to prison of hundreds of thousands of men and women; and of barbarous beating and ill-treatment of prisoners and others. On the other hand, an attempt was made to create divisions in the nationalist ranks by offering bribes and inducements to minority groups, and by consolidating all the feudal, reactionary, and obscurantist elements in the country behind the British Government. The outward symbol of this joining together of the reactionaries was the Round Table Conference in London, and the result of this union was the new "constitution" Act passed by the British Government, which in effect tightens the hold of British imperialism and gives greater importance to the reactionary elements in the country.

Meanwhile new social forces have gathered strength in India and socialistic and Marxist ideas have spread, in both the ranks of organized labour and the National Congress. The Socialist Party forms an important minority in the

National Congress and has an increasing influence. This rise of socialistic ideas has resulted in the development of certain fissiparous tendencies within the Congress, and further developments are likely to make this ideological cleavage more marked. On the whole, the Congress functions as a kind of joint front (including many groups)—a *front populaire*—against British imperialism, whilst in opposition to it is a joint front of the reactionary and feudal elements with that imperialism. The situation is comparable to the anti-fascist and fascist groupings in Europe. In between the two main groups are smaller groups of people who vacillate, though their sympathies are with the national movement.

The present position in India appears to be complex because the country is recovering from the exhaustion of the last civil disobedience movement, and during such periods a certain confusion is inevitable. New ideas find ready acceptance by many and frighten others. In spite of the fact that there is no civil disobedience movement functioning and conditions might be considered normal, the British Government are continuing their severe repression and suppression of civil liberties. In the name of suppressing communism, the labour movement is harassed,[9] many trade unions are declared illegal, labour leaders sent to prison; in the name of suppressing terrorism, political work is stopped in some parts of the country. Many important organizations, political and labour, continue to be banned. A law, which was contemptuously thrown out by the legislature, has been enacted by the Viceroy's executive authority, giving enormous powers to the executive and the police to suppress every form of civil liberty and public activity. Thousands are kept permanently in prison without trial or charge, many other thousands are sent to prison for sedition or other political offences. This is the functioning of British rule in India in normal times. This is also the measure of the strength of the freedom movement in India, as well as of the fear of the British Government of it. For the British Government lives in a continuous state of alarm, and when a government is afraid it acts strangely and wildly.

It is clear that the British Government cannot succeed in putting an end to the freedom movement, it can only keep it down for a while when the nation is exhausted. It is also clear that the new Act has displeased and irritated all active elements in the country, and they can never submit to it willingly. There is more resentment and hostility against imperialist domination in India than at any previous time. Gandhi has for the time being retired from active politics,[10] but he continues to be, and will continue to be, far and away the most dominant

---

[9] The Bombay Special (Emergency) Powers Act was invoked to suppress the strike in the textile industry on 23 April 1934. Legally registered trade unions such as the Young Workers League were banned and the strike leaders were arrested. In July 1934 the Communist Party of India was banned.

[10] On 17 September 1934 Mahatma Gandhi announced his intention to retire from the Congress on the grounds that spinning and khadi were not regarded by all as an integral part of the programme and that many subscribed to nonviolence as a policy and not as a creed.

and influential figure in India, capable of moving millions, and he might return to the political field at any crucial moment. To imagine that he is a back number in Indian politics is the most futile of errors. There are conflicts of ideologies in India and a pulling in different directions, as is natural in a living movement in a great country, but there is unity in the opposition to British imperialism, except in those classes which profit by it, or are the creation of that imperialism. There can be little doubt that the not too distant future will see great changes in India, and the approach to freedom.

All over the world today, behind the political and economic conflicts, there is a spiritual crisis, a questioning of old values and beliefs, and a search for a way out of the tangle. In India also, perhaps more so than elsewhere, there is this crisis of the spirit, for the roots of Indian culture still go down deep into the ancient soil, and though the future beckons, the past holds back. The old culture offers no solution of modern problems: the capitalist West, which shone so brightly in the nineteenth century, has lost its glamour, and seems to be inextricably involved in its own contradictions; the new civilization being built up in the Soviet countries attracts, in spite of some dark patches, and offers hope and world peace, and a prospect of ending the misery and exploitation of millions. It may be that India will resolve this crisis of the spirit by turning more and more to this new order, but, when she does so, it will be in her own way, making the structure fit in with the genius of her people.

6

World Events[1]

We are all engrossed in India at present in the provincial elections that will take place soon. The Congress has put up over a thousand candidates and this business of election ties us in many ways, and yet I would ask you, as I did at Lucknow, to take heed of the terrible and fascinating drama of the world. Our destinies are linked up with it, and our fate, like the fate of every country, will depend on the outcome of the conflicts of rival forces and ideas that are taking place everywhere. Again I would remind you that our problem of national freedom as well as social freedom is but a part of this great world problem, and to understand ourselves we must understand others also.

Even during these last eight months vast changes have come over the international situation, the crisis deepens, the rival forces of progress and reaction come to closer grips with each other, and we go at a terrific pace towards the abyss of war. In Europe fascism has been pursuing its triumphant course, speaking ever in a more strident voice, introducing an open gangsterism in international affairs. Based as it is on hatred and violence and dreams of war, it leads inevitably, unless it is checked in time, to world war. We have seen Abyssinia succumb to it; we see today the horror and tragedy of Spain.

How has this fascism grown so rapidly, so that now it threatens to dominate Europe and the world? To understand this one must seek a clue in British foreign policy. This policy, in spite of its outward variations and frequent hesitations, has been one of consistent support of Nazi Germany. The Anglo-German Naval Treaty threw France into the arms of Italy and led to the rape of Abyssinia.[2] Behind all the talk of sanctions against Italy later on, there was the refusal by the British Government to impose any effective sanction. Even when the United States of America offered to cooperate in imposing the oil sanction, Britain refused, and was content to see the bombing of Ethiopians and the breaking up of the League of Nations system of collective security.

[1] Presidential Address at Faizpur Congress, 27 December 1936. *Eighteen Months in India* (Allahabad, 1938), pp. 69–94. Excerpts.

[2] The treaty of 18 June 1935 permitted Germany to have a navy which was 35% of the naval strength of Britain. This bilateral agreement estranged France and led to a Franco-Italian agreement, which encouraged Italy to invade Abyssinia.

True, the British Government always talked in terms of the Legue and in defence of collective security, but its actions belied its words and were meant to leave the field open to fascist aggression. Nazi Germany took step after step to humiliate the League and upset the European order,[3] and ever the British 'National' Government followed meekly in its trail and gave it its whispered blessing.

Spain came then as an obvious and final test, a democratic government assailed by a fascist military rebellion aided by mercenary foreign troops. Here again while fascist powers helped the rebels, the League powers proclaimed a futile policy of non-intervention, apparently designed to prevent the Spanish democratic government from combating effectively the rebel menace.

So we find British imperialism inclining more and more towards the fascist powers,[4] though the language it uses, as is its old habit, is democratic in texture and pious in tone. And because of this contradiction between words and deeds, British prestige has sunk in Europe and the world, and is lower today than it has ever been for many generations.

So in the world today these two great forces strive for mastery—those who labour for democratic and social freedom and those who wish to crush this freedom under imperialism and fascism. In this struggle Britain, though certainly not the mass of the British people, inevitably joins the ranks of reaction. And the struggle today is fiercest and clearest in Spain, and on the outcome of that depends war or peace in the world in the near future, fascist domination or the scorching of fascism and imperialism. That struggle has many lessons for us, and perhaps the most important of these is the failure of the democratic process in resolving basic conflicts and introducing vital changes to bring social and economic conditions in line with world conditions. That failure is not caused by those who desire or work for these changes. They accept the democratic method, but when this method threatens to affect great vested interests and privileged classes, these classes refuse to accept the democratic process and rebel against it. For them democracy means their own domination and the protection of their special interests. When it fails to do this, they have no further use for it and try to break it up. And in their attempt to break it, they do not scruple to use any and every method, to ally themselves with foreign and anti-national forces. Calling themselves nationalists and patriots, they employ mercenary armies of foreigners to kill their own kith and kin and enslave their own people.

In Spain today our battles are being fought and we watch this struggle not merely with the sympathy of friendly outsiders, but with the painful anxiety of

---

[3] On 16 March 1935 Germany formally denounced the clauses of the Treaty of Versailles imposing disarmament on her; and on 7 March 1936 she occupied the demilitarized zone of the Rhineland.

[4] After 1935, fascism came to be identified with aggression.

those who are themselves involved in it. We have seen our hopes wither and a blank despair has sometimes seized us at this tragic destruction of Spain's manhood and womanhood. But in the darkest moments the flame that symbolizes the hope of Spanish freedom has burnt brightly and proclaimed to the world its eventual triumph. So many have died, men and women, boys and girls, that the Spanish Republic may live and freedom might endure. We see in Spain, as so often elsewhere, the tragic destruction of the walls of the citadel of freedom. How often they have been lost and then re-taken, how often destroyed and rebuilt.

I wish, and many of you will wish with me, that we could give some effective assistance to our comrades in Spain, something more than sympathy, however deeply felt. The call for help has come to us from those sorely stricken people and we cannot remain silent to that appeal. And yet I do not know what we can do in our helplessness when we are struggling ourselves against an imperialism that binds and crushes.

So I would like to stress before you, as I did before, this organic connection between world events, this action and interaction between one and the other. Thus we shall understand a little this complicated picture of the world today, a unity in spite of its amazing diversity and conflicts. In Europe, as in the Far East, there is continuous trouble, and everywhere there is ferment. The Arab struggle against British imperialism in Palestine is as much part of this great world conflict as India's struggle for freedom. Democracy and fascism, nationalism and imperialism, socialism and a decaying capitalism, combat each other in the world of ideas, and this conflict develops on the material plane and bayonets and bombs take the place of votes in the struggle for power. Changing conditions in the world demand a new political and economic orientation and if this does not come soon, there is friction and conflict. Gradually this leads to a revolution in the minds of men and this seeks to materialize, and every delay in this change-over leads to further conflict. The existing equilibrium having gone, giving place to no other, there is deterioration, reaction, and disaster. It is this disaster that faces us in the world today and war on a terrible scale is an ever-present possibility. Except for the fascist powers every country and people dread this war and yet they all prepare for it feverishly, and in doing so they line up on this side or that. The middle groups fade out or, ghost-like, they flit about, unreal, disillusioned, self-tortured, ever-doubting. That has been the fate of the old liberalism everywhere, though in India perhaps those who call themselves liberals, and others who think in their way, have yet to come out of the fog of complacency that envelops them. But we

Move with new desires.
For where we used to build and love
Is no man's land, and only ghosts can live
Between two fires.

What are these new desires? The wish to put an end to this mad world system which breeds war and conflict and which crushes millions; to abolish poverty and unemployment and release the energies of vast numbers of people and utilize them for the progress and betterment of humanity; to build where today we destroy.

7

Spain[1]

In this age when black reaction grips the world, and culture and civilization decay, and violence seems to reign unchecked, the magnificent struggles of the Spanish and Chinese republics against overwhelming odds have lightened the darkness of many a wanderer through the pathless night. We sorrow for the incredible horrors that have taken place, but our hearts are full of pride and admiration for the human courage that has smiled through disaster and found greater strength in it, and for the invincible spirit of man that does not bend to insolent might, whatever the consequences. Anxiously we follow the fate of the people of Spain, and yet we know that they can never be crushed, for a cause that has this invincible courage and sacrifice behind it can never die. Madrid and Valencia and Barcelona will live for ever more, and out of their ashes the Spanish Republicans will yet build the free Spain of their desire.

We who struggle for our own freedom are deeply moved by this epic struggle of the Spanish Republic, for the freedom of the world is imperilled there. The frontiers of our struggle lie not only in our own country but in Spain and China also.

[1] From *China, Spain and the War*, 24 January 1939, pp. 57–8.

8

A World Federation[1]

One of the tragedies of history is the slowness with which people's minds adapt themselves to a changing environment. The world changes from day to day, not so our minds which are peculiarly static and insist on imagining that today is the same as yesterday and tomorrow will not differ greatly. This lag between our minds and reality prevents us from solving the problems of the day and produces war and revolution and much else that afflicts the world. . . .

The old political and economic structure is rotten and moth-eaten and all the king's horses and all the king's men cannot hold it together for long. We discuss the problem of the states as if it was a question of bargaining or give and take between the rulers and the people, with the paramount power taking a share of the spoils. But the States simply cannot fit in the modern world and no amount of argument or soft words can change that fundamental fact. It is on the basis of this fact that they are outworn, decadent systems, which should have been decently buried long ago, that all consideration must proceed. Systems like individuals have their span of life and they cannot go beyond it.

The land system again is intimately connected, or should be connected, with a modern economy. If it is not so connected it must inevitably decay, as it has done. The problem is a scientific, impersonal one and has little to do with our love for the zamindar or the tenant. It is patent that our land system is a drag on the development of the nation and impedes our progress; such systems in other countries have given place to others. So it must inevitably go here also. . . .

Our freedom and our independence must therefore be thought of in terms of the world and of world cooperation. The days of isolated national existence are past beyond recall and the only alternative to world cooperation is world disruption and war and continuous conflicts between nations till they are all involved in a common ruin.

It is difficult to conceive of effective cooperation at present because there are forces and powerful nations which are bent on following a contrary policy. Yet it may be possible to have the right objective and to lay the foundations of such cooperation even now, though it may not be world-wide to begin with.

[1] *National Herald*, 31 May–1 June 1939. Excerpts.

Intelligent opinion all over the world and vast numbers of people are eager and anxious for this to happen, but governments, vested interests and groups come in the way.

A faint glimpse of this world cooperation came to President Wilson twenty years ago and he sought to realize it. But the war treaties and the statesmen of that generation scotched the idea, and the great pile of the League of Nations rises mournfully today in Geneva like a mausoleum enshrining the dead body of a great hope. It had to die as it started under wrong auspices and with the seeds of death within. It was an attempt to stabilize something which could not endure, to protect the imperialisms and special interests of the victor nations.

Its cry for peace meant the continuation of an unjust status quo all over the world, its democracy was a cloak for the subjection of many peoples and nations. It had to die because it was not brave enough to live. There can be no resurrection of that dead body.

But there can be a resurrection of the idea that the League enshrined, not in the limited, twisted and perverse way that took shape in Paris and Geneva, but fuller, more powerful and organic and based on collective peace, freedom and democracy. On no other basis can it seek rebirth or find sustenance.

A world union is necessary today. Unhappily, it will not come because those in authority are children of the old world which has ceased to be and cannot think or act in terms of the new. It will not come before the world is shattered again by war and millions have perished. But it will come because there is no other way out. Such a union can have nothing to do with imperialism or fascism and must be based on the fullest democracy and freedom, each nation having autonomy within its borders, and submitting in international matters to the union legislature to which it sends its representatives. Inevitably it will have to work under a planned and socialized economy in order to end the conflicts of today.

9

A Real Commonwealth[1]

Allahabad, 22 May 1940

Dear Mr. Spalding,[2]

It is clear enough that there can be no independent small states in the future. There may possibly be huge groups of states united together in each group and each group in a state of latent hostility to the other. Though this is a possibility it is obviously a very undesirable possibility and it leads to no stability, but to future wars on a tremendous scale. Therefore we come back to the conclusion that the independent sovereign state must be put an end to, and the political and economic organization of the world must keep pace with the technique of science, which has united the whole earth. That is to say that there should be a real commonwealth of interdependent states, each state forgoing that part of its independence which is necessary for the sake of this commonwealth or federation.

While I accept completely this ideal, I am quite convinced that this ideal cannot be realized through such groupings as the British Empire, even though that empire may change its imperialist characteristics and become a truer commonwealth. I do not think that it is possible for an empire like this ever to shed its imperialism without liquidating its old structure and building afresh on a new basis. So far as India is concerned, it is almost impossible for it to become a really free member of a free British Commonwealth. But India can much more easily become a member of a wider commonwealth which embraces all countries.

Similarly, I do not believe in a united states of Europe or of Europe and America. This will mean ultimately either the exploitation by Europe and America of Asia and Africa or the building up of vast groups of nations hostile to each other. I think therefore that any approach towards the future world commonwealth through either a British group or a European group is fundamentally wrong and will not lead to a real commonwealth. As you have said in

[1] To H.N. Spalding, 22 May 1940. JN Papers, NMML. Excerpts.
[2] Henry Norman Spalding (1877–1953), endowed the Spalding professorship of Eastern Religions and Ethics and a lectureship in Eastern Art at Oxford University.

your letter, India is bound to have the closest relations with her neighbour China and other Asiatic countries. Our contacts with China have already increased greatly and there is a desire on either side to develop them. This cannot happen satisfactorily if we are tied up with any group which excludes China and these countries.

It is worthwhile remembering also the psychological aspect of this question. A long period of British rule and British exploitation of India has put up enormous psychological barriers between us and England. Nationalism is always a somewhat dangerous doctrine. It isolates and is essentially based on an anti-feeling. Fortunately for us in India our whole movement, as directed by Gandhiji, has tried to break down this psychological barrier and to lessen the evils of a narrow nationalism. Still they remain and the only way to break them down completely is to have the feeling of complete freedom from British imperialism. Otherwise these barriers and complexes will continue and embitter our relations.

Yours sincerely,
Jawaharlal Nehru

10

Quatorze Juillet[1]

Quatorze Juillet, the Fourteenth of July, seventeen hundred and eighty-nine. The people of Paris storm the Bastille and capture the old prison and set free the prisoners. But the fall of the Bastille was a symbol and a portent of much else; it broke down many other props and barriers of the old world, and it liberated many forces which would fashion a new order. The Revolution came and the Terror, and then Thermidor and Napoleon. Back again for a while to the Bourbons, and then fresh revolutions and changes, till, in the midst of defeat and disaster, the Third Republic of France was born.

And now the Third Republic is no more, and it would appear that France's ruling class has sold her glorious heritage and magnificent tradition for not even the proverbial mess of pottage. Defeat in battle brings sorrow and humiliation; yet it may be borne if the spirit lives. But what shall we say when the spirit dies and the soul of a country surrenders?

On this fourteenth day of July my thoughts go back a hundred and fifty years and survey the exciting course of French history, since the day that France became the mother of freedom. I have loved that France even in her decay and imagined that, whatever might befall her, her immortal spirit would survive and triumph. On this fourteenth of July, for these hundred and fifty years, the people of France have celebrated the fall of the Bastille. It was their *Fete Nationale*, the Day of the Nation, which symbolized the free spirit of France. There came, a few years ago, the National Front and what a magnificent Fourteenth of July that was, when it was celebrated with an added significance and an overpowering popular enthusiasm.

What is happening in France today, I wonder. For the first time in these hundred and fifty years, there is no *Fete Nationale*, no Fourteenth of July to celebrate. The Bastille fell in 1789, but a hundred and a thousand Bastilles have arisen today, and the lamps of freedom flicker and go out all over the world. And Paris the beautiful is a conquered city, grovelling at the feet of the conqueror.

A few days ago a postcard came to me from a dear friend in Paris,[2] written just before Paris fell. Anguish and sorrow enveloped her at what was happening

---

[1] *National Herald*, 16 July 1940.
[2] Louise Morin.

to her dear land and to the gracious city where she lived. Her bright young son had been torn from college and his fate was uncertain. Yet her faith in France did not fail, and knowing how France was dear to me also, she assured me that all would be well. In the face of adversity, her courage would grow and triumph, as she had so often done in the past when danger overwhelmed her. *"Je me represente,"* so my friend wrote to me, *"l'angoisse et la sympathie avec lesquelles vous devez suivre les evenements actuels. Je pense bien a vous. Le coeur se serre en pensant a tant de souffrances et de ruines. Mais soyez assure que la France voit grandir son courage en face de l'adversite".*[3]

But the France of Petain[4] and Laval[5] did no such thing, and has now forsworn all that the old France stood for. But there is another France, there must be one, for the heritage of a thousand years does not vanish in a night. That other France will rise again and assert the invincible spirit of freedom which made her great. Again we shall hear the stirring strains of the Marseillaise, the song of the Revolution; again she will celebrate the fall of the old Bastille and the new Bastilles that have arisen. Again she will have her *Fete Nationale* on the Fourteenth of July.

And so today, on this great anniversary, let us pay homage to the France of the Revolution, the breaker of the Bastille and of all the bonds that hold the human body and spirit captive.

---

[3] 'I am well aware of the agony and sympathy with which you must be following recent events. I frequently think of you. My heart aches at so much suffering and destruction. But please rest assured that the courage of France increases in the face of adversity.'

[4] Marshal Petain (1865–1951); victor of Verdun in the First World War; collaborated with the Nazis and became head of state, 1940; condemned to death after the war but sentence was commuted to life imprisonment.

[5] Pierre Laval (1883–1945); French politician. As German conquests increased during World War II, sounded various politicians on the feasibility of forming a Petain government to organize a Latin bloc with Mussolini and Franco and leave Britain to deal with Germany. Condemned for conspiracy against the state, collaboration with the enemy and armed action against French resistance movement, was executed by a firing squad on 15 October 1945.

11

Colonialism Must Go[1]

The future of the colonies? The obvious answer is that there is no future for them as colonies, that the whole system known as colonialism has to go. It has to go for a variety of reasons. It is evident that the dependent peoples of the colonial empires are in a rebellious mood and cannot be suppressed for long, and every attempt to suppress them is a drain on the ruling country which weakens it.

It is even more evident that the old-style empires are decadent as empires and show signs of cracking up. In some instances, indeed, they have cracked up and the attempts that are being made to pin together the broken pieces show a lack of wisdom and statesmanship which is amazing. One decadent empire tries to help another still more ramshackle empire and in this process speeds up the process of its own dissolution.

All these are signs of an inevitable change and transition from an era of colonialism to another era which has yet to be given a shape, a form and a name. The fundamental fact behind all this is that colonialism is obsolete in the modern world and does not fit in with the political and economic structure that is gradually evolving.

The problem of the colonies and dependent countries thus is a vital part of the world problem, and an attempt to isolate it results in other problems becoming far more difficult of solution. Behind that problem today lie the passion and hunger for freedom, equality and better living conditions which consume hundreds of millions of people in Asia and Africa. That passion cannot be ignored, for anything that drives vast numbers of human beings is a powerful factor in the dynamics of today.

But essentially it is not the sentimental appeal to freedom that is so important as the lack of food, clothing, housing and of the barest necessities of life which lies behind that urge. This lack can no longer be made good even in part by continuation of colonial administration in any form.

The problem should therefore be considered apart from sentiment in the wider context of world problems, political and economic, because the peace

[1] *The New York Times Magazine*, 3 March 1946. SWJN, Vol. 15, pp. 509–13. Excerpts.

and well-being of the world depend to a large extent on its solution. Colonies and dependencies have been fruitful sources of conflict in the past between acquisitive powers and expanding economics. They lead to an accentuation of power politics. If internal conditions in different countries are in a state of continuous tension and conflict they spread their contagions outside and affect world peace.

It may be difficult to do away with power politics entirely, for they represent to some extent the reality of today trying to find a new equilibrium. But it is certainly possible to lessen their importance and to reduce the area of potential conflict. The elimination of colonialism and imperialism would certainly have this effect and thus help in solving the other major problems of the age. Any variations of the old theme of a covering up of old processes under new names would have the reverse effect and add to the bitterness and conflict.

Effective war today means total war, drawing upon the entire resources of the nation. Effective peace and solution of national and international problems demand also a comprehensive and cooperative effort not only on the part of government but also on the part of the people. Any lack of cooperation between the government and the people leads to failure. There can obviously be no cooperation between an alien and authoritarian government and the people, and hence no proper solution of any problem.

This has been evident in India for a long time past and problems have accumulated till they seem to be almost insoluble. The war accentuated this progress and the Bengal famine was a terribly tragic reminder of the chaos and incompetence that is called government in India today. We are now facing another crisis on an even bigger scale and the shadow of widespread famine darkens the land.

No alien government can deal with this situation satisfactorily, nor can it have the cooperation of the people which is so essential both from the psychological and practical points of view. This is not the game of politics, but something that deeply moves masses of our people. We have seen this government going from disaster to disaster and making a mess of everything.

It is not an easy matter to refashion the destiny of hundreds of millions of people. The uprooting of the British empire, as of other empires, which is happening before our eyes, is bound to lead to numerous upsets and it may take some time to establish a new equilibrium on a surer foundation. The problem of the future of colonies and dependencies is no doubt difficult, as is every major problem today. And yet it is essentially simple, or rather the first big step is a clear renunciation of colonialism and imperialism and recognition of the national independence of the dependent countries within the larger framework of the world order that is slowly evolving. It is only after that unequivocal declaration has been made and immediate steps taken to implement it that other questions can be discussed as between equals.

We do not want any lowering of standards anywhere, even where they are higher than ours. We want to raise our own standards to the highest level. But it is obvious that high standards elsewhere based on an economy which result in low standards in Asian and African counties cannot be allowed. If the people of any country can maintain high standards by their own productive efforts they are welcome to do so, but such standards must not be at the expense of starvation and misery elsewhere.

Indeed low standards and the burden of poverty will tend to pull down standards in other places and will also disturb the economy and peace of the world. We have to aim at the raising of the level of the common man everywhere and for that purpose we have to pay special attention to Asia and Africa which have suffered most in the past. The world has to pull together or not at all.

India is inevitably the crux of the colonial problem by virtue of her size and population, her millennia of cultured life, her contribution to civilization, her capacity and vast resources, her potential power and her strategic position. Historically she has been during the last one hundred and fifty years the classic land of colonial imperialism. . . .

The freedom of colonial and dependent countries will raise many new problems, internal to them as well as external. But there can be no doubt that this would be a powerful stabilizing factor in the world and would tend to reduce the conflicts inherent in power politics by removing some of the major causes. These countries, with their newly achieved freedom, will be intent on their progress for they will have to make up for lost time. Their weight will always be thrown on the side of world peace, for any war would be disastrous to them. India in particular is wedded to peace, and her powerful influence will make a difference.

If, however, freedom is delayed or circumscribed and colonies and dependencies are used as pawns in the game of the power politics of a few great powers, then those dependent or semi-dependent countries will also play their part in power politics to the extent they can, and side with this or that power as suits their convenience and advantage. They will add to the confusion and chaos of a distracted world and be victims, together with others, of the inevitable disaster.

The end of colonialism and imperialism will not mean the splitting up of the world into a host of additional national states intent on their isolated independence. It will lead to a new grouping together of all nations, a new outlook, to cooperation gradually replacing competition and conflict, to the utilization of the wonders of modern techniques and the vast sources of energy at the disposal of man for the advancement of the human race as a whole. It will lead to that one world of which wise statesmen have dreamed and which seems to be the inevitable and only outcome of our present troubles, if we survive disaster.

12

Policy Towards Burma[1]

Peshawar (on Tour), 20 October 1946

My dear Gundevia,[2]

What should be our policy in Burma? We should be perfectly clear about this matter. We need not consider this in any detail but the broad lines should be laid down. Negatively that is not going to be a policy of claiming any special privileges for Indians, particularly for Indian vested interests. In the past a great deal of injury has been done to India's relations with Burma by the insistence of Indian business and other interests for privileged treatment. These interests claimed from England special protection in Burma. That was a foolish and impolite claim even from the point of view of the narrowest self-interest, because in the last analysis England could not protect those interests, but as a matter of fact the British had no desire to do so and they exploited this opportunity for promoting ill will between India and Burma. It must be made perfectly clear that we are not going to appeal anyhow to British authority to protect any of our interests in Burma or elsewhere abroad. We can only protect them in two ways, with the goodwill of the Burmese people and their leaders, or with our own strength, or with both. We cannot have that goodwill if we claim something that gives us a privileged position over them. No Burmese party or group will agree to it, and we are not going to compel them, even if we had the strength to do so, to agree to terms which they thoroughly dislike. Any attempt to coerce them will in all likelihood not succeed and in any event it would be completely opposed to our wider policies.

It must always be remembered that Burma and Ceylon occupy a very special place in regard to India. We may adopt a tough policy in regard to other foreign countries, but we may not do so in regard to Burma and Ceylon because we do not wish to alienate them. They are not completely foreign to us, though in many ways they differ, specially Burma. Our policy must be based therefore on winning them over even though many irritating developments may take place in the present as in the case of Ceylon.

[1] To Y.D. Gundevia. Ministry of External Affairs and Commonwealth Relations. SWJN, Vol. 1 (II series), pp. 526–30. Excerpts.

[2] Y.D. Gundevia was Secretary to the Indian Representative to Burma, 1945–47.

Fortunately the position in Burma is much better, so far as Indians are concerned, than in Ceylon. In Aung San, the dominating personality in Burmese politics, we have a person who is friendly towards India and who wants to develop closer contacts. Not to take advantage of this favourable position will be extreme folly.

Our policy therefore must be definitely based on doing everything in our power to make the Burmese people our friends. This is not desirable from the long distance point of view but also from the narrower point of view of immediate Indian interests. I would be prepared to go some distance in sacrificing some immediate advantage if thereby we bring Burma and the Burmese people nearer to us.

It is clear that in the future Indians in Burma will have to choose between Burmese nationality and Indian nationality. If some choose the former, they are welcome to it, and they should get the normal privileges of Burmese nationals. If they choose to remain Indian nationals, as many no doubt will, they should have all the privileges accorded to the nationals of a friendly country and no more. They cannot have it both ways.

Whether Indians choose to become Burmese nationals or not, they must give the fullest support to the Burmese national movement and the cause of Burmese independence.[3] They cannot make this subject to any conditions in regard to their position or treatment. Any such attempt would be a bad bargain. Indians have every right to look to India as their homeland, to take pride in India and to help, in so far as they can, the cause of India. But however much they may do so, it is their bounden duty as residents of Burma to espouse the cause of Burma and to help it to the utmost of their ability. Otherwise they will remain isolated communities of foreigners cut off from the living currents of Burmese national life and disliked by the Burmese people. I am glad that Indians in Burma joined hands in the recent strikes in Burma.[4] I do not know the merits of these strikes and I cannot pass any judgement upon them, but it was a wise and far-seeing move to fall in line with Burmese sentiment and Burmese activities at this critical juncture.

It is not for Indians to ally themselves as a group with any political party in Burma. Nevertheless it is desirable for them to be as cooperative as possible with Aung San, both because of this dominating position in Burma and his leanings towards India.[5] You have yourself pointed out in your letter how Aung

[3] In his letter dated 5 October 1946, Gundevia had written that a "very large number" of Indians living in Burma had participated in a procession taken out by the A.F.P.F.L. on 29 September.

[4] Gundevia had written that Indians had joined the police strike on 23 September, called by the Joint Services Organisation of Burma to protest against the rising cost of living.

[5] Addressing a mass meeting on 29 September, Aung San had appealed to "all those who called Burma their home" to support him.

San has been copying in some measure what we have done in India. That itself is a favourable sign from our point of view. His letters and messages to me have also been friendly. He is greatly interested in the Inter-Asian Relations Conference we are convening early next year. He has large views, which are unusual among Burmese leaders. His outlook is definitely advanced, politically and economically. So from every point of view we should develop close relations with him.

That again does not mean that we should not remain friendly with other Burmese leaders. But if a choice has to be made we should incline towards Aung San.

Some days ago I sent you a telegram to be communicated to Aung San. This was in regard to the retention of Indian troops in Burma and I invited Aung San and the GOC in Burma to come to India to discuss the matter. I do not know if he will be able to come soon or not. Perhaps it is difficult for him to come soon. But I do hope that he will be able to accept our invitation some time or other. The mere fact of his coming here and discussing our common problems will be a good thing. I should myself like to go to Burma for a few days to meet him and others, but I fear I cannot find the time.

What the future of Indian troops in Burma is going to be, I cannot say at present, except this that we shall try our best to withdraw them from there as elsewhere abroad, as rapidly as possible. Meanwhile we are entirely opposed to the use of Indian troops in any way which is not approved of by the present Burmese Government. If the possibility of any such use arises, you will please inform us immediately. You can make this position quite clear to Aung San whenever opportunity offers itself.

Further you can make clear to Aung San and his Government that the Government of India desire no special safeguards or privileges which may be contrary to Burmese interests for our people in Burma. We have gladly noted the statements made by prominent Burmese leaders that Indians in Burma will receive the same general treatment as the Burmese people. We do not propose to intervene unless we are convinced that injustice is being done to Indians. Even so, it will be our desire to settle the matter amicably as between the two Governments. In no event are we going to seek a privileged position harmful to Burmese interests.

To Indians in Burma we would say that we shall help them in every way to ensure that they enjoy political or commercial privileges such as they are entitled to. But we cannot support them if they demand any special privileges which come in the way of Burmese interests or development. We expect them to live and act in Burma in cooperation with the Burmese people and to advance the cause of Burmese freedom. We would not like them to behave in a manner which will widen the gulf between them and the Burmese, nor do we want to encourage the habit of asking the Government of India for the protection of special rights or safeguards in such matters as separate electorates or reserved seats for Indians. While we cannot give a final opinion unless we see the full picture of any scheme, we want to make it clear that we are opposed to these on principle and because in effect any such device will be injurious to Indian interests. Separate electorates and reservations have failed in India and it has been made clear that they do not protect a minority. They merely isolate it. The position will be much worse in Burma if we make any such demand. We will not get it. What we will get instead is just the ill will of the Burmese people.

It would be desirable for us to encourage contacts with Burma other than merely commercial contacts which can more or less look after themselves. I think it would be a good thing if we made exchanges of students and professors between Burmese and Indian universities, also some development of news services between the two countries. . . .

Our general policy, though one, will have to advance along two parallel lines: closer association between the Government of India and the Government of Burma, and closer association between the people of India and the people of Burma. The former is relatively easy. The latter requires thinking about and activity on many fronts.

Indians abroad seldom succeed in building up an association representing all Indians or all groups. They have an unfortunate tendency to split up in groups. We should help, privately and unofficially, and sometimes even officially, in building up an organization which might be said to represent all Indians. It should have a strong cultural side, a library, reading rooms with plenty of Indian newspapers and periodicals, a kind of club house, etc. This would be a kind of information centre of Indian activities which should be of great help to Indians. The Burmese should be welcome there also.

From all accounts you have done very good work in Burma and carried on during a difficult period with considerable success. I am very glad to learn this. I hope that when Dr. Rauf goes there, the joint efforts of you two will be of great advantage to India and Burma alike and their relations with one another.

Yours sincerely,
Jawaharlal Nehru

13

A United Asia[1]

We stand at the end of an era and the threshold of a new period of history. Standing on this watershed which divides two epochs of human history and endeavour, we can look back on our long past and look forward to the future that is taking shape before our eyes. Asia, after a long period of quiescence, has suddenly become important again in world affairs. If we view the millennia of history, this continent of Asia, with which Egypt has been so intimately connected in cultural fellowship, has played a mighty role in the evolution of humanity. It was here that civilization began and man started on his unending adventure of life. Here the mind of man searched unceasingly for truth and the spirit of man shone out like a beacon which lightened up the whole world.

This dynamic Asia from which great streams of culture flowed in all directions gradually became static and unchanging. Other peoples and other continents came to the fore and with their new dynamism spread out and took possession of great parts of the world. This mighty continent became just a field for the rival imperialisms of Europe, and Europe became the centre of history and progress in human affairs.

A change is coming over the scene now and Asia is again finding herself. We live in a tremendous age of transition and already the next stage takes shape when Asia takes her rightful place with the other continents. . . .

As we meet here today, the long past of Asia rises up before us, the troubles of recent years fade away, and a thousand memories revive. But I shall not speak to you of these past ages with their glories and triumphs and failures, nor of more recent times which have oppressed us so much and which still pursue us in some measure. During the past two hundred years we have seen the growth of western imperialisms and the reduction of large parts of Asia to colonial or semi-colonial status. Much has happened during these years, but perhaps one of the notable consequences of the European domination of Asia has been the isolation of the countries of Asia from one another. India always had contacts and intercourse with her neighbour countries in the north-west, the north-east, the east and the south-east. With the coming of British rule in India, these

[1] Speech delivered at the plenary session of the Asian Relations Conference, 23 March 1947, New Delhi. SWJN, Vol. 2 (II series), pp. 503–9. Excerpts.

contacts were broken off and India was almost completely isolated from the rest of Asia. The old land routes almost ceased to function and our chief window to the outer world looked out on the sea route which led to England. A similar process affected other countries of Asia also. Their common economy was bound up with some European imperialism or other; even culturally they looked towards Europe and not to their own friends and neighbours from whom they had derived so much.

Today this isolation is breaking down because of many reasons, political and otherwise. The old imperialisms are fading away. The land routes have revived and air travel suddenly brings us very near to each other. This Conference[2] itself is significant as an expression of that deeper urge of the mind and spirit of Asia which has persisted in spite of the isolationizm which grew up during the years of European domination. As that domination goes, the walls that surrounded us fall down and we look at each other again and meet as old friends long parted.

In this Conference and in this work there are no leaders and no followers. All countries of Asia have to meet together on an equal basis in a common task and endeavour. It is fitting that India should play her part in this new phase of Asian development. Apart from the fact that India herself is emerging into freedom and independence, she is the natural centre and focal point of the many forces at work in Asia. Geography is a compelling factor, and geographically she is so situated as to be the meeting point of western and northern and eastern and south-east Asia. Because of this, the history of India is a long history of her relations with the other countries of Asia. Streams of culture have come to India from the West and the East and been absorbed in India, producing the rich and variegated culture which is India today. At the same time, streams of culture have flowed from India to distant parts of Asia. If you would know India you have to go to Afghanistan and Western Asia, to Central Asia, to China and Japan and to the countries of south-east Asia. There you will find magnificent evidence of the vitality of India's culture which spread out and influenced vast numbers of people.

There came a great cultural stream from Iran to India in remote antiquity. And then that constant intercourse between India and the Far East, notably China. In later years south-east Asia witnessed an amazing efflorescence of Indian art and culture. The mighty stream which started from Arabia and developed as a mixed Irano-Arabic culture poured into India. All these came to us and influenced us, and yet so great was the powerful impress of India's own mind and culture that it could accept them without being itself swept away or

[2] The main purpose of the conference was to "bring together the leading men and women of Asia on a common platform to study the problems of common concern to the peoples of this continent, to focus attention on social, economic and cultural problems of the different countries of Asia, and to foster mutual contacts and understanding."

overwhelmed. Nevertheless we all changed in the process and in India today all of us are mixed products of these various influences. An Indian, wherever he may go in Asia, feels a sense of kinship with the land he visits and the people he meets.

I do not wish to speak to you of the past but rather of the present. We meet here not to discuss our past history and contacts but to forge links for the future. And may I say here that this Conference, and the idea underlying it, is in no way aggressive or against any other continent or country? Ever since the news of this Conference went abroad, some people in Europe and America have viewed it with doubt imagining that this was some kind of a pan-Asian movement directed against Europe or America. We have no designs against anybody. Ours is a great design of promoting peace and progress all over the world. For too long we of Asia have been petitioners in western courts and chancellories. That story must now belong to the past. We propose to stand on our own feet and cooperate with all others who are prepared to cooperate with us. We do not intend to be the playthings of others.

In this crisis in world history Asia will necessarily play a vital role. The countries of Asia can no longer be used as pawns by others; they are bound to have their own policies in world affairs. Europe and America have contributed very greatly to human progress and for that we must yield them praise and honour, and learn from them many lessons they have to teach. But the West has also driven us into wars and conflicts without number and even now, the day after a terrible war, there is talk of further wars in the atomic age that is upon us. In this atomic age Asia will have to function effectively in the maintenance of peace. Indeed, there can be no peace unless Asia plays her part. There is today conflict in many countries and all of us in Asia are full of our own problems. Nevertheless, the whole spirit and outlook of Asia are peaceful, and the emergence of Asia in world affairs will be a powerful influence for world peace.

Peace can only come when nations are free and also when human beings everywhere have freedom and security and opportunity. Peace and freedom, therefore, have to be considered both in their political and economic aspects. The countries of Asia, we must remember, are very backward and the standards of life are appallingly low. These economic problems demand urgent solution or else crisis and disaster might overwhelm us. We have, therefore, to think in terms of the common man and fashion our political, social and economic structure so that the burdens that have crushed him may be removed, and he may have full opportunity for growth.

We have arrived at a stage in human affairs when the ideal of 'one world' and some kind of a world federation seems to be essential, though there are many dangers and obstacles in the way. We should work for that ideal and not for any grouping which comes in the way of this larger world group. We, therefore, support the United Nations structure which is painfully emerging from its infancy. But in order to have 'one world' we must also, in Asia, think of the countries of Asia cooperating together for that larger ideal. . . .

We seek no narrow nationalism. Nationalism has a place in each country and should be fostered, but it must not be allowed to become aggressive and come in the way of international development. Asia stretches her hand out in friendship to Europe and America as well as to our suffering brethren in Africa. We of Asia have a special responsibility to the people of Africa. We must help them to take their rightful place in the human family. The freedom that we envisage is not to be confined to this nation or that or to a particular people, but must spread out over the whole human race. That universal human freedom also cannot be based on the supremacy of any particular class. It must be the freedom of the common man everywhere and full opportunities for him to develop.

We think today of the great architects of Asian freedom—Sun Yat-sen, Zaghlul Pasha, Ataturk Kemal Pasha and others, whose labours have borne fruit. We think also of that great figure whose labours and whose inspiration have brought India to the threshold of her independence—Mahatma Gandhi. We miss him at this Conference and I yet hope that he may visit us before our labours end. He is engrossed in the service of the common man in India, and even this Conference could not drag him away from it.

All over Asia we are passing through trials and tribulations. In India also you will see conflict and trouble. Let us not be disheartened by this; this is inevitable in an age of mighty transition. We find a new vitality and powerful creative impulses in all the peoples of Asia. The masses are awake and they demand their heritage. Strong winds are blowing all over Asia. Let us not be afraid of them but rather welcome them, for only with their help can we build the new Asia of ours dreams. Let us have faith in these great forces and the dream which is taking shape. Above all, let us have faith in the human spirit which Asia has symbolized for these long ages past.

14

Sympathy for Jews[1]

New Delhi, 11 July 1947

My dear Professor Einstein,

I appreciate very much what you say about the recent decision of India's Constituent Assembly to abolish untouchability.[2] This indeed has been our policy for many years past and it is a matter of deep satisfaction to us that what we have been trying to do in many ways will soon have the sanction of law, as embodied in the Constitution, behind it. You say very rightly that the degradation of any group of human beings is a degradation of the civilization that has produced it. Ever since Mahatma Gandhi began to play a role in Indian politics and social affairs, he has laid the greatest stress on the complete liquidation of untouchability and all that goes with it. He made it part of our freedom struggle and emphasized that it was folly to talk of political freedom when social freedom was denied or restricted for a large number of persons.

You know that in India there has been the deepest sympathy for the great sufferings of the Jewish people. We have rejected completely the racial doctrine which the Nazis and the fascists proclaimed. Unfortunately, however, that doctrine is still believed in and acted upon by other people. You are no doubt aware of the treatment accorded by the Union of South Africa to Indians there on racial grounds. We made this an issue in the United Nations General Assembly last year and achieved a measure of success there. In raising this question before the United Nations we did not emphasize the limited aspect of it, but stood on the broader plane of human rights for all in accordance with the Charter of the United Nations.

What has happened in recent years, more especially since the rise to power of Hitler in Germany, was followed by us with deep pain and anxiety. You are quite right in thinking that India has mourned the horrors which resulted in the death of millions of Jews in the murder machines which were set up in Germany and elsewhere. That was terrible enough, but it was still more terrible to

---

[1] To Albert Einstein. JN Papers, NMML. SWJN, Vol. 3 (II series), pp. 393–6. Excerpts.

[2] The Constituent Assembly of India declared unlawful the practice of untouchability on 29 April 1947.

contemplate a civilization which, in spite of its proud achievements, could produce this horror.

I need not assure you, therefore, of our deepest sympathy for the Jews and for all they have undergone during these past years. If we can help them in any way I hope and trust that India will not merely stand by and look on. As you know, national policies are unfortunately essentially selfish policies. Each country thinks of its own interest first and then of other interests. If it so happens that some international policy fits in with the national policy of the country, then that nation uses brave language about international betterment. But as soon as that international policy seems to run counter to national interests or selfishness, then a host of reasons are found not to follow international policy.

We in India, engrossed as we have been in our struggle for freedom and in our domestic difficulties, have been unable to play any effective part in world affairs. The coming months, and possibly years, will not free us from these grave problems of our own country; but I have no doubt that we shall play a progressively more important part in international affairs. What that part will be in future I can only guess. I earnestly hope that we shall continue to adhere to the idealism which has guided our struggle for freedom. But we have seen often enough idealism followed by something far less noble, and so it would be folly for me to prophesy what the future holds for us. All we can do is to try our utmost to keep up standards of moral conduct both in our domestic affairs and in the international sphere.

The problem of Palestine, you will no doubt agree with me, is extraordinarily difficult and intricate. Where rights come into conflict it is not an easy matter to decide. With all our sympathy for the Jews we must and do feel that the rights and future of the Arabs are involved in this question. You have yourself framed the question: "Can Jewish need, no matter how acute, be met without the infringement of the vital rights of others?" Your answer to this question is in the affirmative. Broadly put, many may agree with you in that answer, but when we come to the specific application of this answer, the matter is not at all simple.

But, legalities apart and even apart from the many other issues involved, we have to face a certain existing situation. I do not myself see how this problem can be resolved by violence and conflict on one side or the other. Even if such violence and conflict achieve certain ends for the moment, they must necessarily be temporary. I do earnestly hope that some kind of an agreement might be arrived at between the Arabs and the Jews. I do not think even an outside power can impose its will for long or enforce some new arrangement against the will of the parties concerned.

I confess that while I have a very great deal of sympathy for the Jews I feel sympathy for the Arabs also in their predicament. In any event, the whole issue has become one of high emotion and deep passion on both sides. Unless men are big enough on either side to find a solution which is just and generally agreeable to the parties concerned, I see no effective solution for the present.

I have paid a good deal of attention to this problem of Palestine and have read books and pamphlets on the subject issued on either side; yet I cannot say that I know all about it, or that I am competent to pass a final opinion as to what should be done. I know that the Jews have done a wonderful piece of work in Palestine and have raised the standards of the people there, but one question troubles me. After all these remarkable achievements, why have they failed to gain the goodwill of the Arabs? Why do they want to compel the Arabs to submit against their will to certain demands? The way of approach has been one which does not lead to a settlement, but rather to the continuation of the conflict. I have no doubt that the fault is not confined to one party but that all have erred. I think also that the chief difficulty has been the continuation of British rule in Palestine. We know, to our cost, that when a third party dominates, it is exceedingly difficult for the others to settle their differences, even when that third party has good intentions—and third parties seldom have such intentions!

It is difficult for me to argue this question with you who knows so much more than I do. I have only indicated to you some of my own difficulties in the matter. But whatever those difficulties might be, I would assure you, with all earnestness, that I would like to do all in my power to help the Jewish people in their distress, in so far as I can do so, without injuring other people.

The world is in a sorry mess and the appetite for war and destruction has not been satisfied yet. Here in India we stand on the verge of independence for which we have struggled for so long, and yet there is no joy in this country at this turning-point in our history and there will be no celebrations of this historic event next month, for we are full of sorrow for what has happened in our country during the past year and for the cutting away of a part from the parent country. This was not how we had envisaged our freedom. What is most distressing is the background of all these events, the bitterness, the hatred and violence that have disfigured the face of India in recent months. We have a terribly hard task before us, but we shall face it, of course, with the confidence that we shall overcome these difficulties, as we have overcome others in the past.

Yours very sincerely,
Jawaharlal Nehru

15

Basic Principles[1]

Our performance in the General Assembly has of course to be in tune with our foreign policy.

India's foreign policy is in the process of being formulated. Indeed there can be no finality about it. While it is to be, or should be, based on certain fundamental principles, it is also something which is to be evolved in the light of experience, something which is to be adjusted to changing circumstances. In a world that is continually changing this latter part of the foreign policy must also necessarily be dynamic.

Foreign policy normally has a long-distance objective as well as short-distance objectives. The latter must be generally in keeping with the former. The latter may occasionally vary, in the light of experience and circumstances, but even while varying, they must keep the former in view.

What is our long-distance objective? Apart from maintaining the independence of India, her rapid economic and social progress, India, by virtue of her position and resources, is bound to play an increasing part in world affairs. This part in world affairs can be divided up into:

(1) Asian Affairs:
    (a) in South East Asia,
    (b) in China and Far East,
    (c) in the Middle East and Western Asia, and
    (d) in the Soviet part of Asia.
(2) General world affairs.

We are most intimately concerned with South East Asia and we should therefore develop these contacts as much as possible. This means that we should particularly help in every way in the freedom of the countries of South East Asia and their closer cooperation with India in political and economic matters, and ultimately in defence. South East Asia would include Australia and New Zealand.

[1] Guidelines for the session of the United Nations General Assembly held on 12 September 1948. JN Collection. NMML. Excerpts.

In regard to China and the Far East, nothing much can be done at present except to maintain friendly relations. China is in a state of utmost turmoil.[2] We should not attach ourselves too closely to any party in China so as to make the other party hostile to us. Naturally as a government we incline towards the present Government of China. In regard to Japan our general policy is to welcome the growth of the Japanese economy.

The Communist movements and revolts[3] in South East Asia are so tied up with the movements for independence that it is difficult to separate them. While we must condemn acts of terrorism and the like, we cannot take part in any measures to suppress these movements. In fact we are not in a position to do so, and any attempt to do so would merely make us vastly unpopular with large masses of people in South East Asia.

India is the natural leader of South East Asia if not of some other parts of Asia also. There is at present no other possible leadership in Asia, and any foreign leadership will not be tolerated. Nevertheless it is entirely wrong for any representative to talk in terms of India being the leader in any part of Asia or to discuss the formation of any Asian bloc. This does not help us in any way and merely irritates others and creates suspicion.

The Middle Eastern countries are very difficult to deal with at present. They want our help and we have certain ties with them which we wish to retain and strengthen. Still, it is probable that as a result of Pakistan coming into existence and the growth of an Islamic sentiment, the Middle Eastern countries will tend to become somewhat hostile to India. Probably these Islamic countries are not in a position to play an important part in world affairs. The importance they have thus far has been largely adventitious and partly due to the rivalries of western powers. Our general policy in regard to them should be one of friendship as well as firmness. There is no reason why we should vary our basic policy just to please these Middle East countries. But we must remember that apart from the Islamic sentiment, there are some reasons which would incline these countries towards India if they take a long view. Afghanistan, being anti-Pakistan, automatically is a little more friendly to India. We should take full

[2] The civil war in China which had been temporarily suspended after the defeat of Japan in 1945, broke out again. Mismanagement and corruption resulted in widespread popular discontent with the Nationalist regime of Chiang Kai-shek and enabled the communists to extend their influence in the countryside. The communist blockade from 29 June to 2 July 1948 of Manchuria and Changchun had starved 800,000 civilians. Nanking charged on 1 July that Government troops had killed 5000 Government troops and workers during their occupation of Kaifeng during 22–25 June.

[3] Communists were involved in every front in South East Asia. In April 1948, the Burmese Communist Party revolted against the Government headed by Thakin Nu. In June, the Malaysian communists took up arms against the British Government. In September, a coup was attempted in Java. In India the communists came into open conflict with the Government.

advantage of this fact. Turkey also is not very much affected by the Islamic sentiment.

As for Soviet Asia, this is part of the larger world problem and need not be treated as an Asian problem.

In world affairs generally we should stand for everything that promotes peace and avoids war and everything that puts an end to any imperialist domination of one country over another. At the same time we should work for close cooperation between nations with a view ultimately to help in the establishment of some world order.

We have repeatedly stated that India should not ally herself with any of the power blocs. This policy fits in with our basic principles and is at the same time beneficial even from the narrow opportunist point of view. Indeed there is no other policy which we can pursue with any advantage. The idea that we can gain some immediate end by alignment with one of the power blocs is essentially wrong. If once we do so, we will even lose our bargaining power, though we may gain some petty temporary advantage. If India ceases to have a neutral policy in regard to these power conflicts, many other countries would also be forced to line up with this or that power bloc. There would be no neutral countries left and no lead in any direction away from war. Indeed India's lining up might bring the world war nearer.

Our proclaimed neutrality apparently has little effect on the cleavage among nations, and sometimes results in our being isolated and gaining the ill will of both sides. That perhaps is to some extent inevitable and need not alarm us. If we adhere honestly and consistently to the policy we have laid down, we shall certainly gain the respect of most countries. India may not count today from the point of view of defence forces or industrial capacity, but India does count in the eyes of other countries because of her potential capacity and the certainly that she is going to play an important role in the future.

There is a psychological reason also for our continuing our policy of neutrality at the present juncture in world affairs. Any deviation from it will weaken us and will make us camp-followers of some group. We will not think of relying on our own strength but will progressively place our reliance on some other country which may or may not help us in time of need, and which will no doubt extract its pound of flesh whenever it can. We will cease to be looked upon as a possible leader of Asian as well as some other nations.

Therefore in the many questions that arise—in Germany,[4] in Greece,[5] in

[4] Berlin remained the storm centre of East-West relations. On 7 June 1948, the western allies announced their intention to create a federal state in their zones and, on 20 June, introduced a currency reform. The Soviet Government rejected it and started a land blockade of Berlin. The western powers fed Berlin by air.

[5] A civil war was going on since 1946 in Greece between the troops of a right-wing government led by the Populist Party and the communist guerrillas. With British and American assistance the Greek army was able to repulse the guerrillas.

China, in Korea,[6] over the Veto,[7] over the Interim Committee, and over the Atomic Energy issue—India must decide her attitude from the long-distance point of view and on the merits of each question. Of course certain minor variations may be made in order to suit circumstances.

During the recent months we have had evidence of a certain coolness towards India both in the USA and the USSR. This is regrettable, but we need not get alarmed or excited about it. On the whole with the UK our relations have improved, though it is yet too early to say how long this improvement will last. Generally speaking, our trade and economic contacts, and even to some extent cultural contacts, are with the western world. There is no reason why we should not maintain and encourage these economic contacts. If ultimately there is some kind of tenuous political bond between India and the UK, this will also encourage contacts. But such contacts should not lead to any political or military subservience or commitments. Nor should it lead to the development of any economic vested interests of foreign countries in India. In other words, while we should develop all these contacts with the UK, the USA and other countries of the western world, we should avoid any alignment with them on world issues.

With the USSR we can try to develop such trade or cultural relations as are possible. But we must keep clear of political entanglements. Russia's policy usually swings between two extremes and it is a little difficult to become really friendly with a country which adopts a hostile attitude or which expects you to become just a camp-follower. That we are not prepared to do on any account. It is probable, however, that the USSR might realize that the policy they have recently pursued towards India does not pay, and they might change that policy somewhat though not very greatly. In any event our attitude to the USSR should be as friendly as possible subject to all this. We are not getting tied up in any way with its world policies, some of which we disapprove. Even if Russia adopts an offensive policy against us, we should meet it with firmness but without any attempt to retaliate in the same way.

We should avoid, in the case of the UK or the USA or the USSR, adopting a self-righteous pose and making remarks and aspersions, which may wound the self-respect of nations and individuals. On no account must we reduce ourselves to the position of a satellite of any country.

In our talks with representatives of other powers we should be frank about

[6] The National Assembly in Seoul adopted on 12 July 1948 a constitution for a Democratic Republic of Korea. But a North Korea broadcast the same day announced plans for a rival constitution of a Democratic Korean People's Republic and for elections on 26 August.

[7] Russia, Britain, the US, France and China disagreed on the principle governing the exercise of the right of veto in the Security Council. The US and Britain opted for conditional use, but Russia adhered to the "rule of unanimity". This had been a subject of heated debate since 1946.

our general position and policy. We are too busy with our own country to desire any entanglements elsewhere. We want peace and avoidance of world war. (The fact that we are carrying on little wars in India or roundabout obviously weakens our position.) To the UK we should make it clear that while maintaining our full independence even as a Republic, we want close relations with what is now called British Commonwealth. We may even think of some vague bond. To the UK and the USA we should however make it clear that in the world as it is today there is not the least chance of our lining up with the Soviet in war or peace. To the USSR we should point out that while we have every intention of maintaining an independent policy, we have no hostility towards it and would like to maintain our neutrality in case of conflict.

Obviously if any country carries on a hostile policy against India, whether this is governmental or apparently non-official, the reactions of India would lead against that country. We are not only newly independent but are sensitive about such matters, and we have not the mentality of submitting to coercion.

In our talks with representatives of other powers we should try to understand their points of view and try to meet them as far as possible without compromising our basic attitude.

16

Note on Foreign Policy[1]

During its long history of struggle for the attainment of India's freedom, the National Congress was naturally absorbed in this struggle and could not pay much attention to foreign affairs. Nevertheless as far back as the early twenties we find the Congress passing resolutions about foreign policy. In spite of our absorption in our national struggle we always viewed it as a part of the struggle of all oppressed and colonial people. Because of this we sympathized with all other peoples in the world who might be suffering from exploitation or the domination of a foreign power. We were anti-imperialist not only in India but in the rest of the world also. Inevitably we become anti-fascist. Whether it was in China or Spain or Abyssinia or Czechoslovakia, the National Congress raised its voice against imperialist and fascist forces and governments.

Inevitably, as a non-official organization, the Congress could only lay down general policies and was not concerned with any specific problem. It was concerned directly with Indians overseas. It was also concerned both directly and indirectly with the problem of racial equality.

Now that India is an independent country, the Government has to face world problems not only on the basis of principle but also on the far more difficult plane of application of a principle in a complicated situation. Normally India does not wish to interfere with other countries, just as India would resent the interference of any other country in its own affairs. But the world today, in spite of friction and conflict, is an interrelated organism and it is impossible for any country to remain in isolation.

Independence brings rights and privileges; it also brings responsibilities and duties which always accompany rights and privileges. It is an inevitable consequence of independence that we should develop foreign relations, have representatives in foreign countries, and take part in foreign affairs. In any event this would be so, but in view of the fact that large numbers of Indians live abroad, it becomes our duty to take interest in them. Also our trade requires foreign contacts and foreign relations. We have today unfortunately even to

[1] 2 December 1948, New Delhi. JN Collection, NMML. This was drafted by Jawaharlal Nehru and sent to Dr. Pattabhi Sitaramayya and used in its entirety by him in his presidential address to the Jaipur Congress on 18 December 1948.

buy foodstuffs from abroad; we have to buy many other things such as capital goods and machinery for the development of our country. But above all we have to participate in this growing structure of a World Order. Not to do all this would mean that we relied on others to do it on our behalf which again means dependence on others and not independence.

India, therefore, as an independent country has naturally developed these foreign relations, sent her representatives abroad to many countries, and taken a full part in international conferences and more especially the United Nations Organization which is gradually and painfully staggering along towards that conception of World Order and cooperation which is embodied in the fine language of its Charter. Some of these international conferences, more especially those dealing with Asia, are finding their way to Indian soil because inevitably India is becoming the focal point of many activities in Asia.

What should our foreign policy be? Broadly speaking the old principles which we have laid down so many times should govern our present policy also. That is to work for the ending of all imperialisms and the domination of one country by another, the ending of racial discrimination and the establishment of racial equality, and world peace and cooperation aimed at ultimately the development of a World Order or One World. These are general policies but in their application many difficulties arise specially in the world today which is suffering from an excess of fear and suspicion and so soon after the last Great War, is again thinking of yet another and a vaster and more terrible war. Groups of powers face each other in their embattled might and try hard to develop their warlike resources.

In this hard world of war and strife India cannot be a weak and helpless spectator. She has to guard her freedom but she will guard it badly if she forgets the essential principles for which she has stood under the guidance of the Father of the Nation.

India's policy has been laid down as one of avoidance of attachment to any bloc of powers which is antagonistic to another bloc. This is a difficult position to maintain and sometimes it brings odium from all the contending parties. Yet, not only on the ground of high principle, but also from the point of view of practical necessity and the good of India as well as of the world, it is the only policy that India can adopt. India must therefore ceaselessly strive to develop friendly relations with not only her neighbour countries but also with the countries of the world and exercise such weight and influence as she possesses to lessen international rivalries and prevent the drift to war. In the recent session of the United Nations, held in Paris, India has played no mean part in following this policy and has shown to the world that she can be friendly and cooperative with other nations without becoming a hanger on of this or that bloc. If India left this policy, then indeed there would be little hope, for only warring factions will remain.

India is more specially interested in what is happening in Asia. I should like specially to refer to the grave crisis in Indonesia where a brave and gallant people fighting for their freedom have been harassed and threatened continuously by an imperialist power. I should like to send my greetings to the Government and people of the Republic of Indonesia and to assure them that our entire sympathy is with them. We are convinced that whatever the immediate future may hold, there can be no doubt that ultimately the free Republic of Indonesia will triumph. Indeed I might say that the process of eliminating imperialism from Asia cannot be stopped and must go on. Every foreign power that holds dominion in any part of Asia must depart.

Africa is in a somewhat difficult position, but the same principle holds good there although it may take somewhat longer to apply. To the people of Africa I should also like to extend our warm sympathy and I want to make it clear that we do not want any Indian vested interest to grow or to exploit the African people. We want Indians in Africa to cooperate with the people there for the advancement of those people. We stand for no domination over any other country and no exploitation of any other people by our people.

The question has arisen as to India's future relationship with the Commonwealth which used to be called the British Commonwealth of Nations. It is clear that India is going to be a free, sovereign, independent Republic in no way subservient to or dependent on foreign authority. That Republic will draw its power and authority from the people of this country. Those people will owe no allegiance to any foreign country or authority. That is clear enough. At present we are passing through a transitional stage of Dominionhood. Dominion Status has certainly meant in practice independence in domestic and external policy. Nevertheless the concept of the Dominion cannot be fitted in with that of a Republic. Therefore Dominion Status must go. The question then arises as to whether it is possible and desirable for the free Indian Republic to have some relationship with the United Kingdom and other countries associated with her. This relationship cannot be that of a Dominion. It can only be the association of free and independent countries agreeing to have certain reciprocal relations which do not limit in any way their freedom to domestic or international policy.

It is within these limiting factors that the question has to be considered. I have said above that India cannot remain in isolation from the rest of the world. It is to the advantage of India, as it will be to the advantage of other countries, to have closer contacts and associations. This may help us in many ways and this may also help the cause of world peace. But whatever associations may be built up, they must in no way derogate from the complete independence of India and the freedom of the policy that she pursues. India is too big and important a country to be swept away any more by the gust of wind from foreign shores. We stand firmly on our soil, receptive to all the good that can come to us, cooperative with others but not allowing ourselves to be pushed about in any direction against our will.

The old world in which we have lived so long is rapidly changing before our eyes. India is changing. We cannot therefore think in terms of the past, even of the immediate past, for if we do so we shall forget the present and we shall not be prepared for the future. Therefore, all questions have to be considered in the light of this new world that is growing up and changing conditions that we are in. In these conditions we should seek cooperation wherever we can have it, while maintaining our freedom and dignity. There are enough forces in the world today breaking up and destroying. We should stand on the side of the builders, not of the destroyers.

17

The Occident and the Orient[1]

A great deal has been said in the past about the Occident and the Orient, the East and the West and the like. I myself have not understood this and all that has been said. At any rate, I have not appreciated them. It is obvious that there are differences between countries, differences of historical background and difference of cultural traditions and so forth. But this business of difference between the Occident and the Orient I have not understood. I don't understand where the line is exactly to be drawn and how. There have been even in the past and now, centres of civilizations. If I may mention them, they are China, India and West Asia, all acting and interacting with each other with different historical backgrounds and yet with many common features. And in Europe and America too, you find these centres of civilization; but the difference has been the fact that for a hundred or hundred and fifty years certain countries in Europe and America have had an intensive career of development of industrialization which has brought in its train many things and which has naturally accentuated this so-called difference between the Occident and the Orient.

It is not the nature of the Occident and the Orient to differ but the fact of industrial development and technical processes have naturally affected tremendously western civilizations and it is affecting the eastern civilizations also. Of course, there is the time-lag between them. The difference is not so much between the Occident and the Orient but as between the centres of civilizations, between areas that have often enough somewhat different psychological backgrounds.

There is far too much tendency today to think, even in advanced countries, about their own psychological background and not try to understand the psychological backgrounds of other countries, with the result that in spite of complete knowledge of political and economic data they completely fail to understand each other. This is because understanding is something much more than memorizing facts of history and geography. Ultimately understanding comes from certain emotional appreciation of other people, of how an individual or a nation functions. As a matter of fact, I may tell you there are so many

[1] Address to Consular Corps, Calcutta, 14 January 1949. From *Hindustan Standard*, 15 January 1949. Excerpts.

people including highly qualified professors of history, who know all the facts and yet do not understand anything at all. So it seems to me to be necessary for the world today to have an emotional, psychological understanding of each other, regardless of the fact whether you accept that psychological outlook or not. Having understood that, the second phase arises.

It is not for you or for me to try to change the powerful psychological backgrounds of the nations, because a deliberate attempt to do so leads to conflicts which are totally unnecessary. As a matter of fact, all the forces of the world today are moving towards a certain uniformity. This is because of communications, wireless, radio, cinema, etc. There is this development of science. How far they will produce this uniformity I do not know. I think it would be a pity if the world became regimented to a single pattern. It will be a dull world then, an unprogressive world.

In India, if I may venture to say so, the whole background of Indian culture has been in the past, I do not speak about the future, an emphasis on the unity of India regardless even of political splitting up. And in the past political splitting in India has been considerable. But there has been much more cultural unity than political or even economic unity.

Together with the idea of unity there has been always an extraordinary diversity and variety in India and no attempt has been made in the past to put an end to that diversity. Provided the essential conditions of unity were acknowledged, that variety was not only tolerated but even encouraged. So, India had tried in the past and succeeded in maintaining a certain unity in outlook and culture, at the same time maintaining the variety of its different cultures in different parts.

I think in the larger context of the world while we are moving and must move towards the conception of world unity—you may call it the one world idea—at the same time it is even more essential that varieties should be maintained and acknowledged as such and no attempt should be made to regiment them to a single pattern. That is to say, we should have a psychological understanding of the other party. If that is done, many of our problems will be far easier of solution. There is far too much of misunderstanding today.

18

An Independent Foreign Policy[1]

We have often thought of Gandhiji and his great doctrine, of his great message and while we praised it often enough, we felt, 'Are we hypocrites, talking about it but being unable to live up to it? Are we deluding ourselves and the world?' Because if we were hypocrites, then surely our future is dark. We may be hypocritical about the small things of life, but it is a dangerous thing to be hypocritical about the great things of life. And it would be the greatest tragedy if we exploited the name and prestige of our great leader, took shelter under it and denied in our hearts, in our activities, the message that he had brought to this country and the world. So we have had these conflicts in our minds and these conflicts continue, and perhaps there is no final solution of these conflicts except to try continually to bridge the gulf between that idealism and that practice which is forced down upon us by circumstances. For, after all if we are in charge of any work, if we are in seats of authority and responsibility to face a particular situation, we can only do so, on the one hand according to the way that we think will meet that situation. We cannot—and I am quite positive that our great leader would not have had us—function as blind automatons just doing the same thing which he had said without reference to changes in events. On the other hand, we have to keep in mind those very ideals to which we pledged ourselves so often. There is always a great difference between the approach to a problem of a prophet and a great statesman, and so we cannot be judged by that high standard. All we can say is that we should do our utmost to live up as far as we can to that standard, but always judging a problem by the light of our own intelligence, otherwise we will fail. . . .

The problems we have to face in world affairs at the present moment bear a great deal of relation to the conflicts that are going on. We have stated repeatedly that our foreign policy is one to keep apart from big blocs of nations—rival blocs—and to be friendly to all countries and not become entangled in any alliances, military or other, that might drag us into any possible conflict . . . We have very strictly followed that policy of not getting entangled in any kind of

[1] Speech during the debate on demands for grants relating to the Ministry of External Affairs and Commonwealth Relations, 8 March 1949. *Constituent Assembly (Legislative) Debates, Official Report.* JN Papers, NMML. Excerpts.

commitment—certainly not military—the question does not arise—with any other power or group of powers, and we propose to adhere to that policy, because we are quite convinced that that is the only possible policy for us at present and in the future. That does not, on the other hand, involve any lack of close relationship with other countries. . . .

We are associated today in the United Nations with a great number of countries in the world. Anything else that we might do will naturally have to be something that does not go against our association with the United Nations—that is within its structure. We have been associated with the Commonwealth that used to be called the British Commonwealth of Nations in the past in a way which was entirely unsatisfactory and we fought to get out of it, until we have completely achieved our objective in regard to independence. In practice, and in theory also, we shall achieve it completely and fully in the course of the next few months. Now, it is only in terms of independent nations cooperating together that we can consider the problem of our association with the Commonwealth. There may be, as some people have suggested, alliances with this or that nation. Alliances usually involve military and other commitments and they are more binding. Other forms of association which do not bind in this manner, but which help in bringing together nations for the purpose of consultation and, where necessary, of cooperation are, therefore, far more preferable than any form of alliance which does bind. . . .

Fortunately we enter upon our independence as a country with no hostile background in regard to any country. We are friendly to all countries. Our hostility during the last 200 years was mainly directed towards the dominating power here and because of India's independence that hostility has largely vanished, though it may survive in some people's minds, but that is not important. So we approach the whole world on a friendly basis and there is no reason why we should put ourselves at a disadvantage, if I may say so, by becoming unfriendly to any group. I think that India has a vital role to play in world affairs. . . .

What are we interested in world affairs for? We seek no dominion over any country. Our main stake in world affairs is peace; our main stake in world affairs is to see that there is racial equality; our main stake in world affairs is that people who are still subjugated should be free. For the rest we do not desire to interfere in world affairs and we do not desire that other people too should interfere in our affairs. If, however, there is interference with us, whether military, political or economic, we shall resist it.

19

The Problem of Burma[1]

New Delhi, 14 April 1949

My dear Thakin Nu,

It was a great pleasure to meet you again and to have full and frank talks with you. You know how vitally interested I am in the future of Burma. This is not merely because I wish Burma well, as indeed I do, but also because what happens in Burma affects India and the whole of Asia. The crisis in Burma is, therefore, of vital significance to all of us and we have anxiously watched it during these past many months.

That crisis, of course, has a military aspect and it is obvious that your Government must meet rebels with force. It follows that you must strengthen your armed forces and keep them disciplined. You have asked us on several occasions for equipment and other supplies and we have tried our best to send them to you. I know that we have not been able to fulfil all your demands. I explained to you the great difficulties that we were experiencing. These difficulties flowed from the partition, which split up our Army, our Air Force, our Services, our communications and almost everything. Immediately after, we had to deal with vast scale civil conflict in northern India and huge migrations of human beings. Soon after came the Kashmir war. For a state, newly free, these problems were colossal and it would not have been surprising if that new state collapsed under their burden. However, we survived and gradually gained strength. But as a result of all this, our resources were strained to the utmost. More especially our army supplies came down to rock-bottom level and because of the difficulty in getting spare parts, much that we had could not be used. We have recently sent a special military mission to Europe and America to get supplies and spare parts.

These have been our extraordinary difficulties and I think it is some credit to our Government that we have pulled through them and made good. But our present position is such that we just cannot find adequate supplies for you. We are trying to collect what we can and you will have them. I hope you will understand our position and realize that we are doing our utmost for you.

---

[1] To U.Nu, JN Collection, NMML. Excerpts.

I have said above that one aspect of the problem in Burma is a military one. It is clear that there are other aspects also and in the long run these other aspects are even more important. I should like you to look at this whole picture, not only in Burma but in Asia and the world. It is an extraordinary picture, both fascinating and disturbing. The whole of Asia is in a state of turmoil and revolution in various stages. I am not afraid of revolution, but I do not want widespread ruin in large parts of Asia, for that would mean delaying progress for a generation or two, apart from the terrible misery that it will bring. To imagine that a mere upsetting of existing governments and institutions necessarily leads to a betterment of the people, is surely not right. It may well lead, as it has led in many places, to a tremendous setback and ruin and misery.

During the past year and a half we in India have had to face exceedingly difficult situations. We have been accused of not being progressive enough in our legislation or our practices. Perhaps some of the accusations have a degree of truth in them. But all this must be measured from the point of view of maintaining stability and security in the state. If this is not done, then chaos follows. We have succeeded not only in maintaining this stability and security but in making progress in that direction, and that is no small gain. For now we are in a position to go ahead fairly fast. Otherwise India would have been split up into numerous fragments or economically and politically broken up, resulting in far lower standards for our people. The hope of progress would have had to be given up for a long time to come. As it is, India is considered to be about the only stable and strong state in a great part of Asia and more and more other states of Asia look up to it for cooperation and guidance.

I mention all this in order to show that we have barely escaped disaster ourselves during the past year and a half and that it is only a long-distance view that has kept us going and prevented our country from going to pieces. We have often had to face even popular disapproval of our action, because we were convinced that any other course would be injurious to the nation. We have looked at the problem of India in the larger context of Asia and world peace and we have gradually evolved a strong integrated India. Vast problems still remain, but we are confident of solving them.

Because we looked ahead and were not afraid of a little unpopularity for the time being, we did may things for which we were criticized. We were anxious that during this period of change-over from British rule to independence, we should take no risks and should in no way encourage disruptive tendencies. Deliberately we decided to keep Lord Mountbatten as Governor-General, although we could have easily chosen one of four own colleagues. Deliberately now we have expressed our willingness to remain associated with the Commonwealth, even though we are going to become a Republic. We have done all this with the one intention of not weakening the stability of the country and gradually forging ahead and building up strength till we can stand completely alone, if necessary.

Burma has unfortunately had to face a succession of troubles and conflicts ever since it became independent. You lost, by horrible assassination, your great leader, Aung San. I had looked to him not only for great leadership in Burma but in Asia also and it was a terrible loss for all of us.

Now you are the leader of Burma and, if I may say so, Burma is very fortunate in having you, because you have wider vision and you are absolutely straight and have no personal axe to grind. Your vision and your high integrity are tremendous assets to Burma. Personally, I have come to believe that straightness and integrity in politics are more important than any other quality. Little-mindedness never makes a nation great.

The present position in Burma is a serious one both from the political and the military point of view. It is clear that the only possible stable government is your Government. The only alternative to this is chaos. If there is this chaos, that is an open invitation to others to come to Burma, whether these others come by sea or over land. Time is running short and danger surrounds Burma. Though Burma is independent, it should never be forgotten that independence is not a question of passing a law or resolutions or slogans, but is dependent entirely on the inner strength and cohesion of the people. If that cohesion is lacking, even military victories will not carry one far. Time is important, I have said, because the situation in Asia is developing rapidly.

Among the various insurgent groups, it is clear that your Government can have little to do and can have little in common with the Communists in Burma or the P.V.Os.[2] Communism in Burma has little to do with real communism. Its name is exploited and violent deeds are indulged in. The Karens, on the other hand, can make suitable allies for you in the future. Any attempt to fight on all fronts is not likely to succeed and may well end in very serious loss. In politics as in warfare, one takes up one's enemy one by one. The Burmese Government has been caught in a bad strategy when it has to face many enemies at the same time. Of all these present insurgents, the Karens are the only ones that really count and that can make a difference in the future.

I know that the Karens have behaved very badly and that there is a great deal of ill feeling and anger against them. But we cannot judge long-distance policies by present-day passion.

It is clear that an outstanding military victory against all the insurgents is unlikely for a long time. This period may well see very serious developments and if Burma is still tied up with its inner revolts, then Burma will become helpless before others from outside.

If this line of reasoning is correct, as I think it is, then it becomes incumbent to stop this civil conflict so far as the Karens are concerned. Of course this can only be done by terms, fair and honourable. It is not for me to suggest what steps are possible or should be taken. Of that only you and your colleagues can be the

[2] People's Volunteer Organization.

judges. All I wish to emphasize is that from the point of view of a longer strategy and of avoiding imminent dangers, it seems essential that everything in reason should be done to put an end to the conflict with the Karens. If this is done, then immediately, other results follow. The country's morale and discipline go up, and your Government's hands are free to deal with other troublesome elements. Your prestige goes up before other countries and financial and other help can follow more easily. You get breathing time to build up your strength, political, economic and military, and it will not be difficult for you then to meet any fresh dangers that might arise. There is, in other words, an immediate change in the situation to your Government's advantage.

What is the alternative to this? Weary dragging on of civil wars for months and months with progressive deterioration. We have seen in Malaya how difficult it is to put an end to civil disturbances. The British Government there has a large and well-equipped army and air force, and yet their success has been very slow. So that one cannot rely upon purely military solutions of these problems. War goes on resulting in more and more disintegration, economic and political. Ultimately there is danger of foreign intervention. This foreign intervention can be from the North, that is, China, or from across the sea by other powers. In either event it will be unfortunate for Burma and her freedom will be put in peril.

Another possible alternative is for some kind of an alliance or cooperation between those who are supporting you and the communists and the P.V.Os. Any such development, I think, would be very disastrous. The so-called communists in Burma are hardly Communists and most of them function as freebooters and terrorists. The P.V.Os. appear to be completely indisciplined and rather opportunist with no particular principle. Any alliance with these elements would lead to rapid disintegration. It would also mean further isolation from the rest of the world, which will be even more chary of giving any help. As a result again, there may be foreign intervention either from the north or from the south.

I have referred to China above. I am not alarmed because of developments in China. I think that they had become inevitable. I cannot say what a new regime in China will be like. But I imagine that it will be very much Chinese and will not function merely at the dictation of others. I do not think this regime will deliberately seek conflict with Burma or try to invade any part of Burmese territory. But if Northern Burma is in a state of disruption and chaos, roving bands from China are likely to enter Burma to take advantage of the situation there. This will lead to further complications.

With the development of the situation in China, Indo-China and Siam are likely to be affected. As it is the French in Indo-China are in a weak position and they are bound to be pushed out sometime or other. In Siam the position is also very unstable. It thus appears that on several sides of Burma there is likely to be violent upheaval and unless Burma is stable then, with a strong government, surrounding upheavals will also tend to disrupt Burma. I have not referred to the world situation as a whole. But everyone knows that it is tense. I do not myself think that a major war is likely to come for a few years, but no one can be certain. The path of prudence lies, in being prepared for any development.

It is on this basis that we are proceeding in India. We want to do everything in our power to prevent another war from taking place, because such a war would be disastrous for humanity. But, at the same time, we are anxious to build up our country and attain strength before a world upheaval takes place. So we are hard at work at this process of building up.

This argument applies even more to Burma. It has to make good from the point of view of the world and the tension that exists there, and more particularly, it has to recover stability before its northern and eastern borders are powerfully affected. The later development may take place within months or so and thus the time at our disposal is strictly limited. Hence the importance of this time factor and your viewing the Burma situation in terms of these possible developments and dangers. Forgetting this imminent future and functioning only in the present will not be the path of wisdom, for that future is going to be the present fairly soon.

From the financial point of view, your country's situation will naturally deteriorate, if hostilities go on. That is always the result of war. In Burma you started from scratch without much in the way of reserves. Indeed you are a debtor country. We would gladly help you financially if we could. But our financial position is a very peculiar one. On the one side we are a creditor country. The UK Government owes us a large sum of money which is locked up in frozen sterling balances. Pakistan owes us a large sum of money which we cannot touch for at least three years and I do not know what will happen afterwards. Burma owes us also a large sum and that we are not likely to touch for some time. On the other hand we have had to face heavy deficit budgets and inflation. If we once give in to this inflation, our economic position would deteriorate rapidly and go towards some kind of a collapse. We do not intend to permit this to happen and we are going to try our utmost to stop inflation, reduce prices, promote industrial development and have rising standards of living. Cash we simply have not got. The only possibility of our helping you financially is, if the UK Government releases some of our frozen sterling balances with them.

The only chance of financial help is thus from the UK Government in cooperation with some other Commonwealth governments. We can join in this, subject to our frozen sterling balances being released. The other Dominion governments may help partly, but only if the UK Government takes the lead. The UK Government has made it clear that they cannot consider loans, unless the main hostilities cease. So we get back into a vicious circle. I do not think the USA is going to help at all in the present circumstances and certainly not, if the UK Government is averse to helping. The USA have received a bad shock in China where they poured in money and are not likely to try again. The result of all this is that financial help appears to be dependent on a cessation of hostilities.

I have placed the broad facts of the situation, as they appear to me, before you. The immediate problems in Burma are known to you much better than to me. Even those immediate problems have to be regarded in that larger context that I have mentioned. You have to consider the two together and find a way out which is honourable to your Government and country and is conducive to peace coming soon and with it financial help and consolidation. The methods of approach must also be decided by you and your colleagues. Sometime ago, you will remember that the Government of India suggested some kind of a mediation. At that time you did not think it appropriate or feasible. I want to make it quite clear what our idea of mediation was. It was not, in any sense, to encourage the Karens or to consider them as equal parties to a dispute. It was and is our firm conviction that the only possible approach in Burma must be one which strengthens your Government's hands. We want your Government to be even more firmly established, because there is no alternative to it in Burma. Therefore, any step that we could take, could only be after full consultation with you and in accordance with your wishes. As a matter of fact, we think that your proposals to the Karens were eminently reasonable and fair and I do not see how you could go much further.

The issue before us was of a somewhat different kind. No principles were involved, no recognition of the Karens or encouragement of them. But it sometimes happens that a third party approach breaks the ice and makes the consideration of a problem easier. We were prepared to make that third party approach, provided you were willing. As you were not willing then, naturally we could take no step. We would ourselves greatly prefer not to take any step in Burma. We do not wish to interfere in any way or to assume any responsibility. But if it was thought that some kind of an approach from us might be helpful to you, we would have undertaken it in order to clear the ground for you to deal with the situation directly.

We are always prepared to do this and to help you in any other way possible to us. I mentioned to you that if real necessity arose, I would myself be prepared to go to Burma. Frankly I would not like to do so at the present moment, as my going there might introduce an element of confusion. But if there was real need and a prospect of my visit doing good, I would put aside all my engagements here and visit Burma for a few days. Even so, of course, the ground would have to be prepared for my visit in some way or other. All I could do or all that any colleagues of mine would do would be just to clear the ground a little and remove a psychological barrier among those who may doubt the bona fides of the Burma Government that the Burma Government's word would be carried out to the letter. I know very well that what you say, you will do, whatever happens.

This has become a very long letter and you will forgive me, I hope, for its length. The length of this letter is some evidence of our deep anxiety to help you and Burma. Trouble and difficulty have brought us even closer together than in the past and we have to hold together. For our part, we want to do so and you can rest assured that we shall remain good friends of the Burmese people and try to help them to the best of our ability. . . .

I have written to you not in an official capacity but as a friend and a colleague. I have therefore written perfectly frankly.

Yours very sincerely,
Jawaharlal Nehru

20

Cooperation in the Commonwealth[1]

I agree that it must be of the essence of an association like the Commonwealth that its members should consult one another on all matters of common concern and cooperate with one another to the fullest possible extent. I must point out, however, that their cooperation would be determined not by any formal commitments accepted in advance, but by their friendly and understanding approach to common problems. The world situation is very complex, for example, the present situation in China. Although countries of the Commonwealth should be prepared to defend themselves against aggression, it would be a mistake to base their policies primarily on the need for mutual assistance in such defence. If war were imminent, preparation for defence would be inevitable. But the first object of their policy should be to prevent war, for experience after two world wars has shown that war can only intensify the very conditions which create that social dissatisfaction and unrest on which communism flourishes. The handling of nationalist movements in Indonesia and Indo-China by the Dutch and the French respectively are example of policies calculated to encourage those forces which aim at the violent overthrow of European domination in Asia. The removal of these irritants to public opinion in Asia would make a much greater contribution to the cause of international security than any military precautions which could be taken.

Political developments in Asia over the next few years will have an important influence throughout the world and the Commonwealth must take note of the obvious moral, namely, that developments in Asia would turn very largely on the attitude of the masses who are not already committed to any particular ideology, and therefore, it is vitally important that the democratic countries should do nothing at this stage which might cause these people to look elsewhere for inspiration and assistance. Throughout Asia, and even in India, there is still suspicion of European domination, though in India there has been a remarkable change during the past two years in the attitude of public

[1] London, 27 April 1949. Intervention at a meeting of the Commonwealth Prime Ministers and the Secretary of State for External Affairs, Canada. Extracts from a report on the Commonwealth Conference. Cabinet Secretariat Papers.

opinion towards the United Kingdom. It is against this background of suspicion that the Commonwealth policy will be judged in India. Unless these
susceptibilities are kept constantly in mind, the influence of the Commonwealth
in Asia cannot be strengthened.

21

Relations with the Soviet Union[1]

New Delhi, 7 May 1949

My dear Radhakrishnan,[2]

I appreciate all that you have written and the many important activities in which you are engaged. I would have hesitated to draw you away from them, or rather some of them. But after giving the most careful thought to this matter, we came to the conclusion that you could do work of the most vital importance for India in the Soviet Union. If I had not thought so, I would not have approached you. Recent developments, that is, the agreement arrived at at the Commonwealth Conference about the Indian Republic remaining in the Commonwealth, make our approach to the Soviet even more important. It is in fact a fundamental and basic one from the point of view of the world situation.

We have three very important posts abroad—London, Moscow and Washington. Each is different from the other. Although all three are of equal importance, the Moscow one is the most delicate and, for the moment, the most important. It is true that the type of work there is not so much the normal routine work in an embassy, though there is some of that of course. It is much more a psychological approach to the Soviet mind and an attempt to make them realize that we mean what we say. In spite of bitter criticisms they have made of India and the present Government of India,[3] we still want to be friendly with them and to help in the preservation of peace in which they are so very much interested. All our foreign policy is directed to that end, and one of the main reasons why I agreed to the recent London settlement was because I

[1] To S. Radhakrishnan. File No. 1(73) Eur. II/49, Ministry of External Affairs, National Archives of India.

[2] Sarvepalli Radhakrishnan (1888–1975) scholar and statesman who was President of India from 1962–67. He served as Indian Ambassador to the Soviet Union from 1949–52.

[3] The Soviet Union condemned the Indian Government as "lackeys of imperialism". A.M. Diakov, a leading Soviet Indologist, declared Jawaharlal Nehru as a demagogue and Gandhism as a reactionary movement and "a most important ideological weapon in the hands of the Indian bourgeoisie for keeping the masses under its influence."

thought this would help in the preservation of peace and would give India a chance to make her influence felt a little more than otherwise. I think it will have that result. To put this across to the Soviet Government is of vital importance. It is just possible that a right approach from us may ultimately make a big difference in world affairs. If our bona fides are accepted, then we can be helpful in easing the tensions that exist in the world.

Thus, in a sense, our activities in Moscow bear directly on our work for world peace. Whether they will succeed or not, is more than anyone can say. But I have a feeling that they will make good. Because of this, after long thought, I came to the conclusion that you would make the most suitable ambassador. My sister has, on the whole, done remarkably well there in difficult circumstances. Owing to various factors I felt that she might not have suitable opportunities for being able to do something fresh in this direction. A person like you, well-known internationally in non-political activities and with broad nationalist and humanist views, would be welcomed in the Soviet Union and would start off with an initial advantage, which most others would not. What positive results you might be able to achieve, it is difficult to say, because such results depend on so many factors outside our control. One thing, however, is certain that we will then prevent the situation from deteriorating and might well help somewhat in bettering it. That in itself would be a big thing in this delicate and complicated world situation.

In spite of our many failings in India, the world is opening out to us and recognizing some quality in us. It is up to us to try our best to take advantage of this, for the future may well be affected by it, our own and that of the world. So the question of appointment to Moscow cannot be treated as just that of any other appointment.

In your letter you say that "If there is the slightest chance of doing any good there (Moscow), it should not be thrown away." I have indicated above that there is very much more than the slightest chance and it would be wrong for you and me to throw this away. You have been good enough to say that. After reading your letter and realizing how you feel about the matter, if I still decide that you should go, you will do so for the period of one year. I am clearly of opinion that you should accept this ambassadorship and go to Moscow. I presume therefore that you will agree. Could you please let me know immediately?

Yours sincerely,
Jawaharlal Nehru

22

Commonwealth
Prime Minister's Conference[1]

Personally I am convinced, even more than before, that our foreign policy of not linking up with any power group is the only correct policy for us to follow. Both in Asia and in the world at large circumstances have made it inevitable that we should have certain economic and commercial bonds with the Commonwealth countries as well as the USA. These will no doubt continue. Also there will be a measure of consultation between the Commonwealth countries. This need not deflect our policy. It may, on the other hand, succeed in deflecting others' policies, more specially in relation to Asia.

I think it is justifiable for us to say that India will be in a freer position to follow any external policy now than it might have been if it had broken the link completely with the Commonwealth. In the latter event, she would have been isolated as there was no other country or group to which it could align itself without detriment. As a result, circumstances might well have forced her to adopt a very cautious and restricted foreign policy, or inevitably to stoop in some particular direction. This latter course would have meant commitments from which we are free now. Thus, oddly enough, outside the Commonwealth we might have lost somewhat our freedom of action.

Certain immediate advantages flow from our continued association with the Commonwealth. These are well known and need not be reiterated. Certain immediate disadvantages would have also resulted from our breaking with the Commonwealth. These are also fairly well known. One of these, however, might be mentioned and that is the position of nine million Indians overseas, chiefly in the British colonies and protectorates. The position of these Indians would have become anomalous if we had completely separated from the Commonwealth. They would have become aliens in the countries they inhabit and would have had to choose between Indian nationality, with the consequent result of deprivation of citizenship rights in the countries they live in, or a denial of Indian nationality. This was a serious matter for such a large number of persons and new and difficult problems would have arisen.

[1] Note written on 7 May 1949. JN Collection, NMML. Excerpts.

Whatever the advantages in remaining in the Commonwealth and whatever the disadvantages in breaking from it, it was clear to me that in no event could we agree to the slightest abrogation or limitation of full sovereignty and independence as a republic.

On the whole, therefore, I feel convinced that we have every reason to be gratified at the result of this meeting.[2] What we do in future will depend upon ourselves and on the strength of India. The main thing, therefore, is to build up that strength and, so far as our foreign policy is concerned, to adopt a friendly attitude towards all other countries, avoid entanglements and commitments and, more specially, remain aloof from any power blocs. I need hardly add that the Commonwealth association is one which is terminable at the pleasure of any party at any time.

[2] Meeting of the Commonwealth Prime Ministers which took place in London from 21 April to 27 April 1949.

23

A Voyage of Discovery[1]

It is true that India's voice is somewhat different; it is not the voice of the old world of Europe but of the older world of Asia. It is the voice of an ancient civilization, distinctive, vital, which at the same time, has renewed itself and learned much from you and the other countries of the West. It is, therefore, both old and new. It has its roots deep in the past, it also has the dynamic urge of today.

But, however the voices of India and the United States may appear to differ, there is much in common between them. Like you, we have achieved our freedom through a revolution, though our methods were different from yours. Like you we shall be a Republic based on the federal principle, which is an outstanding contribution of the founders of this great Republic. In a vast country like India, as in this great Republic of the United States, it becomes necessary to have a delicate balance between Central control and state autonomy. We have placed in the forefront of our Constitution those fundamental human rights to which all men who love liberty, equality and progress aspire—the freedom of the individual, the equality of men and the rule of law. We enter, therefore, the community of free nations with the roots of democracy deeply embedded in our institutions as well as in the thoughts of our people.

We have achieved political freedom but our revolution is not yet complete and is still in progress, for political freedom without the assurance of the right to live and to pursue happiness, which economic progress alone can bring, can never satisfy a people. Therefore, our immediate task is to raise the living standards of our people, to remove all that comes in the way of the economic growth of the nation. We have tackled the major problems of India, as it is today the major problem of Asia, the agrarian problem. Much that was feudal in our system of land tenure is being changed so that the fruits of cultivation should go to the tiller of the soil and that he may be secure in the possession of the land he cultivates. In a country of which agriculture is still the principal industry, this reform is essential not only for the well-being and contentment of the

[1] Address to the US House of Representatives, Washington DC, 13 October 1949. AIR and PIB tapes, NMML. Excerpts.

individual but also for the stability of society. One of the main causes of social instability in many parts of the world, more especially in Asia, is agrarian discontent due to the continuance of systems of land tenure which are completely out of place in the modern world. Another and one which is also true of the greater part of Asia and Africa, is the low standard of living of the masses.

India is industrially more developed than many less fortunate countries and is reckoned as the seventh or eighth among the world's industrial nations. But this arithmetical distinction cannot conceal the poverty of the great majority of our people. To remove this poverty by greater production, more equitable distribution, better education and better health, is the paramount need and the most pressing task before us and we are determined to accomplish this task. We realize that self-help is the first condition of success for a nation, no less than for an individual. We are conscious that ours must be the primary effort and we shall seek succour from none to escape from any part of our own responsibility. But though our economic potential is great, its conversion into finished wealth will need much mechanical and technological aid. We shall, therefore, gladly welcome such aid and cooperation on terms that are of mutual benefit. We believe that this may well help in the solution of the larger problems that confront the world. But we do not seek any material advantage in exchange for any part of our hard-won freedom.

The objectives of our foreign policy are the preservation of world peace and enlargement of human freedom. Two tragic wars have demonstrated the futility of warfare. Victory without the will to peace achieves no lasting result and victor and vanquished alike suffer from deep and grievous wounds and a common fear of the future. May I venture to say that this is not an incorrect description of the world of today? It is not flattering either to man's reason or to our common humanity. Must this unhappy state persist and the power of science and wealth continue to be harnessed to the service of destruction? Every nation, great or small, has to answer this question and the greater a nation, the greater is its responsibility to find and to work for the right answer.

India may be new to world politics and her military strength insignificant in comparison with that of the giants of our epoch. But India is old in thought and experience and has travelled through trackless centuries in the adventure of life. Throughout her long history she has stood for peace and every prayer that an Indian raises, ends with an invocation to peace. It was out of this ancient and yet young India that Mahatma Gandhi arose and he taught us a technique of action that was peaceful; yet it was effective and yielded results that led us not only to freedom but to friendship with those with whom we were, till yesterday, in conflict. How far can that principle be applied to wider spheres of action? I do not know, for circumstances differ and the means to prevent evil have to be shaped and set to the nature of the evil. Yet I have no doubt that the basic approach which lay behind that technique of action was the right approach in human affairs and the only approach that ultimately solves a problem satis-factorily. We have to achieve freedom and to defend it. We have to meet aggression and to resist it and the force employed must be adequate to the purpose. But even when preparing to resist aggression, the ultimate objective, the objective of peace and reconciliation, must never be lost sight of and heart and mind must be attuned to this supreme aim and not swayed or clouded by hatred or fear.

This is the basis and the goal of our foreign policy. We are neither blind to reality nor do we propose to acquiesce in any challenge to man's freedom from whatever quarter it may come. Where freedom is menaced or justice threatened or where aggression takes place, we cannot be and shall not be neutral. What we plead for and endeavour to practise in our own imperfect way is a binding faith in peace and an unfailing endeavour of thought and action to ensure it. The great democracy of the United States of America will, I feel sure, understand and appreciate our approach to life's problems because it could not have any other aim or a different ideal. Friendship and cooperation between our two countries are, therefore, natural. I stand here to offer both in the pursuit of justice, liberty and peace.

24

Exclusion of Some Countries from the UN[1]

The proposal[2] to limit the United Nations by the exclusion of some nations has surprised me greatly. Indeed it seems to forget the very purpose and the very name of the United Nations. It is true that the high hopes with which the United Nations Organization was started have not been fulfilled. At the same time there can be no doubt that by the mere fact of its existence, it has saved us from many dangers and conflicts. Also there is no doubt that in the world today it offers the one hope of finding some way for peaceful cooperation between nations. If the United Nations ceases to be, or if it radically changes its position and nature, then there is nothing left which might inspire that hope for the future and we shall have to go through other terrible experiences and face disasters before we again come back to something which offers a forum for all nations, even though they differ from each other. The whole conception of One World, however distant that One World may be, involves an organization like the United Nations. To imagine that by strict conformity to a single doctrine or approach, we can solve the problems of the world, is to forget the lessons of history and to ignore the realities of today. However difficult the path, it has to be pursued by repeated attempts at cooperation between all nations. Once that attempt is given up, the consequence can only be preparation for conflict on a worldwide-scale and the conflict itself.

It is thought by some people that in the circumstances of today it is quite inevitable for the world to be divided up into two parts, hostile to each other, and for every country to line up on this side or that. There is undoubtedly that hostility, but there is also undoubtedly a refusal on the part of many countries

[1] Message for the United Nations Radio Department broadcast in a special United Nations programme by the Mutual Broadcasting Company, 5 May 1950. Published in the *National Herald*, 8 May 1950.

[2] Herbert Hoover, President of the United States from 1928 to 1932, had proposed on 27 April 1950 that the UN should be "reorganized without the communist countries in it" or "a definite new united front should be organized of those people who disavow communism."

to line up in this way. These countries imagine neither the pressure of world events nor their own destiny requires this lining up on either side and they will, therefore, maintain their separate identity and viewpoint and thus serve the causes they have at heart.

If any attempt is made to change the essential nature of the United Nations, it will not lead to another or a more powerful organization which can work for peace. It would only mean the break-up of something that is actually and potentially valuable with nothing to take its place. I think, therefore, that the proposal to exclude any independent country from the United Nations is unwise and harmful.

25

World Affairs[1]

New Delhi, 21 July 1950

My dear Prime Minister,

I am grateful to you for the two messages that you have sent me through your High Commissioner here. They were delivered to me on the 19th July and we have naturally given the most careful consideration to them. I have already sent you a brief reply in acknowledgment as well as copy of my reply to Mr. Acheson.

I am now venturing to write to you, because I am greatly distressed at the turn events are taking. I agree with much that is contained in the two messages you have been good enough to send me. I had not overlooked the main factors mentioned by you in my approach to Moscow and Washington. I have decided not to pursue my suggestion further, at least at this stage, but I am still convinced that certain basic and important aspects of the crisis that faces us have not been fully appreciated.

I am quite clear that North Korea, probably with the connivance of the Soviet Government and certainly after full preparation, deliberately committed aggression on South Korea. Because of this, the United Nations were fully justified in declaring North Korea as an aggressor and we supported them in this decision, even though all the available information at our disposal about South Korea is not to its advantage.

It appears to be common ground that we should endeavour to limit the area of hostilities to Korea; further that we should try to bring them to a satisfactory end as soon as possible. There should be no question of surrender to aggression. All this is agreed to. But how are we to achieve this, and how are we to prevent hostilities from spreading and even taking the shape of a world war? It would be poor logic that leads us inevitably to such a war, a war which would be disastrous for everyone.

It seems to me that there has not been any clear realization of the position in Asia by the countries of the West. An attempt is no doubt made to understand the new forces at work in Asia, but the process of adaptation lags behind

[1] To C.R. Attlee. V.K. Krishna Menon Papers, NMML.

and events occur, which continually take people by surprise and upset pre-conceived plans. We never seem to catch up with events. You will forgive me, I hope, if I say that there has been a consistent record of failure in the policies adopted in the Far East and in parts of South East Asia by western powers. That failure was due, I think, to a complete lack of understanding of these vast dynamic forces that are at work in Asia. To a small extent, we in India are in a somewhat better position to judge of these forces. We are more directly and closely affected by them and so we have given a great deal of thought to them. The first fact to be borne in mind is that Asia is undergoing vast revolutionary changes. Those changes, before they appear on the surface, have already taken place in the minds of millions of people. These people are not communist. But they seek social change, more especially in the agrarian sphere, and they are not prepared to put up with existing conditions. In particular, they are intensely opposed to any form of colonial control. If a choice is to be made by them, they prefer communism to colonial control. To talk to them of the dangers of communism does not frighten them at all. Any help or encouragement given to a colonial or a socially reactionary regime immediately produces a powerful reaction in them against the country that gives that help. I am merely stating facts, not expressing an opinion.

If this is the state of mass opinion in most of the countries of Asia, it has to be dealt with in some other way than a rather naive condemnation of communism. As we have seen in China, military strength and money cannot win in the end, if they are opposed to these basic urges of the people.

It was with this background in view that we urged, towards the end of last year, the recognition of the People's Government of China. I spoke at length on this subject to Mr. Acheson in Washington in October last. I also spoke on the same lines to Mr. Bevin when I met him in London last November on my return journey from America. Later, India recognized that government and I was happy to find that the UK Government also gave it recognition. Recognition by itself had little meaning and could not bring the advantages that should have flown from it, unless certain other natural consequences followed. These did not follow and a crisis occurred in the United Nations because of the non-inclusion of the People's Government of China.

Again in Indo-China, a curious situation has existed for some time. The more the help that is given to the French there, the more the people become hostile to the French and their supporters. There may be ultimately a French military victory in Indo-China. But it will be at the cost of a hostile population. How long can that victory endure? Step by step, we are getting entangled and there is no clear way out even by victory in war.

This is the position in a great part of Asia. The approach of the western powers makes no appeal to a great majority of people in Asia because it lacks understanding of what those people desire and there is a general impression that the western powers support reaction. The Soviet Government and its allies generally appear to support what might be called the progressive forces in most countries. I know very well that the Soviet Government is probably playing its own expansionist game and that it would be disaster if it succeeded in that. Nevertheless, the fact remains that the western powers, by their policies in Asia, indirectly help the Soviet in Asia. The continued exclusion of the new China from the U.N. helps to increase sympathy for the People's Government in Peking among vast numbers of Asian peoples and distrusts of the policies of western powers.

I have little doubt that the North Koreans will be driven out of South Korea in the end.[2] What will happen then? The moment foreign troops are withdrawn, the same position would arise again or perhaps a worse one. The alternatives thus will be: armies of occupation and full control on colonial lines of these countries or leaving them to shift for themselves and drift inevitably to communism. The former alternative appears to me out of the question for any length of time and the longer it endures, the more we strengthen communism there. If this analysis is correct, then the policy adopted by the western powers does not and cannot lead to any solution, which is satisfactory to them, or what is no less important, conducive to world peace. In a sense this argument may apply to Japan also.

There is another aspect to the general world situation to which, I think, I should make at least passing reference. It is conceivable that, in the event of the military campaign in Korea being prolonged, the western powers may get involved in deeper commitments along the periphery of the Soviet. The Soviet Union may not be directly engaged in these conflicts and its striking power will thus not be affected. In this way also a world war might be brought nearer.

If there is world war, that will be a disaster for everyone. But apart from the disaster, what will even victory in it lead to? War, of course, cannot be avoided, if there is aggression and there is no other way out. But war is meant to help in achieving a certain objective. That objective is not merely the defeat of the enemy but something more positive. If that positive objective disappears, then the sole redeeming feature of a war also disappears and we have not only the disaster of a war but also complete failure afterwards, in spite of military victory.

These are rather trite and obvious remarks and you will forgive me for making them. But I do feel that we are drifting fast in a wrong direction, which can only lead to evil results. There is too facile an impression that military strength and economic resources will solve the problem in the end to our

[2] In spite of the resistance offered by the armed forces of the United Nations the North Korean Army continued to advance in the initial stages of the war. They overran almost all South Korea except for the small perimeter around Taegu and Pusan. Then in September, General MacArthur landed US forces on Inchon and by cutting off the supply lines compelled the North Korean forces to retreat behind the 38th Parallel.

advantage, but it seems to me perfectly clear, in Asia at least, that something more is required than military and economic strength. That something at the present moment is lacking in the approach of the western powers. They have forgotten that millions of people in Asia have strong feelings and cannot be suppressed for any length of time. We cannot outlive the past easily, nor can we cure the evils of the past by the methods of the past.

Yours sincerely,
Jawaharlal Nehru

26

Annexation of Tibet[1]

New Delhi, 1 November 1950

My dear Chief Minister,

The outstanding events in foreign affairs during the last fortnight, so far as India is concerned, have been the developments in Tibet. There had been repeated rumours of Chinese troop movements on the Tibetan border since July last and this led us to draw the attention of our Ambassador in Peking and, through him, of the Chinese Government to the desirability of having peaceful negotiations for the settlement of the problem.[2] No precise information was available about these border movements and often they were denied or explained as movements on the other side of the border. There is an intermediate area between China and Tibet proper which China has considered as part of one of her western provinces and in which China had a right by a treaty[3] to keep garrisons. Many of these movements appeared to be in this middle area. Communications are difficult in Tibet and news travels slowly. So it was not easy to know what was happening.

On our part, we drew the attention of the Chinese Government repeatedly to this matter and pressed them to rely on peaceful methods. They replied that they were prepared for peaceful negotiations and the Tibetan delegates should go to them for this purpose. At the same time, statements were made about an army being prepared for the "liberation" of Tibet, and this was publicly announced as early as August last. We had hoped that, in view of our friendly advice as well as the international situation, military operations against Tibet would be avoided.

We advised the Tibetan delegates to go to Peking and, after some hesitation, they had agreed to do so.

[1] To Chief Ministers. JN Papers, NMML. Excerpts

[2] K.M. Panikkar met the Chinese Vice-Foreign Minister on 13 August 1950 at Peking and communicated the Indian viewpoint.

[3] The sparsely populated and mountainous area in Outer Tibet adjacent to the western sovereignty. The Convention of 1890 between Britain and China authorized China to post her troops in Outer Tibet.

When news came to us that the Chinese Government had formally announced military operations against Tibet, we were surprised and distressed. Immediately we sent a note of protest[4] and requested the Chinese Government not to proceed with these operations and wait for the Tibetan delegates. Their answer was rather curt and laid stress on Tibet being an integral part of China and thus a domestic affair. No outside country, according to them, had a right to interfere in this domestic matter. They still expressed their willingness for peaceful negotiations, but said nothing about halting the advance of their troops. We have again addressed them on this subject and our correspondence will be published before you get this letter.[5]

I must say that this action of the Chinese Government has hurt us considerably and has appeared to us as an act of discourtesy to us in view of our prolonged correspondence on this subject. It has also seemed to us an essentially wrong act and one that might well add to the tensions existing in the world. To use coercion and armed force, when a way to peaceful settlement is open, is always wrong. To do so against a country like Tibet, which is obviously not in a position to offer much resistance and which could not injure China, seemed to us to add to the wrongness of this behaviour. From the international point of view, it was bound to react against China's own interests. Why then should she do it? It is not for me to guess, but it seems clear that owing to the development of the war situation in the Far East, and the accounts of repeated bombing of Manchurian towns,[6] the Chinese Government believed that they were threatened with war by their enemies. A temper arose there full of fear and apprehension and resentment against those real or fancied enemies and this led possibly to a change in policy or to a speeding up of what might have taken much longer to develop.

Whatever the reason may be and whatever their motives may be, the Chinese Government has, in our opinion, acted not only wrongly but foolishly and done injury to itself, to some extent to us, and, I think, to the cause of world peace. As you know, we have consistently tried to be friendly to the new China and have championed her interests in the United Nations and elsewhere. Thus, the new developments must necessarily affect our friendly relations. We do not intend to change our general policy because that is based on certain principles, as well as our judgement of the world situation. We do not even wish to do injury to China in any way, but we shall have to consider carefully every step that we may have to take in the future.

[4] Message to Chou-En-Lai dated 26 October 1950.

[5] The correspondence exchanged between China and India on Tibet was published on 3 November.

[6] On 28 August, China complained to the Security Council about the bombing of Manchurian towns by US aircraft, demanded condemnation of the USA and sought prompt withdrawal of US forces from Korea.

There has sometimes been reference in the press to the consequences on our own frontiers of China's occupation of Tibet.[7] From a military point of view, this has no great consequence and involves no particular danger to India. Tibet is a very difficult country with an average altitude of 12,000 feet and then there is the great Himalayan barrier. It is an exceedingly difficult matter for any considerable body of men to cross to India over the barrier. But in any event we shall always keep proper watch on our extended frontiers to prevent any incidents happening.

[7] *The Statesman* editorial of 29 October cautioned that "even if the threat to the sub-continent should evaporate or, on examination, proves less immediate than some may dramatically suppose, it obviously now can be disregarded by neighbouring non-communist States only at their close peril."

27

World Today[1]

New Delhi, 6 August 1951

Nan dear,

In the world today, more and more, extremists are lining up against each other. On the one side there are of course the communists; on the other the democracies and other countries rely increasingly on the old fascists, Nazis and militarists for their defence. There is the question of rearming Germany and Japan, the aid to Spain, and generally supporting reactionary and semi-fascist regimes. Apart from one's likes and dislikes, even from the narrowest point of view of opportunism, this is a dangerous policy for the democracies. There is still strong feeling in Europe and elsewhere against fascism and Nazism. This is roused up by their pro-fascist policy, and the communist countries take advantage of this. The US, looking at everything from a purely military point of view, misses, or deliberately ignores, this major psychological factor which ultimately affects the morale of nations and of armies. As a matter of fact, I doubt very much if a rearmed Germany, or rearmed Japan will be pillars of strength to the US or to the UK. They might well turn against them. But, in any event, large numbers of other people turn against them because of the encouragement of fascism and the appeal of democracy grows feeble.

The result of all this is that moderate tendencies and really democratic ways and policies find less scope and the fascists and the communists hold the field against each other, ultimately probably leading to war. So far as we are concerned, we want to keep out of this and while we are certainly not lining up with the communist countries, we have an equal distaste for the fascists. Any other policy might mean disruption in India.

It is from this larger point of view that the Japanese peace treaty[2] should be considered. You advised us to sign this treaty. Our ambassadors in Peking and Moscow and London advised us very strongly not to do so and gave plenty of reasons for this. You know the answer we have sent to the State Department suggesting various major changes. There is no likelihood at all of those changes being adopted. In effect, therefore, we will not be in a position to sign the treaty.

[1] To Vijayalakshmi Pandit. JN Collection, NMML. Extracts.
[2] See post, pp. 276–9.

In this matter my mind is quite clear. To accept the Japanese treaty as it is now is to put an end to our present policy and, in fact, turn a political somersault. It might mean almost, though not quite a political break with China. We would have no logic left in any policy that we pursue. This goes against my grain completely. . . .

I need not go into all the arguments, but I want you to appreciate the far-reaching consequences of our signing the treaty. It means a reversal of what we have been saying and acting upon thus far. It means a submission, under pressure or fear, to American policy in the Far East and Asia. The consequences of not signing it means greater ill will in the United States. I realize that, but still my mind is clear that we cannot sign this treaty. No doubt the treaty will be signed without us and will take effect. We cannot stop it and do not come in the way. But I see no reason whatever why we should be, in a sense, guarantors of the treaty and of the many provisions in it which we utterly dislike. We would prefer to sign a simple treaty with Japan.

With love,
Jawaharlal Nehru

28

Japanese Peace Treaty[1]

The Government of India have the honour to acknowledge the reply to their note of the 23rd August 1951, received yesterday afternoon by telegraph from their Charge d'Affaires in Washington[2] to whom it was delivered. While the Government of India are glad of the assurance that the reply of the United States Government has been made in the same spirit of frankness and friendship that animates our note of August 23rd, they regret to have to draw the attention of the United States Government to the note of resentment and reproach in the latter's reply for which they can find no justification in the spirit or phraseology of their own note.

The Government of India welcome the assurance that the overriding desire of the Government of the United States is peace in Asia. The Government and people of India have striven to this end, to the best of their ability, because they consider peace of paramount importance to the world and, more especially, to the countries of Asia, which have suffered for many generations under alien domination. Nothing could be more disastrous for Asia than war which would make impossible of early fulfilment the hopes of development that fill the minds of the people of this great continent. It is with this single aim of preserving peace that the Government of India have considered every problem with which they have been confronted. In the task of maintaining peace and developing the nations of Asia, they would always gladly cooperate with the United States and with other countries.

The Government of India also welcome the assurance of the Government of the United States that they do not want to be a party to colonialism or imperialism. Opposition to colonialism and imperialism has been the basis of India's struggle. Having experienced the burden and the injury that flow from both, the people of India are convinced that continuance of them in any form and in any part of the world cannot lead to peace or progress or to the happiness of the people concerned. World peace can only be assured when the domination of one country over another ceases.

---

[1] Drafted by Jawaharlal Nehru, New Delhi, 27 August 1951. JN Collection, NMML.
[2] M.K. Kripalani was Minister in Washington.

Turning to certain specific points relating to the treaty which arise out of the reply of the Government of the United States, the Government of India wish to make the following observations:

(1) The Government of the United States have expressed the belief that their view of the proposed treaty is shared by the Government and the people of Japan. The Government of India regret that they cannot share this view; such information as they have received does not confirm the appreciation of the situation by the United States Government.

(2) Commenting upon the Government of India's suggestion that the treaty should restore in full Japan's sovereignty "over territories of which the inhabitants have a historical affinity with her (Japan's) own people and which she has not acquired by aggression from any other country", the Government of the United States point out that the Government of India have never questioned the Postdam terms of surrender during the five-and-a-half years during which India has served as a member of the Far Eastern Commission, which was established to ensure the fulfilment of those terms. In suggesting the return of the Ryukyu and the Bonin groups of islands to Japanese sovereignty, the Government of India are not challenging the Postdam terms of surrender. As the Government of the United States have themselves pointed out, those terms left room for the addition, by agreement, of some minor islands to the islands of Honshu, Hokkaidu, Kyushu and Shikoku, over which Japan was to be allowed to exercise sovereignty. Nor have the Government of India any intention whatsoever of applying dissimilar principles to different parts of territories which have a historical affinity with Japan and which Japan did not wrest from any of its neighbours. If they excepted the Kurile Islands from the scope of their suggestion, it was because the Yalta Agreement provided, without any reservation, that 'the Kurile Islands shall be handed over to the Soviet Union". The Government of India cannot be held responsible for an inconsistency, which is the result of the Yalta Agreement.

(3) In discussing the Government of India's views regarding defensive arrangements to be made by Japan, the Government of the United States describe them as tantamount to leaving Japan defenceless against proved aggressors. The Government of India fail to find any warrant for such a conclusion from anything that they have said. The draft treaty recognizes that Japan as a sovereign nation possesses the inherent right of individual or collective self-defence and that Japan may voluntarily enter into collective security arrangements. Adequate provision is thus made for Japan independently to make whatever

arrangement she considers necessary for her self-defence as soon as she has signed the peace treaty and it is not clear to the Government of India why there should be any "period of total defenselessness" for Japan.

(4) In regard to Formosa, the Government of India have suggested that, in keeping with international obligations, it should be stated clearly in the treaty that it would be returned to China. That would determine the future of Formosa leaving the time and manner of such return to be settled at a future date. The Government of India have been and are of opinion that a declaration that Formosa shall be returned to China will help in creating conditions for a settlement in the Far East. But the Government of India has at no time insisted or even suggested that a Japanese peace treaty should be deferred until there is final agreement with respect to the future of Formosa.

(5) The Government of India have been anxious that a peace treaty with Japan should be signed and the military occupation of Japan terminated at the earliest possible moment. All that they have urged is that what they consider to be imperfections of a major character in the draft treaty should be removed, so that the terms of the treaty may promote the prospects of a peaceful settlement of outstanding issues in the Far East. The Government of India do not wish to come in the way of any nation which is satisfied with the terms of the present treaty and are prepared to sign it. They only claim for themselves their inherent and unquestionable right not to sign a treaty with the terms of which they are not fully satisfied. Of there own resolve to establish the friendliest possible relations with Japan, they have already given proof for, as they have informed the Government of the United States, they intend to terminate the state of war with Japan and to establish normal diplomatic relations with her as soon as possible.

The Government of India have no intention of proposing to Japan a treaty of peace, which would in any way be controversial or which would run counter to the provisions of the draft treaty of peace. Their action in not being represented at the San Francisco Conference and in making a separate treaty of peace with Japan, should not, therefore, adversely affect either the friendly relations that exist between the Government of India and the Government of the United States or the cooperation of the two Governments in everything "which is practical and fruitful for peace."

The Government of India hope that the observations made in the foregoing paragraphs reveal a unity of outlook between them and the Government of the United States in many vital matters that affect the future of the people of Asia and of humanity in general. The differences that exist between them are differences of method and approach. On international issues of high moment, such divergences of opinion are bound to occur even amongst the friendliest nations. The most effective way to prevent them from coming in the way of continued cooperation is to avoid the intrusion of acrimony into the discussion of issues over which differences arise. The Government of India feel sure that the Government of the United States concur in this conclusion.

29

The Nonviolent Struggle in South Africa[1]

The All-India Congress Committee has viewed with the deepest interest and pride the great satyagraha movement against racialism in South Africa[2] and sends its fraternal greetings and good wishes to all those Africans and Indians who are participating in it and who have by their discipline, courage and nonviolence, shown themselves to be worthy followers of the great leader, who first gave this new message to the world in South Africa forty-five years ago. It is fitting and of historic significance that it should be in South Africa again that Africans and Indians and others should battle nonviolently for the affirmation of the basic human right of racial equality and against the doctrine of a master race dominating over others.

This challenge of racial arrogance and domination was one of the causes of the last great war. Yet racialism in its most extreme and repugnant form flourishes in South Africa and crushes the great majority of the population there. It is India's basic policy to stand for racial equality and national freedom without which there can be no peace in the world. The great continent of Africa has suffered more than any other part of the earth's surface from the domination of one race over others. Having patiently endured this for generations its people have now shown their strength and wisdom not only in challenging this vicious doctrine but doing so in a civilized and peaceful way. Any other course would lead to widespread and terrible bitterness and sorrow. It is for all the peoples of the world to appreciate the significance of this great happening in Africa and to lend the weight of their moral support to this righteous struggle.

In Africa, as elsewhere, it is not by the domination of one racial or religious group or community over another that a peaceful and progressive society can be built up, but by cooperation between the different elements in the population

[1] Resolution on satyagraha in South Africa drafted by Jawaharlal Nehru for the AICC meeting at Indore, 12 September 1952. The resolution was moved by Govind Ballabh Pant and seconded by Morarji Desai. *The Hindu*, 13 September 1952.

[2] The struggle against apartheid in South Africa had in September entered its fourth month with the arrests of about 2500 people.

in order to build up a multi-racial society in which all have equal opportunities of growth.

The AICC is particularly gratified at the cooperation of Africans and the people of Indian descent in Africa in this struggle. It reaffirms the policy of the Congress that Indians abroad should demand no special privileges at the expense of the inhabitants of the country in which they live. In Africa, the interests of the Africans must be paramount and it is the duty of Indians there to cooperate with them and help them to the best of their ability.

The basic principles[3] of the Charter of the United Nations have been and are being violated in South Africa, and barbarous methods of suppression are being employed against a peaceful population. It is for the conscience of the world to take heed and to prevent this struggle from developing into something which might endanger world peace.

---

[3] Under Article 55 of the Charter, the UN is authorized to promote "higher standards of living, full employment and conditions of social progress and universal respect for and observance of human rights and fundamental freedoms for all without distinction as to race, sex, language or religion."

30

An Overburdened World[1]

I am accused of a certain, perhaps, shall I say, pride in the foreign policy. There is no question of pride in changing it. Any person who thinks of foreign policy or any policy in terms of unchangeability is likely to be wrong at any time, more especially in a dynamic and changing period like the present. But I do feel that many of our critics—not all—look at it in these very terms of an unchangeable viewpoint and outlook. I submit that whether that viewpoint occasionally may be right or may be wrong, it gives a wrong perspective and therefore the results that flow from that approach are likely to be right or wrong.

I have to choose whether I should enter into a large number of details which have been referred to in the course of the debate or rather concentrate on certain major facts. One thing I might say. The honourable member, Mr. Jaipal Singh, said something about appointments or delegations, and something about our foreign policy not being a party policy.[2]

Well, I entirely agree with him. A foreign policy can hardly ever be, if it is at all fully thought out, a party policy. It may be wrong: that is another matter. But it can hardly be a policy which is a purely party policy. Otherwise, no country can have any consistency in its policy. There has to be a certain continuity, at the same time a certain flexibility in that policy. I would submit that the kind words that many honourable members have said about me in regard to this matter of foreign policy are rather beside the point, I am grateful to them, of course, for their sentiments.

I am convinced that whoever might have been in charge of the foreign policy of India during these years could not have but followed more or less the broad policy that we have pursued, because it did not come out of my head or anyone else's head; it came out of the circumstances in which we live and the background of our history and the present context of events. It is the inevitable

[1] Statement in Parliament, 17 March 1953. *Parliamentary Debates (House of the People), Official Report*, 1953, Vol. II, Pt. II, cols 2229–47. Excerpts.

[2] Jaipal Singh of Jharkhand Party said on 17 March during the debate that foreign policy "is above party politics," and it was a "national policy." He also found members guilty of dealing with the foreign policy as a party affair. He further said that: "Again and again I see that there are certain types of people who are sent abroad and others are completely neglected . . . We must see to it that every deputation is of the right type when it is sent abroad."

policy, barring variations here and there, barring certain emphasis here and there. There could be no other foreign policy and I am quite convinced that if by some remote and unlikely chance, honourable members opposite have the sharing of this policy, or the conduct of it, they would inevitably have to follow something like this foreign policy—the emphasis might vary. I am rather doubtful if that statement would apply to the honourable members of the Communist Party opposite. It is possible that they may vary.

Let us consider the question of foreign policy not in a party sense, but really in a national sense and to a certain extent in an international sense. After all we live in a rather difficult and trying period of history, and seeing the changes from day to day, it is not an easy matter even to keep up with those changes. It is an extraordinary thing that while almost everything that we see around us in this world is ultimately the product of human minds, nevertheless human minds lag behind their own products. Events take place, changes take place and the average human mind remains behind it and cannot catch up with the very thing that it itself has created. Whether it is the developments due to the pace of technological progress, which are tremendous today, or whether it is other things, we lag behind: even the so-called advanced countries lag behind, mentally speaking: much more than other countries, who, technologically speaking, are not advanced.

That applies very much to the political sphere at present. It is a good thing to judge of a statement or a speech and find out if that speech would have been in keeping with events, say, ten years ago, or five years ago. I think one will find that many a speech delivered might well have been the same five years ago, or ten years ago. The passage of time or circumstances has made no difference. That itself means that there is a certain static character about the thinking behind it. It is not in keeping or in turn or parallel with reality. Therefore, let our foreign policy be considered as a national policy, as a continuing policy except for the inevitable variations and changes that may come into it from time time.

31

South African Situation[1]

New Delhi, 11 May 1953

My dear Prime Minister,[2]

In the course of my speech,[3] I referred to the turmoil and serious situation developing in various parts of the African continent and expressed my grave apprehension in regard to it. I considered it as a matter which might well affect world peace in the future. I first referred to South Africa and the extreme racial policies being followed by the Government of the Union there, which I considered not only highly objectionable but also opposed to all the conceptions and ideals underlying the Charter of these United Nations. I referred then to recent painful developments in Kenya where as stated I think by the Colonial Secretary in London, a kind of civil war is going on. I made mention of the Gold Coast and Nigeria, where certain steps have been taken by the UK Government which I thought were in the right direction.

Finally I referred to the proposal for a Central African Federation, and I pointed out that this was being imposed on the African population there against their expressed wishes,[4] and was likely to lead to the formation of a

[1] To Godfrey Huggins, File No. AII/53/1423/29-30, MEA. Excerpts.

[2] Godfrey Martin Huggins, FRCS, 1908; served in two hospitals in the UK before migrating to Southern Rhodesia in 1911; general practitioner and surgeon, 1911–21; served in the War, 1914–17; Member, Legislative Assembly of Southern Rhodesia, 1923–44, and Prime Minister since 1934.

[3] Higgins wrote that he was disturbed on reading the report of Jawaharlal Nehru's speech of 13 April. He had the impression that Nehru might have been misled by the information he had been receiving about Southern Rhodesia, so he enclosed the official reports of the Parliament debates of 23 June 1952 when the motion of Federation in Central Africa was introduced.

[4] The formation of Central African Federation was an attempt to overcome the balkanization of Africa. The Federation, initiated during 1945–51 by the British Labour Party, consisted of three territories—Southern Rhodesia (Zimbabwe), Northern Rhodesia (Zambia) and Nyasaland (Malawi). The whites of the North under Roy Wellensky and of the South under Godfrey Huggins favoured the Federation plan. For Southerners, Federation was the means to secure revenue from the copper wealth of the North to meet the rising cost of its rapidly increasing white settlement. The Africans of Zambia and Malawi opposed Federation fearing further loss of community lands to the whites and perpeutation of colour

dominion which might follow the racial and other policies of the South African Union. I felt that, even if this was not the present intention, this development was natural if a small minority of the population, racially different, governed the great majority.

I then explained what our policy was insofar as Indians in any part of the country or elsewhere abroad, were concerned. We had consistently advised them that they must not claim any privilege which was against the interests of the Africans. They had every right to demand equality of treatment, but they had no business to profit at the expense of the indigenous inhabitants of the continent. They must make friends with them and try to help them in such ways as they could, otherwise they would have no place in Africa in the future.

That was the main line of my argument. There had been a good deal of discussion of these subjects in the Indian press for many months past. Indeed, the South African issue has deeply stirred Indian opinion for years past. It has became a test case for them, and one of our basic policies is the recognition of racial equality. I do not mean to say that all races or all individuals are equal or have the same capacity, but we do feel strongly that there should be a basic recognition of equality and that equal opportunities should be given to all. Indeed, we thought that that was one of the basic criticisms against Hitler's racial policy and the idea that a master race should dominate the world. The Charter of the United Nations had laid down in clear terms that principle of equality or of equal opportunity. I know that the Africans are backward and that they cannot suddenly get out of this backward condition. They will require time to do so and every kind help.

We have all along stood, therefore, for the development of a multi-racial society in Africa. I am glad to find that you have used these words yourself in your speech, but evidently this concept of a multi-racial society can be interpreted in many ways.[5] The way we interpret it is that the Africans must have first place in their country with others also having an honoured place. In your own speech you have indicated that you cannot foresee any time when the Africans will have that position or authority in their own countries.

In your speech you have discussed the concept of democracy and set out your political philosophy, and have stated that you reject the idea of domination

---

bar in the copper belt. In 1948, to resist amalgamation they set up a Federation of Welfare Societies which in 1951, was rechristened Northern Rhodesia African National Congress under Harry Nkumtula, to resist the Federation scheme.

[5] Huggins further wrote that their problems were those of a truly multi-racial country and added: "It is quite wrong to apply the term 'colonialism' to them. Each of the three countries in this part of Africa contains Europeans, Indians and Africans, and all these races are here to stay. To refer to the Europeans and Indians as 'settlers' is to ignore facts, because these people are no less permanent inhabitants of these territories than are the Africans, who themselves only came to this part of Africa comparatively recently."

of one race by another. But I do not myself see how the proposal, for a federation can result in anything but the domination of one race by another. Obviously, the basis of any such proposal, or the building up of a multi-racial society, must be confidence and cooperation between the various elements that go to build up that society. If any such proposal is imposed against the wishes of the great majority of the people, that can only lead to increasing hostility, suspicion and bitterness. That will not only come in the way of the building up of friendly inter-racial relations but will inevitably make the dominant minority dislike the majority and try to safeguard its own interests by all the means in its power. We see that happening in other parts of Africa where a measure of political consciousness has grown among the Africans. The result is thus conflict in Africa and unhappy reactions in many other parts of the world.

We in India have no desire to interfere in other countries' internal affairs. I have deliberately refrained from discussing internal conditions in other countries, but where world issues of importance are involved, and when deep passions are aroused even among our own people, I have sometimes discussed these matters as moderately as I could, to give a right direction to people's thinking and not allow it to express itself in extreme forms. The basic thing in regard to any proposal is that it should come from goodwill and consent. Any other approach is not only opposed to the spirit of the times but is likely to lead to unfortunate consequences.

No one can be opposed to the concept of a federation and it is perfectly true that small backward countries cannot easily develop.[6] The modern trend is for larger groups or federations to function together. But the element of consent among the people concerned appears to me to be essential. As far as I know, there is almost complete unanimity among the Africans in their opposition to the Federation scheme. No inter-racial society can grow up with this background, more especially when the colour bar operates both in the social and economic fields and legislative and executive authority is concentrated in the hands of a relatively small group of different people. With the best will in the world, this cannot lead to the realization of the ideal of a cooperative multi-racial society.

Any full consideration of this subject leads one into many avenues of thought and a variety of other world problems are affected by it. Indeed, it becomes part of the complex and confusing picture of the world today. This picture has to be seen as a whole even in order to understand a part of it. Among the major events of recent times have been the changes in Asia and the continuing ferment all over this great continent. Many things are happening in Asia which are good, many are not good. It is not so much a question of liking or

[6] Huggins mentioned that they had in the Federation of these three territories, three races of permanent inhabitants and that those races must live together, and make the best of it. Apart from any other consideration, the real interests of the Africans demanded that the three countries be federated.

disliking them, as of 'understanding a tremendous, dynamic and historic process that is going on. To some extent, this applies to the continent of Africa, though in a different measure, as conditions there are different. Nevertheless, there is dynamism in Africa also, and it requires the most careful and gentle handling. I deplore the violence that is being indulged in by certain African tribes in Kenya. I think that will injure them more than anything else. But I deplore also any idea of crushing the whole people by the coercive apparatus of the state.[7] That will sow the seeds of infinite conflict in the future. The Africans are, I suppose, a somewhat immature people with the virtues and failings which accompany immaturity. But they are to some extent aware today and a measure of political consciousness is coming to them. In the context of the world now, this political consciousness can neither be ignored nor suppressed, quite apart from the merits of the question. The only way appears to me to be to make a friendly and cooperative approach and try to help them to train themselves to assume responsibilities.

Looking at this world picture, I am greatly concerned. More and more I feel that no major problem in the world is going to be solved by war or by coercion on a large scale. Owing to the development of worldwide communications, there are reactions in different places of everything that happens anywhere.

I think that the biggest hopeful event of recent times was the friendly settlement between India and the UK which led to the independence of India and Pakistan as well as Burma and Ceylon. That was a wise and statesman-like gesture and it has resulted in something that is very remarkable. All the piled up bitterness of generations of conflict has been largely put an end to. One can say with confidence that the relationship of India with the UK is essentially one of friendship today because there is no element of compulsion about it and the settlement was brought about in a friendly and cooperative way. I wish other problems in the world could be dealt with in that way.

Yours sincerely,
Jawaharlal Nehru

[7] Nairobi on 24 April 1953, western and south-western forest reserves on 20 May and Tinderet forest reserves on 29 May were declared "special" areas, i.e., anyone failing to halt when challenged could be shot at. In 1953, all territory occupied by the Kikuyu, Meru and Embu tribes was declared "closed", i.e., official permission was required to go out or come into these areas. From 30 April, bombs were used against Mau Mau. In an official announcement made on 9 July, it was stated that during the past ten weeks, 183 sorties had been flown against 85 different targets: 1096 bombs had been dropped and 96,000 rounds of ammunitions fired.

32

The Great Adventure of Man[1]

Mr. President, Members of the National Assembly
of the Federal Peoples' Republic of Yugoslavia,

For thousands of years, Man has been engaged in a great adventure. He has
seen many ups and downs but, nevertheless, he has built up great civilizations
and, what is even more important, certain standards and values of human
conduct which are the essence of civilization. He has taken advantage of science
and technology to unveil the secrets of nature and thus increase his own
strength and power. That power has been used for the advancement and progress of humanity. Unfortunately, it has also been used for evil purposes and
for destruction. Power is a dangerous companion, and sometimes it tends to
ignore and suppress the very values for which man has struggled through the
ages.

Today, we are on the threshold of what has been called the atomic age.
Great advances in physics and the other sciences have changed our conceptions
of the physical world we live in and given us some glimpses of the vastness of
time and space and their inter-relation to each other. This progress of science
has brought new visions and new ideas and is gradually changing the way men
think of the world and even of themselves. Science has also released atomic
energy, a mighty force which may bring untold happiness to humanity or
unimaginable misery and destruction. Thus, we stand not only on the threshold of great happiness but also are faced by a tremendous choice. Which way
do we go, what choice do we make at this critical juncture in the history of man?

While science has done all this and may do much more, it is extraordinary
that men's thinking has not kept pace with it and men's eyes are still blind to
the visions that are being unfolded. Most of us still function in the old ruts and
think along old grooves, which have little relation to the facts of life today.
Some even think of the possibility of war in this atomic age, a war which will
certainly bring ruin to all and destroy civilization and its values, which have
been built up through the struggle of ages. If that is to be the ultimate fate of
humanity, then surely it matters little what ideologies are pursued, what

[1] Beograd, 2 July 1955. Speech at the joint meeting of both Chambers of Federal Peoples'
Assembly. JN Papers, NMML. Excerpts.

objectives we may have, for the end will be the same and it will be a common ruin.

Therefore, the first thing to be clear about is that in the modern age, war is out of the question. It is a relic of a barbarous past which has no meaning today for intelligent human beings.

If war and the way of violence are ruled out, then the only other way is that of peaceful coexistence between nations and an attempt to solve our problems peacefully and by negotiation. Can we do this? Are the difficult world problems of today capable of such treatment? How can we get rid of the fears and suspicions, the hatred and the lack of security that many nations feel, which have led to colossal armaments?

These are difficult questions, and I have no easy remedy to suggest. We have always thought of them with a certain humility of spirit and endeavoured to do our utmost to serve the cause of peace, cooperation, the betterment of human relations and the progress of humanity. I cannot presume to advise other countries because I know that conditions differ and national backgrounds are not the same. All I can venture is to put before you such thoughts as I have for my own country.

I believe ardently in the freedom and independence of my own country as well as that of others. I believe in the freedom of the individual and in the democratic system of working. I think that the suppression of a nation is an evil thing and prevents its growth. Each nation and each and every people must find their soul and function according to their genius. They may be helped in this process by the cooperation of other countries, but essentially they must rely upon themselves, and any imposition from outside suppresses that soul of the nation and stunts its growth. Sometimes, the nation finds its soul in a struggle for its freedom, at other times in constructive and creative endeavour to build itself up. Yugoslavia faced many heavy trials and tribulations during the last World War but, in the very resistance it offered to that brutal invasion, she found her soul.

It is my belief that evil has to be opposed and must not be willingly tolerated, but that evil cannot be opposed by a greater evil, nor can violence or hatred be overcome by greater violence and hatred. Nearly two thousand years ago, it was said by a very great man that those who take to the sword shall perish by the sword. We have seen that happening in actual practice during these last two great wars. In India, our symbols in our long past have not been great military commanders but men like the Buddha and, in our own times, Gandhi, both messengers of goodwill and peace.

There is much talk of peace, and the word is often used as a slogan. There is danger that even good words and good ideas might lose their values by wrong use. Peace should be peaceful. It should not shout or use the language of threat or condemnation. None of us is free from blame, and it does not help much to condemn and criticize, even though something is worthy of condemnation or criticism. Peace should speak in a gentle voice and with understanding.

We often hear of the iron curtain. I think there is some truth in this, but the greatest iron curtain of all is the one we put around our own minds. Indeed, many a wall is put up around our minds, which prevents us from looking at the world as it is. How, then, are we to understand the world or solve its problems? Even though these mental walls are unsubstantial, they are solid enough to prevent any possible entry of a new idea. Because they are unsubstantial, it is even more difficult to deal with them than if they were of brick and stone. It may not be easy to demolish them. Let us at least open some windows in them which will bring some fresh air and light from outside and enable us to have a look at the outside world.

I come from Asia, a continent which has long been in travail and which is today resurgent and dynamic. Yet, many people in other continents do not fully realize this fact and continue to think more or less in the old way. There is the unhappy continent of Africa which is also in a state of deep ferment. The peoples of this continent have suffered untold agony during past centuries and their agony continues even today. Can we solve the problems of the world by ignoring the wisdom of the peoples of Asia and Africa? It is obvious that this cannot be done, and yet attempts are continually being made to do so.

The major problems before the great statesmen of the world today are those of the Far East, Germany and disarmament. Undoubtedly, these problems are of vital importance. But, even here, one sees how many people refuse to face the most obvious facts. There is the great country of China which is denied admittance in the United Nations. Anything more absurd than this seems to me difficult to imagine.

The world has infinite variety, and it is as well that it has this variety which gives richness and charm to it. So, I believe, truth, reality and beauty have infinite variety. We may see some aspect of these but that is only a part of the whole. It may be that someone else sees another aspect of them which is equally true. We must, therefore, learn to be tolerant of others and not seek to impose ourselves upon them. At the same time, the world has grown too narrow for any nation to live a life apart. There has to be intimate cooperation.

We have decided in India to build up a socialist pattern of society. I cannot say exactly what shape this will take. It will have to grow according to objective reality and the needs of the people. It need not be exactly the same as elsewhere but, in any event, it should do away with vested interests, privilege and inequality, and bring freedom, access to knowledge and opportunity to all. It should naturally take full advantage of the power that science and technology give, but at the same time it should retain the creative spirit and the great values of civilization, the belief in truth and beauty, tolerance and gentleness.

Wherever I travel, I see eager bright-faced children, and boys and girls and youths, full of hope, on the threshold of the adventure of life. For us, of our generation, they are a great trust. What future are we going to give them? Are they doomed to perish in war and its terrible consequences, or can we assure them a life of peace and happiness, of creative activity, of contributing further to the progress of humanity and the great adventure of Man?

33

Bulganin, Khrushchev Visit[1]

Your Excellencies, Ladies and Gentlemen,

This is not a mere formal matter of welcome. Events have demonstrated that there is a deeper friendship and understanding between the peoples of our two great countries which are more significant than the formality of welcome. That understanding and friendship have progressively grown, even though the paths we have pursued in our respective couturiers have varied. But in spite of this difference in approach in dealing with our problems, which was inevitable in the circumstances which conditioned our countries and our peoples, there has been no element of conflict between us and there has been an approach to one another in many important fields of human activity. I am happy that this should be so not only for the present, but in the future to come. We are neighbour countries and it is right that there should be a feeling of neighbourliness and friendship between us for the mutual advantage of both our countries and our peoples. I believe also that this friendship is good for the larger causes of the world and, more particularly, for the most vital cause of all, the peace of the world.

We, in India, have been conditioned by our heritage and by our great leaders as well as by the peaceful methods we adopted in our struggle for freedom. Much more so, therefore, do we believe in world peace and cooperation. Indeed for us, as for many other countries, this is a matter of the most vital significance. For, if war descends upon the world with all its terror and terrible disaster, then the great work that we have undertaken to build up our country will come to an end. . . .

It is only eight years since we became sovereign and independent and these eight years have been spent by us in facing, with all our strength, the manifold problems that confront us. They are great problems, for they involve the future well-being of 370 million people who have suffered for long from poverty. We are confident that we can solve these problems and build up a socialist structure of society in our country giving opportunities of well-being and progress to

[1] Speech in Hindi at Banquet in honour of Soviet leaders, N.A. Bulganin and N.S. Khrushchev at Rashtrapati Bhavan, New Delhi, 20 November 1955. JN Papers, NMML. Excerpts.

every single individual. But we know that the task is hard and takes time. Nevertheless, no task is too hard for a people determined to succeed. We are so determined and we have faith in our people.

We believe not only that the ends to be achieved should be good, but also that the means employed should be good, or else new problems arise and the objective itself changes. We believe also that the great cause of human progress cannot be served through violence and hatred and that it is only through friendly and cooperative endeavour that the problems of the world can be solved. Hence, our hand of friendship is stretched out to every nation and every people.

We welcome the cooperation and friendly assistance of other countries. But we realize that a nation develops by its own labours and by its own strength. It was by relying upon ourselves that we gained independence and it is by doing so that we hope to advance to the new objectives that we have placed before ourselves. We are not strong in a military sense or in the world's goods, but we are strong in our faith in our people. In this world of fear and apprehension, I should like to say with all humility, we are not afraid. Why should we be afraid when we wish to be friendly with others? Why should we be afraid when our people have faith in themselves?

We have no ambitions against any other country or people. We wish them all well and we are anxious that freedom and social and economic progress should come to all countries. The denial of this freedom, as well as racial discrimination, are not only improper, but are the seeds from which grows the evil tree of conflict and war.

We do not presume to advise others, but we are convinced that it is not by military pacts and alliances and by the piling up of armaments that world peace and security can be attained. Not being military-minded, we do not appreciate the use of military phraseology or military approaches in considering the problems of today. There is talk of cold war and rival camps and groupings and military block and alliances, all in the name of peace. We are in no camp and in no military alliance. The only camp we should like to be in is the camp of peace and goodwill which should include as many countries as possible and which should be opposed to none. The only alliance we seek is an alliance based on goodwill and cooperation. If peace is sought after, it has to be by the methods of peace and the language of peace and goodwill.

34

Saudi Arabia[1]

14 October 1956

My dear Chief Minister,

Since I wrote to you last, I have paid a brief visit to Saudi Arabia. This was a new type of country for me, new not because it was largely desert, but because of the impact of dollars and a money economy on an ancient, simple and virile people. I saw a great deal of construction, big solid buildings growing up and broad roads being built, where there had been small straggling towns containing chiefly mud houses. These new houses were full of air-conditioners and electric coolers and many other gadgets which contrasted strangely with the bare and bleak country around. I was given a very friendly and cordial welcome not only by the King, but by the people wherever I went, and I liked the people. But, always, I was thinking of how this intrusion of dollars would affect the life of the people, and I was not a little apprehensive that that effect might not be all to the good. Indeed, I mentioned it to my hosts there and asked them if there was not any danger of the people growing soft and losing the qualities which had enabled them to maintain their freedom and their distinctive way of living. The desert, like the mountains, breeds hardy people. They have to contend against the harsher aspects of nature and their very survival demands physical toughness and a capacity for endurance. Civilization has developed chiefly in the richer valleys and the plains where nature is soft and man has had greater leisure to lead an easier life. But that easy life itself has led to a softening of his fibre, even though there has been intellectual growth.

In Saudi Arabia there is not only the great and inhospitable desert, but also the stern, puritanical tenets of the Wahabi sect of Islam, to which the ruling family belongs. In theory and, presumably, in practice, the law is the old Mosaic law as interpreted by the Muslim law-givers of old in the Shariat. It is a hard law which does not deal leniently with a transgressor. It is perhaps not difficult to impose such a law in the broad stretches of the desert where life is simple and temptations are extremely limited. What will happen when life becomes complicated and temptations grow with the advent of what is called modern civilization? How long will the old restraints continue then? The other Arab

[1] To Chief Ministers. JN Papers, NMML. Excerpts.

countries—Syria, Lebanon and Egypt—have had a taste of modern civilization to a far greater extent and, in the course of a hundred and fifty years or so, have gradually adapted themselves to it. In Saudi Arabia the impact is sudden and is likely to be overwhelming. . . .

My visit to Arabia was a great experience for me which I liked. It had also certain desirable political consequences and brought our country and Saudi Arabia a little nearer to one another. Arabia, though backward and undeveloped, still remains the ancient homeland of the Arab race and it was from Arabia that they spread out more than 1300 years ago to conquer vast stretches of Africa and the Eurasian continent. Not only because of the holy places of Islam being situated in Arabia, and the annual Haj pilgrimage which brings large numbers of Muslims to Mecca, but because of innumerable emotional attachments, it has a great pull on Muslims everywhere. Politically, it has some importance of course, but Egypt is at present and has been for some time the premier Arab country. The newspapers of Cairo go all over the Arab world and they have a much larger circulation than Indian newspapers. Egypt, as well as Lebanon and Syria, have been the meeting place of modern Europe with the Arab world and western Asia. In a sense, it has been a meeting place for many centuries. The old Crusades were fought in what is Palestine and Syria and Lebanon now. Most of us have read about these Crusades from books written by western authors with a natural bent towards the Christian West against the Islamic East. More neutral accounts have rather tilted this balance and shown that western Asia was more developed and civilized at the time of Crusades than Europe. In fact, the main effect of the Crusades, apart from the final defeat of the Crusaders, was the influence of western Asian civilization on Europe. Many arts and even luxuries crept into Europe then.

There was another powerful influence on Europe coming from Arab Spain. Cordoba was a great centre of philosophy, medicine and arts and sciences during the middle ages when Europe was supposed to be going through a period of intellectual darkness. Professors from Cordoba went to the Sorbonne in Paris and to other great universities of Europe. Even today Spain bears the impress of the long period of Arab rule there.

After a bright period, during which Baghdad and Corboda were the centres of civilization and culture, there was decay. The Arabs were driven out from Spain, and the Arab empire, of which Baghdad was the Capital, went to pieces. It did not recover. The Ottoman Turks came there and the period of Turkish rule of the Arab countries in western Asia was not noted for any growth or advance and the Arabs were treated as a subject race by the Turks. The Europeans then came there, as they came to many other parts of Asia, and established their dominion. The new and vital Europe with its growing science and industrial civilization became dominant. In Syria and Lebanon the influence was chiefly French. In Egypt it was British.

An American University in Beirut played an important part in not only building up a new middle class but also helped in reviving Arabic as a literary language. In this way Cairo and Beirut and Damascus became the new centres of a mixed culture which affected other Arab lands. Even today university trained people from Cairo and Beirut spread out over Arabia and other Arab countries as engineers, doctors, teachers, etc.

I should like to make clear that Arabia and Saudi Arabia are not synonymous terms. Saudi Arabia is of course for the biggest part of Arabia, but there are other independent or semi-independent states also. When I was at Riyadh, the capital, and Jeddah, the port on the Red Sea, I was not far from the Suez canal. This issue was dominant. . . .

This brings me to the problem of the Suez Canal[2] which has been a dominant international issue during the past two-and-a-half months. We have just heard that some temporary agreement has been arrived at on some basic issues between Egypt on one hand and the western countries on the other in the Security Council. This does not take us very far, and yet it is an important development and one can hardly conceive now of a complete break in the future. I need not tell you that in this matter India has played a part which has been considerable though rather behind the scenes. The attitude of Egypt, throughout these negotiations has appeared to me to be restrained and reasonable. It is on the other side that there has been lack of restraint. Whatever one may think of the original and rather sudden action of Egypt in nationalizing the Suez Canal Company overnight, subsequent to that Egypt has functioned with commendable moderation.

[2] Gamal Abdel Nasser, President of Egypt nationalized the Suez Canal on 26 July 1956 as a reaction to the American and British decision going back on their promise to finance the construction of the Aswan Dam. Nasser declared Martial Law predicting that the tolls collected from passing ships will pay for the Dam. British, French and Israeli attempts to regain control and depose Nasser were not successful.

35

A World of Unreality[1]

Mr. President, Excellencies, Distinguished Delegates,
Ladies and Gentleman,

Man does not live by politics alone, nor, indeed, wholly by economics. And so the UNESCO organization came to represent something that was vital to human existence and progress. Even as the United Nations General Assembly represented the political will of the world community, the UNESCO tried to represent the finer and the deeper sides of human life and, indeed, might be said to represent the conscience of the world community.

I should like to remind you of the preamble to the constitution of this great organization. This embodies a declaration on behalf of the Governments of the states and their peoples and lays down—"that, since wars begin in the minds of men, it is in the minds of men that the defences of peace must be constructed; that ignorance of each other's ways and lives has been a common cause throughout the history of mankind of that suspicion and mistrust between the peoples of the world through which their differences have all too often broken into war; that the great and terrible war which is now ended was a war made possible by the denial of the democratic principles of the dignity, equality, and mutual respect of men and by the propagation in their place, through ignorance and prejudice, of the doctrine of the inequality of the men and races; that the wide diffusion of culture and the education of humanity for justice and liberty and peace are indispensable to the dignity of man and constituted a sacred duty which all the nations must fulfil in a spirit of mutual assistance and concern; that a peace based exclusively upon the political and economic arrangements of governments would not be a peace which would secure the unanimous, lasting and sincere support of the peoples of the world; and that the peace must therefore, be founded, if it is not to fail, upon the intellectual and moral solidarity of mankind." Here is laid down in clear and noble language the basic approach of this organization and the way it was to travel if it was to realize its objectives of international peace and the common welfare of mankind.

[1] Speech at the Inauguration of the Tenth Annual Session of UNESCO, 5 November 1956, New Delhi. JN Papers, NMML. Excerpts.

The preamble of the UNESCO constitution says, as I have quoted, that wars begin in the minds of men. We have been living through a period of cold war which has now broken out into open and violent warfare. If we have closed the minds of men with thoughts of cold war, can we be surprised at its inevitable result?

You will forgive me, I hope, if I speak with some feeling. I would be untrue to myself or to this distinguished gathering, if I did not refer to something which has moved us deeply and which must be in the minds of all of us here. We use brave phrases to impress ourselves and others, but our actions belie those noble sentiments, and so we live in a world of unreality, where profession has little to do with practice. When that practice imperils the entire future of the world then it is time that we come back to reality in our thinking and in our action.

At present it would appear that great countries think that the only reality is force and violence and that fine phrases are merely the apparatus of diplomacy. This is a matter which concerns all of us in whichever quarter of the world we may live in. But, in a sense, it concerns us in Asia and Africa more, perhaps, than in other countries for some of our countries have recently emerged into freedom and independence and we cherish them with all our strength and passion. We are devoting ourselves to serve our people and to better their lives and make them grow in freedom and progress. We have bitter memories of the past when we were prevented from so growing and we can never permit a return to that past age. And yet we find an attempt made to reverse the current of history and of human development. We find that all our efforts at progress might well be set at nought by the ambitions and conflicts of other peoples. Are we not to feel deeply when our life's work is imperilled and our hopes and dreams shattered? . . .

I have called this great assembly the conscience of the world community. The problems we have to face, many and complicated as they are, will never be solved except on the basis of good morals and conscience. It is for this reason that I beg of you, distinguished delegates from the nations of the world, to pay heed to this collapse of conscience and good morals that we see around us, for unless we do so all our fine ideals and the good work you have done will be shattered into nothingness.

36

Suez Crisis[1]

I am happy to find that the Anglo-French and Israeli troops will at long last be withdrawn entirely from Egyptian territory. I feel sure that this would not have been possible had not world public opinion overwhelmingly stood by Egypt. It was a great relief to us to find that despite their long and close alliance in many matters of international policy, the United States of America also stood firm on the question of the withdrawal of the aggressor forces from Egyptian soil. While we can permit ourselves the hope that the worst will soon be over, there will be need for continuous vigilance for some months to come at least. I am anxious that the revulsion of feelings caused by aggression against Egypt should not be sidetracked by extraneous factors. As it is, developments in Hungary have to an extent come in the way of concerted action against aggressors in Egypt. I feel, therefore, that it is more than ever important to prevent other things coming in the way of the sympathy of the world expressing itself fully in favour of Egypt.

In this context I venture to draw your attention to the reports which are circulating abroad that considerable pressure, direct and indirect, is being brought to bear on the large number of British and French nationals and persons of Jewish origin in Egypt. Some of the latter have, I am told, been resident in Egypt for generations. As you may be aware, I asked our Chargé in Egypt to mention the matter informally to your Government and I am told that he has already done so and had a discussion with Ali Sabry. I would repeat the assurance which Rajwade has already given to Ali Sabry that it is farthest from our mind to interfere in any matter which is in the full discretion of the Egyptian Government. But, Mr. President, I feel sure that you will be concerned as much as I am at anything being done which might create an unfortunate impression on world opinion and alienate sympathy from Egypt at a time when most countries in the world are supporting your cause. You have in the recent past shown exemplary patience in the most provocative circumstances. If I may say so, this has impressed the world almost as much as your courage throughout this critical period. I would request you, therefore, not to take steps which would compel a large number of persons to leave Egypt in penurious circumstances. Considerations of security have of course to be borne in mind. But it

[1] Telegram to Nasser, 5 December 1956. JN Collection, NMML.

would not be in the interest of Egypt herself to allow impression to grow that an attempt was being made to recoup losses suffered by Egypt as a result of aggression by UK, France and Israel by sequestrating the properties of British and French nationals. Action is certainly justified against those who have abused the hospitality of Egypt by subversive activities. But the large majority of the people are, I believe, innocent victims of the wrongs committed by their governments and I would request you to show them compassion. If you do not wish any British or French national to remain in your country, they might, I suggest, be given reasonable time to wind up their affairs and not be forced to leave immediately. Even from the short-term point of view a little patience and tolerance at this stage would help in the discussion of bigger issues concerning Egypt in the United Nations and elsewhere. I would not have made this appeal to you had I not felt sure that you would not misunderstand me.

With kind regards,
Jawaharlal Nehru

37

Non-aggression and Non-interference[1]

Through the centuries, India has preached and practised toleration and understanding, and has enriched human thought, art and literature, philosophy and religion. Her sons journeyed far and wide, braving the perils of land and sea, not with thoughts of conquest or domination, but as messengers of peace or engaged in the commerce of ideas as well as of her beautiful products. During these millennia of history, India has experienced both good and ill but, throughout her chequered history, she has remembered the message of peace and tolerance.

In our own time, this message was proclaimed by our great leader and master, Mahatma Gandhi, who led us to freedom by peaceful and yet effective action on a mass scale.

Nine years ago, we won our independence through a bloodless revolution, in conditions of honour and dignity both to ourselves and to the erstwhile rulers of our country. We in India today are children of this revolution and have been conditioned by it. Although your revolution in America took place long ago and the conditions were different here, you will appreciate the revolutionary spirit which we have inherited and which still governs our activities.

Having attained political freedom, we are earnestly desirous of removing the many ills that our country suffers from, of eliminating poverty and raising the standards of our people, and giving them full and equal opportunities of growth and advancement.

India is supposed to be given to contemplation, and the American people have shown by their history that they possess great energy, dynamism and the passion to march ahead. Something of that contemplative spirit still remains in India. But, at the same time, the new India of today has also developed a certain dynamism and a passionate desire to raise the standards of her people. But with that desire is blended the wish to adhere to the moral and spiritual aspects of life.

We are now engaged in a gigantic and exciting task of achieving rapid and large-scale economic development of our country. Such development, in an

[1] Radio Broadcast in the United States, 18 December 1956. JN Papers, NMML. Excerpts.

ancient and underdeveloped country such as India, is only possible with pur-
posive planning. True to our democratic principles and traditions, we seek in
free discussion and consultation, as well as in implementation, the enthusiasm
and the willing and active cooperation of our people. We completed our first
Five-Year Plan eight months ago, and now we have begun, on a more ambitious
scale, our second Five-Year Plan, which seeks a planned development in agriculture and industry, town and country, and between factory and small-scale
and cottage production.

I speak of India because it is my country, and I have some right to speak
for her. But many other countries in Asia tell the same story, for Asia today is
resurgent, and these countries, which long lay under foreign yoke, have won
back their independence and are fired by a new spirit and strive toward new
ideals. To them, as to us, independence is as vital as the breath they take to
sustain life, and colonialism in any form, or anywhere, is abhorrent.

The vast strides that technology has made have brought a new age, of which
the United States of America is the leader. Today, the whole world is our neighbour, and the old divisions of continents and countries matter less and less.
Peace and freedom have become indivisible, and the world cannot continue for
long partly free and partly subject. In this atomic age, peace has also become a
test of human survival.

Recently, we have witnessed two tragedies which have powerfully affected
men and women all over the world. These are the tragedies in Egypt and
Hungary. Our deeply felt sympathies must go out to those who have suffered
or are suffering, and all of us must do our utmost to help them and to assist in
solving these problems in a peaceful and constructive way.

But even these tragedies have one hopeful aspect, for they have demonstrated
that the most powerful countries cannot revert to old colonial methods, or
impose their domination over weak countries. World opinion has shown that
it can organize itself to resist such outrages. Perhaps, as an outcome of these
tragedies, freedom will be enlarged and will have a more assured basis.

The preservation of peace forms the central aim of India's policy. It is in
the pursuit of this policy that we have chosen the path of nonalignment in any
military or like pact or alliance. Nonalignment does not mean passivity of mind
of action, lack of faith or conviction. It does not mean submission to what we
consider evil. It is a positive and dynamic approach to such problems that
confront us.

We believe that each country has not only the right to freedom, but also
to decide its own policy and way of life. Only thus can true freedom flourish
and a people grow according to their own genius.

We believe, therefore, in non-aggression and non-interference by one
country in the affairs of another, and the growth of tolerance between them and
the capacity for peaceful coexistence. We think that, by the free exchange of

ideas and trade and other contacts between nations, each will learn from the other, and truth will prevail.

We, therefore, endeavour to maintain friendly relations with all countries— even though we may disagree with them in their policies or structure of government. We think that, by this approach, we can serve not only our country but, also the larger causes of peace and good fellowship in the world.

Between the United States and India, there had existed friendly and cordial relations even before India gained her independence. No Indian can forget that, in the days of our struggle for freedom, we received from your country a full measure of sympathy and support. Our two Republics share a common faith in democratic institutions and the democratic way of life, and are dedicated to the cause of peace and freedom. We admire the many qualities that have made this country great, and, more especially, the humanity and dynamism of its people and the great principles to which the fathers of the American revolution gave utterance. We wish to learn from you, and we plead for your friendship and your cooperation and sympathy in the great task that we have undertaken in our own country.

38

Racial Discrimination[1]

So take this question of racial discrimination. A question which has been before us, before the United Nations for many, many years. Now, it seems to me always that this question can only lead, if not solved, to disasters of the first magnitude. The great part of the world recognizes that and has come to the conclusion that racial discrimination must be ended, even though they have not altogether been able to put an end to it. But what are we to say where racial discrimination with all its evils is the official policy of states, not something due to human weakness which we try to better or remove? Basically that type of thinking can never be resolved by half measures that will lead to greater conflicts than even what are called conflicts due to nationalist upsurges; because they are a mixture of both nationalism and other things. Here are these tremendous problems for this seminar and elsewhere which have to be considered—difficult problems, because we have to deal not with some theoretical proposition but with vast numbers of human beings—human beings whose minds are in a state of ferment and a state of revolutionary upheaval, and who have to be dealt with not by chiding them, scolding them or trying to oppress or suppress them. Oppression or suppression may succeed in a small measure for a small period of time, but the time has gone by when they can really succeed, and any attempt to do that will only lead to greater upheavals and will leave trails of bitterness behind, which will be bad for the future of those countries and other countries in the world at large.

So, here is this tremendous problem for you to consider, as calmly as you can, because after all we aim, wherever possible, we should aim, at friendly solutions, cooperative solutions. We aim at solutions which do not leave those tremendous hatreds behind which embitter relations and which stop the growth of man. . . . We have to live together, and we have to live together intimately, in contact with each other because with all these modern developments, each country is the neighbour of another country. No country is far away. We live on the threshold of each other's countries and we either live at peace or at

[1] Speech at a Seminar on Problems of Emergent Africa, 17 February 1961, New Delhi. JN Papers, NMML. Excerpts.

war. . . . We have to recognize that no people in this world are going to put up with the domination of other people and with suppression, racial, political, economic or any other. We have to recognize, of course, that there are countries in this world which are highly developed in many ways, others less developed. They are not all the same, but all of them are human beings, trying to live with the dignity of man and not putting up with anything else. That is certain. Keeping that in mind and keeping in mind that ultimately we have to evolve a peaceful order, we should try to aim at steps which will help in that, rather than to some extent, give up the future for some temporary advantage of today; but after all, we live for the future.

39

The Chinese Aggression[1]

Comrades, friends and fellow countrymen,

I am speaking to you on the radio after a long interval. I feel, however, that I must speak to you about the grave situation that has arisen on our frontiers because of continuing and unabashed aggression by the Chinese forces. A situation has arisen which calls upon all of us to meet it effectively. We are men and women of peace in this country, conditioned to the ways of peace. We are unused to the necessities of war. Because of this, we endeavoured to follow a policy of peace even when aggression took place on our territory in Ladakh five years ago.[2] We explored avenues for an honourable settlement by peaceful methods. That was our policy all over the world, and we tried to apply it even in our own country. We know the horrors of war in this age today, and we have done our utmost to prevent war from engulfing the world.

But all our efforts have been in vain in so far as our own frontier is concerned, where a powerful and unscrupulous opponent, and not caring for peace or peaceful methods, has continuously threatened us and even carried these threats into action.

The time has therefore come for us to realize fully this menace that threatens the freedom of our people and the independence of our country. I say so, even though I realize that no power can ultimately imperil the freedom we have won at so much sacrifice and cost to our people after long ages of foreign domination. But, to conserve that freedom and integrity of our territory, we must gird up our loins and face this greatest menace that has come to us since we became independent. I have no doubt in my mind that we shall succeed. Everything else is secondary to the freedom of our people and of our motherland and if necessary everything else has to be sacrificed in this great crisis.

I do not propose to give you the long history of continuous aggression by the Chinese during the last five years and how they have tried to justify it by speeches, arguments and the repeated assertion of untruths and a campaign of

[1] A Broadcast to the Nation, 22 October 1962. JN Papers, NMML.
[2] Chinese forces had seized a portion of Ladakh and built a road across the occupied territory to connect Sinkiang with Tibet.

calumny and vituperation against our country. Perhaps there are not many instances in history where one country, that is India, has gone out of her way to be friendly and cooperative with the Chinese Government and people and to plead their cause in the councils of the world, and then for the Chinese Government to return evil for good and even go to the extent of committing aggression and invade our sacred land. No self-respecting country and certainly not India with her love of freedom can submit to this whatever the consequences may be.

There have been five years of continuous aggression on the Ladakh frontier. Our other frontier at NEFA remained largely free from this aggression. Just when we were discussing ways and means of reducing tension and there was even some chance of the representatives of the two countries meeting to consider this matter, a new fresh aggression took place on the NEFA border. This began on September 8 last. This was a curious way of lessening tension. It is typical of the way the Chinese Government have treated us.

Our border with China in the NEFA region is well known and well established from ages past. It is sometimes called the McMahon Line. This line which separates India from Tibet was the line of the high ridges which divided the watershed.

This has been acknowledged as the border by history, tradition and treaties long before it was called the McMahon Line. The Chinese have in many ways acknowledged it as the border, even though they have called the McMahon Line illegal. The Chinese laid claim, in their maps, to a large part of the NEFA which has been under our administration for a long time. The present Chinese regime was established about 12 years ago. Before that, the Tibetans did not challenge it. Even the maps that the Chinese produced were acknowledged by them repeatedly to be old and out-of-date maps which had little relevance today.

Yet on this peaceful border where no trouble or fighting had occurred for a long time, they committed aggression and this also in very large numbers and after vast preparations for a major attack.

I am grieved at the setbacks to our troops that have occurred on this frontier and the reverses we have had. They were overwhelmed by vast numbers and by big artillery, mountain guns and heavy mortars which the Chinese forces have brought with them. I should like to pay a tribute to our officers and men who faced these overwhelming numbers with courage. There may be some more reverses in that area. But one thing is certain that the final result of this conflict will be in our favour. It cannot be otherwise when a nation like India fights for her freedom and the integrity of the country. We have to meet a powerful and unscrupulous opponent. We have, therefore, to build our strength and power to face this situation adequately and with confidence. The conflict may continue for long. We must prepare ourselves for it mentally and otherwise. We must have faith in ourselves and I am certain that that faith and our preparations will triumph. No other result is conceivable. Let there be this faith and fixed determination to free our country from the aggressor.

What then are we to do about it? We must steel our wills and direct the nation's energy and resources to this one end. We must change our procedures from slow moving methods of peacetime to those that produce results quickly. We must build our military strength by all means at our disposal.

But military strength is not by itself enough. It has to be supported fully by the industry of the nation and by increasing our production in every way that is necessary for us. I would appeal to all our workers not to indulge in strikes or in any other act which comes in the way of increasing production.

That production has to be not only in the factory but in the field. No anti-national or anti-social activities can be tolerated when the nation is in peril.

We shall have to carry a heavy burden whatever our vocation may be. The price of freedom will have to be paid in full measure and no price is too great for the freedom of our people and our motherland.

I earnestly trust and I believe that all parties and groups in the country will unite in this great enterprise and put aside their controversies and arguments which have no place today and present a solid united front before all those who seek to endanger our freedom and integrity.

The burden on us is going to be great. We must add greatly to our savings by the purchase of bonds to help finance production and meet the increasing cost of national defence. We must prevent any rise in prices and we must realize that those who seek to profit at a time of national difficulty are anti-national and injure the nation.

We are in the middle of our Third Five-Year Plan. There can be no question of our giving up this plan or reducing any important element of it. We may adapt it to the new requirements here and there. But essentially the major projects of the plan must be pursued and implemented, because it is in that way that we shall strengthen our country not only in the present crisis but in the years to come.

There are many other things that our people can do and I hope to indicate some of them at a later stage. But the principal thing is for us to devote ourselves to the task of forging the national will to freedom and to work hard to that end. There is no time limit to this. We shall carry the struggle as long as we do not win because we cannot submit to the aggression or to the domination of others.

We must avoid any panic because that is bad at any time and there is no reason for it. We have behind us the strength of a united nation. Let us rejoice because of this and apply it to the major task of today, that of preserving our complete freedom and integrity and the removal of all those who commit aggression on India's sacred territory. Let us face this crisis not light-heartedly but with seriousness and with a stout heart and with firm faith in the rightness of our struggle and confidence in its outcome. Do not believe in rumours. Do not listen to those who have faint hearts. This is a time of trial and testing for all of us, and we have to steel ourselves to the task. Perhaps, we were growing too soft and taking things for granted. But freedom can never be taken for granted. It requires always awareness, strength and austerity.

I invite all of you, to whatever religion or party or group you may belong, to be comrades in this great struggle that has been forced upon us. I have full faith in our people and in the cause and in the future of our country. Perhaps that future requires some such testing and stiffening for us.

We have followed a policy of nonalignment and sought friendship of all nations. I believe in that policy fully and we shall continue to follow it. We are not going to give up our basic principles because of the present difficulty. Even this difficulty will be more effectively met by our continuing that policy.

I wish you well and, whatever may befall us in the future, want you to hold your heads high and have faith and full confidence in the great future that we envisage for our country. *Jai Hind.*

40

The Proclamation of Emergency[1]

For five years, we have been the victims of Chinese aggression across our frontiers in the north. That aggression was, to begin with, rather furtive. Occasionally there were some incidents and conflicts. These conflicts might well be termed frontier incidents. Today, we are facing a regular and massive invasion of our territory by very large forces. . . .

This strange twist of history has brought us face to face with something that we have not experienced in this way for over a hundred years or more. We had taken it almost for granted that despite some lapses in recent years, as in the Suez affair, that this type of aggression was almost a thing of the past. Even the Chinese aggression on our borders during the last five years, bad as it was, and indicative of an expansionist tendency, though it troubled us greatly, hardly led us to the conclusion that China would indulge in a massive invasion of India. Now, we have seen and experienced this very invasion, it has shocked us, as it has shocked a larger number of countries.

History has taken a new turn in Asia and perhaps the world, and we have to bear the brunt of it, to fight with all our might this menace to our freedom and integrity. Not only are we threatened by it, but all the standards of international behaviour have been upset and so all the world is affected by it, apart from the immediate consequences. No self-respecting country which loves its freedom and its integrity can possibly submit to this challenge. Certainly, India, this dear land of ours, will never submit to it whatever the consequences. We accept the challenge in all its consequences, whatever they may be. . . .

Even the McMahon Line which the Chinese have called illegal was laid down 48 years ago, in 1914, and that was a confirmation of what was believed in then. Legal or not, it has been a part of India for a long number of years and certainly, let us say, for 50 years or so, apart from its previous history which is also in our favour. Here then is a boundary which for nearly 50 years has been shown to be our northern frontier. I am limiting what I say to 50 years for the sake of argument; really it was even before that. Even if the Chinese did not

[1] A Statement in the Lok Sabha, 8 November 1962. JN Papers, NMML.

accept it—and I would like to say that the objection they raised in 1913 to this treaty was not based on their objection to the McMahon Line; it was based on their objection to another part of the treaty which divided Inner Tibet and Outer Tibet, the McMahon Line did not come in that; however, it is a fact that they objected to the whole treaty because of that other objection—even if the Chinese did not accept it then, this has been in existence now in our maps, in our practice, in our Constitution, in our organization, administration, etc., for nearly 50 years. Even the non-accepting of it, can it entitle them to undertake an armed invasion to upset it? Even the Chinese know and say that independent India has been in possession of this territory right up to the Himalayan watershed. . . .

Here, I may say, it has been unfortunate, in this as in so many other cases, that the present Government of China is not represented in the United Nations. Honourable Members are surprised when we have supported the Chinese representation—the representation of the People's Government of China—in the United Nations. We have supported it in spite of this present invasion, because we have to look at it this way: it is not a question of likes or dislikes. It is a question, which will facilitate Chinese aggression; it will facilitate its misbehaviour in the future. It will make disarmament impossible in the world. You might disarm the whole world and leave China, a great, powerful country, fully armed to the teeth. It is inconceivable. Therefore, in spite of our great resentment at what they have done, the great irritation and anger, still, I am glad to say that we kept some perspective about things and supported that even now. The difficulty is one cannot call them up before any tribunal or world court or anywhere. They are just wholly an irresponsible country believing, in war as the only way of settling anything, having no love of peace, and with great power at their disposal. That is a dangerous state of affairs not only for India but for the rest of the world. . . .

May I add that there has been a great deal of talk about our unpreparedness? I think most of it is based on ignorance. . . .

There is always a choice and there has been a choice in this and other matters for us to buy arms from abroad or to make them ourselves. Obviously it is infinitely better to make them ourselves, because that strengthens the country, industrially and otherwise and secondly, you cannot altogether rely on outside supplies; any moment they may fail you and economically it is bad to get them from outside. So, our practice has been to try to build up our arms, the industry and the like in the country and we have done fairly well. We might have done better; I do not know. All kinds of difficulties arise, because the development of one industry depends on the whole industrial background of the country. We have laid stress on that. I would not go into that.

A great deal was said about arms, automatic rifles and the rest. For the last three or four years, we have been trying to make them and various difficulties arose about patents, this, that and the other and sometimes about our own difficulties in finding enough foreign exchange. This has been a continuing difficulty, as to how much we should spend in the shape of foreign exchange. Ultimately, we got over these difficulties and we started their manufacture, I forget the date, but sometime this year and we are now making them.

The only alternative was previously for us to get a large number of those weapons from abroad. We hesitated; we wanted to make them ourselves. Undoubtedly, we could have got them, but remember this. If we had tried to get all those weapons from abroad in what might be called relatively peaceful times, we would have had to spend enormous sums of money.

41

A Popular Upsurge[1]

4 December 1962

Dear Lord Russell,

I have given much thought to what you have written. I need not tell you that I am much moved by your passion for peace and it finds an echo in my own heart. Certainly we do not want this frontier war with China to continue and even more certainly we do not want it to spread and involve the nuclear powers. Also there is the danger of the military mentality spreading in India and the power of the army increasing.

But there are limits in a democratic society to what a government can do. There is such strong feeling in India over the invasion by China that no government can stand if it does not pay some heed to it. The Communist Party of India has been compelled by circumstances to issue a strong condemnation of China. Even so, the communists here are in a bad way, and their organization is gradually disappearing because of popular resentment.

Apart from this, there are various other important considerations which have to be borne in mind in coming to a decision. If there is a sense of national surrender and humiliation, this will have a very bad effect on the people of India and all our efforts to build the nation will suffer a very serious setback. At present the popular upsurge all over India can be utilized for strengthening the unity and capacity for work of the nation, apart from the military aspect. There are obvious dangers about militarism and extreme forms of nationalism developing, but there are also possibilities of the people of our country thinking in a more constructive way and profiting by the dangers that threaten us.

If we go wholly against the popular sentiment, which to a large extent I share, then the result will be just what you fear. Others will take charge and drive the country towards disaster.

The Chinese proposals, as they are, mean their gaining a dominating position, specially in Ladakh, which they can utilize in future for a further attack on India. The present-day China, as you know, is probably the only country which is not afraid even of a nuclear war. Mao Tse-tung has said repeatedly that he does not mind losing a few million people as still several hundred

[1] To Bertrand Russell. JN Papers, NMML.

millions will survive in China. If they are to profit by this invasion, this will lead them to further attempts of the same kind. That will put an end to all talks of peace and will surely bring about a world nuclear war. I feel, therefore, that in order to avoid this catastrophe and, at the same time, strengthen our own people, quite apart from arms, etc., we must not surrender or submit to what we consider evil. That is a lesson I learned from Gandhiji.

We have, however, not rejected the Chinese proposal, but have ourselves suggested an alternative which is honourable for both parties. I still have hope that China will agree to this. In any event we are not going to break the cease-fire and indulge in a military offensive.

If these preliminaries are satisfactorily settled we are prepared to adopt any peaceful methods for the settlement of the frontier problem. These might even include a reference to arbitration.

So far as we are concerned, we hope to adhere to the policy of non-alignment although I confess that taking military help from other countries does somewhat affect it. But in the circumstances we have no choice.

I can assure you that the wider issues that you have mentioned are before us all the time. We do not want to do something which will endanger our planet. I do think, however, that there will be a greater danger of that kind if we surrender to the Chinese and they feel that the policy they have pursued brings them rich dividends.

VOL. II

III
India, Pakistan and Kashmir

1. Kashmir   317
2. The Trial of Sheikh Abdullah   320
3. The Kashmir Crisis   322
4. Broadcast on Kashmir   326
5. Frontier Province   330
6. Kashmir Plebiscite   332
7. Kashmir and the United States   335
8. Arbitration on Kashmir Issue   338
9. Plight of Minorities   341
10. At the Edge of a Precipice   347
11. The Basis for Conflict   352
12. Military Confrontation   355
13. Indo-Pak Situation   358
14. Keeping Vigilant   363
15. The Question of Plebiscite   370
16. The Kashmir Policy   372
17. Kashmir and Indo-Pak Relations   375
18. The Good of Kashmiris   378
19. Collective Aggression   380
20. The Question of Kashmir   381

1

Kashmir[1]

Yea, in my mind these mountains rise,
Their perils dyed with evening's rose;
And still my ghost sits at my eyes
And thirsts for their untroubled snows.

Nearly six years ago I quoted these lines from Walter de la Mare as I sat in prison writing the story of my life and thinking of my last visit to Kashmir. In prison or outside, Kashmir haunted me, and, though many years had passed since I had set eyes on its valleys and mountains, I carried the impress of them on the tablets of my mind. I yearned to visit them again, and struggled against this yearning. Was I to leave my work that took all my time, play truant to it, to satisfy the hunger of my eyes and the desire of my heart?

But days passed and months and years, and life is short, and a fear gripped me with this passing of time. Age may have its advantages, and the Chinese, above all other people, have praised them. It gives, or should give, stability and equilibrium to the mind, a sense of poise, an appearance of wisdom, even a keener appreciation of beauty in all its forms. But age is stiff and crabbed and unimpressionable and reacts slowly to outside stimuli. It cannot be moulded easily; its emotional reactions are limited. It looks to comfort and security more than to the fine frenzy of enthusiasm. While it gives its sober and reasoned appreciation to the beauty of nature and art, it does not mirror this beauty in its eyes or feel it in its heart. It makes all the difference in the world whether one visits Italy, not fascist Italy, but the Italy of song and music and beautiful art, of Leonardo and Raphael and Michaelangelo, of Dante and Petrarch, in one's youth or in later years. Besides, what can age do to a mountain except sit and gaze in silent wonder?

So with the passing of time and the slow but irresistible coming of age over me, I began to grow afraid lest I might no longer be capable of experiencing that emotional reaction to the beauty of Kashmir when at last I went there again. . . .

I took the route *via* Abbottabad and the Jhelum Valley, a pleasant route with the panorama of the valley slowly unfolding in all its charm and beauty.

[1] Published in the *National Herald* in six parts between 24–31 July 1940. Reprinted as foreword in *Kashmir: Eden of the East* by S.N. Dhar, pp. 1–27. Excerpts.

But perhaps it would have been better if I had gone via Jammu and over the Pir Panjal. This is dull going most of the way, but as one crosses the mountain and goes through a long tunnel the sight that meets the eye is overpowering in its magic beauty. Out of the darkness one comes into the light, and there, far below, lies the vale of Kashmir, like some wonderland of our dreams, encircled by high mountains that guard it jealously from intrusion.

I did not go this way, and my approach was more sober and the change was slower. But my mind was filled with the excitement of my return and it pleased me to be welcomed everywhere as a brother and a comrade, who, in spite of long absence, was still of Kashmir and was coming back to his old homeland. With joy I saw the reality of the pictures in my mind which I had treasured for long years. I emerged from the mountains and the narrow valley, down which the Jhelum roared and tumbled in youthful abandon, and the vale itself spread out before me. There were the famous poplars, slim and graceful sentinels, beckoning a welcome to you. There was the lordly chenar in all its majesty, with centuries of growth behind it. And there were the beautiful women and bonny children of Kashmir working in the fields.

We approached Srinagar, and there was cordial welcome and friendly faces greeted me everywhere. Up the river we went in a stately barge with numerous *shikaras* following, and the riverside steps and houses filled with cheering men and women and children. I was moved, as I have seldom been, by this affection that was showered upon me, and I became tongue-tied by the emotions that surged within me as the panorama of Srinagar passed by. Hari Parvat was in the background, and Shankaracharya or Takht-e-Suleiman loomed in the distance. I was in Kashmir.

I spent twelve days in Kashmir, and during this brief period we went some way up the Amarnath Valley and also up the Liddar Valley to the Kolahoi glacier. We visited the ancient temple at Martand and sat under the venerable chenar trees of Brijbehara, which had grown and spread during four hundred years of human history. We loitered in the Moghal Gardens and lived for a while in their scented past. We drank the delightful water of Chasme Shahi and swam about in the Dal Lake. We saw the lovely handiwork of the gifted artisans of Kashmir. We attended numerous public functions, delivered speeches, and met people of all kinds.

I tried to give my mind to the activity of the moment, and perhaps, in a measure, succeeded. But my mind was largely elsewhere, and I went through my engagements and the day's programme, and functioned on the public stage, like one who is absorbed in some other undertaking or is on a secret errand whose object he cannot disclose. The loveliness of the land enthralled me and cast an enchantment all about me. I wandered about like one possessed and drunk with beauty, and the intoxication of it filled my mind.

Like some supremely beautiful woman, whose beauty is almost impersonal and above human desire, such was Kashmir in all its feminine beauty of river and valley and lake and graceful trees. And then another aspect of this magic beauty would come to view, a masculine one, of hard mountains and precipices, and snow-capped peaks and glaciers, and cruel and fierce torrents rushing down to the valleys below. It had a hundred faces and innumerable aspects, ever-changing, sometimes smiling, sometimes sad and full of sorrow. The mist would creep up from the Dal Lake and, like a transparent veil, give glimpses of what was behind. The clouds would throw out their arms to embrace a mountain-top, or creep down stealthily like children at play. I watched this ever-changing spectacle, and sometimes the sheer loveliness of it was over-powering and I felt almost faint. As I gazed at it, it seemed to me dream-like and unreal, like the hopes and desires that fill us and so seldom find fulfilment. It was like the face of the beloved that one sees in a dream that fades away on awakening.

2

The Trial of Sheikh Abdullah[1]

Kashmir has been very much in the news for some months past. Ordinarily looked upon as a tourist resort, a country famous throughout history for its loveliness and climate, it has attracted an increasing number of people from year to year.

But it was not its beauty or its attraction for the tourist that brought it in the news in the spring and summer of 1946. Another aspect of this mountain country, which nature has placed like a crown on the brow of India, was constantly thrust before the eyes of millions in the rest of India and even abroad. This was not a thing of beauty. It was ugly in the extreme for this aspect was compounded of extreme poverty and misery, of authoritarian and despotic rule in the interest of a few while crushing the many, and of a fierce suppression of the unhappy people of the State.

Anything that happens in Kashmir has a certain importance for the rest of India, but recent events there have had an even greater importance, for the people's struggle and its fierce repression became symbols of a larger struggle for emancipation. Thus Kashmir became symbolic of the States in India where there is ferment and seething discontent, both political and economic, against the autocratic and often feudal rule that prevails there. The people of other States looked with sympathy towards the people of Kashmir and there was a feeling of solidarity between them. The Rulers of many States, no doubt, sympathized with and encouraged the Kashmir authorities and felt that their own interests were tied up to some extent with the fate of this struggle in Kashmir.

Popular movements which have any reality and strength behind them usually throw up personalities who typify and symbolize that movement. Thus Sheikh Mohammad Abdullah became the living and outstanding symbol of the urge of the Kashmiri people for their freedom. Thus also the trial of Sheikh Abdullah became something much more than the trial of an individual; it was the trial of a whole people. Or perhaps it would be more correct to say that, in the ultimate analysis, it was the trial before the bar of public opinion of the State

[1] New Delhi, 24 September 1946. Introduction to *Kashmir on Trial* (Lahore, 1947). SWJN, Vol. 1 (II series), pp. 294–5.

authorities who had tried to stem the flowing river of the great popular movement.

It is extraordinary how those in authority become blind to the lesson of history; how they cannot even understand current happenings. Just when we find that India is on the verge of independence, we find the Kashmir authorities, totally oblivious of this fact, seeking to crush their own people and their desire for freedom. A real people's movement can never be crushed in this way, much less can it be crushed when India herself is putting an end to foreign rule.

Because of all these factors, recent events in Kashmir have assumed an all-India importance and the trial of Sheikh Abdullah has a particular significance. I am glad that a record of this trial is being published, for this will bring many new facts before the public and help them to understand what has been happening in Kashmir and what happens or may happen in many another State in India.

The story of this brave struggle against the armed forces of the State has not ended by this trial. That story will go on till it reaches the logical end which can only be the establishment of freedom in Kashmir within the larger framework of a free and independent India. Meanwhile Sheikh Abdullah and many of his colleagues lie in prison and to them we send our comradely greetings.

3

The Kashmir Crisis[1]

2 November 1947

My dear Prime Minister,

In my letter to you, dated the 15th October, I said that we had turned the corner and are in a position to face the future with confidence, though unceasing vigilance was still necessary. I little realized then how quickly our vigilance would be tested.

2. You must have followed developments in Kashmir. It is extraordinary how these developments remind one of the technique adopted by Hitler. Indeed, the whole policy of the Muslim League during the past few years has been singularly reminiscent of the Nazi tactics. The Kashmir incidents are a kind of climax to this policy.

3. I am enclosing a copy of a draft which I have prepared for my broadcast[2] on Kashmir and this will give you some picture of the situation. I have not emphasized in this broadcast the part which Pakistan has obviously played in this whole affair. But there can be no doubt about it that the so-called raiders are well-armed and even possess small artillery. They have competent leadership and probably officers of the Pakistan Army have helped in organizing them. The actual tribesmen among the raiders are probably limited in numbers, the rest are ex-servicemen. Part of the Muslim element in the Kashmir forces has also gone over to them. Their equipment is good and they have a large number of lorries. It is impossible to conceive that all this could be done without the full connivance and help of the Pakistan authorities.

4. Our own information is that a Pakistan Army brigade was kept ready at the frontier near Kohala and another brigade was kept at Sialkot near the Jammu frontier. The idea was that as soon as the raiders captured Srinagar, they would announce accession to Pakistan and then the regular Pakistan Army would march in and take possession. It has even been suggested that Mr. Jinnah was thinking of some kind of a triumphal entry.

5. Another feature of Pakistan attack on Kashmir, which also reminds one of Nazi Germany, is the fierce, blatant and false propaganda that has been carried on by their radio and press. All this should put us on our guard. We may

[1] To Chief Ministers, JN Papers, NMML. Excerpts.
[2] See post, pp. 326–9.

have to face a difficult situation in Hyderabad and the Ittehad-ul-Muslimeen[3] is a well-organized fanatical body which may cause trouble. Bombay, Central Provinces and Madras have to be particularly watchful. Needless to say the Government of India is fully conscious of the dangers and is carefully watching the situation. We should like the help of the adjoining provinces, especially in this matter.

6. One of the features of the Kashmir situation which is worthy of notice is the complete disintegration of the Kashmir administration at a moment of crisis. The Maharaja suddenly left Srinagar in the middle of the night accompanied by his Ministers. Most of the other officers also disappeared and there was no constituted authority left at all. The army itself, which was supposed to be strong, somehow faded away. About a quarter of it went over to the invaders, or deserted. The rest was caught in small pockets and generally did not put up any good show at all. It was the National Conference under Sheikh Abdullah's leadership that saved the situation. Our troops could have done nothing but for the stand of the National Conference. Even now the defence of Kashmir is largely based on the cooperation of our troops with the civil population which we are partly arming for the purpose.

7. The example of Kashmir shows how feeble the administrative apparatus is in the States and how rapidly it may collapse in a real emergency. Some of the States, especially in Rajputana and in East Punjab, have been behaving in an undesirable manner. There are cries of a Sikh State of Rajasthan and Jatsthan and the Rulers have taken advantage of the communal troubles to suppress the popular movements. Provincial administrations, especially those adjoining the Indian States, have to tighten up their own administrative machinery and keep it thoroughly efficient. Trouble may come from the States and we have to stop it immediately.

8. Recent events in Kashmir and partly our action in Babariawad and Mangrol have been a severe blow to the Pakistan Government.[4] They have a terrible sense of frustration. Already they were being overwhelmed by their problems. The vast numbers of Muslim refugees who have gone to Pakistan are a terrible burden on them and they cannot look after them. Because of all this they are suffering from the delusion that the Government of India are conspiring to destroy Pakistan. That, of course, is completely false. There is no conspiracy and there is no desire to destroy their state in any way. Any such attempt would lead to grave injury to us. War is a dangerous thing and must be

[3] A communal organization which was demanding an independent State of Hyderabad.

[4] On 1 November 1947, the Government of India sent a small force accompanied by a civil administrator to take over the administration of Babariawad and Mangrol in the Kathiawar region. Babariawad was a group of fifty-one villages held by Mulgirasias, the original landholders, and Mangrol was a small Princely State situated between Porbandar and Junagadh.

avoided. Even to talk of war is not healthy. Only those who do not understand it or its consequences talk lightly of war. From the military point of view there is little doubt that if there was war between India and Pakistan, Pakistan as a state would perish. But, undoubtedly, India would suffer very great injury and all our schemes of progress would have to be pushed aside for many, many years. Therefore, we must do our utmost to avoid war, and that is our definite policy. We cannot be driven into extreme courses simply because thoughtless people shout and become bellicose. We must all, in our own way, try to make people understand the situation and to reduce the tension so that normal relations might be maintained with Pakistan. Both statesmanship and expediency, as well as humanity, require this. That, of course, does not mean that we should surrender our honour or self-respect in the slightest. The danger really is not from any well-thought-out action, but from acute despair on the part of Pakistan, for their leaders have put themselves in a hole and do not know how to get out of it.

9. It is essential for each province to develop its home guards and to strengthen its police service. We must not demand the military to keep law and order. They must be reserved for special occasions only and for the purpose they are intended. I might draw your attention to the fact that in recruiting for the home guard or the police the ex-INA personnel might well be used. They are trained soldiers and would easily fit in and do good work. I know that there has been some prejudice against them in recent months because of some occurrences in Bihar and elsewhere. It is also true that the INA people functioned on both sides during the Punjab disturbances. Also, that the Kashmir raiders are led by a prominent INA officer, Major-General Kiani. But all this can be said of our police force also, as well as parts of our Army who have not been able to retain their discipline and impartiality in the stress of events. I think it would be definitely desirable to use selected INA personnel for the home guard and the police. They should normally be mixed with others and not kept as a separate unit.

10. I should like to say that our Indian Army has, on the whole, kept its balance very well. This cannot be said of the Pakistan Army which has rather gone to pieces and has not got too much discipline left. Our officers in the Army are a fine set of young men. They have had to face suddenly the Kashmir emergency, many of them without any experience of the kind, and they have shown great resource and courage, sometimes bordering on rashness.

11. I should like to draw your attention specially to the necessity for developing intelligence services. This is very important both from the provincial and the Central point of view. It is not easy to develop a good intelligence service suddenly as the men employed must be carefully chosen. Our old intelligence system has more or less broken down as it was bound to, because it was meant for other purposes, chiefly for tracking Congressmen and the like. The

new intelligence service will have to be built differently. There are at present many dangerous tendencies and trends in the country which may broadly be called fascist. They are not only Muslim but also Hindu and Sikh. We should know all about this. The trouble in Delhi was largely due to lack of information in time.

12. The Information Films of India, which was started during war time, but was abolished in April 1946, is now being revived and it is hoped that by the beginning of next year Government's films and news-reels will again be in circulation. The Ministry of Information and Broadcasting have written to your Chief Secretary to insert a condition in the licence of exhibitors in your province enjoining compulsory exhibition of films approved by the Central Government and Provincial Governments. As documentary films and news-reels are not commercially a paying proposition, commercial production and distribution is at present practically non-existent in India. I hope your Government will utilize this powerful medium to reach the masses, more especially for them to understand the various development plans that you are undertaking. Those films will also help to develop a social consciousness and a sense of corporate endeavour. I earnestly hope that your Government will accept the suggestion of the Ministry of Information.

Yours sincerely,
Jawaharlal Nehru

4

Broadcast on Kashmir[1]

Friends and Comrades,

I want to speak to you tonight about Kashmir, not about the beauty of that famous valley, but about the horror which it has had to face recently. We have passed through very critical days and the burden of taking vital and far-reaching decisions has fallen upon us. We have taken those decisions and I want to tell you about them.

Our neighbouring Government, using language which is not the language of governments or even of responsible people, has accused the Government of India of fraud and violence in regard to the accession of Kashmir to the Indian Union. I cannot emulate that language nor have I any desire to do so, for I speak for a responsible government and a responsible people. I agree that there has been fraud and violence in Kashmir, but the question is: who is responsible for it? Already considerable parts of the Jammu and Kashmir State have been over-run by raiders from outside, well-armed and well-equipped, and they have sacked and looted the towns and villages and put many of the inhabitants to the sword. Frightfulness suddenly descended upon this lovely and peaceful country and the beautiful city of Srinagar was on the verge of destruction.

I want to say at once that every step that we have taken in regard to Kashmir has been taken after the fullest thought and consideration of the consequences and I am convinced that what we have done was the right thing. Not to have taken those steps would have been a betrayal of a trust and cowardly submission to the law of the sword with its accompaniment of arson, rapine and slaughter.

For some weeks past we had received reports of infiltration of raiding bands into the State territory of Jammu Province. Also of a concentration of armed men near the border of Kashmir with the North West Frontier Province. We were naturally concerned about this not only because of our close ties with Kashmir and her people but also because Kashmir is a frontier territory adjoining great nations and therefore we were bound to take interest in developments there. But we were anxious not to interfere and we took to step whatever to intervene even though a part of Jammu Province was overrun by these raiders.

[1] Broadcast from Delhi, 2 November 1947. AIR tapes, NMML.

It has been stated that there were raids from the Jammu side across the Pakistan border and that there was communal trouble in Jammu and Muslims were killed and driven away. In the past we have not hesitated to condemn evil whoever might have committed it, whether Hindu or Sikh or Muslim; and so if Hindus or Sikhs or any functionaries of the State misbehaved in Jammu Province certainly we condemn them and regret their deeds.

But I have before me a detailed list of 95 villages in the Jammu Province which have been destroyed by the raiders from Pakistan. Bhimbar, a considerable town, has also been sacked and destroyed. Other towns are besieged and a considerable part of Poonch and Mirpur areas is in possession of the raiders. Does this indicate that aggression took place from the Kashmir side into West Punjab or does it not show that there has been continuous and organized aggression from West Punjab into Kashmir State? These raiders possess the latest type of modern arms. It is reported they have used flame-throwers and a disabled tank has been discovered with them.

About this time we were asked by the Kashmir State to provide them with arms. We took no urgent steps about it and although sanction was given by our States and Defence Ministries, actually no arms were sent.

On the night of the 24th October I learnt of another raid, this time from the Abbottabad-Mansehra road which enters Kashmir near Muzaffarabad. We were told that armed and well-equipped persons in over one hundred lorries had broken in, had sacked Muzaffarabad and killed many persons there including the District Magistrate, and were proceeding along the Jhelum Valley road towards Srinagar. The State forces were spread out in small numbers all over the State and they could not stop this armed and well-organized raid. The civil population, Hindu and Muslim, fled before the raiders.

It was on the 24th night that for the first time a request was made to us on behalf of the Kashmir State for accession and military help. On the 25th morning we considered this in the Defence Committee, but no decision was taken about sending troops, in view of the obvious difficulties of the undertaking. On the 26th morning we again considered this matter. The situation was even more critical then. The raiders had sacked several towns and had destroyed the great power house at Mahura which supplies electricity to the whole of Kash-mir. They were on the point of entering the valley. The fate of Srinagar and the whole of Kashmir hung in the balance.

We received urgent messages for aid not only from the Maharaja's Government, but from representatives of the people, notably that great leader of Kashmir, Sheikh Muhammad Abdullah, the President of the National Conference. Both the Kashmir Government and the National Conference pressed us to accept the accession of Kashmir to the Indian Union. We decided to accept this accession and to send troops by air but we made a condition that the accession would have to be considered by the people of Kashmir later when peace and order were established. We were anxious not to finalize anything in a moment of crisis and without the fullest opportunity to the people of Kashmir to have their say. It was for them ultimately to decide.

And here let me make it clear that it has been our policy all along that where there is a dispute about the accession of a state to either Dominion, the decision must be made by the people of that State. It was in accordance with this policy that we added a proviso to the Instrument of Accession of Kashmir.

We decided to send troops on the afternoon of 26th October. Srinagar was in peril and the situation was urgent and critical. Our staff worked hard that day and night and at daybreak on the 27th our troops went by air. They were small in numbers to begin with, but immediately on arrival they rushed into action to stop the invader. Their gallant commander, a brave officer of our army, was killed the next day.[2]

Since then troops and equipment have been flown over daily and I should like to express my high appreciation and the appreciation of my Government for the fine work which our staff have done as well as the pilots and the air crews who have thrown themselves into this adventure with heart and soul. The airlines have cooperated with us fully and to them also I am grateful. Our young men have shown how they can rise to the occasion in a moment of crisis to serve their country.

Srinagar was in peril and the invader was almost on its door step. There was no administration left there, no troops, no police. Light and power had failed and there was a vast number of refugees there and yet Srinagar functioned without obvious panic and shops were opened and people went about the streets. To what was this miracle due? Sheikh Abdullah and his colleagues of the National Conference and their unarmed volunteers, Muslim and Hindu and Sikh, took charge of the situation, kept order and prevented panic. It was a wonderful piece of work that they did at a moment when the nerves of most people might have failed them. They did so because of the strength of their organization, but even more so because they were determined to protect their country from the ruthless invader who was destroying their country and trying to compel them by terrorism to join Pakistan. Whatever the future may hold, the people of the Valley of Kashmir have exhibited during these past few days remarkable courage, capacity for organization and unity.

It would be well if this lesson was understood by the whole of India which has been poisoned by communal strife. Under the inspiration of a great leader, Sheikh Abdullah, the people of the Valley, Muslim and Hindu and Sikh, were together for the defence of their common country against the invader. Our troops could have done little without this popular support and cooperation.

[2] Lieutenant-Colonel Dewan Ranjit Rai was killed in action on the outskirts of Baramula on 27 October.

The Maharaja of Kashmir deserves to be congratulated on his decision to make Sheikh Abdullah the head of the administration at this critical juncture. That was a wise step which other Rulers might well follow, making their people trustees and defenders of freedom.

It must be remembered, therefore, that the struggle in Kashmir is a struggle of the people of Kashmir under popular leadership against the invader. Our troops are there to help in this struggle and as soon as Kashmir is free from the invader our troops will have no further necessity to remain there and the fate of Kashmir will be left in the hands of the people of Kashmir.

We have passed through days of peril not only for Kashmir but for the whole of India. That peril is less now but it is by no means over and many dangers confront us. We have to be very vigilant and well prepared for whatever may happen. The first step in this preparation is to put an end completely to every manner of communal strife in India and to stand up as a united nation to face every danger which might threaten our freedom. External danger can only be faced effectively when there is internal peace and order and an organized nation.

We talk about the invaders and raiders in Kashmir and yet these men are fully armed and well trained and have competent leadership. All of these have come across and from Pakistan territory. We have a right to ask the Pakistan Government how and why these people could come across the Frontier Province or West Punjab and how they have been armed so effectively. Is this not a violation of international law and an unfriendly act towards a neighbour country? Is the Pakistan Government too weak to prevent armies marching across its territory to invade another country, or is it willing that this should happen? There is no third alternative.

We have asked the Pakistan Government repeatedly to stop these raiders from coming and to withdraw those who have come. It should be easy for them to stop them for the roads into Kashmir are very few and have to pass over bridges. We on our part have no intention of using our troops in Kashmir when the danger of invasion is passed.

We have declared that the fate of Kashmir is ultimately to be decided by the people. That pledge we have given, and the Maharaja has supported it, not only to the people of Kashmir but to the world. We will not and cannot back out of it. We are prepared when peace and law and order have been established to have a referendum held under international auspices like the United Nations. We want it to be a fair and just reference to the people and we shall accept their verdict. I can imagine no fairer or more just offer.

Meanwhile we have given our word to the people of Kashmir to protect them against the invader and we shall keep our pledge.

5

Frontier Province[1]

My dear Nawabzada,

I am writing to you after considerable hesitation. Indeed it is only after some weeks of thought that I have at last decided to write to you on this subject. I hesitated because I was afraid that I might be misunderstood. But I feel so strongly on this subject that I am impelled to write to you.

I am writing about conditions[2] in the Frontier Province which, from all accounts, are very bad. I have no desire whatever to interfere in any way in Pakistan's internal affairs. But I would be less than human if I was not powerfully affected by the kind of news that is reaching us, of the oppression and persecution of the Khudai Khidmatgars in the Frontier Province and more specially of Khan Abdul Ghaffar Khan, Dr. Khan Saheb and other old colleagues of ours, who have played such a notable part in the struggle for the independence of this country. Men of their stature compel respect and if they are treated with cruelty, all those who respect them and have affection for them must necessarily suffer pain.

Allegations have been made by the Pakistan Government about the Khan Brothers and the Khudai Khidmatgars keeping contacts with us here, receiving money, and being encouraged by us to adopt a rebellious attitude towards Pakistan. These allegations have been made without any reference to us or enquiry from us. If you had enquired, we would have told you that these allegations are completely without foundation. Even before the partition took place, our advice to them was to accept it fully and to function in accordance with it. Since the partition there have been no contacts at all between us and the Khan brothers. Because of old friendship and comradeship I would have

[1] To Liaquat Ali Khan, JN Collection, NMML.

[2] The Khudai Khidmatgars refused to collaborate with the Frontier Muslim League and became the volunteer corps of the Pakistan People's Party which had been founded in March 1948 and which elected Abdul Ghaffar Khan as its President. The Frontier Government arrested on 15 June Ghaffar Khan and his son, Wali Khan, on charges of sedition, and sentenced them to three years' imprisonment. On 8 July 1948, the Government outlawed the Khudai Khidmatgars and imprisoned a thousand of them. The police opened fire on their demonstrations and gatherings and in one incident alone over a hundred were killed. Dr. Khan Saheb and Abdul Ghani were arrested soon after. With such repression unrest spread in Waziristan where the Pathans, while accepting Pakistan, sought autonomy.

liked to write to them and receive letters from them. But I refrained from writing as I thought this might lead to misunderstanding. Whether you believe it or not, I can assure you that there have been no contacts between them and us.

But contacts or no contacts, we cannot forget old friendship, nor can we remain unaffected that our old comrades should be subjected to unfair and harsh treatment. The accounts that reach me of the state of affairs in the Frontier Province amaze me, for this appears to be worse than at any time under British rule.[3]

You have often addressed me in regard to reports of persecution of Muslims in India. I do not know what source of information you may have. But I do know that the situation in India has improved beyond recognition and there is no persecution of Muslims anywhere in India. Petty incidents may occur in some places and they are dealt with immediately and sternly. I am happy to say that Hindu-Muslim relations in India have stabilized themselves after the shock of the events that followed partition, and that they are improving with marked rapidity. I have no apprehension on that score, though even so we keep vigilant.

I have denied in public and I wish to deny again in private that India has no aggressive intentions against Pakistan. It grieves me to see baseless reports made about conditions in India, or India's intention to be aggressive. The Pakistan press is full of these baseless reports put forward in a manner which is astonishing. One has the impression of a deliberate campaign being waged to worsen Indo-Pakistan relations and perhaps to bring about a conflict. So far as we are concerned, our policy is entirely opposed and we shall avoid conflict. All this, however, leads to distrust, ill will, fear and an excited state of mind. This is not a good background for any country.

I would repeat again that I am full of apprehension and am greatly concerned about the Khan brothers and the Khudai Khidmatgars. I am writing to you in my personal capacity and I am thinking of this problem not as a political one but as a human one. I trust that you will take this letter in the spirit in which it is written and will pay attention to the conditions in the Frontier Province, which cannot redound to the credit of Pakistan and which may well lead to very grave bitterness and the consequences of such bitterness.[4]

Yours sincerely,
Jawaharlal Nehru

[3] On 8 July 1948, the North West Frontier Province Government, by an ordinance, assumed extraordinary powers to deal with persons and organizations suspected of subversive activities. Indiscriminate arrests were made on the basis of false allegations.

[4] In his reply dated 15 November 1948, Liaquat Ali Khan stated that the action against the Khan brothers and the Khudai Khidmatgars by the local authorities had been taken "after the most careful consideration" and also having in view the internal security and integrity of Pakistan.

6

Kashmir Plebiscite[1]

Your telegram Nos. 249-D[2] and 255-D dated December 3rd received. Matter requires very careful consideration. Some of those I wish to consult out of Delhi. Hope to send you full reply on Tuesday.

2. Would like you to return as early as possible. You may convey our full reply to Commission and then return immediately. I have been terribly overworked not only because of various difficult problems but also Constituent Assembly and coming Congress session.

3. Meanwhile I am conveying to you my reaction for the present to all this business of Commission's talks and proposals. I am dissatisfied and disturbed at the way Commission and Security Council function and I dislike intensely being pushed about from position to position and asked to commit myself without anything being done by Pakistan. I am disgusted by the way representatives of Pakistan go on behaving in Paris and in India and yet both Commission and Security Council accept all this and even call us to the bar to answer charges and make vague commitments. Nothing is said about Pakistan's invasion or their subsequent behaviour in spite of findings of Commission. Throughout the period Commission was here and subsequently Pakistan has been carrying on aggression in Kashmir State pouring in men and supplies, infiltrating into new areas and going on far into Ladakh. We have no complaint because we are too decent to go on doing so all the time. When we met this aggression and stratagem of Pakistan's plans, then there is shouting and cursing and we are asked to explain why we did it. It seems to be forgotten that we are defending our people and our country against brutal and unscrupulous invaders. Zafrullah Khan[3] now threatens aggressive action. It must be made clear that if any such step is taken we shall meet it with all our strength. In view of these threats, any talk with Commission about plebiscite is completely unreal.

[1] Cable to G.S. Bajpai, New Delhi, 5 December 1948. V.K. Krishna Menon Papers, NMML. This cable was repeated to V.K. Krishna Menon.

[2] In this cable Bajpai enclosed the Commission's proposals of 3 December regarding a plebiscite and conveyed Josef Korbel's request that Jawaharlal Nehru consider them sympathetically.

[3] Zafrullah Khan M. was Foreign Minister of Pakistan, 1947–54.

4. Pakistan has been carrying on her vicious and indecent campaign against us and Kashmir Government. It is difficult for us to deal with people who behave in this way, while in private they try to be reasonable. We are not going to allow this kind of indecency in Kashmir.

5. Except for border areas and some sparsely populated mountain tracks, Kashmir is being governed by legal and constitutional government. Peaceful conditions prevail. Agrarian reforms being given effect to and development schemes undertaken. We are unable to understand or accept any suggestion of parity in treatment of Kashmir Government with Azad Kashmir or Pakistan. Indeed we do not propose to allow Pakistan to intervene in any way in Kashmir. We cannot barter away people of Kashmir who have trusted us and to whom we have pledged our honour, nor can we ignore Jammu and Kashmir Government which must have the final say in any matter affecting Kashmir.

6. It is bad enough for attempts to be made to settle intricate problems in Paris and by telegram. It is worse where we have hardly the chance to consult Kashmir Government.

7. It must be remembered that we have to keep in view dangerous aspects of every problem. In view of developments in China,[4] Ladakh assumes special importance. Chaotic conditions in Ladakh and north-east regions as were being produced by Pakistan are likely to lead to dangerous consequences. We cannot permit such developments.

8. We have made it clear right from the beginning that we cannot commit ourselves to any proposals without fullest discussion in India and we suggested that Commission might come here for the purpose. We are now presented with the progressively detailed scheme with all kinds of vague commitments which we must accept by telegram or else we are threatened with some unfavourable development. No responsible Government can tolerate such treatment at any time and more specially when it is the injured party which has suffered invasion and aggression.

9. In considering this matter and bona fides of Pakistan's attitude other matters have also to be kept in view. Pakistan's repeated attempts to bring Hyderabad before Security Council demonstrates its utter lack of bona fides and its venom and enmity against India. Evidence is forthcoming of their part secret intrigues with Hyderabad and their acceptance of large sums of money.

10. I shall let you have my detailed answer to proposals later. But I must make it clear that we are unable to agree to any step being taken regarding proposed plebiscite such as appointment of Plebiscite Administrator before

[4] The armies under Mao Zedong were increasingly successful and were only 25 miles away from Nanking, the capital, where in fact no civil government was functioning as Sun Fo, nominated Prime Minister, was unable to form a cabinet. Both Nanking and Shanghai were in the grip of a panic which had sent up prices sharply high and provoked a mass exodus of people to the south.

Parts I and II of Commission's resolution have been fully implemented. Nor can we agree to ceasefire unless every Pakistan soldier and tribesman withdraws. We are not going to trust Pakistan's word for anything and we are not going to commit ourselves to anything till Pakistan shows by its action that it is carrying out Commission's resolution.

7

Kashmir and the United States[1]

I confess that I am not at all satisfied with the memorandum[2] the US Ambassador gave to you conveying the views of the State Department in regard to the Kashmir issue and more especially the attitude India had taken. You have dealt with this matter fairly exhaustively in your conversation with the Ambassador.[3] I am inclined to think that it might be worthwhile sending some kind of a brief written reply.

The criticism made by US officials that we have unduly emphasized the legal and military security aspects of the problem, seems to me to proceed from a certain ignorance of or ignoring the whole basis and inception of this problem. As you have pointed out, we have not been legalistic at all and we have agreed to many things which may be said to have weakened our legal position. The basic fact is that Pakistan encouraged and helped the invasion of Kashmir and thus committed an act of aggression. It is not denied and it is inferentially admitted by the Commission that from any point of view, legal or moral, this was an act of aggression. Pakistan denied this and actually sent their own regular army within Kashmir State territory. When this could no longer be hidden,

[1] Note to Secretary-General, 10 August 1949. File No. 52/339/NGO-55, M.E.A.

[2] Loy W. Henderson submitted a memorandum on 9 August 1949 on behalf of the State Department expressing their concern about the slow progress of the truce agreement in Kashmir. "Stress on military security factors", the memorandum stated, "makes it appear that the Government of India lacks confidence in the United Nations' ability to implement a peaceful settlement of the dispute." It further alleged that the refusal of the Government of India, in connection with the Commission's truce proposals of 28 April, to permit the Commission prior to signing of the truce agreement to inform the Government of Pakistan of the Indian schedule of troop withdrawals reflected an emphasis on both security and legal aspects. The oversensitiveness from the Indian side was also said to indicate "the possibility of renewed hostility in Kashmir."

[3] The US memorandum was in response to Henderson's meeting with Bajpai on 29 July 1949. The meeting was held at the request of Bajpai who wanted to clarify the doubts of American officials that India was not acting in good faith regarding Kashmir and was endeavouring to avoid a plebiscite. Henderson emphasized the need for conciliatory attitude on the part of India and Pakistan Governments in solving the Kashmir problem as it was coming in the way of "effective economic assistance to India" from the United States.

they had to admit it. Both the legal and moral issues as well as questions of security become of high importance to us. There can be no decision about Kashmir to which we can agree unless this moral issue is disposed of.

As for security, we are not for the moment thinking in terms of some third power invading India or Pakistan. We are definitely thinking of the danger of Pakistan invading or helping to invade our territories. The fact that they have done so and have persisted in this invasion would be quite enough to justify our fears. Continuous press propaganda to this effect, unchecked by the Pakistan Government, and statements by responsible Pakistan ministers, continually referred to aggressive war. Right at the beginning, when we referred this matter to the UN Security Council we drew attention to this moral aspect as well as to the security aspect. No clear decision has been given to us on these issues. Even while the UN Commission was functioning, further invasion continued. The State Department says that they cannot believe that responsible statesmen in either India or Pakistan hold the disastrous view that their two countries will resort to war to resolve their differences. Certainly we do not wish to resort to war for this purpose. But the fact is that Pakistan has actually been carrying on war admittedly in our territory and threatens to continue it. This has been done in spite of the functioning of the UN Commission. It is not quite clear how we can rely for the security of Kashmir on the United Nations in these circumstances.

Partly conscious of this fact the UN Commission laid down in their resolution[4] that the Pakistan forces, regular and irregular, should leave Kashmir State territory. They further recognized the sovereignty of the Kashmir Government over the whole State. While these conversations were going on, Pakistan has not only increased its forces in Kashmir, but has trained and armed larger numbers of so-called 'Azad Kashmir' forces. These forces are a continuing threat to the security of Kashmir. No responsible statesman can view this prospect with equanimity or take any step which might leave Kashmir unguarded from these irregular armies of Pakistan or predatory bands encouraged by them.

The Ambassador's reference to the possibility of wholesale massacres in India and Pakistan seems to me completely unjustified. I do not think there is any such possibility. Is it suggested that because of this possibility, we should surrender to the threats of Pakistan and not only give up our legal and moral

---

[4] On 11 December 1948 proposals were put before the two governments and incorporated in the resolution of 5 January 1949. The new proposals accepted a free and impartial plebiscite; demanded that Pakistan should implement Part I & II of the Commission's resolution of 13 August; and said that the plebiscite administrator would deal only with the organization of the plebiscite. The term "freedom of speech" should not imply the right to play upon religious fanaticism or tend to disturb law and order; large-scale disarming and disbanding of the 'Azad Kashmir' forces should be accomplished and ordinary offenders not be regarded as political prisoners.

position but endanger the security of large numbers of people in Kashmir State who look to us for protection? It is certain that if we did so, there would be far greater upheavals both in Kashmir and elsewhere than if some other development took place.

We appreciate what the State Department says about their neutrality in this matter and their attempt to hold the balance even between India and Pakistan. We should, however, like to know if in the view of the State Department, legal and moral considerations have no particular weight and an invasion of friendly territory should be accepted as an accomplished fact. Do they consider that India and Pakistan are equally guilty in this matter? If not then subsequent developments have to be judged accordingly. Apart from legal and moral issues, the practical aspect also has great importance. Acceptance of aggression at any time and more especially in the present circumstances, means encouraging it for the future and has very far-reaching consequences. In India no government can stand if it failed in its primary duty to protect those who have looked up to it for protection and who have the legal and moral right to do so. It is then that upheavals might take place in India, which should be avoided.

8

Arbitration on Kashmir Issue[1]

8 September 1949

My dear Mr. President,

I greatly appreciate the friendly solicitude which prompted you to write and particularly welcome your frankness because it enables me to write with equal candour. Since India became independent, and the creation of Pakistan was part of the scheme of transfer of power by Great Britain, we in India have been conscious of the need for peace and cooperation between ourselves and Pakistan. One striking example of the genuineness of our desire to be friendly to Pakistan was the transfer to its Government of the equivalent of approximately 150 million dollars at a time when we knew that Pakistan was aiding and abetting the invasion of Jammu and Kashmir and might use this money to further this aggression against India. I could cite other instances but do not wish to overweigh this letter with detail.

Kashmir undoubtedly is a cause of acute tension between Pakistan and us. But, as we have already pointed out to your Ambassador, there are other causes as well, the root cause being the emotional climate of Pakistan whose people are being constantly encouraged by its Government and leaders to pursue a policy inspired by fear of and hatred towards India in the false belief that India seeks to destroy this new state. Apart from other considerations, it is not to India's interest to have any such aim. Her paramount need is peace in the world, of which the maintenance of friendly relations with her neighbours is an essential condition. In particular, the maintenance of such relations with Pakistan is of the greatest importance because of historical, geographic, economic and other factors.

You have referred to the inability of my Government and the Government of Pakistan to agree through negotiations with the assistance of the United Nations Commission on the terms of truce in Jammu and Kashmir. We have, since the Commission first visited this subcontinent last year, given manifold proof of active cooperation with that body. The last example was our readiness to discuss truce terms, under the auspices of the Commission, with representatives

[1] To Harry S. Truman. JN Collection, NMML.

of Pakistan. It was a matter of painful surprise to us that the Commission decided to abandon the idea of a conference, in our view primarily because Pakistan refused even to discuss some matters to which we attach importance, particularly the large-scale disbanding and disarming of the so-called 'Azad Kashmir' forces, a step to which, according to assurances given to us, the Commission has agreed. As we have repeatedly stated to the Commission, firm decisions to implement this assurance are a condition precedent to the withdrawal of our forces. Without satisfactory arrangements for large-scale disbanding and disarming of the 'Azad Kashmir' forces, the withdrawal of Indian forces will gravely imperil the security of the portion of the State held by us. And, unless there is this large-scale disbanding and disarming of the 'Azad Kashmir' forces, the conditions for a free and impartial plebiscite cannot come into being.

As regards the Commission's proposals for arbitration, I should like to state, at the outset, that India is not opposed to the principle of arbitration. Arbitration is, under Article 33(I) of the Charter of the United Nations, one of the methods of achieving a peaceful solution of a dispute which is likely to endanger the maintenance of international peace and security, and India is a firm believer in the principles embodied in the Charter. The reference to arbitration should, however, be on a precise and defined issue which, if settled by that method, will have the effect of creating conditions for ending a dispute that threatens international peace and security. The proposal for arbitration as presented to us by the Commission does not satisfy the necessary condition and we have found ourselves unable to accept it for reasons which are briefly set out below:

(1) According to the interpretation given to us, the Arbitrator would have the authority not only to arbitrate but would also be free to determine the points on which he should arbitrate. So far as the Government of India are aware, this procedure is novel and without precedent and could hardly be justified.

(2) The main difference between us and the Government of Pakistan is about the disbanding and disarming of the 'Azad Kashmir' forces. The Commission has given us an assurance that there is to be large-scale disbanding and disarming of these forces. If steps to implement the assurance are not taken immediately, it will be impossible for us, consistently with the necessity of safeguarding the portion of the Jammu and Kashmir State against a repetition of the horrors of the invasion of the valley in October 1947, to withdraw the bulk of our forces. Moreover, if there is to be no large-scale disbandment and disarming of the 'Azad Kashmir' forces, one of the essential conditions for holding a free and impartial plebiscite will not be satisfied. As we explained to the Commission's principal representative, Dr. Lozano, when he discussed with us the draft of what subsequently became the

Commission's Resolution of 5th January 1949, with such a large number of members of the 'Azad Kashmir' forces under arms, it will be impossible for a substantial number of persons normally resident in the so-called 'Azad Kashmir' area, who are not refugees, to express their opinion freely regarding the future of the state.[2] The large-scale disbanding and disarming of the 'Azad Kashmir' forces is, therefore, not a matter of arbitration but for affirmative and immediate decision.

I would also like to draw your attention to the fact that since the assurance regarding the disbanding and disarming of 'Azad Kashmir' forces was given to us by the Commission, the number of these forces has been increased by Pakistan considerably. For all practical purposes, they form a part of the Pakistan Army. The mere withdrawal of the regular Pakistan Army from the territory of Jammu and Kashmir state will thus leave a large and well-trained army, under Pakistan's leadership, behind in the state territory. That will be contrary to the basis of the Resolution of the UN Commission of the 13th August 1948, and will create a new situation full of peril to the state. It is for this reason that we have laid stress on the interdependence of the phasing of the withdrawal of their forces from the State with the disbanding and disarming of the 'Azad Kashmir' forces.

In conclusion, I wish to assure you that India does not wish the Kashmir or any other dispute to be settled by the sword. She will always be ready to consider a solution by any method that would lead to a peaceful settlement of the entire dispute.

May I ask you, Mr. President, to accept the best wishes of the Government and people of India for the great nation of which you are the chosen head and, for yourself, the assurance of my most friendly sentiments and my highest consideration.

Yours sincerely,
Jawaharlal Nehru

---

[2] For aide memoire of the meeting with Alfredo Lozano and Eric Colban from 20 to 22 December 1948, see SWJN (II Series), Vol. 9, pp. 219–24.

9

Plight of Minorities[1]

New Delhi, 20 March 1950

My dear Attlee,

You have enough burdens to carry and I have no desire to add to them. And yet I feel that I should write to you and put you in touch with recent happenings in India in regard to Indo-Pakistan relations. A great deal of importance has been attached in the past two years or more to the Kashmir affair, and undoubtedly, it was and is important. From our point of view, it could have been settled long ago and much more easily, if it had been dealt with properly, but unfortunately, some of the basic facts of the situation were repeatedly ignored and we managed to get more and more entangled in details.

However, it is not about Kashmir that I am writing, but about something which is far more important and dangerous in its consequences. This is the Bengal situation, as it has arisen in the course of the past three months. I am writing to you not with the object of asking you to do anything in this matter, but rather to keep you informed of the background and the present state of affairs. I feel I owe this to you.

We accepted Pakistan and the partition of India with great reluctance, but nevertheless firmly, in the hope that this would give us peace and an opportunity of devoting ourselves peacefully to the many problems that we had to face. We hoped that Pakistan would do likewise and, as old-time passions cooled, there would progressively be more and more cooperation between India and Pakistan. Immediately after partition came the terrible killings and the huge migrations in the Punjab. More than ten million people were uprooted from Pakistan and India and a legacy of passion and hatred was left by these terrible happenings. That was a time of great trial for us. Fortunately for us we had Gandhiji with us then and, largely because of him, we stopped this madness from spreading much beyond the Punjab. And then we set ourselves to find another equilibrium and to heal the deep wounds that had been caused.

Partition left huge minorities on either side, though larger in India than Pakistan. It was assumed, as the very basis of partition, and assurances to this

[1] To C.R. Attlee. V.K. Krishna Menon Papers, NMML.

effect were freely given, that the minorities on both sides would be given full protection. We hoped that after the tremendous upheaval in the Punjab to which I have referred, the minorities would find a secure and honourable place in both countries. We tried our utmost in India, both in theory and practice, to give the Muslim minority the same position and opportunity as others had. Muslims occupied and occupy the highest places in the state, memberships of the Central and Provincial Cabinets, Governorships, Ambassadorships, Federal Court Judgeships, High Court Judgeships, high executives offices and the like. They were and are members of our political parties like the Congress. In Pakistan the Hindus did not and do not occupy any important place and cannot even be members of the Muslim League Party which controlled the Government. That party itself is communal and thus there is not even a chance for a non-Muslim to influence its work or decisions.

As a result of the migrations after the partition, the Frontier Province and West Punjab were almost completely cleared of Hindus and Sikhs. East Punjab was also almost completely cleared of Muslims. But we made a great effort and brought back many Muslims to the East Punjab and I believe there are over 100,000 of them there now. Many thousands of Muslims, who had gone away from Delhi, also returned. It was Gandhiji's policy that we should try to bring back as many people as possible.

The provinces of Sind and East Bengal were not affected, to any great extent, by those early migrations. But conditions in both these provinces continued to be such that non-Muslims felt unhappy there and saw no chance of fitting into the new order. About 27 per cent of the population of Sind were Hindus, who were largely professional and business people—lawyers, doctors, teachers, engineers, merchants, etc. In East Bengal about a third of the population, numbering 16 million were Hindus. Many people believe that the Pakistan Government deliberately followed a policy in both Sind and East Bengal of squeezing out the Hindus. Whether they did so or not, many of their minor officials functioned in that way, and there was the continuous pressure from the Muslim refugees who had come from India, mainly from the East Punjab. Even apart from this, the whole conception of the state in Pakistan, that is a theocratic Islamic state, was such that non-Muslims could only have some kind of inferior position in it. The atmosphere was oppressive and religious bigotry and hatred of the Hindus were the prevailing sentiments.

And so, a gradual migration of the Hindus started from Sind and East Bengal. Occasionally some incident took place, which accelerated this process. This went on till Sind had practically no Hindu population left, except for the sweepers, who were not permitted to leave by the Government there, as their services were required. Sind was thus added to West Punjab and the Frontier Province as an area where the minority problem had practically been solved by the elimination of the minority.

Meanwhile, the gradual migration of Hindus from East Bengal also continued, in spite of our attempts to stop it. We discouraged it in every way, because the prospect of over 10 million people coming over was frightening. Any such migration would have involved terrible misery for vast numbers of human beings and would have created almost insoluble problems. It would have upset the whole economy and social set-up of India and it would have created difficulties in the way of the nearly 40 million Muslims who are our countrymen in India. In spite of our efforts, people came over. Ultimately, about the middle of 1949, this stream lessened and almost stopped for a while. By then nearly two million non-Muslims had come over from East to West Bengal.

During this period, there was no major migration from India to Pakistan. Some Muslims undoubtedly went over. But a very much larger number came back to India, because they found conditions here secure and satisfactory. Hardly any Hindu who came over from Pakistan went back.

This was the state of affairs, when sometime last December certain incidents happened in Khulna district in East Bengal which led to an influx of refugees into Calcutta. The stories that these refugees brought led to trouble in Calcutta, and a kind of chain reaction was started. Immediately after, widespread trouble took place in Dacca, Barisal, Bakarganj, Feni, Chittagong and many other places in East Bengal. It was rather extraordinary how this trouble took place more or less at the same time in a number of widely separated areas of East Bengal. There was heavy killing, arson and looting and abduction of women and forcible conversion. Bengal is peculiarly susceptible to any attacks on women and forced conversions. Tension increased greatly and incidents occurred in some parts of the U.P. and Bombay also. Early in March, tribal people in some parts of Assam, incited by some refugees from East Bengal, swept down over the Muslim population of that area and committed widespread arson and drove about 40,000 Muslims across the border into East Pakistan. Since then there has been no major incident either in Pakistan or India. But minor incidents, such as occasional stabbing or arson, have occurred.

I do not wish to draw a balance-sheet of evil deeds, as it serves little purpose to do so and the information at our disposal is still far from complete. But my own belief is, from such facts as we possess, that the killing in East Pakistan was far greater. Also that there was no rape or abduction of women or forced conversions in West Bengal. On both sides passions have been roused and there is a sense of insecurity both in East and West Bengal. In East Bengal it may be said with some assurance that hardly a single Hindu wants to remain there. For some time after the disturbances, travel was limited and obstructions were placed in the way of people coming from East to West Bengal. The result of this was to increase panic and a feeling of being in a trap. Much as we dislike big migrations, we felt that it was essential to open the door to these people coming over and to ask the Pakistan Government to give full protection during travel. This protection was necessary, because some horrible train outrages had occurred, when large numbers of people were killed in railway trains. As soon as train services and steamers were resumed, though on a restricted scale the migrations started. Over 200,000 Hindus have come over from East Bengal, usually with little or nothing even in the shape of personal belongings. At the same time over 100,000 Muslims have left West Bengal for East. Probably most of these are permanent residents of East Bengal who worked in Calcutta and the neighbourhood. Some of the Muslims left Calcutta for other parts of India, like the U.P. and Bihar. These migrations continue and are limited only by the transport available.

I have recently visited Calcutta twice and seen the stream of refugees collecting in camps and other places. I have also seen, at close quarters, the intense emotion and anger of the people in Calcutta. It must be remembered that a very large number of people in East and West Bengal are related to each other and thus any tragic happening has an intimate significance for people on either side. We are trying to do our best for the refugees and to lessen the panic and the anger. We have felt that it is better to allow people to come to West Bengal or to go away from it without let or hindrance, in order to remove a feeling of being shut in, as if in a trap. I do not know how long this migration will continue. We have controlled the situation wherever any trouble has occurred and punished the trouble-makers. We are trying to help Muslims who have suffered. Meanwhile, reports reach us of petty incidents happening and of people travelling from East Pakistan to India being harassed in many ways and deprived of their belongings. Large numbers of Hindus in camps in East Bengal are in great distress because adequate food is not supplied.

I made various proposals to the Prime Minister of Pakistan, including one for a joint visit by him and me to both East and West Bengal, also about joint commissions of the Governments of East and West Bengal, inclusive of Ministers, visiting the affected areas. Neither of these proposals was accepted. We then discussed the desirability of issuing some kind of a joint declaration. On the whole we agreed to most of its terms; the most important part of these was free movement of people from one country to another. But such a declaration has no great importance now, because people have lost all faith in declarations and assurances.

We have to face today a problem of colossal magnitude and complexity. We can hardly think in terms of vast transfers of population which may last years before they are completed and which would upset completely the economy of both countries. It would be a continuing evil, with refugees spreading all over the country carrying their tales of woe and becoming sources of further infection. At the same time we cannot think of preventing people, who find it impossible to remain in Pakistan, seeking succour from us. The problem has many aspects, but perhaps the most important is the psychological one. That derives, I think, from that unfortunate conception of an Islamic theocratic state which Pakistan professes.[2] That in itself prevents minorities in Pakistan from settling down and tension and trouble continue. We cannot spend the rest of our lives in facing this and in meeting year after year huge migrations of people. We cannot also just ignore what happens to our kith and kin on the other side. There can be no peace or equilibrium in India till the fullest protection and opportunity are given to the minorities both in Pakistan and India. We have set ourselves to do that and I think, by and large, we have succeeded, though occasionally we have failed. At any rate our policy is clear. On the Pakistan side, their policy influenced by the idea of a theocratic state, itself tends to push out the non-conformists. As these people come to India, they create difficulties for our Muslim countrymen.

My colleagues and I have done our utmost to face this difficult situation and to stand our ground against heavy pressure for some kind of direct action aimed at protecting the non-Muslim minority in East Bengal. How long we can stand that pressure will depend on happenings in East Pakistan. So long as the mentality that led to the creation of Pakistan, namely the hatred of the Hindus and India lasts and expresses itself in violence or in continued pressures on the Hindu minority, so long will there be not only no easing of the tension between the two countries but an ever-present risk of sudden conflict. It is my considered opinion that the fair and just treatment of the minorities in both Pakistan and India is far more important for the maintenance of peace than the settlement of the Kashmir dispute. Unlike Kashmir, this problem of the minorities involves no dispute over territory. And yet, as large numbers go over from one side to another, questions of having additional territory for them are put to us.

What we need for a satisfactory solution is to put our conceptions of the state on a right basis and to put an end to distrust and hate. India, as I have repeatedly said, has no designs upon the territorial integrity or the independence of Pakistan. We seek nothing more than to be left free to develop in our own way and to do so in friendship and peace with Pakistan. But Pakistan continues to be influenced by that communal spirit which led to its creation and which influences still its policy even towards its non-Muslim minority. If there is to be real peace between us, this mentality must come to an end.

This has become a long letter and I must apologize for having taken up so much of your time. I have written with no desire to blame Pakistan or to throw upon other shoulders the responsibility which, in the last resort, only the two Governments directly concerned must bear. The purpose of this letter is to give

[2] Attlee in his reply of 29 March agreed about the difficulty caused by theocratic states and wrote that Europe was full of examples. "We have two on our doorstep Eire and Northern Ireland." He emphasized that toleration was the essence of democracy.

you, as objectively as I can, an account of recent happenings and their effect on Indo-Pakistan relations. We are thoroughly alive to the perils that face us and are anxious to avert them. But success in this extremely difficult task cannot be achieved by our efforts alone.[3]

Yours sincerely,
Jawaharlal Nehru

[3] Attlee replied that in the general tense situation some incident might precipitate a serious conflict whose results in the world situation would be incalculable. He expressed concern for India and wrote that Labour's policy towards India had made a very strong appeal to the majority of people in Britain and "we have gained strength to go forward in other parts of the Commonwealth and Empire". But he feared that this policy would be attacked if it went wrong in the subcontinent as the British—being practical people—judged by results.

10

At the Edge of a Precipice[1]

I beg to place on the Table of the House an Agreement signed by the Prime Minister of Pakistan and by me on behalf of our respective Governments. This Agreement[2] was signed on Saturday afternoon, after discussions lasting for a full week. I shall not read out this Agreement, as copies of it are going to be given to Members of the House. I shall only refer to some of its salient features and I earnestly hope that this House and the country will give full support to this Agreement and to the policy which underlies it. We have had many agreements in the past and we have had many breaches of agreements also. I think I may say with justice that this particular Agreement, both in regard to its contents and its timing, has a peculiar significance and importance. Our future depends upon the measure of compliance in Pakistan and India.

During the past weeks and months, the whole country, and more particularly Bengal, have faced tragedy and disaster and it is not surprising that people's mind should have been excited and passion let loose. Yet the disaster that came and the tragedy that overwhelmed vast numbers of people appeared to be a prelude to an even greater catastrophe. As I sat, hour after hour, discussing these matters of grave import with the Prime Minister of Pakistan, I saw an unending stream of unhappy, fear-stricken refugees, uprooted from their homes, facing a dark and unknown future. I experienced their sorrow and misery and I prayed for guidance as to how this could be stopped. All the ideals I had stood for since fate and circumstance pushed me into public affairs, appeared to fade away and a sense of utter nakedness came to me. Was it for this that we had laboured through the years? Was it for this that we had had the high privilege of discipleship of the Father of the Nation?

We have to grapple with material facts, but even more so we have to grapple with immaterial things in people's minds and hearts. We have to deal with fear and passion and prejudice. As the House knows, scenes of horror have been enacted in many places. News of this had unnerved and angered many people.

[1] Jawaharlal Nehru's statement in Parliament on the Agreement signed between India and Pakistan, 10 April 1950. *Parliamentary Debates*, Vol. IV, Part II, 1950, pp. 2675–8.

[2] For the text of the Agreement between India and Pakistan see *Parliamentary Debates*, Vol. IV, Part II, 1950, pp. 2678–80.

The time had come when we had to make a final effort to stop this rot or to drift inevitably towards catastrophe. Formal state communications were too slow and too barren of results. It became essential that there should be some personal touch and a frank discussion of the situation and the problems, and an earnest attempt to solve them.

I invited the Prime Minister of Pakistan to come to Delhi and he was good enough to accept this invitation. For seven days we discussed the Bengal situation as well as many other matters which have poisoned the relations of India and Pakistan. Both of us were burdened with a heavy sense of responsibility for the fate of our countries and of many millions therein was involved in these discussions. The matter was not merely a political one or an economic one, but essentially a human problem in which human lives and human suffering were involved in a measure that was almost unthinkable. The problem was not a mere Bengal one but essentially all-India. Indeed its repercussions went far beyond the borders of India and Pakistan. Because of this, the world took deep interest in this meeting and its result.

The first part of the Agreement deals with certain fundamental democratic rights of all citizens and nationals and it is declared therein that minorities must have complete equality of citizenship, irrespective of religion, a full sense of security in respect of life, culture, property and personal honour, freedom of movement within each country, freedom of occupation, speech and worship, equal opportunity to participate in the public life of the country, to hold political or other office, and to serve in the country's civil and armed forces.

All this has been laid down, as the House knows, in our Constitution and it was not necessary for us to repeat it. It became necessary however to say so, because doubts had arisen in people's minds, and these doubts had been frequently expressed, that the Pakistan state was based on a certain communal idea and therefore could not give equality of citizenship to its minorities. The Prime Minister of Pakistan repudiated this with force and said that in the constitution they were framing, it was their intention to lay down these democratic rights, as we had done in our constitution. Indeed this had been stated already in the Objectives Resolution adopted by the Constituent Assembly of Pakistan. He assured me that his Government believed in the modern conception of a democratic state and that indeed there could be no other form of state under modern conditions. This assurance is embodied in Part A of the Agreement.

We have called our state a secular state, and there has been some misunderstanding of this, as if it was something opposed to religion or morality. Some misguided people in our country have even demanded something in the nature of a communal state here. But so far as this House is concerned and the vast majority of the people in our country, we have definitely adopted the idea of a secular state and we intend to adhere to it in full measure. This does not mean that religion ceases to be an important factor in the private life of the individual.

It means that the state and religion are not tied up together. It simply means the repetition of the cardinal doctrine of modern democratic practice, that is the separation of the state from religion and the full protection of every religion. The Prime Minister of Pakistan has made it clear in the Agreement that his state is based on these modern democratic ideas.

Part B of the Agreement deals more especially with the migrants from East and West Bengal, Assam and Tripura. We have ensured in this that these migrants should have freedom of movement and protection in transit and that they shall be free to remove as much of their moveable personal effects, household goods and personal jewellery, as they may wish to take with them; also a fixed quantity of cash. Further that the migrant may deposit his or her jewellery or cash in a bank and facilities would be provided to him or her for their transfer to him or her, subject, as regards cash, to exchange regulations.

There has been much complaint about harassment by customs authorities and others. In order to prevent this, it has been agreed that liaison officers of the other Government shall be posted at these Customs Offices.

While freedom of movement from one country to another has been assured, it has been laid down that migrants can return to their homes when they choose. If they return by the end of this year, that is 31st December 1950, they will be entitled to the restoration of their immoveable property, house or land. In the case of a migrant who decides not to return, ownership of all immoveable property shall continue to vest in him and he shall have unrestricted right to dispose it off by sale, exchange or otherwise. Arrangements will be made for trustees to hold this property and to recover rent and necessary legislation will be passed to enable this to be done.

This last provision, that is the retention of the ownership of immoveable property and the right to sell or exchange it, will apply to all the migrants who have left East Bengal or West Bengal or Assam since the 15th August 1947. Thus this provision will include those 15 lakhs of persons who have come away from East Bengal in the course of the last two years and a half. This provision will also include the migrants who have left Bihar for East Bengal owing to communal disturbances.

Part C of the Agreement deals with the restoration of normal conditions, the punishment of all those who are found guilty, collective fines and special courts. It deals also with the setting up of agencies for the recovery of abducted women and for the non-recognition of forced conversion and the punishment of people who are found guilty of converting people forcibly. I should like specially to mention to the House that it is laid down that any conversion effected during a period of communal disturbance shall be deemed to be a forced conversion.

It is proposed to set up Commissions of Enquiry to report on the causes and extent of the recent disturbances and to make recommendations with a view to preventing them in future. Further, it is stated that prompt and effective steps will be taken to prevent dissemination of news and mischievous opinion calculated to rouse communal passion. Propaganda in either country directed against the territorial integrity of the other or purporting to incite war between them will also not be permitted.

All this is specially applicable to the affected areas in East and West Bengal and Assam. But some of it is of general application to any part of Pakistan or India.

Each Government has decided to depute a Minister to remain in these areas. These Central Ministers will be charged with the responsibility to help in restoring confidence, so that the refugees may return to their homes and in generally supervising the implementation of this Agreement.

It is also proposed to include in the Cabinets of East Bengal and West Bengal a representative of the minority community.

In order to assist in the implementation of this Agreement it has been further decided to set up Minority Commissions in East Bengal, West Bengal and Assam. The Central Ministers will have the right to attend and participate in any of the meetings of any Commission. Either of them may call for a joint meeting of any two Minority Commissions. These Commissions will be charged with the implementation of this Agreement and to report from time to time thereon.

In the event of the Central Ministers supporting any recommendation, they will be normally given effect to. If there is disagreement between the two Central Ministers, the matter shall be referred to the Prime Ministers of India and Pakistan who shall either resolve it themselves or determine the agency and procedure by which it will be resolved.

This, in brief, is the substance of the Agreement that has been arrived at. I think it may be said with justice that this Agreement should bring immediately a certain relief from the tension that has persisted for some time. The problem of Bengal and Assam will not be solved by this Agreement alone, but for millions of people there it will not only bring some immediate relief but also a ray of hope for the future. It depends, on the two Governments and the peoples of Pakistan and India as to how far that ray can be extended into the full flood of the light of the sun.

The problem before us has many aspects, but perhaps the most important is the psychological and human aspect. Conditions have been created which make it difficult, if not impossible, for people to live in their homelands and so vast numbers of them have preferred to leave everything they possessed and go to distant places rather than live always with insecurity and fear as their companions. Unless this fear and insecurity are removed completely and normal civilized conditions of life prevail, this problem will not be solved in spite of all agreements. An agreement is a step, and a step only, in a certain direction. It has to be followed up by many other steps and more particularly by a change in the very conditions of life. By this Agreement the Governments of Pakistan and India have pledged themselves to take those other steps also and I feel sure that this House will give its full support to this great enterprise, which means so much to millions of our countrymen. To the people of East and West Bengal and Assam, I would make a special appeal, for they have suffered most from these tragic upheavals and they are concerned most with the implementation of this Agreement. The whole of India has not only sympathized with them but has shown that sympathy in many ways. Their cause has become the cause of the whole country. So far as the refugees are concerned, the Government of India has undertaken unlimited responsibilities for their welfare. But while we shall undoubtedly look after, to the best of our ability, those unhappy persons who come as refugees and try to rehabilitate them, it is clear that this is no satisfactory solution of this great problem. The only solution is to produce proper conditions to live in their homelands, wherever they may be and to put an end to the barbarism and inhuman behaviour that we have witnessed during these past weeks. If one thing is certain, it is this: that we shall not serve our people or our country or the cause of humanity by encouraging private violence and inhuman behaviour. That is the way of degradation and weakening of the nation.

The brief course of our history as an independent nation has been bedevilled by our strained relations with Pakistan and the conflicts that have resulted from them. Those conflicts led to this disaster in Bengal and we came on the verge of something far greater even than that. We have stopped ourselves at that edge of a precipice and turned our backs to it. That by itself is, I submit, a definite gain. It is now up to us, as it is up to the Government and people of Pakistan, to live up to our professions and to face all our problems with sanity and goodwill and the fixed determination to put an end to the vicious atmosphere that has surrounded us for these two-and-a-half years.

11

The Basis for Conflict[1]

Unfortunately, the passions and manoeuvres that led to the partition did not die away and subsequent events rather added to them. It is said that Kashmir is the basic difficulty which comes in the way of cooperative relations between India and Pakistan. It would be more correct to say that the problem of Kashmir is the resultant of that basic inner conflict between the two countries. India stands for a secular state and for freedom of its component parts to live their autonomous lives. Pakistan continues to be a communal state, which, by the very nature of its objectives and ideology, is aggressive in its outlook. Such an ideology appears strange in the world today and it is difficult to conceive of a modern state which makes a large number of its citizens feel that they are inferior citizens and cannot be treated as equals.

In India there are some people who in their unwisdom and lack of vision represent the communal policy of Pakistan in reverse. In doing so, they support that policy and weaken the basic conception of the Indian state. They have even stated that they want to put an end to the partition. This is the height of folly. Fortunately such people are few and have little influence, and our state policy, as well as the wishes of the great majority of our people, are quite clear on this subject. We desire no ending of the partition for that can only bring infinite trouble to all concerned. This has been repeatedly stated and must be clearly affirmed again, so that there remains no shadow of doubt about it.

In Pakistan it is the state policy that represents the old two-nation theory and the same narrow communalism which the Muslim League did. While we have no desire to interfere with the inner workings of Pakistan, we cannot ignore the effect of this on millions of people in Pakistan and indirectly in India. It is a disruptive and subversive policy.

In East Pakistan and West Bengal a very grave situation arose early in 1950.[2] Fortunately an agreement arrived at with the Prime Minister of Pakistan

[1] Report to AICC, 6 July 1951. JN Collection, NMML. Excerpts.

[2] Reports of alleged ill-treatment of Hindus in certain districts of East Pakistan led to communal disorders in a number of districts in West Bengal from January 1950. Then followed riots in Calcutta and Dhaka. The situation was finally controlled by the signing of the Delhi Agreement between Nehru and Liaquat Ali Khan on 8 April 1950.

was of great help in resolving that immediate crisis. That, of course, was no solution of the basic problem. But it brought relief to millions of people and vast numbers of migrants returned to their original homes. Nevertheless, the fact remains that the position of the minority community in Eastern Pakistan (in Western Pakistan it hardly exists) is one of peculiar difficulty. The middle-class elements, which were the backbone of education and trade and the professions, have practically been driven out, and the others remain full of fear and apprehension about their future. Recently, the flow of non-Muslim migrants from Eastern Pakistan to West Bengal has increased substantially and created a grave problem.

Kashmir has been wrongly looked upon as a prize for India or Pakistan. People seem to forget that Kashmir is not a commodity for sale or to be bartered. It has an individual existence and its people must be the final arbiters of their future. It is here today that a struggle is being fought, not in the battlefield, but in the minds of men. That struggle started many years before partition. As the communal movement grew in India under the leadership of the Muslim League, and the two-nation theory was propounded, attempts were made to capture this beautiful valley of Kashmir by the proponents of that theory. They failed then and Kashmir developed a strong nationalist movement with a certain ideology which was socially advanced. The National Conference of Kashmir led this movement and it found common ground in many matters with the National Congress and the Indian States People's movement. So, in the thirties and in the forties, the link of common ideals and the bond of comradeship in a common cause bound us together, whether we were Hindus or Muslims or Sikhs or others. It was natural, therefore, for the people of Kashmir to resist later the narrow communalism of Pakistan which sought to thrust itself by violence and force upon them. It was natural and inevitable for the people of India to stand by them in their agony.

Thus this question of Kashmir is of deep significance to India as it is to Pakistan. But its significance is felt most of all by the people of Kashmir who wish to live their lives according to the ideology and nationalist feeling that they have themselves developed. During the past three-and-a-half years of conflict and continuous tension, it is surprising to note the progress that the State of Jammu and Kashmir has made. In some matters, such as agrarian legislation,[3] it has gone ahead of India, and brought about a change in the economy of the great majority of people, which is truly revolutionary. How can the people of

[3] On 13 July 1950, the Kashmir Government enacted the Abolition of Big Landed Estates Act, 1950, which made individual holdings of more than 182 *kanals* (about 23 acres) illegal, the rest being transferred to peasant-tillers who would be turned into peasant-proprietors, paying their revenue directly to the Government. The Distressed Debtors' Relief Act was passed in 1950 and Debt Conciliation Boards were established to relieve the debtors of their indebtedness in case the principal, and 50 per cent interest, had already been paid.

this state, with their socially advanced ideology, look forward except with dismay towards the communal, reactionary and authoritarian regime of Pakistan. India's position in regard to Kashmir has been repeatedly and firmly stated and we stand by it.

In this connection our minds naturally go to one of the finest men that India has produced, a great leader in our struggle for freedom and a man whose whole life was dedicated to this struggle and to the service of the common man. This man is Abdul Ghaffar Khan. He and his brave comrades continue their lives in prison in Pakistan year after year, even though it is said that freedom has come to their country. This is not only significant but also symbolic of the type of freedom which awaits brave and freedom-loving spirits in Pakistan.

It is not Kashmir, therefore, but rather a much deeper conflict that comes in the way of friendly relations between India and Pakistan and the situation is a grave one. We cannot give up the basic ideals which we have held so long and on which the whole conception of our state is founded. We cannot encourage anything which breaks up the national unity of India. We cannot submit to a continuation of the old policy of disintegration and aggression. This must be clearly understood. We realize the necessity of friendly relations with Pakistan and we shall continue to strive for them, but that friendship can only come if the spirit of aggression is given up by Pakistan.

Plate 1

Plate 2: With defence personnel

Plate 3: With Chairman Mao Tse-tung of China, Peking, 21 October 1954

Plate 4: With Albert Einstein at Princeton, New Jersey, 5 November 1949

Plate 5: With Indira Gandhi

Plate 6: With Queen Elizabeth II, New Delhi, 26 January 1961

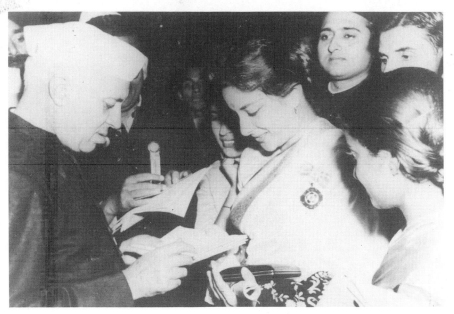

Plate 7: With Nargis

Plate 8: On horseback as Prime Minister

12

Military Confrontation[1]

This morning's paper contained a statement by the Prime Minister of Pakistan, Mr. Liaquat Ali Khan, in which he accused India of thinking in terms of aggression on Pakistan and of amassing her troops on Pakistan's borders and of doing many other things which he did not appear to like.[2]

It is a gross falsehood for anyone to suggest that India has any intention to attack Pakistan or any other country. There is no country and no government in the world which does not abhor the idea of war as much as India. As evidence of this we had demobilized a considerable section of our army last year,[3] and we had hoped that this would have some effect on Pakistan. Instead of this Pakistan has been adding to her defence forces feverishly and, what is much worse, there has been a continuous, intensive and vicious propaganda for war in Pakistan during the last six months and more.[4] Hardly a day goes by when the Pakistan newspapers do not demand war against India. Responsible leaders of Pakistan, including Ministers in Government demand war. I do not know of any other state where such propaganda is being carried on for war anywhere else at any time. We have repeatedly drawn attention to this of the Pakistan Government and at the United Nations. Yet this has continued. Either the Pakistan Government are responsible for it and encouraging it or are incapable of checking it.

During the last month a number of aggressive raids have taken place on Indian Union territory in Kashmir State from Pakistan. We have drawn the

[1] Speech at a public meeting, Bangalore, 16 July 1951. AIR tapes. Extracts.

[2] On 15 July 1951, Liaquat Ali Khan told a press conference at Karachi that 90 per cent of the Indian Army had been concentrated within striking distance of the borders of West and East Pakistan, constituting a grave threat to Pakistan's security, the interests of neighbourly relations between the two countries and to international peace. He said that he had asked Jawaharlal Nehru to remove this threat and had also informed the Security Council of this development.

[3] India had reduced its army by 52,000 in 1950.

[4] Preparations for organized raids and sabotage in Indian Union territory had been made in Pakistan and armed forces in both West and East Pakistan, massed near the Indian frontiers had been augmented greatly. The Pakistan Government had asked factories in Pakistan to stock coal for six months' consumption. It had also enjoined on its fighting personnel not to ask for leave.

attention of the United Nations to this also.[5] We know also that organized preparations for raids and sabotage in the Indian Union territory have taken place from Pakistan. My Government would have been failing in their duty if they did not take adequate measures to meet this grave situation. We are taking all such measures. On no account will India attack Pakistan but if Pakistan indulges in any aggression against India in any part of her territory this will be met adequately. We want to make this perfectly clear.

It is intolerable for continuous propaganda for *jehad* to be carried out in Pakistan, month after month without check or hindrance, and then for the Prime Minister of Pakistan to tell us that India is at fault and that he wants good neighbourly relations with India. We want good neighbourly relations but not at the price of aggression, insult and calumny and continuous threat of war. Mr Liaquat Ali Khan refers to a "no-war declaration."[6] It was we who suggested it repeatedly and pressed for it and yet this was rejected by Pakistan on flimsy grounds repeatedly.[7] As I have said, we reduced our army last year I should like to know whether the defence forces of Pakistan were reduced or increased during the past year. I should like to know whether these forces have not been added to greatly in both western and eastern Pakistan and if they are not amassed near the borders of Indian territory.

We are engaged today in preparation for the most colossal democratic election in history. Only a day or two ago the Congress party finalized the manifesto for these elections after open discussions in which we re-emphasised the need for peace and friendly relations with all our neighbours including Pakistan.[8] We agree that the maintenance of a peaceful atmosphere is desirable. We have done our utmost for this.

The answer from Pakistan has been the cry of *jehad* and threat of war. It ill becomes the Prime Minister of Pakistan to talk of good neighbourly relations or of peace when his Government, his ministers and his newspapers, and many

[5] On 5 July 1951, the Government of India drew the attention of the Security Council to three incidents which took place on Indian territory between 23 and 26 June 1951. Two Indian soldiers were killed in Jammu Province, 800 yards inside the ceasefire line. One Indian soldier had been killed and three wounded when patrols were fired on shortly after in the same area. Three more Indians were killed when patrols were fired on in the Titwal area. In addition, Pakistani forces also opened fire on two occasions on the Indian patrols in the Uri area.

[6] Liaquat Ali Khan had recently suggested a five-point peace package: the withdrawal of troops to normal peace-time stations; a reaffirmation that the Kashmir issue would be decided by plebiscite and that all differences in this regard should be settled by the Security Council; the renunciation of the use of force for settlement of disputes; a reaffirmation that propaganda against the other country would not be permitted; and a no-war declaration.

[7] India had first proposed through diplomatic channels in December 1949, a joint 'No-War Declaration' by India and Pakistan.

[8] See Volume I, Chapter 5, pp. 367–71.

of his people are continually talking of war and preparing for it. I regret to have to say that the activities of British military advisers and officers and ex-officers in Pakistan have added greatly to the prevailing tension.

Mr. Liaquat Ali Khan has referred to Kashmir. He seems to forget that Pakistan's aggression still continues in Kashmir and that a part of Kashmir State territory, which is Indian Union territory, is still occupied by his troops. I have yet to learn under what law or equity this can be justified.

Meanwhile, the present game of raiding Indian territory from Pakistan continues. If this is Mr. Liaquat Ali Khan's idea of promoting a friendly atmosphere with a neighbour country it is not ours. I repeat that we shall commit no aggression on Pakistan on any account, but if Pakistan attacks any part of the Indian Union territory we shall repel this attack with all our strength.

13

Indo-Pak Situation[1]

New Delhi, 30 July 1951

My dear Dickie,

As you are naturally very interested in the rather critical situation that has arisen between India and Pakistan, I am giving you my appraisal of the latest situation. Personally, I do not think that there is any real chance of war. For one thing, there can be no sudden move and any attempt to do so will mean a big-scale war. That itself is a restraining factor. Secondly, there has been so much shouting about it and so much attention has been drawn to it that it is more difficult now to start shooting.

The contrast between Pakistan and India today is striking. In Pakistan they are having blackouts, A.R.P., all kinds of volunteers enrolled, defence days, people writing their names with blood to affirm their determination, and so on and so forth. At public gatherings cries are raised: "On to India. Let us conquer India". The whole thing is so infantile, and yet there are elements of tragedy in it. In India there is not the slightest difference in our normal lives and practically no excitement whatever. There is no talk of blackouts or A.R.P. or any other defence measures, civil or military. Except for the fact that we sent our Armoured Division across the two rivers of the Punjab and made some other minor dispositions, we have done nothing else. We did not shout about this. Why did we send this Armoured Division across the rivers? As I have told you, there has been a continuous call for jehad in Pakistan and the press has been full of it for many months past. We had definitely decided to reduce our army by 100,000 this year. We had decided also to send away our Armoured Division from Meerut to Jhansi, where there are better quarters. Jhansi is of course much further away from the frontier and we were told it would take an extra month for it to move up to the frontier from there. Then we became slightly anxious. There was the daily propaganda in Pakistan, there were statements by ministers there, there were rather serious raids into Kashmir, and there was information received by us that there was an organized plan for a big-scale and sudden attack in Kashmir in order to achieve some quick and substantial result. We also got

[1] To Lord Mountbatten, JN Collection, NMML. Excerpts.

evidence of attempts being made by people from Pakistan to commit sabotage on a big-scale in the valley. We had actually reduced our forces in Kashmir very considerably. We had left many important points very thinly protected. Our army people told us that they were not in a position to ensure safety. The story was that immediately Graham went away, there would be this attack. This was supported by all kinds of odd bits of information that we got from Pakistan.

What were we to do? We were told that if we wanted to send our Armoured Division to the Punjab border, it would take some six weeks to do it properly. There are two rivers to cross in the Punjab with narrow bridges. This business of crossing the rivers took time. If, by any chance, those bridges were destroyed, then it would become exceedingly difficult to cross the rivers at all. This was too grave a risk to run and so we decided, very reluctantly, to cancel our orders for the transfer of the Armoured Division to Jhansi and send it instead to East Punjab across those rivers. I do not see how any government could have acted otherwise. Indeed I felt sure that our lack of proper defence on our frontiers would itself be an invitation for an attack. So we sent these troops there and there they will remain till we are assured that there is no danger.

As a matter of fact, normally the main concentrations of Pakistan troops are always near the Indian border from Rawalpindi, Sialkot, Jhelum to Lahore. We have not shouted about this. They can attack us suddenly and without notice, as they can attack parts of Kashmir, because they are right near. Indeed the question arises whether normally we can leave our frontier inadequately guarded. In the old days, as you know, most of the Indian army was concentrated in or near the North West Frontier. But in any event, it seems to us fantastic that we should be asked to withdraw our troops from the border when this raging, tearing campaign for war is going on in Pakistan.

We have reacted very calmly to this and I must say that our people, both in the Punjab and in Delhi, have also shown no excitement. The only thing that is rather alarming is the new exodus of Hindus from East Bengal to West Bengal. Between one and two thousand come daily. These belong to the real agricultural classes who had stuck there till now in spite of provocation. They are leaving their lands either because of fear or because conditions have become intolerable or because of both.

Western Pakistan was practically cleared of non-Muslims from 1947 onwards. Out of millions there, only a few thousand remain, mostly the scheduled classes. I am not referring to the major migrations from August or October 1947, but to the subsequent squeezing out of Hindus from Sind which took place later. This process took place more slowly in East Bengal. It became very rapid last year when I had the Agreement with Liaquat Ali Khan. This Agreement had a good effect and many people went back. Now for the last six weeks, this has started again and it is increasing in volume. There is no counter-movement on any big scale. Many people think that ultimately, all or nearly all the Hindus of East Pakistan will be driven out. This means 11 or 12 millions of people. Even if this number is reduced to half, it is terrific. What are we to do with them, and imagine the reactions of this process.

I am a little tired of receiving from and sending long messages to Liaquat Ali Khan. I am afraid I have come to the conclusion that most of the leaders of Pakistan are crooked in their dealings. Yet, of course, I shall continue because there is no other way. . . .

Kingsley Martin[2] is of course a good friend, but he has an extraordinary capacity for getting muddled. His thinking about India recently has been far from straight, probably because his correspondents here are not particularly intelligent. I do not know who they are. I regret I do not agree with him about Kashmir. I think this business would have been long over more or less to the satisfaction of the parties concerned, if there had not been a continuous instigation of Pakistan by the authorities and the press in England and of course of the USA. I have been amazed to read much that has been written in the British press about Kashmir. There has been so much venom and anger in it. It is evident that the UK Government as well as the USA Government and their press had long ago decided that Kashmir should go to Pakistan and they are greatly disappointed that we do not fall in with their wishes. In this matter, as in some others, no arguments are needed or are helpful when one starts with the wrong premises and the wrong convictions. I have not a shadow of doubt that the people of Kashmir proper are overwhelmingly with Sheikh Abdullah. Apart from everything else, his land reforms have made a great change. The difference between the valley of Kashmir, etc., and the 'Azad Kashmir' areas is tremendous. On the one hand, there is a progressive, autonomous and well-running government, which has shown quite substantial results in many ways; on the other hand, there are backward and rather primitive conditions. Apart from anything else, this is a clear case of conflict between progress and reaction.

The Pakistan army has been rather shaken up by the conspiracy trials. Some of their own best officers are under trial. I think the case against them is greatly exaggerated. There was no question of their murdering anybody, but they were greatly worked up about what they considered the reactionary policies of their government. In fact one of their cries was that Pakistan was becoming a kind of joint colony of the UK and USA.

You refer to Auchinleck and Gracey.[3] Some days ago at Bangalore, I said that "the activities of British military advisers and officers and ex-officers in Pakistan have added greatly to the prevailing tension." Attlee has been answering questions about this in the House of Commons and has repudiated

[2] (1897–1969): editor, *New Statesman and Nation*, 1930–60.

[3] Mountbatten wrote that he had been worried about the warlike preparations between India and Pakistan. He had in a hand-written note to Attlee, told him that Gracey and Auchinleck were the two officers whom Jawaharlal Nehru had in mind.

the insinuation. As a matter of fact, I used moderate language. I did not accuse anyone of positive action. What I said was there was the reaction to these activities, which added to the tension. There is not a shadow of doubt about this. Regardless of the motives of anybody, the fact is that all our army officers are talking about it and feeling angry and the general public is referring to it.

When I said this, I had Auchinleck and Gracey in mind certainly, but I had much else in mind also. Pakistan and Karachi are full of British officers, military and civil. It is our misfortune that every one of them is bitterly anti-India. We receive constant reports of what they say in private and sometimes in semi-public. They attend Indo-Pakistan conferences over some particular issue. Almost invariably the British officer is more difficult than the Pakistan representatives at the conference. Our evacuee property problem might have been much nearer solution but for the fact that Moss[4] used to represent Pakistan at our conferences. Moss was the person who once sentenced me to four years for a speech. Many of those officers who had, according to us, a very bad record in India, were later absorbed by Pakistan and they have been more against us than any Pakistani can be.

I remember an Inter-Dominion Conference in Lahore, when Mudie was there. Liaquat Ali practically agreed to our propositions, when Mudie openly asked him not to give in. There was a luncheon interval and afterwards Liaquat Ali changed his attitude completely and the conference was a failure. Gracey, you will remember, was the person who advised the Pakistan Government early in 1948 to send their army inside Kashmir. Is it surprising that all this should create a powerful impression on the Indian mind? Many of our officers meet Pakistani officers on various occasions and they get on well together. But they tell us that when the British officers of Pakistan are there, then relations become stiff immediately.

The UN observers, many of whom are drawn from the US, are notoriously and sometimes openly against us. Part of the reason at least is that we are not supporting US policies elsewhere in the world. One of them referred to me in a private letter as "that prize bastard, Nehru, who comes in the way of a settlement." This is not conducive to our faith in the UN observers.

I wish people in England would realize that this Kashmir question is not a matter of territory or profit, at least so far as we are concerned. It is a matter of the most vital principle. If we accept the Pakistani thesis, which is supported by the UK Government, that Kashmir being Muslim must be presumed to go to Pakistan, then we give up every principle that we have stood for and make the position of 40 million Muslims of India very difficult. That does not mean that we should impose our will on Kashmir. But that does mean that the decision about Kashmir will have to be political and economic and not on the

---

[4] Eric Moss (1896-1981); joined Indian Civil Service, 1923; district magistrate and collector of Gorakhpur, 1940-42. He sentenced Nehru at Gorakhpur in 1940.

basis of religion. What Pakistan wants is to have an opportunity of bringing in all its religious bigotry and hatred into Kashmir, and thus having a kind of civil war all over the place which, it thinks, will bring it advantage. We are not going to permit that.

We are a little tired of the advice being given to us from time to time in minority language from the US and the UK. They seem to forget that we are not some little Central American Republic or some Balkan country which can be cowed down or won over by money. Even if we were a small country, that has not been our past.

There is a great deal of talk about the Indian army's presence in Kashmir and very little talk of the fact that the Pakistani army sits in Kashmir territory. The very first thing decided by the UN Commission was that the Pakistani army and auxiliaries should withdraw. Other steps followed. Well, they have not withdrawn and they have added to their strength and entrenched themselves. Whatever right there may or may not be in favour of the Indian army being there, there is not a shadow of justification for the Pakistani army to be in Kashmir territory.

14

Keeping Vigilant[1]

New Delhi, 1 August 1951

My dear Chief Minister,

In my last letter to you, I referred to the growing tension, almost amounting to a crisis, in Indo-Pakistan relations. Since then, there has been an exchange of telegrams between Mr. Liaquat Ali Khan and me.[2] These telegrams have been published in the newspapers and you must have seen them. In a sense, the critical situation has worsened because of the continuous warlike propaganda in Pakistan and their blackouts, civil defence measures, and the like.[3] On the other hand, it may be said to have rather stabilized itself, as people get used to a repetition of threats and hysterical utterances. I think it is generally recognized, even by those who have been unfriendly to us in the United Kingdom and elsewhere, that Pakistan has overshot the mark and its attention has been drawn to this.[4] The patent contrast of warlike Pakistan and peaceful India is too obvious not to be noticed by even the casual observer. Gradually it is sinking into the consciousness of outside observers that there is something wrong about the tumult and shouting in Pakistan.

But the fact remains that the situation is serious and we must be vigilant all the time and not be caught unawares. I think there is little chance of that

[1] To Chief Ministers. File No. 25(6)/1951, PMS. JN Collection, NMML.

[2] The developing crisis produced an exchange of telegrams between Nehru and Liaquat Ali Khan from 15 July to 11 August 1951. Jawaharlal Nehru in his cable to Liaquat Ali Khan on 24 July reaffirmed that nothing in the way of a plebiscite could possibly take place until Pakistan had "vacated its aggression" in Kashmir by withdrawing all forces from the disputed territory. "The question of Kashmir", Nehru said in another cable to Liaquat Ali Khan on 29 July 1951 "would have been decided peacefully long ago in accordance with the wishes of the people there had it not been "for the major fact that Pakistan first encouraged, and then actively took part in violent aggression against the State and its people." This offence against the norms of international behaviour should be set right.

[3] Trial blackouts were carried out in Lahore, Rawalpindi and Karachi between 23 July and 5 August 1951. By an ordinance promulgated on 26 July, the Pakistan Government assumed powers to prepare civil defence and take other precautionary measures including requisitioning of property and on 27 July, four battalions of the Pakistan National Guards were incorporated into the Pakistan army.

[4] On 30 July, Krishna Menon reported from London that "Pakistan has been repeatedly told that they are playing with fire and that the war and jehad talk is highly injurious."

happening, and it is because of this that I think the chances of war taking place are not great. In Pakistan, there is a full realization that we are earnest and there is no bluff about what we have done or said. We have been studiously moderate in our utterances, or at any rate, most of us, but there has been no lack of firmness about what we have said. We have sometimes been criticized for not taking special measures in regard to what is called civil defence. That is so. Civil defence measures become necessary in case of war, although some of them adopted in England at the time of the last War are inapplicable or of not much use in India in present circumstances. There is far too great a tendency for people to think in terms of imitating what was done in western countries during the Great War. But some such measures certainly would be necessary if war came. We have to decide whether we should take them as a precaution now or avoid them. I am quite clear that we should do nothing which leads to public excitement and an expectation of war. The harm that it does is far greater than the possible good it might do. It interferes with the normal life of the community, with trade and commerce, and tends to produce a psychosis, which Pakistan has been deliberately encouraging and which we wish to avoid. If, unfortunately, necessity drives us to some such recourse, we shall undoubtedly have to take such measures and take them speedily and efficiently. But for the present, all that is necessary is to be clear in our minds as to what may be required in an emergency, so that we might be prepared for it. No public steps should be taken.

Apart from defence preparations, involving the army, etc., the most important element in a conflict is the morale of the people. I am happy to tell you that the morale of our people, all over northern India, is excellent. There is not the least sign of panic or even of obvious excitement. This is not due to a lack of appreciation of the seriousness of the situation, but rather to the wish to avoid war, and to a feeling of calm strength that if danger comes, it will be faced without flinching and with confidence. Three days ago, I addressed a public meeting in Delhi. That was one of the most exhilarating experiences I have had. It was, of course, an open air meeting and a vast crowd, estimated at 200,000, had gathered. Throughout the meeting, it rained continuously, and sometimes heavily. And yet, that tremendous audience not only stood the rain but was cheerful throughout. I spoke to them about this serious situation and told them all what Pakistan was saying and doing and of the steps we had taken. I dealt with the situation as objectively and calmly as I could and I watched carefully the reaction of that great crowd. I have a sense of crowds, and of mass feeling and the reactions I got, pleased me. We have heard a great deal during past months about our internal troubles and disintegrating forces and the like in our public life. And yet, when I saw that vast multitude under most unfavourable circumstances, I had the consciousness of buoyant strength without any bluster. My comparison of the 'clenched fist' of Pakistan with the Asoka Chakra, our symbol of peace and righteousness, evoked the loudest applause.

I would therefore suggest to you to deal with the present situation in a way which demonstrates to the people that we are not in the slightest upset by it and that we are going to carry on our work in the normal way, and in effect better than the normal. We should, of course, keep wide awake and follow events carefully. We should have in our minds what we should do in case any particular emergency arises. But we should not do anything which might lead the public to think that war is on the doorstep. I do not, in fact, think that it is anywhere near. But I cannot and you cannot relax our vigilance.

As usual, we have received, and I suppose Pakistan has received also, communications from the UK and USA Governments, pointing out to us the dangers of the situation and stressing the need for peace. Good advice is always welcome though sometimes it may not be appropriate. Our desire for peace with Pakistan would not have arisen but for the policies pursued by the UK and USA Government in regard to the Kashmir dispute. They have consistently encouraged the intransigence of Pakistan. Is it surprising then that Pakistan, so encouraged, has gone far in the wrong direction?

Nothing has surprised me so much during the past months or even years than the deliberate policy pursued by the UK and USA Governments, in the Security Council of the UN and elsewhere, in regard to Kashmir. I hope I am not entirely incapable of taking an objective view of the situation. I have tried to do so and I cannot understand why some foreign countries should be so hostile to us in this matter. There must be some basic cause for it, which has little relation to the merits of the dispute. It is clear that long ago the UK and the USA Governments came to the conclusion that Kashmir must go to Pakistan. That had nothing to do with the merits of the case. Having come to that conclusion, naturally the policy they have pursued have been meant to further that objective. Why did they start with this premise? If we trace this, perhaps we will have to go back to pre-partition days when the British Government encouraged the Muslim League and separatism in India. We shall also have to go back and try to understand the policy of the UK, which led them to support feudal and reactionary regimes in the Middle East and sometimes even favour the idea of Pan-Islamism or an Islamic bloc. In the old days, this was against Czarist Russia. Later, Communist Russia became a major danger. Of course, there was oil in the Middle East and the routes to India and the Far East had to be protected. After the First World War, the whole of the vast area from Afghanistan to Turkey was more or less under British occupation and Mr. Winston Churchill even suggested the creation of a Middle Eastern Empire. But other developments took place. There was the new Soviet Russia, weak and facing a civil war, but nonetheless a power, with a new kind of strength. Kemal Ataturk[5] drove out the Allied occupation forces from Turkey and later defeated the Greek army, which was supported by the British. Reza

[5] Mustafa Kemal Pasha.

Shah Pahalvi[6] became dominant in Iran. In the Arab countries, all kinds of new situations arose. Iraq remained largely under British control.

Even so, the attempts to keep some kind of control of the Middle Eastern regions continued. It was little realized by the diplomats and the policy-makers of western countries that new and powerful forces were rising all over Asia and that they could not be dealt with in the old way, either by military pressure or financial inducement. It seems astonishing how lacking in awareness western nations have been and, to some extent, even are today, about these forces. They seem to think that their analysis of the situation is complete when they talk of the communist danger which must be met.[7] Undoubtedly, communist expansion must be met. But it cannot be met adequately with the support of reactionary and feudal regimes. It is there that European and American policies have failed. The US supported the reactionary Kuomintang regime in China and came to grief. Even now they support the remnants of that regime in Formosa.

It is in this context of Middle Eastern policy that one can fit in the old British policy in India, of encouraging separatism and ultimately building up of Pakistan. Pakistan was to become a part of this Middle Eastern Islamic bloc. It was not realized that while Islam is undoubtedly a great force, the new nationalisms of Asian countries were, on the political plane, a much greater force. India was and is considered very important, as it undoubtedly is. But there was no uncertainty about India's policy, as it followed an independent line of its own. Pakistan, for all its loud talk, was a much more pliable instrument and easy to control. Hence Pakistan was to be the centre of this Islamic block of nations in western Asia and it was through Pakistan that this block could be most easily controlled. It became important therefore to build up Pakistan for this purpose, both internally and externally. The vast and well-established publicity machine of the UK worked to this end. Pakistan publicity had little to do, because others did its work much more efficiently and thoroughly. All it had to do was to make clear that it would fit in with the general policies laid down for it. Inside Pakistan, there continued, both in the defence forces and the civil service, a considerable number of British officers, nearly all of them of the old colonial type. They influenced policies there and even day-to-day activities.

If Pakistan had to be built up, then it became necessary that Kashmir should go to Pakistan both to give it additional strength and so that the borderland touching the Soviet Union should be under control. Hence the basic policy of the UK in regard to Pakistan. This flows from the old policy and it

---

[6] (1877–1944); Prime Minister of Iran (Persia), 1923–25; Shah of Iran, 1925–41.

[7] On 20 July, George M. McGee, Assistant Secretary of State, told the Foreign Affairs Committee of the House of Representatives that the United States proposed to spend $540 million in military and economic aid to West Asia and Africa in view of the Soviet intentions to dominate that region.

is easy to justify it on the simple plea that Kashmir is predominantly Muslim and therefore it should go to Pakistan.

The USA did not have this background of Middle Eastern and Indian policies of the UK. But in such matters, they followed the UK's advice and lead. This was all the more easy because they felt with the UK, and perhaps even more so, that Pakistan was easy to keep within their sphere of influence in regard to wider policies, while India was an uncertain and possibly not reliable quantity in this regard. Because of this also, both the UK and the USA have been irritated with Afghanistan, which does not fit in with their idea of how Pakistan should develop, and have continually brought pressure to bear upon it to fall in line with Pakistan. Afghanistan has refused to do so and continues to be hostile to Pakistan because of the Pakhtoonistan issue.

This whole policy which the UK and the USA have pursued in varying degrees in Asia may meet with some success in some places and on some occasions. But it is basically misconceived, because it fails to take into consideration the major factor, that is the new urges that move masses of men and women in the different countries of Asia. In the Far East this policy has led to an impasse; in Iran it has created great difficulties for the UK. As I pointed out to you in my last letter, the oil dispute in Iran is but the outward manifestation of something much bigger.

I hope that the analysis I have made of the past and present policies will help us a little to understand the situation in relation to India, and especially Kashmir. We are often blamed for our propaganda and some of the criticism is no doubt justified. We are, of course, at the same time told to economize and not to waste money in foreign countries. We cannot have it both ways. As a matter of fact, Pakistan throws money about in foreign countries on its propaganda and uses many methods which we do not consider desirable. But, in the main, they have the benefit of vast propaganda machines of other countries which we do not and cannot have, if we pursue our independent policy. This is, of course, a simplified way of describing a complicated situation. In the final analysis, however, it is thoroughly understood in the UK as well as in the USA, that India counts far more than Pakistan.

There is another aspect of the situation which is perhaps not kept in mind by us as much as it ought to be. Our frequent declarations that we are a secular state are appreciated abroad and raise our credit. But they are not wholly believed in and it is often thought that a few leading personalities represent this viewpoint, and not the mass of the people or even many important organizations. This picture of India that most people abroad have had is that of a caste-ridden country split up into innumerable social compartments with large numbers of untouchables and the like. Our social habits are not understood and are disliked. We do not mix easily with people. We do not generally eat and drink with them, as Pakistanis do. And so there is a general feeling of dislike and distaste in regard to India. It is little realized here what great injuries to our credit abroad is done by the communal organizations of India, because they represent just the things which a western mind dislikes intensely and cannot understand. When these communal organizations attack openly the secular idea of the state this is supposed to represent a prevailing sentiment among Hindus especially and all our protestations about the secular state fail to convince. The recent inauguration of the Somnath temple,[8] with pomp and ceremony, has created a very bad impression abroad about India and her professions. Pakistan, of course, has taken full advantage of this and made it one of the principal planks of its propaganda.[9]

Thus, in our contacts and propaganda abroad, we have to contend against a positive, widespread and well-organized propaganda machine of great countries working for Pakistan and often against us; and on the other hand, in negative dislike and distaste for the social habits and many things that are observed in India. In addition to this, the money we spend in propaganda is strictly limited and trained persons with a full appreciation of historical trends and political issues are also not easy to find. Propaganda abroad is not merely a part of an efficient newspaperman but requires, in addition, other qualities.

I have mentioned the disabilities we suffer from abroad. There are advantages also and they are by no means negligible. The story of India's long struggle for freedom under Gandhiji has powerfully impressed the world and, more especially, the Asian countries as well as the people of Africa. That tradition and Gandhiji's name are tremendous assets. In the eyes of large numbers of people we have stood for certain principles and we have adopted a certain technique and policy which brought us success. Because of that, they still look to our country for a certain kind of lead and for advice based on experience. In the past, India was the chief example of the new colonialism and it was partly because of India that other countries also suffered subjection, because they lay on the route to India. Then India became a symbol of a struggle for freedom against that colonialism, carried on against great odds, without stooping to objectionable methods. In many ways we influenced the nationalist movements of other countries and they looked up to us. They still do so, to some extent. The independent policy that we have pursued in foreign affairs has helped to maintain that old tradition and to add to our credit abroad. Also the mere fact of our great potential resources, our geographical position, and the belief that we are destined to play an important role and perhaps make some difference in world affairs, adds to the respect which comes to us.

[8] On 11 May 1951 by President Rajendra Prasad.
[9] For example, on 12 May 1951, a resolution was passed at a public meeting in Karachi denouncing the renovations at the Somnath temple as an insult to Muslims and an act of aggression against Pakistan "as Junagadh is part of Pakistan's territory."

All these are valuable assets provided only that we ourselves maintain that old tradition, adhere to our principles and our independent policies. But it is not merely enough to repeat old truth and slogans. We have to live up to them. This is the great test for us. Unfortunately there are many people in the country who repeat those old principles and act in opposition to them. There are still others who denounce those principles and openly proclaim something entirely different. Whatever harm communalism may do in India, and it can do great harm because it is a disruptive and degrading force, the harm it does to India in other countries is tremendous. Immediately the high edifice that we have built up in their eyes begins to crack up and totter and we appear to them as narrow-minded bigots following social customs which nobody in the world understands or appreciates. We talk of high philosophies and our ancient greatness but act in narrow grooves and show intolerance to our neighbour. These are basic questions for us to keep in mind, for our future depends on the answer that we give to them.

Yours sincerely,
Jawaharlal Nehru

15

The Question of Plebiscite[1]

The House will remember that a few days ago I made a fairly lengthy statement[2] in this House about the affairs of Jammu and Kashmir State. . . .

For the last five years now we have been seized of this problem and it has been one of the heaviest burdens that the Government has had to carry. It has been a heavy burden, because the problem was a complicated one, a problem in which our saying 'aye' or 'nay' was not enough. Other factors were involved . . .

We have tried to fashion our action in regard to this problem, keeping in view always certain obligations and responsibilities that we had. What were those obligations and responsibilities? Number one: To protect and safeguard the territory of India from every invasion. That is the primary responsibility of the state. Secondly, to honour the pledge we gave to the people of Jammu and Kashmir State. And that pledge was a two-fold pledge. One was, again, to protect them from invasion and rape and loot and arson, and everything that accompanied that invasion. That was one part of the pledge. The second part of the pledge was unilaterally given by us that it will be for them to decide finally what their future is to be. That is the second obligation. The third was to honour the assurances we gave to the United Nations. And the fourth was to work for a peaceful settlement. That was no pledge to anybody, but it was the policy we have tried to pursue right from the beginning, because it is in the nature of things that we should pursue that policy being wedded to the ideals of peace. And apart from that it was necessary that we should do so because in this world, as I have just hinted to this House, we live, we appear to live, on the edge of a precipice, and one has to be very careful in taking any step which might perhaps make the world tumble over that precipice. . . .

Some friends have advised us to withdraw this matter from the United Nations. I am not quite sure if they have studied this subject or considered how it is possible to withdraw this, or any such matter from the United Nations. When the United Nations is seized of such a matter, it was seized of it at our

---

[1] Speech while moving the motion regarding Jammu and Kashmir State, 7 August 1952. *Parliamentary Debates,* (House of the People), Vol. IV, Part II, cols. 5775–85. Excerpts.

[2] For statement of 24 July 1952 see SWJN, Vol. 19 (II series), pp. 219–38.

instance. That is true, but if we had not moved the United Nations, others might have moved it and others can move it. It continues to be seized of it. If we said, "we withdraw from the United Nations", it would only be a sign of impatience and temper on our part without resulting in what perhaps some people hope. Therefore, the question of withdrawal from there does not arise, unless of course, this House wishes that we, the Government of India and the Union of India itself, withdraw from the United Nations and face all the consequences that it brings. . . .

Therefore, it would be wrong, I submit to this House, for us to do anything to weaken those beginnings of a world structure that we see, even though we may disagree with it, and even though we may sometimes criticize it, as we have done. Therefore, for these and other reasons, I do not understand this cry of our withdrawing this matter of Kashmir from the United Nations. It is not a question of withdrawing it from some law court to the other. This matter is not before the United Nations as a forum. It is before the nations of the world, whether they are united or disunited and whether they are a forum or not. It is an international matter. It is a matter in the minds of millions of men. How can you withdraw it from the minds of millions of men by some legal withdrawal or otherwise from some forum?

16

The Kashmir Policy[1]

New Delhi, 18 August 1953

My dear Bakshi,

The situation that you and we have to face is indeed a difficult one. Nobody ever thought that it would be easy, but certain new factors have made it even more difficult than we might have expected. We have now, with the experience gained, to think fully of our policy and line of action, keeping not only the immediate present in view but also the probabilities of tomorrow and the day after. After making some kind of appraisal of these future possible developments, we should mould our policy from now onwards accordingly. Naturally, nobody can speak with certainty about the future and we shall have to keep wide awake at every step. . . .

The situation in Kashmir and as between India and Pakistan has become a very dynamic and indeed an explosive one. It cannot be treated in a static way. We have to consider the various forces at work and, understanding them, try to fashion our policy so as to get the best advantage out of it. In particular, we have to look a little ahead and think of the future. Only then can we function satisfactorily in the present. Every course that we may adopt is beset with difficulties and risks. We cannot avoid them. We have to choose the lesser evil and we have to choose a path which not only promises the greatest advantage but is dignified and in keeping with our general policy.

As you know, Pakistan has behaved very wildly and hysterically during the last week or more. In fact there has been some reality in tales of war. A break of diplomatic relations was definitely talked about. It was odd that just at this time Mahomad Ali should have come here and that the people of Delhi should have given him an astonishingly warm welcome.[2] No one that I can remember has ever had such a tremendous welcome from Delhi, apart from Gandhiji. Obviously, this welcome was not particularly to an individual. It was due to a

---

[1] To Bakshi Ghulam Mohammad. JN Collection, NMML. Excerpts.

[2] The Prime Minister of Pakistan, Mahomad Ali and his wife, on their arrival at Delhi airport on the 16th evening, were greeted by a large crowd with enthuisiastic shouts of "Mahomad Ali *Zindabad*" (Long live Mahomad Ali) and "Pakistan *Zindabad*" (Long live Pakistan) and showered with garlands and flowers. At a civic reception accorded to him at the Red Fort

desire for peace and a settlement of various issues and it was due to a recognition that Mahomad Ali was honestly aiming at peace and settlement. The contrast between the wild outpouring of jehad, etc., in Pakistan and this wonderful welcome was extraordinary and significant.

This welcome has undoubtedly helped in creating a better atmosphere and it is not only right but also wise on our part to take advantage of this atmosphere. That will affect the Kashmir situation also to a great extent and ease many tensions. We have to think of our problems not only in the narrow governmental way, which of course we must, but also from the broader psychological point of view. We have to deal with masses of human beings and ultimately it is these masses who make a difference in a critical situation. We have to deal with foreigners whose weight can be cast for us or against us at a particular moment, and that also makes a difference.

You have a number of good ideas for the reform of the Kashmir administration for relieving the burdens on the poor. The sooner you give effect to them the better and we shall help you in that. But you will only succeed in doing that in the measure that tension is lessened. Otherwise, the atmosphere for constructive work will be absent and your energies will be absorbed by day-to-day difficulties. A lessening of tension between India and Pakistan will inevitably lessen tension internally in Kashmir and give you that chance of working which you must have.

Keeping all this in view, we have thought that we should take some slightly positive step in our talks with Mahomad Ali in regard to Kashmir. I think that this step should be our agreement to select a Plebiscite Administrator by some provisional date, say, the end of April next. That means about eight months from now. Meanwhile, we should agree to try our best to settle some of the preliminary problems that have confronted us with the UN. I do not want the UN to come into the picture at this stage, or, as far as possible, even at later stages. Also I want to make it clear that such a Plebiscite Administrator should come from a small and neutral country of Asia or Europe, not the big powers like America or England. After such a Plebiscite Administrator is selected and appointed (he would necessarily have to be appointed formally by the Kashmir Government), he will have his work cut out. It will be a difficult job which will take at the very minimum a year and probably nearly two years. That means that, before a possible plebiscite takes place, about two years from now will elapse or possibly more.

It is true that the appointment of a Plebiscite Administrator will somewhat create a disturbance in peoples' minds. On the other hand, not to say that we

---

on 19 August, Mahomad Ali was cheered lustily and repeatedly by a crowd of over 10,000 people who had gathered there defying heavy rain. He said on the occasion that the "capital of Republican India" had given him a "right royal reception" and acknowledged that never before had he received such a memorable welcome.

will take such a step next year will itself create a further disturbance and conditions will remain abnormal and difficult. In the balance therefore, it seems to us desirable that we should accept this position and take this step and thus lessen tension all round and then work to the best of our ability. That is the general line of our thinking; Ajit Prasad will develop this further.

It is important that whatever agreements we should arrive at with Mahomad Ali here should have your and your Government's full approval, publicly given. That will strengthen you and help you greatly. Any other line would obviously be harmful and would encourage your opponent. . . .

With all good wishes.

Yours sincerely,
Jawaharlal Nehru

17

Kashmir and Indo-Pak Relations[1]

Michael Brecher: Well, aside from the fact that Kashmir has legally acceded to India, what makes Kashmir so important to India? Does it have any implications for India's efforts to establish a secular state and to maintain communal harmony in this country?

Jawaharlal Nehru: Yes, that is probably the most important aspect of it. There is a sentimental aspect, not so important. Kashmir has been intimately connected with India, culturally and otherwise, for 2000 or 3000 years. It has been a great centre of Indian culture, it has been a great centre of Buddhist culture, it has been a great centre of Islamic culture. Probably in Kashmir more than anywhere else in India there has been less of what is called communal feeling, and Hindus and Muslims and others have very rarely quarrelled. And even if they have quarrelled, it has been of short duration. Their lives are generally more or less alike. Their culture is alike, their language, eating habits, and whatever goes to make a culture. And they have lived happily together even if there has been trouble in India. Now, we have never accepted, even when partition came to India, the two nation theory, that is, that the Hindus are one nation and the Muslims are another. If Muslims want to go out of India, that is a different matter, that is, a certain area of India votes itself out. But we did not accept it and, even if every Muslim says so—every Muslim did not say so—I say we cannot accept that because once we accept that nationality goes by religion, we break up our whole conception of India. India is a country with many religions. Maybe one is larger than the others, but there are fairly big religions here, any number of them. And, as in any other country, nationality has to be based on others factors, not on religion, of course giving freedom to various religions to function. Pakistan came into existence and a large number of Muslims decided that way when we accepted it. Many went there, and many Hindus came here. Nevertheless, thirty-five million Muslims remained in India. Today there are more Muslims in India than there are in West Pakistan.

MB: A fact that is generally unknown.

JN: Unknown, because Pakistan is in two bits. In Kashmir, even before the partition, there was, as you must know, a struggle for the mind and heart of

[1] *National Herald*, 2 November 1956.

Kashmir between the Muslim League and the national movement of Kashmir. We did not come into the picture then. Later, we came in, and the national movement of Kashmir deliberately rejected the Muslim League idea of the two-nation theory. That was before partition and, naturally, we welcomed it and we cooperated with them in the larger national movement. Then came the partition and the struggles in India. There were no troubles in Kashmir. And, when Kashmir joined India, both in the constitutional sense, through the Maharaja who had the right to do so, and in a popular sense through the organization, well, apart from political and other aspects, it was very important for us because it helped our thesis of nationalism not related to religion. If the contrary thesis were proved in Kashmir, it would affect somewhat—I don't say it would break up India—but it would have a powerful effect on the communal elements in India, both Hindu and Muslim. That is of extreme importance to us—that we don't, by taking some wrong step in Kashmir, create these terribly disruptive tendencies within India. . . .

MB: In view of the tragic aftermath of partition, Mr Prime Minister, in the form of communal riots, the Kashmir problem and other unresolved issues between India and Pakistan, is it visionary, do you think, to expect a genuine rapprochement between the two countries in the foreseeable future?

JN: Before I answer that question I shall say something about a related matter. Many people think and say that the Kashmir problem is a major problem which comes in the way of good relations between India and Pakistan. That is true, in a sense, but not basically true. What I mean is this: the Kashmir problem is a result of other conflicts between India and Pakistan, and even if the Kashmir problem were solved, well, not in a very friendly way, those basic conflicts would continue. If it were solved in a really friendly way, then, of course, it would help. But it is a friendly approach to the problem that is important, not a forcible solution, which gives rise to other problems.

MB: Yes, I think most people would agree but what are these basic conflicts?

JN: I should say, basically, they are ideological. And we go back again to what I was just talking about, this business of the two-nation theory, what is nationalism and all that. Also, I am sorry to refer to it, there is an unfortunate tendency—not of Muslims as such—but of some people, saying: 'We were the rulers of India before the British came, why shouldn't we again be rulers over India? We shall capture Delhi, we shall do this!' Of course, it is rather fantastic and nonsensical but this kind of thing produces action and reaction. I would also say that so far as the people of Pakistan and the people of India are concerned, they are in a much better and more friendly frame of mind today than they were some years ago at partition time. Conditions have improved very greatly. There really is hardly any prejudice against each other qua individuals or qua groups. As a nation the political issue may come up or some other issue, or they may be excited about some religious story. But when Indians go to Pakistan in groups, they are welcomed and embraced. When the Pakistanis come here they are welcomed and embraced too. You see, we have the same language, so many things in common.

MB: What effect, if any, Sir, does the current political crisis in Pakistan have on the establishment of more friendly relations between the two countries?

JN: It is difficult to answer. When a country is afraid, it is afraid of taking any step forward. . . .

MB: Because it doesn't feel that its own foundations are secure?

JN: Yes, it is afraid and they have fed themselves on fear of India. This is totally unjustified because under no circumstances whatever, even from the view of the narrowest national interests, do we wish to interfere in Pakistan. We want them to be an independent country and a flourishing country. It is not good for us to have a country that is not flourishing because that leads to political crisis, conflicts and all kinds of things. And when Pakistan, either politically or economically, grows weak, the fear element increases and is played upon deliberately, so as to divert people's attention. And one is always afraid of adventurist action, that kind of thing. It stops a natural development—it has taken place in the past—of more friendly relations between India and Pakistan.

18

The Good of Kashmiris[1]

The basic thing about Kashmir is the good of the people of Kashmir. Nothing else counts. The major consideration for me and for my Government has been the good of the people of Kashmir.

India agreed to a plebiscite in Kashmir on certain conditions and in a certain context of events. The very first condition was the withdrawal of Pakistan armies from the territory of Jammu and Kashmir State which they had invaded. They have not done it even today.

Any such conditional offer—it is strictly conditioned—cannot last for ever and ever. I have no doubt in my mind that under fair and peaceful conditions and in conditions where religious fanaticism is not allowed to play, a great number of people in Kashmir in a plebiscite would decide for India. We laid stress always that elections and plebiscite must be on political and economic issues. We do not want communal riots and call it a plebiscite. I do not want Kashmir in the name of plebiscite to be the scene of fratricidal war which will spread to India and upset the delicate balance that has been established here. If I am convinced that I have not honoured any international commitments in regard to Kashmir, I will either honour them or resign my Prime Ministership.

The recent developments in the Kashmir problem has caused us some concern and distress because it seems to us that this serious problem which has existed for nine years now was dealt with very casually recently in the Security Council. Wisdom requires something more than casual consideration and casual decision while dealing with the Kashmir problem with its strong emotional background in India and Pakistan involving all kinds of consequences.

I am not personally conscious of any double or separate standards. If I judge deliberately the Kashmir issue by any different standard, then I would stand condemned not only before other countries but before my own people and even more so before myself, my mind and heart. I think if moral issues come in, India stands rather well over the Kashmir matter. . . .

The question of Kashmir, apart from the good of the people of Kashmir, has become deeply significant, because if any wrong step is taken it will upset

[1] Speech at Island grounds, Madras, 31 January 1957. *National Herald*, 1 February 1957. Excerpts.

many things in the whole of India. We have never accepted it and we do not propose to accept the two nation theory on which Pakistan was founded.

The five-power resolution was pushed through and hustled through in the Security Council even without trying to understand what the position was.[2] The resolution was drafted and was in existence even before the Security Council took the trouble of hearing our representative. That is the most casual way of dealing with an important question.

There has been a great fuss made about Jammu and Kashmir framing its Constitution and its accession to India. So far as I remember the Pakistan Constitution has incorporated that part of Jammu and Kashmir which is under her control in her state. Nobody shouted about it. The Security Council did not move. When this fact was mentioned in the Security Council it did not apparently create any impression. It is an extraordinary thing that they did not apply their mind to it.

[2] The Anglo-US resolution of 30 March 1951 on the Kashmir issue envisaged (i) the possibility of not treating the state as a single entity for allocation of areas to the two countries; (ii) stationing of a UN force; and arbitration. Though India rejected the resolution, the Security Council adopted it and appointed Frank Graham as its representative to bring about an agreement between India and Pakistan on the procedure for demilitarization and a plebiscite.

19

Collective Aggression[1]

Are we wrong in assuming that the attitude of some countries in the Security Council is one of deliberate hostility to India, ignoring patent facts and past history and even forgetting the provisions of the Charter of the United Nations? We are told that the four-Power resolution was meant to lead to a just and fair solution and to prevent mistrust and misunderstanding. If that is so, then words have lost their meaning or there is a singularly perverse attempt not to understand what has happened or what is taking place now.

We have stated categorically that in no event will we allow any foreign forces to set foot on Indian territory and yet this has been mentioned in the four-Power resolution as a matter for consideration. I do not know if this is supposed to lessen tension or help in removing mistrust. We can only look upon it as an act of hostility to India and a breach of the UN Charter.

In the old days we struggled against the attempts of the British Government in India to encourage divisions and separations in India in order to weaken the Nationalist movement. We refused to accept the two-nation theory and later gave a secular basis to our Constitution. After independence we tried to forget the past and laboured not without success for close and friendly relations with the United Kingdom. Now the old past raises itself again and policies are being pursued by other countries which promote separation and imperial India. I am convinced that, as in the past, so now, peaceful settlement and friendly relations between India and Pakistan are possible if other countries do not interfere and encourage aggression and a policy of hatred, fanaticism and violence.

We are committed to peace and the ways of peace. But if our freedom is threatened, then we must protect it in every way open to us. While India talks of peaceful solutions, military aid flows into Pakistan and the campaign of hatred and threats of war continue to fill the air.

We have been told that the five-Power resolution is in furtherance of collective security. It looks to us perilously like collective aggression or collective approval of aggression.

[1] Press Interview aboard the PM's plane, 21 February 1957. *The Hindu*, 22 February 1957. Excerpts.

20

The Question of Kashmir[1]

Question: You said that Kashmir is part of India. When did it become part of India?

JN: A few hundred years ago, and Kashmir has always been in history for thousands of years, not always a political part but essentially a part of India and for hundreds of years a political part of India long before the British came. It has been essentially and culturally one of the biggest seats of Indian culture and learning. Some of the finest books about Indian history have been written in Kashmir. Then came the partition of India and certain rules were laid down about it. According to the rules, Kashmir acceded to India and became part of the Indian Union as an autonomous state of the Indian Union. That is why I say that Kashmir is as much a part of India as Calcutta or Bombay or Madras. At that time, Kashmir was invaded through Pakistan and later by Pakistan.

I don't think it is possible for anyone, even a Pakistani, to say that that was not aggression. There have been a number of cases of aggression in the world in the last ten years or so. There has been no case of clearer and more flagrant aggression than that of Pakistan over Kashmir territory which was Indian Union territory. Now, whatever legal or other arguments one may have about Kashmir in the Indian Union, there is not a shadow of doubt over the argument in favour of the presence of Pakistani troops in Kashmir and that aggression is continuing today. Over one-third of the territory of Jammu and Kashmir State is in the occupation of the Pakistan Army. My friend reminds me that one-third in population and nearly one-half in area, is in the possession of Pakistan. It is a continual aggression, and there is absolutely no kind of justification. One justification Pakistan has put forth is that the majority of the people in Kashmir are Muslims. Now, that is a very odd argument. Once we admit that states are formed on the basis of religion, we go back to the Middle Ages in Europe or elsewhere. It is an impossible argument. If we admit it, then, within India, as it is today after partition, there are 40 million Muslims. Are they Pakistani citizens and do they owe allegiance to Pakistan? Every village in India has Muslims. There are also Christians. Is there Christian nationality or Muslim nationality or Buddhist nationality, a Hindu nationality? It is an impossible

---

[1] *The Journal of the Indo-Japanese Association*, July-November 1957.

proposition so that the present position is that Kashmir is, undoubtedly, that is, legally speaking, historically speaking, constitutionally speaking, a part of India, a part of the Union of India.

The Jammu and Kashmir State has been invaded, aggression committed against it by Pakistani forces who are still continuing that aggression by occupying it. It is only a country like India, peacefully inclined, that would have stopped its military operations against the aggressor and decided to deal with it peacefully and I would be very much surprised if any other country would have done that. In keeping with our tradition of peace and what Mr. Gandhi taught us we were anxious to stop it. We stopped at cease-fire even though the aggression is continuing and we said that we would decide it by peaceful methods and that is our present policy. We wanted to decide every question by peaceful methods but that does not mean and will not mean our submission to aggression, and I regret that this fact has not been adequately appreciated by some of the great powers, who talk about aggression in other places. But in Kashmir where there is an act of international gangsterism they support it; I am astonished. I wish to make it perfectly clear that whatever happens we shall never submit to this aggression and it does not matter what powers in the wide world support it, we will not accept it. I think it is a shameful thing that this fact is slurred over. The matter is coming up before the Security Council in a day or two and I want, therefore, to make it perfectly clear that this fact is slurred over and privately we are told one thing and publicly another attitude is adopted by some of the great powers. I have seldom come across such double standards as in this matter of Kashmir. Here is the barest and the most blatant piece of aggression and continuing aggression and we are told: Oh, forget the past, forget the past, whatever it was. Well, well, if we are prepared to forget the past, the history of the world today will be very different from what it was.

Q: What is India's position in regard to the Pakistani offer to withdraw its troops from Kashmir if there is a United Nations-supervised plebiscite in both parts of the country?

JN: It is very kind of Pakistan to make offers. The only thing I want from Pakistan is to get out of Kashmir. I want no offers from them. They have been committing aggression on my territory, on India. What business have they to tell us that you do this or that? We will admit no foreign troops in any spot of India, one inch of India, it does not matter whatever happens to India and whether you call them United Nations troops or any other troops. I have just explained to you that we have had enough experience of foreign troops in India and come what will, we will not admit foreign troops. Just because Pakistan commits aggression, has it got the right to invite other troops to aid its aggression or to shelter its aggression? We admit no foreign troops, whether in Pakistani part of any other part. We will not be willing to do that. As for the national plebiscite, it is up to us to decide what is going to happen in Kashmir. We will have two elections in Kashmir—two general elections in our part of Kashmir. Pakistan talks about the plebiscite in Kashmir and for the last ten years it has not had any election in Pakistan itself. I think it is monstrous the way this question has been dealt with by some people without understanding.

IV

War, Peace
and Disarmament

1.	The Danger of War	387
2.	The Betrayal of Czechoslovakia	389
3.	The Hoax	392
4.	The New Europe	395
5.	World Politics	397
6.	Destiny	399
7.	Treachery and Betrayal	400
8.	A Crumbling World	401
9.	Nonviolence and the State	404
10.	India's Day of Reckoning	408
11.	The Death Dealer	417
12.	An Age of Crises	419
13.	The Role of the United Nations	421
14.	Ends and Means	425
15.	India's Policy	431
16.	Need for a Temper of Peace	432
17.	World Power Equilibrium	435
18.	The New Spirit of Asia	439

19. Formosa   442

20. World Peace and Cooperation   444

21. War, Peace and Cooperation   452

22. The International Scene   462

23. The Abolition of War   465

24. A Creeping Sickness   472

25. Weapons of Destruction   475

26. Disarmament   477

27. Solving World Problems   480

1

The Danger of War[1]

This session of the Indian National Congress will have many important resolutions to consider and adopt. But I venture to say that not one of them will be more important than the one I have just now placed before you.[2] It is important because any war nowadays is an international disaster. It must result in terrible slaughter and destruction. It must let loose, as the last war let loose, the floodgates of hatred and barbarism. When all countries and all nations are linked together and cannot be separately considered it is inconceivable, even if a war is fought outside the frontiers of India, that it would leave India untouched. We have intimate connection with any such war because it is likely to be fought very near our frontiers and India is very likely to be involved in it. If there is such a war, you and I will not sit peaceably holding our conferences and congresses. Indeed, we may ourselves hear the roaring of cannons and we may see bombshells dropping from aeroplanes upon our peaceful villages. It is very important also because such a war may result—I hope it does not result—in strengthening British imperialism to such an extent that it may make it more difficult for us to achieve freedom. It may remove for a generation or two our hope of freedom, so that in any event we cannot ignore any preparations for war or any chance of war.

[1] Speech at the A.I.C.C. Session, Madras, 26 December 1927. JN Papers, NMML. Excerpts.

[2] Jawaharlal Nehru had moved: "This Congress has noted with grave concern the extraordinary and extensive war preparations which the British Government is carrying on in India and in the Eastern Seas, specially in the North West Frontier of India. These preparations for war are not only calculated to strengthen the hold of British imperialism in India in order to strangle all attempts at freedom, but must result in hastening a disastrous war in which an attempt will be made to make India again a tool in the hands of foreign imperialists.

The Congress declares that the people of India have no quarrel with their neighbours and desire to live at peace with them, and assert their right to determine whether or not they will take part in any war.

The Congress demands that these war preparations be put an end to; and further declares that in the event of the British Government embarking on any warlike adventure and endeavouring to exploit India in it for the furtherance of their imperialist aims, it will be the duty of the people of India to refuse to take any part in such a war or to cooperate with them in any way whatsoever."

No man or woman can ignore it, least of all an Indian who desires to achieve freedom for his country. It is a well-known fact that all countries are preparing more or less for war. It is not only England; it is every country because in Europe today there is fear. Europe is in the grip of fear and out of fear comes hatred and out of that comes violence and barbarism. Every country in Europe hates every other country. The most feared and hated country in Europe is England. There is talk of disarmament, there is talk of peace. But those of you who have taken the trouble to study what has been happening at Geneva and elsewhere will realize that all this talk of disarmament is mere camouflage. Today, Europe is perhaps a greater powder magazine than it was in 1914 when the last Great War broke out. War has not broken out yet because all nations are exhausted. But all the seeds of war are present and at present in greater number than they were thirteen years ago. When you look at the Balkans, Poland, Italy, Czechoslovakia, Lithuania and Russia, everywhere there is preparation for war, and there is chance of war. Let us see what attitude the country with which we have most relations has taken in these war preparations and in this talk of peace and disarmament. We are specially interested in Britain's attitude. We have had in recent times various disarmament conferences at Geneva. There was a Naval Disarmament Conference also. But these conferences failed largely because Britain could not agree to proposals made by other countries. Indeed in the past Britain has definitely refused to accept the principle of compulsory arbitration with a little country like Switzerland because it may be giving up a dangerous principle! It has stood for its right to wage war without any reference to the League of Nations or to any other authority. At the last meeting of the Assembly of the League of Nations, Sir Austen Chamberlain made an extraordinary speech on behalf of England. He stated that he was not prepared to sacrifice the empire for the vague ideals of peace and disarmament of the League of Nations. For him the British Commonwealth was a greater thing than those ideals.

2

The Betrayal of Czechoslovakia[1]

As an Indian, intensely interested in Indian independence and world peace, I have followed recent developments in Czechoslovakia and Spain with anxious interest. For some years past the Indian National Congress has criticized and dissociated itself from British foreign policy, which has seemed to us consistently reactionary and anti-democratic, and an encouragement to fascist and Nazi aggresion.[2] Manchuria, Palestine, Abyssinia and Spain agitated the people of India. In Manchuria the foundations were laid for encouraging triumphant aggression, all covenants and rules of international law were ignored, and the League of Nations sabotaged. With all our sympathy and goodwill for the Jews in their distress in the face of fierce and inhuman persecution in Europe, we considered the struggle in Palestine as essentially a national struggle for freedom which was suppressed by violence by British imperialism in order to control the route to India. In Abyssinia there was a gross betrayal of a brave people. In Spain little was left undone in order to harass the Republic and encourage the insurgents. Having decided that the Spanish Government should lose, or was going to lose, the British Government tried in a variety of ways to hasten the desired end—and even insult, injury and gross humiliation by the insurgents were endured.

The fact that everywhere this policy has been a disastrous failure has not and does not discourage the British Government from continuing to pursue it. The consequences of the rape of Manchuria we see all around us in the world today. The problem of Palestine grows worse from day to day and violence counters violence and the Government uses ever-increasing military forces and coercion in an attempt to subdue a people. It is not always remembered that the problem is largely the creation of the British Government and it must shoulder the responsibility for much that has happened. Abyssinia, as your correspondent points out, still remains unconquered and is likely to remain so. In Spain a

[1] Letter to the editor, London, 8 September 1938. *Manchester Guardian*. Reprinted in *The Unity of India*, pp. 284–7.

[2] Britain had persuaded France to join her in an effort to induce Czechoslovakia to transfer to Germany all territories where more than 50 per cent of the population was German-speaking.

heroic people have refused to fall in with the wishes of the British Government and have demonstrated that they will not be and cannot be crushed or subdued.

It is a remarkable record of failure. And yet the government of Great Britain is not capable of learning from it and mending its ways. It pursues even more intensively its policy of encouraging aggression and giving support to General Franco and the fascist and the Nazi powers. No doubt it will carry on in this way if allowed to do so, till it puts an end to itself as well as the British Empire, for overriding every other consideration are its own class sympathies and leanings towards fascism. That would certainly be a service it will render, howsoever unwittingly, to the world, and I would be the last person to object to an ending of imperialism. But I am deeply concerned with the prospect of world war and it distresses me exceedingly to realize how British foreign policy is directly leading to war. It is true that Herr Hitler has the last and determining word in this matter but Herr Hitler's decision itself will largely depend on the British attitude. This attitude has so far done everything to encourage him and to bully and threaten Czechoslovakia. So if war comes, the British Government can have the satisfaction or otherwise of feeling that they were largely responsible for it, and the people of Britain, who have put this Government in power, can draw what comfort they can from this fact.

I had thought that nothing that this Government did could surprise me (unless it suddenly turned progressive and worked for peace). But I was mistaken. Recent developments in Czechoslovakia and the way the British Government, directly and through its mediators, has baulked and threatened the Czech Government at every turn has produced a feeling of nausea in me, and I have wondered exceedingly how any Englishman with any trace of liberal instincts or decency could tolerate this. I have wondered still more how those who talk so loudly of peace could have supported, actively or passively, this obvious invitation to war.

Recently, I spent some time in Czechoslovakia and came in contact with numerous people, both Czech and German. I returned full of admiration for the admirable temper of the Czech people and the democratic Germans who, in face of grave danger and unexampled bullying, kept calm and cheerful, eager to do everything to preserve peace, and yet fully determined to keep their independence. As events have shown they are prepared to go to extraordinary lengths to satisfy every minority claim and preserve peace but everybody knows that the question at issue is not a minority one. If it was the love of minority rights that moved people why do we not hear of the German minority in Italy or the minority in Poland? The question is one of power politics and the Nazi desire to break up the Czecho-Soviet alliance,[3] to put an end to the democratic

[3] By the Soviet-Czech treaty of May 1935, each country was committed to join France in aiding the other state if it were attacked. But during the Czech crisis of 1938 neither France nor the USSR came to the assistance of Czechoslovakia.

state in central Europe, to reach the Rumanian oil fields and wheat, and thus to dominate Europe. British policy has encouraged this and tried to weaken that democratic state.

In any event, we in India want no fascism or imperialism and we are more convinced than ever that both are closely akin and dangers to world peace and freedom. India resents British foreign policy and will be no party to it, and we shall endeavour with all our strength to sever the bond that unites us to this pillar of reaction. The British Government has given us the final and unanswerable argument for complete independence.

All our sympathies are with Czechoslovakia. If war comes, the British people, in spite of their pro-fascist government, will inevitably be dragged into war. But, even then, how will this government, with its openly expressed sympathies for fascist and Nazi aggression or a like government, advance the cause of democracy and freedom? So long as this Government endures, fascism will always be at the doorstep.

The people of India have no intention of submitting to any foreign decision on war. They alone can decide and certainly they will not accept the dictates of the British Government which they distrust utterly. India would willingly throw her entire weight on the side of democracy and freedom but we heard these words often enough twenty years ago and more. Only free and democratic countries can help in freedom and democracy elsewhere. If Britain is on the side of democracy then its first task is to eliminate the empire from India. That is the sequence of events in Indian eyes and to that sequence the people of India will adhere.

3

The Hoax[1]

The tragic drama of Europe unfolds itself and each day brings further news of the dismemberment of the continent as we have known it. Czechoslovakia, from being a proud free nation, a citadel of democracy, is now a country sunken in sorrow and despair, with hungry wolves snarling and biting off bits of it, and its shrunken remains becoming almost a colony of Nazi Germany. South-east Europe trembles and falls into the Nazi orbit. There is trouble brewing in Danzig[2] and in Alsace-Lorraine.[3] Violence reigns supreme in Europe. No other way seems to be known here except aggressive violence or pitiful surrender.

The great War cut up Europe anew; we have now a fresh refashioning of the continent. And how far this will go on no one can tell. The two redeeming features are Spain and Russia. In spite of all the attempts of the British and French Governments to betray Spain, the Spanish people have refused to surrender to fascism and Nazism, and today, in spite of daily bombardments from the air, they hold aloft the torch of freedom and democracy. And Russia stands as a mighty bulwark against advancing Nazism.

While Europe shakes and trembles, the British Parliament is on holiday and the Prime Minister of Britain goes afishing. And *The Times*, that thunderer of old, has sunk to the level of Herr Hitler's own well-managed press and sings his praises from day to day. Even *Punch*, that very respectable organ of the British middle classes, has lost its temper with *The Times*, and in biting satire of a *Times* leader writes:

> Justice alone was yielded
> And everyone was right;
> The sword that Hitler wielded
> Was not a sword of might.
> The French and we were tender
> And took the kindliest course;

[1] Signed article written at London, 15 October 1938. *National Herald*, 25 October 1938.

[2] After Munich, Germany demanded that Poland should cede Danzig and grant Germany extra-territorial routes across the corridor.

[3] After annexing the Sudetenland, Nazi Germany mounted its pressure on the Balkan states. Hitler also stepped up propaganda activities in Alsace-Lorraine.

The Czechs did not surrender
To fear nor yet to force.
Lord! I could write a column
Of tripe to this intent,
As smooth-as suave-as solemn-
If England gave up Kent.

What has been at the back of British foreign policy during these past months? To imagine that Mr. Chamberlain was suddenly faced with the alternative of war and a humiliating peace is to delude oneself. Even to the last moment he held the important cards in his hands and could have imposed an honourable peace, or, at any rate, a much better agreement. No one can doubt that this was certain a few weeks earlier. But every such policy involved a measure of cooperation with Russia and a certain opposition to Hitler. Mr. Chamberlain's fundamental policy has been opposed to both these developments and he has consistently followed it ever since he came to power. That policy has been one of encouraging the growth of the Nazi power and of functioning almost as an ally of Hitler.

In order to follow this policy more effectively, he got rid of a popular Foreign Secretary, Mr. Eden. He even removed the permanent head of the foreign office, Sir Robert Vansittart, and took to Sir Horace Wilson instead.[4] In Spain, he tried his utmost to smother and kill the republic. In Czechoslovakia, he brought all the strength of his government to support the Nazi ultimatums and threatened the Czechs with all manner of penalties if they did not submit. It was not merely that he deserted the Czechs in their time of need. The reality was far worse. By sending Lord Runciman to Prague and his consistent pressure he acted throughout as the faithful friend and ally of Herr Hitler. Mr. Churchill has pointed out that, but for Britain's intervention, the Czechs could have got, at any time previously, much better terms.

At no time had Mr. Chamberlain thought in terms of a conflict with Germany. Hence the total unpreparedness of Britain when the question became a vital one. Even the A.R.P. preparations were farcical and apparently meant to create panic. Mr. Chamberlain had decided to give a triumph to Herr Hitler and he succeeded in his endeavour, probably more than he intended.

The past is done with; it is the future that concerns us. But in understanding the future we must have a clear understanding of the motives of Mr. Chamberlain and the British Government. Munich has not changed them. These motives are to build up a fascist-imperialist alliance to resist democracy all over the world, and in particular to oppose the Soviet power. Ultimately to restrict democracy in England itself and to hold down the colonial countries with a firmer grip.

[4] (1882–1982); chief industrial adviser to Chamberlain's government; appointed adviser on foreign affairs, 1938; accompanied Chamberlain to Munich.

As events have turned out, such an alliance would be dominated by Nazi Germany with England as a junior partner. Mr. Chamberlain, no doubt, would have preferred to accept a subordinate position. The alternative of joining hands with Soviet Russia and the democratic forces is repugnant to him, for that would mean the end of Nazism and fascism and ultimately even imperialism.

A crisis is always a testing time for individuals and parties and their polities, and the recent crisis has at least done this much good that it has cleared the air and shown us where everyone stands. Mr. Chamberlain and his government are obvious partisans of fascism though the garb they would put round it would have a semi-democratic appearance. It is interesting to notice how the British Parliament is receding into the background. It does not meet when critical decisions have to be taken. It only gives its subsequent approval. The cabinet as such hardly counts or is even mentioned; it is the Prime Minister who counts. Mr. Chamberlain arrives at vital decisions without reference to his cabinet; he defends them in Parliament as his decisions, and not as the corporate decisions of the cabinet. Parliament gradually approximates to the Reichstag, and Mr. Chamberlain is beginning to fancy himself as a Fuehrer.

Attempts to suppress personal and civil liberty are becoming increasingly common in England, and the freedom of newspapers is interfered with. It is well known that, in case war had begun, the Government had decided to suppress all anti-government newspapers and criticism.

The Labour Party has not distinguished itself during the crisis. It played an utterly ineffective and insignificant role and did not seem to know its own mind when immediate and effective action was called for. One can expect little from it in the future, unless it changes greatly.

The pacifists behaved strangely. The more I see them here the more I realize the difference between them and the dynamic and effective pacifism of Gandhiji. Gandhiji has taught us not to submit to evil whatever the consequences, and he has shown us a way of combating evil. Pacifists in Europe seem to believe that the best way to avoid war is to submit to the threat of war. Thus, in effect, they become the supporters of those who threaten violence. Some pacifists here went to extraordinary lengths in their support of Herr Hitler in Czechoslovakia.

For me the greatest shock came from some of the leaders of the Independent Labour Party. They stood up in Parliament to praise Mr. Chamberlain as the man who brought peace. There was not a word of criticism of his policy. There was some vague talk of capitalism and socialism and of the evils of the present order. But in this grave crisis, their forces, such as they were, were lined with the serried ranks of the reactionaries. It was not surprising that they were cheered by the Conservatives.

I wondered at this strange exhibition of those who considered themselves revolutionaries and socialists. Words seem to have little meaning; it is after all action that counts, and it is by our actions that we shall be judged.

4

The New Europe[1]

A quick nemesis is overtaking those who played with war and peace during these fateful days and betrayed friends and allies. The assurance that war was not imminent, that this terrible danger was past for the time being at least, brought a tremendous feeling of relief to the millions. They rejoiced, as well they might, and Mr. Chamberlain basked in the sunshine of their joy. Was he not the peacemaker, who had averted war single-handed? And yet in his heart he knew, and his well-drilled battalions knew, that peace was a far-off dream, and a war more terrible than ever, and far more dangerous for them, was lurking round the corner. The price they had paid in dishonour and faithlessness gave neither peace nor respite, and so they cry now: "to arms, to arms, let us work night and day for the war that is to come."

For a looker-on, these days of destiny have been full of meaning. Yet none of us can be a looker-on when the fate of the world hangs in the balance. Emotions crowd upon us; hope and fear and anger and disgust come in quick succession. Vast forces, opposing ideals were in conflict and for some days we stood on the edge of a razor, precariously balancing ourselves on the fleeting moment and peering into the dark and unknown future.

Strange that at this hour of destiny a Chamberlain and a Daladier should occupy the centre of the stage. We had long heard and we knew that Britain's government was the poorest that she had had since the days of Lord North.[2] And now these very men had to face destiny and the world witnessed their crumpling up and their utter poverty of thought or deed. Was it their fault, one wondered, or the fault of the people whom they represented and who cheered them after a deed of shame and sorrow? Or was it the death-gasp of democracy itself, as we had known it?

For years we had been watching the gradual betrayal of democracy and all the fine ideals that had gone to build up a League of Nations. We protested and condemned British policy in Manchuria, in Abyssinia, in Spain, in China again. We could hardly believe that it could go further, that Britain and France

[1] *National Herald*, 18 October 1938.
[2] Guilford Frederick North (1732–1793); British Prime Minister, 1770–82; responsible for the policy which led to the loss of the American colonies.

would themselves murder the democracy which had been their pride for so long. Yet Mr. Chamberlain and his colleagues gave that stab to the plaudits of the multitude.

On Tuesday, fascism trembled and Hitler, for all his brave words, thought of retreat. The people of Germany began to move and hold peace demonstrations. In Italy there was trouble.[3] Then at that critical moment Mr. Chamberlain came to the rescue. On Thursday, the Munich agreement was signed and fascism was triumphant.

The old Europe was dead and a new continent was taking shape. Herr Hitler swept not only into Czechoslovakia with his legions but spread out his wings far and wide. Like a terrifying avalanche fascism spread and countries and governments bowed to its will. Poland, Lithuania, Hungary, the Balkans and Turkey, all looked to Berlin for orders. France became a second class power, England a junior partner in the fascist game. Hitler now dares to issue orders to England as to who should be her ministers and leaders, for no anti-fascists can be tolerated. England may not, except at the cost of provoking war with Germany, presume to have a Labour government.

And Czechoslovakia? "Farewell, France," she says, "Goodbye, England, you have crucified us to save yourselves. But do you imagine that even the price of dishonour and betrayal that you have paid will save you? Your time will come soon."

Most tragic and heart-rending of all is the fate of hundreds of thousands of German democrats handed over to Hitler.[4] Many have committed suicide, many have already been shot, and concentration camps grow up to swallow and engulf thousands.

France passes into the background, her noble history darkened by this last act of base betrayal. England is yet counted among the great powers, and she will not succumb totally without struggle. But her greatness has left her and under the Chamberlains and Halifaxes her decline is inevitable.

[3] Germany was alarmed by the mobilization of the British fleet which followed the British communique of 26 September 1938 that a German attack on Czechoslovakia would compel France, Britain and Russia to come to her assistance. Mussolini too cancelled orders of general mobilization.

[4] It was reported that Hitler had demanded the immediate surrender of all non-Nazi Sudetens including about ten thousand members of democratic organizations.

5

World Politics[1]

The past weeks of crisis and disaster have shaken all of us. War was happily avoided for the moment, but disaster came nevertheless, and the future is dark with possibilities of war and something that is worse even than war. When the time of trial came in Europe, it was obvious that the forces of real peace and progress were not strong enough or determined enough to face the issue. It was not the enemy abroad that mattered so much, but his reactionary allies at home, who stabbed democracy and freedom from behind, and thus ensured the triumph of brutal reaction and violence in Europe. Perhaps what moved these reactionary governments in so-called democratic countries was not fear of defeat but fear of victory, for that victory would have been a victory of real democracy and possibly an end of fascism in Europe. Fascism had to be kept going in Europe, whatever the cost. That cost has been a heavy one and the bills will continue to be presented and paid till disaster overwhelms the world.

The people of India have followed the course of events with pain and anguish. Wedded to peace and democratic freedom, they have watched the complete surrender of democracy with shock after shock of surprise. They have one consolation. They were no parties to this betrayal and dishonour.

Today the prestige of England and France has vanished utterly from all over the East. Unfortunately even the progressive forces in these countries have suffered because of this and little reliance is placed on them. When crisis came they failed to make any impression or even to pull together, and even now the lesson has not been sufficiently learnt. India feels more than ever that the only way to gain her objective of independence is by her own organized strength and will to freedom and through such sacrifices as may be demanded of her. She is not weak today; she is self-reliant and is conscious of her growing strength, and she has learnt not to surrender to evil or to superior physical might, whatever the consequences.

Inevitably we shall rely on ourselves but it is foolish to think on narrow national lines in this world today, especially after Munich and the triumphant domination of fascism over Europe. If the progressive forces all over the world

[1] London, 23 October 1938. *The Tribune* (London), 28 October 1938.

cannot even now pull together they are doomed to annihilation and they will deserve that doom. Therefore, India must necessarily pursue this policy of cooperation with those who stand for freedom. What will others do?

Recent events have demonstrated with startling clarity that freedom is indivisible. We cannot have a static world in which freedom and democracy exist in some parts and a total denial of freedom in other parts. There will be conflict between the two, for the very presence of democratic freedom is an offence in the eyes of fascism and ultimately undermines it. Therefore, there is a continuous attempt by fascism to put an end to free conditions in other countries. This can either be met by a policy of surrender and a progressive suppression of liberties or by facing aggression and refusing to submit to it. The policy of the British Government is apparently the former one, or perhaps this is not surrender for them as they themselves approve of fascism. This simply cannot be the policy of those who care for freedom and democracy. What are these to do?

"To resist is to conquer" is the slogan of the Spanish Republic and they have lived up magnificently to that slogan. Alone in Europe, they have shown that democracy, if it so wills, can defend itself successfully even against overwhelming odds. Powerful states have collapsed and proud empires have been humbled by methods of gangsterism. But the people of Spain·stand unconquered and unsubdued, and out of the very horror they have gone through, they have built up a new Spain which fills all friends of democracy with hope.

If we are to face fascism, it is in that spirit that we have to do it. To hold hard to our principles and to freedom and to refuse to surrender even unto death. But if we compromise with those principles, and carry on our own imperialism while we combat fascism, we lose both friends and supporters as well as all the strength and enthusiasm that come from fighting for a worthy cause. If England really fought for democracy, she would have the world's sympathy and support. But who would sympathize with an imperialist England fighting to keep her colonies?

6

Destiny[1]

The ides of March brought disaster to Europe and to democracy, and Czecho-slovakia vanished from the map of the world. Yet war did not come. Stunned and full of fear, the countries of Europe waited for yet another spring of the beast of prey. It came soon enough, and Memel was the victim. Yet war did not come. We were told that the spring campaigns and offensives were over and peace would reign in Europe till the far-off autumn at least. But autumn was still far off when Easter came with its message of goodwill, and Good Friday saw the rape of Albania. Yet war did not come.

War has not come yet, but who can tell when it will descend on us? Who dare say that peace is assured till the autumn or even till the hot summer enve-lops us? There is marching and stamping of millions of armed men in Europe, and night and day men and women turn out engines of destruction and dig trenches and erect barricades, and the sky is covered with the messengers of death. Who dare say that the thin thread that holds back these forces will not snap and unleash destruction and doom on hapless mankind? Peace, so-called peace, holds today; what of tomorrow or the day after?

Like some pre-ordained tragedy, inevitable and inescapable, war pursues us and will seize us by the throat. We shall not escape our destiny.

[1] *National Herald*, 19 April 1939.

Treachery and Betrayal[1]

It is an interesting and instructive exercise for the student of history to collect and read the various declarations of war aims which conquerors and governments have made throughout the ages. Always he will find a justification on the highest moral grounds, either religious or political; every aggression is justified, every brutality is condoned for the preservation of some high principle. Often he will discover that it is only the love of ultimate peace that urges the conqueror and aggressor onward. Has not even Herr Hitler said so? Recently a fascinating anthology of declared war aims was published in England and this went back two thousand years. It was astonishing to read the very same language, the same fervent love of peace, in these declarations made a hundred or a thousand years ago by kings and emperors who launched a war, as we read today. One could almost imagine, with a few verbal changes, that it was Mr. Neville Chamberlain who was speaking and not a medieval ruler.

The anthology dealt with the countries of the West, but we have no doubt that a similar collection can be made from the declarations of eastern rulers. The desire to hide one's real motives under cover of fine phrases and pious doctrine is a human failing common to the East and the West. There have been few among the rulers of men who have not been guilty of it and who have not sought to cloak their misdeeds in this manner. Once there was in India, two thousand years ago, the great Asoka who, unique among his kind, felt the horror of war in the full tide of conquest and laid bare his heart.

Looking at this past record of declarations and justifications a measure of despair seizes one, or we grow cynical. Is humanity always to go through the self-same round of deceit; must there always be this vast gap between the spoken word and the shady deed? Yet hope fills up every time these brave declarations are made and we try to believe, against all past experiences, that this time at least the word will be translated into the deed. So it was in 1914 and after, and millions believed, and believed in vain, that the war was to end war and to establish peace and freedom on this unhappy planet of ours. We know the heritage of that war; we know the deceit and treachery and betrayal of politicians; we know well the horror that has pursued us since then.

[1] *National Herald*, 19 October 1939.

8

A Crumbling World[1]

During the last few weeks India has suddenly been forced to think hard about international happenings and their reactions on her. Some of us have been dabbling in international affairs for many years, and occasionally a passing interest was aroused among large numbers of people in the country in the fate of Abyssinia, Palestine, Czechoslovakia, Spain, and China.

Fundamentally, however, we were, as a people, far too much absorbed in our own national problems. The coming of the war in Europe led inevitably to a deeper interest in events abroad. Even so, the struggle was a distant one, and our excitement was that of an onlooker. May 10th, a date famous in Indian history, brought the invasion of the Low Countries of western Europe, and the rapid developments that have followed each other since then have galvanized our minds and brought the possible consequences of the war very near to us. New problems suddenly confront us, entirely novel situations have to be faced.

The last two meetings of the Congress Working Committee met under these difficult conditions and tried to adjust themselves to them. The public has seen their resolutions and there has been some argument about them. It would be worthwhile, however, for us to consider dispassionately what has happened in Europe, with all its future implications, if we are to understand the curious and changing world that we live in. Wishful thinking is at any time an unhelpful occupation; today it is full of peril. All of us are much too apt to remain in the old ruts, to think the old thoughts, to utter the old slogans, even though everything else may have changed beyond recognition. Fundamental principles and objectives must have a certain stability and continuance, but in other ways reality demands that we adapt ourselves to it.

What has happened? The map of Europe has changed utterly and many nations have ceased to be. Poland went, Denmark and Norway succumbed, Holland collapsed, Belgium surrendered, France fell suddenly and completely. All these went into the German orbit. The Baltic countries and Bessarabia have been more or less absorbed by Soviet Russia.[2]

[1] Lucknow, 16 July 1940. *National Herald*, 17 July 1940.

[2] The Soviet Union occupied Bessarabia on 28 June 1940 and incorporated the Baltic states on 14 July 1940.

These are mighty changes and yet it is being increasingly realized that they are but the prelude to what is to come. We are not merely witnessing a great and overwhelming war with all its destructive horror. We live today in the midst of a revolutionary epoch of vast significance, more important and far-reaching perhaps than any given in recorded history. Whatever the outcome of this war may be, this revolution will complete its appointed course, and till this takes place there will be no peace or equilibrium in this planet of ours.

We must realize that the old world dies, whether we like it or not. Already those who were most representative of it have become phantom figures, ghosts of a yesterday that is no more.

If the Nazis win through, as they well might, there is little doubt of what they would try to make of Europe and the world. They will create a new type of European union under German leadership and control, a Nazi empire of Europe. The small states would go and so would democracy, as understood by us, and the capitalist system as it has prevailed. A form of state capitalism would flourish in Europe and big industry would be concentrated in the Germanic lands, the other countries, including France, being reduced largely to an agricultural status. This system would be based on a collective supernational economy and would be subject to authoritarian control. The Nazi empire would have its colonies, chiefly in Africa, but it would also try to control the economy of other non-European countries and harness the labour power of their peoples. The economic weight of such a mighty authoritarian union would be tremendous and the rest of the world would have to adapt itself to it.

Such is the Nazi thesis. What of England if this happens? If there is a complete German victory, England ceases to be a power that counts. In Europe she has no influence left; she loses her empire. It is almost immaterial whether she joins the Germanic-European union or not. The centre of gravity of the British race shifts elsewhere, most probably to Canada and they become closely allied to, or even absorbed in, the United States of America.

Much will depend upon Soviet Russia. There is little doubt that she dislikes intensely the rapid growth of Nazi power which may threaten her later. Nevertheless she will adapt herself to the change unless the war draws on for a lengthy period and brings exhaustion of the combatants. A swift German victory would thus lead to a Nazi empire in Europe with outlying possessions. This may be allied to Japan in the East. Two other great federations will remain—Soviet Russia and the United States of America, both essentially hostile to Germany. The war may have ended, but the seeds of future wars will remain between these mighty groups.

What happens if the Nazis do not win within the next few months? Probably a long and exhausting war in which both combatants suffer greatly and are completely exhausted. The economic structure of England and Europe collapses and the only possible future is one of large federations of nations, or of a world federation, based on a different economy and on strict world control of production, transport and distribution. The present-day capitalist system goes. The British Empire ends. Small states cannot exist as independent units. Possibly even the conception of money changes.

In any event, therefore, this war will bring about a fundamental political and economic change, a change that will be more in keeping with modern conditions which demand closer intercourse between nations and a breaking down of international barriers. The strength of Germany today lies not so much in her ruthless efficiency and military machine as in the fact that, perhaps unconsciously, she has become the agent of a historic process. She is trying to turn it in an evil direction; she may even succeed in this for a while. The weakness of France and England was essentially due to their desire to hold on to forms and structures which were doomed to disappear. They represented something that was dying, whether in their empires or in their economic system. They had repeated chances during the past twenty years of putting themselves in step with history, of being the leaders in building up a real international order based on social justice and national freedom. They preferred to hold on to their past gains and vested interests and empires and now it is too late and everything slips out of their hands.

France passes away for a while. But England still fails to learn the lesson. Still she talks in terms of empire and seeks to preserve her special interests. It is sad to see a great people so blind to everything except the narrow interests of a class, and risking everything but not taking the step which would put them right with the world and with the great historic processes that are marching on with giant strides.

9

Nonviolence and the State[1]

There has been much argument on the question of nonviolence and the application of this principle to the governance of a state. A difference of opinion appears to have arisen over this question between Mahatma Gandhi and some members of the Working Committee. This difference may be due largely to misunderstanding. In order to remove any misunderstandings and to facilitate a clarification of the issues involved, the various points that have to be considered are noted below.

This note deals only with the application of this principle to a state and, in particular, to the use of armed forces for the purposes of repelling external invasion or quelling internal disturbances.

As the question has arisen for our consideration, it has two parts: the general principles which should govern our policy as a state and as Congress, and the situation created by the Delhi resolution, subsequently confirmed at Poona. We shall consider these separately.

1. Both because of our adherence to the principle of nonviolence and from practical considerations arising from our understanding of world events, we believe that complete disarmament of all national states should be aimed at, and is in fact an urgent necessity if the world is not to be reduced to barbarism. (It is manifestly impossible for disarmament or even a reduction of armaments to take place while the war is going on. The question can only be considered on a world basis when peace is re-established. But even while the war is being carried on, the objectives of full disarmament should be kept in view, so that public opinion may be cultivated.)

2. Complete disarmament means in essence the ending of wars between national states. This will only take place when the causes of such wars have been eliminated or reduced very greatly. If the causes remain, there will be continuous conflict, political and economic, and this will lead to wars. Therefore, if real disarmament is to come, it is essential to tackle this problem and to remove these causes of conflict and war.

[1] Confidential note written at Wardha, 25 August 1940. JN Papers, NMML.

These causes are many, but briefly they may be summed up as the suppression of one nation by another, of large masses of people by privileged groups, of the uneven distribution of the world's resources which are essential to modern life in any state, of inequalities between nation and nation and group and group, of haves and have-nots as between nations as well as between groups or classes. There may also be religious or racial causes or historical animosities, but these are likely to die out if the more fundamental causes are removed. Over-population may also be a cause.

3. The most important causes of recent wars have been the desire of industrialized nations to get raw material cheap and markets for manufactured goods. The easiest way to get both of these is to take possession of a country or to get an economic stranglehold over it. This has led to the recent phase of imperialism. This again has led to the latest phase of financial imperialism (like that of the United States of America) where actual possession of territory is not necessary but an economic empire is established. Heavy investments are made in the colonial and subject country and thus vested interests are created to the disadvantage of that subject country. These vested interests require the protection of armed forces. Two kinds of conflicts or wars take place due to rivalries between imperialist powers which lead to major wars, and the suppression of a colonial people, which is usually called a colonial campaign or just police measures against rebellious people.

4. This question is too vast for any detailed consideration here but the main facts stand out. Disarmament ultimately depends on far-reaching changes in the political and economic structure of the world, leading to a removal of the basic causes of war. So long as this is not done, the conflicts continue and lead to wars. Even the existence of entirely independent national states leads to conflict between them, and some kind of world union or federation will have to be evolved.

5. The question of complete disarmament thus becomes tied up with fundamental political and economic changes in the world. It cannot be tackled, much less solved, by itself.

6. It is said that actual disarmament must be preceded by moral, disarmament. There is some truth in this but, as a matter of fact, there is widespread horror of war among the people of all countries, and disarmament would be immensely popular. Only some privileged or interested groups as well as governments may feel differently. As a result of the present war the revulsion for war is likely to be tremendous. But one must not forget that even this feeling lessens and fades away and hatred and the desire to revenge remain, if there is no proper settlement and the seeds of war remain.

7. There is another important aspect of disarmament. What exactly is disarmament? Not to keep an army, or navy, or military aeroplanes may be the obvious answer, yet this is totally insufficient. In modern warfare armies have become secondary factors. The air arm counts for most. Even if military aeroplanes are abolished, civil and commercial planes can very easily be converted for use as bombers. And every chemical factory can produce bombs at a moment's notice. Thus even if a country disarms totally in the ordinary sense of the world, it may be potentially armed and capable of offensive and destructive warfare. It is obviously out of the question to put an end to all chemical factories, which produce essential products for human needs, or to stop commercial and civil flying altogether. Even if this was done outwardly, a country which possessed scientific and technical skill could arm rapidly. It does not cost much, relatively speaking, to produce aeroplanes or bombs.

8. Thus the question of disarmament is full of difficulty and we come back to the prior necessity of removing the causes of war. This means the evolution of a new world order based on a different political and economic system which avoids conflict. This must lead to a world federation and the distribution of the world's resources fairly among different countries and peoples.

9. Another aspect is that, as the world is constituted today, no country can be isolated from the others, nor can it for long follow a policy which is totally at variance with that of others, however much it might try to do so. A country may go one step ahead and give a lead to others but the gap cannot be great.

10. Even if there is total disarmament, it is too much to expect that all antisocial elements in various countries will disappear. Such elements will try to take advantage of the disarmament of a state to seize power by force. It will be necessary, for a longish transitional period, to keep an international police force (apart from national police) to deal with such aggressors.

11. In India a method of meeting armed aggression by nonviolent direct action has been evolved. This may in theory be applicable to a state defending itself, but it obviously requires a high stage of development among considerable numbers of people. If that stage is not reached, then it may not only fail, but lead to disastrous results—hypocrisy, meanness, cowardice and a servile mentality. To say that it must be applied even if the people are not ready for it, means the degradation of the people.

12. On the other hand, India cannot at present imaginably become a military power of first class importance. It can at best become a third rate

power and that too at a cost which is almost unbearable for a poor country. It is therefore essential for India that world disarmament should take place.

13. The policy that India should pursue, therefore, is:

i) To stand resolutely for complete world disarmament.

ii) To state that she is even prepared to take a lead in this, if this is at all possible, even though other countries hesitate.

iii) At the same time to realize that an absolute commitment is not possible, as any action taken must depend on external as well as internal factors.

iv) To take every step towards this end, that is possible, during the transitional period, realizing that full achievement may not come immediately and some steps may be necessary.

v) To train people, psychologically and otherwise, in nonviolent direct action.

vi) Even if an army has to be tolerated during the transitional period, to give it progressively more of the character of a militia or national police force.

vii) To develop the physique of the people and train them in drill and methods of organized action. This is necessary also from the point of view of giving an outlet for the suppressed militarism of the people.

viii) To build up a civil and commercial air service.

ix) To endeavour by all means in her power to help in bringing about a new political and economic order in the world and thus remove causes of war. In particular, to follow such an economic policy within the country, and a foreign policy to fit with this abroad . . .[2]

---

[2] Incomplete in the original.

10

India's Day of Reckoning[1]

I welcome the opportunity of writing in the columns of *Fortune* on the vital problems that confront India. These problems are no longer our concern only; they are of world concern, affecting the entire international situation today. More so will they affect the shaping of future events.

Whether we consider them from the point of view of the terrible world conflict that is going on, or in terms of the political, economic, and commercial consequences of this war, the future of 400 million human beings is of essential importance. These millions are no longer passive agents of others submitting with resignation to the decrees of fate. They are active, dynamic, and hungering to shoulder the burden of their own destiny and to shape it according to their own wishes.

The Indian struggle for freedom and democracy has evoked a generous response from many an American, but the crisis that faces us all is too urgent for us merely to trade in sympathy or feel benevolent towards each other. We have to consider our major problems objectively and almost impersonally and endeavour to solve them, or else these problems will certainly overwhelm us, as indeed they threaten to do. That has been the lesson of history and we forget it at our peril. It is, therefore, not merely from a humanitarian point of view, though humanitarianism itself is good, but rather in the objective spirit of science that we should approach our problems.

The next hundred years, it has been said, are going to be the century of America. America is undoubtedly going to play a very important role in the years and generations to come. It is young and vital and full of the spirit of growth. The small and stuffy countries of Europe, with their eternal conflicts and wars, can no longer control the world. Europe has a fine record of achievement of which it may well be proud. That achievement will endure and possibly find greater scope for development when its accompaniment of domination over others is ended.

If the next century is going to be the century of America, it is also going to be the century of Asia, a rejuvenated Asia deriving strength from its ancient culture and yet vital with the youthful spirit of modern science.

[1] *Fortune* (Chicago), March 1942. SWJN, Vol. 12, pp. 168–77.

Most of us are too apt to think of Asia as backward and decadent because for nearly two hundred years it has been dominated by Europe and has suffered all the ills, material and spiritual, which subjection inevitably brings in its train. We forget the long past of Asia when politically, economically and culturally it played a dominant role. In this long perspective the past two hundred years are just a brief period that is ending, and Asia will surely emerge with new strength and vitality as it has done so often in the past.

One of the amazing phenomena of history is the way India and China have repeatedly revived after periods of decay, and how both of them have preserved the continuity of their cultural traditions through thousands of years. They have obviously had tremendous reserves of strength to draw upon. India was old when the civilization of Greece flowered so brilliantly. Between the two there was intimate contact and much in common, and India is said to have influenced Greece far more than Greece did India. That Grecian civilization, for all its brilliance, passed away soon, leaving a great heritage, but India carried on and her culture flowered again and again. India, like China, had more staying power.

Asia is no suppliant for the favours of others, but claims perfect equality in everything and is confident of holding her own in the modern world in comradeship with others.

The recent visit of Generalissimo Chiang Kai-shek and Madame Chiang to India was not only of historic significance but has given us a glimpse of the future when India and China will cooperate for their own and the world's good. The Generalissimo pointed out a remarkable fact: that India and China, with a common land frontier of 3000 kilometres, had lived at peace with each other for a thousand years, neither country playing the role of aggressor, but both having intimate cultural and commercial contacts throughout these ages. That in itself shows the peaceful character of these two great civilizations.

Keeping this background in mind, it will be evident how unreal and fantastic is the conception of India as a kind of colonial appendage or offshoot of Britain, growing slowly to nationhood and freedom as the British dominions have done. India is a mother country, which has influenced in the past, vast sections of the human race in Asia. She still retains that storehouse of cultural vitality that has given her strength in the past, and at the same time has the natural resources, the scientific, technical, industrial and financial capacity to make her a great nation in the modern sense of the world. But she cannot grow because of the shackles that tie her down, nor can she play her part, as she should, in the war crisis today. That part can be a great one not only because of the manpower at India's disposal but because, given a chance, she can rapidly become a great industrial nation.

The World War is obviously part of a great revolution taking place throughout the world. To consider it in only military terms is to miss the real significance of what is happening. Causes lie deep, and it would be foolish to imagine that all our present troubles are due to the vanity and insatiable ambition of certain individuals or peoples. Those individuals or peoples represent evil tendencies. But they also represent the urge for change from an order that has lost stability and equilibrium and that is heartily disliked by vast numbers of people. Part of the aggressors' strength is certainly due to their challenge to this old system.

To oppose these inevitable changes and seek to perpetuate the old, or even to be passive about them, is to surrender on a revolutionary plane to the aggressor countries. Intelligent people know these aggressors are out to impose tyranny far worse than any that has existed, and therefore they should be opposed. To submit to them is to invite degradation of the worst type, a spiritual collapse far worse than even military defeat. We see what has happened in Vichy, France. We know what has happened in Central Europe and in Northern China. And yet that fear of possible worse fate is not enough, and certainly it does not affect the masses of population who are thoroughly dissatisfied with their present lot. They want some positive deliverance to shake them out of their passivity, some cause that immediately affects them to fight for. A proud people do not accept present degradation and misery for fear that something worse may take its place.

Thus the urgent need is to give a moral and revolutionary lead to the world, to convince it that the old order has gone and a new one really based on freedom and democracy has taken its place. No promises for the future are good enough, no half-measures will help, it is the present that counts, for it is in the present that the war is going to be lost or won, and it is out of this present that the future will take shape.

President Roosevelt has spoken eloquently about this future and about the four freedoms,[2] and his words have found an echo in millions of hearts. But the words are vague, and do not satisfy, and no action follows those words. The Atlantic Charter is again a pious and nebulous expression of hope, which stimulates nobody, and even this, Mr. Churchill tells us, does not apply to India.

If this urgent necessity for giving a moral and revolutionary lead were recognized and acted upon, then the aggressor nations would be forced to drop the cloak that hides many of their evil designs, and new forces of vast dimensions would rise up to check them. Even the peoples of Europe now under Nazi domination would be affected. But the greatest effect would be produced in Asia and Africa. And that may well be the turning point of the war. Only

[2] In a message to the US Congress on 6 January 1941, Roosevelt had stated that Four Freedoms should prevail throughout the world—freedom of speech and expression, freedom of worship, freedom from want, and freedom from fear. These were substantially incorporated in the Atlantic Charter.

freedom and the conviction that they are fighting for their own freedom can make people fight as the Chinese and Russians have fought.

We have the long and painful heritage of European domination in Asia. Britain may believe or proclaim that she had done good to India and other Asiatic countries, but the Indians and other Asiatics think otherwise, and it is after all what we believe that matters now. It is a terribly difficult business to wipe out this past of bitterness and conflict, yet it can be done if there is a complete break from it, and the present is made entirely different. Only thus can those psychological conditions be produced that lead to cooperation in a common endeavour and release mass effort.

It was in this hope that the National Congress issued a long statement in September 1940, defining its policy in regard to the European war and inviting the British Government to declare its war aims in regard to imperialism and democracy, and, in particular, to state how these were to be given effect in the present.

For many years past the Congress had condemned fascist and Nazi doctrines and the aggressions of the Japanese, Italian and German Governments. It condemned them afresh and offered its cooperation in the struggle for freedom and democracy.

But it is stated: "If the war is to defend the status quo of imperialist possessions and colonies, of vested interests and privilege, then India can have nothing to do with it. If, however, the issue is democracy and world order based on democracy, then India is intensely interested in it. The Committee is convinced that the interests of Indian democracy do not conflict with the interests of British democracy or world democracy. But there is an inherent and ineradicable conflict between democracy for India, or elsewhere, and imperialism and fascism. If Great Britain fights for the maintenance and extension of democracy, then she must necessarily end imperialism in her own possessions and establish full democracy in India, and the Indian people must have the right of self-determination to frame their own constitution through a constituent assembly without external interference and must guide their own policy. A free democratic India will gladly associate herself with other free nations for mutual defence against aggression and for economic cooperation."

That offer was made two-and-a-half years ago and it has been repeated in various forms subsequently. It was rejected in a way that angered India. The British Government has made it clear beyond a doubt that it clings to the past; and present and future, in so far as Britain can help it, will resemble that past. It is not worthwhile to dwell on the tragic history of these two and a half years that have added to our problems and the complexity of the situation. Events have followed each other in furious succession all over the world and, in recent months, parts of the British Empire have passed out of England's control. And yet, in spite of all this, the old outlook and methods continue and England's statesmen talk the patronizing language of the nineteenth century to us. We are intensely interested in the defence of India from external aggression but the only way we could do anything effective about it is through mass enthusiasm and mass effort under popular control.

We cannot develop our heavy industries, even though wartime requirements shout for such developments, because British interests disapprove and fear that Indian industry might compete with them after the war. For years past Indian industrialists have tried to develop an automobile industry, aeroplane manufacture and shipbuilding—the very industries most required in wartime. The way these have been successfully obstructed is an astonishing story. I have been particularly interested in industrial problems in my capacity as Chairman of the National Planning Committee. This Committee gathered around it some of the ablest talent in India—industrial, financial, technical, economic, scientific— and tackled the whole complex and vast problem of planned and scientific development and coordination of industry, agriculture, and social services. The labours of this Committee and its numerous sub-committees would have been particularly valuable in wartime. Not only was this not taken advantage of but its work was hindered and obstructed by the Government.

Two-and-a-half years ago we had hoped to be able to play an effective role in the world drama. Our sympathies were all on one side, our interests coincided with these. Our principal problem is after all not the Hindu-Muslim problem, but the planned growth of industry, greater production, just distribution, higher standards, and thus gradual elimination of the appalling poverty that crushes our people. It was possible to deal with this as part of the war effort and coordinate the two, thus making India far stronger, both materially and psychologically, to resist aggression. But it could only have been done with the driving power that freedom gives. It is not very helpful to think of these wasted years, now that immediate peril confronts us and we have to meet this peril differently now, for in no event do we propose to submit to aggression.

It is said that any transfer of power during wartime involves risks. So it does. To abstain from action or change probably involves far greater risks. The aggressor nations have repeatedly shown that they have the courage to gamble with fate, and the gamble has often come off. We must take risks. One thing is certain that the present state of affairs in India is deplorable. It lacks not only popular support but also efficiency. The people who control affairs in India from Whitehall or Delhi are incapable even of understanding what is happening, much less of dealing with it.

We are told that the independence of Syria is recognized,[3] that Korea is

---

[3] On 28 September 1941, the independence and sovereignty of the Syrian Republic was promised. Syria was to be an ally of Free-France and the Allies. Independence was granted to Syria by the British on 28 October 1941.

going to be a free country.[4] But India, the classic land of modern imperialist control, must continue under British tutelage. Meanwhile daily broadcasts, from Tokyo, Bangkok, Rome, and Berlin, in Hindustani announce that the Axis countries want India to be independent. Intelligent people know how false this is and are not taken in. But many who listen to this, contrast it with what the British Government says and does in India. We have seen the effect of this propaganda in Malaya and Burma. India is far more advanced politically and can, therefore, resist it more successfully. She is especially attracted to China and has admired the magnificent resistance of the Russian people. She feels friendly towards the democratic ideals of America. But with all that she feels helpless and frustrated and bitter against those who have put her in her present position.

Some of the problems are of our own making; some of British creation. But whoever may be responsible for them, we have to solve them. One of these problems, so often talked about, is the Hindu-Muslim problem. It is often forgotten that Muslims like Hindus also demand independence for India. Some of them (but only some) talk in terms of a separate state in the north-west of India. They have never defined what they mean and few people take their demand seriously, especially in these days when small states have ceased to count and must inevitably be parts of a larger federation. The Hindu-Muslim problem will be solved in terms of federation but it will be solved only when British interference with our affairs ceases. So long as there is a third party to intervene and encourage intransigent elements of either group, there will be no solution. A free India will face the problem in an entirely different setting and will, I have no doubt, solve it.

What do we want? A free, democratic, federal India willing to be associated with other countries in larger federations. In particular, India would like to have close contacts with China and Soviet Russia, both her neighbours, and America. Every conceivable protection, guarantee and help should be given to our minority groups and those that are culturally or economically backward.

What should be done now? It is not an easy question for what may be possible today becomes difficult tomorrow. But this war is not going to end soon, and what happens in India is bound to make a great difference. The grand strategy of war requires an understanding of the urges that move people to action and sacrifice for a cause. It requires sacrifice not only of lives of brave men but of factual prejudices, of inherited conceptions of political or economic domination and exploitation of others, of vested interests, of small groups that hinder the growth and development of others. It requires conception and

[4] On 1 March 1942, the Korean Independence Army in Chungking thanked Roosevelt for his initiative for Korean independence and promised help to the Allies and the Chinese against the Japanese. The Cairo Conference in 1943 recognized the independence of Korea.

translation into action, in so far as possible, of the new order based on the political and economic freedom of all countries, of world cooperation of free peoples, of revolutionary leadership along these lines, and of capacity to dare and face risks. What vested interests are we going to protect for years to come when the interests of humanity itself are at stake today? Where are the vested interests of Hong Kong and Singapore?

It is essential that whatever is to be done is done now. For it is the present that counts. What will happen after the war nobody knows, and to postpone anything till then is to admit bankruptcy and invite disaster.

I would suggest that the leaders of America and Britain declare: First, that every country is entitled to full freedom and to shape its own destiny, subject only to certain international requirements and their adjustment by international cooperation. Second, that this applies fully to countries at present within the British Empire, and that India's independence is recognized as well as her right to frame her own constitution through an assembly of her elected representatives, who will also consider her future relations with Britain and other countries. Third, that all races and peoples must be treated as equal and allowed equal opportunities of growth and development. Individuals and races may and do differ, and some are culturally or intellectually more mature than others. But the door of advancement must be open to all; indeed those that are immature should receive help and encouragement. Nothing has alienated people more from the Nazis than their racial theories and the brutal application of these theories. But a similar doctrine and its application are in constant evidence in subject countries.

Such a declaration clearly means the ending of imperialism everywhere with all its dominating position and special privileges. That will be a greater blow to Nazism and fascism than any military triumph, for Nazism and fascism are an intensification of the principle of imperialism. The issue of freedom will then be clear before the world and no subterfuge or equivocation will be possible.

But the declaration, however good, is not enough, for no one believes in promises or is prepared to wait for the hereafter. Its translation into present immediate practice will be the acid test. A full changeover may not be immediately possible, yet much can be done now. In India a changeover can take place without delay and without any complicated legal enactments. The British Parliament may pass laws in regard to it or it may not. We are not particularly interested as we want to make our own laws in the future. A provisional National Government could be formed and all real power transferred to it. This may be done even within the present structure, but it must be clearly understood that this structure will then be an unimportant covering for something that is entirely different. This National Government will not be responsible to the British Government or the Viceroy but to the people, though of course it will seek to cooperate with the British Government and its agents. When opportunity offers in the future, further changes may take place through a constituent assembly. Meanwhile it may be possible to widen the basis of the present Central Assembly to which the provisional National Government will be responsible.

If this is done in the Central Government, it would not be at all difficult to make popular governments function in the provinces where no special changes are necessary and the apparatus for them exists already.

All this is possible without upsetting too suddenly the outer framework. But it involves a tremendous and vital change, and that is just what is needed from the point of view of striking popular imagination and gaining popular support. Only a real changeover and realization that the old system is dead, past revival, that freedom has come, will galvanize the people into action. That freedom will come at a moment of dire peril and it will be terribly difficult for anyone to shoulder this tremendous responsibility. But whatever the dangers, they have to be faced and responsibility has to be shouldered.

The change suggested would give India the status of an independent nation, but a peaceful changeover presumes mutual arrangements being made between representatives of India and Great Britain for governing their future relations. I do not think that the conception of wholly sovereign independent nations is compatible with world peace or progress. But we do not want international cooperation to be just a variation of the imperial theme with some dominant nations controlling international and national policies. The old idea of Dominion Status is unlikely to remain anywhere and it is peculiarly inapplicable to India. But India will welcome association with Britain and other countries, on an equal basis, as soon as all taint of imperialism is removed.

In immediate practice, after the independence of India is recognized, many old contacts will continue. The administrative machinery will largely remain, apart from individual cases, but it will be subject to such changes as will make it fit in with new conditions. The Indian army must necessarily become a national army and cease to be looked upon as a mercenary army. And future British military establishment would depend on many present and changing factors, chiefly the development of the War. It cannot continue as an alien army of occupation, as it has done in the past, but as an Allied army its position would be different.

It is clear that if the changes suggested were made, India would line up completely with the countries fighting aggression. It is difficult, however, to prophesy what steps would be most effective at this particular juncture. If the military defence of India now being carried on beyond her frontiers proves ineffective, a new and difficult military situation arises that may require other measures. Mahatma Gandhi, in common with others, has declared that we must resist aggression and not submit to any invader; but his methods of resistance, as is well known, are different. These peaceful methods seem odd in this world of brutal warfare. Yet, in certain circumstances, they may be the only alternative left to us. The main thing is that we must not submit to aggression.

One thing is certain: whatever the outcome of this war, India is going to resist every attempt at domination, and a peace that has not solved the problem of India will not be long purchased. Primarily this is Britain's responsibility, but its consequences are worldwide and affect this war. No country can, therefore, ignore India's present and her future, least of all America on whom rests a vast burden of responsibility, and towards whom so many millions look for right leadership at this crisis in world history.

11

The Death Dealer[1]

I was asked today what my reactions were to the atom bomb experiment.[2] For the moment I did not say anything, but my mind became more and more occupied with this latest "advance" of our civilization and numerous pictures of what might happen came before me.

First of all, it seemed very odd to me that this experiment should take place in the way it did, with all the fanfare of publicity for which America is famous. Normally war offices do not shout about their latest weapons and indeed try their utmost to keep them secret. It is true that probably such an experiment could not have been kept wholly secret. But still there was no obvious necessity for deliberate publicity unless some definite objective was being aimed at.

What could this be? Surely to announce to the world and to all to whom it may concern of this might of the United States of America and their readiness to blow up any people or country who came in the way of their policy. It was a challenge and a threat. It was a reminder of the stark reality behind all the talks of the foreign ministers and the UNO. It was the dark shadow of approaching war—World War III.

This is not the way to lay the foundations of peace or to remove the fear in people's minds which leads so often to war. Inevitably that fear would grow and grip nations and peoples and each would try frantically to get this new weapon or some adequate protection from it.

Peace seems far distant now, a dream that has faded, and mankind apparently marches ahead to its doom. For though the atom bomb has come to blast the world, no bomb has yet touched the minds of our statesmen and men of authority, who cannot get out of their old ruts, and still want to preserve their old world. We have heard much of the Four Freedoms and of the brave new world to come, and yet the only freedom that the mass of humanity is likely to possess is the freedom to die and to be blown to bits; of course, to preserve democracy and liberty and the Four Freedoms.

Have words lost all their meaning and have men's minds lost all anchorage? For this surely is the way to madness, and the great men who control our

[1] Editorial, 1 July 1946. *National Herald*, 2 July 1946.
[2] The US tested an atomic bomb at Bikini Islands on 1 July 1946. It damaged more ships than were ever before damaged by a single explosion.

destinies are dangerous self-centred lunatics, who are too full of their conceit and pride of power that they will rather rain death and destruction all over the world than give up their petty opinions and think and act aright.

It is an astonishing and shameful thing that people should put up with this madness, especially when the world seemed so near to achieving what it has desired and dreamt of for ages past. Peace and cooperation and well-being for all the peoples of the world were well within grasp. But the gods perhaps envied the lot of man and drove him mad.

Whether madness and death are the fate of man in the near future, or something better, no one can say. But it is certain that the way of the atom bomb is not the way of peace or freedom. The only useful purpose it can serve is to put an end to the power-mad people in authority, to those who wish to dominate over others, to the race-proud who deny equality to others, to the men of privilege who rest on others' labour and suffering, to those who prosper when others starve and die.

12

An Age of Crises[1]

We live in an age of crises. One crisis follows another and even when there is some kind of peace, it is a troubled peace, with fear of war and preparations for war. Tortured humanity hungers for real peace, but some evil fate pursues it, and pushes it further and further away from what it desires most. Almost it seems that some terribles destiny drives humanity to ever-recurring disaster. We are all entangled in the mesh of past history and cannot escape the consequences of past evil. In the multitude of crises, political and economic, that face us, perhaps the greatest crisis of all is that of the human spirit. Till this crisis of the spirit is resolved, it will be difficult to find a solution for the other crises that affect us.

We talk of world government and one world, and millions yearn for this. Earnest efforts continue to be made to realize this ideal of the human race which has become so imperative today, and yet those efforts have thus far proved ineffective, even though it becomes ever clearer that if there is going to be no world order, then there might be no order at all left in the world. Wars are fought and won or lost and the victors suffer almost as much as the vanquished. Surely, there must be something wrong about our approach to this vital problem of the age, something essentially lacking.

In India during the last quarter of a century and more, Mahatma Gandhi made an outstanding contribution not only to the freedom of India but to that of world peace. He taught us the doctrine of nonviolence, not as a passive submission to evil, but as an active and positive instrument for the peaceful solution of international differences. He showed us that the human spirit is more powerful than the mightiest of armaments. He applied moral values to political action and pointed out that ends and means can never be separated, for the means ultimately govern the end. If the means are evil, then the end itself becomes distorted and at least partially evil. Any society based on injustice must necessarily have the seeds of conflict and decay within it so long as it does not get rid of that evil.

[1] Recorded on 19 March 1948 for broadcast to the United States on 4 April 1948. AIR tapes, NMML.

All this may seem fantastic and impractical in the modern world, used as it is to thinking in set grooves. And yet we have seen repeatedly the failure of other methods and nothing can be less practical than to pursue a method that has failed again and again. We may not perhaps ignore the present limitations of human nature or the immediate perils which face the statesman. We may not, in the world as it is constituted today, even rule out war absolutely. But I have become more and more convinced that so long as we do not recognize the supremacy of the moral law in our national and international relations, we shall have no enduring peace. So long as we do not adhere to right means, the end will not be right and fresh evil will flow from it. That was the essence of Gandhi's message and mankind will have to appreciate it in order to see and act clearly. When eyes are bloodshot, vision is limited.

I have no doubt in my mind that world government must and will come for there is no other remedy for the world's sickness. The machinery for it is not difficult to devise. It can be an extension of the federal principle, a growth of the idea underlying the United Nations, giving each national unit freedom to fashion its destiny according to its genius, but subject always to the basic covenant of the world government.

We talk of rights of individuals and nations but it must be remembered that every right carries an obligation with it. There has been far too much emphasis on rights and far too little on obligations; if obligations were undertaken, rights would naturally flow from them. This means an approach to life different from the competitive and acquisitive approach of today.

Today fear consumes us all, fear of the future, fear of war, fear of the people or nation whom we dislike and who dislike us. That fear may be justified to some extent. But fear is an ignoble emotion and leads to blind strife. Let us try to get rid of this fear and base our thoughts and actions on what is essentially right and moral, and then gradually the crisis of the spirit will be resolved, the dark clouds that surround us may lift and the way to the evolution of world order based on freedom will be clear.

13

The Role of the United Nations[1]

I am grateful for the opportunity that has been given to me to address this great Assembly. I feel a little embarrassed and a little overwhelmed by this occasion because this Assembly represents the world community, and, whether we who are present here are big men and women or small, we represent a mighty cause, and something of the greatness of that cause falls upon us too and makes us, for the moment, greater perhaps than we are.

Therefore, in venturing to address this Assembly, I feel embarrassed. You have been dealing with intricate and difficult problems, and I do not, and I would not, venture on this occasion to say anything about those great problems that confront you. You carry the burdens and the sorrow of the world. But I have often wondered whether, in dealing with those problems, the approach that is normally made to them is a right one or not. The Charter of the United Nations, in noble language, has laid down the principles and the purposes of this great organization. I do not think it would be possible to improve upon that language. The objectives are clear; your aim is clear; and yet, in looking at that aim, we lose ourselves often, if I may venture to say so, in smaller matters and forget the main objective that we were looking at. Sometimes it seems that the objective itself gets a little clouded and lesser objectives are before us. . . .

This Assembly took shape after two mighty Wars and as a consequence of those Wars. In the Preamble of your Charter you recount these. What has been the lesson of those Wars? Surely the lesson of those Wars has been that out of hatred and violence you will not build peace. It is a contradiction in terms. The lesson of history, the long course of history, and more especially the lesson of the last two Great Wars which have devastated humanity, has been that out of hatred and violence only hatred and violence will come. We have got into a cycle of hatred and violence, and not the most brilliant debate will get you out of it, unless you look some other way and find some other means. It is obvious that if you continue in this cycle and have wars which this Assembly was especially meant to avoid and prevent, the result will not only be tremendous

[1] Address to the third session of the U.N. General Assembly, at Palais de Chillot, Paris, 3 November 1948. JN Papers, NMML. Excerpts.

devastation all over the world but the non-achievement by any individual power or group of its objective.

How, then, are we to proceed? It may be that it is difficult to get this hatred and prejudice and fear out of our minds. Nevertheless, unless we try to proceed in this way, to cast out this fear, we shall never succeed. Of that I am quite convinced.

You meet here representatives of all the nations of the world, or nearly all. Inevitably, you have before you the immediate great problems that confront more especially Europe, which has suffered so much.

May I say, as a representative from Asia, that we honour Europe for its culture and for the great advance in human civilization which it represents. May I say that we are equally interested in the solution of European problems; but may I also say that the world is something bigger than Europe, and you will not solve your problems by thinking that the problems of the world are mainly European problems. There are vast tracts of the world which may not in the past, for a few generations, have taken much part in world affairs. But they are awake; their people are moving, and they have no intention whatever of being ignored or of being passed by.

It is a simple fact that I think we have to remember, because unless you have the picture of the world before you, you will not even understand the problem, and if you isolate any single problem in the world from the rest you do not understand the world problem. Today, I do venture to submit that Asia counts in world affairs. Tomorrow it will count much more than today. Asia, till recently, was largely a prey to imperial domination and colonialism; a great part of it is free today; part of it still remains unfree; and it is an astonishing thing that any country should still venture to hold and to set forth this doctrine of colonialism, whether it is under direct rule or whether it is indirectly maintained in some form or other. After all that has happened, there is going to be no mere objection to that, but active objection, an active struggle against any and every form of colonialism in any part of the world. That is the first thing to remember.

We in Asia, who have ourselves suffered all these evils of colonialism and of imperial domination, have committed ourselves inevitably to the freedom of every other colonial country. There are neighbouring countries of ours in Asia with whom we are intimately allied. We look to them with sympathy; we look at their struggle with sympathy. Any power, great or small, which in that way prevents the attainment of the freedom of those peoples does an ill turn to world peace. . . .

There is another question to which I want to draw attention—that is the question of racial equality, which is something which is laid down in the provisions of the United Nations Charter. It is well to repeat that, because after all this question of racial equality has frequently been spoken about in the Assembly of the United Nations.

I do not think I need dwell on any particular aspect of that question, but I would remind this Assembly of the worldwide aspects of this question. Obviously there are large regions of the world which have suffered from this racial inequality. We also feel that there is no part of the world where it can be tolerated in the future, except perhaps because of a superior force. If racial inequality is practised, if it is a menace to world peace and if it violates the principles of United Nations Charter, to tolerate it is obviously to sow seeds of conflict. . . .

It is a strange thing, when the world lacks so many things, food and other necessities, in many parts of the world and people are dying from hunger that the attention of this Assembly of Nations is concentrated on a number of political problems. There are economic problems also. I wonder if it would be possible for this Assembly for a while to take a holiday from some of the acute political problems which face it, and allow men's minds to settle down and look at the vital and urgent economic problems, and look at places in the world where food is lacking.

I feel that today the world is so tied up in fears, apprehensions, some of them justified no doubt, but where a person feels fear, evil consequences follow. Fear is not a good companion. It is surprising to see that this sense of fear is pervading great countries—fear, and grave fear of war, and fear of many things. . . .

We are all guilty men and women. While we are seeking points where error occurs, we should not forget that there are none of us who is exempt from blame.

If we proceed to this problem, and discuss in peace the psychology of fear, if we realize the consequences of what is happening, it is possible that this atmosphere of fear may be dissipated. Why should there be this fear of war? Let us prepare ourselves against any possible aggression, let no one think that any nation, any community can misbehave. The United Nations is here to prevent any fear of hurt; but at the same time let us banish all thought of an aggressive attitude whether by word or deed. I ask this Assembly to remember that such great problems cannot be solved if our eyes are bloodshot and our minds are obscured by passion.

I have no doubt that this Assembly is going to solve our problems. I am not afraid of the future. I have no fear in my mind, and I have no fear, even though India, from a military point of view, is of no great consequence. Still I am not afraid of the bigness of the great powers, and their armies, their fleets and their atom bombs. That is the lesson which my master taught me. We stood as an unarmed people against a great country and a powerful empire. We were supported and strengthened because throughout all this period we decided not to submit to evil, and I think that is the lesson which I have before me and which is before us today. I do not know if it is possible to apply this to the problems which face the world today. It is a terrible problem, but I think if we banish this fear, if we have confidence, even though we may take risks of trust rather than to risk violent language, violent actions and in the end war, I think those risks are worth taking. . . .

It is perhaps not very proper for me to address this great Assembly on such matters, because I have not been associated with it or with all these different problems in any intimate degree. However, there would have been no point in my addressing you merely to repeat certain pious phrases. I feel strongly about this matter, and that is why I should like to present the views and wishes of the Indian people. And the Indian people happen to be three hundred and thirty millions in number; it is well to remember that. We have had a year of freedom and a year of difficulty. We have overcome many of those difficulties and we shall overcome the others. We propose to go ahead at a rapid pace. We propose to build and construct and be a power for peace and for the good of the world. We propose to meet every aggression, from whatever quarter it comes, in every possible way open to us. However, we do not think that the problems of the world or of India can be solved by thinking in terms of aggression or war or violence.

14

Ends and Means[1]

In this world of incessant and feverish activity, men have little time to think, much less to consider ideals and objectives. Yet, how are we to act, even in the present, unless we know which way we are going and what our objectives are? It is only in the peaceful atmosphere of a university that these basic problems can be adequately considered. It is only when the young men and women, who are in the university today and on whom the burden of life's problems will fall tomorrow, learn to have clear objectives and standards of values that there is hope for the next generation. The past generation produced some great men but as a generation it led the world repeatedly to disaster. Two World Wars are the price that has been paid for the lack of wisdom on man's part in this generation. It is a terrible price and the tragedy of it is that, even after the price has been paid, we have not purchased real peace or a cessation of conflict and an even deeper tragedy is that mankind does not profit by its experience and continues to go the same way that led previously to disaster. We have had wars and we have had victory and we have celebrated that victory; yet, what is victory and how do we measure it? A war is fought presumably to gain certain objectives. The defeat of the enemy is not by itself an objective but rather the removal of an obstruction towards the attainment of the objective. If that objective is not attained, then that victory over the enemy brings only negative relief and indeed is not a real victory. We have seen, however, that the aim in wars is almost entirely to defeat the enemy and the other and real objective is often forgotten. The result has been that the victory attained by defeating the enemy has only been a very partial one and has not solved the real problem; if it has solved the immediate problem, it has at the same time, given rise to many other and sometimes worse problems. Therefore, it becomes necessary to have the real objective clear in our minds at all times whether in war or in peace and always to aim at achieving the objective.

I think also that there is always a close and intimate relationship between the end we aim at and the means. If the means are wrong, it will vitiate the end or divert us in a wrong direction. Means and ends are thus intimately and

[1] Address at Columbia University, New York, 17 October 1949. AIR and PIB tapes, NMML. Excerpts.

inextricably connected and cannot be separated. That, indeed, has been the lesson of old taught to us by many great men in the past but unfortunately it is seldom remembered.

I am venturing to place some of these ideas before you, not because they are novel but because they have impressed themselves upon me in the course of my life which has been spent in alternating periods of incessant activity and conflict and enforced leisure. The great leader of my country, Mahatma Gandhi, under whose inspiration and sheltering care, I grew up, always laid stress on moral values and warned us never to subordinate means to ends. We were not worthy of him and yet, to the best of our ability, we tried to follow his teachings. Even the limited extent to which we could follow his teachings yielded rich results. After a generation of intense struggle with a great and powerful nation, we achieved success and, perhaps, the most significant part of it, for which credit is due to both parties, was the manner of its achievement. History hardly affords a parallel to the solution of such a conflict in a peaceful way, followed by friendly and cooperative relations. It is astonishing how rapidly bitterness and ill will between the two nations have faded away, giving place to cooperation. And we in India have decided of our own free will to continue this cooperation as an independent nation.

I would not presume to offer advice to other and more experienced nations in any way. But may I suggest for your consideration that there is some lesson in India's peaceful revolution which might be applied to the larger problems before the world today? That revolution demonstrated to us that physical force need not necessarily be the arbiter of man's destiny and that the method of waging a struggle and the way of its termination are of paramount importance. Past history shows us the important part that physical force has played. But it also shows us that no such force can ultimately ignore the moral forces of the world; and if it attempts to do so, it does so at its peril. Today, this problem faces us in all its intensity, because the weapons that physical force has at its disposal are terrible to contemplate. Must the twentieth century differ from primitive barbarism only in the destructive efficacy of the weapons that man's ingenuity has invented for man's destruction? I do believe, in accordance with my master's teachings, that there is another way to meet this situation and solve the problem that faces us.

I realize that a statesman or a man who has to deal with public affairs cannot ignore realities and cannot act in terms of abstract truth. His activity is always limited by the degree of receptivity of the truth by his fellowmen. Nevertheless, the basic truth remains and is always to be kept in view and, as far as possible, it should guide our actions. Otherwise we get caught up in a vicious circle of evil when one evil action leads to another.

India is a very old country with a great past. But she is a new country also with new urges and desires. Since August 1947, she has been in a position to pursue a foreign policy of her own. She was limited by the realities of the situation which she could not ignore or overcome. But even so, she could not forget the lesson of her great leader. She has tried to adapt, however, imperfectly, theory to reality insofar as she could. In the family of nations she was a newcomer and could not influence them greatly to begin with. But she had a certain advantage. She had great potential resources that could, no doubt, increase her power and influence. A greater advantage lay in the fact that she was not fettered by the past, by old enmities or old ties, by historic claims or traditional rivalries. Even against her former rulers there was no bitterness left. Thus India came into the family of nations with no prejudices or enmities, ready to welcome and be welcomed.

Inevitably, she had to consider her foreign policy in terms of enlightened self-interest but at the same time she brought to it a touch of her idealism. Thus, she has tried to combine idealism with national interest. The main objectives of that policy are: the pursuit of peace, not through alignment with any major power or group of powers but through an independent approach to each controversial or disputed issue, the liberation of subject peoples, the maintenance of freedom both national and individual, the elimination of racial discrimination and the elimination of want, disease and ignorance which affect the greater part of the world's population. I am asked frequently why India does not align herself with a particular nation or a group of nations and am told that because we have refrained from doing so we are sitting on the fence. The question and the comment are easily understood, because in times of crisis it is not unnatural for those who are involved in it deeply to regard calm objectivity in others as irrational, short-sighted, negative, unreal or even unmanly. But I should like to make it clear that the policy India has sought to pursue is not a negative and neutral policy. It is a positive and vital policy that flows from our struggle for freedom and from the teachings of Mahatma Gandhi. Peace is not only an absolute necessity for us in India in order to progress and develop but is also of paramount importance to the world. How can that peace be preserved? Not by surrendering to aggression, not by compromising with evil or injustice, but also not by talking and preparing for war.

Aggression has to be met, for it endangers peace. At the same time, the lesson of the last two Wars has to be remembered and it seems to me astonishing that, in spite of that lesson, we go the same way. The very process of marshalling the world into two hostile camps precipitates the conflict which it has sought to avoid. It produces a sense of terrible fear, and that fear darkens men's minds and leads them into wrong courses. There is perhaps nothing so bad and so dangerous in life as fear. As a great President of the United States said,[2] there is nothing really to fear except fear itself.

[2] Franklin D. Roosevelt on 4 March 1933.

Our problem, therefore, becomes one of lessening and ultimately putting an end to this fear. That will not happen if all the world takes sides and talks of war. War becomes almost certain then.

We are a member of the family of nations and we have no wish to shirk any of the obligations and burdens of that membership. We have accepted fully the obligations of membership in the United Nations and intend to abide by them. We wish to make our full contribution to the common store and to render our full measure of service. But that can only be done effectively in our own way and of our own choice. We believe pasionately in the democratic method and we seek to enlarge the bounds of democracy on both the political and the economic plane, for no democracy can exist for long in the midst of want and poverty and inequality. Our immediate needs are economic betterment and raising the standards of our people. The more we succeed in this, the more we can serve the cause of peace in the world. We are fully aware of our weaknesses and failings and claim no superior virtue; but we do not wish to forfeit the advantage that our present detachment gives us. We believe that the maintenance of that detachment is not only in our interest but also in the interest of world peace and freedom. That detachment is neither isolationism nor indifference nor neutrality when peace or freedom is threatened. When man's liberty or peace is in danger we cannot and shall not be neutral; neutrality then would be a betrayal of what we have fought for and stand for.

If we seek to ensure peace we must attack the root causes of war and not merely the symptoms. What are the underlying causes of war in the modern world?

One of the basic causes is the domination of one country by another or an attempt to dominate. Large parts of Asia were ruled till recently by foreign and chiefly Europeans powers. We ourselves were part of the British Empire, as were also Pakistan, Ceylon and Burma. France, Holland and Portugal still have territories over which they rule. But the rising tide of nationalism and the love of independence have submerged most of the western empires in Asia. In Indonesia, I hope that there will soon be an independent sovereign state.[3] We hope also that French Indo-China will achieve freedom and peace before long under a government of its own choice. Much of Africa, however, is subject to foreign powers, some of whom still attempt to enlarge their dominions. It is clear that all remaining vestiges of imperialism and colonialism will have to disappear.

Secondly, there is the problem of racial relations. The progress of some races in knowledge or in invention, their success in war and conquest, has tempted them to believe that they are racially superior and has led them to treat other nations with contempt. A recent example of this was the horrible attempt,

[3] The Netherlands transferred full sovereignty to Indonesia on 27 December 1949.

so largely successful, to exterminate the Jews. In Asia and Africa, racial superiority has been most widely and most insolently exhibited. It is forgotten that nearly all the great religions of mankind arose in the East and that wonderful civilizations grew up there when Europe and America were still unknown to history. The West has too often despised the Asian and the African and still, in many places, denies them not only equality of rights but even common humanity and kindliness. This is one of the great danger points of our modern world; and now that Asia and Africa are shaking off their torpor and arousing themselves, out of this evil may come a conflagration of which no man can see the range of consequences. One of your greatest men said that this country cannot exist half slave and half free.[4] The world cannot for long maintain peace if half of it is enslaved and despised. The problem is not always simple nor can it be solved by a resolution or a decree. Unless there is a firm and sincere determination to solve it, there will be no peace.

The third reason for war and revolution is the misery and want of millions of people in many countries and, in particular, in Asia and Africa. In the West, though the war has brought much misery and many difficulties, the common man generally lives in some measure of comfort—he has food, clothing and shelter to some extent. The basic problem of the East, therefore, is to obtain these necessaries of life. If they are lacking, then there is the apathy of despair or the destructive rage of the revolutionary. Political subjection, racial inequality, economic inequality and misery, these are the evils that we have to remove if we would ensure peace. If we can offer no remedy, then other cries and slogans will make an appeal to the minds of the people.

Many of the countries of Asia have entered the family of nations; others we hope will soon find a place in this circle. We have the same hopes for the countries of Africa. This process should proceed rapidly and America and Europe should use their great influence and power to facilitate it. We see before us vast changes taking place, not only in the political and economic spheres but even more so in the minds of men. Asia is becoming dynamic again and is passionately eager to progress and raise the economic standards of her vast masses. This awakening of a giant continent is of the greatest importance to the future of mankind and requires imaginative statesmanship of a high order. The problems of this awakening will not be solved by looking at it with fear or in a spirit of isolationism by any of us. It requires a friendly and understanding approach, clear objectives and a common effort to realize them. The colossal expenditure of energy and resources on armaments is an outstanding feature of many national budgets today but that does not solve the problem of world peace. Perhaps, even a fraction of that outlay, utilized in other ways and for other purposes, will provide a more enduring basis for peace and happiness.

[4] Abraham Lincoln on 16 June 1858.

That is India's view, offered in all friendliness to all thinking men and women, to all persons of goodwill in the name of our common humanity. That view is not based on wishful thinking but on a deep consideration of the problems that afflict us all, and on its merits I venture to place it before you.

15

India's Policy[1]

Peace cannot be purchased by compromise with evil or by surrender to it. Nor can peace be maintained by methods that themselves are the negation of peace. During our long struggle for freedom, we never surrendered and we did not compromise at any time with what we considered evil. Yet, under Gandhiji's guidance, we tried to follow the methods of peace and were friendly even to those who tried to crush us. He taught us the peaceful, yet unyielding approach; he taught us how to preserve the temper of peace even in a struggle.

Today, if we talk of peace, sometimes people mistake it for appeasement of evil. The temper of peace is completely absent today and the only alternative to a surrender appears to many people to be war with all its terrible consequences. Surely, there are other alternatives which are far removed from surrender and yet lead to the objective aimed at. It is in this spirit that we have tried to approach the world's problems. We are not pacifists. We keep an army and a navy and an air force and if danger threatens us we shall use them. But we seek no dominion over other people. Our sole object is to be left in peace ourselves to solve our own problems and, where possible, to help and cooperate with others. In doing so, we try not to be swept away by passion and anger but to maintain the temper of peaceful approach. It is in this spirit and with all humility and prayerfulness that I have endeavoured to guide India's policy. I have done so in the belief that I have the trust and goodwill of my countrymen behind me. That has fortified me and given me strength even when the outlook was dark.

[1] Broadcast to the Nation, 31 December 1950. JN Papers, NMML. Excerpts.

16

Need for a Temper of Peace[1]

Of my generation many have lived the greater part of our lives and only a few years remain to us. It matters little what happens to our generation; but it does matter a great deal what happens to hundreds of millions of others, and to the world at large. Today, these hundreds of millions all over the world live under some kind of suspended sentence of death, and from day to day an atmosphere is created in people's minds of the inevitability of war. Helplessly we seem to be driven towards the abyss. More and more people in responsible positions talk in terms of passion, revenge and retaliation. They talk of security, and behave in a way which is likely to put an end to all security. They talk of peace, and think and act in terms of war.

Are we so helpless that we cannot stop this drift towards catastrophe? I am sure that we can, because vast masses of people in every country want peace. Why, then, should they be driven by forces apparently beyond their control in a contrary direction? Politicians and statesmen strive for peace through the technique of politics which consists in devising carefully worded formulae. During the last ten days the Commonwealth Prime Ministers have wrestled with this problem of world peace. All of us earnestly seek peace. I hope that our labours will help in producing the desired result. But something more is necessary than mere formulae. It is a passion for peace and for civilized behaviour in international affairs that is necessary. It is the temper of peace and not the temper of war, even though peace is casually mentioned.

It is to this temper of peace that I want especially to direct my mind and your mind. We are in the midst of an international crisis, and perhaps an even greater crisis that confronts us today is the crisis in the spirit of man. We have built up a great civilization whose achievements are remarkable and which holds the promise of even greater achievement in the future. But while these material achievements are very great, somehow we appear to be slipping away from the very essence of civilization. Ultimately, culture and civilization rest in the mind and behaviour of man and not in the material evidence of it that we see around us. During war the civilizing process stops and we go back to some

[1] Broadcast from the B.B.C., London, 12 January 1951. JN Papers, NMML.

barbarous phase of the human mind. Are we speeding back to this barbarism of the mind?

If we desire peace, we must develop the temper of peace and try to win even those who may be suspicious of us or who we think are against us. We have to try to understand others just as we expect them to understand us. We cannot seek peace in the language of war or of threats. You will all remember the magnificent example of which both England and India have reason to be proud. Both of us, in spite of long continued struggle, approached our problems with this basic temper of peace, and we not only resolved them, but produced at the same time an abiding understanding and friendship of each other. That is a great example which we might well bear in mind whenever any other crisis in the relations of nations confronts us. That is the civilized approach to problems which leaves no ill will or bitterness behind.

I am not a pacifist. Unhappily the world of today finds that it cannot do without force. We have to protect ourselves and to prepare ourselves for any contingency. We have to meet aggression or any other kinds of evil. To surrender to evil is always bad. But in resisting evil we must not allow ourselves to be swept away by our own passions and fears and act in a manner which is itself evil. Even in resisting evil and aggression, we have always to maintain the temper of peace and hold out the hand of friendship to those who, through fear or for other reasons, may be opposed to us. That is the lesson that our great leader Mahatma Gandhi taught us and, imperfect as we are, we draw inspiration from that great teaching.

In Asia, as you know, great changes have taken place. I fear that most of us, and perhaps more particularly you of the West, do not realize the vastness of these changes. We are living through a great historic process which has created a ferment in the minds of hundreds of millions of people and which can be seen at work in political and economic changes. Asia has a very long history behind it and for long ages it played an outstanding part in the world. During the last two or three hundred years it suffered eclipse. Now it is emerging from colonial status. Inevitably this is making a great difference to the balance of forces in the world. The old equilibrium has been upset and can never come back again. That is a basic fact to remember. Asia is essentially peaceful, but it is also proud and sensitive and very conscious of its newly-won freedom. In its exuberance it may go wrong occasionally. It has mighty problems of its own and wishes to live at peace with the rest of the world, but it is no longer prepared to tolerate any domination or threat of domination, or any behaviour after the old pattern of colonialism. It demands recognition of its new position in the world. Therefore, I would like you to look with understanding and sympathy on these historic changes which are taking place in Asia, for it is of the utmost importance that Europe, America and Asia as well as other parts of the world should understand each other. Nor should we forget the millions of people who are still under colonial status in Africa and elsewhere. Outworn formulae of a past age will not help. A new approach and understanding are needed, and if these are forthcoming I feel sure that Asia will respond with all friendship. The countries of Asia need and seek friendship and cooperation, for they have tremendous problems to solve. These problems are concerned with the primary needs of their people—food, clothing, housing and the other necessities of life. They are too busy with these problems to desire to be entangled in international conflicts. But against their will they are dragged into them.

Great nations have arisen in Asia with long memories of the past they have lived through, and with their eyes fixed on a future of promise. India, Pakistan, Burma, Ceylon and Indonesia have recently acquired their freedom. China has taken a new shape and a new form. But, whether we like that shape and form or not, we have to recognize that a great nation has been reborn and is conscious of her new strength. China in her new-found strength has acted sometimes in a manner which I deeply regret. But we have to remember the background of China, as of other Asian countries—the long period of struggle and frustration, the insolent treatment that they have received from imperialist powers, and the latter's refusal to deal with them in terms of equality. It is neither right nor practical to ignore the feelings of hundreds of millions of people. It is no longer safe to do so. We in India have two thousand years of friendship with China. We have differences of opinion and even small conflicts, but that long past comes up before us and something of the wisdom of that past also helps us to understand each other. And so we endeavour to maintain friendly relations with this great neighbour of ours, for the peace of Asia depends upon these relations.

The immediate problem of today is the problem of the Far East. If that is not solved satisfactorily, trouble spreads to Europe and to the rest of the world. And perhaps Europe, with her magnificent record of progress, not only in material achievements but also in the culture of the mind and spirit, will suffer most if war comes. Therefore, we must come to grips with this Far Eastern problem with the firm determination to solve it. We can only do so with the temper and approach of peace and friendliness, and not by threats. The time when threats were effective is long past. No question of saving face or prestige should come in the way of this human and civilized approach to the problems of our age.

Our task is the preservation of peace and indeed of our civilization. To this task let us bend our energies and find fellowship and strength in each other.

17

World Power Equilibrium[1]

Kashmir, 26 August 1952

My dear Chief Minister,

I have often written to you about foreign affairs and our foreign policy. There is far too great a tendency, even among eminent statesmen abroad, to simplify the issues and to talk in terms of some crusade, either for communism or anti-communism. This makes an understanding of the real situation much more difficult. Whatever our views may be about economic problems and policies, the first thing to remember is that it is not on account of these ideologies that this world crisis has arisen. Because of various historical reasons, two tremendous world powers dominate the scene today—the USA and the USSR. The other countries are either attached to one or the other in a subordinate capacity or play a rather passive independent role. In effect, each of the two great world powers struggles to obtain a predominant position in the world.

What can be the outcome of this historical process that has practically eliminated the other great and small powers? That historical process has been conditioned by many factors, chiefly technological developments. Will this process continue till one great power practically dominates the world? These technological developments in the science of warfare and rapid transport and communications have made it possible for such widespread and distant dominion to be exercised.

But before any such development takes place, there is bound to be war, because neither of the two great powers will submit to the other's dominion. We may calculate the relative strength of the two and their allies. In doing so, I think it would be true at this stage to say that the strength of the American group is greater, because they possess the more advanced technological processes and their industrial production is colossal. On the other side also, there is continuous technological progress and they have masses of human beings at their disposal. In any event, it can no longer be said that either side has a preponderating advantage which can result in a smashing and fairly quick

[1] To Chief Ministers, JN Papers, NMML. Excerpts.

victory. Thus, a world war now would not only be a prolonged affair, but would bring mutual destruction on a colossal scale. It would make little difference as to who is the victor and who is the vanquished, when the world lies in ruins.

It is for this very practical reason, apart from any theoretical or ethical approach, that every effort has to be made to prevent such a war from happening. What is the alternative?—some kind of adjustment between the great blocs of powers. If that adjustment is not possible, then war is inevitable and means a defeat for modern civilization and the very causes for which people will fight. The great question therefore is whether such an adjustment is possible. Considering the tremendous issues at stake, statesmanship must come to the conclusion that an adjustment must be made. Any other approach leads to disaster.

Most statesmen recognize this patent fact, but they often say that they will deal with the other party when they are strong enough to impose their will. That presumes that while one party adds to its strength, the other will remain quiescent. Of course, that is not going to happen. Indeed, it may well be that the other party grows more in strength during the interval and so the relative position either remains the same or worsens.

At the end of the last World War it was generally thought that the possession of the atomic bomb by the USA gave them a tremendous advantage over their adversaries. That advantage no longer exists in that measure now, and if there is a war, both sides may well use the atomic bomb. In the same way, it will be difficult for one party to have a major advantage for long and the other will catch up soon enough. Therefore, this talk of dealing with strength has no meaning. It simply leads to a policy of drift while conditions become worse.

If some kind of mutual adjustment and the creation of a new balance of power is the only way out, then countries like India can play a role which might help in bringing about that adjustment. We must not exaggerate this and imagine that we can do much. But we should not underrate the possibility either. Because of this, we have tried from time to time to help in bringing about conditions for a settlement in Korea. We have not succeeded. But that is no reason why we should despair or give up, for the consequences of no settlement are terrible to contemplate.

Few people realize fully how the old balance of power has been completely shattered. We either create a new balance or go to war. Mere piling up of armaments does not create a balance. It adds to the fear that leads to hatred and utter lack of understanding. It is not enough for us to talk vaguely of peace and put forward high ethical and moral principles. We have to understand the position objectively and practically in all its implications and then come to decisions. None of us, however powerful we may be, can mould the world after our pattern. There are inherent limitations in the power of the greatest country and it is dangerous to overestimate one's own power and to underestimate the power of the adversary. We have to keep this in view ourselves in regard to our limited commitments, whether they are military or financial. It is extraordinary how some people, who should be presumed to be responsible, talk irresponsibly of war, as if war was the solvent of all ills. One of our gravest problems is that of minorities in East Bengal. There is no doubt that the Pakistan Government has, in the past, followed a policy of squeezing out the middle classes especially. The April 1950 Agreement[2] certainly brought about some improvement, but the process continues and there is a great deal of distress. We try to deal with this problem on the diplomatic plane. The only other plane is that of war which, I am convinced, will not solve that problem, whatever else it might do. Yet, leading personalities talk about our adopting methods which can only lead to war.[3] I cannot imagine anything more irresponsible from every point of view and, more especially, that of the minorities concerned. We are accused sometimes of a policy of appeasement and are asked to get tough with Pakistan. The toughness that our accusers exhibit is the use of strong and offensive language. That is not how a civilized nation acts, nor is that the way of statesmanship. A nation conserves its strength and, because of that strength, can sometimes afford to take strong action. Even that action is inevitably limited by the strength and resources of that nation. It does not issue threats and use offensive language.

In the world today we live in some kind of a twilight between peace and war. The old balances having been completely upset, no new equilibrium has taken their place. For a long time Europe was the political centre of the world. Then America came into this picture and Europe and North America became the two main centres. Now western Europe has receded into the background and the two principal centres of power are supposed to be Washington and Moscow. At the same time, great changes and revolutions in Asia have taken that vast continent, to a large extent, outside the purview of colonial politics. China has emerged as a great power and, because of its alliance with the Soviet, has added greatly to the weight of Moscow in the world affairs. It must be remembered, however, that China and Russia need not pull together in every matter, because there are bound to be occasional conflicts in their national interests.

As the atomic age advances, war ceases to be a means of furthering a foreign policy, because war becomes an instrument of universal destruction. If there can be any justification for war today, it can only be in pure self-defence or self-preservation against aggression. Where there is such an aggression and a challenge to the very existence of a nation, that challenge has to be met. Or else, the nation disintegrates.

In this dangerous and threatening state of the world, what are we to do? We

---

[2] See ante Chapter 3, item 10, p. 347.

[3] S.P. Mookerjee, speaking at Pune on 25 August, asked the Government to follow the advice of Mahatma Gandhi which according to him had been that the life and property of the Hindus in Pakistan should be protected even if it meant using force.

cannot play a major part, but we can, perhaps, play some small part in either hastening or averting catastrophe. If we line up with either of the major contestants for world supremacy, we give up such little influence that we might possess in averting catastrophe and in that sense we hasten it. Keeping apart, we, and such other countries as function in the same way, at least keep an area free from the fever of war and view events with some calmness and objectivity, and occasionally throw our weight on the side of peace. Thus, whether we look at this question from the point of view of narrow national interest or the larger one of world peace, the only policy we can pursue is one of nonalignment with the power blocs and trying to maintain friendly relations with all countries.

Yours sincerely,
Jawaharlal Nehru

18

The New Spirit of Asia[1]

Mr. Mayor and Citizens of Peking,

I came to this great country of China, which is itself a little world, from another great country, which is also a little world of its own. Both have long roots in the past. Going back to the dawn of history, both have received through the ages innumerable streams of thought and culture from outside and have absorbed them and made them their own, giving them the impress of their own powerful personalities. They have changed and adapted themselves from time to time, and now, after long years of suppression, they have changed again and are blossoming out in various ways. These new and revolutionary changes in China and India, even though they differ in their content, symbolize the new spirit of Asia and the new vitality which is finding expression in the countries of Asia. Both our countries as well as the other countries of Asia have tremendous problems to face and we face them with assurance and self-confidence and with the firm desire to build our countries and bring happiness and contentment to our vast populations. That is the desire of every country in Asia.

We bear no ill will to any other country or people and desire to live at peace with the world. Although we have suffered at the hands of others in past years, I hope that we will bear no grudge against them and that no others will interfere with us.

Each of our countries was conditioned in its own way by its natural genius and the circumstances that faced it. We attained our freedom pursuing different paths. In India we were fortunate in achieving independence through peaceful methods and by a peaceful settlement and today we have no ill will against those who, in previous years, dominated over us. China's struggle was more arduous and more full of conflicts.

The emergence of China and India as free and sovereign countries, as well as the freedom that has come to other countries in Asia, has changed the face of this ancient continent. The old balance of forces, which resulted in the domination of Asia, has gone and a new equilibrium is gradually arising through pain and turmoil.

[1] Speech at Peking, China, 23 October 1954. Prime Ministers Office, File No. 8/294/-54-PMP. JN Papers, NMML.

While these great changes have taken place in the political, economic and social spheres, another mighty revolution is gradually taking shape. We stand at the threshold of a new age when man will command the tremendous forces released by atomic energy. Even as the Industrial Revolution, which began nearly 200 years ago, changed the face of the world, we are likely to see a greater change in the present generation.

It is in this mighty context and in this perspective that we have to look at the problems of today. These great forces can destroy the world and can also advance humanity to unimaginable levels of human well being.

It is this vital choice that the world has to make today. The choice is between peaceful progress and war, a war that will not be like the wars of old, but something infinitely worse and more destructive, something that might destroy civilization as we know it and degrade human beings to the level of the beast.

There can be only one answer to this question. But the mere avoidance of war is not enough. We have to remove the causes that lead to war and promote actively a climate of peace and goodwill. Fear and hatred and violence have darkened man's horizon for many years. Violence breeds violence, hatred degrades and stultifies, and fear is a bad companion. We have to get out of the vicious circle of conflict and try to build a new world based on friendly cooperation, where there is no domination or exploitation of one country by another, of one class by another, of one race by another. In our endeavours to build this new world, I earnestly hope that our methods will be those of peace and cooperation, for, I am convinced, that evil and violent methods cannot lead to good results.

China is a proud country with the culture of ages behind her. She rejoices in her new-found freedom and strength and looks forward with hope and confidence to the future. As an individual I may count for little, but I am also proud of my country and my heritage and, as a representative of my country and people, I can speak with strength and confidence in the future. But it is with no sense of pride but rather of humility that I face these great problems which confront us and which demand not pride of spirit and national vainglory and assertiveness, but rather the spirit of accommodation and friendly cooperation between all nations, great and small, to whatever continent they may belong. In this approaching atomic age, the rivalries and conflicts of the past have no place and we have to think and act in a different way, if this world and what it has achieved are to survive.

Great nations are today ranged against each other and there is said to be a conflict between East and West. We talk of disarmament, but each country adds to its armed strength and new and terrible weapons of war are forged. That is not the way to peace. We must recognize that the only way to live in this world is through coexistence and cooperation and recognition of the right of each country to live its own life. There can be no East and West ranged against each other in the future. There could be only one world devoting itself in friendly cooperation between its different parts to the advancement of humanity. The recent agreement in Geneva, in which the representatives of China played such a distinguished part and which brought peace to Indo-China, has shown us the way to peaceful settlements by negotiation of difficult problems.[2] There is no reason why we should not apply this method to other problems also, even though there are difficulties and the way may be long. That is the only path we can tread.

The five principles declared on behalf of China and India lay the foundations of this new approach. I earnestly trust that they will be accepted and acted upon not only by the countries and peoples of Asia but also by other countries and peoples. Thus we shall enlarge the area of peace and remove the fear of war and the tensions that exist today.

I have come to you as a messenger of peace and goodwill and I have found here both the spirit of peace and goodwill. So I have felt in harmony with my surroundings and my faith in the future has strengthened.

[2] The conflicts in Vietnam, Laos, Thailand and Cambodia with the principal involvement of France and later United States were known as the Indo-China wars. An agreement was signed at the Geneva Conference in July 1954.

19

Formosa[1]

New Delhi, 23 February 1955

My dear Chief Minister,

The Commonwealth Prime Ministers' Conference in London coincided accidentally with the development of a grave crisis in the Far East. This was in connection with Formosa and the off-shore islands of China.[2] It was natural, therefore, for the Prime Ministers' Conference to pay much attention to this crisis. We discussed it at some length and there was some difference of opinion. But there was also a measure of agreement. All of us were very anxious to help in lessening the tension and finding some way which might lead to negotiation between the parties concerned. We did not succeed in this. Nevertheless, it did all of us good to hear the viewpoints of the others. Thus, we could form a better picture of the situation.

It was natural for the United Kingdom, Canada, Australia and New Zealand to be nearer to the American viewpoint and to understand it better. China was still a far-off country to them, which had indulged in a revolution producing awkward situations. To some extent, it fell to me to represent what might be called the Asian point of view. I am not referring particularly to the question of Formosa but rather to the general ferment in Asia which is one of the striking features of the present age. I pointed out that this basic upheaval of men's ideas and their urges in Asia must be understood. It did little good to think of Asia as it was previously, rather static and unchanging. Asia was dynamic today and, to some extent, even explosive and unless we understand this, we shall be unable to deal with any of its problems adequately. It was in this context that I wanted the Far East situation to be considered. Pakistan and Ceylon were partly in agreement with what I said, though they did not lay so much stress on this aspect.

So far as the Formosa situation was concerned, for a country that had

---

[1] To Chief Ministers. JN Papers, NMML. Excerpts.
[2] Formosa (Taiwan) was ceded to China after World War II. Following Communist victory on the mainland in 1949 the Nationalist government and its supporters, led by General Chiang Kai-shek, fled to Formosa. In 1954 the Nationalist government and the United States signed a mutual defence treaty and Formosa received military and economic support from the USA.

recognized the new China, it followed naturally that Formosa should be part of it. That indeed was in keeping with the numerous statements made during and after the world war. At the same time, present facts had to be recognized and some peaceful way out found for a negotiated settlement. That was our attitude. Most of the countries did not go quite so far as this and did not wish to commit themselves in regard to Formosa's future. They considered it undetermined although, I have little doubt, they felt that ultimately it would have to go to China. The fact, however, of the United States' strenuous objection to the very idea of Formosa going to China was an effective barrier to their thinking. The result was that they concentrated on the coastal or off-shore islands and wanted these islands to be evacuated by the Kuomintang troops. If this was done without conflict, the chances of untoward incidents would lessen very greatly. There would then be nearly a hundred miles of sea between China and Formosa, and further developments could be considered at leisure. We were all agreed that these off-shore islands, more especially Quemoy and the Matsu islands, should be evacuated as soon as possible.

The American attitude was by no means clear. Recently Mr. Dulles has spoken at some length and has perhaps clarified the US position a little, though even now it is full of ambiguity. He has stated that Quemoy and Matsu islands are not necessary for American strategy, but he has added that if they are attacked, the US Navy would defend them. He has further made it clear that the Kuomintang Government of Formosa is not willing to evacuate them. There the matter rests at present. The situation is obviously full of danger. On the one side, the Chinese proclaim loudly and repeatedly that they will attack and seize not only these islands but Formosa itself. On the other hand, the Americans appear to be determined to prevent this. Meanwhile, attack and counter-attack continue in some small measure. There is always a danger of something happening which may lead to an explosion on a bigger scale. President Eisenhower has referred to Formosa as the spearhead of their strategic defence. If that is so many thousands of miles away from the United States, then it is legitimate for the Chinese to think that Formosa is much more necessary for their defence.

I think that the Americans are afraid that if the coastal islands are evacuated, the Kuomintang forces in Formosa would be demoralized and might even crack up. This is certainly a possibility. This indicates that the present regime in Formosa has little inner strength and is bolstered up by external forces. One might perhaps compare it, though the parallel is not exact, to an old Indian State or some other kind of subordinate state. It is difficult to imagine that this kind of situation can last or be stabilized for long, more especially in the Asia of today.

Yours sincerely,
Jawaharlal Nehru

20

World Peace and Cooperation[1]

Mr. Chairman,

   . . . We have just had the advantage of listening to the distinguished leader of the Turkish Delegation who told us what he, as a responsible leader of the nation, must do and must not do. He gave us an able statement of what I might call one side representing the views of one of the major blocs existing at the present time in the world. I have no doubt that an equally able discourse could be given on the part of the other bloc. I belong to neither and I propose to belong to neither whatever happens in the world. If we have to stand alone, we will stand by ourselves, whatever happens (and India has stood alone without any aid against a mighty empire, the British Empire) and we propose to face all consequences.

What has the "reality" led us to? What has the reality of the peace that followed the last War led us to? I would like the honourable delegates to realize that, to appreciate that. This so-called realistic appreciation of the world situation, where has it led us to? It has led us to the brink of war, a third world war. It has been stated by eminent persons who know about it that if there is another war there will be total destruction of mankind. That is to say, a third world war would bring us not only to the abyss of civilization and culture but would mean total destruction. We have to face that.

The delegate for Turkey has gone through the history of the past ten years. Perhaps that history could be, here and there, interpreted differently. Much of it may be true and much of it may be interpreted differently. It is hardly possible for us to discuss the history of the past ten years because we have been living in revolutionary times. Following this last World War, in Asia great things have happened. There is that great nation, China, which has risen after hundreds of years of strife and oppression. That is a major fact of the situation. There is India which does not presume to possess any military might but presumes to have the strength to face any danger, whenever it may come.

We do not agree with the communist teachers, we do not agree with the anti-communist teachers, because they are both based on wrong principles. I never challenged the right of any country to defend itself; it has to. We will

[1] First part of the speech in the closed session of the Asian-African Conference at Bandung, 22 April 1955. JN Papers, NMML. Excerpts.

defend ourselves with whatever arms and strength we have, and if we have no arms we will defend ourselves without arms. I am dead certain that no country can conquer India. Even the two great power blocs together cannot conquer India; not even the atom or the hydrogen bomb. I know what my people are. But I know also that if we rely upon others, whatever great powers they might be if we look to them for sustenance, then we are weak indeed.

True our outlook is different. Ideologies are talked about. Let us not talk about ideologies. What did the Hon'ble delegates from Turkey talk about ideology? He talked about it all the time. If I am to talk about another ideology, the Gandhian ideology, I can go on for hours, but I do not want to impose it on honourable members here. I know that Gandhi won my freedom. I am afraid of nobody. I suffer from no fear complex; my country suffers from no fear complex. We rely on nobody except on the friendship of others; we rely on ourselves and none others.

I do not want to take up the time of honourable delegates here but I wish to tell this House that I neither believe in the communist nor the anti-communist approach to this question. So far as we are concerned, we have adopted a line of action and we propose to adhere to it, come what may. But let us examine the situation as it is today. What does it lead to? Some delegates have pointed out the dangers of the situation. One side says, "Let us arm, and arm and arm because the other party is arming" and the other party says "Let us arm, and arm and arm because the other party is arming." So, both sides go on making arms.

My country has made mistakes. Every country makes mistakes. I have no doubt we will make mistakes; we will stumble and fall and get up. The mistakes of my country and perhaps the mistakes of other countries here do not make a difference; but the mistakes the Great Powers make do make a difference to the world and may well bring about a terrible catastrophe. I speak with the greatest respect for these Great Powers because they are not only great in military might but in development, in culture, in civilization. But I do submit that greatness sometimes brings quite false values, false standards. When they began to think in terms of military strength—whether it be the United Kingdom, the Soviet Union or the USA—then they are going away from the right track and the result of that may be that the overwhelming might of one country will conquer the world. Thus far the world has succeeded in preventing that; I cannot speak for the future. But you have today two mighty colossuses, neither of whom can put an end to the other but obviously they can ruin each other and the rest of the world. There is no other way out. Everybody recognizes it; the great statesmen of England, Russia and America recognize it. Let us admit that we have all committed mistakes. Let us admit that one has committed more mistakes than the other. However, that is immaterial, except in academic debate.

We have to face the position as it is today, namely, that whatever armaments one side or other might possess, war will lead to consequences which will result in not gaining an objective but ruin. Therefore, the first thing we have to settle is that war must be avoided. Naturally war cannot be avoided if any country takes to a career of conquest and aggression. Secondly, the countries of Asia have to consider whether we can, all of us put together—certainly not singly prevent the great powers or big countries going to war. We certainly cannot prevent the big countries going to war if they want to but we can make a difference. Even a single country can make a difference when the scales are evenly balanced. What are we going to do? Are we going to throw our weight in the scales on the side of peace or war? It is no use blaming the Soviet Union or America. It is perfectly true that at the present moment we, not only in Asia but in Europe as well, have every reason to dislike and oppose, not only external aggression but internal subversion and all the rest of it.

Let us then talk of the steps we can take. The first step is to make our view clear that these things should not happen. So far as I am concerned, it does not matter that war takes place; we will not take part in it unless we have to defend ourselves. If I join any of these big groups I lose my identity; I have no identity left, I have no views left. I may express it here and there generally but I have no views left. If all the world were to be divided up between these two big blocs what would be the result? The inevitable result would be war. Therefore, every step that takes place in reducing that area in the world which may be called the "unaligned area" is a dangerous step and leads to war. It reduces that objectivity, that balance, that outlook which other countries without military might can perhaps exercise.

Honourable members laid great stress on moral force. It is with military force that we are dealing now but I submit that moral force counts and the moral force of Asia and Africa must, in spite of the atomic and hydrogen bombs of Russia, the USA or another country, count. Unfortunately, in discussing this very desirable proposition put forward by the Prime Minister of Burma, we have drifted to all kinds of other things. On the face of it, nobody can challenge the proposition of the Prime Minister of Burma. All that may be said of it is that it does not go far enough, that it is rather reiterating, even repetitive, of the Charter. Every truth that you say is likely to have originated somewhere or other. The point is that a certain truth has a certain application at a particular moment. If it has no application at a particular moment, it will be forgotten. Why does this simple word "coexistence" raise all sorts of turmoil in people's minds? Because it has a significance in the present state of the world. Otherwise everybody recognizes it. What is the alternative to peaceful coexistence? There may be coexistence, not peaceful, but something in the nature of Cold War. Why then be afraid of the word? Are we choosing war deliberately or moving unconsciously towards war, which cold war implies. I say that there is no alternative for any country, unless it wants war, but to accept the concept of peaceful coexistence. In some countries the very word peace is looked upon with horror. It is most amazing. That word is considered dangerous! So I submit, let us consider these matters practically, leaving out ideologies. Many members present here do not obviously accept the communist ideology, while some of them do. For my part I do not. I am a positive person, not an "anti" person. I want positive good for my country and the world. Therefore, are we, the countries of Asia and Africa, devoid of any positive position except being pro-communist or anti-communist? Has it come to this, that the leaders of thought who have given religions and all kinds of things to the world have to tag on to this kind of group or that and be hangers on of this party or the other carrying out their wishes and occasionally giving an idea? It is most degrading and humiliating to any self-respecting people or nation. It is an intolerable thought to me that the great countries of Asia and Africa should come out of bondage into freedom only to degrade themselves or humiliate themselves in this way. Well, I do not criticize these powers. They are probably capable of looking after themselves and know what is best for themselves. But I will not tie myself to this degradation. Am I to lose my freedom and individuality and become a camp-follower of others? I have absolutely no intention of doing that.

A reference was made to these various attacks made in the Middle East, South-East Asia and so on. The whole course of the discussion has proceeded on that theme. Mr. Mohamed Ali put forward an excellent resolution. Certainly the first four points in that resolution are acceptable to us all. The fifth deals with self-defence, singly or collectively. I do not deny the right of any country to defend itself. It is a natural right that cannot be denied. Then why is it put there? It has been put there because of these pacts that have been organized in western and eastern Asia. If that is the position I am not prepared to accept it. If that point is put there to cover those pacts, how can we accept it? I do not challenge Mr. Mohamed Ali's right to enter into any pacts although I may disagree with him, but under cover of words to ask this conference to accept the principle of those pacts is, I submit, something that should not be done. It is open to him to have those pacts. It is open to me not to have them. But to bring in this way the collective defence pacts made in the last year is going far beyond our subject and bringing in things which are highly controversial and which tend to lead to fundamental differences of opinion.

I submit to you, every pact has brought insecurity and not security to the countries which have entered into them. They have brought the danger of atomic bombs and the rest of it nearer to them than would have been the case otherwise. They have not added to the strength of any country, I submit, which it had singly. It may have produced some idea of security, but it is a false security. It is a bad thing for any country thus to be lulled into security.

The distinguished delegate of Turkey referred to NATO. I have nothing to say against NATO. It is open to the European countries to join it for self-defence. I cannot challenge it in the slightest. But I should like to point out to this assembly that this conception of the NATO has extended itself in two ways. It has gone far away from the Atlantic and has reached other oceans and seas. Leave that alone, Secondly, do honourable members of this conference realize that the NATO today is one of the most powerful protectors of colonialism? I say that explicitly. I am not saying that indirectly, but directly and explicitly. Here is the little territory of Goa, in India, which Portugal holds. We get letters from the NATO powers—mind you, Portugal is a member of NATO—and Portugal has approached its fellow members in the NATO on this point— telling us "You should not do anything in regard to Goa, you should not do this and that." I will not mention these powers; they are some of the so-called Big Powers. It does not matter what powers they are, but it is gross impertinence. The new Republic of India told them that it is gross impertinence on their part. Let there be no doubt about it, we shall deal with this little matter in the way we like.

The distinguished delegate of Iraq was eloquent about Morocco, Algeria and Tunisia. Does he realize that these three territories would probably have been independent if it were not for NATO? Today because of the assistance given by these Great Powers NATO has bases for various purposes in these parts of the world. So we must take a complete view of the situation and not be contradictory ourselves when we talk about colonialism, when we say 'colonialism must go', and in the same voice say that we support every policy or some policies that confirm colonialism. It is an extraordinary attitude to take up.

So I do submit that we must for the moment leave out past history, as to what happened in Potsdam, at the Cairo Conference and at Yalta, as to what President Roosevelt said or Winston Churchill said and what somebody else did. All post-war confusion has arisen from all kinds of steps taken, right or wrong, in the past. And we have to suffer today because of this confusion, because it clouds our view of the total world situation. Turkey said that the US and other powers disarmed rapidly after the War. Let us admit that. What happens today? Can we forget that the situation we have to face today is that the world, a good part of it, is ranged with one big bloc or other, both having a certain ideology? I do not know the ideology of the western bloc. Certainly it is not one single ideology; those in it differ, but in a military sense they hold together. There are other countries in the world which have not aligned themselves in this way. Some may sympathize with this bloc or the other, and some may not. Two big colossuses stand face to face with each other, afraid of each other. Today in the world, I do submit, not only because of the presence of these two colossuses but also because of the coming of the atomic and hydrogen-bomb age, the whole concept of war, of peace, of politics, has changed. We are thinking and acting in terms of a past age. No matter what generals and soldiers learned in the past, it is useless in this atomic age. They do not understand its implications or its use. As an eminent military critic said: "The whole conception of war is changed. There is no precedent." It may be so. Now it does not matter if one country is more powerful than the other in the use of the atomic bomb and the hydrogen bomb. One is more powerful to cause ruin than the other. That is what is meant by saying that the point of saturation has been reached. However, powerful one country is, the other is also powerful. It is the world that suffers; there can be no victory. It may be said perhaps rightly that owing to this very terrible danger, people refrain from going to war. I hope so. The difficulty is that while governments want to refrain from war, something suddenly happens and there is war and utter ruin. There is another thing: because of the present position in the world there is not likely to be aggression. If there is aggression anywhere in the world, it is bound to result in world war. It does not matter where the aggression is. If one commits aggression there is world war.

I want the countries here to realize it and not to think in terms of any limitations. Today, a war however limited it may be, is bound to lead to big war. Even if tactical atomic weapons, as they are called, are used, the next step would be the use of the big atomic bomb. You cannot stop these things. In a country's life-and-death struggle, it is not going to stop short of this. It is not going to decide on our or anybody else's resolutions but it would engage in war, ruin and annihilation of others before it allows itself to be annihilated completely. Annihilation will result not only in the countries engaged in war, but owing to the radioactive waves which go thousands and thousands of miles it will destroy everything. That is the position. It is not an academic position; it is not a position of discussing ideologies; nor is it a position of discussing past history. It is looking at the world as it is today.

The leaders of the great nations like the President of the United States have to carry a world of responsibility in having to face this position. So do the leaders of United Kingdom and Russia. It is a tremendous burden. I do not know at what time an error might be made this way or that way which would lead to war.

Now, therefore, are we, the Asian and African countries, going to look on it passively or are we going to take a step which will upset the balance on one side or the other? This is not a question of security. Will not security be damned if war comes? Who is going to protect us if war comes and if atomic bombs come? Of course, every country will look after itself, but it will be difficult to do that with atomic bombs, radioactive waves and all that. Therefore, I would beg this conference to appreciate the gravity of this situation. It is a very grave situation indeed. We have not discussed Formosa and the rest, nor is it necessary for us to discuss the merits of the question. But the fact is that in the Far Eastern countries the situation is very grave. One does not know where it will lead to. Therefore, can we not in our own way say something peacefully, and in a friendly way, firmly declaring something, which will set the scales in favour of peace? That is the problem.

I do submit that the so-called five principles (whatever the number may be, they have more or less been included in the resolution of the Prime Minister of Burma) is not a magic formula which will prevent all the ills of the world. But it is something which meets the needs of the day. It lessens tension; it does not harm anybody, criticize anybody, condemn anybody. And I assure you, broadly speaking, President Eisenhower is in agreement with those principles. I know that the present Prime Minister of England has said so in a public address given to our Members of Parliament. Some of us here may disagree with it, but surely that is the reverse of the right step for us to take. I therefore beg of this conference to consider the matter in the light of the actualities of today. I am entirely one with the Honourable Head of the Turkish delegation when he says that we must take a realistic view, a view which is related to facts of today, not yesterday or the day before yesterday.

Between the day before yesterday and today there have been war and vast revolutions have taken place; many changes have taken place and all kinds of things have been happening. So that one must consider things as they are today. If the Hon'ble delegate of Iraq represents the right viewpoint, I can say that the world is going to ruin. It is not an approach to this question and his speech is full of irritation, hatred and disregard. His whole speech is a tirade, It is not a balanced speech. Let us not align ourselves as independent nations of Asia and Africa, but take a line of our own. I do not say that it should be a single line. I do submit that the Resolution put forward by the Burmese Prime Minister is the correct solution. A word may be changed here and there. It works on a correct basis, a friendly basis for all countries. It does not say anything which might irritate anybody.

The Prime Minister of Pakistan says that it is good but not enough, and he wanted to add many things. There is some Resolution which he had about colonialism. We have dealt with it already. You take away the force of the Resolution if you add all these things. He said something about the peaceful solution of disputes. Have a Resolution or an amendment; but he has referred to all kinds of things. Some people have said: "Let us have the Charter". As a matter of fact, some of the Hon'ble delegates were not present when the Prime Minister of Burma proposed his Resolution. So, Mr. President, with your permission, I shall read it out again.

The nations assembled at the Asian-African Conference declare that their relations between themselves, and their approach to the other nations of the world, shall be governed by complete respect for the national sovereignty and integrity of other nations. They will not intervene or interfere in the territory or the internal affairs of each other or of other nations, and will totally refrain from acts or threats of aggression. They recognize the equality of races and of nations, large and small. They will be governed by the desire to promote mutual interest and cooperation, by respect for the fundamental Human Rights and the principles of the Charter of the United Nations.

I do submit that there is not a word in this Resolution to which anybody can object. As a matter of fact, the word "coexistence" is not used at all, although we are discussing this Resolution under that head. Unless one thinks that there is no alternative to this except war, and to be prepared for war, this resolution has to be accepted.

21

War, Peace and Cooperation[1]

Mr. Chairman,

During the few days we have been here we have had important discussions, but I doubt if any discussion has been so important as the one we are having today. I am very glad that all of us have spoken frankly and fully upon these vital subjects. May I right from the beginning express my regrets to the distinguished delegate from Iraq for what I said yesterday about his speech exhibiting hatred; his speech I thought exhibited hatred and we were naturally upset about it.

May I also say that when I spoke yesterday I rather criticized the military outlook of some powers here. I do not mean to say that we should all be pacifists. I regret I am no pacifist. I should like to be one, but I am no pacifist in the circumstances of today and because of the responsibilities I have.

I do not believe in weakness, but in the strength of the people. Weakness creates a vacuum which power fills in. The question that arises is not weakness or strength, but what constitutes strength in a nation. Armies and the like are only one factor, if I may say so, a relatively unimportant factor, in the strength of a nation. If we have an army today and no backing, it is of no use. It is the industrial backing that a country wants; if we had no economic power the army would not be able to hold on, because the weapons are made somewhere else. We have to depend on others. Apart from all these factors, there is a certain factor; the morale of the people—the morale which refuses to give in, whatever happens.

We have spoken frankly. Perhaps I spoke with a measure of warmth yesterday, and if any words that I used yesterday seemed disrespectful to any distinguished delegate present here, I apologize wholeheartedly. I spoke with warmth and frankness because I feel strongly about these matters. Here we are meeting in this conference. What does this conference mean? It means many .things. If I may respectfully say, this conference reflects the profound historical changes that are taking place in Asia. It is a vast change that is going on, much bigger than the subjects that we are here discussing. Unfortunately, the thinking of men's minds often lags behind events. It is an odd thing, although events

[1] Second part of the speech in the closed session of the Asian-African Conference at Bandung, 23 April 1955. JN Papers, NMML.

take place because of the human mind, yet the human mind lags behind the very events that take place. So we often think in terms of the past when the present is already different from that past.

Now I have come here naturally in my capacity as a representative of India, but I have come here not merely as an individual or representative of India, but as a part of the revolutionary process that has been going on in India; for I am a child of that revolution. I am no static person; I have been in the market place; I have moved with crowds and seen the vast squalor and the poverty prevailing and so I feel strongly about these matters. We have dreamt dreams and we have partly realized those dreams not only for India but for Asia and the whole world. So if anything happens that seems to come in the way of the realization of those dreams, that seems to shatter them into bits, then naturally we react strongly with all the energy and force at our command.

We have had a very important statement from the Prime Minister of China. He has spoken with full authority and made certain statements. I shall not say much about it except to point out what is obvious: the various things that he has said on behalf of his government and his country deserve the fullest consideration. I shall rather deal with what the distinguished delegates from Iraq, Lebanon and the Philippines said chiefly in dealing with the speech I made yesterday. But before I do that I should like to repeat: the basic fact which troubles me often is the fact of our discussing things in terms of the past, when the present and the future are impinging upon us. We stand everywhere in the world, more so in Asia, on the sword's edge of the present dividing the past from the future. It is a precarious position, an exciting position, a fascinating position. But we have to be careful. We should be careful to preserve the hard-won freedom we have got, careful to see that it is not crushed out of existence, not only by the enemy or opponent of us all, but by world events. So that we have to see this large picture and in looking at it, one sees all kinds of changes. What are they due to? Well, many things. We may criticize communism, Russia, the Soviet Union, America, whatever we like, but all these things are parts of great historical processes—if I may go back 150 or 160 or 170 years—they are the culmination of the Industrial Revolution. This atomic bomb is the culmination of the Industrial Revolution.

Now Asia fell back in the race of life because of the Industrial Revolution which came to Europe first and then to America. Asia became a power vacuum. Now our going to Europe for building our arms and armaments would be of no use unless we build ourselves up on a much sounder basis. Therefore, we are all anxious—each country here—to advance forward in every way—economically, industrially and the like—to build up our source of power, our basic source of power, which, I submit, is morale and elan and the vitality of a nation. Here big countries and small countries can play a tremendous part because of the elan that they possess, because of the spirit of life they possess. Now that almost all countries represented here—big and small—have not been able to keep pace in the race of life, they have now to catch up and catch up rapidly. We have no time to lose; we have to face the technological changes that have brought about all this vast difference in the world. We the countries in Asia have the good in our grasp, but something terrible threatens to smother us, I mean the atomic bomb and the hydrogen bomb. But then this technological advance has also made the world one. We may be jealous of our nationality and sovereignty and independence but as the threat affects the whole world we are really beginning more and more not to consider each one of us as isolated nations. Therefore, we have to bring up our thinking to this technological development.

Now it would be highly improper, for me to criticize ideologies and theories and all that, but, with all deference and humility, I would suggest—I am only expressing my own personal opinion—that the way of approach to these world problems, which the great Powers at present are adopting, whether they are on the communist side or the non-communist side, is completely, out of date and that is why we are faced with all this trouble, all this confusion, because events outpace us—march ahead of us—and we are left behind. I am no believer in the Communist theory—there is much in it which I accept in the economic theory, but basically I think it is out of date today, more especially in this atomic age. I think equally that the opposite theory is out of date in the context of modern world affairs.

Now one thing more. I think the delegate from the Philippines referred to the bigness of India and to the smallness of other countries. May I remind him that all the bigness of India did not prevent India from becoming a subject nation for a long period of time. It is not physical bigness that counts and I venture to repeat what I said yesterday and to give the assurance that India will not do this or do that thing because of its population of 370 millions but because of the quality of the Indian people, not because of their numbers. I believe that that quality has developed in Indonesia and in other countries also. I want to develop that quality and I do not want any country in Asia to be lulled into a sense of, shall I say, dependence upon others, because that saps—that undermines the growth of that elan of a nation—that spirit of self-dependence, of having faith in themselves. That is the basic—if you like, the only—reason why I do not like the business of creating a feeling of dependence. A feeling of cooperation is obviously right and it is necessary in the world of today.

I refer to pacts and other things because they have been directly referred to. Now, obviously it would be highly improper for me to go about criticizing everybody else as if I am a very wise man. I have no such inclination and if I refer to anything I refer to it in the context of world events of today. I cannot say whether what was done yesterday or ten years ago was desirable or not because one has to judge at the moment. The application of certain high principles depends on the historical context of the moment. Therefore, whatever I have said does not apply to the past, we can deal with the past separately. I will deal with the present as it is today and it is in that context that I plead that the military view of the situation—I am not referring to any particular thing—is not correct. It would not have been correct anyhow with the coming of the atomic age. Now, for instance, I am not here to say that the countries of western Europe were unjustified in having the NATO alliance; I cannot say that honestly. I do, as I said yesterday, take exception to the extension of the NATO alliance to the colonial territories because that affects me and all the countries here, but, for self-defence, if they have the NATO alliance, I have nothing to say. When we come to the very edge of the precipice, then we have to be careful what we do, whether what we do does not topple us over the precipice and whether something that we do adds to the security or insecurity of our country. None of the prime ministers, or other ministers, present here can responsibly discharge his task by complacently thinking that all is well. All is not well in the world today; that is the basic position and we have to think how we meet the situation. Anyway people have tried to meet the situation in the past few years. After all what is the history of the past two years. I am not going into history but I may say, with all respect, that it is a history of diplomatic failure. If we ask whether the past few years have taken us towards peace—lessening of tension—or towards war and increase of tension, I say there has been patently a failure. Whoever may be responsible is not the point, but the point is that this diplomatic failure has been leading the world towards war and increase of tension. It has led us nowhere and, if not checked, it will rather lead us to wrong places and it is not wisdom to pursue it.

Let us think afresh. What was wrong with the past, what has led us to the brink of world war? The Hon'ble delegate of Lebanon said that it is easy to quote some scientists or others talking about the destruction of the human race by the new hydrogen bomb and it is equally easy to quote people, equally distinguished, who would minimize the effects of that bomb. He is completely right. We can quote authorities for either side, but I say that if there is a danger of that, we must naturally see what is going to happen to our countries in the context of the present world conditions and I venture to say that no scientist in the world can say definitely what will be its precise effect because certainly we are piercing the curtain of the known and peering into the unknown. Nobody knows yet what the effect of these radioactive substances is likely to be. Some say it will have a disastrous effect; others say it might not be so, but the fact is that we have arrived at a stage when we do not know how deep would be its effect.

In fact, as everyone knows, one of these hydrogen bomb experiments has surprised the very persons, the very scientists, who were behind it, because it was much worse than they thought. We cannot say what is going to happen, but we are all agreed on the enormous danger of this new invention. As to what is the extent of that danger, we may differ in our estimation.

Now, Sir, with your permission, I shall take up some of the points that the distinguished delegate from Iraq has raised in a very cogent and logical speech. He said that there are two camps in the world today, which, of course, is known to all of us, and that there are three possibilities—passive and negative resistance and peace through strength. We understand Sir Winston Churchill's peace-through-strength approach, universal disarmament, international control, etc.

Now, as I have just said, my attitude or India's attitude, is certainly not passive. It is certainly not a negative attitude. I have to take India ahead. I have to increase the strength of India, and I presume everyone feels that way about his own country. It is definitely a positive attitude, realizing that the objective should be peace and that we should positively and actively work for peace and try to counter everything that takes one to war. Now the attitude of peace-through-strength of Sir Winston Churchill is true in a sense. Of course, as I said, weakness is the greatest crime that a country or a people can have, but I would beg to say that the strength at any time—much more so today—cannot be measured by military standards alone. Anyhow, a country—in fact most countries, apart from very, cannot really even take part effectively in a big war in regard to atomic weapons and the like. They cannot measure themselves and their strength by means of atomic weapons that they possess. So let us build up our strength, but the obvious answer to all this talking about peace through strength is for every power to talk of peace through strength. So both sides go on stressing strength for peace, with the result that armaments grow more and more and consequently the danger also grows. That way you are not solving the question at all. It is getting worse and worse. When arms grow fears also grow more and then there should be more arms to encounter the fears till the whole thing topples down. It is logical that every country wants to achieve strength and work for peace, but the whole context of it is that if peaceful strength is talked about and worked for in a sense which frightens the other party, then obviously the other party reacts exactly in the same way and if you build up 50 per cent or more of strength, the other person has also built up 50 per cent or more of strength. That is the present position. How to meet it? Well, if you have arrived at this stage, the only way to meet it is to prevent a war, to promote confidence and to lessen tension.

Now much has been said about disarmament. Some members have studied this question deeply. I do not pretend to be an expert, but I have studied it ever since the old League of Nations considered the question of disarmament year after year in Geneva and they appointed a Preparatory Committee on Disarmament which sat for three years. I myself am in favour of disarmament—of every type of armament. Let us realize that from the point of disarmament it is not very logical to speak of only one weapon and leave somebody else in possession of another weapon. One has to see the whole picture. But what is this disarmament? Some people say let us have disarmament first, then talk about coexistence.

I am sorry I used the world 'coexistence', because that word seems to bring up all kinds of frightening pictures before people's minds. A delegate, with great knowledge of past history referred to what happened in 1924. I am not aware of that. It is true that we have got into the practice of using words, slogans and cliches that confound our thought and limit our logical processes of thinking and the sooner we do away with them the better it will be. Then what are we to do if somebody used the word in a wrong or mischievous sense? How do we give up that word? I doubt if any word has been so misused as peace. Have we to give up peace? That is the position. Somebody used it the wrong way. Let us use it in the right way and stop the person using it in the wrong way. Similarly, the word 'coexistence' has come up for so much discussion that it has lost its significance.

I was talking about disarmament. Some people said that before you accept the principle of living together peacefully, we must disarm ourselves. That is perfectly true. On the other hand, it is equally true to say that nobody can disarm till the fears and tensions are removed. So you get into a vicious circle which goes on. Is it possible for advance to be made on both fronts? Let us try to advance on both fronts. No country, it is obvious, is going to take the risk; no responsible government can take the risk. On the other hand, not doing something in itself is a tremendous risk; it is the greatest risk of war. Therefore, we have to balance these risks. Let each country strengthen itself so far as it can, but strenghtening itself should not take place in the manner which increases apprehensions and fears. There have been open threats and open challenges that if you do not do this, we will come and hit you on the head and invade your country. Is this a search for peace? Peace as a word has itself assumed the likeness of war today. I would submit that we should not indulge in this, because it is not creating peace; whatever the countries may feel and whatever their views and ideologies, we should not use the word which frightens others. Great things are happening in the world today. So far as I can help it, I do not go about denouncing a thing if I do not agree. Because one denunciation brings about another. It is no use slinging mud at each other.

I go back again to disarmament as a whole, but one should really create lessening of tension. The moment the tension is lessened, disarmament becomes easier. I think in the last few years it has made some advance. How far this would go, I do not know. This is the state of affairs in the world today and we have to be realistic in facing the existing problems. What does disarmament mean? It means not having weapons for the purposes of war; but we must realize the fact that all these countries of the world are gradually being industrialized, they are having factories, chemical factories, and they can produce arms and ammunition at short notice. They may not be able to produce atomic bombs in a short time; but the hydrogen bomb is easier to make. It is an easy matter for the scientists. Therefore, we should not forget that in advanced countries, industries can make all these things at a short notice, even if you decide to disarm those countries. And, that was exactly the difficulty which faced the League of Nations too in disarming the different nations; it is so very difficult to talk of

disarmament in the case of highly industrialized countries. If it comes to anything, these countries can produce all these things in a week's time. Therefore,
I would pose a question to the delegates here: Are you going to stop industrialization of the various countries so as to disarm them? I feel that we cannot hold
that view because we have to make progress in the industrial field and thereby
also improve our economic fabric which is the most important and baffling
problem facing us today. So, the question of disarmament is a complicated
question in which we cannot easily come to fruitful decision. We can discuss
it and it must be discussed, but for us merely to say that we should disarm ourselves, would not help us.

Now, I come to the few possibilities that the delegate from Iraq mentioned.
The first possibility that he suggested was that we should be passive, which
means that the people of a country are not a live people. We have been passive
too long in Asia; it is about time that we gave up passivity and came to live like
active people in the world. So, I completely disagree with his first proposition.

The second was peace through strength. Well, I doubt very much if many
countries here can ever acquire strength at least for a long time to come to resist
any of the Great Powers of the world. That is not possible. We certainly require
strength to protect our liberty, but then our strength will be dependent on
industrialization. We have to industrialize the countries as much as possible.
The whole industrial background of various countries represented here has to
be given a new outlook and finally and most important, it depends on the
improvement of the economic fibre of the country. Well, now for instance, you
cannot make a country strong by supplying it arms and deadly weapons like
atom bomb and hydrogen bombs, because until such time as it is industrialized
and able to produce these weapons itself, you will have to go on supplying
weapons. So, the position does not change at all. The balance is the same.
Therefore, it does not help us to talk about peace through strength. So, actually
disarmament is the only remedy that we have in view, but that has got to be
achieved through international control. We quite realize that a highly industrialized country is an armed country because it can produce all types of arms
including hydrogen bombs at a short notice while others are not. So, therefore,
we have to approach this question in its proper perspective and certainly we can
industrialize each and every country for peaceful purposes to keep up the moral
fibre of the nation at its highest pitch. It is necessary to make every country
realize that it would be a stiff job to adopt aggressive motives against any country.

Then, the honourable delegate from Iraq said that we should all be united
in one single block as there was great danger of obliteration to the small nations
if they are left single by themselves. I have never suggested that we should not
organize for self-defence. But, what I said was that if you organize in a way
which does not solve the problem, you are constantly in danger. Today, what
is the nature of war? In this atomic age, havoc can be played within a very short

time. There cannot be real defeat or real victory in war in the present-day world of scientific development. Therefore, I say that we should not involve ourselves into a common danger by forming a separate block of nations. Really, small nations have greater chance of survival if they keep away from military alliances. Therefore we have to think and think very seriously before we form ourselves into a common bloc. By all means, if you all think in terms of forming a bloc of small nations, you can do so, but there are grave dangers involved in it as I feel that we are in a stage where we cannot help each other effectively. I do not quite understand how we can reduce the tension which exists today by making military alliances.

I am all for ideological disarmament; it is quite true that ideological disarmament can bring about harmony and peace but, for that, we have to work. We have to stop cursing each other, we have to stop using the language of war. In this connection a reference was made to the Cominform.[2] Well, there is no doubt about it—and I admit it quite frankly—that any organization like the Cominform cannot in the nature of things fit in with peaceful coexistence. That is to say, any organization with the object of carrying aggressive and interfering propaganda in other countries obviously goes against the idea of two countries existing peacefully together; it obviously goes against the principle among the so-called five principles of non-interference; it is entirely opposed to them.

China mentioned other organizations in the world of different kinds, but aiming at internal interference. It is perfectly true. All countries here have had the experience not only of the activities of the Cominform organizations. And we have to deal with both in India and we do so effectively, I hope. If anybody misbehaves, we ask him to behave, and if he does not, we ask him to go away, communist or anti-communist. I entirely agree that if there is to be peaceful coexistence, if we have to adopt the principle of non-interference, with each other, then any interference, whether it is Communist or anti-Communist, must stop, and each country should develop according to its own notions. But you cannot put a wall against ideas. Ideas grow. I do not mind ideas coming. You cannot stop them. It is not the ideas that I object to, but it is the foreign interference in a country, doing aggressive propaganda this way and that way.

The delegate from Lebanon referred to my speech yesterday about my saying something about pacts. I do not remember my words but I am sure I had not meant exactly that. What I said was for any country of Asia putting itself in a position where it is dictated to in its affairs, is, personally speaking, a humiliating spectacle. That was my point. It is far too much for any country, whether it is on the Communist side or the non-Communist side, being bound hand and foot and not being able to act as it likes.

[2] Communist Information Bureau, or Cominform was set up in 1947 by the USSR to coordinate the exchange of information between East European and some West European Communist parties.

One of the necessary steps that the world should take in order to bring about lessening of tension is to encourage trade. Yet there are all kinds of embargoes on trade. Many countries desiring trade are compelled and coerced into not going in for it, thereby not only acting against their wishes but I feel acting against the interest of peace. So I ventured to say yesterday that there was great danger in Asia—great danger because we are trying to stand up on our feet to stand firmly on our ground—if we begin to align ourselves with Big Power blocs.

The Honourable delegate from Philippines referred to the Manila Agreement and pointed out that it was purely defensive and aimed at economic development. I entirely agree but I would ask you, with all respect, to remember its timing. It was soon after the Geneva Agreement. What was the threat in South East Asia then and where did it come from? There was not the slightest fear of aggression to any of the countries of South East Asia. I saw none and see none. It was thought that the threat might come from a big country called China. True it is a big country. But, was there any threat then? Actually at that time there had been a lessening of tension because of the Geneva Agreement. And yet some people rushed to Manila and had this treaty. They may have given economic help but this occasion was rather extraordinary. It seemed to be an angry reaction to what had happened in Geneva. It has made no difference to anybody; it had not strengthened even the military potential or the economic potential of South East Asia; it had not added to the security even in a military sense. It added rather to the insecurity of the region because it has put others on guard that here is an organization which is a military pact.

Fear exists on both sides. The Geneva Agreement had gone a long way in lessening the tension. A horrible war was going on for seven long years; it stopped the war. It did much more. Why did the Geneva Agreement succeed? Because in Geneva all the Great Powers came up against the terrible threat of war. If the Geneva Agreement had not come off, war would have started in Indo-China, a war not only in Indo-China but inevitably on a bigger scale which would have developed into a world war. The Geneva Agreement laid down that the Indo-China States should not be aligned with any of the big blocs. Now observe these Great Powers coming to an agreement, because they were up against this grave danger of a terrible war. They chose the way of nonalignment not for themselves but for the Indo-China States. If any of the Indo-China States aligned themselves, let us say, to the Communist bloc, then obviously the western Powers feared that Communism would spread all over Asia. China was apprehensive of the Indo-China States becoming a base for the western Powers. So if either of the eventualities happened, there was the danger of war. Therefore, the only way out was to prevent either bloc from sitting down in Indo-China and using it as a jumping-off ground. Therefore, circumstances compelled the Great Powers, all of them, to agree to a policy of coexistence and nonalignment for the Indo-China States.

It is a very good and significant example of how to deal with situations like this. We have heard the representative of Cambodia stating quite frankly what the position was. He said that press correspondents asked him: "Are you lining up with America or China?" He replied that he was lining up with Cambodia.

The only way, therefore, open is the way of the Geneva Agreement which is the way of nonalignment and friendly cooperation and peaceful existence. There is no other way.

Now let us try this example in the wider field. Please remember that I am not saying that you lay down your arms. You will have to be awake, wide awake. That is perfectly true but at the same time you must realize that the policies that countries like America and Russia are pursuing in the past two years have brought us to this. For us the best course would be to be friendly with them. Of course we can evolve our own policies independently, put them before them, discuss with them and not by way of arms. We should influence them in two ways. First of all we should put them in a friendly way. The arguments put forward now usually are not put forward in a friendly way, they are threats. Even good arguments are put forward as threats and the other party also puts forward equal threats. But if you say in a friendly way we are not their enemies, they will consider, because whatever our present position may be, we do represent potentially a mighty force that is Asia. It is a tremendous thing. Therefore, we have got this great opportunity, unique opportunity of playing a constructive, peaceful role in the world today in a friendly way, not that we like everything that happens in the Soviet Union or in America. We should not increase the feeling of dislike and hatred. If you do things in the right manner, people will respond, and you will have good results. The results may not be there immediately. I submit therefore that the policy that this Conference should pursue is that of friendly coexistence.

22

The International Scene[1]

New Delhi, 26 August 1955

My dear Chief Minister,

During the post-War years, we have had to deal with two sets of circumstances: One is the outstanding and dominant position of two great countries, the USA and the USSR, and their hostility and fear of each other. Round these countries gathered others and so two major groups opposed to and afraid of each other dominated international affairs with their fears and rivalries. The second factor was a kind of epidemic of revolutionary movements in various parts of the world, notably in Asia and Africa. These revolutionary movements were the result of internal and sometimes long-distance causes, as well as the upset caused by the Second World War. This War put an end to the old balance of power in the world or, perhaps, it would be more correct to say that the nineteenth century balance had been upset by the First World War and ever since then no real equilibrium had been established. The period between the World Wars was a troubled period. There were plenty of petty wars and major upheavals in China and Spain. There was Mussolini and later Hitler. Unable to find an equilibrium, events marched to the dreadful climax of the Second World War.

This second great War brought about even greater upsets than the first had done and, ever since then, the world has vainly sought some kind of a balance or equilibrium. Meanwhile, powerful movements, national or with a social purpose, have affected many countries. They have taken many shapes. Some have been clearly nationalistic; others have appeared to be communist or, at any rate, they have been dominated by communists. But, even there, nationalism and the desire to put an end to foreign and colonial rule has been evident. In India, we achieved our freedom in our own peaceful way, by agreement. Largely as a consequence of India's independence, Pakistan, Burma and Ceylon also became independent. Indonesia followed and, then, that vast country, China, suddenly emerged as a powerful nation under communist rule. Meanwhile, war

[1] To Chief Ministers. JN Papers, NMML. Excerpts.

continued in the states of Indo-China and Koreas. In North Africa, there were nationalist movements and sporadic uprisings. In the rest of Africa, there was a new awakening of the African people.

Many of these national movements were believed to have been caused by international communism. This is a very limited reading of the situation. Communism undoubtedly encouraged some of them and, in others, it came into conflict with nationalism, but, essentially, these revolutionary movements were born of the soil and of the conditions that had prevailed there. They would have happened anyhow, though it is possible that they might have taken a somewhat different turn in some places but for this new factor of communism.

Thus, there was a great upheaval in the relationships of nations, and this upheaval continued without settling down. In Europe, there was no fighting, but the problem of Germany was far the most important and dangerous problem in the world, and events appeared to march slowly towards some inevitable doom. This happened also in the Far East where the whole balance had been upset by the emergence of China. In Asia, there was turmoil of various kinds, sometimes influenced by Communist activities, but principally representing the urge for freedom from colonial rule. Africa was less developed politically, but it was obvious to any clear-sighted individual that there were the rumblings there of a mighty earthquake.

Generally speaking, however, international affairs were dominated by the conflict between the two major groups and, between these two, tension increased and preparations for war became more and more hurried and dominant. People's minds, in spite of their fear and dislike of war, came to accept this horror as an inescapable calamity. A large number of countries were committed to this group or that. Others, though uncommitted and unaligned, gave their sympathy to one or the other. That sympathy was partly based on some ideological foundations but largely on the expectation that one or the others group would lead them to the freedom they desired.

In this tremendous confusion and outpouring of hatred and violence, it was difficult for the voice of peace to be listened to. It is true that the word 'peace' was shouted aloud, just as 'democracy' was bandied about. But these slogans themselves were used in a context of hatred and war. India's voice was a thin, small one, criticized, decried, laughed at and disliked. It was one of the turning-points of history for that voice suddenly to assume a certain importance in world affairs. That was not because of India's strength but, rather, because of the rightness of that policy. The only alternative to it was war, and there can be no doubt that nearly all the peoples of the world did not want war.

During the last year or more, a gradual change has come over the international scene. It may be said to have begun with the armistice in the Korean War and more so by the Geneva Agreements of a year ago when opposing parties met together and found some way of cooperating, even though in a limited field. The pressure of events drove them, almost against their will, to this Agreement.

Other things happened. After Stalin's death, changes began in the Soviet Union. The atom and hydrogen bomb became realities in the public mind and it began to dawn on people everywhere that war was not inevitable and could possibly be avoided. In effect, the idea of peaceful coexistence became practical. The German problem today is far from solution, but nobody imagines that there is going to be war over it and the partition of Germany is accepted for the present and for the foreseeable future. In the Far East, the decision of the United States to contain Chiang Kai-shek and practically give up the idea of attacking the mainland of China was itself an indirect acceptance of the People's Government of China. Even in Korea, the partition appears to be accepted and in Vietnam some countries would rather have two Vietnams than have a conflict over them or even an election. All this means an acceptance of the status quo in areas of imminent danger. That acceptance is by no means permanent, but it is preferred to the alternative of war. In other words, the Great Powers are more or less agreed today that force will not be used to change the status quo. This is not a formal agreement of course, but nevertheless this may be said to be the present position.

Such a result is of high significance and naturally lessons tensions and the fear of war. It leads people to think more realistically in terms of negotiated settlements. We may still be very far from such settlements. But at least we look in that direction now and have turned away from thinking continually of an approaching cataclysm.

23

The Abolition of War[1]

I agree with Professor Sawer that while each of the authors urges[2] judgement on "the ancient and complex institution known as War according to their particular specialities", they all come to the same conclusion, viz., the abolition of war. Mankind today echoes this sentiment and yet our civilization has to find the ways and means of achieving this end and of releasing itself from fear and the passions, the complexities and the uncertainties which they have created and sustain.

Mankind, and the world's statesmen, must however find a way out; for, in this day and age, a global war means unprecedented destruction if not annihilation.

There are few problems that call for more calm judgement than the issue of war. Yet, the approach to, and consideration of, this problem is more often than otherwise in the context of emotion, passion or prejudice, or at best in terms of pious virtue and sentiment. This is true whether it be of its causes and, as some argue, its justification, or, as humanity ardently desires, to bring about the end of war. I rather agree with Professor Oliphant when he says: "A pious or well-intentioned belief in peace is merely irritating unless inner conviction is backed by real knowledge of the causes of war with some idea of how peace might be maintained."

It is unrealistic, and indeed perilous, to rest in the belief that this world of ours would be rid of the scourge of war and that war would be abandoned as a method of settling disputes and problems, merely because there is the general desire for peace. Too often this desire is coupled with placing the onus of existing tensions and threats to peace and of their calamitous prospects on others—individual national leaders, nations or groups of them. The plea for peace has thus become inseparable from political acrimony, and the language of war is almost used to promote peace! All this is part evidence that possibly the desire for peace, though well nigh universal, is not yet an informed and instructed desire, nor is it free from some of the very factors that threaten

[1] Foreword to *Paths of Peace* by Victor H. Wallace, 12 August 1956. Excerpts.
[2] Geoffrey Sawer, Dean of the Research School of Social Sciences, Australian National University, Canberra. He had written the concluding chapter of the book.

civilization with a holocaust. To this attention is paid in this study. They are referred to as the causes of war. This may be a somewhat simplified approach. For, even if we are able to discover and formulate all these causes, and do so, we cannot get rid of them by pulling them out as it were, each one by their root and trunk. The economic, ideological, social, racial and other factors are so woven into our institutions that they cannot be readily isolated only in regard to their evil aspects! We cannot therefore uproot them as it were.

This means, therefore, that we have to use our informed thinking to understand and assess these causes, and their relation to war and war institutions, their place in national and international politics, economy and thought, and seek to adapt and orient them in terms of our evaluation in relation to war or its avoidance. It also means that the process of the outlawing of war, in effective terms, requires institutional forms and changes, which would render national policies and the trend of civilization becoming oriented away from conflict.

That institutional changes and arrangements are necessary to this end is recognized by nations and governments. So is the war danger itself and all its ominous implications. But, side by side with this realization is also the persistence and often the accentuation of frustrations, fears—economic, racial and political—which lead in the opposite direction. These baulk purposeful policies and condition the attitude towards institutional remedies. The approach to them tend to share the characteristics of conflict rather than cooperation.

The United Nations and its predecessor, the League of Nations, were conceived and they emerged as a result of the recognition to which I have referred. There have been earlier efforts also in the direction. We in the world of today, however, continue to encounter and be dominated by these same opposite forces and tendencies.

The Charter of the United Nations opens with the words in the preamble: "We the peoples of the United Nations determined to save succeeding generations from the scourge of war", and sets out as its purpose in Article 1 as the maintenance of peace and security, the development of friendly relations among nations based on respect for the principle of equal rights and self-determination of peoples, the achievement of international cooperation and harnessing the action of nations to attain these ends.

This is the primary and fundamental aim of the world organization. Since its foundation, many and varied have been its activities to relieve mankind of many pressures and menaces in the economic and social fields, and its efforts even in the field of war prevention and cessation of armed conflicts have had some modest successes. The fact, however, remains that a decade after its foundation the world is more armed, more war-prepared, more sharply divided into camps, each claiming that its armed strength is for collective defence. Today, we are face to face with the potential of the hydrogen bomb and worse to come!

This then is our problem. In viewing it, would it not be right for us to consider, what in essence, creates and sustains this contradiction? There can be no short and conclusive answer to this question. To attempt any such would be to disregard the realities and the complexities which now govern power relationships and which have governed ill-poised equilibria during inter-war years in the modern world.

Yet, we should search our minds to discover and assess some of the basic factors in this contradiction. If these were understood, it would help to orient institutional changes for the better and for approaches and efforts to them to be more purposefully inspired. Again, it would profit us to examine and evaluate some of the bases on which present-day international thinking and alignment rest. This latter, the authors have sought to do, and I shall also endeavour to reflect on them.

The main factor which underlies the contradiction to which I have referred and which impedes, if not nullifies, progress towards peace, and the idea of a cooperating world is the hiatus and the divergence between the end—the abolition of war—and the means adopted to achieve it, which latter constitute the core of the foreign policy of the major powers. Means have to be equated with ends. They should share the essential quality of the ends; otherwise the approach to the problem itself is one of conflict, and a hiatus between what we avowedly desire and what we do to attain it.

Peace and cooperation must therefore be sought not by war-preparedness as an effective or constructive instrument for their attainment. I can understood a case for nations being prepared for their own defence, and also of collective defence, if attacked. The Charter of the United Nations (Art. 51) provides for this. But to seek to establish an equilibrium, or an orientation towards peace, by each party seeking to maintain a disequilibrium in its own favour is to contradict and nullify the very purpose this policy seeks to achieve.

This, however, is the pattern of power relations and the approach to peace in the world of today. The balance of power is often spoken of as an "equilibrium". The world has, however, been tilted from this "equilibrium" by one side tipping the scales against the other, and being always alerted to do so. This does not save us from "the scourge of war", nor can it hope "to save succeeding generations" from it. As a basis of international policy which would rid the world of war its impotence stands proven.

For the last three hundred years, since the emergence of Nation States in the modern world, nations have relied for survival or fulfilment by this process of mobilized antagonisms. All these years, the nations of the world have been engaged in wars with brief intervals during the greater part of which war clouds gathered on the horizon.

There is, however, a significant difference between power balances, as it used to be and as they are in the world today! Hitherto, there were several rival power groups, the alignment of one or more of which to one or other of the prospective contenders would have tilted the balance against the opponent. The uncertainty of that alignment, or sometimes, the prospect or threat of one of them joining the opposite camp was a deterrent. To that extent, the balance of power finds its historic justification.

Today, however, the "Balance" rests on a bipolarity. There are the two blocs; the western alliance and the Soviet group with no other power grouping, either powerful enough or placed geographically and politically to render its alignment on one side or the other a deterrent. To a certain extent the old position may still be the case, when there is only a cold war and the relations of some countries to either of the groups are not exclusive, and some countries like my own remain uncommitted to the rivals in the bipolarity. But this ceases to have any value, or any great power of deterrence, in a major crisis.

The balance of power today, therefore, is devoid even of that amount of breaking power that a group of countries may have been able to exercise on the mounting momentum to conflict as between two rival alliances in a multiple balance system. The bipolarity not merely totally discredits the balance approach, but it makes it ominous and the portent of catastrophe.

The advent of thermo-nuclear power and the weapons of mass destruction as part of the armoury of the Great Powers has totally deprived any validity that might have existed in the conception and policies of Balance of Power and has rendered it a menace instead of a means of security in the world of today. This is the case both in regard to the nations concerned on either side in the present bipolarity as well as for the rest of mankind. These weapons and the magnitude in which they will be employed have erased the differences between the capacity to inflict punishment and of receiving the same; for the side that employs them is not immune from the lethal effects of their own offence. They have no defence before the proximate and almost instantaneous retaliation any more than the enemy had against the attack delivered on him.

It is argued that the accumulation of destructive power and the military alliance which subserve them are purely "defensive" and therefore politically and morally justified. They are argued to be part of the mechanism of world peace. In its political aspect this argument cuts right across the conception, the purpose, the procedures and the machinery provided and contemplated in the Charter of the United Nations. It takes away from the world organization not merely the control but the decision for the use of sanctions and, therefore, the way to collective peace or security. It is also argued that the power grouping enables negotiating with the other side from positions of strength, an argument that fails to be convincing when it is realized that each side considers it has, or seeks to attain, superiority in this respect.

There are those again who have begun to look on the hydrogen bomb and the capacity for mass destruction as a "deterrent" to war. It may be conceded that this may be the case in the beginning and in the short term. But fear is no' basis on which to build peace and, what is more, we cannot be certain that the hydrogen bomb will function as a deterrent against the use by the possessor of it. Some miscalculation, panic or some internal changes within a country, and even fear over-reaching itself, can trigger this force. Nothing deters global conflict thereafter. If the hydrogen bomb is thus elevated to the level of being the custodian of peace, the inter-war nuclear race would claim that it stands justified as a peace agent.

A divided world is also argued on ideological grounds. No doubt, differences in ideologies, national backgrounds and in moral or social values engender and sustain differences between nations. This aspect of the causes of war has been examined in this study. The conclusion is that "the view that the conflict between ideologies is the main source of international conflict is not supported by historical evidence". Ideological differences there always have been. It is a reflection of the diversities in civilization and history. Ideas, however, have greater potency than the means adopted to destroy them. War and even less the threat of war do not stifle ideas or their extension. The contention that the present world division is due to ideological conflict, justifies the propaganda in this regard and psychological warfare, fear and suspicion, as the normal mechanism of international behaviour. The ideological aspect today, however, is more the instrument than the cause of our divided world.

International cooperation means international tolerance. We are today, by and large, sufficiently civilized in the context of our national communities to regard tolerance as the basis of communal life within our national societies. Without it, national groups and certainly democratic institutions cannot survive. For nations to learn to tolerate, to coexist peacefully, is but the extension of this idea into international relations. It means an attitude of live and let live and a belief in the power of example and persuasion rather than in arbitrament by force. We must take down our fences, at least to some extent, for he who sets himself against being persuaded cannot hope to persuade another.

The hydrogen bomb is not an instrument of persuasion. Yet it dominates the thinking and behaviour in world politics and, as I said before, is set out to be regarded as an instrument of peace. The world must outlaw these weapons if it is to survive. Their outlawing would in itself promote confidence. They do not add to the sense of security. Is it not odd that the most powerful nations of today feel the most insecure, and therefore seek even more power, and in turn feel still more insecure?

Disarmament, therefore, is not merely a desirable alternative to the present competitive arming, it is an imperative if we are to survive. The nations accept this in principle and the United Nations has been discussing disarmament for a decade. The world's armament stocks and destructive power, however, have grown more and more, during the same period.

I do not propose to enter into the controversies surrounding this problem and the different disarmament plans. It is, however, a reflection on the statemanship and wisdom of our age that we seem to be bogged down by this problem and drawn deeper and deeper into the tragic pool of the Balance of Power and the doctrine of "Peace by horror". I would like to say, however, and briefly, that while we argue, we drift perilously into greater complexities. We should therefore view the problem of world disarmament not as one of producing a perfect system for it, but as a process which we must begin now, and seek to hasten building up confidence and agreements as we go on and not plead disagreements on ultimate plans barring our objective. We could make a beginning even now if the Great Powers would agree to the cessation of explosions of weapons of mass destruction by the stopping of further manufacture of the weapons of mass destruction and also by making at least a token beginning in the abandoning of these weapons by publicly dismantling at least a few of them by the atomic powers. We could all agree to submit our military budget figures to the United Nations. We could each aim at some reductions even unilaterally. We could utilize the areas of agreement in the disarmament controversy instead of stressing disagreements alone.

. . . Nations by cooperating with one another, in tolerance, and recognizing diversities, by respect for one another as sovereign nations, by not interfering in one another's affairs, can survive, progress and advance to greater and greater degrees and spheres of cooperation. Such peaceful coexistence in our time is the forerunner of one human race and one world. We frustrate our destiny if we continue to base our hopes on a divided world, resting on fear and armed might; and each of us arrogate to ourselves the larger share, if not the monopoly, of virtue or of national, racial or moral superiority. We can then only see the rest of the world as evil to be exorcized! Fortunately we are not in this extreme state of intolerance in the world of today.

Happily we, as though moved by some elemental forces or destiny, move towards world cooperation. Ours is a shrunken world. Science, trade and commerce, communications and the march and impact of ideas have made nations and peoples, often despite adverse circumstances, belong more and more to one another. Sentiment, the world over moves us in that direction too, despite all fears and inhibitions. In this scientific age both vistas hitherto unknown and unimagined by man, and terrors not dreamt of by him which cast the menace of annihilation on him and his world are before us. We, the peoples and nations of the world, and our statesmen and governments must make conscious and intelligent efforts to solve those problems that challenge the survival of humanity and civilization.

The paths to peace are difficult, but pursue them we must. They alone enable survival and fulfilment. The journey calls for patience and tolerance and the belief in our objectives. They demand, more than all, an equation of means and ends. The call for the endeavours of us all.

24

A Creeping Sickness[1]

16 March 1957

Dear Norman Cousins,

I am not, I think, a pessimist. Indeed, I do not think that any person can function effectively if he has no hope for the future. I have hope both for the world and for my own country, India, which I seek to serve. And yet, as I indicated to you in my previous letter, I have a feeling of depression growing within me, a feeling that the good things of the world are gradually being pushed out, that some slow disintegration is taking place in the collective mind of man in spite of the great advances that we see.

You refer in your article to this new possibility of our present generation having the power to put an end to everything that history has achieved. That is a terrible thought. What is worse, I think, is a creeping sickness of humanity which gradually leads it to this final destruction. Ultimately, this is of the mind, as I think the UNESCO constitution says: 'Wars begin in the minds of men.' In spite of the patent fact that a nuclear war may well end everything that humanity stands for, most people take preparations for it for granted, even though they wish to avoid it. Why do they do it? They go back to this all-pervading fear, which appears to them to make it incumbent on them not to be left behind in the race for the latest type of death-dealing machinery. The whole approach is patently illogical, and yet there appears to be no escape from it. Essentially, the problem becomes one of psychology or of some kind of moral or ethical approach.

Politicians, however good they may be, do not frame their policies on this basis, even though they talk a great deal about morality. An individual might and does sometimes rise to high levels. But the mass thinks chiefly in terms of self-preservation and is much more prone to fear and anger and violence. Even the great advance of education has not got rid of these ever-present dangers, so far as the mass mind is concerned. Fear feeds upon fear, as violence feeds upon violence.

Oddly enough, in a democratic society, while the dangers of any sudden and terrible action are limited, the leader's ability to control the mass is also limited. There may be occasional exceptions for limited periods. Any political leader has to function under these limitations. Occasionally, he may override

[1] To Norman Cousins. JN Papers, NMML. Excerpts.

them. But we seldom have a single leader with that power. So a leader must not only feel what is right, but has also to convince masses of people about it. Thus he tends to compromise or else he would cease to be the leader. The only example in current history that I know of a leader who refused to compromise on what he thought was right, is Gandhi, and Gandhi was assassinated in the end, as prophets often are. He was a rare combination of a political leader who had something of the prophetic instinct in him.

I suppose the approach to the great problem of today has to be twofold. There should be the moral approach or the prophet's and there has to be the political leader's approach. The latter should be in tune with the former, though it may not go that far. At any rate, every step taken, however short it may be, should be towards that moral goal preached by the prophet. It depends on the leader and the circumstances he has to face, as to how big the step he takes is. But, in any event, he should not go back or take a step in a wrong direction. It is not feasible to ask the leader to take a step which he cannot give effect to, because public opinion is not ripe for it. In educating public opinion, both the prophet and the leader have to help in their respective ways.

All this is very well. But time is short, and disaster hangs over us. Two Great Wars have brutalized humanity and made them think more and more in terms of violence. What progress, scientific and cultural, and in human values, we have made, is somehow twisted to the needs of violence. I think that the major disservice that Marxism and communism have done to the world, is the encouragement of violence to achieve political or economic ends. But, of course, it is not Marxism alone that has done this. Fascism was, I think, even worse in this respect because it did not have the ideological element of communism. But, apart from communism and fascism, there is quite enough of this violent approach to problems even by others. I know that, the world being what it is, it is not possible to do away with some violence or coercion. At the same time, I have become more and more convinced that the way of violence and hatred is not the way of solving any problem. That is why I think that the 'cold war' is something that is essentially bad, whatever the reasons of expedience that might be advanced for it. It takes us in a wrong direction.

Taking a practical view of things as they are, we see these two very powerful countries, the USA and the USSR, opposed to each other. Regardless of right or wrong, although we cannot, of course, ignore them, it seems obvious to me that the Cold War only aggravates their conflicts and spreads fear more and more. Some approach other than that of the cold war has to be found, some approach other than that of military alliances.

As a politician, I cannot suggest, as Gandhi might have done, that a country should be brave enough to do away with armed forces for its defence. I recognize the inevitability at present of providing for defence and not leaving a vacuum which might tempt an evil-doer. Even so, I do not understand how defence is helped by the tactics of the Cold War or by the propagation of hatred and fear.

It should be possible to take adequate steps for defence and yet seek for a removal of tensions and a friendly atmosphere in the world. After all, the great masses of people everywhere want that friendly atmosphere and to avoid all horrors of war.

This leads one to the question of disarmament. Again, it is not feasible to talk about this in absolute terms. But there may be progressive steps, the main value of each step being a lessening of fear. Disarmament must inevitably take into consideration nuclear weapons. What can we do about them? I would suggest that two things can be done. One is stopping any further experiments, the other is stopping any further production of atomic or hydrogen bombs. This may be difficult now, but it is going to be much more difficult in the future, when a number of countries can produce them. At present, there are apparently only three, the USA, the USSR and the UK. Within a few years, it is likely that the process will become simpler, though the products will remain equally terrible, and a number of other countries might be able to make these bombs. Thus, delay in taking any effective steps makes the position increasingly more difficult.

In regard to experimental explosions, I am convinced that these are a crime against humanity. . . . The rival powers or groups of powers are such today that neither of them can think of defeating the other without being largely destroyed itself. If that is so, then one has to accept a policy of tolerance of each other, of live and let live, and hope that the new atmosphere that is created may lead to a progressive lessening of tensions and fear. This, again, might and should lead to a lessening of the coercive apparatus of the state in authoritarian countries, that is, to greater individual freedom. We shall not get that individual freedom in these states by threatening them. In fact, this policy of threats will inevitably result in a continuation of coercion and deprivation of freedom.

Instead of military pacts aimed against each other, one would imagine that a more sensible way would be for pacts between rival powers, something in the nature of the old Locarno Treaty between Germany and the other western countries. It is true that the Locarno Treaty did not bring peace, and Hitler came. That was not the fault of Locarno, and other circumstances prevailed. Anyhow, I see no other way except that there must be an agreement on the basis of live and let live, and that this should be backed by the United Nations. If any country breaks that agreement, then presumably the other countries will pull it back or deal with it. I know that no agreement is foolproof, and it is very difficult to trust some countries. Nevertheless, the position created by this mutual bond backed by the UN cannot possibly be worse than what we have today, and it will surely lessen tensions and fear, which will then enable the world to look at the problem in a more reasonable way.

Yours sincerely,
Jawaharlal Nehru

25

Weapons of Destruction[1]

Our earth has become too small for the new weapons of the atomic age. While man, in the pride of his intellect and knowledge, forces his way into space and pierces the heavens, the very existence of the human race is threatened. There are enough weapons of mass destruction already to put an end to life on earth. Today, America and Russia possess them in abundance, and England also has them. Tomorrow, it may be that other countries will possess them, and even the capacity to control them will go outside the range of human power. Nuclear test explosions take place, contaminating air and water and food, as well as directly injuring the present and future generations of mankind.

No country, no people, however powerful they might be, are safe from destruction if this competition in weapons of mass destruction and Cold War continues.

Apart from these dangers ahead, the civilization which thousands of years of human effort have built up is being corroded and undermined by fear and hatred, and will progressively wither away if these trends continue. All the peoples of the world have a right to life and progress and the fulfilment of their destiny. They have the right to peace and security. They can preserve these rights now only by living peacefully together and by solving their problems by peaceful methods. They differ in their creeds and beliefs and ideologies. They cannot convert each other by force or threats of force, for any such attempt will lead to catastrophe for all. The only way is to exist peacefully together in spite of differences, and to give up the policy of hatred and violence.

The moral and the ethical approaches demand this. But practical common sense points this way even more.

I have no doubt that this can be done. I have no doubt that America and Russia have it in their power to put an end to this horror that is enveloping the world and darkening our minds and our future.

Millions of people believe in what is called Western capitalism; millions also believe in communism. But there are many millions who are not committed to either of these ideologies, and yet seek, in friendship with others, a better life and a more hopeful future.

[1] Statement to the Press, New Delhi, 27 November 1957. JN Collection, NMML.

I speak for myself, but I believe that I echo the thoughts of vast numbers of people in my country as well as in other countries of the world. I venture, therefore, to make this appeal to the great leaders, more especially of America and Russia, in whose hands fate and destiny have placed such tremendous power today to mould this world and either to raise it to undreamt-of heights or to hurl it to the pit of disaster. I appeal to them to stop all nuclear test explosions and thus to show to the world that they are determined to end this menace, and to proceed also to bring about effective disarmament. The moment this is done, a great weight will be lifted from the mind of man. But it is not merely a physical change that is necessary, but an attempt to remove fear and reverse the perilous trend which threatens the continued existence of the human race. It is only by direct approaches and agreements through peaceful methods that these problems can be solved.

26

Disarmament[1]

I have listened attentively and with respect to many of the speeches made here, and sometimes I have felt as if I was being buffeted by the icy winds of the Cold War. Coming from a warm country, I have shivered occasionally at these cold blasts.

Sitting here in this assembly chamber, an old memory comes back to me. In the fateful summer of 1938, I was a visitor at a meeting of the League of Nations in Geneva. Hitler was advancing then and holding out threats of war. There was mobilization in many parts of Europe, and the tramp of armed men was being heard. Even so, the League of Nations appeared to be unconcerned and discussed all manner of subjects, except the most vital subject of the day. The War had not started then. A year later it descended upon the world with all its thunder and destructive fury. After many years of carnage, that war ended, and a new age—the atomic age—was ushered in by the terrible experience of Hiroshima and Nagasaki.

Fresh from these horrors, the minds of men turned to thoughts of peace, and there was passionate desire to put an end to war itself. The United Nations took birth on a note of high idealism embodied in the noble wording of the Charter. But there was also a realization of the state of the post-War world as it was. Therefore, provision was made in the structure of the organization to balance certain conflicting urges. There were permanent members of the Security Council and there was provision for unanimity amongst the great powers. All this was not very logical. But it represented certain realities of the world as it was, and because of this, we accepted them. . . .

Unfortunately, we live in a split world which is constantly coming up against the basic assumptions of the United Nations. We have to bear with this and try to move even more forward to the conception of full cooperation between nations. That cooperation does not and must not mean any domination of one country by another, any coercion or compulsion forcing a country to line up with another country. Each country has something to give and something to take from others. The moment coercion is exerted on a country, not only is its freedom impaired but its growth suffers.

[1] Speech at the UN General Assembly, New York, 3 October 1960. JN Papers, NMML. Excerpts.

We have to acknowledge that there is great diversity in the world and that this variety is good and is to be encouraged, so that each country may grow and its creative impulse might have full play in accordance with its own genius. Hundreds and thousands of years of history have conditioned us in our respective countries, and our roots go deep down into the soil. If these roots are pulled out, we wither. If these roots remain strong and we allow the winds from four quarters to blow in upon us, they will yield branch and flower and fruit.

Many of the speakers from this forum have surveyed the world scene and spoken on a variety of problems. I would like to concentrate on what I consider the basic problem of all. My mind is naturally filled with problems of my own country and our passionate desire to develop and to put an end to the poverty and low standards of living which have been a curse to hundreds of millions of our people. To that end we labour, as indeed other underdeveloped countries are doing. Even so, there is something else which we consider is of greater importance. That is peace. Without peace all our dreams vanish and are reduced to ashes. The Charter of the United Nations declares our determination to save succeeding generations from the scourge of war and to reaffirm faith in fundamental human rights, and for these ends to practise tolerance and live together in peace with one another as good neighbours.

The main purpose of the United Nations is to build a world without war, a world based on the cooperation of nations and peoples. It is not merely a world where war is kept in check by a balancing of armed forces. It is much deeper than that. It is a world from which the major causes of war have been removed with social structures built up which further peaceful cooperation within a nation as well as between nations.

In the preamble to the constitution of UNESCO it is stated that war begins in the minds of men. That is essentially true; and ultimately it is necessary to bring about the change in our minds and to remove fears and apprehensions, hatreds and suspicions. Disarmament is a part of this process, for it will create an atmosphere of cooperation. But it is only a step towards our objective, a part of the larger effort to rid the world of war and the causes of war.

In the present context, however, disarmament assumes a very special importance for us, overriding all other issues. For many years past, there have been talks on disarmament and some progress has undoubtedly been made in so far as the plans and proposals are concerned. Still we find that the race of armaments continues, as also the efforts to invent ever more powerful engines of destruction. If even a small part of these efforts was directed to the search for peace, probably the problem of disarmament would have been solved by this time.

Apart from the moral imperative of peace, every practical consideration leads us to that conclusion. For, as everyone knows, the choice today in this nuclear age is one of utter annihilation and destruction of civilization or of some way to have peaceful coexistence between nations. There is no middle way. If war is an abomination and an ultimate crime which has to be avoided, we must fashion our minds and policies accordingly. There may be risks, but the greatest risk is to allow the present dangerous drift to continue. In order to achieve peace we have to develop a climate of peace and tolerance and to avoid speech and action which tend to increase fear and hatred.

It may not be possible to reach full disarmament in one step, though every step should be conditioned to that end. Much ground has already been covered in the discussions on disarmament. But the sands of time run out, and we dare not play about with this issue or delay its consideration. This, indeed, is the main duty of the United Nations today and if it fails in this, the United Nations fails in its main purpose. . . .

The question of disarmament has been considered at various levels. There is general disarmament and the ending of test explosions of nuclear and thermonuclear weapons. . . .

Disarmament must include the prohibition of the manufacture, storage and use of weapons of mass destruction, as well as the progressive limitation of conventional weapons. It is well to remember that there is a great deal of common ground already covered, and the various proposals made by different countries indicate this common ground, but certain important question have not yet been solved. Behind all this lies the fear of a surprise attack and of any one country becoming stronger than the other in the process of disarmament. It is admitted that disarmament should take place in such stages as to maintain broadly the balance of armed power. It is on this basis only that success can be achieved and this pervading sense of fear countered.

There is an argument as to whether disarmament should precede controls or whether controls should precede disarmament. This is a strange argument, because it is perfectly clear that disarmament without controls is not a feasible proposition. It is even more clear that controls without disarmament have no meaning. The whole conception of control comes in only because of disarmament. It is not proposed, I hope, to have controls of existing armaments and thus in a way to perpetuate those armaments. It must therefore be clearly understood that disarmament and a machinery for control must go together, and neither of these can be taken up singly. It seems very extraordinary to me that great nations should argue about priorities in this matter and make that a reason for not going ahead. Therefore, both questions should be tackled simultaneously and as parts of a single problem.

Success may not come immediately, but it is, I think, of the greatest importance that there should be no gap, no discontinuity, in our dealing with this problem. Once there is discontinuity, this will lead to a rapid deterioration of the present situation and it will be much more difficult to start afresh.

27

Solving World Problems[1]

These last years of difficulty and crisis have brought out more than ever before the importance of this organization. Indeed, one wonders what the world would be like if the United Nations ceased to be or did not function. Therefore, it is of the highest importance that this great organization should not only function but should function with effectiveness and with the support of the countries represented here.

. . . The General Assembly and the Security Council took many steps in the last year or more in regard to these matters and thereby somewhat enlarged the functions of the organization and showed what it could do. Unfortunately, those steps did not immediately yield the results that we had hoped for, and that was true because of various difficulties and the somewhat obstructive methods which were employed by some. But I trust that in future we shall work with greater unanimity and effectiveness in carrying out the decisions of the United Nations.

In one place, the Congo, the United Nations has undertaken a great responsibility, and on the success of that venture of the United Nations depends in many ways the future of the United Nations itself, or its future effectiveness. It may continue, of course, even after a lack of success there, but it would then continue as an ineffective body whose mandate does not run far. Therefore, it is of the utmost importance that the work that this great organization has undertaken in the Congo should succeed and should yield results. All the countries represented here are interested in this vital problem. We in India are to some extent a little more interested than some others, because, at the invitation of the United Nations, we have placed some of our resources and some of our armed forces at the disposal of the organization for service in the Congo, and we are naturally interested that their functioning should yield success.

I have referred to the Congo—and I am not going to refer to each individual problem facing the United Nations—because the Congo has become

[1] Speech at the UN General Assembly, New York, 10 November 1961. JN Collection, NMML. Excerpts.

the symbol and the touchstone of success for the activities of the United Nations.

During the last year, many additions have been made to the membership of this General Assembly. New countries have come here, chiefly from Africa, and I am happy about this enlargement. More particularly, I should like to mention the name of just one country because, for years, we have been suggesting that name and hoping that that country will be admitted. I refer to Outer Mongolia, and I am happy that at last that country has found a place in this Assembly.

When future historians write about this period in which we are living, they may well say that an outstanding feature of this period was the emergence of African countries, the new life that is coursing through the veins of Africa, which I think is, historically speaking, of vital importance today.

Because of that vitality and tremendous urge in the various countries of Africa, we find problems arising that are problems of a new vitality, and not problems of a decadent people. They are the problems of a new life emerging. Sometimes they are troublesome problems, but we must recognize that they are problems of growth and therefore problems which should encourage rather than discourage us.

In Africa, there is the Congo, to which I have referred, and there is the near-by country of Angola under Portuguese rule. It is well to remember that while colonialism is a fading institution and, historically speaking, is a disappearing one; nevertheless today a fairly big empire remains in Africa and elsewhere under Portuguese rule when bigger empires have ceased to be. Apart from this theoretical question, practically speaking, what we heard of events in Angola has been distressing in the extreme. If it is distressing to us, we can imagine how much it must distress people in Africa. I earnestly hope that this remnant of colonialism will also peacefully change.

In the Congo there have been difficulties. The Security Council decided about eight or nine months ago on two basic principles about the Congo: one was the unity of the Congo, a Republic, and the other was the removal of foreign mercenary elements. I have no doubt, and probably other members here present have no doubt, that much of the trouble in the Congo has been due to external encouragement and interventions. If this kind of activity continues, the problems will become more difficult of solution. Therefore, it is incumbent that the problem should be solved as soon as possible and that these foreign elements should be removed or should be made to leave Katanga province and other parts of the Congo. There is really no half-way house to this: one either has unity in the Congo or not. If there is no unity, the Congo will split up and instead of one problem we shall have to face many problems, each more difficult than the other, and not only will the Congo split up but the United Nations will suffer a serious setback. Therefore, I would beg this great organization to consider what steps should be taken which would be effective and which would yield quick results.

There are other colonial problems, of course. There is Algeria. I can only say that the terrible sufferings that the people of Algeria have undergone during the last eight years must find fulfilment. I am sure they will, but I would hope that they will do so soon and that the story of their agony should not drag on. There are some indications that perhaps this may happen soon. I hope those indications point in the right direction.

I do think that at this stage of the world's history it has become impossible for colonies to continue without creating complications which may lead to major conflicts in the world. While that is so, it is a fact that as we stand or sit here today, the world is facing even graver problems, the problems of world survival, the problems of war and peace, and unless they are dealt with wisely and in a statesmanlike manner, the future that faces us is a very painful one.

More and more we live under a kind of regime of terror. Terror of what? Terror of some kind of catastrophe like war descending upon us, some kind of disaster when nuclear weapons are used and the future of the world's survival is imperilled. It is an odd circumstance that in spite of this general knowledge, the full realization of this basic fact today perhaps has not come to us and is not appreciated by many governments. The choice today before the world is a choice which has never come to it before: it is a choice of self-extinction, practical extinction or survival. Many people think and talk about escaping from the disaster of a nuclear war by burrowing under the earth and living like rats in a hole. Surely it is a strange commentary on our times that we should be driven to that conclusion instead of diverting all our energies and all our strength to the prevention of that catastrophe.

The first thing to be realized is that there can no longer be any kind of normal existence unless we get rid of this terror that hangs over us. How can that terror go? There are basic problems before us—the German problem, the problem of the city of Berlin and other problems elsewhere which I believe are capable of solution, because I am convinced that no country deliberately desires war. I am convinced that the people all over the world are passionately in favour of peace. Why then are we unable to solve these problems?

It is difficult for me to say. The problems are difficult and they cannot be easily solved; nevertheless, the alternative to not solving anything is infinitely worse. No country, great or small, can easily agree to something which wounds its honour and self-respect. Even a small country cannot easily be offended today, that is, its honour cannot be offended, much less a great country. No solution can therefore be found which is based on the wounding of the honour or self-respect of a country.

We talk about many problems like disarmament, and sometimes one has the feeling that although there is apparent agreement, really behind it there is not that faith in disarmament that is necessary, and that talks are more of some kind of attempt to put the other party in the wrong rather than to achieve something, while it is of the utmost importance that that achievement should take place. I am convinced that the modern world cannot continue for long without full disarmament. All these problems have come up again and again. Ultimately it is perhaps true that the material advance which has taken place in the world, and that is magnificent, has gone far ahead of the development of human minds, which lags behind. They do not fit in with the modern age and the mind still thinks in its narrow terms of 100 or 200 years ago, of how nations function, how diplomats function, and how wars took place. We know, we have heard and we have read about the new possibility of a nuclear war. Nevertheless, emotionally, we do not understand it fully; otherwise it seems to me impossible that there should be these continuing deadlocks and impasses because the fact is that under modern conditions war must be ruled out, or the world or civilization or humanity has to submit to the ending of all it has laboured for thousands of years.

If that is true, then surely it is important and urgent that we should approach this question with speed, deliberation, and a determination to solve it rather than merely show that the other party is wrong.

I mentioned disarmament. This Assembly last year, I think, decided almost unanimously in favour of general, widespread disarmament. The great nations of the world have all committed themselves to that. The United States, through its President, recently put forward proposals which are in line with what this Assembly has decided. The Soviet Union has put forward proposals to the same effect, varying slightly but essentially aiming at the same thing: even in broad outline there is a good deal of commonness about them.

If that is so, what comes in our way? Why should we not grasp this opportunity when there is so much agreement, and remove this fear and terror from people's minds and devote all the great energies and resources of the people to world advancement?

I do not know; except what I have said, that we are quite unable to get out of old ways of thinking which ought to have no place in the modern world, old ways of hatred and violence, not realizing that violence today is not the violence of yesterday but a violence which could exterminate all of us, not realizing that there is no victory today for any country in a major war—only defeat and extermination for all.

If that is so, then surely this major and outstanding question must be dealt with with speed and those great countries, especially those which have the greatest responsibility because they possess the biggest weapons of warfare—nuclear weapons—should address themselves again and again to negotiations, to talks, to the consideration of this problem together to find some remedy, with the determination that they will not separate until they have come to some agreements, of course.

Those agreements cannot be merely agreements of some countries, however great. They must represent all the members of this United Nations in this great body. But I do think that it is better for those countries—a few of them—to deal with this problem rather than for a larger body to deal with it, to begin with.

I feel rather strongly on this question although we in India are not situated in the major theatres of a possible war—probably not. Nevertheless, I feel that everything that man has striven for in the past thousands of years is at stake today. As strongly as I feel about these colonial matters, about the freedom of colonial countries and others, I do think that the major question and the biggest question today is this question of war and peace and disarmament. There is no conflict between those. In fact, the whole atmosphere of the world will change if disarmament comes in and these present problems go towards solution.

How then are we to do it? I do not know. The President was good enough to refer to the wisdom of the East or to my wisdom. It was kind of him to make that reference to me, but I possess no greater wisdom than each one of us here; only perhaps in some matters some of us may feel a little more. Some of us who have experienced many ups and downs in our lives may think more deeply about them. But if it is wisdom that we want, it is the common wisdom that should come to everyone. It is no mystery. In the problems before us there are no mysteries. They are obvious problems, and the fear of war is obvious; the fear that grips mankind is obvious. How can we go on dealing with the secondary question of the world, discussing them, etc., when this basic problem deludes us?

As a part of this question of disarmament there is the particular question today of nuclear tests. The General Assembly passed a resolution recently about them. It was, I think, a great misfortune that after a period of abstinence from nuclear tests there was a resumption. There can be no doubt that that turned the attention of the world in a wrong direction, apart from the harm it might do. Immediately the idea of a possible war became more prevalent. Immediately it became more difficult to have treaties for ending nuclear tests because while treaties are essential, are necessary for this, when the whole atmosphere becomes one of fear and apprehension, it becomes more difficult to get a treaty.

I do think, and I would beg the countries concerned to realize, that they are doing a grave disservice to the world, to their own countries even, by not putting an end to this business of nuclear tests and putting an end to it by treaty as rapidly as possible.

The Assembly has passed a resolution in favour of some kind of moratorium. No one imagines that a voluntary moratorium is going to solve this question. There must be stricter controls by treaty and otherwise. But while that should be aimed at and worked for and achieved as rapidly as possible, one should not leave the door open, while you discuss it, for those nuclear tests to go on. Arguments may be raised that one party or one country gets an advantage over the other and these arguments may have substance. Yet my own reaction to these nuclear tests is a very strong one. I think they are basically evil; they encourage evil. Therefore, the sooner this evil is dealt with the better.

I cannot suggest any rapid or magic ways of dealing with the problems of the world. But I find that perhaps the worst difficulty we have to face is something you cannot grip: an atmosphere, the imponderables of life, how people are suddenly filled with fear, passion and hatred. How can we deal with them? We live in this world of conflicts and yet the world goes on, undoubtedly because of the cooperation of nations and individuals. The essential thing about this world is cooperation, and even today, between countries which are opposed to each other in the political or other fields, there is a vast amount of cooperation. Little is known or little is said about this cooperation that is going on, but a great deal is said about every point of conflict, and so the world is full of this idea that the conflicts go on and we live on the verge of disaster. Perhaps it would be a truer picture if the cooperating elements in the world today were put forward and we were made to think that the world depends on cooperation and not on conflict.

A proposal has been made by various people to the effect that more attention should be directed to these cooperative ventures, especially for peace and in the interest of peace, so that more positive thinking may take place on this subject and people should realize that this cooperation is already taking place and it can be extended. Some years ago it was resolved to have an International Geophysical Year. That was a specific subject, but it has been suggested that perhaps this Assembly might resolve to call upon all countries of the world to devote a year, not to speeches about peace—I do not think that is much good—but to the furtherance of cooperative activities in any field—political, cultural and whatever fields there may be, and there are thousands of fields. That perhaps would direct some of our energy and some of our thinking to this idea of cooperation, which would create an atmosphere for solving the problems more easily. That by itself will not solve any problem but it will lessen this destruction and conflict which now afflict the world. I make this suggestion to you not in any detail but broadly, so that this Assembly might consider it and, if it is worthwhile, perhaps appoint a committee to consider it further and make suggestions as to how this might perhaps be done.

As you will have noticed, the words are amusing and can easily be called hackneyed phrases and hackneyed thinking. There is nothing new or wonderful about them. There is nothing new or wonderful about the truths of the world, and the truth is that violence and hatred are bad—bad for individuals and bad for everybody. The great men of the world have been those who have fought hatred and violence and not those who have encouraged it—even in some supposedly worthwhile cause, and we have arrived at the stage where this, I feel, has to be checked. It really requires a new way of thinking, a new development of humanity. Possibly we are going through that process and possibly this very crisis will wake up the mind of man and direct it to this new way of thinking. The old way of thinking has landed us in this disastrous situation, even though, as I said, the world has made tremendous progress in many ways, progress which manifestly can cure the material ills of the world. But what shall it profit the world if it conquers the material ills and then commits suicide because it has not controlled its own mind?

VOL. II

V

Language

1. On Translation   489

2. Lingua Franca of India   493

3. The Question of Language   495

4. Power of Words   498

5. A Poetic Testament   499

6. The Language Controversy   500

7. The Function of Language   502

8. The National Language   505

9. Translation of the Constitution   511

10. Linguistic Provinces   513

11. The Place of English   516

1

On Translation[1]

To translate from one language to another language is a very difficult task. The fact is that real translation of even slightly profound thought is just impossible. What is the function of a language? It helps us to think. Language is semi-frozen thought—imagination converted into statues. Its second function is to enable one to express one's ideas and convey them to others, so that we may exchange thoughts. There are others uses of language too, but we need not now go into them. A word or a phrase comes to our mind in the form of a certain image. Simple and straight words like table, chair, horse and elephant form easy and clear images and when we utter these words listeners also form in their minds images, almost of the same type. We can then say that they have understood our meaning.

But the moment we step ahead of these simple and easy words complications set in. Even an ordinary phrase produces many pictures in the mind and it is possible that in the listener's mind different pictures are produced. Much depends upon the mental faculties of the speaker and the listener—their education, their experiences, knowledge, inspirations and feelings. Now proceed a step further and take abstract and complicated words such as truth, beauty, ahimsa, dharma, *mazhab*. So very often during the day do we use these words, but if asked to explain their meaning fully we may face a lot of difficulty. Sometimes some words will not produce identical images in the minds of two people. Although both uttered the same word different things are meant. The more complicated and abstract the ideas put forward, the more these difficulties increase. It is also possible (and it has happened) that because of such misunderstandings we may quarrel and smash each other's skulls.

Such difficulty can arise between two persons who speak the same language, are literate and civilized and brought up in the same culture. If one is literate and the other illiterate and crude, the difference between them is wider and it is impossible for them to understand each other fully. They live in two worlds. But these difficulties look small when compared to those of two persons who speak two different languages and do not know much about the cultures of each

[1] Almora District Jail, 1 August 1935. JN Papers, NMML. Original in Hindi.

other. Their mental ideas and images differ as heaven and earth. They hardly understand each other. What surprise, then, if they do not trust each other and are afraid of and quarrel with each other?

A philologist, Professor J.S. Mackenzie, who has deeply studied languages and their relations, has written, "an Englishman, a Frenchman, and an Italian cannot by any means bring themselves to think quite alike, at least on subjects which involve any depth of sentiment: they have not the verbal means." This despite the fact that an Englishman, a Frenchman, a German and an Italian are the products of one culture and their languages are closely related. Even so, it is said that on any abstract topic, they cannot by any means think alike because their languages differ! If this is their condition, what will be the relation between the languages of an Indian and an Englishman? By wearing dhoti and kurta an Englishman does not start thinking like an Indian just as the latter cannot understand the civilization of Europe by putting on a coat and trousers and eating with knives and forks.

When such are the problems in people understanding one another, what should the poor translator do? How should he deal with these problems? He should first of all realize these difficulties and know that translation does not mean looking at words in the dictionary. He has to know the two languages very well and also the cultures behind them. He should try to forget himself and become one with the ideas of the author and then put these ideas in his own words in the other language.

I think our translators rarely try to reach this depth and mostly translate as in the newspapers. Often I have come across words and phrases in Hindi that have stunned me. Trade union translated as *vyapar sangh* is correct from the literary point of view. But can anyone, who does not know, understand that *vyapar sangh* stands not for traders but for labourers? The phrase, trade union, has a history of over a hundred years behind it. Those who know will realize how this name was given. In France this is not the name, nor is that the translation. They call it *syndicat* (from which syndicate has been adopted in English). Suppose we are translating from French to Hindi, shall we translate it as syndi-cate or something like that? This is a simple example—the real problem arises when more complicated words occur.

Secondly, translators should, as far as possible, use easy and simple words which do not have many meanings and do not mislead. Long phrases should be avoided. Well-known literary works of all the existing languages of the world have been translated, and translated very well, in many languages. There is no reason why in Hindi also there should not be such good translations. I am sure when our translators give their attention to this matter, this urgent work also will be successfully done. Our big problem is that the BAs and MAs of our universities know very little English and no other foreign language at all.

Ordinary literary books can be translated but the correct translation of books of religion, philosophy and such abstract subjects seems to be impossible. There the words carry very different meanings, like a dress that is worn by dozens of men; how is one to make a distinction between the various meanings? It is one word but still not one, and conveys different images in the mind—such as beauty, truth, religion, *mazhab*. Take beauty for example—the beauty of a woman, of nature, of an idea, of art, of truth, of a phrase, of character, of a novel and so many more can be added—what is common between them all? Stating that a thing that is liked and which pleases people is beauty is somewhat confusing; and there can be no agreement on this.

There are many such confusing words which convey many meanings, in every language. There are some words which are obsolete and mean nothing. Some words are mendicants and about them Matthew Arnold had said— "terms thrown out, so to speak, as a not fully grasped object of the speaker's consciousness." Some words are known as 'nomads', they wander, and do not mean anything special. Such words are to be found in every language and those persons specially who have no clarity of thought use them. They hide their weaknesses in long, confusing and to some extent meaningless words. That prose in which such words are used profusely (I do not at the moment mean such words as beauty, truth) becomes weak. Such writing has not a razor's edge nor can it attain its objective as does an arrow from a bow.

We can try to see that these obsolete, mendicant and nomad words are not used, as far as possible, in our speech and writing. The fault is not of the poor words, but of our minds, semi-learned and less disciplined. One affects the other. Those who speak and those who write make the language, but, then, it leaves a similar effect on those new persons who use it. In old languages like Sanskrit, Greek and Latin, looseness of thought or word is rarely allowed. They seem well-knit, sharp as a weapon and devoid of useless words. This gives them a glamour and a dignity which leaves a peculiar impression. Of current languages, French perhaps is the most trim and the French people are known for their mental discipline and chastity of expression.

The somewhat useless words, then, can be tackled in this way, but what are we to do about our abstract words of a higher level? We love them, they are necessary for us and often help make us prominent. But still, they are confusing and sometimes mean so much that they become meaningless. Take for example the idea of God. In every religion and language thousands of words are attributed in his praise. It looks as if man's mind could not comprehend this idea and to hide its weakness, opened the dictionary and hurled all the turgid and impressive words that one could lay one's hands upon, over his head. It was beyond the mental faculty to understand the meanings of those words, but having said and written a lot, a sort of consolation was gained that we have done our duty and that God should have no grudge against us at least. Thousands are the names of Allah, as if by adding the names the reality becomes clearer.

In English they describe God as absolute, omnipotent, omniscient, omnipresent, perfect, ultimate, immutable, eternal, etc. All this no doubt sounds frightening, but if impertinently one ponders over these words, one gets nowhere. The renowned American philosopher William James[2] has written thus about it: "The ensemble of the metaphysical attributes imagined by the theologian is but a shuffling and matching of the pedantic dictionary adjectives. One feels that in the theologian's hands they are only a set of titles obtained by a mechanical manipulation of synonyms: verbosity has taken the place of vision, professionalism that of life."

Similarly the Italian philosopher, Croce,[3] in disgust, explained the word 'sublime' thus: "The sublime is everything that is or will be so called by those who have employed or shall employ the name." There is hardly anything left to say after this and everyone should be convinced.

These high-class sublime matters are undoubtedly beyond the layman's reach, and we should let the pundits and learned decide, when to use the abstract words and how to translate them. All the same, we laymen should not forget that words are dangerous things and the more abstract, the more deceptive. And the most dangerous words, perhaps, are dharma and *mazhab*. Everyone in his heart understands them in his own way. In everyone's heart they form new impressions. Some will think of a temple, mosque or church; the others of a few books, or of some religious oblations, statute, philosophy, customs or of mutual disagreements. In this way one word will produce hundreds of different pictures in the minds of men, and that will bring out a variety of thoughts. It seems to be the weakness of the language that one word can produce such a varied effect. A word should, actually, connote just one picture. It means that dharma or *mazhab* has a hundred facets, each of which should have a separate word for it. They say there were more than two hundred words used for making love in the old American Maya language. How can we now translate all those words correctly?

In the use of words Mahatma Gandhi too is guilty to some extent. In general whatever he speaks or writes is precise and effective—no superfluous words and no attempt at a flowery style. This trimness is his power. But whenever he talks of God, the truth or ahimsa—and that he does very often—then that mental precision is lessened. God is truth, truth is God, nonviolence is truth, truth is nonviolence—all this he has said. It must mean something but it is not quite clear what. To me at least, such use of words suggests that injustice is being done to them.

---

[2] (1841–1910); author of *The Varieties of Religious Experience*.
[3] Benedetto Croce (1866–1952).

2

Lingua Franca of India[1]

One of the legends about India which our English rulers have persistently circulated all over the world is that India has several hundred languages—I forget the exact number. For proof there is the census. Of these several hundred, it is an extraordinary fact that very few Englishmen know even one moderately well, in spite of a lifelong residence in this country. They class the lot of these together and call them the 'vernacular', the slave language (from the Latin *varna*, a home-born slave), and many of our people have, unknowingly, accepted this nomenclature. It is astonishing how English people spend a lifetime in India without taking the trouble to learn the language well. They have evolved, with the help of their *khansamahs* and *ayahs*, an extraordinary jargon, a kind of pidgin-Hindustani, which they imagine is the real article. Just as they take their facts about Indian life from their subordinates and sycophants, they take their ideas about Hindustani from their domestic servants, who make a point of speaking their pidgin language to the sahiblog for fear that they would not understand anything else. They seem to be wholly ignorant of the fact that Hindustani, as well as the other Indian languages, have high literary merit and extensive literatures. . . .

Some people imagine that English is likely to become the *lingua franca* of India. That seems to me a fantastic conception, except in respect of a handful of upper-class intelligentsia. It has no relation to the problem of mass education and culture. It may be, as it is partly today, that English will become increasingly a language used for technical, scientific and business communications, and especially for international contacts. It is essential for many of us to know foreign languages in order to keep in touch with world thought and activities, and I should like our universities to encourage the learning of other languages besides English—French, German, Russian, Spanish and Italian. This does not mean that English should be neglected, but if we are to have a balanced view of the world we must not confine ourselves to English spectacles. We have already become sufficiently lopsided in our mental outlook because of this concentration on one aspect and ideology, and even the most rabid of our

[1] From An Autobiography, pp. 452–5.

nationalists hardly realize how much they are cribbed and confined by the British outlook in relation to India.

But however much we may encourage the other foreign languages. English is bound to remain our chief link with the outside world. That is as it should be. For generations past we have been trying to learn English, and we have achieved a fair measure of success in the endeavour. It would be folly to wipe the slate clean now and not to take full advantage of this long training. English also is today undoubtedly the most widespread and important world language, and it is gaining fast on the other languages. It is likely to become more and more the medium of international intercourse and radio broadcasting, unless 'American' takes its place. Therefore we must continue to spread the knowledge of English. It is desirable to learn it as well as possible, but it does not seem to me worthwhile for us to spend too much time and energy in appreciating the finer points of the language, as many of us do now. Individuals may do that, but to set it as an ideal for large numbers is to put a needless burden on them and prevent them from progressing in other directions.

3

The Question of Language[1]

We have had during recent months a revival of the old controversy between Hindi and Urdu, and high excitement has accompanied it and charges and counter-charges have been flung about. A subject eminently suited for calm and scholarly consideration and academic debate has been dragged down to the level of the market-place, and communal passions have centred round it. Inevitably, many of the champions who have entered the field of battle have little to do with scholarship or the love of a language for its own sake; they have been chiefly concerned with the government orders and court procedure. Those who loved language as the embodiment of culture, of any thought caught in the network of words and phrases, of ideas crystallized, of fine shades of meaning, of the music and rhythm that accompany it, of the fascinating history and associations of its words, of the picture of life in all its phases, those to whom a language is dear because of all this and more, wondered at this vulgar argument and kept away from it.

And yet we cannot keep away from it or ignore it, for the question of language is an important one for us. It is not important because of that cry of the ignorant that India is a babel of tongues with hundreds and hundreds of languages. India, as everyone who looks round him can see, has singularly few languages considering its vast size, and these are intimately allied to each other. India has also one dominant and widespread language which, with its variations, covers a vast area and numbers its votaries by the hundred million. Yet the problem remains and has to be faced.

It has to be faced for the moment because of its communal and political implications. But that is a temporary matter and will pass. The real problem will remain: as to what policy we shall adopt in a scheme of general mass education and the cultural development of the people; how shall we promote the unity of India and yet preserve the rich diversity of our inheritance?

The question of language is ever one of great consequence for a people. Almost exactly three hundred years ago Milton, writing from Florence to a

[1] Allahabad, 25 July 1937. *The Bombay Chronicle*, 11–13 August 1937. Reprinted in *The Unity of India*, pp. 241–61. Excerpts.

friend, emphasized this and said: "Nor is it to be considered of small conse-quence what language, pure or corrupt, a people has, or what is their customary degree of propriety in speaking it . . . for let the words of a country be in part unhandsome and offensive in themselves, in part debased by wear and wrongly uttered, and what do they declare, but by no light indication, that the inhabi-tants of that country are an indolent, idly yawning race, with minds already long prepared for any amount of servility? On the other hand, we have never heard that any empire, any state, did not at least flourish in a middling degree as long as its own liking and care for its language lasted."

A living language is a throbbing, vital thing, ever changing, every growing and mirroring the people who speak and write it. It has its roots in the masses, though its superstructure may represent the culture of a few. How, then, can we change it or shape it to our liking by resolutions or orders from above? And yet I find this widely prevalent notion that we can force a language to behave in a particular manner if we only will it so. It is true that under modern con-ditions, with mass education and mass propaganda through the press, printed books, cinema, and the radio, a language can be varied much more rapidly than in past times. And yet that variation is but the mirror of the rapid changes taking place among the people who use it. If a language loses touch with the people, it loses its vitality and becomes an artificial, lifeless thing instead of the thing of life and strength and joy that it should be. Attempts to force the growth of a language in a particular direction are likely to end in distorting it and crushing its spirit.

What should be the policy of the state in regard to language? The Congress has briefly but clearly and definitely stated this in the resolution on fundamental rights: "The culture, language and script of the minorities and of the different linguistic areas shall be protected." By this declaration the Congress is bound, and no minority or linguistic group can require a wider assurance. Further, the Congress has stated in its constitution, as well as in many resolutions, that, while the common language of the country should be Hindustani, the pro-vincial languages should be dominant in their respective areas. A language cannot be imposed by resolution, and the Congress desire to develop a com-mon language and carry on most of our work in the provincial languages would be pious wishes, ignored by the multitude, if they did not fit in with existing conditions and the needs of the situation. We have thus to see how far they so fit in.

Our great provincial languages are no dialects or vernaculars, as the ignorant sometimes call them. They are ancient languages with a rich inheritance, each spoken by many millions of persons, each tied up inextricably with the life and culture and ideas of the masses as well as of the upper classes. It is axiomatic that the masses can only grow educationally and culturally through the medium of their own language. Therefore it is inevitable that we lay stress on the pro-vincial languages and carry on most of our work through them. The use of any other language will result in isolating the educated few from the masses and in retarding the growth of the people. Ever since the Congress took to the use of these provincial languages in carrying on its work we developed contacts with the masses rapidly and the strength and prestige of the Congress increased all over the country. The Congress message reached the most distant hamlet and the political consciousness of the masses grew. Our system of education and public work must therefore be based on the provincial languages.

4

Power of Words[1]

22 February 1944

Darling Indu,

What strange and mysterious things are words! The spoken word is powerful enough but even more so is the written word, for it has more of permanence. Images of thoughts and impresses, of the treasures of memory and stored fancies, the prelude and foundation of action, an idol with clear outlines or shapeless, and yet full of the breath of life! As with so many things to which we grow accustomed—the stars in the heavens, and flowers and green grass, and mountains, and the gentle rippling flow of water, murmuring as it goes—and growing accustomed to them, our senses are dulled to their astonishing beauty, so also with words. But when, in the morning of the world, words and language first burst upon the mind of man, how great must have been the joy of this discovery, with what reverence he must have looked upon this mighty thing, coming to him out of the unknown! Inevitably, he praised the Gods he worshipped and called this new power of expression the language of the Gods. Carefully he treasured it in his memory and handed it on from generation to generation, and out of that arose the books he called sacred, the scriptures of various lands and religions.

Sacred they were, as every word of power is sacred, as every attempt of man to understand and mystery of life and of his own nature, as the unfolding of his mind and intelligence, as his ceaseless challenge and struggle against the powers and principalities that would ignore him and suppress him. But words have become too common coin today, debased and often counterfeit, fit emblems of many of the human beings who use them.

Papu

[1] To Indira Gandhi. JN Collection, NMML. Excerpts.

5

A Poetic Testament[1]

A language is something infinitely greater than grammar and philology. It is the poetic testament of the genius of a race and a culture, and the living embodiment of the thoughts and fancies that have moulded them. Words change their meanings from age to age and old ideas transform themselves into new, often keeping their old attire. It is difficult to capture the meaning, much less the spirit, of an old word or phrase. Some kind of a romantic and poetical approach is necessary if we are to have a glimpse into that old meaning and into the minds of those who used the language in former days. The richer and more abundant the language, the greater the difficulty. Sanskrit, like other classical languages, is full of words which have not only poetic beauty but a deep significance, a host of associated ideas, which cannot be translated into a language foreign in spirit and outlook. Even its grammar, its philosophy, have a strong poetic content; one of its old dictionaries is in poetic form.

It is no easy matter, even for those of us who have studied Sanskrit, to enter into the spirit of this ancient tongue and to live again in its world of long ago. Yet we may do so to a small extent, for we are the inheritors of old traditions and that old world still clings to our fancies. Our modern languages in India are children of Sanskrit, and to it owe most of their vocabulary and their forms of expression. Many rich and significant words in Sanskrit poetry and philosophy, untranslatable in foreign languages, are still living parts of our popular languages. And Sanskrit itself, though long dead as a language of the people, has still an astonishing vitality.

[1] From *The Discovery of India*, pp. 165–6. Excerpts.

6

The Language Controversy[1]

In the India of today and tomorrow, there will be infinite opportunities and openings for those who are fit and competent. Young men should face this prospect with enthusiasm and zest and in a spirit of adventure, without giving way to frustration or a sense of despondency at things which might have gone wrong in the past.

No individual can guarantee for himself success, but every individual can guarantee for himself a good effort, a good run and good work in life whatever might be the result. We have done our job and we have had the joy of it. This is the spirit in which all should work.

The question of language is a subject of great argument today, but unfortunately the argument seems to be conducted mostly by people who know nothing about language. When a question like this comes up in the political arena, other issues are introduced and it becomes impossible to consider it on merits and take a right decision. It seems to me that generally the position that we have to carry on in our own language is obviously correct. It is also obvious that India must keep intimate contact with foreign countries and her people must know foreign languages. Equally also, a language widely known in India will be difficult to give up or replace. The real argument, however, seemed to take place over Urdu and Hindi and Hindustani, particularly in the northern parts.

No real language can be a sort of made-to-order business. A language grows but it may be helped to grow in a particular direction by educational methods. In the past, literary forms of languages were largely sequestered round select circles. Today, that is not so and it is going progressively to be less so in the future. Today in any democratic society language tends to change very greatly, sometimes it even deteriorates in the sense of purity, but, at the same time it, becomes more vigorous. While in literary style you may have a fine and attractive vehicle though not very vigorous, under democratic development, language gets a certain crudity but vigour and strength also. Of course, we should like to have both but ultimately you have to choose which side you will stress a little more than the other.

[1] Speech at a special convocation held by the Osmania University, Hyderabad, to confer the honorary degree of Doctor of Law, 26 December 1948. From *The Hindu*, 27 December 1948. Excerpts.

Take English which is one of the most powerful languages. It is not as graceful as some other languages but it has a certain vigour. One of the reasons for this is that it is progressively ceasing to be English and becoming American. Personally educated in an English University, I do not myself like many of these Americanisms very much but I think these developments are putting new vigour into the English language and numerous words have come into its vocabulary.

All the people who argue about Hindi and Urdu think in terms of importing new terms and expressions or in static terms and opposing all change. Both are incorrect prejudices. People talk about a national language as if a national language was ever made by statute. No doubt a state language can be laid down by law but a national language grows automatically into a national language. You cannot call a language the national language if it is not so in actual fact. It amazes me how many people argue in their ignorance. Anything they do not understand they call Sanskrit or Persian. Instead of owning ignorance they start complaining. The first sign of decay is when we shut the door and shut ourselves in.

At every stage of India's greatness the windows of her mind were wide open. In language also it is more so. Anybody who wants to limit a language kills that language. I find protagonists of Hindi and Urdu always thinking in terms of limiting the language and not expanding it. That is a dangerous thing. For my part I think there is no need for state action in the matter at all. I am quite sure that out of the masses of India the real national language will arise. I realize that after all the masses cannot give fine literary flourishes or touches of beauty to language. That is to be done by the elite. But if the language is to be vigorous, it has to be understood largely by the people.

I do not know how many of you remember that when Kemal Pasha wanted to develop Turkish—he did not like the use of Arabic words in Turkish. He appointed a commission to tour villages and collect good village words and see that these were incorporated and popularized in schools and colleges. This strengthened Turkish tremendously and brought literally Turkish in common touch with the people. That shows that if a language is cut off from the people it will not grow. It might be used in courts among courtiers but it cannot grow in these days of democracy, popular assemblies and parliaments. Those literary cliques and coteries which think in terms of pure Urdu and Hindi are really killing language.

I do not know much about linguistics. But I do know something as to what is beautiful in languages. It takes my breath away when I see these people producing something which they call pure Hindi or pure Urdu which is something as near bombastic nonsense as I can imagine. We have to evolve and create conditions for evolving a powerful language which must have its windows and doors open and imbibe wholesome influences.

The Function of Language[1]

I believe that a language is a greater test of a nation's character than almost anything else. If a language is strong and vigorous, so are the people who use it; if it is rather superficial, ornate and intricate, the people reflect it. Of course this may be more correctly put the other way about, for it is the people who create the language. But there is some truth also in the language moulding the people. A language which is precise makes the people think precisely. Lack of accuracy and precision in meaning leads to muddled thinking and, consequently, confused action.

A language which is confined in a strait-jacket, with no doors and windows open for progressive change, maybe both precise and graceful, but is apt to lose touch with a changing environment and the mass of the people. This inevitably leads to a loss of vigour and a growth of a certain artificiality. At any time this would not be good, but in the present dynamic age, with almost everything changing round about us, a straitjacket will deaden a language. The courtly languages of previous ages had much to commend them. But they are totally unsuited to a democratic age, where we aim at mass education. A language, therefore, must fulfil two functions: it must base itself on its ancient roots and, at the same time, vary and expand with growing needs and be essentially the language of the mass of people and not of a select coterie. This is all the more necessary in this age of science and technology and world communication. In so far as possible, that language should have common or similar words with other languages in regard to scientific or technical terms. It must, therefore, be a receptive language, accepting every word from outside that fits into its general structure. Sometimes that word may be slightly varied to suit the genius of the language.

Classical languages have played a very great part in the development of human society. At the same time they have rather impeded the growth of popular languages. So long as the learned thought and wrote in the classical language, there was no real growth of the popular language. In Europe, Latin came in the way of growth of the European languages till about the sixteenth

[1] 13 February 1949. *National Herald.* Excerpts.

century. In India Sanskrit had such a dominating influence that the Prakrits, and what subsequently became provincial languages, were rather stunted. Later, Persian also became a language of the learned in large parts of India and this also came in the way of the growth of popular languages in some parts of India.

In India we are rightly committed to the growth of our great provincial languages. At the same time we must have an all-India language. This cannot be English or any other foreign language, although I believe that English, both because of its world position and the present widespread knowledge of it in India, is bound to play an important part in our future activities. The only all-India language that is possible is Hindi or Hindustani or whatever it is called.

These are certain basic propositions which we must bear in mind in considering this vital question. We must remember that any hurried decision on it on a political plane or under the influence of momentary passions or prejudices, may well prove harmful. We have to build for the future and a false foundation may well stunt our future growth not only linguistically but in the wider domain of culture and human advancement. It is far better to go slow and avoid every kind of rigidity. Language is a very delicate instrument, evolved in its higher aspects by fine minds and strengthened by the popular use of it. It grows like a flower and too much external compulsion retards that growth or twists it into a wrong direction.

It is not very material what we call this language, whether Hindi or Hindustani, except for the fact that every word has a history behind it and connotes something very definite, which limits its meaning. What we must be clear about in our minds is the inner content of the language and the way it looks at the world, that is, whether it is restrictive, self-sufficient, isolationist and narrow, or whether it is the reverse of this. We must deliberately aim, I think, at a language which is the latter and which has therefore a great capacity for growth. The English language, probably more than any other today, has this receptiveness, flexibility and capacity for growth. Hence its great importance as a language. I should like our languages to face the world in the same way.

I am distressed at the way this question of language is considered and debated in India today. There is little of scholarship behind this argument and less of culture. There is no vision or thought of the future. Language is looked upon more as a kind of extended journalese, and a perverted nationalism demands that it should be made as narrow and restricted as possible. Any attempt to expand it is branded as a sin against this form of nationalism. Beauty in a language is often supposed to be an extreme ornateness and the use of long and complicated words. There is little vigour or dignity in evidence and one gets the impression of extreme superficiality and shallowness. Just as poetry is not a mere collection of rhymes and metres, so also a language is not just a display of intricate and difficult words. Recent attempts to translate well-known common words from English are fantastic in the extreme. If this tendency persists, that surely is murder of a fine vehicle for the expression of thought.

If I was asked what is the greatest treasure that India possesses, and what is her finest heritage, I would answer unhesitatingly it is the Sanskrit language and literature and all that this contains. This is a magnificent inheritance and so long as this endures and influences the life of our people, so long will the basic genius of India continue. Apart from its being a treasure of the past, it is, to an astonishing degree for so ancient a language, a living tradition. I should like to promote the study of Sanskrit and to put our scholars to work to explore and bring to light the buried literature in this language that has been almost forgotten. It is surprising that while we talk so much of language in terms of an extreme nationalism, only lip homage is paid to it or it is exploited for political ends. Very little is done to serve it as a language should be served. Whether in Sanskrit or in the modern Indian languages, constructive work is rare. We often follow a dog-in-the-manger policy of disliking any other growth and at the same time not doing anything ourselves. A language will grow ultimately because of its inherent worth and not because of statutes or resolutions. Therefore the true service of a language is to increase its value, practicability and inherent worth.

8

The National Language[1]

Mr. President,

There has been a great deal of debate here and elsewhere, and much argument over this question. . . .[2]

Now I am not going to talk about any of the various amendments that are before you or even analyse the amendments that I am supporting.[3] Rather I wish to draw your attention to certain other aspects, certain basic things which perhaps are presented by this conflict on the issue either in the House or in the country. After all it is not a conflict of words, though words may represent that conflict here. It is a conflict of different approaches, of looking perhaps in somewhat different direction.

We stand—it is a platitude to say it—on the threshold of a new age, for each age is always dying and giving birth to another. But in the present context of events all over the world and more so perhaps in India than elsewhere, we are participating both in a death and in a birth and when these two events are put

[1] Speech in the Constituent Assembly, 13 September 1949. *Constituent Assembly of India Debates, Official Report*, Vol. IX, 30 July 1949 to 18 September 1949, pp. 1409–16. Excerpts.

[2] Since July 1949 there was opposition to the inclusion in the Draft Constitution of the Article which proposed Hindi and Devanagri as official language and script of India respectively and English as an additional language for ten years. The opposition came from (1) a group which did not want any official language to be prescribed by the Constitution; (2) a group which wanted adoption of Hindustani and not Hindi as official language; and (3) a group which wanted English to be the official language for 15 years to be replaced thereafter following a national debate. There was also a controversy on the adoption of the form for the use of numerals.

[3] The amendment of Gopalaswami Ayyangar proposed that the official language of the Union should be Hindi in the Devanagari script, the numerals to be used for the official purposes of the Union should be the international form of Indian numerals, English should continue to be used for all official purposes of the Union for a period of 15 years, the President be authorized during that period to sanction the use of Devanagari numerals in addition to international numerals for any of the official purposes of the Union, and that English should continue in the form of bills and laws and their interpretations in Courts for a period much longer than 15 years as Hindi lacked precision.

together then great problems present themselves and those who have to solve them have to think of the basic issues and not be swept away by superficial considerations. Whether all the Honourable Members of this House have thought much of these basic issues or not I do not know. Surely many of them must have done so. But there are those basic issues. What is our objective? What are we going to do? Where do we want to go to?

Language is a most intimate thing. It is perhaps the most important thing which society has evolved, out of which other things have taken growth. Now language is a very big thing. It makes us aware of ourselves. First, when language is developed it makes us aware of our neighbour, it makes us aware of our society, it makes us aware of other societies also. It is unifying factor and it is also a factor promoting disunity. It is an integrating factor and it is a disintegrating factor as between two languages, as between two countries. So it has both those aspects and when therefore you think in terms of a common language here you have to think of both those facts.

All of us here, I have no doubt, wish to promote the integrity of India. There are no two opinions about it. Yet in the analysis of this very question of language and in the approaches to it one set of people may think that this is going to be a unifying factor, another may think that if approached wrongly it may be a disintegrating factor, and a disruptive one. So I want this House to consider this question and therefore it has become essential for us to view it in this larger context and not merely be swept away by our looking for this or that.

A very wise man, the Father of our Nation, thought of this question, as he thought of so many important questions affecting our national future. He paid a great deal of attention to it and throughout his career he went on repeating his advice in regard to it. Now that showed that, as with other things, he always chose the fundamentals of our national existence. Almost every thing he touched you will remember, was a basic thing, was a fundamental thing. . . .

Now the first thing he taught us was this: that while English is a great language—and I think it is perfectly right to say that English has done us a lot of good and we have learnt much from it and progressed much—nevertheless no nation can become great on the basis of a foreign language. Why? Because a foreign language can never be the language of the people, for you will have two strata or more—those who live in thought and action of a foreign tongue and those who live in another world. So he taught us that we must do our work more and more in our own language. . . .

Secondly, he laid stress on the fact that that language should be more a language of the people, not a language of a learned coterie—not that it is not valuable or is not to be respected—we must have learning, we must have poets, great writers and all that; nevertheless, in the modern context, even more than in the past, no language can be great which is divorced from the language of the people. Ultimately a language grows in greatness and strength if there is a proper marriage between those who are learned and the masses of the people. . . .

The last thing in this matter to which the Father of the Nation drew our attention was this, that this language should represent the composite culture of India. Insofar as it was the Hindi language it should represent that composite culture which grew up in northern India where the Hindi language specially held sway; it should also represent that composite culture which it drew from other parts of India. Therefore he used the word 'Hindustani' not in any technical sense, but in that broad sense representing that composite language which is both the language of the people and the language of various groups and others in northern India, and to the last he drew the attention of the people and the nation to that. . . . For the last thirty years or so, in my own humble way, I stood by that creed in regard to language and it would be hard for me if this House asked me to reject that thing by which I have stood nearly all my political life.

Not only that, but I do think that in the interests of India, in the interests of the development of a powerful Indian nation, not an exclusive nation, not a nation trying to isolate itself from the rest of the world but nevertheless aware of itself, conscious of itself, living its own life in conformity and in cooperation with the rest of the world, that approach of Mahatmaji was the right approach . . .

Now, we stand on the threshold of many things and this Resolution itself is the beginning of what might be termed a linguistic revolution in India, a very big revolution of far-reaching effects, and we have to be careful that we give it the right direction, the right shape, the right mould lest it goes wrongly and betrays us in wrong directions. Men shape a language, but then that language itself shapes those men and society. It is a question of action and interaction and it may well be said that if a language is a feeble language or an imprecise language, if a language is just an ornate language, you will find those characteristics reflected in the people who use that language. If the language is feeble those people will be rather feeble; if it is just ornate and nothing else they will tend to ornateness. So it is important what direction you give to it. If a language is exclusive those people become exclusive in thought and mind and action.

That is what I meant when I said at the beginning that perhaps behind all this argument and debate there are these different approaches. Which way do you look? As you stand on the threshold of this new age, do you twist your neck back and look backwards all the time, or do you look forward? It is an important question for each one of us to answer because there is, inevitably perhaps, a tendency in this country today to look back far too much. There is no question of our cutting ourselves away from our past. That would be an absurdity and a disaster because all that we are we have been fashioned by that past. We have our roots in that past. If we pull ourselves out of that past, we are rootless. We cannot go far merely by imitating others, but there is such a thing as having your roots in the soil but growing up to the sky above and not always looking down to the soil where your roots are. There is such a thing as marching forward and not turning back all the time. In any event, whether you want it or not, world forces and currents will push you forward but if you are looking back you will stumble and fall repeatedly.

Therefore, that is the fundamental thing in approaching this problem: which way are you looking, backward or forward? People talk about culture, about *Sanskriti*, etc., and rightly, because a nation must have a sound basis of culture to rest itself, and as I have said that culture must inevitably have its roots in the genius of the people and in their past. . . .

Now, whatever might have been the case in the past, in the present—today—there can be no doubt whatever that there is a powerful international culture dominating the world. Call it, if you like, a culture emanating from the machine age, from industry and all the developments of science that have taken place. Is there any Honourable Member present here who thinks that if we do not accept that culture—adapt it if you like, but accept it fundamentally—that we can make much progress merely by repeating old creeds? If I may venture to say, it is because at a previous period of our history we cut ourselves off from the culture of the rest of the world and in this culture I include everything including the art of war—we became backward and we were overborne by others who were not better than us but who were more in step with the culture of the time. They came and swept us away and dominated us repeatedly. The British came and dominated over us. Why? Because in spite of our ancient *Sanskriti* and culture, they represented a higher culture of the day—not in those fundamental and basic things which may be considered eternal, if you like—but in other things, the culture of the age, they were superior to us. They came and swept us away and dominated over us for all this long period.

They have gone. Are we going to think of going back in mind, thought and action to that type of culture which once brought us to slavery? . . .

Again, look at this language problem from another point of view. Till very recently—in fact, I would say a generation ago—French was the recognized diplomatic and cultural language of Europe and large parts of the earth's surface. There were other great languages—there was English, there was German, there was Italian, there was Spanish—in Europe alone, apart from the Asian languages. Yet French was the language in Europe, certainly of culture and diplomacy. Today it has not got that proud place. But even today, French is most important in diplomacy and public affairs. Nobody objected to French. No Englishman, or Russian, or German or Pole objected to French. So all those other languages were growing and today it might be said that English is perhaps replacing French from that proud place of diplomatic eminence.

Before French, in Europe, the language of diplomacy was Latin just as in India the language of culture and diplomacy for a vast period of time was

Sanskrit, not the language of the common people but the language of the learned and the cultured and the language of diplomacy, etc. And not only in India, but the effect of that, if you go back to a thousand years, you find in almost all of South East Asia, not to the same extent as in India, but still Sanskrit was the language of the learned even in South East Asia and to some extent even in parts of Central Asia. The House probably knows that the most ancient Sanskrit plays that exist have been found not in India but in Turfan on the edge of the Gobi desert.

After Sanskrit, Persian became the language of culture and diplomacy in India and over large parts of Asia—in India due to the fact of changing rule but apart from that, Persian was the diplomatic language of culture over vast parts of Asia. It was called—and it is still called—the "French of the East" because of that. These changes took place while other languages were developing, because of the fact that French in Europe and Persian in Asia were peculiarly suited for this purpose. Therefore, they were adopted by other countries and nations too. India may have adopted it partly because of a certain dominating influence of the new ruler, but in other countries which were not to dominated, they adopted Persian when it was not their language because it was considered as suitable for that purpose. Their languages grew.

We took to English obviously because it was the conqueror's languages, not so much because at that time it was such an important language, although it was very important even then—we took to it simply because we were dominated by the British here, and it opened the doors and windows of foreign thought, foreign science, etc., and we learnt much by it. And let us be grateful to the English language for what it has taught us. But at the same time, it created a great gulf between us who knew English and those who did not know English and that was fatal for the progress of a nation. That is a thing which certainly we cannot possibly tolerate today. Hence this problem.

However good, however important, English may be, we cannot tolerate that there should be an English-knowing elite and a large mass of our people not knowing English. Therefore, we must have our language. But English—whether you call it official or whatever you please, it does not matter whether you mention it in the legislation or not—but English must continue to be a most important language in India which large numbers of people learn and perhaps learn compulsorily. Why? Well, English today is far more important in the world than it was when the British came here. It is undoubtedly today the nearest approach to an international language. . . .

All these factors have been borne in mind in this amendment that Shri N. Gopalaswami Ayyangar has placed before the House. I do not know what the future will be for this language. But I am quite sure that if we proceed wisely with this Hindi language, if we proceed wisely in two ways, by making it an inclusive language and not an exclusive one, and include in it all the language elements in India which have gone to build up with a streak of Urdu or a mixture of Hindustani—not by the state, remember, but by allowing it to grow normally as it should grow and if, secondly, it is not, if I may say so, forced down upon an unwilling people, I have no doubt it will grow and become a very great language. How far it will push out the use of the English language I do not know; but even if it pushes out English completely from our normal work, nevertheless, English will remain important for us in our world contacts and in the international sphere.

So, to come back to the basic approach to this problem: Is your approach going to be a democratic approach or what might be termed an authoritarian approach? I venture to put this question to the enthusiasts for Hindi, because in some of the speeches I have listened here and elsewhere there is very much a tone of authoritarianism, very much a tone of the Hindi-speaking area being the centre of things in India, the centre of gravity, and others being just the fringes of India. That is not only an incorrect approach, but it is a dangerous approach. If you consider the question with wisdom, this approach will do more injury to the development of the Hindi language than the other approach. You just cannot force any language down the people or group who resist that. You cannot do it successfully. You know that it is conceivably possible that a foreign conqueror with the strength of the sword might try to do so, but history shows that even he has failed. Certainly in the democratic context of India it is an impossibility. You have to win through the goodwill of those people, those groups in India in the various provinces whose mother tongue is not Hindi. You have to win the goodwill of those groups who speak, let us say, some variation of Hindi, Urdu and Hindustani. If you try, whether you win or not, if you do something which appears to the others as an authoritarian attempt to dominate and to force down something then you will fail in your endeavour. . . .

We stand on the threshold of a new age. Therefore it is important that we should have this picture of India clearly in our minds. What sort of India do we want? Do we want a modern India—with its roots steeped in the past certainly insofar as it inspires us—do we want a modern India with modern science and all the rest of it, or do we want to live in some ancient age, in some other age which has no relation to the present? You have to choose between the two. It is a question of approach. You have to choose whether you look forward or backward.

9

Translation of the Constitution[1]

My dear Mr. Speaker,

. . . I am grateful for the trouble you have taken to write to me at length on the subject of translation of the Constitution. . . .

I am writing more as a lover of language as such than as a politician. I am eager that Hindi should develop and become more and more the common all-India language. But I am afraid that the method adopted by the enthusiasts for Hindi is likely to hamper this development and at the same time, to make Hindi not a living, growing and vital language, but rather a stilted and artificial one.

In regard to a common script, I can understand that Gujarati and Marathi should be written in the Devanagari script. But to write Urdu, at this stage, in Devanagari will be to produce something which is of use to nobody. Those who know Devanagari will read the original Hindi. Those who do not know it, will not be able to read the Urdu in Devanagari script. Each and each language has a genius of its own. Hence the objection to Hindi being written in the Roman script. Urdu has a flavour which cannot easily be put in Nagari script. It represents also centuries of contact with Persian, and to some extent, Arabic. It would be a pity to break those contacts.

I fear my views on the language question do not represent what might be called the majority opinion in India and are not very popular. But it has been a matter of sorrow to me that in such a vital question as language we should forget all artistry and all beauty and become the slaves of some pedagogues and grammarians who have no conception of art or beauty or the music of words. Each word is a thing of power with a history behind it, calling up images in one's mind. No word can ultimately be translated with accuracy into any other language. One can only find some synonym for it which does not convey the exact sense. Translation becomes, therefore, if it is to be good, something divorced from the grammarian and the man with a literal mind. Otherwise it

[1] To G.V. Mavalankar. File No. 32(98)/48–PMS. SWJN, Vol. 14 Part I (II series), pp. 360–1. Excerpts.

is dull and without effect or even real meaning. It seems to me a tragedy that our beautiful languages should be strangled in this way. A language, more than anything, represents the character of a people. Milton wrote long ago: show me the language of a people and I shall tell you who and what they are without knowing more about them. I think this is perfectly true.

I am a great admirer of Sanskrit, though I know little of it. I hope that Sanskrit will be studied largely in the future not only because of its treasures but also because of its conciseness. The history of Sanskrit literature is revealing. It might almost be the history of the Indian people from the earliest ages to recent times. I am not for the moment referring to the content of the language, but rather to the structure and vocabulary. We begin with Vedic Sanskrit with its amazing power compressed into a few words. This develops in the lovely classical Sanskrit, a thing of beauty and conciseness. Later this conciseness fades away and long and ornate sentences come in. Vigour gradually diminishes and is replaced by an artificial elaborateness. So one can imagine the Indian people gradually losing their pristine strength and vigour and getting lost in loose and elaborate thinking without much result.

We had and have an ideal opportunity for building up Hindi as well as all our other languages, so as to make them both beautiful and vigorous, expressive and concise. We are wasting that opportunity, I feel, and going in the wrong direction.

Yours sincerely,
Jawaharlal Nehru

10

Linguistic Provinces[1]

I am not greatly interested where a particular state boundary is situated, and I find it very difficult to get passionate or excited about it. I have my preferences, naturally, but it does not make much difference to me where the internal boundary of a state is drawn. Infinitely more important is what happens on either side of the boundary, what happens within the state—more especially in the great multilingual or bilingual areas—and what happens to people inside a particular state who may, linguistically or in any other sense, form a minority. Once we lay down these basic principles correctly and act up to them, then the vast number of problems and difficulties and legitimate grievances that arise will automatically disappear. . .

May I also suggest, for the consideration of this House, that while members here represent their constituencies, they represent something more? Each member is not only a member for this or that area of India, but a member for India as a whole. He represents India, and at no time can he afford to forget this basic fact that India is more than the little corner of India that he represents. This is all the more necessary when we have to face certain forces which may be called separatist. People's attention is being diverted to local, parochial, state and provincial problems and they are forgetting the larger problems of India. . . .

I am constantly compelled to think in larger terms, not only in national terms but in international terms. I see the picture of India in that larger context. Perhaps, my travel has helped me to see events in the true perspective. As I travel about India I feel excited by its moving drama. There are of course many things I do not like; but it is inspiring to see India moving today as if by the dictates of some preordained fate and destiny towards its goal. . . : There are many people in the wide world who also are beginning to feel the drama and adventure of what is happening in India. They see how we have got over great problems and great difficulties. It is true that we have even greater problems ahead, but we are judged in the measure in which we have succeeded in the past. We may argue about the boundary of Bihar or Bengal or Orissa. We may regard

[1] Speech in the Lok Sabha, 21 December 1955. JN Papers, NMML. Excerpts.

the question as important, but the word 'important' is a relative word. There may be things which are more important, and we must not lose ourselves in passionate excitement over the boundary of a state. We must take a total view of India. We must, by constitution, convention or otherwise guarantee that a person, whether he lives on this side of the border of a state or the other, will have the fullest rights and opportunities of progress according to his own way. . . .

I recognize that the language of the people is a vital matter for their development, whether it is education, administration or any other matter. But there is a distinction between developing the language to the fullest extent, and this passion for building a wall around a linguistic area and calling it a border. I completely accept the statement that people cannot really grow except through their language, but it does not follow that in order to make them and their language grow, a barrier must be erected between them and others. The various language areas in India represent the development of history through the ages. But drawing a hard and fast line between two areas is, I think, carrying it too far. As a matter of fact, it just does not matter where you draw your line. If you judge a border purely from the linguistic point of view, you will be going against the wishes of many people. Invariably there are bilingual areas. As long as you cannot prevent people of one state from going to another, there will always be bilingual areas. Are you going to stop, contrary to the dictates of the constitution, the movement of workers or of other people from one state to another? You cannot. Therefore, whatever fixed line you may draw, people on one side may be attracted to the other and move there, and thus change the linguistic composition of the state or of the border area. Are we going to sit down every few years and say, "The language ratio of this particular *tehsil* or *taluk* has changed and, therefore, it should be taken out of this state and put into another?" You must realize that while there are clearly marked linguistic regions, there are also bilingual areas and even trilingual areas between two such regions. And wherever you may draw your line, you do justice to one group and injustice to another. . . .

This question of language has somehow come to be associated with the question of states' reorganization. I repeat that I attach the greatest importance to language but I refuse to associate it necessarily with a state. In our country there are bound to be states where a single language is predominant. But there are also bound to be areas where there are two languages. In such instances, we should encourage both of them. We should make it perfectly clear that the dominant language of that state should not try to push out or suppress in any way the other language of the state. If we are clear about this, then the language issue does not arise.

Connected with language are other cultural issues which should also be treated on the same basis. That is to say, every culture and every manifestation of culture should be encouraged. There is no exclusiveness about culture. The more inclusive you are, the more cultured you are. The more barriers you put up, the more uncultured you are.

Thinking the way I do in this matter, I personally welcome the idea of bilingual or multilingual areas. For my part, I would much rather live and have my children brought up in bilingual and trilingual areas than in a unilingual area. In that manner, I think, I would gain a wider culture and wider understanding of India and of the world. . . .

I would say that the first and most important question in this entire Report is the last portion in which certain safeguards are mentioned. We should have these clear safeguards laid down possibly in the constitution or in some other way, so that a fair deal is given to every language in this country. We should not say: "We are in a majority and therefore our language should prevail." Every language has an equal right to prevail, even if it is a minority language in the country, provided it is spoken by a good number of people. I understand that the Bombay Municipal Corporation has schools in fourteen languages, because Bombay is a great city with many language groups.

Secondly, if I may venture to lay down a rule, it is the primary responsibility of the majority to satisfy the minority in every matter. The majority, by virtue of its being a majority, has the strength to have its way; it requires no protection. It is a most undesirable custom to give statutory protection to minorities. It is sometimes right that you should do that to give encouragement, for example, to backward classes, but it is not good in the long run. It is the duty and responsibility of the majority community, whether in the matter of language or religion, to pay particular attention to what the minority wants and to win it over. The majority is strong enough to crush the minority which might not be protected. Therefore, whenever such a question arises, I am always in favour of the minority.

Talking about religion in the broad sense of the word, the votaries of the Hindu religion in our country greatly outnumber the others. Nobody is going to push them from that position; they are strong enough. Therefore, it is their special responsibility to see that people following other religions in India feel satisfied that they have full freedom and opportunity. If this principle is applied, most of these troubles and grievances will disappear.

11

The Place of English[1]

Dear Ramdhari Sinha Dinkar,

I am convinced that real mass progress in India can only be made through our own languages and not through a foreign language. I am anxious to prevent a new caste system being perpetuated in India—an English-knowing caste separated from the mass of our people.[2] That will be most unfortunate. This in fact happened during the British period. It could happen then because education was very limited. It cannot happen now, when education is becoming widespread.

I cannot conceive of English being the principal medium of education in India in the future. That medium has to be Hindi or some other regional language. Only then can we remain in touch with our masses and help in a uniform growth.

But there are other aspects. One, I have mentioned above, about the necessity of knowing English or any other foreign language for scientific and technological purposes. Also, if I may say so with all respect, we are a narrow-minded people and are apt to live in our own shells. There is the danger of our getting cut off from the world of thought in all its aspects and becoming complacent in our own little world of India. For this reason also contacts with foreign languages are essential.

Thus I think that Hindi must be given every encouragement to grow and to be used for educational and administrative purposes, provided always that it grows on sound lines and not on superficial, journalistic lines. Secondly, Hindi (or some other regional language) has to be the medium of education.

Thirdly, English should be a compulsory second or third language. It is of course not necessary or possible for everybody in India to know English. But a very large number should know it for the reasons I have stated above. They can know it in two ways. One is a fully adequate knowledge of the language. The other is to know it as a language of comprehension, that is, to be able to

[1] To Ramdhari Sinha 'Dinkar', PM's Secretariat, File No. 40(99)/56-PMS.

[2] In his letter of 5 September 1956, Dinkar had said that persons like him had become very much afraid of the Government's policy regards Hindi in view of the speeches of Jawaharlal Nehru and Maulana Azad at the conference of Education Ministers.

read books and periodicals in it without perhaps being able to speak it easily. On the whole I am inclined to think that English as a compulsory subject in our schools (the medium being Hindi) is desirable. The schools will give some basic knowledge, enough perhaps for comprehension. After that, a relatively small number will proceed to a more thorough knowledge of English. It is obvious that English cannot be taken at the university stage. Universities are meant for specialized subjects, not for elementary teaching.

So far as teaching science and technology is concerned, I think that even there the medium should be Hindi in our schools. At a later stage English would be necessary for some years to come. Even when English is not necessary for the advanced teaching of science, it will nevertheless remain necessary for that wider contact with scientific literature.

Yours sincerely,
Jawaharlal Nehru

VOL. II

VI

Science and Technology

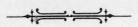

1. The Spirit of the Age   521

2. Science and the Community   522

3. Atomic Energy   526

4. The Responsibility of Scientists   528

5. The Spirit of Science   533

6. Technology and Man   536

7. Nuclear Energy   538

8. Temper of Science   540

9. The Creator and the Destroyer   542

1

The Spirit of the Age[1]

Most of us unhappily are too much engrossed in the business of politics to pay much attention to the finer and more important aspects of life. That is natural perhaps in a nation which struggles for national freedom and to rid itself of the bonds that prevent normal growth. Like a person in the grip of a disease it can think only of how to gain health again, and this obsession is a barrier to the growth of culture and science. We are entangled in our innumerable problems; we are opposed by the appalling poverty of our people. But if we had a true standard of values we would realize that the silver jubilee of the Indian Science Congress this year is an event of outstanding importance. For that Congress represents science, and science is the spirit of the age and the dominating factor of the modern world. Even more than the present, the future belongs to science and to those who make friends with science and seek its help for the advancement of humanity. . . .

Though I have long been a slave driven in the chariot of Indian politics, with little leisure for other thoughts, my mind has often wandered to the days when, as a student, I haunted the laboratories of that home of science, Cambridge. And though circumstances made me part company with science, my thoughts turned to it with longing. In later years, through devious processes, I arrived again at science, when I realized that science was not only a pleasant diversion and abstraction, but was of the very texture of life, without which our modern world would vanish away. Politics led me to economics and this led me inevitably to science and the scientific approach to all our problems and to life itself. It was science alone that could solve these problems of hunger and poverty, of insanitation and illiteracy, of superstition and deadening custom and tradition, of vast resources running to waste, of a rich country inhabited by starving people. . . .

If science is the dominating factor in modern life, then the social system and economic structure must fit in with science or it is doomed.

[1] Allahabad, 26 December 1937. Message for the silver jubilee celebrations of the Indian Science Congress at Calcutta, 3–9 January 1938. *The Hindustan Times*, 8 January 1938. Excerpts.

2

Science and the Community[1]

I do represent in some small measure something of the new India that you see rising about us. I think it is right and proper and very necessary for the world of science to be in intimate contact with the new India. It is also essential that new India should also come in intimate contact with the world of science. Because if science—whatever progress it may make—is isolated from the living currents it will not go very far. . . .

Surely, science is not merely an individual's search for truth. It is something infinitely more than that if it worked for the community. Its objective must be to remove the ills of the community. It must have a social objective before it. For a hungry man or a hungry woman, truth has little meaning. He wants food. For a hungry man, God has no meaning. He wants food. And India is a hungry, starving country and talk of truth and God and even of many of the fine things of life to the millions who are starving is a mockery. We have to find food for them, clothing, housing, education, health—all the absolute necessaries of life that every man should possess. When we have done that we can philosophize and think of God. So, science must think in terms of the 400 million persons in India. Obviously, you can only think in those terms and work along those lines on the wider scale of coordinated planning. . . .

What the future will bring I do not know; I can neither foretell the future, nor have I any authority to bind my country down to what it may or may not do in future, but in these days, so soon after the last war, when people again think of wars and when scientists are yoked into work in preparation for future wars, I think it is desirable and necessary that men and women of science should also think about the way they are often misused and exploited for base ends and should make it clear that they do not want to be so exploited.

Anyway, I do hope that India in future will not allow herself to be dragged into wars which are likely to be far more terrible than any that we have experienced thus far.

[1] Presidential address at the Thirty-fourth Indian Science Congress, Delhi, 3 January 1947. From the *Proceedings of the Thirty-fourth Indian Science Congress, Delhi, 1947* (Calcutta, 1948), pp. 1–4, and from *The Hindustan Times—Science Congress Supplement*, 4 January 1947. Excerpts.

I say that, and yet I know how difficult it is for a line to be drawn between scientific work for peace and for war. This great force—atomic energy—that has suddenly come through scientific research may be used for war or may be used for peace. We cannot neglect it because it might be used for war; obviously in India we want to develop it, and we will develop it to the fullest. Fortunately we have eminent scientists here who can do so. We shall develop it, I hope, in cooperation with the rest of the world and for peaceful purposes.

It is a tragedy that, when these enormous forces are available in the world for beneficent purposes and for raising human standards to undreamt of heights, people should still think of war and conflict and should still maintain economic and social structures which promote monopoly and create differences in standards of wealth between various groups and peoples. It is a tragedy, whatever other people might say about it, and no man of science should accept it as a right ordering of events. So in India today, while we are busy with our own political and economic problems, we have inevitably begun to think more and more of the vaster problems that face us and in the resolution of which science must inevitably play a big part.

I invite all of you who are present here, young men and old in the field of science in India, to think in these larger terms of India's future and become crusaders for a rapid bettering of the 400 millions in India, and crusaders of peace in India and the world and international cooperation for peace and progress.

I do believe firmly that the only right approach to the world problems and to our national problems is the approach of science, that is to say, of the spirit of science and method of science. Somehow eminent men of science when they come out of their study or laboratory forget the approach and method of science in other fields of life. While in our particular field, we may be meticulously careful, when we come out into the social and economic fields, we forget the scientific approach. I firmly believe that it is through the method and spirit of science that we can ultimately solve our problems. All over the world it is because we forget the scientific approach that many of our troubles arise.

While you must discuss your particular problems I want that you should not ignore the picture as a whole. There has been a tendency in the last few generations towards greater and greater specialization. It has yielded rich results but it has led to the narrowing of vision of the average person. Perhaps some of our troubles are due to this fact, and also because you can never understand a picture fully unless you have a conception of the whole.

You cannot divorce science from social and political happenings and from the economic structure of the world. Therefore, perhaps it is time that science developed a certain philosophy and unity, if I may put it so. It had this quality in the olden days when science presented a smaller picture than it does now. That gave a certain organic unity to it. Now with each department going its own way, it has become difficult. I do think that in the present circumstances of the world we should develop something of that unity of outlook and appreciation of the world problems. Nearly two years ago a bomb burst in Hiroshima. It created inevitably a great deal of excitement. It seemed to me to herald all kinds of enormous changes, constructive as well as destructive. It produced a conflict in people's minds as to where we were going, rather where civilization was going, what things could happen. Whether it was necessary or not I do not know, but obviously it led to one question which troubled a large number of people. The question was whether to gain a certain end any means and every means possible should be adopted because the means adopted at Hiroshima were horrible beyond words. Maybe the end desired was achieved, but it is a question which every scientist has to consider.

Science has two faces like Janus: science has its destructive side and a constructive, creative side. Both have gone on side by side and both still go on. No one knows which will ultimately triumph. Hiroshima became a symbol of this conflict and, in spite of all the decisions of the Atomic Energy Commission of the United Nations[2]—and we welcome those decisions, of course, in so far as they go—the doubt remains in one's mind as to where we are speeding.

On the other hand, apart from the atomic bomb aspect of it, we are obviously on the threshold of a new age in the sense of enormous power resources being put at the disposal of humanity and the community. Will this new age change—and I think it will change—enormously the whole structure of society? My mind goes back to the time when gunpowder burst upon the world. Gunpowder at any rate pushed the Middle Ages away completely and fairly rapidly, in course of time, brought or helped to bring about a new political and economic structure.

Of course, there were many forces at work. Nevertheless, gunpowder did produce that powerful effect on society and ultimately out of the feudal order a new capitalist order gradually developed. Now I wonder whether this so-called atomic bomb is not also the herald of a new age, of a new structure of society, which has to be established in order to fit in with present conditions. All these thoughts come to my mind because I want to understand this picture in this broad way and not to be lost in the argument. I myself am convinced that there is going to be no very great progress either in science or in other ways unless certain fundamental changes take place in the social structure. Here in India we have a peculiar structure. You can see in different places different types of social structures. You can see social structures approximating to those in the early Middle Ages as well as to those of the twentieth century. This picture which is

[2] On 30 December 1946, the United Nations Atomic Energy Commission adopted an American plan recommending a treaty, binding on all members of the United Nations, for peaceful uses of atomic energy. The plan also suggested the setting up of an international authority to give effect to the treaty.

rapidly changing even the twentieth century structure does not seem to answer the present needs.

So personally I feel convinced that a radical change must come, a radical change in the direction of allowing the whole community to develop and not only a small group on top. I do not think that the enormous big projects that we have in view in India can really succeed without the cooperation of the people at large. I think we shall be able to turn these vital currents in the right direction and mould them on scientific lines.

3

Atomic Energy[1]

Sir,

I move: That the Bill to provide for the development and control of atomic energy and for purposes connected therewith, be taken into consideration.

Unfortunately, the first use that atomic energy has been put to has somewhat clouded the other manifold uses that it is likely to be put to in the future. Most people probably think of atomic energy in the sense of something producing atomic bombs for the destruction of human beings. But, probably, even the great destruction of that atomic bomb will be forgotten, while the use of atomic energy may in future powerfully influence the whole structure of the world. No one can say when that use will be perfected or brought into the common life of man. But the tempo of change and progress is so great nowadays that it is quite possible that within our lifetime we may see the whole world change because of the use of this enormous power being released for human purposes. Therefore, it is not from the point of view of war that I am placing this Bill before this House but rather from the point of view of the future progress of India and the Indian people and the world at large. If we do not set about it now, taking advantage of the processes that go towards the making of atomic energy, and join the band of scholars and researchers who are trying to develop it, we will be left behind and we shall possibly only just have the chance to follow in the trail of others. That is not good enough for any country, least of all for a country with the vast potential and strength that India possesses. Fortunately for India we have most of the material that is needed—the minerals that are essential and the human material, which is perhaps even more essential. All that is necessary is that we should put them together and the state should give every facility for this development.

Now, because of this association of atomic energy with war, inevitably the matter has become a highly secret matter and most of the countries advanced in research are jealous that the results of their research should not be known to others, unless, of course, there is some kind of mutual exchange. We have,

[1] Speech moving the Atomic Energy Bill in the Constituent Assembly (Legislative), 6 April 1948. *Constituent Assembly of India (Legislative) Debates, Official Report*, Vol. V, 1948, pp. 3315–34. Extracts.

therefore, ourselves proceeded somewhat cautiously, that is to say, in a sense that our research work cannot be as public as normal scientific research or scientific work ought to be. Firstly, because if we did that, the advantage of our research would go to others before we reaped it, and, secondly, it would become impossible for us to cooperate with any other country which is prepared to cooperate with us in this matter, because it will not be prepared for the results of their research to become public. Therefore, this Bill lays down that this work should be done in privacy and in secrecy.[2] There is no other way of doing it. It is not that we desire secrecy and privacy. We should rather wish that all scientific work and scientific research were public and that the world could take advantage of it. I am entirely opposed to any secrecy in science, just as I am entirely opposed to the pernicious system of patent medicines that has spread, whether they are the western type of patent medicines or Unani or Ayurvedic or any other. I think secrecy in science or in the art of cure is a dangerous thing. So it is not our desire to keep these processes secret but we are compelled by circumstances to proceed along these lines; otherwise there can be no progress at all.

So this Bill gives certain powers to the Atomic Energy Board that we have already got, subject, of course, always to the supervisory and superintending power of the Government, to carry on these researches in non-public and secret way and to concentrate more or less all the researches in it and bring them more or less together into its own domain.

[2] Clauses 11, 14 and 15 laid down restrictions on information, offences and penalties.

4

The Responsibility of Scientists[1]

You have been welcomed by the Governor and by the Premier[2] of this province and I have come here on behalf of the Government of India to bid you a warm welcome to this Science Congress and to assure you, if an assurance is needed, of our interest in your work and achievements. I am also here in my personal capacity as a citizen of Allahabad to express my pleasure at the meeting of this distinguished Congress in my home town of Allahabad. Reference has been made to this city as a centre of intellectuality and as a place where for ages past people came for learning and also as a place where people come to die. When these compliments are paid to this city of Allahabad I do not take them at their face value. So far as the question of dying is concerned, I prefer to live in a place where people go to live and not to die. But when Allahabad is said to be the seat of intellectuality, it almost leads me to think that it has no other claim left, having been deprived of most of the other things that originally belonged to her. Fortunately, the university is still here in Allahabad and presumably will continue. Fortunately, the rivers Ganga and Jamuna are also here and presumably will continue. Therefore, in the final analysis, the citizens of Allahabad need not despair and so long as we have Ganga and Jamuna we can carry on.

We are happy to see amidst us Dr. C.V. Raman, one of the most eminent Indian scientists who recently celebrated his sixtieth birthday. Sixty years are not very much in a man's life and we hope that he will be spared for many more years of service in the cause of science and in the cause of India.

Undoubtedly, science has done tremendous good to the world and to India. We have to concentrate on the advancement of scientific research and the application of science. The Government is building up laboratories, institutes and the like to give opportunities to youth to further the cause of science, because we realize that a country must be good in regard to scientific research and application of science if it is to play its proper part in the world,

[1] Inaugural address at the thirty-sixth session of the Indian Science Congress, Allahabad, 3 January 1949. *Proceedings of the Thirty-sixth Indian Science Congress* (Calcutta), 1949, pp. 31–5.

[2] Sarojini Naidu and Govind Ballabh Pant respectively.

and because we also realized that we cannot solve our problems, economic or otherwise, without the help of science. Science must progress and we, as a Government, are certainly going to do our utmost to give it an opportunity but ultimately it is the human being who counts in an institute and not the money which flows into it from the exchequer. If India has human being of the right calibre who can take advantage of these opportunities, it will be well and good. I am quite convinced that many of our younger men in the scientific field are of the right calibre and are bound to make good, if they are given opportunities.

I have come to think that quality is far more important than quantity in scientific knowledge. It is true that out of quantity comes quality, or the opportunity comes if the masses of India have sufficient opportunities for their training, and I have no doubt that a vast number of competent, able and talented young men and women will come out in every field of activity and more especially in science. Giving them opportunity is where quantity comes in, but if we are content with quantity only then I fear we will remain secondary in the field of science. Therefore, quality becomes essential and I lay stress on this because I fear that during the past two or three years when we talked to much of scientific advance we laid stress on quantity more than on quality.

I am not satisfied with the quality and output in the field of science in India. Frankly speaking, I think that we are not quite so big in the scientific field as we say we are. Somehow we are getting lost in smaller thing, in mutual debates and arguments and not concentrating on that type of scientific work which is of a basic nature, and out of which all other types of scientific activities grow. I like to see more of fundamental work and less of what I may call rather superficial work. In fact, more of that spirit of true science which should animate and inspire us and lead us to bigger achievements.

The problems we have to face in the world and in India today are overwhelming. In India the economic problem is dominant and we have to think of ways to solve it. Unfortunately, even the cause of science is suffering in India because of our economic difficulties. The economic problem is a big one and it is not directly concerned with your work in the Science Congress. What should scientists do and to what end should they work?

Obviously, men of the highest calibre must be given a chance to work as they choose and it is no good third-rate men trying to do the work of first-rate men. Really first-rate men in the field of science, and indeed in any field, must be given a fair amount of latitude to do just what they like. They may fail or they may succeed, but if they are not given this latitude, they may miss something very great. The problem that troubles me is how, in the final analysis, science is helping us today in the solution, not of the thousand and one problems of the world, but of what I shall call the one single fundamental problem of this world. In spite of its very great scientific achievement today, the world is obviously in a bad way and there is something very wrong about it. There are plenty of men of ability and talent and even genius, plenty of men of goodwill and yet the world goes wrong.

What are they going to do about it? Peoples say they are in an age of transition, but every age is an age of transition. What do men of science propose to do about it? Whether they are scientists or not, they cannot escape the consequences of this conflict of spirit that is going on all over the world and certainly in India. I do not think that mere scientific advance, however great it may be, gives an answer to this major problem. Indeed, scientific advance rather intensifies that problem unless they find some other ways and means of solving it. The shake-up of the world, when industrial civilization began about two hundred years ago, had continued in varying degrees. As soon as places where industrialization had not spread became fewer and fewer, the crisis became more and more acute. It led to the First World War, which led then in a more acute form to the Second World War, and today it is leading to some frightful catastrophe. The lack of adjustment, caused by industrialization spreading and not being properly balanced with other conditions, had led to the crisis that enveloped them. The odd thing is that scientists added to that crisis by finding out more and more ways of advance in this particular field. Unless the scientists finds out ways of balancing that advance, he adds to the crisis and the result is that he speeds the possible destruction of his own work in a big way.

How exactly any scientist is going to deal with this tremendous problem I do not know. A scientist, like any other person, must develop some kind of organic knowledge of human history and human advance. He must develop some perspective and try to see how things have developed, how humanity has been affected in its various phases of existence, how it has profited by science and how it has not profited, not because of a lack of science but because of a lack of adjustment of what science produced. We have numerous examples of the highest scientific advance in a country being utilized for wrong purposes. While scientists must necessarily specialize, they must look at their problem in its wider perspective, as part of the human problem, in the historical as well as in the human perspective and then perhaps they may see it in its right place. Thus when they make their new discoveries, they may also think of the factors of balancing their discoveries. There should be an attempt to preserve everything that they have gained today and to add to it. There should be a further attempt to balance their gains in various ways, in the social and economic spheres and in the realm of spirit.

I would like you scientists to think about this aspect of the problem, because it affects all of us very greatly and all our achievements may be swept away by the great world disasters and catastrophes, simply because we work in our grooves and others work in their grooves and great forces work in contrary directions and are not balanced. The Governor appealed to you, men of science, not to help the forces of evil and destruction. That applies to each one of us, wherever we may be, and we should endeavour not to ally ourselves in any way with the forces of evil destruction. It is no good getting excited against this nation or that as most people do. Most people and most nations are alike more or less. They have their good and bad points. In a way, the problem has to be looked at impersonally, objectively and scientifically to understand the various forces that are at work today in the world. Know men's minds, understand them and try to help the right forces and the right urges.

Air travel takes us quickly from one part of the world to another and there are no political frontiers in the air. It is the mind of man that has achieved everything and developed everything. The mind of man is still probing into the mysteries of nature and the universe and probing with success. Most of the people in most parts of the world have not quite adapted themselves to the great achievements of science which they use daily. They use them just as so many people use the aeroplane in India, but they are as far removed to everything which an aeroplane signifies or means as anything can possibly be.

Today there is very little poise left in the nations and even statesmen go about openly cursing each other in conferences and in other places with the result that they live in an atmosphere of extreme tension with possibilities of wars or domestic conflict. Surely there is something very wrong about the world where all these conflicts and tensions take place, and if they do not understand what is wrong and help to the extent they can in setting it right, they are living in an artificial atmosphere. It should be the job of science or particularly some departments of science to try to solve these problems by developing to some extent a philosopher's bias in addition to the scientist's outlook. It requires in every field of life, especially for men at the top, a touch of philosophy, not too much of metaphysics which is most dangerous, but understanding problems of human life and applying science to the solution of those problems. This is not merely a question for the politicians or the scientists, it is a question for every sensitive, thinking human being. Obviously, scientists are both sensitive and thinking and, therefore, it is a question for them. They put up a vast number of laboratories and produce results which help them to meet this problem or that problem and then some overwhelming catastrophe comes which puts an end to their laboratories and to their work. It is an astounding position and I can hazard a few guesses as to the reason for it. A high degree of specialization has produced highly talented persons and even persons of genius, but often enough a person who is a very bad citizen in the real sense of the word. Each person works in his special groove, but there is very little of coordination between different grooves and all his work is upset from time to time by great forces, of which he has no understanding because he does not even try to understand them as they fall outside his groove. They have to understand these great forces, control them or divert them along right channels. If there is a conflict today in the world between forces of destruction and forces of construction, they must try to encourage and support and help in every way the latter.

5

The Spirit of Science[1]

In the course of less than four months, we have put up, and declared open or rather wished to declare open three national laboratories,[2] and I suppose, before this year is out, some more national laboratories will also be started. This is a great venture, testifying to the faith, which our scientists and our government, I hope, have in science. Of course, the putting up of fine and attractive buildings certainly does some services to science, I suppose, but nevertheless, buildings do not make science as Dr. Raman[3] has often reminded us. It is human beings who make science, not brick and mortar, but buildings help the human beings to work efficiently and with proper equipment. Therefore, it is desirable to have these fine laboratories, so that trained persons may work there, and persons may be trained for future work.

Now, why do we put up these laboratories, these research institutes and the like? Of course, everyone says, to advance the cause of science. Why so? You, Sir,[4] referred to the spirit of science. I wonder exactly what that spirit is, or whether we have the same ideas about that spirit or whether many of us differ? Is science, as is often supposed, a handmaid to industry? Certainly, it wants to help industry. Why? Because it wants to create, help in creating greater wealth, for the nation, for the people. It wants to increase, to have better living conditions for the people, greater opportunities of growth and so on and so forth. That I suppose, will be agreed to. But there is something more about it, I think, than this. What ultimately does science represent? I suppose, the active principle of science is discovery. Discovery, I said. You Sir,[5] just referred to scientists declaring war on nature. May I put it in a different way, that we seek the cooperation of nature, we seek to uncover the secrets of nature, to understand them and to utilize them, for the benefit of humanity. Anyway, the active principle of science is discovery. Now, what is, if I may say so, the active principle

[1] Speech at the opening of National Fuel Research Institute, Digwadih, Dhanbad, 22 April 1950. AIR tapes, NMML. Excerpts.

[2] Jawaharlal Nehru inaugurated the National Chemical Laboratory at Pune on 3 January 1950 and the National Physical Laboratory at New Delhi on 21 January 1950.

[3] C.V. Raman.

[4 & 5] Rajendra Prasad, the President of India.

of any social framework of society? Normally it is conservatism, of remaining where we are, of not changing, of carrying on, no doubt with improvement, no doubt, adding to it something or other. But, nevertheless, it is the principle of continuity, rather than of change. So we come up against a certain inherent conflict, between that principle of society, which is one of continuity and of conservatism and the principle of science, which is of discovery, which brigs about change, and which challenges that continuity. So, with the result, that the scientific worker, although he is praised and patted on the back, is nevertheless, not wholly approved of, because he comes and upsets the status quo.

And we see, that, normally speaking, science seldom really has the facilities that it deserves, except when some misfortune comes to a country in the shape of war. Then everything has to be set aside and science has its way for an evil purpose; nevertheless, it has its way. Now it is interesting to see this apparently inherent conflict between the normal conservatism of a static society and the normal revolutionary tendency of the scientists' discoveries, which changes often enough the basis of that society, because it changes living conditions, changes conditions governing human life, human survival and the rest. Now, I take it that most people who talk glibly of science, including our great industrialists, think of science as a kind of handmaiden to make their work easier. Well, so it is of course, it does make their work easier. Something which adds to the wealth of the nation, something which betters conditions. All that science does do. But surely science is something more than that, and the history of science shows that it does not just merely better the old but it sometimes upsets the old. It not only merely adds new truths to old, but sometimes the new truth it discovers, disintegrates some parts of the old truth, and thereby upsets not only the way of men's thinking, but the way of their lives too. So it is not merely a question of repeating the old in better ways, adding to the old, but creating something that is new. That is new to human consciousness.

Now, if we pursue this line of thought, then what exactly does the spirit of science mean? It means not only accepting the fresh truths that science may bring, not only improving the old but to be prepared to upset the old, if it goes against that spirit. To accept the new, to accept the disintegration of the old, not to be tied down to something that is old, because it is old, not to be tied down to a social fabric, or an industrial fabric, or an economic fabric, simply because you have carried on with it, although it goes contrary to the spirit of science, or to a new discovery of science—it means all that. Now most countries, whatever they may say, normally do not like to change. The human being is essentially a conservative animal. He dislikes change. He is used to certain ways of life, and any person trying to change them, meets with his disapproval. Nevertheless, change comes and people have to adapt themselves to it as they have, in the past. Now all countries, as I said, are normally conservative. But I imagine that our country, India, is more than normally conservative, and it is, therefore, that I have ventured to place these thoughts before you, because there is a curious hiatus, I find in people's thinking, if I may say so, in even scientists thinking, who praise science and practise science in the laboratory, but who discard the ways of science and the methods of approach of science and the spirit of science in everything else that they might do in life, and they become completely unscientific about it.

Now, if you approach science in that way, it no doubt does some good, it will always do some good. It teaches us new ways of doing things. It improves, may be, our conditions of industry or life, but the basic thing that science should do is to teach us to think straight and to act straight, and not to be afraid of anything, of discarding anything or accepting anything provided we have sufficient reason to do so. I should like our country to understand that, to appreciate that idea more because our country in a sense, in the realms of thought, has been singularly free in the past and it has not hesitated to look down the deep well of truth whatever it might contain. Nevertheless, with a mind so free in social practice, it encumbered itself so much that it came in the way of its growth, and it comes in the way of its growth today, in a hundred ways; our customs, our ways of looking at things, the little things that govern our lives, which have no real importance. But nevertheless they come in our way, and now that we have attained independence, naturally, there is a resurgence of all kinds of new forces, good and bad. Good forces, of course, are let loose by a sense of freedom. But also a number of rather narrowing forces, which narrow our minds, narrow our outlooks, which under the guise what people call culture, really mean a restriction of culture and a denial of any kind of real culture, because culture is a widening of the mind and of the spirit. Culture is never a narrowing of the mind or a restriction of the spirit of a man or of a country.

Therefore, if we look at science in the real way, and if we think of these research institutes and laboratories in a fundamental sense, then these are something more than just finding out little ways of improving things. . . . But they have to gradually affect our minds, the minds not only of those who work here, the young men and young women who might work here, but the minds of others too, and the minds of the rising generation more especially, so that the nation may grow up, imbibing the spirit of science and be prepared to accept a new truth, even though it has to discard something of the old in doing so. Only then, will this approach to science bear true fruit.

6

Technology and Man[1]

Technological developments bring about huge changes. Today we take trains, aeroplanes, radio, etc., for granted. But we have not yet got what is called an industrial background. Whether it is good or bad, it is a fact. That background exists in America, which is the world's most highly industrialized country. Its background is technological and industrial, so much so that the machine begins to become almost human in the way in which it works and while this happens, the human beings become more like machines. I am not considering the good and the evil of it. I am just trying to analyse what is happening.

The basic fact is that the tremendous pace of technological advance that has forced itself upon the people, whether they like it or not, because technological advance represents power. It represents military power. If you have not got it, well, you cannot protect yourself; you become a subject or a slave country. That is why Abdul Hamid of Turkey in spite of all hatred for the western civilization, adopted western military methods. Japan did it deliberately. It did not take western culture but it took western technology and western warfare methods and it became a great power. It is this technological development which has changed the entire face of the world.

Most of us are not conscious of this when we see the technological advances made by America and Europe; we do not realize what all this means. In a sense, our minds function in an agricultural or pre-industrial age. The pace of change is so great that we begin to wonder.

I want you to realize this extraordinary fact that while all these technological and other changes come out of the mind of man, nevertheless, the mind of man very often lags behind them. There was the French Revolution over 160 years ago with its war cries of Liberty, Equality and Fraternity and it was based on a generation or two of previous mental preparation of the people. The Industrial Revolution followed which was in fact a much bigger thing in the way in which it changed the entire outlook of the people; but even when the Industrial Revolution had advanced in Europe for 60 or 70 years, the minds of men were

[1] Speech at a meeting of State Development Commissioners, New Delhi, 18 April 1953. JN Collection. Excerpts.

still concerned with the French Revolution, not realizing that the world was changing rapidly under the impact of the Industrial Revolution. I am pointing out how events were marching in those days and are now marching more swiftly than men's minds. We have to be very wide awake about it. First of all we should try to understand them—not necessarily to accept everything, not necessarily to be blown off our feet but to try and understand them, because if we did not do so, whether we like it or not, we may be thrown off our feet, we may be submerged in some wave.

Perhaps these are more than what is required to be said on this occasion, which has no direct relevance, but I am saying all this to make you think, to broaden your outlook. It amazes me that while mighty problems are cropping up in the world, mighty forces are at work and tremendous technological changes are talking place, change that I find in our country, is on the communal plane which is fantastic nonsense to me. It shows the utter immaturity of the individual or the group that talks and argues in that way. It has no relation to the present-day world, I mean the talks about Hindu, Muslim and Sikh communalism. It just shows that they are completely backward in their thinking, in their minds. They never grasp the march of events in the centuries past and in the era they live in. Our country as a whole will be doomed and will continue to be a backward country as in the past while other countries will go ahead.

Everybody will agree, even the rank communalist, that we must be technologically advanced, we must have a modern, up-to-date army, we must have the latest aeroplanes, even the atom bomb. But it is not realized that the latest types of aeroplane and armies are the outcome of certain mind, of a certain mental approach. You cannot have the medieval mind and have the latest type of aeroplanes too. You cannot have modern development, modern technology with a medieval mentality behind it, which is represented in many ways in India but which is represented more than in anything else, by what is called the communal outlook. Of course, any kind of narrow outlook is bad in itself.

7

Nuclear Energy[1]

In the last generation or two, there have been certain explorations of the remotest frontiers of human knowledge which are leading us to many strange discoveries and strange consequences. Max Planck's Quantum Theory and, later on, Albert Einstein's Theory of Relativity changed the whole conception of the universe. Soon came the atom bomb with its power to kill. . . . The human mind and human efforts are unleashing tremendous powers without quite knowing how to control them. They cannot be controlled by a mere desire or demand for banning them. Nobody can really control the human mind from going on unleashing new forces. One of the political problems of the day is how to approach this problem of control which is of vital consequence. Such an approach presupposes some measure of lessening of tension in the world, some measure of mutual confidence on the part of the great nations, some agreement to allow each country to live its own life. The only alternative is conflict, and if the idea of conflict is in the minds of nations, then the atom bomb will undoubtedly remain.

Let us consider the possible issues. It is perfectly clear that atomic energy can be used for peaceful purposes, to the immense advantage of humanity. It may take some years before it can be used more or less economically. I should like the House to remember that the use of atomic energy for peaceful purposes is far more important for a country like India, whose power resources are limited, than for a country like France, an industrially advanced country. Take the United States of America which already has vast power resources of other kinds. To have an additional source of power like atomic energy does not mean very much for them. No doubt they can use it; but it is not so indispensable for them as for a power-starved or power-hungry country like India or like most of the other countries in Asia and Africa. I say that because it may be to the advantage of countries which have adequate power resources to restrain and restrict the use of atomic energy because they do not need that power. It would be to the disadvantage of a country like India if that is restricted or stopped. We should remember this very important aspect of the so-called international

[1] Speech in the Lok Sabha, 10 May 1954. JN Papers, NMML. Excerpts.

control. Who is to control atomic energy internationally? Which are the nations that are going to control it? One may say, the United Nations. Obviously, there is no other organization approaching the United Nations in its international jurisdiction. And yet, the House knows, the United Nations as it is does not include in its scope even the big nations of the world. Some of the biggest are kept out. The United Nations can control only itself. It cannot control any nation which is not in it, which it refuses to admit and with which it would not have anything to do. The result will be that though it may control a great part of the world, still there is a part of the world which is not controlled by it. That part over which there is no control, may make all the mischief. Therefore, the question of international control becomes difficult.

8

Temper of Science[1]

In the old days, long long ago, I suppose that learned men and high priests used to gather, from time to time, to share experiences and to try to probe into the mysteries of nature. It may be that modern scientists, or some of them, may rather look down upon those ancient efforts, though I hope very few do so, because after all even those, what you might consider from your modern stand-point as unscientific efforts, were the basis for further advance, even though they might have dealt with alchemy or metaphysical research or something with a much broader basis, that is philosophy. Anyhow, the high priests of those days, presumably, dominated the scene, and they may sometimes have exploited their position and misled the multitude; they may have tried to instill the fear of certain mysteries in the multitude, so as to keep up their vested interests as high-priests. Nevertheless, basically, that was a search for truth, to understand the nature of things, the nature of the practical world, as well as to explore the nature of some other worlds, if there are such, or wherever they may be. Now, gradually those times led, through many many steps, to the beginnings of science as we see it today and science developed, and now it overshadows the world, not only in its external achievements but in men's thinking, and the scientists of today now occupy the position of the high-priests of the mysteries. It is true that the true scientists does not function, and does not want to function, in a mysterious way and science and knowledge is largely an open secret to those who care to see and understand it, as it should be. Nevertheless, it becomes so complicated that·few people, perhaps, have the capacity to understand it, or have the will to take the trouble to understand it, and for most it becomes some kind of a mystery which is beyond their reach. Nevertheless they profit by it, of course, suffer from it, or both, and the world as we see it becomes, essentially, something that has grown out of science or its application, and science is likely to dominate us more and more in the future. Therefore, it is a thing of the highest importance, what scientists do, in what atmosphere and temper they work, how far scientists help a certain direction in the world's development, in the world's thinking, and how far they give it a wrong direction.

[1] Address at the forty-third session of the Indian Science Congress, Agra, 2 January 1956. AIR tapes, NMML. Excerpts.

Scientists, presumably, are searchers after truth and truth is a difficult thing to aim at. And if you search after truth you must not be afraid of the consequences of that search, even though it may sometimes force you to look down into the pit of hell. If you are afraid of the consequences of your search then you cannot go too far. That is so. You search for it, whether it is good or bad. Nevertheless, I take it, that such a thing as pure objectivity in any individual, even in a scientist, is not quite possible or, if I may say so, desirable. You cannot isolate yourself from the life of the world, from the joys and sorrows, from the possible dangers to the world or the possible benefits that might come to the world from your activity. You must have some function in life, to aim somewhere, not merely to look with wide open eyes at what is happening, in fact, to give some turn to events where you can. The moment we become functionless, we become rather passive spectators of events than have any hand in directing them. I do not suppose that scientists would like to be called merely passive spectators, or anyone for that matter. Therefore, some kind of broad ideal has to be before us, apart from, of course, the search for truth. What is that broad ideal?

Well, there may be many ideals, but obviously that ideal must have some relation to the problems of today. Let us put it in the narrowest way, a problem that Indian scientists have to deal with is, the development of the Indian people, the betterment of the Indian people, raising their standards, increasing their wealth and removing inequality. Planning, if you like, in its widest sense to help in that process, to direct it properly, that is a big problem which takes all our time and energy, or ought to take. Or let us go a step further and think of certain world problems. Now, I am not going to discuss these great world problems, and I think all of us are too apt to express our opinions in regard to them with a measure of arrogance, as if we could solve the problems of the world, if only our views were accepted by the world. That is not a becoming attitude for anyone however wise he might consider himself. Nevertheless, to surrender to the problems of the world and feel helpless is also not becoming. But without considering any particular problem, big as they are, we can, all of us, and more especially men and women of science, can perhaps consider the basic approach to those problems.

What do I mean by the basic approach? Shall I say, the basic temper in which those problems should be approached; the temper of science, the temper of reasonableness, the temper of finding out the truth or, whether that is a temper of science or not I do not know, the temper of peace. I think that really is more important, the more I think of it, than any positive step that might be taken towards the solution of a problem.

9

The Creator and the Destroyer[1]

Science has driven out, one might say, broadly speaking, many of the gods before whom people bowed and itself assumed a godlike pose. Like Janus, the god of the month of January, it has two faces, the face of the creator and the face of the destroyer and both faces look down upon us and often, perhaps, we have to make a choice as to which face we like and which we are going to encourage. On the one hand, we have this magnificent and majestic sweep of science, advancing onwards, bringing more and more power to human beings; on the other, somehow we see the misuse, or the possible misuse, of this power for destructive purposes. For the first time in human history it can be said with some confidence that mankind has the capacity and the power to get rid of the physical ills that humanity suffers from, to bring about a measure of welfare to all the thousands, millions, of inhabitants of this world which nobody could dream of previously. That is a possibility and a thing that can be done, provided, of course, one tries to do it in the right way. On the other hand, one also sees the terrible picture of science the destroyer, and the very weapons, the very power that it gives to humanity, being trained for the use of such destruction as the world has never seen. . . .

It is obvious that science and technology in the last two hundred years or so have changed the world, changed it for the better—I don't think very much for the better. It is obvious that that process is going to continue. It is going to continue whether we like it or not anyhow. I think we should like it and try to direct it into right channels and if in the last two hundred years it has effected amazing changes in the structure of the world, of society, the pace of that change has become much greater today. That too is obvious. Therefore we must realize that in the next generation, maybe a little more or little less, vast changes will keep coming here, changing the way of life. The way we live affects our thinking—the way we think. Are we, therefore, at the dawn of a new civilization or is this the twilight of the old or both? Do we see round about us in all this toil and trouble the birth pangs of a new order or something almost resembling the death agony of the old? I do not know. . . . I remember the great scientist,

---

[1] Speech at the Indian Science Congress, New Delhi, 21 January 1959. JN Papers, NMML. Excerpts.

who is supposed to have brought out or produced the first atomic bomb, when he saw that first experimental explosion, suddenly thinking of some word in our *Gita* about the splendour of a thousand suns blazing out suddenly all together in the sky, the splendour of a thousand suns which was used for destructive purposes, not for the glory of the earth, or mankind and all the time there was conflict in his mind which way we go with everything and all the riches and the greatness in the shape of welfare and progress before us. Yet, must we go the wrong way or must we take these mighty risks that we have to take today? I do not know, of course. But I do know this—there is no getting away from science and the march of science. It is only through that that we can not only solve our problems but even the world's problems. But in doing so, those who are the high priests of science must also realize that there is something as a social consequence of their scientific work and discovery, something very big. But there is even in science some moral issue involved. . . . But in pursuing science, surely we have to keep in view certain fundamental aspects and realities which we value. Is truth or the pursuit of truth to be tied up with the pursuit of hatred and violence, or should it accompany charity and compassion? There are ways of doing the same thing, I suppose; even for scientists, there are two ways open for making these approaches and the choice has to be made in this present generation of ours, I think, lest all this majesty of science may go the wrong way when it was open to us and it seems not so difficult to go the right way.

VOL. II

VII

Youth and Education

1. Awakening in the Youth   547

2. On the Mission of Youth   548

3. Breaking Shibboleths   550

4. Students and Politics   557

5. Halls of Learning   560

6. Another Casualty   564

7. Nationalism and Internationalism   566

8. The Time for Hard Labour   569

9. The World Around Us   576

10. The Need for Discipline   579

11. The Strength of the Unafraid   581

12. The Purpose of Education   583

13. Universities   585

1

Awakening in the Youth[1]

Ever since my return from Europe eleven weeks ago I have seen and felt a new awakening in the youth of India. After long suppression, the spirit of youth is up in arms against all forms of authoritarianism and is seeking an outlet in many ways and in many directions. Youth leagues have sprung up in all parts of the country and individual young men and young women, weary of the continual and barren strife of many of their elders, are groping for a path which might lead them to a fuller realization of themselves, a better and more prosperous India and a happier world. They are beginning to realize that communalism is the very negation of what we should strive for and the attempts that are made to remove this canker from our body politic, well meant as they are and sometimes productive of good results, seldom touch the roots of the problem.

It is felt by many that religion, as preached and practised in India, has become a grave danger to the state and octopus-like it spreads its tentacles into every department of life whether it is political, economic or social. The rules and regulations laid down in a bygone age and for an entirely different society are sought to be applied now in all their rigidity to modern life and conditions, with the inevitable result that there is a hiatus, and friction and unhappiness are the common lot of life in India. Like the old man of the sea, religion has mounted our backs and effectively prevented all progress and advancement. Religion was not meant to be this and if it continues to encroach on other departments of life, the reaction may engulf it utterly.

Thinking men and women, and the young specially, cannot help being distressed at the present inequalities between man and man, class and class. Gross and vulgar luxury on the one side and abject misery on the other must produce, in all who are sensitive and those who themselves suffer under the existing system, a feeling of intense bitterness and revolt. The present system has been admittedly a failure and is condemned. As to what should take its place opinions differ but whatever it may be it should provide for the removal of, or at any rate tend to remove, inequalities of class and caste and wealth. It should result in equal opportunities for everyone and not the grossly unfair lack of opportunities which is the lot of most people today.

[1] Letter to the Editor, *The Leader*, 24 March 1928.

2

On the Mission of Youth[1]

I have visited many foreign countries, and everywhere I found this kind of talk about each country being a chosen country with a special mission. I found it in England where Englishmen regard themselves as chosen by God to civilize the earth. I found it among the French with their invincible pride talking about a mission of France. You have heard about German *Kultur.*

Russia says she has a special task in solving the world's problems. It all strikes me as very curious. Frankly I do not believe in it. No country, however great, can be regarded as a chosen country or a race of chosen people. Historically countries have grown great at one time and have taken dominating roles in shaping world destinies. Apart from that there is nothing chosen about them. And I regard it as a dangerous way of looking at it.

Then there is good deal of talk about differences between the East and the West. I confess I fail to see it. China and India differ in their habits, customs and outlook from each other as much as they differ from any western country but they are grouped together as against Europe. There is much difference between Europe and Asia today because Europe is industrialized and Asia is not. Europe of the Middle Ages was much the same as Asia of the Middle Ages. And I see no particular reason to pride ourselves on our peculiarities, angularities and insularities. I always feel irritated when anybody talks of our immortal past. I am not unconscious of the greatness of our past. But when I study our later history and survey our present condition I see very little of the chosen people about us.

Much is said about the superiority of our religion, art, music and philosophy. But what are they today? Your religion has become a thing of the kitchen, as to what you can eat, and what you cannot eat, as to whom you can touch, and whom you cannot touch, whom you could see and whom not.

What is our music? Our national music is nothing more than infernal din and painful noises which are a nuisance on our roads. Even this sometimes assumes communal aspects and not infrequently results in deplorable tragedies. What is our art? What is there that is beautiful in the homes of our countrymen?

[1] Speech at a students' meeting at Bombay, 20 May 1928. *The Tribune*, 22 May 1928. Excerpts.

Why, even in your own homes? What is India's national literature? As far as I know, much of what goes under the name of modern literature in Hindi and Urdu is sloppish and soppy.

Indian civilization today is stagnant. It is the duty of youth to convert this stagnant pool into a moving stream. The test of youth is action, rebellion in every sphere. Every youth must rebel. Not only in the political sphere but in social, economic and religious spheres also. I have not much use for any man who comes and tells me that such and such thing is said in the *Koran*. Everything unreasonable must be discarded even if they find authority for it in the Vedas and in *Koran*. I know there are difficulties in pursuing this path but these difficulties are infinitely better than inaction.

Looking at the present conditions everywhere we see that fear is the dominating feeling. It is so in Europe. Everybody is afraid of everybody else. And they are going on arming themselves in the fear that somebody would attack them. It is the same in India. Every group, every community is afraid of the other, each thinks that at the next opportune moment the other would swallow it. . . . This feeling of want of security must go. If Indian youth must achieve India's destiny it must be in the words of the great leader of the French Revolution, "daring and daring and still more daring".

3

Breaking Shibboleths[1]

Young men and women of Bengal,

. . . I am no weaver of the fine phrases or trafficker in eloquence. To Bengal, justly known for her warm-hearted eloquence and love of art and beauty and passionate emotionalism, you have invited a dweller from the colder and sometimes much hotter regions of the north, whose ancestors came not so very long ago from the barren and snow-covered mountains that overlook the vast India plain, and I am afraid I carry with me something of the coldness and hardness of that mountain climate. A very great leader of Bengal[2] and of our country, whose memory we revere today, once called me very justly "cold-blooded". I plead guilty to the charge, and since you have taken the risk of inviting me you will have to bear with my cold-bloodedness.

I have begun by drawing your attention to certain minor differences between us, a Kashmiri settled in the heart of Hindustan, which is now called the United Provinces, and the residents of Bengal—and yet you all know how unimportant these differences are and how strong are the common bonds that tie us—the bonds of a common legacy from the past, of common suffering and the hope of building up a great future for this country of yours and mine. And, indeed, you can carry the comparison a little farther across the artificial frontiers that separate country from country. We are told of vital differences of race and character. Such differences there undoubtedly are but how many of them are purely accidental due to climate and environment and education and how liable to change are they? You will find that the common bond is greater and more vital than the differences, though many of us may not realize the fact.

It is the realization of the common bond of humanity that has given rise to the great youth movement of today. Many of you may be too young to remember the despair and feeling of revolt in the minds of youth during, and specially after, the Great War. Old men sat in their comfortable cabinets and banking houses and hid their selfishness and greed and lies under a cover of fine phrases and appeals for freedom and democracy. And the young, believing in

---

[1] Presidential Address at the All–Bengal Students' Conference, Calcutta, 27 September 1928. *The Searchlight*, 28 September 1928.

[2] C.R. Das.

these fine phrases, went out by the millions to face death, and few returned. Seventy million of them were mobilized and of the fifteen million that actually served on the front, over eight million died and over five-and-a-half million were maimed for life. Think of these terrible figures and then remember that they were all young men with their lives stretching out in front of them and their hopes unfulfilled. And what did this awful sacrifice bring forth? A peace of violence and an aggravation of all the ills that the world was suffering from. You remember well that the first fruits of peace in India were the Rowlatt Act and Martial Law. You know also how the fine principle of self-determination, which the Allies shouted from the house-tops, has been applied to India and to other countries. A new cloak for the greed of the imperialist powers was created in the shape of mandates and in awarding mandates the "principal consideration" was to be the preference of the inhabitants. This preference was shown unaccountably by rebellion against the British in Mesopotamia and rebellion against the French in Syria. But the aeroplane and the bomb was the British answer in Iraq and the ancient and beautiful city of Damascus was reduced to ruins[3] by the French. In Europe itself the peace created far more problems than it solved.

Is it any wonder that the youth of the world rebelled and cast out their old-time leaders on whom even the terrible lesson of the war was lost, and who still went on intriguing in the old way, and prepared for yet another and a greater way? Youth set about organizing itself and set out to find the ways and means of establishing an order of society which would put an end to the misery and conflicts of today.

And so the youth of the world probed deeper into the cause of present-day misery. They studied the economic and the social conditions of the people, and they saw that although science and the changes that science had brought, had in a few generations covered the track of centuries, the minds of men still lagged behind the thought in terms of a dead past. Science had made the world international and interdependent, but national rivalries continued and resulted in war. Science had vastly increased production and there was enough for all and to spare but poverty continued and the contrasts between luxury and misery were more marked than ever before. But if mankind is foolish and errs, facts do not adapt themselves to errors and the world of our imagination conflicts with the world of reality; and is it any wonder that chaos and misery result?

Facts are not to blame for this. The troubles and the difficulties lie rooted in our misconception of them and our misinterpretation of them. Our elders fail frequently because they are rigid in their minds and unable to change their mental outlook or adapt themselves to changing facts. But youth is not hidebound. Youth can think and is not afraid of the consequences of thought. Do

---

[3] The French twice bombarded Damascus in 1925 to put down a revolt.

not imagine that thought is an easy matter or that its consequences are trivial. Thought is not or should not be afraid of the wrath of heaven or the terrors of hell. It is the most revolutionary thing on earth. And it is because youth dare think and dare act that it holds out the promise of taking out this country and this world of ours from the rut and the mire in which they have sunk.

Are you, young men and women going to dare to think and dare to act? Are you prepared to stand shoulder to shoulder with the youth of the world, not only to free your country from an insolent and alien rule but also to establish in this unhappy world of ours a better and a happier society? That is the problem before you and if you wish to face it sincerely and fearlessly, you will have to make up your mind to rid yourselves and your country of every obstacle in your path whether it is placed by our alien rulers or has the prestige of ancient custom.

You must have your ideal clear-cut before you. How else can you hope to build the great structure of your dream? Can you build a palace on the foundations of a mud hut, or a fine bridge with straw? With definite ideas of your goal you will gain clearness of purpose and effectiveness of action and each step that you take will carry you nearer to your heart's desire.

What shall this ideal be? National independence and perfect freedom to develop on the lines of our own choosing is the essential requisite of all progress. Without it there can be no political, economic or social freedom. But national independence should not mean for us merely an addition to the warring groups of nations. It should be a step towards the creation of a world commonwealth of nations in which we can assist in the fullest measure to bring about cooperation and world harmony. . . .

But there can be no world cooperation as long as one country dominates over and exploits another and one group or class exploits another. Therefore, we shall have to put an end to all exploitation of man by man or woman. You cannot have a purely political ideal, for politics is after all only a small part of life, although situated as we are under alien rule, it dominates every branch of our activity. Your ideal must be a complete whole and must comprise life as it is today, economic, social as well as political. It can only be a social equality in the widest sense and equality of opportunity for everyone. It is notorious that we have neither of these today.

Our womenfolk, in spite of the great examples of old that we are so fond of repeating, are shackled and unfree. Large classes of our countrymen have been deliberately suppressed by us in the past and denied all opportunities of growth in the name of religion and ancient practice. And all over India, we see today millions toiling in field and factory and starving in spite of their toil. How can we rid these millions of their dire poverty and misery and make them share in the freedom to come? We hear of the service of the poor and sometimes even of the exaltation of the poor. And by a little act of charity or service we imagine that our duty is done. Having reserved very magnanimously the kingdom of heaven for the poor we take good care to keep the kingdom of the earth for ourselves. Youth at least should be above this hypocrisy. Poverty is not a good thing; it is not to be exalted or praised but an evil thing which must be fought and stamped out. The poor require no petty services from us or charity. They want to cease to be poor. That can only come by your changing a system which produces poverty and misery.

In the course of the last few months you have seen the whole of India convulsed in labour troubles. Lock-outs and strikes and shootings have followed one after another. It is amusing, do you think, to the worker to strike and starve and perhaps be shot? Surely no one does so unless his lot becomes unbearable. And indeed the lot of the Indian today in factory or field is past all endurance. In the jute mill of your province, profits and reserve accumulations in ten years before 1926 amounted to nearly 440 crores of rupees. Think of this enormous figure and then see the condition of poor workers in these mills. And yet the jute workers, miserable as they are, have gone there because there was no room for them on the land or their conditions on the land were even worse. Can you expect any peace in the land when there is so much misery and so much contrast between wealth and abject poverty.

You cannot ignore these problems or leave them to a future age for solution. And if you are afraid of tackling them, you will find that facts can only be ignored at your peril. We are sometimes told that we must do justice between landlord and tenant and capitalist and worker, and justice means the maintenance of the status quo. It is the kind of justice the League of Nations gives when it maintains the present status quo with the imperialist powers dominating and exploiting half the earth. When the status quo itself is rank injustice, those who desire to maintain it must be considered as upholders of that injustice.

If your ideal is to be one of social equality and a world federation, then perforce we must work for a socialist state. The word socialism frightens many people in this country but that matters little for fear is their constant companion. Ignorant of everything important that has happened in the world of thought since they left their school books, they fear what they do not and will not understand.

It is for you, the youth of the country, to appreciate the new forces and ideas that are convulsing the world and to apply them to your own country. It is interesting to note that during the Great War when a great crisis threatened to engulf the nations of the West, even the capitalist countries of Europe were forced to adopt socialistic measures to a large extent. This was not only done internally in each country but, unable to resist the pressure of events, even internationally. There was cooperation in many fields and national boundaries seemed to recede into the background. There was economic cooperation of the closest kind and ultimately even the armies of many nations became one army under a single head. But the lesson of the war has been lost and again we drift towards a greater disaster.

Socialism frightens some of our friends, but what of communism? Our elders sitting in their council chambers shake their grey heads and stroke their beards in alarm at the mere mention of the word. And yet I doubt if any of them has the slightest knowledge of what communism is. You have read of the two new measures which are being rushed through the Assembly—one of them to throttle the trade union movement, and the other to keep out people whom the Government suspects of communism. Has it struck you that it is a very curious thing that the mighty British Empire with all its tanks and aeroplanes and dreadnoughts should be afraid of a few individuals who came to spread a new idea? What is there in this new idea that the British Empire should collapse like a pack of cards before this airy nothing? Surely you could not have better evidence of the weakness of this giant empire which sprawls over the fairest portions of the earth's surface. It is a giant with feet of clay. But if an idea is a dangerous thing, it is also a very elusive thing. It crosses frontiers and customs barriers without paying any duty and bayonets and men of war cannot stop it. The Government of India must be strangely lacking in intelligence if they imagine that they can stop any ideas from entering India by legislation.

What is the communist idea before which the British Empire quakes? I do not propose to discuss it here, but I wish to tell you that though personally I do not agree with many of the methods of the communists, and I am by no means sure to what extent communism can suit present conditions in India, I do believe in communism as an idea of society. For essentially it is socialism, and socialism, I think, is the only way if the world is to escape disaster.

And Russia, what of her? An outcast like us from nations and much slandered and often erring. But in spite of her many mistakes she stands today as the greatest opponent of imperialism and her record with the nations of the East has been just and generous. In China, Turkey and Persia of her own free will she gave up her valuable rights and concessions, while the British bombarded the crowded Chinese cities and killed Chinamen by the hundreds because they dared to protest against British imperialism.

In the city of Tabriz in Persia, when the Russian ambassador first came, he called the populace together and on behalf of the Russian nation tendered formal apology for the sins of the Tzars. Russia goes to the East as an equal, not as a conqueror or a race-proud superior. Is it any wonder that she is welcome?

Some of you may go in after years to foreign counters for your studies. If you go to England, you will realize in full measure what race prejudice is. If you go to the continent of Europe, you will be more welcome whether you go to France or Germany or Italy. If any of you go to Russia, you will see how racial feeling is utterly absent and the Chinamen who throng the universities of Moscow are treated just like others.

I have placed before you the ideals of internationalism and socialism as the only ideas worthy of the fine temper of youth. Internationalism can of course come to us only through national independence. It cannot come through the British Empire or the British Commonwealth of Nations, call it what you will, for that empire is today the greatest foe of internationalism. If in future England chooses to enter a real world federation none will welcome her more than we, but she will have to shed her imperialism before she can enter. Our quarrel is not with the people of England but with the imperialism of England.

I have laid stress on internationalism although it may be a distant ideal for us. But the world is already largely international, although we may not realize it. And situated as we are, the reaction against foreign rule is apt to make us narrowly national. We talk of the greatness of India, of her special mission to the world and we love to dwell on her past. It is well that we remember our past, for it was great and worth remembering. But it is for the aged to look back; youth's eyes should be turned to the future. And I have often wondered if there is any country in the world, any people who do not fancy that they have a special mission for the world. England has her white man's burden which she insists on carrying in spite of the ungrateful people who object and rebel; France has her *mission civilisatrice*; America is God's own country; Germany has *Kultur*; Italy has her new gospel of Fascism; and Russia her Communism. And it has been so always. The Jews were the elect of the Lord, and so were the Arabs. Does it not strike you as strange that every country should have the identical notion of having a special mission to reform the world, to enrich its culture in some way, and none need lay claim to being the chosen of the Lord?

Self-admiration is always a dangerous thing in an individual. It is equally dangerous in a nation, for it makes it self-satisfied and indolent and the world passes by leaving it behind. We have little enough reason to be satisfied with our present lot, with many of our customs, with our excessive religiosity, with the sad lot of our women and the terrible condition of the masses. What good does it do us to waste our energy and our time in chanting praises of the dead past when the present claims our attention and work awaits us? The world changes and is changing rapidly and if we cannot adapt our society to the new conditions, we are doomed to perish. We have seen what can be done in a brief span of years and even months by a Kemal Pasha or an Amanullah who were not afraid to break through ancient custom and prejudice. What has been done in Turkey and backward Afghanistan can be done in India. But it can only be done in the manner of Kemal Pasha or Amanullah, by fearlessly facing obstacles and removing them and not waiting till the crack of doom for slow reform. It is not a choice for you as it was not a choice for Turkey or Afghanistan, between extinction and immediate action. Turkey and Afghanistan chose the latter path and are reckoned today as great nations. What will your choice be?

The world is in a bad way and India especially is in a perilous state in spite of the glitter and superficial splendour of our great cities. There are rumours of war and awful prophecies that the next war may result in irretrievable disaster to civilization. But the very excess of evil may hasten the cure.

Does not our own Gita state:

यदा यदा हि धर्मस्य ग्लानिर्भवति भारत।
अभ्युत्थानम अधर्मस्य तदात्मानं सृजाम्यहम्।।
परित्राणाय साधूनाम् विनाशाय च दुष्कृताम्।
धर्मसंस्थापनार्थाय संभवामि युगे युगे।।[4]

You and I are Indians and to India we owe much, but we are human beings also and to humanity we also owe a debt. Let us be citizens of the commonwealth or empire of youth. This is the only empire to which we can owe allegiance, for that is the forerunner of the future federation of the world.

---

[4] "Yada yada dharmasya glanirbhavati Bharata
Abhyutthanam adharmasya tadatmanam srijamyaham.
Paritranaya sadhuam vinashaya cha dushkritam
Dharma samsthapanarthaya sambhavami yuge yuge."

[Chapter IV, Verses 7 & 8]

Whenever there is a decline of righteousness and rise of unrighteousness, O Bharata (Arjuna), then I send forth myself.

For the protection of the good, for the destruction of the wicked and for the establishment of righteousness, I come into being from age to age.

4

Students and Politics[1]

India at present is a peculiar country and the questions that are raised surprise one. Some even argue that the independence of India is bad for India; that something less than independence is in reality more than it. Not being metaphysically inclined, I find some difficulty in understanding these abstruse problems. Yet another peculiar question relates to students and politics. Students must not take part in politics, some say. What is politics? According to the usual interpretation in India (official India), to assist or support the government in any way is not politics; but it is politics to criticize or work against the existing order in India.

Who are the students? They may be children in the elementary schools or young men and women in colleges. Obviously the same considerations cannot apply to both.

Quite a large number of senior students today possess a vote for the coming provincial elections. To vote is to take part in politics; to vote intelligently necessitates the understanding of political issues; to understand political issues results usually in accepting a certain political policy; and if one accepts that policy it is the duty of the citizen to push that policy, to try to convert others to it. Thus inevitably a voter must be a politician, and he should be an ardent politician if he is a keen citizen. Only those who lack the political or social sense can remain passive and neutral or indifferent.

Even apart from his duty as a voter, every student must, if he is properly trained, prepare himself for life and its problems. Otherwise his education has been wasted effort. Politics and economics deal with these problems and no person is properly educated unless he understands them. Perhaps it is difficult for most people to see a clear path through life's jungle. But whether we know the solution of the problem or not, We must at least know the nature of it. What are the questions that life puts to us? The answers may be difficult, but the curious thing is that people seek to answer without knowing the real questions. No serious or thinking student can take up this futile attitude.

The various isms that play such an important part in the world today—

[1] From *Eighteen Months in India* (1938), pp. 51–5.

nationalism, liberalism, socialism, communism, imperialism, fascism, etc.—are efforts on the part of various groups to answer these questions. Which answer is correct? Or are they all steeped in error? In any event we have to choose, and in order to choose we must know and have the capacity to choose correctly. This cannot be done if there are repressions and suppressions of thought and action. It cannot be done properly if High Authority sits on us and prevents the free play of the mind.

Thus it becomes necessary for all thinking individuals, and more so for the student than for others, to take the fullest theoretical part in politics. Naturally this will apply to the senior students at life's threshold rather than the junior ones who are still far from these problems. But a theoretical consideration is not enough for a proper understanding; even theory requires practice. From the point of view of study alone the student must leave his lecture halls and investigate reality in village and town, in field and factory; to take part to some extent in the various activities of the people, including political activities.

One has ordinarily to draw the line somewhere. A student's first business is to train his mind and body and make them efficient instruments for thought, understanding and action. Before he is trained he cannot think or act effectively. Yet the training itself comes not from listening to pious advice, but by indulging in action to some extent. That action, under normal conditions, must be subordinated to the theoretical training. But it cannot be eliminated or else the training itself is deficient.

It is our misfortune that in India our educational system is thoroughly lopsided. But an even greater misfortune is the highly authoritarian atmosphere that surrounds it. Not in education alone, but everywhere in India, red-liveried, pompous and often empty-headed authority seeks to mould people after its own pattern and prevent the growth of the mind and the spread of ideas. . . .

They do not like the qualities that are encouraged in free countries, the spirit of daring, the adventures of the soul in uncharted regions. Is it surprising then that we do not produce many men and women who seek to conquer the Poles or Everest, to control the elements and bring them to man's use, to hurl defiance at man's ignorance and timidity and inertia and littleness and try to raise him up to the stars?

Must students take part in politics? Must they take part in life, a full wholesome part in life's varied activities, or be of the clerkly breed, carrying out orders from above? As students they cannot keep out of politics; as Indian students, even more so they must keep in touch with it. Yet it is true that normally the training of their minds and bodies must be their principal consideration during this period of their growth. They must observe a certain discipline but that discipline should not be such as crushes the mind and kills the spirit.

So, normally. But abnormal conditions come when all normal rules are swept away. During the Great War, where were the students of England,

France, Germany? Not in their colleges but in the trenches, facing and meeting death. Where are the students of Spain today?

A subject country is always to some extent in an abnormal condition. So India is today. And in considering these problems we must also consider our environment and the growing abnormality in the world. And as we seek to understand it, we are driven to take part, however little it might be, in the shaping of events.

5

Halls of Learning[1]

I have not been a stranger to the halls of learning, for many years my path branched off from them and took me to strange and dusty byways. Often I had dipped into those wells where lie imprisoned the thoughts and dreams and experience of past ages, but fate and circumstances conspired together to drag me away from that pleasant and ordered life and cast my lot among the vast unlearned of this country. I met multitudes of men and women, the vast majority of whom had never known school or college, nor had they ever been touched in any way by the education that the state or private enterprise had organized.

I felt attracted by your invitation for what is there more attractive and vital today than education? In this warring world, full of sorrow and conflict, with a thousand problems oppressing us, how shall we find peace and a solution for these problems except through right education?

So I have come to you to wish you well and to commend your labours. It would ill become me, a layman and an amateur, to discuss the intricate problems which are meant for experts. But there is danger in the expert's specialized way of looking at things, for he may lose the right perspective and forget to see life as a whole. That danger has to be guarded against especially now when the very foundations of life are challenged and are at stake. What is your objective, your aim in education? Surely you train the rising generation for life. What pattern of life do you envisage, for unless you have that clear picture in your minds, the education that you give will be superficial, faulty and aimless, and your problems and difficulties will ever increase. You will go on lecturing on navigation while the ship is going down.

The ideal of education has long been the improvement of the individual. That ideal must inevitably hold, for without individual advancement there can be no social progress. But even that care of the individual must today be considered in terms of the mass of the people or else the enlightened individual will be submerged in the unenlightened mass. And, in any event, is it right or just

[1] Inaugural address at the All India Educational Conference, Baradari, 27 December 1939. *National Herald,* 28 December 1939. Excerpts.

that a group of individuals should have opportunities of advancement and growth which are denied to the many?

But even from the standpoint of the individual, a vital question has to be faced. Can an individual truly advance, except in the rarest cases, if the environment that surrounds him is pulling him back all the time? If this environment is evil or injurious to him, the individual battles in vain against it and must inevitably be crushed by it. What is this environment? It consists of inherited ideas, prejudices and superstitions which restrict the mind and prevent growth and change in a changing world. It is the pressure of political circumstances that keeps the individual and the group in enforced subjection and thus starves his soul and crushes his spirit. It is, above all, the stranglehold of economic conditions which denies opportunity to vast masses of people. It is this complex of prejudice and superstition, political and economic conditions, that form our environment which holds us in its grip.

Through your educational system you may teach all the well-known virtues, but life today teaches something else, and the voice of life is louder and more effective. You may teach the advantages of cooperative effort, but our social structure is based on cut-throat competition, and each one tries to rise on the dead selves of others. The glittering prizes go to him who is most successful in knocking down and crushing his rivals. Is it any wonder that our youth should be attracted by these glittering prizes, and should hold acquisitiveness as the most desirable quality in an acquisitive society?

We swear by nonviolence in this country, yet violence envelops us not only in its more obvious forms of warring nations but in the very social structure in which we live. Out of this violent environment no real peace or nonviolence can ever come, unless we change that environment itself.

Our educational system, in spite of the ideals which it may profess, is itself an outcome of and a part of this environment. It seeks sustenance from it and, consciously or unconsciously, supports it. Yet if there is anything clear in the world today, it is this: that this environment is the cause of most of our troubles, and to leave it as it is, is to head straight for disaster.

Indeed, it may already be too late to prevent that disaster, and the war that is raging in Europe may yet shatter the edifice of modern civilization. We shall not escape this tragedy, and even if we survive this general collapse our own problems threaten to overwhelm us, unless we see aright and act aright. Recent events have shown how strong the forces of evil and disruption and narrow-minded bigotry are in this country. We have seen also how the dominant political and economic interests resent and combat change.

These are larger problems which will not come up before this conference, and yet they affect our education vitally and all our educational efforts will be in vain if these problems do not find proper and early solution. But even apart from the problems of the moment, no educationist can ignore the vital question of what education should aim at in the social and economic sphere. All education must have a definite social outlook and must train our youth for the kind of society we wish to have. Politicians may strive for political and economic changes in order to bring that society into existence, but the real basis of that society must be laid in the teaching of our schools and colleges. The real change will have to come in the minds of men, though that change can and will be helped greatly by external changes in the environment. The two processes go together and should help each other.

Our present-day social fabric is a decadent and dying thing, full of its own contradictions, and leading continually to war and conflict. This acquisitive and competitive society must be ended and must give place to a cooperative order, where we think in terms not of individual profit but of the common good; where individuals cooperate with each other and nations and peoples work in cooperation for human advancement; where human values count for more and there is no exploitation of a class or group or nation by another.

If this is the accepted ideal of our future society then all our education must be fashioned to that end and must not ay homage to anything that is against this conception of the social order. That education will always have to think in terms of the hundreds of millions of our people, and not sacrifice their interests for any group or class. The teacher will then be not just a follower of a profession which gives him a livelihood, but one who has chosen his vocation in the ardent spirit of a missionary in a sacred cause which fills his being.

Recently much thought has been given in India to educational progress and people's mind are astir and expectant and full of hope in this world of today which has so little hope. You will no doubt consider the new Basic Scheme of education. The more I have studied this and watched it grow, the more fascinated I have been by it. Further experience will no doubt bring changes and variations but I have little doubt that we have found in this scheme the path that leads to mass education on the right lines, when education keeps in tune with life and prepares for life. Particularly, it is suited to a poor country like India.

As I have wandered about India and seen her millions of unhappy, sorrow-laden people, with sunken eyes and hopeless look, I have felt overwhelmed with the tragedy of India. Yet I have always sensed the tremendous vitality of our people and felt confident that they will pull themselves out of this miserable condition and recover the bright and happy faces and hopeful eyes that should be the birthright of every individual. They hunger and have not the wherewithal to eat, they seek work and find none, their bare bodies shiver in the cold, their homes are mud huts, continually tumbling down, bright-eyed opportunity never comes their way.

All this is tragedy and must be remedied. But the greatest tragedy is the

killing of the spirit, when there is no hope or sense of adventure or pride left
in them. It is this that we have to end before India is reborn.

Let not young souls be smothered out before
They do quaint deeds and fully flaunt their pride,
It is the world's one crime its babes grow dull,
Its poor are ox-like, limp and leaden-eyed.
Not that they starve, but starve so dreamlessly,
Not that they sow, but that they seldom reap,
Not that they serve, but have no gods to serve,
Not that they die but that they die like sheep.

It is pleasant for intellectual and enlightened people to discuss calmly the
affairs of a troubled and distant world. They feel secure and well-contented in
their limited spheres, cut off from reality. But reality is upon us now and the
troubled world is no longer distant but threatens to envelop and overwhelm us.
Those who are frightened of this unpleasant reality, and seek refuge from it,
struggle helplessly and bitterly against fate and function more and more like
marionettes controlled by unseen forces. None of us dare to act in this weak
ineffectual way when everything that is worthwhile in life calls to us to clear
thought and brave deeds. The world is unpleasant; let us realize it and then, like
men, seek to change it and make it a pleasanter, juster place for all of us to live
in.

6

Another Casualty[1]

Truth, they say, is the first casualty in war. There are many other casualties, apart from the human beings who kill each other and die in their millions. Some casualties are unavoidable, others may be avoided, yet others are totally unnecessary.

I do not know in which category education will fall. In Spain, right in the midst of the civil war, I saw the Republic Government building new schools and pushing forward its educational programme with all speed. In China, also, after years of horrible war, I noticed an enthusiasm for education and every effort to further it.

Not so in India. Here education is apparently considered a luxury in wartime by the military or civil authorities. Already many schools have been closed and probably many more will suffer the same fate. In the Central Provinces I found that the only teachers' training college and a number of normal schools had been closed. In my own city of Allahabad some of our biggest schools have had to close down and their buildings have been taken possession of by the military. The CAV High School had seven hundred and fifty pupils. An order came for immediate evacuation. After much persuasion a day's reprieve was granted, possibly because the next was a Sunday. The Vidya Mandir High School consisting of four hundred students was served with a similar order. When it was pointed out that it was not possible to leave the building within a few hours, I am told that the furniture and belongings of the school were forcibly taken out and deposited in the open.

The Kayastha Pathshala School, the Majidia School and the Anglo-Bengali Intermediate College have also been taken over and occupied, presumably by the military.

I cannot judge of the urgent military necessity which led to these extraordinary happenings. But I cannot conceive of anything which can justify this indecent behaviour. If schools have to be evacuated let this be done properly and decently and full arrangements be made for their continuance elsewhere. Only a very stupid soldier acts in this way.

[1] Article printed in the *National Herald*, 5 July 1942.

Another significant fact is that only Indian schools, and in Allahabad, only private schools have been evacuated in this way. There seems to be some law of fate that almost every activity of the present government in India should be wrong, unjust and partial.

It is rumoured that the Allahabad University is also going to get notice to quit and that it might have to move to Haridwar.

My mind goes back to China where bright-faced boys and girls continued their studies though Japanese bombs came down from the skies almost every day; where universities functioned in spite of every difficulty; where it was universally felt that whatever was sacrificed to war, education must be preserved and expanded. For, on education depended the growing generation, and on that growing generation depended the future of the country.

7

Nationalism and Internationalism[1]

It is obvious that nationalism by itself, unconnected with some wider concept, is a narrow creed. It is also obvious that without nationalism we are rootless. We just have no deep roots anywhere. On the other hand internationalism is not only good but essential in the world today. And yet some kind of vague internationalism, without definite contacts and bonds with nationalism, is almost an airy nothing. How to combine the two? What are the essential features of the two? And what are the conflicts between the two? Apparently there are, though possibly in reality there are not. You know in the past many years internationalism has grown as life's activities have tended that way with the increase not only of rapid communication, but with the growth of almost everything that we see around us today.

So people think that nationalism is something fading off and giving place to internationalism. We see internationalism in many aspects, even in the activities of what I might call proletarian elements of the world. On the other side of the scale we see internationalism developing perhaps more concretely, though with less shouts, in the realm of finance, trade and commerce and cartels, and in between we see this internationalism in the development of science, in the new commerce of ideas, in so many ordinary things which meet us at every turn of the road, the radio, cinema, etc.

People think that internationalism is obviously the thing of the future, and nationalism must fade away. And there is a great deal of truth, I suppose, in this and yet whenever a country or the world faces a crisis, nationalism becomes immediately dominant. We have had a very big crisis during the last five or six years of the world war. One of the lessons of this crisis is how, when deeply stirred, the people turn to nationalism immediately. Every country that was involved in this war became tremendously nationalistic. It forgot its internationalism. Even in cases of countries with proletarian bias, which thought and believed in terms of internationalism and workers of the world holding together against other elements oppressing them, nationalism is intensely a dominant passion.

[1] Convocation address at Viswa Bharati University, Santiniketan, 24 December 1945. *Amrita Bazar Patrika*, 25 December 1945. Excerpts.

In spite of this development of internationalism all over the world, which is an inevitable development influencing human life, man's mind continues to function to a very large extent, especially in times of crisis, on a nationalistic basis. So, I suppose, one of the problems of today and tomorrow is how to fit in these two conceptions—nationalism and internationalism. Nationalism obviously is something deep down in human nature. We cannot uproot it and there is no reason why we should try to uproot it, because nationalism ultimately depends on all that is best in us.

How can we get rid of it without cutting off ourselves from our deep moorings? If we do it we would probably become superficial. But why should nationalism come into conflict with internationalism? I find attempts are being made at Santiniketan and Viswa Bharati to combine the two. Your attempts may not find a perfect solution, but even grouping towards a proper answer and succeeding in some measure in this attempt to my mind is a great achievement.

Then again there is another aspect, the proper integration of the old and the new. Here again we belong to the old, each one of us wedded to the old, or rather it would be more correct to say, we would prefer to say, we do not belong to the old but rather the past belongs to us. To belong to the old means that we are old but the old belongs to us means that we have it in us and yet we are in the present looking forward to tomorrow. This integration of the past and the present and the future is again a difficult problem. It is extraordinary that many of us who live in the present are hardly conscious of it, but wrapped up in the past. Now the past is not enough, although the past is an absolutely essential thing for the present. Man's life changes as everything changes in this world from day to day, from hour to hour. But, curiously enough, man's mind does not change. Always there is a lag, the mind remains tied up in the face of changes all round. It may be that it is one of the causes of lack of integration and of many of the conflicts of today. So while holding on to the past we have to hold on and keep changing and understanding the changes of the present and so fit in ourselves for the future. In ancient countries like India and China, where we have a tremendous cultural tradition which inspires and sometimes pulls us back, the need for a proper integration of the past with the present and the future becomes even more important.

There is perhaps today, more so than in the past, the necessity for greater integration between the outer life and the inner life of man. The absence of integration leads to all problems and upsets. Seldom, I suppose, has life all over the world lacked in poise as it is today. We may develop extraordinary equilibrium and poise but persons, more especially in the highly industrialized countries of the world, have no inner equilibrium. Now, this may or may not be the necessary consequences of industrialization as such, but it has been a consequence of the kind of life that has resulted from it. In our own case in India, there is also this want of integration, not because of industrialization but because of many other reasons. Obviously unless there is harmony between the outer life and the inner life, man is a battle ground most of the time.

It seems to me that Santiniketan and Viswa Bharati tackle all these problems and try to solve them in some way. As I said, perfect solution is perhaps difficult or almost impossible of achievement in this world of ours, but it is something that fills one with hope that there should be a place which at any rate thinks of these problems, considers them and tries to solve them to the best of its ability. But the fact that you have become symbols and emblems of those who try to solve these problems is in itself a measure of the achievement of Santiniketan and Viswa Bharati.

8

The Time for Hard Labour[1]

Your Excellency, Mr. Premier, Vice Chancellor,[2] Members of the University and Friends,

You have had a great deal of eloquence today, and you have seen many eminent persons, and I am not quite sure if it is not an imposition on you to listen to another address. Yesterday, I am told, you listened to a very eloquent address from Dr. Radhakrishnan.[3] I have the misfortune not to have been present. It is too much of giving you addresses and perhaps too much of giving you good advice which may not be good for the giver or the listener. Nevertheless, I have to perform the function and a duty, and I suppose it is your function and duty at present to listen to me.

I have to thank you for the honour you have conferred upon me.[4] I shall say frankly that I have had so much honour and love from my people that a little addition to it does not make much difference. . . .

. . . When this young generation on whose shoulders the great task of carrying India a stage further in her long journey is going to fall, when this young generation behaves in a manner which is incomprehensible to me, it amazes me. And when they talk about taking part in politics or this or that, I am amazed that the whole of India is shouting for work, shouting for labour, shouting for building, and when doing things they think in other directions and they work in other directions, they talk some language which I do not understand. Have I got old, then I wonder, am I cut off from this younger generation? Am I right or are they right? Who is right and who is wrong? I do not

[1] Speech at the Silver Jubilee Convocation of Lucknow University, 28 January 1949. AIR tapes, NMML. Excerpts.

[2] Mrs Sarojini Naidu was the Governor of U.P. and Chancellor of the University, G.B. Pant, the Premier and Acharya Narendra Deva, the Vice Chancellor.

[3] On 27 January 1949, Radhakrishnan in his Convocation address advised the students to contribute to the building up of the country and to guard themselves against the 'dangers of private ambitions and personal selfishness'. He said that, "what we need today is not merely a kind of external arrangement but a kind of internal growth."

[4] Jawaharlal Nehru received the degree of Doctor of Literature (*Honoris Causa*) along with Radhakrishnan, Maulana Azad and twelve others.

know. Perhaps, I may be wrong. Anyhow I can only work according to my own lights.

Here is a time when work is required, labour is required, peace is required, cooperative effort is required. Nevertheless, when I look around me, I see not an atmosphere of work, not a psychology of things being done, but only thought of criticism and running down and finding fault, petty factions and the like. I see them in all grades, above and below, the younger generation and the older generation, everywhere, and then as I said, a slight feeling of uneasiness comes over me, a malaise, because after all, I may have a few more years to labour and the only ambition that I have is that to the end of my days I should work my hardest and then when I have done my job I should be thrown on the scrap heap. . . .

Look at this problem. Just for a moment forget India, and look at the broad aspect of this problem in the sweep of history. Where have we arrived? I won't go too far back, but a hundred and fifty years ago or longer than that we saw the beginning of the Industrial Revolution in the western world, and that progressed for a hundred years or more. It was based on a certain development, a new form of capitalist structure or society. Industrial capitalism—now what did the industrial capitalism seek to do? What did it aim at? It aimed at the greater production of wealth. Before that the world was very poor, production was limited. It had stabilized itself at a poverty level. Industrial capitalism sought to increase the wealth of the world by new means of production. It had in it the seeds of certain difficulties and contradictions—but leave that out— industrial capitalism, for a variety of reasons, progressed and solved the problem it had set to itself. Remember that capitalism has been one of the greatest successes of the past. It solved the problem of production, but in solving it, it produced other contradictions and other difficulties.

. . . It was the First World War that upset the more or less stabilized or what appeared to be stabilized economy of the world. Since that First World War there has been no settling down and there is going to be no settling down, perhaps, for a long time to come till a large number of adjustments are made. And essentially the question of settling down is not only growth of production but also the solution of the problem of equitable distribution.

Now, I am purposely not using terms which have definite connotations in your minds—socialism, communism, capitalism, and the like. Try to think of what the problem is and not get vaguely lost in a term which may have a hundred meanings. So you had the second war following upon the first, because of this maladjustment and lack of adjustments. And I do not know, you may even have a third war, although the odd thing is that each war does not help to solve the problem but makes it infinitely more difficult. I referred to a possible third war—I do not, I might add—personally think that there is any prospect, or probability of war in the near future or well, shall I say, in two or three years.

So do not be frightened that the war is just next door. Nevertheless, nobody can say that war is outlawed or outmoded or will not take place. Now just keep a picture in your mind of what the business of war means or a new war. If there is a war then there can be little doubt that war will mean the most tremendous destruction on the widest scale, infinitely more than any past war has done. It will mean—apart from destruction of humanity, of cities, etc., what the human race has built up through ages—it will mean the limiting of food production. Now ever since the last war food has been a big problem in the world. As you know in India it has been one of our major problems. If there is another war, food production will be so limited that there probably will be death by starvation by millions all over the world. People think rather lightly of war. The next war, a world war, is going to be the greatest disaster that humanity has ever experienced, and do not imagine that India or any part of the world is going to escape that disaster—some may have more of it, some may have less. It just does not matter who is going to be the winner in that war—because this destruction will be a common factor, this tremendous loss will be a common factor all over the world. . . .

One of the changes that the development of science has brought about in the world has been the addition of a tremendous deal of knowledge, a vast quantity of which very few people, if any, can wholly grasp. It is too much for the human mind to grasp. Perhaps some prodigies may grasp it, but normally, even for the intelligent people, it is too much. Leave out the whole field of human knowledge which is vast—take the field of scientific knowledge, take even the field of a particular branch of science—so much is there that each individual has to specialize, if he has to be good at his branch. He specializes, he becomes an authority on his subject, but at the expense, perhaps, of his not knowing much about other departments of life. A highly specialized individual scientist or technician may be ignorant of many important aspects of life, may, in other words, be a bad citizen, although he is a very, very good scientist. Specialization has grown so much with the growth of knowledge that a synoptic view of human life, what might be called the philosopher's view of human life with all its problems, has receded to the background. Our politicians too may be persons specialized to win elections or to deal with the immediate problems of the day, but they have neither the time nor the leisure to consider these problems in their broader aspects.

Now, how are we to get over this, I do not know. I put this difficulty before you. Take a country like the United States of America, which is technologically speaking the most advanced country, and therefore, from the point of view of material resources the most powerful country. It can produce wealth and where there is wealth there is power. . . . Take an American engineer, an American doctor—he is very good at his job. But he is so good that he has no time to be good at anything else. Now America is a good example to understand this, because America has the highest development of a certain type towards which the world has been going. Others have also gone that way but not quite so far.

Now we, who are in India, are bound to be industrialized; we are trying to be industrialized; we must be industrialized for greater wealth, greater production. That is true, but are we going just to create a number of specialized agencies and specialists and thus think that we are solving the problem? We have to create specialists, but we must have an understanding of the problem, not only in its wide context today, but somewhat in the wide sweep of history. . . .

Now we have to face a refugee problem of vast dimensions. Six million people to be looked after—all kinds of people, middle-class people, working class people, peasants, people who have never done a stroke of work in their lives, peoples who had worked and can not find work and so on. Just remember all these problems when you sit down and criticize the Government of India or the Government of U.P.

See first what the achievement is and then see what the lack of achievement is, and then, thinking both of the achievement and the lack of achievement, let us try our hardest. After all, you must understand that in a democratic country or in any country of course, much more so in a country with some kind of a democratic government, you cannot expect the government to do everything for you.

. . . And I tell you also that even a feeble government, even a bad policy of government, can yield greater results in the country if people cooperate to that end. So the essential thing is how to develop that psychology, the psychology of work and cooperation among the people. Today, if we are suffering from anything in India, it is that the right psychology is not present. Whether it is in the worker or the owner of the factory, or whether it is the younger generation, it is entirely a wrong psychology. It is a psychology of thinking that they can achieve ends by threats and demonstrations and the rest. And I am sorry to say that people, who ought to know much better, somehow are taken in by it and encourage this kind of thing. Now, I tell you that I consider nothing more dangerous for India's present or India's future than the continuance of this psychology.

As a person responsible for the fate of India I dare not enfeeble my nation and give a chance to evil-minded countries and evil-minded forces to come in add and play havoc in this country. Thereby my freedom may be imperilled not only politically or from the military point of view, but from the economic point of view also. If you are enfeebled and are helpless and our millions are in a starving condition, we cannot do anything. We may take out our processions and shout out slogans, but how are we to feed those millions when there is no food and we have gradually arrived at that low level? Well, we are too weak really to stand up in the world today. I tell you, an almost inevitable consequence, whatever the final emergence may be, of any process which aims at smashing up the present structure completely is the enfeebling of the nation and imperilling of our freedom, and evil people, evil forces, evil countries taking advantage of it and exploiting the situation for their own profit and advantage. I do not want that to happen. I think that this generation, and when I say this generation I mean not my generation, but the generation of the young men and young women who are sitting here, having taken their degrees, and who are going out in the life tomorrow and the day after—that this generation will be a ruined generation, if the smashing up process takes place. . . . Therefore, you have to proceed on the lines of not smashing up the structure, but changing it, and changing it as rapidly as you can. . . .

No government can take risks with violence. And I tell you from such accounts as I have heard that the Government of U.P. has been too weak in dealing with the situation here. There has been a lot of loud criticism about what is happening. If I had been in charge, I would have taken stronger action against those who have been misbehaving in the streets of Lucknow. What is this business of young men and women attacking the police and slapping them and throwing bombs and playing about with lathis.[5] Are our young men and women degraded to this level of vulgarity and indiscipline and lack of understanding that they behave in this way and call it freedom? . . . A government can go, another government can take its place. But if a government sees violence being done before its eyes it must suppress that violence, and it will suppress it. Let there be no doubt about it. Whether men or women or children, whoever does it will be picked up. You as citizens cannot allow it, because if you do it the police will come. I want to congratulate the police of Lucknow for the way they have behaved here and the restraint they have shown. If we are slapped in the face, shall we turn the other side as Christ said? Well, if we all could do that the world would be a different place to live in. But obviously a police force is not supposed to turn the other side when it is slapped. So please understand this, please recognize these enormous problems that we have to face here, the problems that require hard work.

. . . Now India is going to be run by a large number of trained people in the future, by a relatively small number of 'A' class men in every sphere—in technology, science, and other fields. In fact, the more such persons the better. Ultimately a country's standing in the world is obviously determined not by the number of people it has—crores and crores—but by the number of top-ranking men and women it has to show who can give a proper lead and also by the number of other eminent men it has to carry on the work of a large country. It is a certain quality that counts in the end, not quantity, although quantity also is necessary in a certain measure. Now, do you realize that it is out of you are

[5] During a demonstration, in support of the teachers' strike in Lucknow in January 1949, some students were said to be carrying lathis and bombs with them. It was also alleged that one girl had slapped a policeman.

going to come or ought to come those top-ranking men and women? If the time for education is looked upon as a time for demonstration, as I said, it is a time of peril to the nation when everything has to be set aside—then you do not get prepared for the future, and then the problem that I have to face comes up before me.

Well, I tell you my biggest headache is to find 'A-1' persons in India, and sufficient numbers of them. They are very very few. Mind you, I know that there is the best and the most excellent material in India. But where have we got them? I want to tell you of the three branches of the military of which I have some experience, personal experience. I have had a lot to do with the Indian Army and the Navy and the Air Force, and it is my opinion and it has been confirmed by expert foreign opinion, that the young Indian officer in our Defence Services is first class—first class not merely in discipline but in the quality of his mind. That is important. Warfare has ceased now to be merely a matter of gymnastics and drill. It is the quality of the mind that counts in this business, and we have been told by very eminent judges that they have been surprised at the quality of mind of the young Indian officer. Now that is a comfort. I have not mentioned the other qualities like courage and daring. They are very good, they are very necessary, but after all, ultimately it is the quality of mind that counts, even above courage and daring.

Now finally, I want to put before you another aspect of this problem, although it has many aspects, and that is, if I may say so, the moral aspect. It is my belief and conviction that the world's problems today are not just going to be solved by financial or economic means or purely, by what I might call, political means. At the back of them lies a tremendous conflict of the spirit which is reflected in other conflicts, economic or political. Whether it is solved today or tomorrow—unless this conflict of the spirit is solved—there is going to be no peace on earth or in any country. And it is well for us to remember this at all times and especially today.

Day after tomorrow is the first anniversary of the death of Mahatma Gandhi. A year has passed since he died. It has been a hard year for all of us, for the country, and yet, I suppose, his death has made us think of some of the things he stood for even more than when he was alive and I believe that fundamentally what he stood for, unless we understand it and act up to it, we are not going to succeed; or if I may put it positively, that if we understand it and act up to it, we are bound to succeed. So I wish to stress this moral aspect both in its world context and in our more immediate context of India. After all, we have to function in this field. It is a big enough field for India.

There is a great deal of talk of India's leadership here and there. I discourage this talk. It is just pompous nonsense, talking about leadership. Let us look after ourselves, and if we look after ourselves properly we shall have opportunities of serving other countries, not in any terms of leadership and imposing ourselves on them, but because they themselves will come and seek our service. But before we seek to serve others or guide others, we must be in a position to do so. India has attained a great name in the world of today for various reasons, but the most important of those reasons is Mahatma Gandhi. It was he who gave this great stature to India, and that stature was not given because of India's army or navy or wealth but because this giant among men suddenly showed up the moral pettiness of the politicians of the world. So India gained this place because people thought of India in certain moral terms. And they were right in the sense that India had produced Gandhi, though most of us were petty people unworthy even of following him. So let us think of this problem in this context of morality, and again I come back to this that we may differ, as we do, and I do not mind our differing—but whether we differ or not we must be clear in our own mind about this, that we should not stoop to any low or violent means. . . . Therefore, I would beg of you to consider all this and to realize, that if we are living in a time of great moment for our country and the world, a very great responsibility is thrust upon us to understand this question in order to think of how to solve it and act rightly in this context. *Jai Hind.*

9

The World Around Us[1]

Dear Children,

Shankar[2] asked me to write something for the Children's Number of his *Weekly*. In a weak moment, thinking more of the children than of the *Weekly*, I promised to write. But I soon realized that I had made a rash promise. What was I to write about?

I like being with children and talking to them and, even more, playing with them. For a moment I forget that I am terribly old and that it is a very long time ago since I was a child. But when I sit down to write to you, I cannot forget my age and the distance that separates you from me. Old people have a habit of delivering sermons and good advice to the young. I remember that I disliked this very much long ago when I was a boy. So I suppose you do not like it very much either. Grown-ups have also a habit of appearing to be very wise, even though very few of them possess much wisdom. I have not quite made up my mind yet whether I am wise or not. Sometimes listening to others, I feel I must be very wise and brilliant and important. Then, looking at myself, I begin to doubt this. In any event, people who are wise do not talk about their wisdom and do not behave as if they were very superior persons.

So I must not give you a string of good advice as to what you should do and what you should not do. I suppose you have enough of this from your teachers and others. Nor must I presume to be a superior person.

What then shall I write about? If you were with me, I would love to talk to you about this beautiful world of ours, about flowers and trees and birds and animals and stars and mountains and glaciers and all the other wonderful things that surround us in this world. We have all this beauty all round us and yet we, who are grown-ups, often forget about it and lose ourselves in our arguments or our quarrels. We sit in our offices and imagine that we are doing very important work.

I hope you will be more sensible and open your eyes and ears to this beauty and life that surrounds you. Can you recognize the flowers by their names and

[1] New Delhi, 3 December 1949. Children's Number, *Shankar's Weekly*, December 1949.
[2] K. Shankar Pillai, founder-editor of the weekly.

the birds by their singing? How easy it is to make friends with them and with everything in nature, if you go to them affectionately and with friendship. You must have read many fairy tales and stories of long ago. But the world itself is the greatest fairy tale and story of adventure that was ever written. Only we must have eyes to see and ears to hear and a mind that opens out to the life and beauty of the world.

Grown-ups have a strange way of putting themselves in compartments and groups. They build up barriers and then they think that those outside their particular barrier are strangers whom they must dislike. There are barriers of religion, of caste, of colour, of party, of nation, of province, of language, of customs, and of rich and poor. Thus they live in prisons of their own making. Fortunately children do not know much about these barriers which separate. They play or work with each other, and it is only when they grow up that they begin to learn about these barriers from their elders. I hope you will take a long time in growing up.

I have recently been to the United States of America, to Canada and to England. It was a long journey right on the other side of the world. I found the children there very much like the children here, and so I easily made friends with them and, whenever I had the chance, I played with them a little. That was much more interesting than many of my talks with the grown-ups. For children everywhere are much the same; it is the grown-ups who imagine they are very different and deliberately make themselves so.

Some months ago the children of Japan wrote to me and asked me to send them an elephant. I sent them a beautiful elephant on behalf of the children of India. This elephant came from Mysore and travelled all the way by sea to Japan. When it reached Tokyo, thousands and thousands of children came to see it. Many of them have never seen an elephant. This noble animal thus became a symbol of India to them and a link between them and the children of India. I was very happy that this gift of ours gave so much joy to so many children of Japan and made them think of our country. So we must also think of their country and of the many other countries in the world, and remember that everywhere there are children like you going to school and work and play, and sometimes quarrelling but always making friends again. You can read about these countries in your books, and when you grow up, many of you will visit them. Go there as friends and you will find friends to greet you.

You know that we had a very great man amongst us. He was called Mahatma Gandhi. But we used to call him affectionately Bapuji. He was very wise, but he did not show off his wisdom. He was simple and childlike in many ways and he loved children. He was a friend of everybody, and everybody, peasant or worker, poor man or rich man came to him and found a friendly welcome. He was a friend not only to all the people of India but also to all the people in the rest of the world. He taught us not to hate anybody, not to quarrel, but to play with each other and to cooperate in the service of our country. He taught us also not to be afraid of anything and to face the world cheerfully and with laughter.

Our country is a very big country and there is a great deal to be done by all of us. If each one of us does his or her little bit, then all this mounts up and the country prospers and goes ahead fast.

I have tried to talk to you in this letter, as if you were sitting near me, and I have written more than I intended.

Jawaharlal Nehru

10

The Need for Discipline[1]

A question is often raised as to whether students should take part in politics. As far as I am concerned, students should take part in politics subject to certain provisos. Student organizations should not take part in politics, for then they would cease to be student organizations and function for some other purpose completely diverse from the well-being of the student community. I am in favour of students taking part in politics individually or in groups in their personal capacity. In a fast-changing world no one can keep our young people from politics.

There is, however, one important factor for students to consider before engaging their minds in politics. They should remember that they are the future citizens of the country, and the sole responsibility of running the affairs of the country will eventually fall on their shoulders. For this task they must equip themselves first with knowledge and training, and finally with experience. After their academic career they have to face the realities of life and the knowledge they have gained at colleges and universities helps them to become responsible citizens.

. . . One of the world's ailments today is that there are too many old men at the helm of affairs—too many in the rut unable to adjust themselves to the changed conditions. The world will be a better place if the younger generation, active and intelligent, takes over. However, to attain this, youth require training which is uninterrupted by political or ideological influences. If they do not develop mentally or physically during their period of training, they will never do so later. To whatever position they may be pushed up, if they lack experience and knowledge they will speedily fall back.

. . . Preoccupation with power politics during student life is in conflict with your training. It then becomes a gamble for the future. The primary responsibility of the student is to train his body and mind with as close association with public affairs as possible.

I noticed a degradation of human personality in the Indian scene and it distresses me to see various forces, negative and destructive, hampering the progress of the nation.

[1] Speech at the inauguration of the first convention of the National Union of Students, Bombay, 15 September 1950. From *The Hindustan Times*, 16 September 1950.

Every country, whatever may be the ruling political ideology, is guided by certain principles and standards. Standards may not be the same throughout the world. But when standards fall, along with them the nation, the community and the individual go down too.

Work, hard work, not for years but for generations, should be the order of the day if any nation wants to survive. Hard work is essential if the nation is to advance in the economic sphere and if people have to advance well. I am pained to see lack of discipline and character in India. The choice before the country is between becoming a progressive, first-rate nation and a disintegrated, tenth-rate nation. I can never think of India becoming anything but a first-class nation, maintaining a high standard in both internal and external affairs. To become a first-class nation, however, India needs first-grade men. We require the best scientists, engineers, doctors and administrators. You should develop an integrated personality.

. . . Political activity will become barren unless it has some standards or values. Laying of a sound human character is not complete by itself. A conflict between constructive and destructive forces is going on in the country. I have no doubt that in the ultimate analysis the constructive forces will triumph, though I cannot logically prove it. Take up the challenge of the destructive forces and do not fall prey to disruptive tendencies.

11

The Strength of the Unafraid[1]

What a troublesome person Shankar is! Every few days I get a reminder from him that I must write something for the children's number or else he himself appears and looks at me with reproachful eyes. Here I am trying hard to get through a great deal of work before I leave for England on the 1st of January. On top of this, I am expected to write articles. Shankar seems to forget that most of my writing has been done in the leisure of prison. Since I came out of that small prison and entered the larger prison of office, my freedom to read and write has been taken away from me. I cannot do many of the things that I would like to do, and I have to do much that I intensely dislike.

I suppose Shankar knows all this, but he has got an idea into his head that something from me must appear in the Children's Number. Well, I am bound to confess that I like this idea of the Children's Number very much and I should like to help it to grow. I liked the last number and I am almost sure that the next number will be better.

What pleases me most of all is the great interest that children in distant countries have taken in this venture. I was surprised and delighted to visit an exhibition where hundreds of pictures and cartoons sent for Shankar's Children's Number were exhibited.

As I looked at these pictures, I thought of the vast army of children all over the world, outwardly different in many ways, speaking different languages, wearing different kinds of clothes, and yet so very like each other. If you bring them together, they play or they quarrel. But even their quarrelling is some kind of play. They do not think of differences amongst themselves, differences of class or caste or colour or status. They are wiser than their fathers and mothers. As they grow up, unfortunately, this natural wisdom gets covered up often by the teaching and behaviour of their elders. They learn many things at school, which are useful no doubt, but they forget gradually that the first thing to remember is to be human and kind and playful and to make life richer for ourselves and others. We live in a wonderful world, full of beauty and charm

---

[1] Message for children, 27 December 1950. *Shankar's Weekly*, Children's Number, December 1950.

and adventure. There is no end to the adventures that we can have, if only we seek them with our eyes open. So many people seem to go about their lives' business with eyes shut. Indeed, they object to other people keeping their eyes open. Unable to play themselves, they dislike the play of others.

Our own country is a little world in itself with infinite variety and ever so many places which we can discover. I have travelled about a great deal in this country from north to south and east to west, and I have grown in years. And yet I have not seen many parts of this country that we love so much and that we seek to serve. I wish I had more time to visit the odd nooks and corners of India. I would like to go there in the company of bright young children whose minds are opening out with wonder and curiosity, as they make new discoveries. I should like to take them with me not so much to the great cities of India but to the mountains and the forests and the great rivers and the old monuments, all of which tell us something of India's story. I would like them to realize that we can play about in the snow in some parts of India and we can also go to other parts where tropical forests flourish. We would have a voyage of discovery of the beautiful trees in our forests and on the hillsides and the flowers that grace the changing seasons and bring life and colour to us. We could watch the birds and try to recognize them and make friends with them. But the most exciting adventure would be to go to the forests and see the wild animals, both the little ones and the big. Foolish people go with a gun and kill them and thus put an end to something that was beautiful. It is far more interesting and amusing to wander about without a gun or any other weapon and to find that wild animals are not afraid and can be approached. Animals have keener instincts than man. If a man goes to them with murder in his heart, they are afraid of him and run away. But if you go with friendly feelings, they realize that a friend is coming and do not mind him. If you are full of fear, then the animal gets afraid too and, in his fear, he might attack. The fearless person is seldom, if ever, attacked.

Perhaps that lesson might be applied to human beings also. If we meet other people in a friendly way, they also grow friendly. But if we are afraid of them or if we show our dislike to them, then they behave in the same manner.

These are simple truths which the world has known for ages past. But, even so, the world forgets and the people of one country hate and fear the people of another country, and because they are afraid, they are sometimes foolish enough to fight each other.

Children should be wiser. At any rate the children who read Shankar's Children's Number are expected to be more sensible.

12

The Purpose of Education[1]

In the final analysis, no subject is of greater importance than that of education. It is the men and women in a country that make and build a nation and it is education that is supposed to build those men and women.

The process of education, therefore, must help to build men and women suited to the age and the tasks they have to perform. It should presumably deal with certain basic factors in the development of boys and girls to give them strength of character and the right outlook on life. I do not mean by this that they should be conditioned only in one particular way, but rather that they should develop, apart from the essentials of character, a trained, receptive and tolerant mind which is capable of considering problems in their entirety and trying to arrive at solutions. They should in effect develop into integrated human beings. Integration means not only a process within themselves, which of course is highly important, but also a measure of integration with the environment.

The part of training that deals with the environment will necessarily vary with the age and the kind of work that these people may be called upon to do. We live, as is well known, in an intensely transitional age. We cannot go back upon it and we can only try to understand it and look forward to the changes that are likely to come. The Industrial Revolution has changed the face of the world in the course of the last one hundred and fifty years. In a sense it is continuing and tremendous scientific and technological advances are taking place now at an almost unthinkable pace. These will no doubt affect the structure of human life and association. How to fit in with this and yet to retain those fundamental traits of character which are considered essential, is the problem of the age. Probably most of our difficulties are due to the fact that there is lack of concordance between the individual and the environment. This physical environment has changed so rapidly that the human being has not adapted himself to it except, to some extent, externally.

In India we have perhaps to face even greater changes than elsewhere because, whether we will it or not, we cannot cut ourselves off from this powerful

---

[1] Message to the Hindustani Talimi Sangh, 28 November 1957. JN Papers, NMML. Excerpts.

current of changes. We are entering not only the industrial age but the atomic age and perhaps a little later the interplanetary age. We are doing all this before we have found our feet even in the initial stages.

The problem is a colossal one and yet has to be faced. Basic education laid stress on various factors of importance, notably the coordination of the mind with manual work. That is an essential feature which we have to encourage. As a result of this, stress was laid on what are called the development of cottage industries and a seeming contradiction arose between cottage industries and the machine age that we live in. We cannot get out of the machine age and the question is how far such concordance is necessary and to what extent we can bring it about. It is a difficult question to answer for the distant future. But in the present, it is clear that however much we may advance in the technique of the machine age, and I feel sure that we must advance that way, it still remains necessary for us to develop in a large way cottage industries and the like. Also, India can only develop if her villages develop, and too great a hiatus between the village and the city is bad. The whole purpose of the community development scheme is to develop the villages along modern lines but keeping their inner basis to some extent intact.

13

Universities[1]

The question of education has been much in my mind recently. We all realize the importance of it from every point of view and indeed it is essential for our social and economic development. We want mass education as well as higher education, more particularly technical education.

When we talk about the emotional integration of India, we think immediately of the educational process which will help in this integration. No doubt it will do so, and it has become important that our textbooks and course should be prepared accordingly.

And yet, there is an obvious danger that faces us if certain present trends in educational matters are allowed to continue. It may be that these linguistic trends might actually lead to greater provincialism and feelings of separateness among the states. This is not merely a linguistic matter although that is important enough, but certain other trends which lay stress on the state and not on the country as a whole. The gods we pay homage to become tied up with our conception of the state and not the nation.

I am myself convinced that the medium of education must be the mother tongue of the child, boy and girl. Only then can his or her mind develop adequately. But unless the larger ideal of India and its unity is always kept in view, this may well lead us to a form of separatism which will impede both our unity and our progress. Our universities, adopting, if they do, the regional languages, will get more and more isolated from each other. Professors and teaching staff will not be easily exchangeable and generally speaking, the outlook that will inevitably grow out of these surroundings, will be a narrow one and not so much an all-India one. There are, of course, strong urges in favour of Indian unity. I do not mean to suggest that they will be easily overcome, but while intellectually we may continue to think of that unity, emotionally we will be conditioned otherwise.

How are we to get over this dilemma? The universities are supposed to build a certain intellectual atmosphere in the country. If there is no common approach in the universities, then this atmosphere itself will be not a common

[1] Circular, 3 July 1961. JN Papers, NMML.

one but a somewhat disruptive one. As a matter of fact, while standards of education are going up in other advanced countries, our own standards are said to be deteriorating. It has become important to pull these standards up by an attempt at a more effective organization of resources which are in many cases spread out too thinly to be really effective. This is particularly applicable to scientific and technological studies, but it applies to the humanities also.

In science or in any of the higher studies, it is not the brilliant individual who counts so much now, but the team of able men who work together. If we have done well in atomic energy, it is because we have collected a considerable number of able young men and women to work together as a team. In our universities, this kind of thing is lacking, even though they may have individual teachers who are good.

It has been suggested that the way to pull standards up in universities is to encourage this team work by having centres of advanced study in as many universities as possible. That is to say, each centre will be for a particular subject, and it should function on an all-India basis. In regard to scientific and technological subjects, such centres should work in close cooperation with national laboratories and institutes.

Each such centre in a university would have a team of professors, lecturers, research fellows, etc., of outstanding ability and qualifications actively engaged in research and advanced teaching, in a particular branch of study. It is considered important that there should be a combination of research and teaching, thus not only maintaining contact with fresh young minds, but also creating a proper academic atmosphere for serious and sustained work. We have found that we have quite an adequate number of bright young students, and given the chance, they will do very well. But that chance is usually lacking.

All this would mean an addition to our professional and teaching staff. In this matter of team work, a certain minimum number is necessary.

We dare not allow the standards of our universities to go down. For, a university can only justify itself by maintaining high academic and professional standards. It would be an essential part of any such scheme for universities to keep in close touch with each other, exchanging professors, teachers, scholars and senior students, and thus building a corporate intellectual life of India.

If universities are functioning in different languages, how do we bring about this close cooperation and exchange of professors, students, etc., between one region of the country and another? This question has been troubling me and I would like to draw your attention to it. All our progress depends not on the number of factories and plants that are put up, but on the quality of human beings that we produce and train. That quality depends, in the final analysis, on our universities and on their close contact with each other.

I have often noticed that the appointment of vice-chancellors to universities is considered almost entirely from the administrative point of view. Administration is important, but essentially a university is a body of persons devoted to academic pursuits, and this must always be kept in view so that a proper academic atmosphere is maintained and encouraged. If the vice-chancellor, who is the executive head of the university, is merely an administrator, then he cannot enter into that academic life which is so important, nor is he likely to be respected greatly by the large body of students. I think it is essential, therefore, that our vice-chancellors should be men of learning and high academic standards.

VOL. II

VIII
Personal

1. Cambridge   593
2. Finer Side of Life   595
3. Imprisonment   596
4. Lathi Charges   599
5. Human Endeavour   603
6. Bapu's Arrest   605
7. Reaction to Gandhi's Fast   607
8. Aims and Objectives of Life   610
9. Musings   612
10. The Death of Motilal Nehru   613
11. Back in Prison   615
12. Kamala   618
13. Introspection   620
14. Family Ties   624
15. A Solitary Traveller   627
16. A Hundred Pictures   630
17. The True Perspective   635
18. The Call of India   636
19. Dreams and Reality   637

20. A Private Person   638

21. A Bundle of Tempers   639

22. Human Personality   640

23. Restraining Feelings   642

24. Rashtrapati   643

25. Psychoanalyzing Oneself   647

26. Relationships   649

27. A Report on His Own Tour   651

28. Confining Barriers   654

29. Creeping Age   656

30. Writing from Prison   657

31. On Personal Style   660

32. Time   661

33. Voyage of Discovery   662

34. Taking Decisions   664

35. Perceptions   669

36. Mountains and Rivers   671

37. Family as A Unit   673

38. Stray Notes   676

39. Effects of Jail Life   679

40. Cause and Effect   681

41. Bengal Famine   683

42. Philosophy and Life   685

43. Children   688

44. The Moon   690

45. Mental Perturbation   691

46. Beginning of Life   693

47. Philosophy of Life   694

48. Memories and Fancies   703

49. Uncertainties   705

50. Decisions and Responsibilities   706

51. Life   707

52. In Conversation with Norman Cousins   709

53. Kashmir and the Constituent Assembly   726

54. Sense of Ineffectiveness   728

55. Controlling Emotions   730

56. Touring in India   733

57. Mountains   735

58. Laying down Office   736

59. Human Relations   738

60. Will and Testament   740

1

Cambridge[1]

Three years I was at Cambridge, three quiet years with little of disturbance in them, moving slowly on like the sluggish Cam. They were pleasant years, with many friends and some work and some play and a gradual widening of the intellectual horizon. . . .

My general attitude to life at the time was a vague kind of Cyrenaicism, partly natural to youth, partly the influence of Oscar Wilde and Walter Pater. It is easy and gratifying to give a long Greek name to the desire for a soft life and pleasant experiences. But there was something more in it than that for I was not particularly attracted to a soft life. Not having the religious temper and disliking the repressions of religion, it was natural for me to seek some other standard. I was superficial and did not go deep down into anything. And so the aesthetic side of life appealed to me, and the idea of going through life worthily, not indulging it in the vulgar way, but still making the most of it and living a full and many-sided life attracted me. I enjoyed life and I refused to see why I should consider it a thing of sin. At the same time risk and adventure fascinated me; I was always, like my father, a bit of gambler, at first with money and then for higher stakes, with the bigger issues of life. Indian politics in 1907 and 1908 were in a state of upheaval and I wanted to play a brave part in them, and this was not likely to lead to a soft life. All these mixed and sometimes conflicting desires led to a medley in my mind. Vague and confused it was but I did not worry, for the time for any decision was yet far distant. Meanwhile, life was pleasant, both physically and intellectually, fresh horizons were ever coming into sight, there was so much to be done, so much to be seen, so many fresh avenues to explore. And we would sit by the fireside in the long winter evenings and talk and discuss unhurriedly deep into the night till the dying fire drove us shivering to our beds. And sometimes, during our discussions, our voices would lose their even tenor and would grow loud and excited in heated argument. But it was all make-believe. We played with the problems of human life in a mock-serious way, for they had not become real problems for us yet, and we had not been caught in the coils of the world's affairs. It was the pre-War world of the early twentieth century. Soon this world was to die, yielding place

[1] From *An Autobiography*, pp. 19–26.

to another, full of death and destruction and anguish and heartsickness for the world's youth. But the veil of the future hid this and we saw around us an assured and advancing order of things and this was pleasant for those who could afford it.

I write of Cyrenaicism and the like and of various ideas that influenced me then. But it would be wrong to imagine that I thought clearly on these subjects then or even that I thought it necessary to try to be clear and definite about them. They were just vague fancies that floated in my mind and in this process left their impress in a greater or less degree. I did not worry myself at all about these speculations. Work and games and amusements filled my life and the only thing that disturbed me sometimes was the political struggle in India. Among the books that influenced me politically at Cambridge was Meredith Townsend's *Asia and Europe.* . . .

I remember Edwin Montagu, who later became Secretary of State for India, often visiting "The Magpie and Stump." He was an old Trinity man and was then Member of Parliament for Cambridge. It was from him that I first heard the modern definition of faith: to believe in something which your reason tells you cannot be true, for if your reason approved of it there could be no question of blind faith. I was influenced by my scientific studies in the university and had some of the assurance which science then possessed. For the science of the nineteenth and the early twentieth centuries, unlike that of to-day, was very sure of itself and the world. . . .

In the summer of 1912 I was called to the Bar, and in the autumn of that year I returned to India finally after a stay of over seven years in England. Twice, in between, I had gone home during my holidays. But now I returned for good, and I am afraid, as I landed at Bombay, I was a bit of a prig with little to commend me.

2

Finer Side of Life[1]

District Jail, Lucknow
1 September 1922, 6 a.m.

My dear father,

Ever since my return from England I have done little reading and I shudder to think what I was gradually becoming before politics and N.C.O. snatched me away from the doom that befalls many of us. Freedom in many of its aspects is denied us but the freedom and the glory of thought is ours and none can deprive us of it. But the life I led and that so many of us lead, the atmosphere of the law courts, the uninspiring conversation of bar libraries, the continuous contact with the sordid side of human nature—all this and the absence of any organized intellectual life gradually kill this power of free thought. We dare not think or follow up the consequences of our thought. We remain in the ruts and the valleys, incapable almost of looking up towards the mountain tops. And the finer side of life escapes us, we cannot even appreciate art or beauty, for everything that is outside the ruts and the valleys terrifies us. We cling to our physical comfort, and a very second rate, bourgeois comfort at that. We do not even know how to live well or to enjoy ourselves. Few of us have any joie de vivre left. And so we live out our lives with little said or little done that beautifies existence for us or for others, or that will be remembered by anyone after we are dead and gone. That was the fate reserved for us also till the high gods took us in hand and removed us from the ruts and placed us on the mountain side. We may not reach the top yet awhile but the glory of wider vision is ours. We can see the stars better and sometimes the rays of the morning sun reach us sooner than those in the valleys.

[1] To Motilal Nehru. SWJN. Vol. 1, pp. 333–4. Extracts.

3

Imprisonment[1]

We knew that matters had at last come to a head; the inevitable conflict between the Congress and the Government was about to break out. Prison was still an unknown place, the idea of going there still a novelty. I was sitting rather late one day in the Congress office at Allahabad trying to clear up arrears of work. An excited clerk told me that the police had come with a search warrant and were surrounding the office building. I was, of course, a little excited also, for it was my first experience of the kind, but the desire to show off was strong, the wish to appear perfectly cool and collected, unaffected by the comings and goings of the police. So I asked a clerk to accompany the police officer in his search round the office rooms, and insisted on the rest of the staff carrying on their usual work and ignoring the police. A little later a friend and a colleague, who had been arrested just outside the office, came to me, accompanied by a policeman, to bid me goodbye. I was so full of the conceit that I must treat these novel occurrences as everyday happenings that I treated my colleague in a most unfeeling manner. Casually I asked him and the policeman to wait till I had finished the letter I was writing. Soon news came of other arrests in the city. I decided at last to go home and see what was happening there. I found the inevitable police searching part of the large house and learnt that they had come to arrest both father and me. . . .

In 1921 prison was an almost unknown place, and very few knew what happened behind the grim gates that swallowed the new convict. Vaguely we imagined that its inhabitants were desperate people and dangerous criminals. In our minds the place was associated with isolation, humiliation, and suffering, and, above all, the fear of the unknown. Frequent references to gaol-going from 1920 onwards, and the march of many of our comrades to prison, gradually accustomed us to the idea and took away the edge from that almost involuntary feeling of repugnance and reluctance. But no amount of previous mental preparation could prevent the tension and nervous excitement that filled us when we first entered the iron gates. Since those days, thirteen years ago, I imagine that at least three hundred thousand men and women of India

[1] From *An Autobiography*, pp. 79 and 90–8.

have entered those gates for political offences, although often enough the actual charge has been under some other section of the criminal code. Thousands of these have gone in and out many a time; they have got to know well what to expect inside: they have tried to adapt themselves to the strange life there, as far as one can adapt oneself to an existence full of abnormality and a dull suffering and a dreadful monotony. We grow accustomed to it, as one grows accustomed to almost anything; and yet every time that we enter those gates again, there is a bit of the old excitement, a feeling of tension, a quickening of the pulse. And the eyes turn back involuntarily to take a last good look outside at the greenery and wide spaces, and people and conveyances moving about, and familiar faces that they may not see again for a long time. . . .

The nearest approach to privacy that I could get was by leaving my barrack and sitting in the open part of the enclosure. It was the monsoon season and it was usually possible to do so because of the clouds. I braved the heat and an occasional drizzle even, and spent as much time as possible outside the barrack.

Lying there in the open, I watched the skies and the clouds and I realized, better than I had ever done before, how amazingly beautiful were their changing hues.

"To watch the changing clouds, like clime in clime;
Oh! sweet to lie and bless the luxury of time."

Time was not a luxury for us, it was more of a burden. But the time I spent in watching those ever-shifting monsoon clouds was filled with delight and a sense of relief. I had the joy of having made almost a discovery, and a feeling of escape from confinement. I do not know why that particular monsoon had that great effect on me; no previous or subsequent one has moved me in that way. I had seen and admired many a fine sunrise and sunset in the mountains and over the sea, and bathed in its glory, and felt stirred for the time being by its magnificence. Having seen it, I had almost taken it for granted and passed on to other things. But in gaol there were no sunrises or sunsets to be seen, the horizon was hidden from us, and late in the morning the hot-rayed sun emerged over our guardian walls. There were no colours anywhere, and our eyes hardened and grew dull at seeing always that same drab view of mud-coloured wall and barrack. They must have hungered for some light and shade and colouring, and when the monsoon clouds sailed gaily by, assuming fantastic shapes, and playing in a riot of colour, I gasped in surprised delight and watched them almost as if I was in a trance. Sometimes the clouds would break, and one saw through an opening in them that wonderful monsoon phenomenon, a dark blue of an amazing depth, which seemed to be a portion of infinity. . . .

One misses many things in prison, but perhaps most of all one misses the sound of women's voices and children's laughter. The sounds one usually hears are not of the pleasantest. The voices are harsh and minatory, and the language brutal and largely consisting of swear-words. Once I remember being struck by a new want. I was in the Lucknow District Gaol and I realized suddenly that I had not heard a dog bark for seven or eight months. . . .

There is always a feeling of relief and a sense of glad excitement in coming out of the prison gate. The fresh air and open expanses, the moving street scene, and the meeting with old friends, all go to the head and slightly intoxicate. Almost, there is a touch of hysteria in one's first reactions to the outer world.

4

Lathi Charges[1]

The assault on Lala Lajpat Rai, and his subsequent death, increased the vigour of the demonstrations against the Simon Commission in the places which it subsequently visited. It was due in Lucknow, and the local Congress Committee made extensive preparations for its 'reception'. Huge processions, meetings, and demonstrations were organized many days in advance, both as propaganda and as rehearsals for the actual show. I went to Lucknow, and was present at some of these. The success of these preliminary demonstrations, which were perfectly orderly and peaceful, evidently nettled the authorities, and they began to obstruct and issue orders against the taking out of processions in certain areas. It was in this connection that I had a new experience, and my body felt the baton and lathi blows of the police.

Processions had been prohibited, ostensibly to avoid any interference with the traffic. We decided to give no cause for complaint on this score, and arranged for small groups of sixteen, as far as I can remember, to go separately, along unfrequented routes to the meeting place. Technically, this was no doubt a breach of the order, for sixteen with a flag were a procession. I led one of the groups of sixteen and, after a big gap, came another such group under the leadership of my colleague, Govind Ballabh Pant. My group had gone perhaps about two hundred yards, the road was a deserted one, when we heard the clatter of horses' hoofs behind us. We looked back to find a bunch of mounted police, probably two or three dozen in number, bearing down upon us at a rapid pace. They were soon right upon us, and the impact of the horses broke up our little column of sixteen. The mounted policemen then started belabouring our volunteers with huge batons or truncheons and, instinctively, the volunteers sought refuge on the sidewalks, and some even entered the petty shops. They were pursued and beaten down. My own instinct had urged me to seek safety when I saw the horses charging down upon us: it was a discouraging sight. But then, I suppose, some other instinct held me to my place and I survived the first charge, which had been checked by the volunteers behind me. Suddenly I found myself alone in the middle of the road; a few yards away from me, in various directions, were the policemen beating down our volunteers. Automatically,

[1] From *An Autobiography*, pp. 177–81.

I began moving slowly to the side of the road to be less conspicuous, but again I stopped and had a little argument with myself, and decided that it would be unbecoming for me to move away. All this was a matter of a few seconds only, but I have the clearest recollections of that conflict within me and the decision, prompted by my pride, I suppose, which could not tolerate the idea of my behaving like a coward. Yet the line between cowardice and courage was a thin one, and I might well have been on the other side. Hardly had I so decided, when I looked round to find that a mounted policeman was trotting up to me, brandishing his long new baton. I told him to go ahead, and turned my head away—again an instinctive effort to save the head and face. He gave me two resounding blows on the back. I felt stunned, and my body quivered all over but, to my surprise and satisfaction, I found that I was still standing. The police force was withdrawn soon after, and made to block the road in front of us. Our volunteers gathered together again, many of them bleeding and with split skulls, and we were joined by Pant and his lot, who had also been belaboured, and all of us sat down facing the police. So we sat for an hour or so, and it became dark. On the one side, various high officials gathered; on the other, large crowds began to assemble as the news spread. Ultimately, the officials agreed to allow us to go by our original route, and we went that way with the mounted policemen, who had charged us and belaboured us, going ahead of us as a kind of escort.

I have written about this petty incident in some detail because of its effect on me. The bodily pain I felt was quite forgotten in a feeling of exhilaration that I was physically strong enough to face and bear lathi blows. And a thing that surprised me was that right through the incident, even when I was being beaten, my mind was quite clear and I was consciously analysing my feelings. This rehearsal stood me in good stead the next morning, when a stiffer trial was in store for us. For the next morning was the time when the Simon Commission was due to arrive, and our great demonstration was going to take place.

My father was at Allahabad at the time, and I was afraid that the news of the assault on me, when he read about it in the next morning's papers, would upset him and the rest of the family. So I telephoned to him late in the evening to assure him that all was well, and that he should not worry. But he did worry and, finding it difficult to sleep over it, he decided at about midnight to come over to Lucknow. The last train had gone, and so he started by motor car. He had some bad luck on the way, and it was nearly five in the morning by the time he had covered the journey of 146 miles and reached Lucknow, tired out and exhausted.

That was about the time when we were getting ready to go in procession to the station. The previous evening's incidents had the effect of rousing up Lucknow more than anything that we could have done, and even before the sun was out, vast numbers of people made their way to the station. Innumerable little processions came from various parts of the city, and from the Congress office started the main procession, consisting of several thousands, marching in fours. We were in this main procession. We were stopped by the police as we approached the station. There was a huge open space, about half a mile square, in front of the station (this has now been built over by the new station) and we were made to line up on one side of this maidan, and there our procession remained, making no attempt to push our way forward. The place was full of foot and mounted police, as well as the military. The crowd of sympathetic onlookers swelled up, and many of these persons managed to spread out in twos and threes in the open space. Suddenly we saw in the far distance a moving mass. They were two or three long lines of cavalry or mounted police, covering the entire area, galloping down towards us, and striking and riding down the numerous stragglers that dotted the maidan. That charge of galloping horsemen was a fine sight, but for the tragedies that were being enacted on the way, as harmless and very much surprised sightseers went under the horses' hoofs. Behind the charging lines these people lay on the ground, some still unable to move, others writhing in pain, and the whole appearance of that maidan was that of a battlefield. But we did not have much time for gazing on that scene or for reflections; the horsemen were soon upon us and their front line clashed almost at a gallop with the massed ranks of our processionists. We held our ground, and, as we appeared to be unyielding, the horses had to pull up at the last moment and reared up on their hind legs with their front hoofs quivering in the air over our heads. And then began a beating of us, and battering with lathis and long batons both by the mounted and the foot police. It was a tremendous hammering, and the clearness of vision that I had had the evening before left me. All I know was that I had to stay where I was, and must not yield or go back. I felt half blinded with the blows, and sometimes a dull anger seized me and a desire to hit out. I thought how easy it would be to pull down the police officer in front of me from his horse and to mount up myself, but long training and discipline held and I did not raise a hand, except to protect my face from a blow. Besides, I knew well enough that any aggression on our part would result in a ghastly tragedy—the firing and shooting down of large numbers of our men.

After what seemed a tremendous length of time, but was probably only a few minutes, our line began to yield slowly, step by step, without breaking up. This left me somewhat isolated, and more exposed at the sides. More blows came, and then I was suddenly lifted off my feet from behind and carried off, to my great annoyance. Some of my young colleagues, thinking that a dead-set was being made at me, had decided to protect me in this summary fashion.

Our processionists lined up again about a hundred feet behind our original line. The police also withdrew and stood in a line, fifty feet apart from us. So we remained, when the cause of all this trouble, the Simon Commission, secretly crept away from the station in the far distance, more than half a mile away. But, even so, they did not escape the blacks flags or demonstrators. Soon after, we came back in full procession to the Congress office, and there dispersed, and I went on to father, who was anxiously waiting for us.

Now that the excitement of the moment had passed, I felt pain all over my body and great fatigue. Almost every part of me seemed to ache, and I was covered with contused wounds and marks of blows. But fortunately I was not injured in any vital spot. Many of our companions were less fortunate, and were badly injured. Govind Ballabh Pant, who stood by me, offered a much bigger target, being six foot odd in height, and the injuries he received then have resulted in a painful and persistent malady which prevented him for a long time from straightening his back or leading an active life. I emerged with a somewhat greater conceit of my physical condition and powers of endurance. But the memory that endures with me, far more than that of the beating itself, is that of many of the faces of those policemen, and especially of the officers, who were attacking us. Most of the real beating and battering was done by European sergeants, the Indian rank and file were milder in their methods. And those faces, full of hate and blood-lust, almost mad, with no trace of sympathy or touch of humanity! Probably the faces on our side just then were equally hateful to look at, and the fact that we were mostly passive did not fill our minds and hearts with love for our opponents, or add to the beauty of our countenances. And yet, we had no grievance against each other; no quarrel that was personal, no ill-will. We happened to represent for the time being strange and powerful forces which held us in thrall and cast us hither and thither, and, subtly gripping our minds and hearts, roused our desires and passions and made us their blind tools. Blindly we struggled, not knowing what we struggled for and whither we went. The excitement of action held us; but, as it passed, immediately the question arose: To what end was all this? To what end?

5

Human Endeavour[1]

Allahabad, 20 August 1931

Dear Mr. Durant,

Your letter raises fascinating questions—fascinating and yet rather terrible. For your argument leads to the inevitable conclusion that all life is futile and all human endeavour worse than useless. You have done me the honour of putting these questions to me, but I feel my utter incompetence to answer them. Even if I had the time and leisure, which unhappily I have not at present, I would find it difficult enough to deal with the problems you have raised.

Indians are supposed to find pleasure in metaphysics but I have deliberately kept aloof from them, as I found long ago that they only confused me and brought me no solace or guidance for future action. Religion in its limited sense did not appeal to me. I dabbled a little in the various sciences, as a dilettante might, and found some pleasure in them and my horizon seemed to widen. But still I drifted and doubted and was somewhat cynical. Vague ideals possessed me, socialistic and nationalistic, and gradually they seemed to combine and I grew to desire the freedom of India passionately, and the freedom of India signified to me not national freedom only but the relief of the millions of her men and women from suffering and exploitation. And India became a symbol of the suffering of all the exploited in the world and I sought to make of my intense nationalism an internationalism which included in its fold all the nations and peoples that were being exploited.

I was troubled by these feelings and felt my helplessness. There seemed to be no obvious way of realizing my heart's desire. Then came Mr. Gandhi and pointed a way which seemed to promise results, or at any rate which was a way worth trying and afforded an outlet for my pent-up feelings. I plunged in, and I discovered that I had at last found what I had long sought. It was in action that I found this—action on behalf of a great cause which I held clear. Ever since then I have used all my strength in battling for this cause and the recompense I have had has strengthened me, for the reward has been a fuller life with a new meaning and a purpose to it.

[1] To Will Durant. JN Papers, NMML. Excerpts.

This is hardly an answer to your question. But not being a philosopher, but just a man who feels at home in action, I cannot give you a very logical or scientific answer. I have believed in science and logic and reason, and I believe in them still, but at times they seem to lack something and life seems to be governed by other and stronger forces—instinct or an irresistible drive towards something—which for the moment do not appear to fit in with science or logic as we know them. History with its record of failure, the persistence of evil in spite of all the great men and great deeds of the past, the present breakdown of civilization and its old-time ideals, and the dangers that lurk in the future, make me despair sometimes. But in spite of all this I have a feeling that the future is full of hope for humanity and for my country and the fight for freedom that we are waging in India is bringing us nearer the realization of this hope. Do not ask me to justify this feeling that I have for I can give you no sufficient reasons. I can only tell you that I have found mental equilibrium and strength and inspiration in the thought that I am doing my bit for a mighty cause and that my labour cannot be in vain. I work for results of course. I want to go rapidly towards my objective. But fundamentally even the results of action do not worry me so much. Action itself, so long as I am convinced that it is right action, gives me satisfaction.

In my general outlook on life I am a socialist and it is a socialist order that I should like to see established in India and the world. What will happen when the world becomes perfect I do not know and I do not very much care. The problem does not arise today. There is quite enough to be done now and that is enough for me. Whether the world will ever become perfect, or even much better than it is today, I shall not venture to answer. But because I hope and believe that something can be done to better it, I continue to act.

I am afraid I have avoided your principal question—what is the meaning or worth of human life? I cannot answer it except by telling you how I have looked upon life and what motives have driven me to action.

Sincerely yours,
Jawaharlal Nehru

6

Bapu's Arrest[1]

Sept. 22, Thursday

What a capacity Bapu has got for giving shocks to people? A week ago—on the 14th—I read about his decision to "fast unto death" in disapproval of the separate electorates given by Ramsay MacDonald's award to the depressed classes.[2] Suddenly all manner of ideas rushed into my head—all kinds of possibilities and contingencies rose up before me—and upset my equilibrium completely. For two days nearly I was in darkness with no light to show the way out, my heart sinking when I thought of some results of Bapu's action. The personal aspect was powerful enough and I thought with anguish that I might not see him again. It was on board ship that I saw him last, over a year ago, when he was sailing for England. Was that going to be my last sight of him?

And then I felt annoyed with him for choosing a side issue for his final sacrifice—just a question of electorate. What would be the result on our freedom movement? Would not the larger issues fade into the background? And if he attains his immediate object and gets a joint electorate for the depressed classes would not that result in a reaction and a feeling that a result has been achieved and nothing more need be done for a while? And was not his action a recognition and in part an acceptance of the Communal Award and the general scheme of things as sponsored by the Govt.? Was it consistent with noncooperation and civil disobedience? Was there not danger of our movement trailing off into something insignificant after so much sacrifice and brave endurance?

And I felt angry with Bapu at his religious and sentimental approach to a political question. Was he entitled to coerce people in this way? What would happen to this country if the practice spread? And his frequent references to God—God has made him do this—God even indicated the date of the fast &c. were most irritating. What a terrible example to set!

[1] Prison Diary. JN Papers, NMML. SWJN, Vol. 5, pp. 407–8.
[2] The award announced on 10 August 1932 recognized the depressed and scheduled castes as a minority and gave each minority a fixed number of seats with separate electorates.

And I thought of Kamala and mother, feeling sure that they would have a terrible shock if Bapu died—Would they survive?

If Bapu died! What would India be like then? And how will her politics run! There seemed to be a dreary and dismal future and despair seized my heart when I thought of it.

So I thought and thought and confusion reigned in my head and anger and despair and love for him who was the cause of this upheaval. I hardly knew what to do and I was irritable and short tempered with everybody, and most of all with myself.

For two days I felt bad. And then—a strange enough thing for me!—I had quite an emotional crisis and I cried and wept. Somehow the tears took away a great deal of my confusion and worry. I felt calmer and the future not so dark. Bapu had a curious knack of doing the right thing at the psychological moment and it might be that his action—impossible to justify as it was from my point of view—might lead to great results—not only in the narrow field in which it was confined, but in the wider aspects of our national struggle. And even if Bapu died, the great fight will go on. So whatever happened one must keep ready and fit for it instead of behaving like a foolish lovesick girl.

It was strange how rapidly the storm subsided and I felt calm and collected and ready to face the world and all it might offer. I had made up my mind to face even Bapu's death without flinching.

Since then news has come that some settlement will be arrived at and there is no danger of his death. And all over the country there has been an upheaval, the like of which has seldom been seen. On the 20th, when the fast began, there was fasting and hartal all over India—scores of millions must have fasted. Nearly all the jail people—staff, prisoners, politicals, non-politicals—fasted; many for 36 hours. And all over the country temples are being thrown open to "untouchables". There seems to be a magic wave of enthusiasm, running through the Hindu society, and untouchability appears to be on its last legs. What a magician is this little man sitting in Yeravda Jail, and how well he knows how to pull the strings that move people's hearts! What can poor logic and intellect and reason do before him!

But I do wish he would not refer so frequently to the Almighty as if God was personal adviser for every act of his. I find this extraordinarily irritating.

Kamala of course celebrated the receipt of news of Bapu's fast by fainting off immediately!

7

Reaction to Gandhi's Fast[1]

5 May 1933

My dear Bapu,

I feel utterly at a loss and do not know what to say to you.[2]

Religion is not familiar ground for me, and as I have grown older I have definitely drifted away from it. I suppose I have something else in its place, something other than just intellect and reason, which gives me strength and hope. Apart from this indefinable and indefinite urge, which may have just a tinge of religion in it and yet is wholly different from it, I have grown to rely entirely on the workings of the mind. Perhaps they are weak supports to rely upon, but, search as I will, I can see no better ones. Religion seems to me to lead to emotion and sentimentality and they are still more unreliable guides. Intuition—undoubtedly there is such a thing, though where it comes from I cannot say; perhaps from the stored-up experiences at the back of the mind, the subconscious self.

The Harijan question is bad, very bad, but it seems to me incorrect to say that there is nothing so bad in all the world. I think I could point to much that was equally bad and even worse. All over the world there is the same Harijan question in various forms. Is it not the outcome of special causes? Surely it is due to something more than mere ignorance and ill will. To remove these causes or to neutralize their effect appears to be the only way to deal with the roots of the matter. But why should I write of these matters now! I do not want to argue in this letter as the stage for argument seems to be past.

It is hard to be so far from you, and yet it would be harder to be near you. This crowded world is a very lonely place, and you want to make it still lonelier. Life and death matter little, or should matter little. The only thing that matters is the cause that one works for, and if one could be sure that the best service to

---

[1] To Mahatma Gandhi. JN Correspondence, NMML. Excerpts.

[2] In his letter of 2 May 1933, Gandhi wrote: "The Harijan movement is too big for a mere intellectual effort. There is nothing so bad in all the world and yet I cannot leave religion and therefore Hinduism . . . but then I cannot tolerate it with untouchability. Fortunately Hinduism contains a sovereign remedy for the evil."

it is to die for it, then death would seem simpler. I have loved life—the mountains and the sea, the sun and rain and storm and snow, and animals, and books and art, and even human beings—and life has been good to me. But the idea of death has never frightened me; from a distance it seems fitting enough as the crown of one's endeavour. Yet, at close quarters, it is not pleasant to contemplate.

The last fourteen or fifteen years have been a wonderful time for me, ever since I had the good fortune to be associated with you in various activities. Life became fuller and richer and more worthwhile, and that is a dear and precious memory which nothing can take from me. And whenever the future happens to be dark, this vision of the past will relieve the gloom and give strength.

Yours affly.,
Jawahar

8 May, Monday[3]

Bapu has begun his twenty-one day fast today.[4] When the first news of the proposed fast came a week ago I had a shock but I recovered soon. Three days ago came Bapu's letter—typical cry from the heart which bowled me over and I had quite an emotional crisis. I sent him a telegram which I did not like at all. My mind was in a muddle. This was the telegram:

> Your letter. What can I say about matters I do not understand. I feel lost in strange country where you are only familiar landmark and I try to grope my way in dark but I stumble. Whatever happens my love and thoughts will be with you. Jawahar.

4 June, Sunday[5]

I am writing here after a long gap. The great fast is over and Bapu has survived. On the day of his discharge, which was the first day of the fast, May 8th, he suspended civil disobedience for six weeks. I received this announcement with mixed feelings. A shock—and then a willing acceptance of the fast with some misgivings about the phraseology of his statement.[6]

As I watched the emotional upheaval during the fast I wondered more and

[3 & 5] Prison Diary. JN Papers, NMML. Excerpts.

[4] On 1 May Gandhi announced that he would commence a fast for 21 days from 8 May. In a statement issued to the press, Gandhi said the fast was not directed against anybody in particular but was prayer for the purification of himself and his associates.

[6] Gandhi decided to suspend civil disobedience on his release on 8 May in consultation with M.S. Aneg, the acting Congress President. Gandhi had said "How can I take advantage of this release in order to prosecute the civil disobedience or to guide it, as the purpose of the fast will be frustrated if I allow my brain to be occupied by any extraneous matter, that is, any matter outside the Harijan work."

more if this was the right method in politics. It is sheer revivalism and clear thinking has not a ghost of a chance against it. All India, or most of it, stares reverently at the Mahatma and expects him to perform miracle after miracle and put an end to untouchability and get Swaraj and so on—and does nothing itself! And Bapu goes on talking of purity and sacrifice. I am afraid I am drifting further and further away from him mentally, in spite of my strong emotional attachment to him. His continual references to God irritate me exceedingly. His political actions are often enough guided by an unerring instinct but he does not encourage others to think. And even he, has he thought out what the objective, the ideal, should be. Very probably not. The next step seems to absorb him.

What a tremendous contrast to the dialectics of Lenin & Co! More and more I feel drawn to their dialectics, more and more I realize the gulf between Bapu & me and I begin to doubt if this way of faith is the right way to train a nation. It may pay for a short while, but in the long run?

And then I cannot understand how he can accept, as he seems to do, the present social order; how he surrounds himself with men who are the pillars and the beneficiaries of this order. They talk lovingly of 'Bapu' but do not take any risks. How can we get anything worthwhile with these people as our hangers-on? No doubt they will profit and take advantage of both our movement and of any constitutional changes that may come. They always prosper till the final reckoning comes.

I want to break from this lot completely—I want to place our ideal crystal clear before the people. But Bapu always talks of compromise and his sweet reasonableness deludes people and befogs their minds.

There is trouble ahead so far as I am personally concerned. I shall have to fight a stiff battle between rival loyalties. Perhaps the happiest place for me is the gaol! I have another three months here before I go out, and one can always return.

8

Aims and Objectives of Life[1]

13 June 1933

Betty darling,

Physical health is a tremendous help in getting a suitable kick-off in life and some degree of mental equilibrium. Of course mental health does not always follow even physical fitness but it is almost never found with bodily illness or unfitness.

As I read your letter I was suddenly made acutely conscious of a contrast. I felt as if I had been pulled out of my familiar surroundings of thought and ideas and dreams—for action is denied me in the present—and taken to a strange place where phantom figures moved to and fro trying to live the 'gay life' The gay life! The strange quest for something in the market place, something which cannot be measured in terms of gold and silver and is not to be found, search as you may, in the gaily-bedecked stalls, the pursuit of a shadow which eludes us for shadows are always elusive; the frantic attempt to possess the beauty of the living rose by grasping it too tightly and crushing it to death. Mussoorie is but a score of miles away from where I sit and write this letter, and the contrast between life at Mussoorie and life in my little high-walled and thought-infested abode is great enough. But greater still is the contrast, I felt, between the thoughts and desires and passions of the phantom figures that flit on the hilltop and the other phantom that sits and reads and writes and imagines all manner of things. So as I read your letter, reality, if such a thing there is, melted away from me and I fell to musing in a ghostly world of phantoms in which I myself was but a shadow figure. And I saw a procession of Rajas and Ranis and their satellites and parasites dancing away in a veritable *dance macabre* for they danced on a seething mass of hungry and famine-stricken humanity, and their dance led to a sudden precipice over which they toppled, and vanished from the scene. They were rather pitiful figures, relics of a bygone age, trying bravely to keep up appearances but doomed to inevitable extinction.

But then, I wondered, what of the other phantoms? Have they a better fate in store for them? And that led me to strange phantasies, full of an incongruous mixture of doubt and assurance. But why should I inflict my phantasies on you?

[1] To Krishna Nehru. *Nehru's Letters To His Sister* (London, 1963), pp. 29–31. Excerpts.

It seemed to me so strange to read in your letter of people who have no aim in life. Of course, there are many such people but you will find that as a class these people are apt to become or rather to be parasites on society. It is only then that they can afford the luxury of no aim. The vast majority of people have no grand aims but the day-to-day struggle of life absorbs them. And as for others surely the fault is nobody's but their own if they flit about aimlessly and disconsolately. It is not a question of equipment; equipment helps in making one's activities more effective. It is a question of a twist in the mind. Life is not a very gentle or considerate teacher. If one allows oneself to drift about on the surface of the waters, the waves and the tides are apt to knock one against the rocks, but a good swimmer can even ride the storm.

I am myself so consumed by my own aim and objective that I find it extraordinarily difficult to appreciate the want of aim in anybody. Even apart from my personal obsession, I find the world today an absorbing and fascinating place to live in. We live in an age of mighty changes and terrible conflicts, when hope and despair fight for mastery in each thinking mind. A person who is not affected by these events, and who has no desire to take part in them, is hardly a live person intellectually.

None of us can say with assurance what the future will bring. Within the next few years there may even be another mighty war which will reduce modern civilization to dust and ashes. But whatever may happen and whether our dreams come true or remain but dreams, there are some things which help us to guide life's journey. Life is a short enough affair; it is too short for us to make it petty or cheap. Let us not cheapen ourselves but live in the grand manner for the big things in life, and then the vicissitudes of fortune will matter little, and even if we have to go to the guillotine we shall do so like some of the French nobles a hundred and forty years ago (that is the only decent thing they did!) with grace and dignity and a smile on our lips.

Your loving brother,
Jawahar

9

Musings[1]

3 June, Sunday

I am definitely below par, physically & mentally. For many days have been feeling very depressed & poorly. This little yard with its high walls is irritating and so flat & stale. Once a fortnight I go to the jail office to be weighed and this means a little outing from the yard and a walk of fifty yards or so in the fresh air outside. What a change it is! There is freshness & fragrance, & the cool smell of grass & soft earth, and distant vistas.

I suppose it is this close confinement that affects the nerves. And then when any news comes in letters or newspapers that I do not like it upsets me far more than it should. Kamala is again in the grip of her old disease and this news has oppressed me. Indu does not write to me and I get very angry. So during the last few days I have been full of irritation against Kamala & Indu & the world generally. Curious when one is in a bad mood how one finds excuses for it and picks at otherwise trivial matters in the past. It is not Kamala's fault that she is again laid up. What is the poor girl to do? But this means that I shall be lonelier here than ever. And my mind goes back to all the petty grievances I have had against her in the past and dwells on them and this increases my ill humour. I fight against this with little success while it lasts. Gradually it goes away. If I have to write a letter during this fit of ill-humour the letter is bound to be a harsh and unfriendly one. I wrote yesterday to Kamala & others. I had not quite recovered and in spite of all my efforts my letter was harsh and I am afraid will pain her.

---

[1] Prison Diary, 1934. JN Papers, NMML. SWJN, Vol. 6, pp. 255–6.

10

The Death of Motilal Nehru[1]

S.S. "Cracovia", April 21, 1931

Ten days I was with Dadu before he left us. Ten days and nights we watched his suffering and agony and his brave fight with the Angel of Death. Many a fight had he fought during his life, and many a victory won. He did not know how to surrender, and even face to face with death, he would not give in. As I watched this last struggle of his, full of anguish at my inability to help him whom I loved so much, I thought of some lines which I had read long ago in a tale of Edgar Allan Poe: 'Man doth not yield himself to the angels, nor even unto death utterly, save by the weakness of his feeble will.'

It was on the 6th of February, in the early morning, that he left us. We brought his body, wrapped in the flag he loved so well, from Lucknow to Anand Bhawan. Within a few hours it was reduced to a handful of ashes and the Ganga carried away this precious burden to the sea.

Millions have sorrowed for him; but what of us, children of his, flesh of his flesh and bone of his bone! And what of the new Anand Bhawan, child of his also, even as we are, fashioned by him so lovingly and carefully. It is lonely and deserted and its spirit seems to have gone; and we walk along its verandahs with light step, lest we disturb, thinking ever of him who made it.

We sorrow for him and miss him at every step. And as the days go by, the sorrow does not seem to grow less or his absence more tolerable. But, then, I think that he would not have us so. He would not like us to give in to grief, but to face it, as he faced his troubles, and conquer it. He would like us to go on with the work he left unfinished. How can we rest or give in to futile grief when work beckons and the cause of India's freedom demands our service? For that cause he died. For that cause we will live and strive and, if necessary, die. After all, we are his children and have something of his fire and strength and determination in us.

The deep blue Arabian Sea stretches out before me as I write; and on the other side, in the far distance, is the coast of India, passing by. I think of this vast and almost immeasurable expanse and compare it to the little barrack, with

[1] From *Glimpses of World History*, 1934, pp. 55–6.

its high walls, in Naini prison, from where I wrote my previous letters to you. The sharp outline of the horizon stands out before me, where the sea seems to meet the sky; but in gaol, a prisoner's horizon is the top of the wall surrounding him. Many of us who were in prison are out of it today and can breathe the freer air outside. But many of our colleagues remain still in their narrow cells deprived of the sight of the sea and the land and the horizon. And India herself is still in prison and her freedom is yet to come. What is our freedom worth if India is not free?

11

Back in Prison[1]

12 January 1935, Saturday

A terrible and unexpected shock. Early in the morning a telegram came from Nan from Allahabad that Jivraj Mehta had telephoned from Bombay to say that mother had had a stroke of paralysis and was unconscious. Nan was going immediately to Bombay. I held together for a while and then came the thought that I had seen the last of mother. Her face, charged with pain and emotion, as she said goodbye to me on 23 Aug., when I was rearrested and carried off to Naini, rose up before me vividly. As I was getting in the police car she ran up again to me with arms outstretched. That face haunted me. How she loved me and was wrapped up in me. She would ask my advice in the most trivial things and hold on to even a suggestion as if it was the final and inescapable truth. How she had suffered because of my long absences in prison and how she had bravely faced & endured not only this agony but the physical pain of a police lathi charge. She did this more for her love of father and me than for any principle. And yet there was also the pride not to submit.

I collapsed and wept and found some difficulty in pulling myself together. Poor little mother—what a tortured life she had led for many years—all her children in prison and so much happening that was painful. And now the end had come suddenly. Perhaps it was as well that it was sudden and perhaps painless. She would not recover from this stroke of paralysis at her age and in her weak state.

But it was hard to think that I would not see her again. I grow lonelier than ever. The home that father had built up so lovingly goes to pieces. Kamala lies ill in Bhowali—a long long illness with no cure in prospect, mother lying unconscious in Bombay, I in Almora Jail. . . .

I have shivered all day although it has not been as cold as usual. The wind is moaning through the pine trees a dismal note full of desolation. Or is it my mind that is desolate? I am losing most of the footholds I had. India, Allahabad—the mental bonds that tied me to them seem to loosen and I feel

[1] Excerpts from Prison Diaries and Letters. JN Collection, NMML.

like an exile who cannot even look forward to a home anywhere. The moaning wind is a fit accompaniment to my mood. I am weary but there is no rest.

4 February

To Indira Nehru

The clouds are my favourite companions here and I watch them daily. Sometimes they pay me a visit in the shape of mist and they fill my barrack with a damp and sticky feeling, but it is not so bad. Usually they are high up assuming the most fantastic shapes. I fancy I see shapes of animals in them, elephants and camels and lions, and even little pigs. Or they resemble the porpoises that hop about in the sea, or fish lying side by side, almost like sardines in a tin. And then they would change suddenly and coalesce and look like a mighty ocean, and at other times like a beach. The wind rustling through the deodars helps the illusion for it sounds like the tide coming in and the waves breaking on a distant seafront. It is a great game, this watching of the clouds. Once I saw some whiffs of them floating about and I was immediately reminded of Sir Prabhashankar Pattani's peroxide beard. It was really a remarkable likeness and I was highly amused and laughed to myself for a long time. Have you seen this famous beard? It is worth seeing. Puphi—the elder one—knows it well and so you had better tell her of my experience here.

22 February

To Indira Nehru

Why does one read books? To instruct oneself, amuse oneself, train one's mind, etc., etc.—certainly all this and much more. Ultimately it is to understand life with its thousand facets and to learn how to live life. Our individual experiences are so narrow and limited, if we were to rely on them alone we would also remain narrow and limited. But books give us the experiences and thoughts of innumerable others, often the wisest of their generation, and lift us out of our narrow ruts. Gradually as we go up the mountain sides fresh vistas come into view, our vision extends further and further, and a sense of proportion comes to us. We are not overwhelmed by our petty and often transient loves and hates and we see them for what they are—petty and hardly noticeable ripples on the immense ocean of life. For all of us it is worthwhile to develop this larger vision for it enables us to see life whole and to live it well. But for those who cherish the thought of rising above the common herd of unthinking humanity and playing a brave part in life's journey, this vision and sense of proportion are essential to keep us on the right path and steady us when storms and heavy winds bear down on us.

How curious is life! I seem to be learning its mysterious ways still and my wonder grows. It is overwhelming at times and how it mocks! I have returned from Bhowali full of strange thoughts and feelings which I hardly dare put down in black and white. There is a sense of emptiness & loneliness and yet there is also some relief from the tension of past days. At least I feel I know what the trouble is which caused this tension. Understanding is often painful but it is better than a blind search for something which eludes one. And yet I do not know—so many fresh mysteries crop up. So many dark alleys leading I know not where. What can one do except to keep calm and preserve an untroubled exterior and wait for life's playful fantasies to develop? What can one do anyway in prison? At least one can read Blake:

> Never seek to tell thy love,
> Love that never told can be;
> For the gentle wind does move
> Silently, invisibly.

The flowers are in evidence everywhere. The plum trees are covered with white blossoms—the whole tree looks like a bouquet from a little distance. So also the peach tree with its mauve-coloured flowers. And then there is an extraordinary flower, red as blood, growing in bunches on big trees and hanging like a Japanese lantern. It looks so artificial. It is vivid against the greenery of the leaves and one can spot the tree from a considerable distance. There are so many other flowers appearing—buttercups and daisies and *sarson* and others whose names even I don't know.

New birds also are appearing—sometimes strangers visit my barrack—on my way to Bhowali I pass very beautiful Himalayan birds.

Human beings, birds, flowers—each growing in its own way, mysteriously fitting into this strange pattern that is life.

12

Kamala[1]

For the Sword outwears its sheath,
And the soul wears out the breast.

Byron

There she lay frail and utterly weak, a shadow of herself, struggling feebly with her illness, and the thought that she might leave me became an intolerable obsession. It was eighteen-and-a-half years since our marriage, and my mind wandered back to that day and to all that these succeeding years had brought us. I was twenty-six at the time and she was about seventeen, a slip of a girl, utterly unsophisticated in the ways of the world. The difference in our ages was considerable, but greater still was the difference in our mental outlook, for I was far more grown-up than she was. And yet with all my appearance of worldly wisdom I was very boyish, and I hardly realized that this delicate, sensitive girl's mind was slowly unfolding like a flower and required gentle and careful tending. We were attracted to each other and got on well enough, but our backgrounds were different and there was a want of adjustment. These maladjustments would sometimes lead to friction and there were many petty quarrels over trivialities, boy-and-girl affairs which did not last long and ended in a quick reconciliation. Both had a quick temper, a sensitive nature, and a childish notion of keeping one's dignity. In spite of this our attachment grew, though the want of adjustment lessened only slowly. Twenty-one months after our marriage, Indira, our daughter and only child, arrived.

Our marriage had almost coincided with new developments in politics, and my absorption in them grew. They were the Home Rule days, and soon after came Martial Law in the Punjab and noncooperation, and more and more I was involved in the dust and tumble of public affairs. So great became my concentration in these activities that, all unconsciously, I almost overlooked her and left her to her own resources, just when she required my full cooperation. My affection for her continued and even grew, and it was a great comfort to know that she was there to help me with her soothing influence. She gave me

[1] From *An Autobiography*, pp. 561–3.

strength, but she must have suffered and felt a little neglected. An unkindness to her would almost have been better than this semi-forgetful, casual attitude.

And then came her recurring illness and my long absences in prison, when we could only meet at gaol interviews. The civil disobedience movement brought her in the front rank of our fighters, and she rejoiced when she too went to prison. We grew ever nearer to each other. Our rare meetings became precious, and we looked forward to them and counted the days that intervened. We could not get tired of each other or stale, for there was always a freshness and novelty about our meetings and brief periods together. Each of us was continually making fresh discoveries in the other, though sometimes perhaps the new discoveries were not to our liking. Even our grown-up disagreements had something boyish and girlish about them.

After eighteen years of married life she had still retained her girlish and virginal appearance; there was nothing matronly about her. Almost she might have been the bride that came to our house so long ago. But I had changed vastly, and though I was fit and supple and active enough for my age—and, I was told, I still possessed some boyish traits—my looks betrayed me. I was partly bald and my hair was grey, lines and furrows crossed my face and dark shadows surrounded my eyes. The last four years with their troubles and worries had left many a mark on me. Often, in these later years when Kamala and I had gone out together in a strange place, she was mistaken, to my embarrassment, for my daughter. She and Indira looked like two sisters.

Eighteen years of married life! But how many long years out of them had I spent in prison-cell, and Kamala in hospitals and sanatoria? And now again I was serving a prison sentence and out just for a few days, and she was lying ill, struggling for life. I felt a little irritated at her for her carelessness about her health. And yet how could I blame her, for her eager spirit fretted at her inaction and her inability to take her full share in the national struggle. Physically unable to do so, she could neither take to work properly nor to treatment, and the fire inside her wore down the body.

Surely she was not going to leave me now when I needed her most? Why, we had just begun to know and understand each other really; our joint life was only now properly beginning. We relied so much on each other, we had so much to do together.

13

Introspection[1]

It was true that I had achieved, almost accidentally as it were, an unusual degree of popularity with the masses; I was appreciated by the intelligentsia; and to young men and women I was a bit of a hero, and a halo or romance seemed to surround me in their eyes. Songs had been written about me, and the most impossible and ridiculous legends had grown up. Even my opponents had often put in a good word for me and patronizingly admitted that I was not lacking in competence or in good faith.

Only a saint, perhaps, or an inhuman monster could survive all this, unscathed and unaffected, and I can place myself in neither of these categories. It went to my head, intoxicated me a little, and gave me confidence and strength. I became (I imagine so, for it is a difficult task to look at oneself from outside) just a little bit autocratic in my ways, just a shade dictatorial. And yet I do not think my conceit increased markedly. I had a fair measure of my abilities, I thought, and I was by no means humble about them. But I knew well enough that there was nothing at all remarkable about them, and I was very conscious of my failings. A habit of introspection probably helped me to retain my balance and view many happenings connected with myself in a detached manner. Experience of public life showed me that popularity was often the handmaiden of undesirable persons; it was certainly not an invariable sign of virtue or intelligence. Was I popular then because of my failings or my accomplishments? Why indeed was I popular?

Not because of intellectual attainments, for they were not extraordinary, and, in any event, they do not make for popularity. Not because of so-called sacrifices, for it is patent that hundreds and thousands in our own day in India have suffered infinitely more, even to the point of the last sacrifice. My reputation as a hero is entirely a bogus one, and I do not feel at all heroic, and generally the heroic attitude or the dramatic pose in life strikes me as silly. As for romance, I should say that I am the least romantic of individuals. It is true that I have some physical and mental courage, but the background of that is probably pride: personal, group, and national, and a reluctance to be coerced into anything.

[1] From *An Autobiography*, pp. 204–8.

I had no satisfactory answer to my questions. Then I proceeded along a different line of inquiry. I found that one of the most persistent legends about my father and myself was to the effect that we used to send our linen weekly from India to a Paris laundry. We have repeatedly contradicted this, but the legend persists. Anything more fantastic and absurd it is difficult for me to imagine, and if anyone is foolish enough to indulge in this wasteful snobbery, I should have thought he would get a special mention for being a prize fool.

Another equally persistent legend, often repeated in spite of denial, is that I was at school with the Prince of Wales. The story goes on to say that when the Prince came to India in 1921 he asked for me; I was then in gaol. As a matter of fact, I was not only not at school with him, but I have never had the advantage of meeting him or speaking to him.

I do not mean to imply that my reputation or popularity, such as they are, depend on these or similar legends. They may have a more secure foundation, but there is no doubt that the superstructure has a thick covering of snobbery, as is evidenced by these stories. At any rate, there is the idea of mixing in high society and living a life of luxury and then renouncing it all, and renunciation has always appealed to the Indian mind. As a basis for a reputation this does not at all appeal to me. I prefer the active virtues to the passive ones, and renunciation and sacrifice for their own sakes have little appeal for me. I do value them from another point of view—that of mental and spiritual training—just as a simple and regular life is necessary for the athlete to keep in good physical condition. And the capacity for endurance and perseverance in spite of hard knocks is essential for those who wish to dabble in great undertakings. But I have no liking or attraction for the ascetic view of life, the negation of life, the terrified abstention from its joys and sensations. I have not consciously renounced anything that I really valued; but then values change.

The question that my friend had asked me still remained unanswered: did I not feel proud of this hero-worship of the crowd? I disliked it and wanted to run away from it, and yet I had got used to it, and when it was wholly absent, I rather missed it. Neither way brought satisfaction, but, on the whole, the crowd had filled some inner need of mine. The notion that I could influence them and move them to action gave me a sense of authority over their minds and hearts; and this satisfied, to some extent, my will to power. On their part, they exercised a subtle tyranny over me, for their confidence and affection moved inner depths within me and evoked emotional responses. Individualist as I was, sometimes the barriers of individuality seemed to melt away, and I felt that it would be better to be accursed with these unhappy people than to be saved alone. But the barriers were too solid to disappear, and I peeped over them with wondering eyes at this phenomenon which I failed to understand.

Conceit, like fat on the human body, grows imperceptibly, layer upon layer, and the person whom it affects is unconscious of the daily accretion.

Fortunately the hard knocks of a mad world tone it down or even squash it completely, and there has been no lack of these hard knocks for us in India during recent years. The school of life has been a difficult one for us, and suffering is a hard taskmaster.

I have been fortunate in another respect also—the possession of family members and friends and comrades, who have helped me to retain a proper perspective and not to lose my mental equilibrium. Public functions, addresses by municipalities and local boards and other public bodies, processions and the like, used to be a great strain on my nerves and my sense of humour and reality. The most extravagant and pompous language would be used, and everybody would look so solemn and pious that I felt an almost uncontrollable desire to laugh, or to stick out my tongue, or stand on my head, just for the pleasure of shocking and watching the reactions on the faces at that august assembly! Fortunately for my reputation and for the sober respectability of public life in India, I have suppressed this mad desire and usually behaved with due propriety. But not always. Sometimes there has been an exhibition on my part in a crowded meeting, or more often in processions, which I find extraordinarily trying. I have suddenly left a procession, arranged in our honour, and disappeared in the crowd, leaving my wife or some other person to carry on, perched up in a car or carriage, with that procession.

This continuous effort to suppress one's feelings and behave in public is a bit of a strain, and the usual result is that one puts on a glum and solid look on public occasions. Perhaps because of this I was once described in an article in a Hindu magazine as resembling a Hindu widow! I must say that, much as I admire Hindu widows of the old type, this gave me a shock. The author evidently meant to praise me for some qualities he thought I possessed—a spirit of gentle resignation and renunciation and a smileless devotion to work. I had hoped that I possessed—and, indeed, I wish that Hindu widows would possess—more active and aggressive qualities and the capacity for humour and laughter. Gandhiji once told an interviewer that if he had not had the gift of humour he might have committed suicide, or something to this effect. I would not presume to go so far, but life certainly would have been almost intolerable for me but for the humour and light touches that some people gave to it.

My very popularity and the brave addresses that came my way, full (as is, indeed, the custom of all such addresses in India) of choice and flowery language and extravagant conceits, became subjects for raillery in the circle of my family and intimate friends. The high-sounding and pompous words and titles that were often used for all those prominent in the national movement were picked out by my wife and sisters and others and bandied about irreverently. I was addressed as *Bharat Bhushan*—'Jewel of India' *Tyagamurti*—'O Embodiment of Sacrifice'; and this light-hearted treatment soothed me, and the tension of those solemn public gatherings, where I had to remain on my best behaviour, gradually relaxed. Even my little daughter joined in the game. Only my mother insisted on taking me seriously, and she never wholly approved of any sarcasm or raillery at the expense of her darling boy. Father was amused; he had a way of quietly expressing his deep understanding and sympathy.

But all these shouting crowds, and dull and wearing public functions, and interminable arguments, and the dust and tumble of politics touched me on the surface only, though sometimes the touch was sharp and pointed. My real conflict lay within me, a conflict of ideas, desires and loyalties, of subconscious depths struggling with outer circumstances, of an inner hunger unsatisfied. I became a battleground, where various forces struggled for mastery. I sought an escape from this: I tried to find harmony and equilibrium, and in this attempt I rushed into action. That gave me some peace; outer conflict relieved the strain of the inner struggle.

Why am I writing all this sitting here in prison? The quest is still the same, in prison or outside, and I write down my past feelings and experiences in the hope that this may bring me some peace and psychic satisfaction.

14

Family Ties[1]

Darling Indu,

I want you to leave India in a happy and expectant frame of mind. Do not worry at all about me. I am all right. I can manage to find a fair measure of peace of mind wherever I might be. The mind cannot be enchained and I have developed the habit of undertaking great journeys mentally. I am quite sure that I am happier and freer here than great numbers of people who are not physically restricted. My peace of mind would be almost complete if I was assured that mummie and you were faring well in Europe.

Parents are a curious phenomena. They seem to live their lives again in their children. I have many wider interests in life which sometimes envelop me and make me forget much else, but still I am not free from that preoccupation of parenthood and I am vastly interested in your growth and preparation for life. The fact that I cannot help you much personally does not lessen this preoccupation. Parents, again, have a tendency to mould their children after their own fashion and to impress them with their own ideas. To some extent I suppose this is inevitable, and yet the fact is that each individual stands out by himself or herself as a new experiment which life is working out. To force a growing person into a particular mould is to stultify him or her and to prevent growth. Bernard Shaw has called this the greatest of crimes. And so I have tried, with what success I cannot say, not to force my ideas and pattern of life on you. I want you to grow and develop after your own fashion and only so can you fulfil your life's purpose. Inevitably you will carry through life certain hereditary habits and ideas which our home life has impressed upon you in your early days, and I am conceited enough to think that your hereditary background is rather good. But the foreground must be your own creation. I have often asked you what particular subjects of study interest you. The object of my questions was not so much to determine these subjects as to find out how your mind was working. It matters little what subjects you specialize in, provided they are such as interest you. What I am far more interested in is yourself. All round us we see people

[1] To Indira Nehru, Indira Gandhi papers. NMML. Excerpts.

who have had brilliant academic careers and yet who are somehow unable to fit in anywhere. Partly the fault is theirs, but certainly there is something seriously lacking in such a one-sided education.

Right education must be an all-round development of the human being, a harmonizing of our internal conflicts and a capacity to cooperate with others. We are the mirror through which we see others and generally we shall find in others what we look for and expect. If we keep this mirror of our minds and hearts bright and clean, the world and other men and women will have a pleasant aspect to us and we shall be agreeable companions and comrades to them. But if we cloud our mirror and make it murky and smoky how shall we see straight? We shall then become self-centred and selfish, oblivious of our own failings and always finding fault with others. And the others will come to the conclusion that we are highly disagreeable persons and pass us by.

I am afraid I am writing like a professor. Forgive me this while. I do not want to preach or profess but I do want to take you into my confidence. As I grow older and perhaps wiser I attach more and more importance to real education, and by that, you know, I do not mean examinations and the like. I think a proper intellectual training is essential to do any job efficiently. But far more important is the background of this training—the habits, ideals, ideas, objectives, the internal harmony, the capacity for cooperation, the strength to be true to what one considers to be right, the absence of fear. If one attains this internal freedom and fearlessness it is difficult for the world, harsh as it is, to suppress one. One may not be happy in the narrow sense of the word for those who are sensitive can seldom be crudely happy, but the loss is not great for something that is worthwhile takes its place, a sense of inner fulfilment.

For you these questions and problems are yet of the future. Do not trouble about them. It is a little foolish of me to write of them even and thus perhaps to burden your mind when it should be as free of burdens as possible. At your time of life you should grow in happiness for otherwise your youth would be darkened with care and worry. I want you to be happy in your youth for so I renew my own youth and participate in your joy. I do not want you to be a quarrelsome and disgruntled specimen of humanity.

You cannot help carrying the burden of your family with you, not so much in Europe but very much so in India. As it happens, your family has attained a great deal of prominence in the Indian world and this has its advantages and disadvantages for you. I am proud of my father and the example of his life has often inspired me and strengthened me. Trying to judge him not as his son but independently of it, I believe he was a really great man. If your grandfather's example strengthens and inspires you in any way that is your good fortune. If your feelings towards your father or mother also help you in that way, well and good. But your grandfather and father and mother, whatever their virtues may be, have many failings also like all human beings. The public mind, however, especially in India, has a habit of idealizing and dehumanizing the persons it likes and this is apt to irritate, in particular those who are supposed to live up to these imaginary standards. The family and one's forebears thus become a nuisance and a burden. I do not want you to feel this way about us! Do not imagine that the family or family tradition wants you to do this or that or to refrain from doing something else.

You should go the way you think proper and right and if the thought of family tradition helps you in this, well stick to it. Not otherwise. To some extent you cannot get rid of the family tradition for it will pursue you and, whether you want to or not, it will give you a certain public position which you may have done nothing to deserve. That is unfortunate but you will have to put up with it. After all it is not a bad thing to have a good family tradition. It helps us to keep looking up, it reminds us that we have to keep a torch burning and that we cannot cheapen ourselves or vulgarize ourselves.

There is a terrible lot of vulgarity in the world and we see it everywhere in India. And when I talk of vulgarity I do not refer to the poor; they are singularly free from it for they do not try to pose and appear to be something other than they are. It is our middle class that is often vulgar. It has no artistic standards and it has got rather lost between eastern and western culture. It is hardly to blame for it for circumstances have forced this unhappy state of affairs on it. Political circumstances have largely made us what we are and then there is our narrow domestic life. And so when we go out into the world we are often making false gestures which jar on the sensitive. I confess that I find this very painful.

Your loving,
Papu

15

A Solitary Traveller[1]

Almora Jail, 19 July 1935

Dear Kamman,

Along with Indu's last letter, I received a few lines from you also, which you had written before the operation. You had referred in it to my earlier letter in which I had mentioned about my being a solitary traveller. You probably did not understand me properly, and it is also not easy to understand. It is true that I am not very happy. In fact, to be happy in this world is not easy for anyone who is even in the least sensitive, and who looks out of his narrow circle and tries to understand the present world. At the most, he develops in himself an attitude of tolerance and keeping his goal in view, works for it. Only thus can he get satisfaction or happiness, whatever you may call it, but this happiness is not an ordinary worldly happiness. The people who undertake big tasks have to carry heavy burdens. These burdens of mine have gone on increasing—I was not, nor am, bothered much about them, but certainly there has been a change in this during the last two, three years and particularly during the last six months. I have started feeling my loneliness more acutely. That loneliness is of the mind and soul. I know it is my good fortune that a large number of people love me and give me company. But still there is a wide gulf between them and me. Remember that the greatest loneliness is felt amidst a crowd—not in a forest—in a crowd which can neither know nor understand. There is communion of mind and spirit between the people when they can understand each other. Zeal and courage are good things no doubt, but if right thinking is not there, they cannot take you far. Hindus and Muslims who break each other's heads and kill and murder in the name of religion—do they lack in zeal or courage? No knot can be untied by mere zeal and no intricate problem can be solved for the present-day world is full of such knotty problems.

What do we aim at after all? We talk vaguely about freedom and so no two persons can derive the same meaning. Freedom for what and for what purpose? Freedom is not the end. It is the means for achieving another end—what is that?

[1] To Kamala Nehru, Kamala Nehru Papers, NMML. Original in Hindi. Excerpts.

I plunged deeply into politics and obviously became a politician. Yet, my attention was always drawn towards other problems which are the real problems of this world like human relationships, national relations, the relationship between man and man, and between man and woman, or the attitude of adults towards children. Taking together all these relationships, what should be the relationship among the people within a nation? How can there be maximum mutual cooperation, and ultimately, what should be the relationship between nations? These questions are bigger than mere politics. Intelligent people of the world think about these questions, discuss them and try to resolve them. But of what concern are these questions to our country? We are all spiritually enlightened people and want to have direct personal contact with God. Why should we have any concern with men? People here have nothing to do with learning, nor with thinking or understanding. Whatever pictures have been formed in the minds during their childhood stick there till the end. There is not even a desire to understand. They are confident that they know everything and consider those who do not agree with them as obstinate or selfish.

I consider all these things most stupid. Maybe it is my mistake because from the beginning I received a different type of education. The ten or twelve years that I spent in school or college were not of much importance. I got real education later by myself and therefore whatever I am is a result of my own efforts. Man is a mass of ideas. Some people do not outgrow the ideas, formed during their childhood, whatever their age. For more than twenty years, how many battles I have fought and still continue to fight in my mind. The real battlefield is in every person's body and mind and decisions are made there only. Only their shadow falls outside. After these long years of inner turmoil, struggle and deep reflection, I gradually reached certain conclusions. But as I went on untying the knots of my mind, I felt that I was getting further and further away from others. Many of their ideas began to appear to me as absolutely wrong and harmful. The gulf between them and me went on widening. What they considered intelligent I thought to be stupid. And so two ideas took their roots in my mind: first, what is called the religious way is absolutely dangerous for it increases selfishness and suppresses the real matters of spirit. And secondly, there is only one remedy both for the individual and the country, and that is the right education. It is fundamental education which teaches one to think, understand and discriminate. Without this there can be no real progress.

After looking all around me and then at myself, I felt my loneliness more. The journey is not of the body but of the mind and thoughts. One who is not mentally and spiritually one's companion is a stranger. There are lots of fellow-travellers even in trains, but they are strangers. But sometimes you come across a stranger who immediately finds a place in your heart and mind. Sometimes I receive letters from strangers which contain some lines that straightaway appeal to my heart. But I receive these rarely. Very often nobody understands this or even tries to understand it. And when one does not understand another person there is a lack of trust and one fears him and attempts are made to keep oneself away from him or to hide things from him. Where there is no trust, it is difficult for love to sustain.

When I have been observing such things around me then how can they increase my happiness or remove my loneliness? It becomes even difficult for me to act upon the principles I have set for my life. During Papa's lifetime my burden was light and I had no worries about domestic matters. I relied on him for everything. Despite the fact that there was a wide difference in our views, we understood each other a lot and there was no need for us to talk much in order to know what either of us desired. His death removed this great support of mine and one person who understood me somewhat by his love and intellect was no more. Then I felt my loneliness more and also the burden of the household. The burden was not much but some anxiety was there. This anxiety went on increasing because some difficulties came in the way of my following those principles which I wanted to follow.

All these things went on affecting me. After seeing the attitude of my colleagues, I started feeling day by day that I would have to travel alone on my journey. This fact has been emerging more clearly before me for the last six months. It is apparent that this does not mean that I have no companions, no friends to love me or help me when I am tired and exhausted. But there are very few who share with me my thoughts and principles of life. Love,

Yours,
Jawahar

16

A Hundred Pictures[1]

In the long autumn evenings I sat by myself in my room in the pension, where I was staying, or sometimes went out for a walk across the fields or through the forest. A hundred pictures of Kamala succeeded each other in my mind, a hundred aspects of her rich and deep personality. We had been married for nearly twenty years, and yet how many times she had surprised me by something new in her mental or spiritual make-up. I had known her in so many ways and, in later years, I had tried my utmost to understand her. That understanding had not been denied to me, but I often wondered if I really knew her or understood her. There was something elusive about her, something fay-like, real but unsubstantial, difficult to grasp. Sometimes, looking into her eyes, I would find a stranger peeping out at me.

Except for a little schooling, she had had no formal education; her mind had not gone through the education process. She came to us as an unsophisticated girl, apparently with hardly any of the complexes which are said to be so common now. She never entirely lost that girlish look, but as she grew into a woman her eyes acquired a depth and a fire, giving the impression of still pools behind which storms raged. She was not the type of modern girl, with the modern girl's habits and lack of poise; yet she took easily enough to modern ways. But essentially she was an Indian girl and, more particularly, a Kashmiri girl, sensitive and proud, childlike and grown-up, foolish and wise. She was reserved to those she did not know or did not like, but bubbling over with gaiety and frankness before those she knew and liked. She was quick in her judgement and not always fair or right, but she stuck to her instinctive likes and dislikes. There was no guile in her. If she disliked a person, it was obvious, and she made no attempt to hide the fact. Even if she had tried to do so, she would probably not have succeeded. I have come across few persons who have produced such an impression of sincerity upon me as she did.

I thought of the early years of our marriage when, with all my tremendous liking for Kamala, I almost forgot her and denied her, in so many ways, that comradeship which was her due. For I was then like a person possessed, giving

[1] From *The Discovery of India*, pp. 40–6.

myself utterly to the cause I had espoused, living in a dream-world of my own, and looking at the real people who surrounded me as unsubstantial shadows. I worked to the utmost of my capacity and my mind was filled to the brim with the subject that engrossed me. I gave all my energy to that cause and had little left to spare.

And yet I was very far from forgetting her, and I came back to her again and again as to a sure haven. If I was away for a number of days the thought of her cooled my mind and I looked forward eagerly to my return home. What indeed could I have done if she had not been there to comfort me and give me strength, and thus enable me to recharge the exhausted battery of my mind and body?

I had taken from her what she gave me. What had I given to her in exchange during these early years? I had failed evidently and, possibly, she carried the deep impress of those days upon her. With her inordinate pride and sensitiveness she did not want to come to me to ask for help, although I could have given her that help more than anyone else. She wanted to play her own part in the national struggle and not be merely a hanger-on and a shadow of her husband. She wanted to justify herself to her own self as well as to the world. Nothing in the world could have pleased me more than this, but I was far too busy to see beneath the surface, and I was blind to what she looked for and so ardently desired. And then prison claimed me so often and I was away from her, or else she was ill. Like Chitra in Tagore's play, she seemed to say to me: 'I am Chitra. No goddess to be worshipped, nor yet the object of common pity to be brushed aside like a moth with indifference. If you deign to keep me by your side in the path of danger and daring, if you allow me to share the great duties of your life, then you will know my true self.'

But she did not say this to me in words and it was only gradually that I read the message of her eyes.

In the early months of 1930 I sensed her desire and we worked together, and I found in this experience a new delight. We lived for a while on the edge of life, as it were, for the clouds were gathering and a national upheaval was coming. Those were pleasant months for us, but they ended too soon, and, early in April, the country was in the grip of civil disobedience and governmental repression, and I was in prison again.

Most of us menfolk were in prison. And then a remarkable thing happened. Our women came to the front and took charge of the struggle. Women had always been there of course, but now there was an avalanche of them, which took not only the British Government but their own menfolk by surprise. Here were these women, women of the upper or middle classes, leading sheltered lives in their homes—peasant women, working-class women, rich women— pouring out in their tens of thousands in defiance of government order and police lathi. It was not only that display of courage and daring, but what was even more surprising was the organizational power they showed.

Never can I forget the thrill that came to us in Naini Prison when news of this reached us, the enormous pride in the women of India that filled us. We could hardly talk about all this among ourselves, for our hearts were full and our eyes were dim with tears.

My father had joined us later in Naini Prison, and he told us much that we did not know. He had been functioning outside as the leader of the civil disobedience movement, and he had encouraged in no way these aggressive activities of the women all over the country. He disliked, in his paternal and somewhat old-fashioned way, young women and old messing about in the streets under the hot sun of summer and coming into conflict with the police. But he realized the temper of the people and did not discourage anyone, not even his wife and daughters and daughter-in-law. He told us how he had been agreeably surprised to see the energy, courage, and ability displayed by women all over the country; of the girls of his own household he spoke with affectionate pride.

At father's instance, a 'Resolution of Remembrance' was passed at thousands of public meetings all over India on January 26th, 1931, the anniversary of India's Independence Day. These meetings were banned by the police and many of them were forcibly broken up. Father had organized this from his sickbed and it was a triumph of organization, for we could not use the newspapers, or the mails, or the telegraph, or the telephone, or any of the established printing presses. And yet at a fixed time on an identical day all over this vast country, even in remote villages, the resolution was read out in the language of the province and adopted. Ten days after the resolution was so adopted, father died.

The resolution was a long one. But a part of it related to the women of India: 'We record our homage and deep admiration for the womanhood of India, who, in the hour of peril for the motherland, forsook the shelter of their homes and, with unfailing courage and endurance, stood shoulder to shoulder with their menfolk in the front line of India's national army to share with them the sacrifices and triumphs of the struggle. . . .'

In this upheaval Kamala had played a brave and notable part and on her inexperienced shoulders fell the task of organizing our work in the city of Allahabad when every known worker was in prison. She made up for that inexperience by her fire and energy and, within a few months, she became the pride of Allahabad.

We met again under the shadow of my father's last illness and his death. We met on a new footing of comradeship and understanding. A few months later when we went with our daughter to Ceylon for our first brief holiday, and our last, we seemed to have discovered each other anew. All the past years that we had passed together had been but a preparation for this new and more intimate relationship.

We came back all too soon and work claimed me and, later, prison. There was to be no more holidaying, no working together, not even being together, except for a brief while between two long prison terms of two years each which followed each other. Before the second of these was over, Kamala lay dying.

When I was arrested in February, 1934, on a Calcutta warrant, Kamala went up to our rooms to collect some clothes for me. I followed her to say good-bye to her. Suddenly she clung to me and, fainting, collapsed. This was unusual for her as we had trained ourselves to take this jail-going lightly and cheerfully and to make as little fuss about it as possible. Was it some premonition she had that this was our last more or less normal meeting?

Two long prison terms of two years each had come between me and her just when our need for each other was greatest, just when we had come so near to each other. I thought of this during the long days in jail, and yet I hoped that the time would surely come when we would be together again. How did she fare during these years? I can guess but even I do not know, for during jail interviews, or during a brief interval outside there was little normality. We had to be always on our best behaviour lest we might cause pain to the other by showing our own distress. But it was obvious that she was greatly troubled and distressed over many things and there was no peace in her mind. I might have been of some help, but not from jail.

All these and many other thoughts, came to my mind during my long solitary hours in Badenweiler. I did not shed the atmosphere of jail easily; I had long got used to it and the new environment did not make any great change. I was living in the Nazi domain with all its strange happenings which I disliked so much, but Nazism did not interfere with me. There were few evidences of it in that quiet village in a corner of the Black Forest.

Or perhaps my mind was full of other matters. My past life unrolled itself before me and there was always Kamala standing by. She became a symbol of Indian women, or of woman herself. Sometimes she grew curiously mixed up with my ideas of India, that land of ours so dear to us, with all her faults and weakness, so elusive and so full of mystery. What was Kamala? Did I know her? Understand her real self? Did she know or understand me? For I too was an abnormal person with mystery and unplumbed depths within me, which I could not myself fathom. Sometimes I had thought that she was a little frightened of me because of this. I had been, and was, a most unsatisfactory person to marry. Kamala and I were unlike each other in some ways, and yet in some other ways very alike, we did not complement each other. Our very strength became a weakness in our relations to each other. There could either be complete understanding, a perfect union of minds, or difficulties. Neither of us could live a humdrum domestic life, accepting things as they were.

Among the many pictures that were displayed in the bazaars in India, there was one containing two separate pictures of Kamala and me, side by side, with the inscription at the top, *adarsha jori*, the model or ideal couple, as so many people imagined us to be. But the ideal is terribly difficult to grasp or to hold. Yet I remember telling Kamala, during our holiday in Ceylon, how fortunate we had been in spite of difficulties and differences, in spite of all the tricks life had played upon us, that marriage was an odd affair, and it had not ceased to be so even after thousands of years of experience. We saw around us the wrecks of many a marriage or, what was no better, the conversion of what was bright and golden into dross. How fortunate we were, I told her, and she agreed, for though we had sometimes quarrelled and grown angry with each other we kept that vital spark alight, and for each one of us life was always unfolding new adventure and giving fresh insight into each other.

The problem of human relationships, how fundamental it is, and how often ignored in our fierce arguments about politics and economics. It was not so ignored in the old and wise civilizations of India and China, where they developed patterns of social behaviour which, with all their faults, certainly gave poise to the individual. That poise is not in evidence in India today. But where is it in the countries of the West which have progressed so much in other directions? Or is poise essentially static and opposed to progressive change? Must we sacrifice one for the other? Surely it should be possible to have a union of poise and inner and outer progress, of the wisdom of the old with the science and the vigour of the new. Indeed we appear to have arrived at a stage in the world's history when the only alternative to such a union is likely to be the destruction and undoing of both. . . .

As these last days went by a subtle change seemed to come over Kamala. The physical condition was much the same, so far as we could see, but her mind appeared to pay less attention to her physical environment. She would tell me that someone was calling her, or that she saw some figure or shape enter the room when I saw none.

Early on the morning of February 28th, she breathed her last. Indira was there, and so was our faithful friend and constant companion during these months, Dr. M. Atal.

A few other friends came from neighbouring towns in Switzerland, and we took her to the crematorium in Lausanne. Within a few minutes that fair body and that lovely face, which used to smile so often and so well, were reduced to ashes. A small urn contained the mortal remains of one who had been vital, so bright and so full of life.

17

The True Perspective[1]

I do not agree with references to the sacrifices I have made, because I have found myself with a job to do, and when one does the job one wants, there is no sacrifice in doing it. I think of the vast numbers of our people in India, who get no garlands, receptions or mention in newspapers. They also serve. They have made sacrifices and they continue to do so. When I think of the burden that these millions of Indians carry, then I begin to feel myself quite humble, and here in London, this great city of immense wealth, something happens to me. The magnificent buildings and all the signs of civilization disappear and I see in their place the millions of little mud huts back in the motherland. Then I look around the world as it is today and notice the concern of people for what is happening here and there and it seems to me that the only way one can get things in true perspective is to stand on one's head. When I think of what is happening here in England today, I think of the Buddha who once said that the tears that have been shed in the world would fill up all the waters. Some of us have had a strenuous and arduous time in our country, but in other countries also people find it hard, and though it may be difficult not to be bitter, I can assure you there is no bitterness in me, certainly not towards individuals. What bitterness there is in my heart, or in those of my colleagues, is never directed against the human individual but always against systems and machines.

[1] Speech at the Stewart Restaurant, London, 31 October 1935. JN Papers, NMML. Excerpts.

18

The Call of India[1]

21 November 1935

Bharati dear,

I am greedy about books and I buy them rather extravagantly and many friends pamper me by sending them. So I sat surrounded by this pile, glad of the books and also rather envious of them and of the lore they contained, for I doubted if I would have the time to read many of them. And then to the letters.

My present surroundings faded off, my recent memories, powerful as they were, grew dim, and I entered another world—a world of conflict and unhappiness and sordid manoeuvring and gallant endeavour wasted and helpless impotence and doubt and indecision and mutual recrimination—yet, through all this misery, one could glimpse something that was worthwhile. And out of all the jumble of thoughts and emotions that rose within me I began to feel a pull and a call which ever grew stronger. It was the call of India, whatever this may be. And I wondered at this pull and how strongly it influenced me even though spiritually I often felt a stranger in my own country.

Yours,
Jawahar

---

[1] To Bharati Sarabhai. JN Papers, NMML. Excerpts.

19

Dreams and Reality[1]

Bharati dear,

How limited are words and how they hide us from ourselves. Sometimes we seek refuge in their triteness, at other times we lose ourselves in their muse, and ever the reality eludes us, pursue it how we may. And yet, do we really pursue it and seek it? Very few I suppose, have the courage to do so, for reality includes the pit of hell as well as heaven. We avoid it in spite of our brave talk and to escape from it we build up illusions and fanciful castless in the wide expanses of our imagination. Why blame words then? It is we who do not know how to use them rightly or dare not do so.

Does a person ever understand another, or does he understand himself? Individuals meet and pass each other with eyes closed, unknowing and un-known, their drab exteriors covering a deep mystery. Sometimes there is a flash of understanding, a strange revelation and then darkness, though it can never be quite so dark again. And sometimes as a French poet once said, as we gaze into the eyes of our dearest and nearest we find that a stranger is looking at us.

How to bridge the gap between the dreams that fill us and the reality that is so different? How to do it? How? It seems easy when one is young and full of enthusiasm. In our pride of youth we care little for walls and obstacles. It is good that we should feel that way for a while at least during our span of life before weariness and dissolution come. It is good to cling to and lengthen that period of youth. And therefore I wrote to you some time back not to hurry, to linger awhile on the way. And when you pass on to a fuller and more complex life, carry something of the breath of youth with you, something of its idealism, but in place of its egotism try to widen your humanity. Only then can we endeavour to bridge that gap. At best that bridge is a ramshackle affair, liable to collapse at the first touch of storm and tempest. But the effort is always worthwhile; it brings its own reward. And there seems no other way.

Yours,
Jawahar

---

[1] To Bharati Sarabhai. JN Papers, NMML. Excerpts.

20

A Private Person[1]

My dear Psyche,

    Subhas Bose, I found, had taken to describing himself as a writer. Being more modest, I could not quite bring myself to do that. But what am I? In a recent application for a passport, I decided to call my profession 'public affairs', whatever that might mean. I suppose the term is wide enough to cover a multitude of activities, good and evil. And yet, in spite of public exhibitions and the like, I have never ceased to feel a singularly private person.

Yours,
Jawahar

---

[1] To Goshiben Captain, 28 December 1935. JN Papers, NMML. Excerpts.

21

A Bundle of Tempers[1]

12 November 1936

Dear Bebee,

Calcutta after these long years was cordial. The procession was prodigious and excited Bengalis and others shouted and danced with excitement while I adopted the pose of the strong silent man, standing at the back of the car, statuesque, immobile, almost expressionless. I loved to feel the contrast—how terribly vain I am!—and then the humour of it would make me laugh and suddenly thousands would laugh with me, and later grow more excited still. I am never tired of watching a crowd and playing upon its moods and a strange sense of kinship with it comes over me.

. . . I must say that I am myself astonished at the vitality I am showing in spite of my great age. I go on and on and the slight weariness passes soon enough. Almost it was as if some force was pushing me on, not Aurobindo, I am afraid. Like an arrow from the bow I shoot on and I do not know who the holder of the bow was. And the arrow has a bit of flame about it and while it lights others, it consumes itself. But it will last a while still and then one day it will end suddenly. That is the way I should like it to end—a snap and the light goes out. No slow fading out for me I hope. I think I am indifferent as to when this occurs. Life interests me greatly but it has ceased to hold me and so I can venture to play about with it, and when this occurs the burden seems to grow less. How foolishly people talk of sacrifice and suffering. Here am I, a bundle of tempers, pride and a great deal of carelessness, and I am held up as a model of the virtue of self-sacrifice. I really do not care what happens and yet, curiously enough, when I am doing a job I give all my thought to it, concentrate on it, and thus achieve results which would be denied to better and stronger men. Even the passage through a crowd makes me put all my concentrated thought and strength to it, and thus I succeed. How self-centred I am and I go on talking about myself, but you set me to it. Do not worry about me. I shall carry on for a long time yet—that is my fate, and then I shall snap and go on my last procession.

Jawahar

[1]To Padmaja Naidu. JN Papers, NMML. Excerpts.

22

Human Personality[1]

Meerut District (in running car)
22 January 1937

My dear,

I am reduced to such straits, I have to write in a car racing along. Time has become such a precious commodity that one must seize it where one can. . . .

Human personality has fascinated me and I took to the study of psychology and psychoanalysis because of this fascination. What devils and angels we all are, hoplessly mixed up together. And the knowledge of this fact makes one a little more tolerant, a little humbler (a quality, you will tell me, I sadly lack), and there again you will be wrong as in so many things about me. You have built up an idealized picture of me and you are surprised when it does not fit in with reality. And then you rush to the other extreme and suffer pain and are distressed. I am not that idealized picture and I am not as bad as you might sometimes have thought me. I have enough of the devil in me, and it is that perhaps that drives me on, but the angel is there also to curb it and subdue it.

I told you once that sometimes faintly I felt almost capable of murder. Perhaps that was exaggerated for I can't quite conceive myself doing it whatever the provocation. But that faint subconscious feeling makes me understand the murderer. I have no horror of him as I have of the worm-like species of human beings.

And so we swing about from one extreme to another, innumerable personalities tied up together, showing each other at different times and surprising our friends and lovers. Others do not see these changing facets for the mask is on. Be warned therefore and do not be unduly alarmed if you see the devil in me, or even the beast. On the whole I think (conceit) I possess rather less of the beast than most people. But there is enough of the devil. A fortunate chance yoked that devilry to public action which has brought me credit, and yet a little twist and I would have had a mountain of discredit.

What do I know about myself? Little enough. I am, as I suppose others are, a helpless vehicle of strange forces and urges which push us along the road of

---

[1] To Padmaja Naidu, Padmaja Naidu Papers, NMML. Excerpts.

destiny. Yet I would master any destiny. And in my endeavour to do that, I am unthinkingly hard and cruel to others for they pass from my mind and I forget them utterly for a while. Those I love have to suffer most for they attribute all manner of motives to this sudden forgetfulness. It is not my love that wavers but another overmastering passion or obsession that. . . .

(I had to stop suddenly as I arrived at my destination. It was a big meeting and I held forth—felt frightfully sleepy—could hardly keep my eyes open even though my lips were moving. Now I am writing on.)

So the earthly paradise fades away and even while I hold the loved one in my arms my mind wanders away and forgets the present and I become a stranger from another land. I return but it is difficult to capture the old mood—the charm is broken and I look on detached, as through iron bars, on two beings, one being myself. I try to be friendly but friendship is a distant affair. Sometimes the mood returns.

And you, stranger, who are you? I do not know, but I know that I like to see you and be near you and hear your voice, and touch you and to look at your radiant smile. Is that not enough for me? Must I go deeper still? Whether I will or not, unknown depths reveal themselves, and sometimes they please and sometimes they trouble. . . .

My love to you, darling one.

Jawahar

23

Restraining Feelings[1]

Allahabad, 29 September 1937

Bebee—Have you only now realized what a fearful handicap it is to be well brought up? To do what you do not want to do, not to do what you long to do; to hear one's own voice unendingly till one is aweary of it and almost begins to hate it, and yet not to say what one has to say, to repress oneself till one is fit to burst; to meet almost all the dull and uninteresting people of the world and to dream of others who are far away, beyond reach; to look pale and detached when fire rages inside one; to want to kiss soft lips but yet to keep away from them; to yearn to embrace and yet to keep your arms away till they ache. Oh, there are so many things which good breeding brings in its train. You know them, you who are so well-bred. But who told you that I had been well brought up? You presume to know me a little and yet mislead yourself. Neither the governess, nor Harrow, nor Cambridge, nor anything else has taught me good breeding and I am a savage at heart caught and made a prisoner in the mesh of circumstance. From my exalted perch I envy others who are freer.

Jawahar

---

[1] To Padmaja Naidu. Padmaja Naidu Papers, NMML. Excerpts.

24

Rashtrapati[1]

By Chanakya

Rashtrapati Jawaharlal ki Jai.[2] The Rashtrapati looked up as he passed swiftly through the waiting crowds, his hands went up and were joined together in salute, and his pale hard face was lit up by a smile. It was a warm personal smile and the people who saw it responded to it immediately and smiled and cheered in return.

The smile passed away and again the face became stern and sad, impassive in the midst of the emotion that it had roused in the multitude. Almost it seemed that the smile and the gesture accompanying it had little reality behind them; they were just tricks of the trade to gain the goodwill of the crowds whose darling he had become. Was it so?

Watch him again. There is a great procession and tens of thousands of persons surround his car and cheer him in an ecstasy of abandonment. He stands on the seat of the car, balancing himself rather well, straight and seemingly tall, like a god, serene and unmoved by the seething multitude. Suddenly there is that smile again, or even a merry laugh, and the tension seems to break and the crowd laughs with him, not knowing what it is laughing at. He is godlike no longer but a human being claiming kinship and comradeship with the thousands who surround him, and the crowed feels happy and friendly and takes him to its heart. But the smile is gone and the pale stern face is there again.

Is all this natural or the carefully thought-out trickery of the public man? Perhaps it is both and long habit has become second nature now. The most effective pose is one in which there seems to be least of posing, and Jawaharlal has learnt well to act without the paint and powder of the actor. With his

[1] An article written by Jawaharlal Nehru under the pseudonym, Chanakya, 5 October 1937. JN Papers, NMML. He later appended the following note: "This article was written by Jawaharlal Nehru, but it was published anonymously in *The Modern Review* of Calcutta, November 1937. 'Rashtrapati' is a Sanskrit word meaning Head of the State. The title is popularly used for President of the Indian National Congress. Chanakya was a famous Minister of Chandragupta, who built an empire in north India in the fourth centuryBC, soon after Alexander's raid on India. Chanakya is the prototype of Machiavelli."

[2] Victory to President Jawaharlal.

seeming carelessness and insouciance, he performs on the public stage with consummate artistry. Whither is this going to lead him and the country? What is he aiming at with all his apparent want of aim? What lies behind that mask of his, what desires, what will to power, what insatiate longings?

These questions would be interesting in any event, for Jawaharlal is a personality which compels interest and attention. But they have a vital significance for us, for he is bound up with the present in India, and probably the future, and he has the power in him to do great good to India or great injury. We must therefore seek answers to these questions.

For nearly two years now he has been President of the Congress and some people imagine that he is just a camp-follower in the Working Committee of the Congress, suppressed or kept in check by others. And yet steadily and persistently he goes on increasing his personal prestige and influence both with the masses and with all manner of groups and people. He goes to the peasant and the worker, to the zamindar and the capitalist, to the merchant and the peddler, to the Brahmin and the untouchable, to the Muslim, the Sikh, the Christian and the Jew, to all who make up the great variety of Indian life. To all these he speaks in a slightly different language, ever seeking to win them over to his side. With an energy that is astonishing at his age, he has rushed about across this vast land of India, and everywhere he has received the most extraordinary of popular welcomes. From the far north to Cape Comorin he has gone like some triumphant Caesar passing by, leaving a trail of glory and a legend behind him. Is all this for him just a passing fancy which amuses him, or some deep design, or the play of some force which he himself does not know? Is it his will to power, of which he speaks in his *Autobiography*, that is driving him from crowd to crowd and making him whisper to himself:

> I drew these tides of men into my hands
> and wrote my will across the sky in stars.

What if the fancy turn? Men like Jawaharlal, with all their capacity for great and good work, are unsafe in democracy. He calls himself a democrat and a socialist, and no doubt he does so in all earnestness, but every psychologist knows that the mind is ultimately a slave to the heart and logic can always be made to fit in with the desires and irrepressible urges of a person. A little twist and Jawaharlal might turn a dictator sweeping aside the paraphernalia of a slow-moving democracy. He might still use the language and slogans of democracy and socialism but we all know how fascism has fattened on this language and then cast it away as useless lumber.

Jawaharlal is certainly not a fascist, not only by conviction but by temperament. He is far too much of an aristocrat for the crudity and vulgarity of fascism. His very face and voice tell us that:

Private faces in public places
are better and nicer than
public faces in private places.

The fascist face is a public face and it is not a pleasant face in public or private. Jawaharlal's face as well as his voice are definitely private. There is no mistaking that even in a crowd, and his voice at public meetings is an intimate voice which seems to speak to individuals separately in a matter-of-fact homely way. One wonders as one hears it or sees that sensitive face what lies behind them, what thoughts and desires, what strange complexes and repressions, what passions suppressed and turned to energy, what longings which he dare not acknowledge even to himself. The train of thought holds him in public speech, but at other times his looks betray him, for his mind wanders away to strange fields and fancies, and he forgets for a moment his companion and holds inaudible converse with the creatures of his brain. Does he think of the human contacts he has missed in his life's journey, hard-and-tempestuous as it has been; does he long for them? Or does he dream of the future of his fashioning and of the conflicts and triumphs that he would fain have? He must know well that there is no resting by the way in the path he has chosen, and even triumph itself means greater burdens. As Lawrence said to the Arabs: "There could be no rest-houses for revolt, no dividend of joy paid out." Joy may not be for him, but something greater than joy may be his, if fate and fortune are kind—the fulfilment of a life purpose.

Jawaharlal cannot become a fascist. And yet he has all the makings of a dictator in him—vast popularity, a strong will directed to a well-defined purpose, energy, pride, organizational capacity, ability, hardness, and, with all his love of the crowd, an intolerance of others and a certain contempt for the weak and the inefficient. His flashes of temper are well known and even when they are controlled, the curling of the lips betrays him. His overmastering desire to get things done, to sweep away what he dislikes and build anew, will hardly brook for long the slow processes of democracy. He may keep the husk but he will see to it that it bends to his will. In normal times he would be just an efficient and successful executive, but in this revolutionary epoch, Caesarism is always at the door, and is it not possible that Jawaharlal might fancy himself as a Caesar?

Therein lies danger for Jawaharlal and for India. For it is not through Caesarism that India will attain freedom, and though she may prosper a little under a benevolent and efficient despotism, she will remain stunted and the day of the emancipation of her people will be delayed.

For two consecutive years Jawaharlal has been President of the Congress and in some ways he has made himself so indispensable that there are many who suggest that he should be elected for a third term. But a greater disservice to India and even to Jawaharlal can hardly be done. By electing him a third time we shall exalt one man at the cost of the Congress and make the people think in terms of Caesarism. We shall encourage in Jawaharlal the wrong tendencies and increase his conceit and pride. He will become convinced that only he can bear this burden or tackle India's problems. Let us remember that, in spite of his apparent indifference to office, he has managed to hold important offices in the Congress for the last seventeen years. He must imagine that he is indispensable, and no man must be allowed to think so. India cannot afford to have him as President of the Congress for a third year in succession.

There is a personal reason also for this. In spite of his brave talk, Jawaharlal is obviously tired and stale and he will progressively deteriorate if he continues as President. He cannot rest, for he who rides a tiger cannot dismount. But we can at least prevent him from going astray and from mental deterioration under too heavy burdens and responsibilities. We have a right to expect good work from him in the future. Let us not spoil that and spoil him by too much adulation and praise. His conceit is already formidable. It must be checked. We want no Caesar.

25

Psychoanalyzing Oneself[1]

Allahabad, 20 October 1937

My dear,

What am I to write to you? How am I to answer your questions? Surely you did not expect me to psychoanalyse myself in an article, written ostensibly by another for publication? And written at the fag end of a tiring day. But your complaint is a deeper one and no doubt justified. But it is justified only because you will imagine me as something other than I am, something nobler perhaps, more mysterious, more complicated. Have I not warned you against that fatal error? We expect too much from people and then are disappointed. Many things are wrong with me, not only my theoretical knowledge of psychology. That theoretical knowledge is itself a vain delusion. I do not possess it and yet I have somehow managed to impress you with it. The first thing that you must remember about me is that I have a knack of imposing on people (you included, in spite of your insight and perception) and I produce in their minds exaggerated notions about myself. That knack has stood me in good stead in life. Even in examinations I usually did far better than others who were my superiors in knowledge. In life I have done the same because consciously or unconsciously, or both, I always try to create an impression. I succeeded often enough. And so I have succeeded in impressing you with my theoretical knowledge of psychology when as a matter of fact I hardly know anything about it. But you are perfectly right in saying that I have little sense of intuitive perception. Conceited and self-centred people seldom have it.

Again you are wholly right in saying that I have been a failure in my individual relationships—curiously enough there have been singularly few such relationships in my life. Perhaps I felt my weakness, or was afraid of interference with my public activities. To find a reason is rather silly. Such things just happen because one is made that way. My most successful relationships are of a casual variety. I suppose the reason for this failure is my incapacity to give. You mention Bapu, but I am quite sure that I have not given him anything that was valuable or worthwhile. I took much from him; what little I gave was not to him as an individual but to him as an abstraction. This is rather vague and yet it has

---

[1] To Padmaja Naidu. JN Correspondence, NMML.

a positive meaning. I have been and am one of those who take from individuals without giving much in return; if I give at all, it is to the group.

I have begun to discuss myself—I like it, I suppose, and yet it is distasteful. Your questions put me on enquiry and the result of the enquiry was not a pleasing one. When the sanctuaries are empty, what is there to reveal? Out of that barrenness and poverty, what is there to give?

Perhaps I exaggerate but essentially this is true. I do not think I am a secretive individual; I am probably franker about myself than the average man. And there are very few happenings in my life that I would take the trouble to hide. And if I hide them, it is because they are trivial and commonplace and my conceit wants a nobler background. Legend has almost invested me with that background and having got it I do not very much care what it is. I have a measure of restraint but that too is the product of a long loneliness. If thoughts pass through my mind, as they do in abundance, I let them go through and fade away. Some stick or come back again and again. Is it worthwhile giving them the clothing and shelter of words? And how can words imprison the vague fancies of an uncharted mind? Perhaps some sort of intuition might capture them. . . .

Love,

Jawahar

26

Relationships[1]

11 March 1940

Darling,

Your letter of the 20th February has just come. It does not make cheerful reading. I long to help you or to do something for you but I feel so helpless. Not only are you far from me, with a major war coming in the way, but otherwise too I am hardly capable of even advising. Only you can judge or your doctors or others whom you can consult. I wish I could take the burden somewhat from you but I have lost faith in myself in many ways. I am writing to Bhandari and I hope you will also keep in touch with him.

Thinking about you so often, it has struck me how little we have been together during these years, especially since 1930. You were a babe in arms when I became entangled in noncooperation and the like and for some years I saw you irregularly. Then we were together in Geneva for some months before you went to Chesieres. From 1930 onwards I was often in prison and you were first at the Poona school and then at Santiniketan. Later Switzerland, Bristol, Oxford, etc. You came to India in 1937 and I went to Europe in 1938. Again you came to India for a few months but even here you were mostly at Almora. It is almost a year since you went.

. . . Off and on we have met but my mind has been full of you and has formed a thousand pictures which keep me company. Long ago when you were at Mussoorie and I was in Allahabad, I tried to fill the gap created by your absence by writing to you those letters which came out later as a little book. I continued this practice because it soothed me and pleased me and supplied something that I lacked. I seldom thought of writing books, I was thinking of you. But books resulted.

During all these years of separation and thinking of you, you came very close to me, or rather the image I made of you became part almost of me. But then that was a creature of my thought. You were far away.

I moved about in crowds, my days filled with incessant activity. To save myself from being submerged in these crowds I lived my own life of the mind,

[1] To Indira Nehru. Indira Gandhi Papers, NMML. Excerpts.

where I had myself for companion and those pictures of my dear ones which were largely my own creation. The crowds gave something to me of value but they took a lot out of me. Gradually I came to realize that while perhaps I understood crowds a little, I did not understand individuals. Probably this deficiency, which distressed me, was innate in me and had little to do with the crowds or my activity. Only that activity covered and hid it from my eyes. I realized with something of a shock how little one person really knows another, and how often those that are nearest and dearest to us are almost as strangers to us. I had read this somewhere in French poetry and hardly realized its significance. This knowledge with all its disturbing consequences, came to me. I wondered if this was the general rule or at least a common occurrence, or was it peculiar to a few? Meanwhile life passed on leaving many an impress upon me. The crowd ceased to fascinate me as it used to, and I found how utterly alone I was. I had learnt much in the passage of years, but I had failed in the hard test of life. I had proved incompetent and life is hard on the incompetents. Large numbers of people, men and women, came to me or wrote to me for advice about their own personal problems. Because of my political notoriety, they took me to be an expert in matters beyond my ken. The success that had apparently come to me and made me known to large numbers covered a failure in much that counts in the life of the individual.

Public and private life act and react on each other, and this sense of failure has pursued me in almost all I do. With this lack of faith in myself, how can I advise anyone? What right have I to interfere in another's life? I have not made my own a brilliant success and all my good intentions, or so I imagined they were, have not prevented me often from making a mess of things. In my pride I thought that I could do great things, but life has humbled me and shown me the error of my thought.

So, my darling, I am a poor kind of person to seek advice from. Everything that I can possibly give you is yours for the asking, but do not seek advice from me for my mind is disturbed and lacks clarity. Even this letter, I suppose, is a jumble of ill-assorted ideas which will possibly confuse and worry you. I am sorry. But it represents a fraction of my mind. . . .

All my love to you, my dear one,

Your loving,
Papu

27

A Report on His Own Tour[1]

Jawaharlal Nehru returned to Lucknow, late tonight, after concluding a five-day tour of some of the Oudh districts. He spent the day in Bara Banki district, holding meetings at Rudaui, Safdarganj, Haidergarh and Dewa.

The river Gomti had to be crossed by boat in order to go to Haidergarh. This place, being somewhat difficult of access, is seldom visited by outside leaders and Jawaharlal Nehru's visit was, therefore, a great event and attracted a large gathering.

The meeting at Dewa, which is seven miles from Bara Banki town, was unique and memorable. The shades of evening were falling when Jawaharlal Nehru arrived, accompanied by the president and secretary of the District Congress Committee. A vast concourse of people had gathered to hear him.

Many of these had come over from Bara Banki, but the audience was predominantly kisan. Very soon this great audience settled down in an orderly manner and presented a spectacle which will live long in the memories of those who saw it. A sea of heads stretched away into the far distance and lost itself in the gloom. As far as one could see, there were masses of India's kisan humanity, and beyond the range of vision there were still more of them. It is difficult to estimate such a huge crowd, but conservative estimates placed the number at 50,000.

The size of the crowd was impressive and overpowering. Their demeanour was still more impressive. There they sat, row upon row, eager, expectant, a little excited and yet perfectly calm and disciplined.

Jawaharlal Nehru spoke for just an hour and there was perfect silence throughout. Right at the beginning he had asked them not to interrupt his speech by slogans and they carried out his instructions to the letter and held themselves in leash, although their excitement was apparent. Occasionally a quiver of appreciation at something said ran through that mighty gathering.

This was a political gathering, but it was something much more. Jawaharlal Nehru spoke in a serious vein and with feeling. He was evidently moved. There was a sense of vast issues, of great decisions, of the call which might come to

[1] Lucknow, 22 October 1940. This report was written by Jawaharlal Nehru and published in the *National Herald* of 23 October 1940.

anyone at any moment. The multitude of listeners seemed to be in tune with the speaker and seemed to rise above themselves for the moment. There was a hush and a solemnity, which pervaded the atmosphere.

The proceedings began with a very moving poem in Hindi, describing the plight of the kisan in the kisan's own homely language. The audience appreciated this greatly. It struck home. It was obvious that Nehru was moved. This poem set the tone for his speech. He referred to it right at the beginning—to this picture of present-day India.

And then he spoke, with a quiver in his voice, of the dream that had made life worthwhile for him—the dream of the India of tomorrow. He developed this theme and the picture became a living and glowing one. And then, suddenly, he grew sad. For twenty years and more, he said, he had seen this vision and sought to make it a reality. And yet when he saw the condition of the people round about him, their appalling poverty, their miserable environment his heart misgave him. Was this all the result they had obtained after twenty years' travail and labour?

Then again, he changed his mood and spoke triumphantly of the vast inner changes that had come over the people. They were poor still, and overburdened with care and sorrow, but they had got rid of the fear that oppressed them and the hopelessness that enveloped their lives from birth to death. That was a mighty change, which had brought them nearer to Swaraj. And now they stood on the threshold of the future, a future which would mean a changed world and a new India. What this new India would be, he could not say. That would depend on their stout hearts and strong arms. Fate, Destiny, Karma! We were not going to be their slaves, but we would bend them to our will and build India after the picture in our own hearts.

So he spoke on, and that vast audience listened rapt, unmoving but deeply moved. He spoke of Swaraj, panchayati raj and what this was; of the mighty revolution that was taking place all over the world; of the war in Europe and how India was dragged into it; of the satyagraha started at Gandhiji's instance by Vinoba Bhave; of the next step that would follow; of the vast responsibility of each one of us at this tremendous crisis. Be ready and disciplined! Organize yourself, hold to nonviolence, put an end to all internal squabbles and differences and face the future with unity, strength and confidence.

For slightly more than an hour he spoke and he ended by appealing to the audience to give up the habit of touching the feet. They must behave as free men and give up all habits which reminded one of subjection and slavery. Let them hold themselves erect always, bending to no one.

When the meeting ended, Nehru asked the audience to remain seated till he had left and to make a narrow passageway for him to go through. His instructions were carried out and not a single person got up. Right through that mighty gathering he marched, none moving or touching his feet, as they had done when he came. Only their hands were folded in a silent salute and their faces were alight with a new experience. The stars were shining brightly as Nehru motored away to Bara Banki and that multitude of human beings dispersed, filled all the roads, and marched towards their villages.

28

Confining Barriers[1]

5 November 1940

Darling Indu,

And now about you, my darling one. My arrest and sentence must not
make the least bit of difference to what you intend doing. Do not worry in the
slightest. I have deliberately chosen my path, well knowing the consequences,
and have trained myself to it. Age creeps upon me but I am young enough still
in mind and body and hardened to most occurrences. It would distress me
greatly if I felt that the odd things that happen to me upset any plans that you
may make for yourself. I cannot help you much in the making of these plans
and indeed this is not necessary. You are well enough I hope now and will be
quite fit soon. To a large extent circumstances and world happenings control
our lives today. You are tied up in Switzerland and cannot easily get away. The
barriers that confine me are much narrower. We shall put up with these temporary impediments and mishaps without being affected by them too much.
Anyway, my life is on the wane, though it may take an unconscionable time
about it. Yours is to come. Each generation has to solve its own problems, and
that perhaps applies far more today, in this fast-changing world, than ever
before. For a passing generation to impose itself on a new one is bad. Yet we are
always doing it, consciously sometimes, unconsciously most of the time. I have
no doubt that I do it. And yet I do not want to and I would like you to help me
in this. Do not therefore consider me, or what you may think are my wishes in
anything, as a burden and an obstacle in your way. I have almost ceased to have
any wishes about others, individually considered, though I have these wishes
for large impersonal objects. I have learnt from experience that I am not wise
enough to advise others. I find difficulty in deciding many questions for myself;
how can I decide for others, even though they are dear to me?

In the solitude of prison I shall think of you a great deal. I shall sit here wrapped up in my thoughts and you will be a constant companion bringing joy and
solace to me. So I shall not be really lonely, and the years or months that I pass
here will perhaps bring peace to my mind. I shall make friends again with the

[1] To Indira Nehru. Indira Gandhi Papers, NMML. Extracts.

stars and watch the moon wax and wane, and see the pageant of the world, with all its beauty and horror, as an onlooker from a distant place or a different world. I have worked hard during most of my life but I have worked as I wanted to, and life, in spite of many hard knocks, has been gracious to me. I suppose I have hard work still to do. There are no ways of escape from it. But at present I feel somewhat weary in mind. When I feel this way I seek refuge in poetry and the classics. What is wisdom, asks Euripides:

What then is Wisdom? What of man's endeavour? . . .

To stand from fear set free, to breathe and wait,
To hold a hand uplifted over Hate.
And shall not Loveliness be loved for ever?

Do I not betray my age and generation in what I write, and in my quotations? . . .

All my love, *carissima*, and may it be well with you.

Your loving,
Papu

29

Creeping Age[1]

14 November 1940

Today is my birthday—51st. Perhaps a suitable day for beginning a journal. It is a terrifying thought, this creeping on of age. Fifty-one is a goodly age. In China it entitles one to all the respect that is paid to age. I can't get used to the idea that I am getting old, and others help me to delude myself. To some extent I have become associated in the minds of many youth, and, most irrationally, this association continues, even though age may descend upon me heavily. True, I do not particularly feel the weight of it and am still full of vitality. Compared to nearly all my contemporaries, I am younger in appearance and even more so in vitality.

I think I am almost indifferent to death. There are no strong personal bonds which would hold me back if death beckoned to me. In a narrow personal sense I am rather detached, or so I imagine myself to be. And yet I am tied up with so many things and vaguely, at the back of my mind, the idea persists that I have yet to do big work. There is always an element of preparation for this in whatever activity I might indulge in.

[1] Prison Diary. JN Collection, NMML. SWJN, Vol. II, p. 493. Excerpts.

30

Writing from Prison[1]

15 May 1941

Indu,

Letters from prison, with all manner of evilly inclined folk and knaves and fools running their eyes through them and, often enough, blue-pencilling or blacking out passages. How can one write a real, intimate letter under these circumstances? For months I have hardly written a letter from here, except for one or two semi-business communications. I was annoyed at the Govt.'s attitude, irritated at parts of my letters—innocent enough I thought, they were—being blacked out. And so in sheer perversity I did not write just when Govt. relaxed the rule for me and allowed me to write frequent letters. Probably I would still have written to you but you were out of reach and expected every moment to leave England for India.

And yet this business of censorship is no new thing, although jail and CD aggravate it tenfold. During the last twenty years, even since the first CD movement or even earlier, I have always had the idea at the back of my mind that my letters might be read by censors and the like. Even during the slack periods, politically speaking, some kind of censorship always continued. Possibly all our letters were not censored, but some always were, and I could never write as freely and frankly as I wanted to. My political life and methods were such that there was little secrecy about them, though inevitably there were things I did not want to shout from the housetops. But when it came to personal matters it was a different story. Not that there were any great secrets of mine which I wished to hide from the public gaze. But no one likes to undress his mind and soul in public. So, always through all these long years, whenever I took pen in hand to write a letter, subconsciously I kept a check on myself, feeling that strangers would see that letter. I could write with a certain measure of clarity and even my restraint of language gave some evidence of the mind and thought behind. But that could only be a fleeting glimpse and sometimes an irritating one, for there was a suspicion of a veil hiding much.

Perhaps even before these iron bars of censorship enveloped us and made me retire a little more into my shell, I had developed a measure of restraint in

---

[1] To Indira Nehru, Indira Gandhi Papers, NMML. Excerpts.

expression and behaviour. That too, I am inclined to think, was a way of self-protection against a fear I always had of being swept away by too much sentiment. You will be surprised to find me accusing myself of sentiment, for I show precious little of it and am much more of a hard-boiled egg, now at any rate. Yet, I fear, this hardness is only at the surface and underneath lies a sea of sentiment which has often frightened me. A lifetime of disciplined living and deliberate training of the mind and body to make them efficient instruments for the purpose I had in view, has thrown a hard shell over this turbulent mass and on the whole I feel fairly sure of myself. This has given me a certain degree of self-confidence and usually a crisis or difficulty makes me clearer-headed and calmer. Yet on occasions the shell bursts to my great discomfiture.

Apart from this fear of my own tendency to wallow in sentiment, there was another reason which induced me to fortify my shell—that mighty Maginot Line which could after all be so easily turned. I realized that any slackening on my part produced far-reaching reactions on others, and I was alarmed at the consequences. I could not live up to them and indeed I had no intentions of doing so. Thus I caused needless pain to others and I blamed myself for this. And so again I retired into my shell and peeped out of it.

What is Papu driving at, you will say. Why all these patches of early auto-biography? Well, I really do not know myself. My mind cooped up for months past is just bursting and if, by some miracle, I could transfer all those ideas and thoughts to paper suddenly, a fat volume might materialize! The ideas are not methodically arranged as they would have to be if I tried to write a book, and they just tumble over each other and the poor pen cannot possibly keep pace with them. But I am not writing a book and I do not just see myself writing a book for some considerable time. I toyed with this writing idea for weeks and months. I almost sat down to it. But I could not begin and it grows harder to do so, as time goes by.

Why so? Because I cannot write superficially, unless I am writing a political or non-personal article, and even then it is frightfully difficult for a person who is an active politician. He may not say everything he wants to say, he may not discuss frankly his own colleagues or his opponents, for he has to think of a hundred consequences. Every word spoken or written has to be weighed, consciously or subconsciously. How cribbed and confined and imprisoned we are by these iron bars of the spirit.

If this is so about political matters, how much more difficult it is about personal matters. Can anyone be ever really frank about oneself, one's own emotions and mental struggles, one's urges and desires and those half-conscious imaginings which float, dream-like, through the mind?

My *Autobiography* is, I think, about as frank and truthful a document, both politically and personally, as I could make it. Probably it compares favourably with others of its kind in this respect. I poured out myself in it at a time when

I was going through much agony of soul. And yet, in spite of all the pouring out, all the restraints and inhibitions were there, and I suppressed much that filled my mind and heart. To that extent I was untruthful. Especially this was so in the last few chapters dealing with my personal life. It was impossible for me to lay bare my heart before anybody, much less before the world at large.

But these last six years since the *Autobiography* was written have had a powerful effect upon me. I have suffered greatly, experienced many hard knocks in my personal as well as my political life, saw some of my ideals become airy nothings and some of my dearest personal relations fade away. I have survived all this, hardened, matured, call it what you will. I am not just one and fifty years old. Somehow my body keeps healthy and fit in spite of a growing tiredness with it. But I feel as if I was hundreds of years old in mind and the weight of these centuries lies heavily upon me. If this is the beginning of wisdom, then I am on the threshold of Saraswati's haven. But I would barter this wisdom and experience, so dearly bought, for the lighthearted unwisdom of my younger days.

How can I write about these six years with any frankness and throw my naked soul before the public? And if I miss out everything that really mattered to me, what remains that is worthwhile? These six or seven years are bound up in my inner life with Kamala and you. Of course even before this period both of you played a major part in my personal and inner life. But one takes many things for granted in one's younger days; even our struggles have a passing quality. Apart from this, in the twenties I was totally abnormal. I had a flame-like quality, a fire within me which burned and consumed me and drove me relentlessly forward; it made me almost oblivious of all other matters, even of intimate personal relations. I was in fact wholly unfit as a close companion of anyone except in that one sphere of thought and action which had enslaved me. Gradually I woke up to other matters. I realized then, and I realize now even more, what an impossible person I must have been to get on with. My very good qualities which made me an efficient instrument for political action, became defects in the domestic field. Yet I found, to my infinite joy, that those I cared for above all else had gladly and willingly tolerated me and put up with my vagaries. As my awakening proceeded I yearned above all else for those closer human contacts of the spirit with those I loved with all my heart. Unfortunately long and trying periods of jail came, year after year, and normal life and contacts were denied. It was in those days of the early thirties that I wrote those hundreds of letters to you which came out subsequently as *Glimpses*. That was one attempt of mine somehow to quench a little the insatiable thirst that consumed me.

Papu

31

On Personal Style[1]

12 June 1941

Dear Indu,

. . . What is this much-praised style of mine, I begin to think? A certain simplicity and a certain lucidity in short sentences, partly due to clear thinking and having something to say. But partly also, I think, to a certain rhythm and a love of the sound of words. I hate an ill-balanced sentence. It jars. Why this rhythm? I do not know. It is not just an external thing, an ear for it or an eye to balance it. It has to do ultimately with a mental rhythm, or perhaps something even deeper than that. During these past twenty years or so, while you have been growing up, slowly this sense of rhythm in life has grown within me as ideas and actions fitted in, or at least approached each other. It is a soothing and comforting experience and it helps greatly in the tug-of-war of life. The shouting and cursing become unimportant and rather silly, and much of the vulgarity that surrounds us lessens in significance and effect.

It is curious how the manner of writing (even more than the manner of speaking) betrays a person. The style is the man they say. In old China they judged people for high appointments from the style of an essay. Perhaps that is going too far, but there is a lot in it. When outside prison I get a large number of letters from strangers and I have developed a habit of drawing a mental picture of the writer from the few sentences he may have written. Sometimes just one sentence, a few words, give me an intimate glimpse and I feel drawn to the person.

How my letters taper down to absurd topics. But, as I said, when I take pen in hand, it is the tyrant pen that is master and it goes its self-appointed way. And yet what I have written is not so absurd after all. More and more I have come to think that what is important in a person is not what he says or proclaims but what he is and does. There is something after all about these ancient civilizations, like India and China: thousands of years of cultural continuity which has sunk deep into the racial consciousness. Even the poverty-stricken peasant in China and India has some impress of that on his face and in his manner.

Your loving,
Papu

[1] To Indira Nehru, Indira Gandhi Papers, NMML. Excerpts.

32

Time[1]

Dear Bebee,

Two letters from you I have had since I wrote to you last. Both dated May 1941. How helpful these dates are. But they are a definite improvement on 'Thursday' or 'Saturday' which usually adorn a woman's letters. Tell me, why do women deal so casually with Time, the tyrant king of all of us? Is it that they are too afraid of him to approach close to the presence? Or is it that woman lives in the present so much that the day, with its joy or sorrow, is enough for her and the past and future just a blurred outline? Or, perhaps, with her faculty of intuition, she has somehow, instinctively, grasped the idea that there is neither time nor space, but only a mysterious combination of the two, which we, who possess just ordinary three dimensional brains, cannot easily understand? How odd time is. I read once a curious analogy which stuck in my mind. We travel, let us suppose, from Bombay to Calcutta, passing various stations one after the other, and we get the impression that Wardha, Nagpur, Raipur &c. &c. succeed each other in point of time. Yet they are always there. It is only we who somehow sense them in a time sequence. So also the events and happenings of our lives. There they are all the time but we experience them in what we call a time order. The future is there, like the past and the present, but our eyes have not seen it yet. Which all sounds very mysterious and rather silly. But time is odd, I repeat.

Jawahar

[1] To Padmaja Naidu, Padmaja Naidu Papers, NMML. Excerpts.

33

Voyage of Discovery[1]

29 June 1941

Darling Indu,

It might be worthwhile for you to start on a voyage of discovery of India. For many years now I have been travelling in these oceans of time and space. I have seen a great deal of the physical aspect of this country of ours and met thousands, and indeed millions, of its varied people. It is a fascinating journey, not so much in just sightseeing but in its mental aspect, when the past and present get strangely together and the future flits about like an insubstantial shadow, or some image seen in a dream. The real journey is of course of the mind; without that there is little significance in wandering about physically. It is because the mind is full of pictures and ideas and aspects of India that even the bare stones—and so much more our mountains and great rivers, and old monuments and ruins, and snatches of old song and ballad, and the way people look and smile, and the queer and significant phrases and metaphors they use— whisper of the past and the present and of the unending thread that unites them and leads us all on to the future. When I have the chance—and alas! it is not too often—I like to leave my mind fallow and receive all these impressions. So I try to understand and discover India, and some glimpses of her come to me, tantalize me and vanish away.

The real voyage of discovery cannot be confined to books. And yet books are essential for they tell us of the past—of history, of culture, of the way people lived, thought, acted. So why not dip into this treasure and try to understand what our forefathers were?

There are many books which I could suggest to you, though unfortunately good books about India or Indian history and culture have yet to be written. But we cannot wait for them. We must profit by what we have got. Indeed there are far more books now on the subject than there were when I was a boy. I remember well still the excitement with which I saw and read Vincent Smith's *Early History of India.* I was very young then and did not understand all I read. But this book suddenly opened out vast vistas before me and India's past, which

[1] To Indira Nehru. Indira Gandhi Papers, NMML. Extracts.

had been a blank in my mind, became filled with great deeds. That book of Vincent Smith's though far from good (no English I.C.S. man can write a really good book about India) was the first of its kind and it created, not only in me but in others, a new outlook and a certain pride in our past. That book is still a standard book though it is out of date because of recent discoveries. For instance, it does not mention Mohenjodaro. Still it is worth reading and you might get it. Our old copy at Anand Bhawan disappeared long ago and so a new copy had better be purchased. It is worth having and keeping.

Havell's *History of Aryan Rule in India* is not very good history (official historians dislike Havell intensely) but it is a good book, imaginative, understanding and based on the artistic record of India. Havell was an artist. There are many other books I could tell you of but they must wait. One book worth reading for the British period is Thompson & Garrett's *Rise & Fulfilment of British Rule in India*. (Thompson is our old friend of Boars Hill). This is a hefty tome but light reading. We might as well know something of this sorry record of British rule which we want to displace. The book is in Anand Bhawan.

It would also be worthwhile for you to go to our oldest history book—the *Rajatarangini* which Ranjit translated in prison. This book is a big one. Many parts of it are dull reading, some parts are very interesting. As a whole it is a tour de force of Kalhana, the author. Ranjit's translation has many appendices &c., which are important.

Have you read Kalidas's *Shakuntala*? Or the *Mrichhakatika*? The play Ranjit has been recently translating—the *Mudrarakshasa*—should be read also . . . Perhaps he will be able to let you have a spare typed copy when you come next. It is peculiarly interesting just at present as it deals with politics and war and spying and fifth column activity &c.—all over 2000 years ago!

Apart from Ancient Greece, India was the only country which developed a regular drama, which was performed, in the old days. No other country has anything comparable to these two.

Your,
Papu

34

Taking Decisions[1]

Darling Indu,

I have been thinking about our conversation of yesterday's or at any rate of the fag end of it. A little before you went away you put a question to me which rather surprised me in the manner it was put and the impatience that lay behind it. Otherwise there was no occasion for surprise.

I am writing this to you so that you might be able to think about it calmly, have talks with Madan Bhai (to whom you can show this letter if you like) and then, when you come here next, we can have a further talk.

You will remember that when you were going to Calcutta you gave me a note and also said something to the effect that you felt very muddled and helpless in dealing with many things that crop up and wanted my help. That help, my dear, you have always had and always will have so far as I am concerned. It depends upon you to take it and profit by my advice or not. Sometimes I have felt, and indeed you have told me frankly and directly, that you distrusted me and imagined things about me which naturally made it very difficult for me to help you in any way. Those were perhaps moods of the moment which passed. Still, every mood we experience, every thought we have, leaves its impress upon us and moulds our future. It is the letter you gave me on your way to Calcutta that impels me to give you advice again so that your way in life may be as far from difficulty as possible. Life is a difficult enough job and it never forgets or forgives our mistakes.

I have made it clear to you repeatedly that in no way will I obstruct you in following your own decisions about yourself. That is not only a general principle I believe in but I came to this decision about you long ago and have held to it. Naturally as one who is intensely interested in you and attached to you, I have thought about you and your life and future ever since you were a child. I have made innumerable plans about you; I have thought again and again how to help in making you a person who can face life and its problems serenely and with confidence; who can make good in any department of activity that you might take up. What this activity might be, what work you might take up was

---

[1] To Indira Nehru, Indira Gandhi Papers, NMML. Excerpts.

not for me to determine. As you grew up the choice would be made by you. About your marriage I never worried as that, above all, would depend upon your own choice. What I was most interested in was your bodily and mental development, keeping pace and harmony with your emotional development and thus creating and building up what is called an integrated human being. Once that is achieved or partly achieved it does not much matter what one does or who one marries, for one's choice comes out of a well-regulated and ordered scheme of the body, mind and emotions.

I had hoped that after your formal education at a university was completed, you might supplement it by some travel in various countries and especially by specializing in two or three languages, other than English. I wanted you to go to Russia to see things there for yourself. This background of mental training and knowledge would just be the foundation on which you would build your future life and growth. College, etc., does not teach very much but it serves an important purpose by training and developing our minds and making us capable of self-educating ourselves in life's ways later on.

Then with this background of mental training and a wider culture I expected you to return to India and discover the fascinating thing that is India. In this task I wanted to help you personally and I expected you to help me somewhat also. There are very few persons in India, I think, who could give effective help not only in public life but almost for any activity, other than technical, better than I could. Hundreds and thousands of young men and girls have wanted to serve with me as secretaries or in some way to get this training. I have never encouraged anyone and have shouldered my burdens alone, for I had always imagined you to occupy that niche. Till you come, that niche had better be left empty. No one else could take your place.

It was with this idea ever hovering in my mind that I wrote piles and piles of historical and other letters to you. I wanted gently, slowly but yet surely to train your mind in that wider understanding of life and events that is essential for any big work.

Of course I did not think of you just as a secretary to me or otherwise attached to me all the time. That would have been excessively selfish of me. I knew you would marry and I wanted you to do so and thus to live your own life. I only wanted to give you some special training which would stand you in good stead in later life. It was a training for which many people hanker and hanker in vain.

All these and hundreds of other ideas passed through my mind day after day, month after month, during these past years. There were so many inte-resting and odd kinds of work that I could find for you, which would help you in developing and becoming more efficient. So that when the time came you could with assurance tackle any big national job. And the time for this will surely come for our people before long.

Somehow things did not turn out as I had hoped. Your ill health came in the way, your education was interrupted and the world's troubles and wars and conflicts, and our own national difficulties were always intervening. This has to be accepted and all one can do is to adapt oneself to it all and still forge ahead to achievement. Difficulties and obstructions should not frighten us or upset us. Often they train us and harden us much more than the soft things of life.

All this is the past. It is largely over. I mention it so that you may realize how I have pictured you to myself and woven tales about your picture in my hand. It takes a good deal of adjustment for me to throw all these tales and fancies into the scrap heap.

All this again had little to do with the question of your marriage. Having left that to you, I gave no thought to the matter.

Gradually what began to worry me was a feeling that you were very far away from me, from my thoughts, my fancies and ideas, my hopes and dreams. A gulf existed between these thoughts and ideas of you in my mind and you. I thought it was a passing phase and that as soon as we could be together again the gulf would disappear and I could tell you about my dreams and share them with you.

Then I realized that some things that meant a great deal to me had little significance for you. Our sense of values seemed to differ vastly. That hurt. For a sense of values lies at the very basis of life and governs it. All culture is after all a sense of values, certain restraints, certain responsibilities joyfully undertaken.

What pained and surprised me was the casual way in which you were prepared, and even eager, to discard very precious traditions and heritage, some things that were part of my being and which I hoped would be yours. It was rare good fortune for us to have this heritage and I, for one, was proud of it.

Life does not give its gifts over and over again, and we kick away its valuable gifts at some peril to our future.

All this as a background. Now for the present.

I should have thought that the obvious thing for you or anyone else to do on return from abroad, after a fairly long absence, was to look round and get your bearings. Try to understand your environment, the changes that have taken place and so gradually adapt yourself to them, and then go ahead. This was the normal course for any student returning home. It was perhaps more necessary for you and at this particular time of war and conflict. You have been seriously unwell. You require physical and bodily rest. Above all peace of mind to consider all problems especially those relating to your own life, calmly and without excitement. Marriage is an important thing in life. It may make or mar one's life. And yet marriage is something smaller than life. Life is a much bigger thing. It is difficult enough to understand it, still one has to try.

So I had thought it natural for you to have a period of rest from conflict in your mind. Why any conflict? It you want to marry Feroze, well go ahead and do it. No one will stop you. So why worry about it? Therefore no conflict or worry was necessary.

As it happens even your present health indicates, I believe an avoidance of marriage for some time, some months at least. But that is for doctors to say. Apart from that, from most points of view there is an element of absurd haste in your returning from Europe in frail health and suddenly marrying.

It is always important to do a thing in the right way. Indeed how one does anything is as important as the thing itself. If in our attempt to solve a problem we create half a dozen new problems, we have not acted very wisely. Therefore, let us pay heed to the manner of doing it and avoid anything that leads to future difficulty. To create irritations and ill will in others is never worthwhile. Give them time and opportunity to adjust themselves. Avoid also breaking as far as possible with old contacts and ways. You do not know what the new ones will be like and you might well be landed high and dry. I am not referring to Feroze but life's other contacts, including Feroze's family. Of course one does not marry a family; yet one cannot ignore it either and it can make itself pleasant or unpleasant. I know nothing about his family or other contacts.

All these and so many other matters require careful consideration by you. There is too much of casualness in your approach to the question.

If you have decided upon any course of action, it is up to you to inform and discuss it with some of those who are intimately connected with you. Not only courtesy demands it but ordinary good sense. You smooth your way in this manner and if you do not remove oppositions, you tone it down. Also every important matter should always be discussed with others. It does not matter if you agree or disagree with them. The discussion always throws fresh light on many aspects and helps our own thought. To avoid such discussions is to admit the weakness of one's own thoughts and position and allow oneself to drift or be driven—and both are bad. Each one must be master or mistress of one's own fate.

Therefore, do not worry yourself. Remove any burdens you have in your mind and look at the world and everyone with clear and bright eyes, unafraid and uncowed. Remember that every vital decision rests with you, not with others. So why worry? Take your time, develop calmness and restraint and when the moment comes take the step indicated openly and after telling your friends. Any other course will inevitably add to future worries and be a burden to your mind. It is not worthwhile. Also try not to break with your past and the world you have lived in. That will be painful for you and for others and will bring fresh problems in its train. Besides it is not necessary. There is so much worthwhile in that old world, so many people who would do anything to help you, that to walk away from them, as if they did not count for anything, is unjust to you and to them. . . .

When you come to any decision think out the future consequences in detail, in so far as you can. It is not good to jump into any action without previous thought about the consequences.

I have given you above my ideas on the subject. Think about them—discuss them with Madan Bhai—and then forget about it all for the present and do some regular work in Mussoorie.

If you want to discuss this matter with me further when you come next, I shall gladly do so. But I have had my say in this letter and told you how, I think, you should act, feeling as you do. To that for the present I have nothing to add.

Love,

Your loving,
Papu

35

Perceptions[1]

24 July 1941

My dear Bapu,

I have been taught self-restraint about my personal feelings and emotions and the habit of confessing to people or taking them into one's confidence is totally alien to me. I live a lonely personal life and the only person who could occasionally peep into it was Kamala. Few people even know or realize how I felt about Kamala. It seems rather silly to say so and the expression is a trite one, but throughout our married life I was very much in love with her. Why this was so, I do not know; such feelings are spontaneous and often utterly unreasonable. It was not just because she was my wife or because she had certain good qualities. Neither of these facts lead to a man's love for a woman. Affection there may be, a feeling of contentment with each other and all that through close associations and mutual interests. But love as I conceived it and as it came to me was something different, something electric, something often painful. It was not the conception of duty owed or an obligation to be discharged. I would hate to have someone feel that it was his or her duty to love me. I want no such purchase. . . .

My conception of marriage and sex may strike you as odd; they certainly differ from yours. In my own married life there was this unusual fact (I think it is definitely unusual in sedate and long-married people) that while I might be irritated with Kamala or quarrel with her, her touch would always thrill me. I was the worst possible husband for any woman owing to my intense public activities, preoccupations, absences and jail. Yet always there was a certain magic in our relationship. She was a mystery to me and I was a mystery to her and something of the initial novelty and surprise never wore off, and though we grew older in years, we remained very young in our outlook. It is rather odd that I should make this confession to anyone, and more especially to you, whose ideas of the relationship between man and woman seem very extraordinary to me. I am a pagan at heart, not a moralist like you, and I love the rich pagan culture and outlook on life of our ancients, their joy in beauty of all kinds, in

---

[1] To Mahatma Gandhi, 24 July 1941. JN Papers, NMML. Excerpts.

richness of life and a wise understanding of human nature with all its virtues and frailties.

India grows upon me more and more and I am ever discovering something new in her. It is a voyage of discovery which has no end. And yet people call me, because of my ways and outlook, a European and an Englishman. They are right in a way and yet only superficially so. I do believe intensely in India, though it would be hard to define this belief. I have never yet been disappointed in the common people of India perhaps because I did not expect too much from them. But I am irritated and disgusted often enough by our middle classes (my own kind) who have lost all sense of values, of beauty, of what is essential in life. Their vulgarity and weakness and limited outlook apall me. Always they seem to be willing to sell their immortal selves for a dirty mess of pottage.

I am at peace here and, as usual, quite fit and feeling absurdly young for my advanced years. The realization that I am over fifty-one always surprises me. I can't quite believe it! I do not worry at all, or perhaps it would be more correct to say, that I worry seldom. At no period previously in jail have I had this feeling of inner calm. The days pass easily enough with reading, spinning and various other activities. The present does not engage my attention much; whatever I might be doing, my mind tries to probe into the future, to imagine what this mad world will be like tomorrow and how and where India will fit into it. Why do people worry so much about getting something quickly and now, and fear that if they do not get it, it might elude their grasp? Do they not realize that we have come to the end of an age and there is no further room for quibbling and political trickery and manoeuvre and all the arts of the average politician? Only strength counts in this naked age which lays bare all weakness. It may be the strength of armed might, which is above law and lawyers, or some other form of inner strength, which also is above law and lawyers. A people or a nation which still thinks in terms of law and lawyers is lost.

With my love to you,

Yours affectionately,
Jawaharlal

36

Mountains and Rivers[1]

28 July 1941

Darling Indu,

You and I, in our respective abodes, are on the verge of Garhwal. I can see the Garhwal foothills from here and a longish walk will take you to the district boundary. The knowledge of this surpassing beauty so near us and yet so far from this warring world, so peaceful and unperturbed by human folly, excites me. Those strange people who were our ancestors in the long ago felt the wonder of these mountains and valleys and, with the unerring instinct of genius, yoked this sense of awe and wonder to man's old yearning for something higher than what life's daily toil and conflicts offered, something with the impress of the eternal upon it. And so for two thousand years or more, innumerable pilgrim souls have marched through these valleys and mountains to Badrinath and Kedarnath and Gangotri, from where the baby Ganga emerges, so tiny and frolicsome, but to grow and grow in her long wandering till she becomes the noble river that sweeps by Prayag and Kashi and beyond.

Shall I ever go wandering again in these mountains, and pierce the forest and climb the snows and feel the thrill of the precipice and the deep gorge? And then lie in deep content on a thick carpet of mountain flowers and gaze on the fiery splendour of the peaks as they catch the rays of the setting sun? Shall I sit by the side of the youthful and turbulent Ganga in her mountain home and watch her throw her head in a swirl of icy spray in pride and defiance, or creep round lovingly some favoured rock and take it into her embrace? And then rush down joyously over the boulders and hurl herself with a mighty shout over some great precipice? I have known her so long as a sedate lady, seemingly calm, but for all that, the fire is in her veins even then, the fiery vitality of youth and the spirit of adventure, and this breaks out from time to time when her peaceful waters seem angry and tumble over each other and spread out over vast areas.

I love the rivers of India and I should like to explore them from end to end, and to go back deep into the dawn of history and watch the processions of men and women, of cultures and civilizations, going down the broad streams of

[1] To Indira Nehru, Indira Gandhi Papers, NMML. Extracts.

these rivers. The Indus, the Brahmaputra, the Ganga, and also that very lovable river of ours—the Jamuna.

Heigh ho! How many things I would like to do, how much there is to see, how many places to go to! What wonderful dreams we can fashion out of the past and out of the unknown future that is still to be! Men come and men go but man's dreaming and quest go on, and when failing hands can no longer hold the torch, others, more vigorous and straight, take hold of it, and they in their turn pass it on to yet others still.

How I begin musing when I write to you.

Love,

Your loving,
Papu

37

Family as A Unit[1]

28 October 1941

Darling Betty,

My dear, how can I advise you or Raja about family affairs? The decision has to be made by the persons concerned and by no others because it depends entirely on one's own outlook on life as well as one's reaction to what is happening in India and the world. No rule of thumb can be applied. If I had been personally concerned in such a matter, I would have had no difficulty in dealing with it as my mind is quite clear about relative values in life and what my own duties and obligations are. But if the mind is not clear then difficulties arise and endless and inconclusive argument. Going to jail is a trivial matter in the world today which is being shaken to its foundations. As a mere routine it has no doubt some value and I think does one good. But that value is not very great unless there is an inner urge to do it. If an inner urge is present then little else matters, for that represents something vital.

Raja and you should try to be clear in your minds about the kind of future you are arriving at and try to realize that future, in so far as you can. The large and joint families of the past no doubt served a useful purpose and fitted in with the social structure we had evolved through long ages. But that structure is cracking up now and it cannot survive in its old form. It is pulled in two different directions at the same time—the individual asserting his right to his own way of living, and the larger social group, the community or nation, demanding a unified pattern and equal opportunities for all. Between these two pulls, the middle pull of the joint family becomes less and less; it comes in the way of the individual life as well as the large natural life. It does not fit in with the thought and elemental forces that move the world today. So it must fade away, as it is indeed doing. But we are such a huge country and with such deep roots in the past, that major changes take time. Yet in these days time itself moves quickly.

I do believe that the family as a unit is important, especially the smaller family, and fulfils a psychological need. It will survive. But the economic bonds

[1] To Krishna Huthersing. *Nehru's Letters to His Sister*, (London, 1963), pp. 81–5.

that tie up large numbers of persons in a joint family tend to become real bonds, helping the individual often but also suppressing him and preventing growth. Where a common outlook on life is lacking they become a nuisance to all concerned and a constant source of irritation. There is a feeling, and you have mentioned it, that the burden falls on some and not on others, that some are not pulling their weight, that some sow while others reap, and so on. One cannot argue against this for it all depends on our sense of values. Is money-making our test or some other also?

Then again consider even money-making today. Only a fool or an infinitely wise man will dare to prophesy for the future in a changing world. But even a man of average intellect can say that everything is going to change during the next few years all over the world, including India. It is indeed changing before our eyes, and it is quite likely that the millionaire may become a thing of the past. The whole conception of money may change and all our friends who are piling up gold or silver, or mostly paper in the form of securities or currency notes, may suddenly find the bottom knocked out of their treasure chest, and the chest empty. Whoever wins in this war, that may well happen. We shall see before we are much older.

In times of storm and stress the only capital that counts is intelligence, individual capacity to face a crisis calmly and to overcome it. The Bank of France and the French millionaires did not save France—indeed they helped in her downfall—and now they have to part with their millions also. If we in India as individuals and as a nation have the necessary intelligence, moral fibre and staying power, it will go well with us; otherwise not.

Do not forget that India and China, in spite of their present difficulties, have shown tremendous staying power for ages past. They have done so, I believe, because of their sense of moral values.

I have written quite an essay and I could write on almost indefinitely. But I must have pity on you and desist. The point is that a time comes in the life of every individual when there should be some certitude of his way of life—objectives, etc. He may change repeatedly with changing circumstances even afterwards but all the essential adaptations and the background remain much the same, or it changes subtly producing more certainty. Without this there is continuous shifting and consequent distress of mind.

I do not know what life holds for me but I am not afraid of it and I do not think anything is likely to happen to India or the wide world which will bowl me over. At least so I think in my conceit. I am slowly developing a measure of serenity, of poise, of strength of purpose which is impersonal. It does not matter if I die, as die I must some time or other. Millions are dying daily in war or otherwise. The smaller and more personal problems gradually lessen their hold on me and I feel more detached. I want to be unburdened, if not unentangled personally. I do not know that I shall succeed, or indeed that I want to do so.

For I am attached enough to life and its diversity and richness. I am perfectly willing to face it as pleasantly as I can and to take such joy from it as is possible, subject to my own mental limitations. But I want to be equally willing and prepared for the full stop when that comes.

Meanwhile there is much to do and I want to do it with every ounce of energy. And if, as at present, I cannot indulge in activity I prepare myself for it, physically and mentally, and store up energy.

So there! Do not take me too seriously when I begin talking about myself. That comes with age. It is a sure sign—this mounting a pulpit and holding forth. I began by writing about you and drifted inevitably to the first person. I am sorry. I apologize.

But the point is that you people worry too much and often about unimportant matters. Do not do so. It makes one dull and that is bad. One should take life as it is—and it isn't much to shout about—and just refuse to allow petty or big troubles to put us out. It is remarkable how they vanish if one treats them in this way. Just think of the big things and the major upsets that are happening all over the world, and thinking of them you will gain a sense of perspective and your own little troubles will sink into insignificance.

Your loving brother,
Jawahar

38

Stray Notes[1]

Zero hour of the world

Indonesia—Korea—Ceylon—Nepal.
Emotional reactions—debasement of moral standards.
Demoralization—falsehood.
Danger of being swept away by passion.
Go to the people—find out what they feel or say. Not playing politics.

What politics have we played at? =This not the Congress way for 22 years. Many of us would not be on this stage if the game was just a political one— Circumstances have forced us.

Spending our lives in prison=Not the action of the moment but due to deep-seated conviction and urges before which all else is secondary and immaterial. Something more than politics.

Hope when War came—Dashed and broken—and a campaign of misrepresentation and breaking national movement—Congress . . .[2] Britain.

Frustration and desparation and a firm anti-British sentiment—

Lesson of France—Burma &c.

Evacuees.

& how! Government of India—incompetence—corruption &c defeated— lack of will to resist except demand for freedom.

Publication of papers.

मेरे कानों में हिन्दुस्तान की आवाज गूंजी–

दिलों के तूफान

---

[1] Notes made by Jawaharlal during the Congress Working Committee meeting on 5 August 1942. JN Papers, NMML.
[2] One word is illegible.

आर्जू-तमन्ना थी-अब भी वही ही लेकिन
सबसे बड़ी यह के यह सिलसिला ख़तम हो-चाहे
हम ख़तम हों [3]

Past failure—How to remedy? Not by carrying on in the old way—

We do not wish to have dominion over others—but we cannot tolerate dominion over us.

World federation—(Nepal &c.)

Muslim League

Immediate peril to India—how to meet it.

Resistance to Japan or Germany—No submission whatever happens. Real danger to us *now*—later to Britain.

Throwing our bread upon the waters.

Quit India—

Independence—

49 crores

I do charge the British Government with bitter hostility to the people of India, with deliberate falsity and perversion, with every attempt to disrupt India—with enmity to the Congress.

Sowing bitter seeds of hatred and now the harvest approaches.

Every fibre of my body rebels against the British Government.

British Labour Party

Change in me
Rajaji

Tagore Centenary [*sic*]. His last message—
Crisis in Civ[lization]. [4]

---

[3] Echoed in my ears the voice of India—The storms raging in people's hearts! A yearning, an aspiration was there. And it is there, there still. But the most important of all—This chain must break, even if we break!

[Note:—Literal translation from Hindi. This does not appear to be a quotation but Jawaharlal's own thoughts in semi-verse style.]

[4] Tagore's last message was read out in Santinketan on 14 April and later printed as a booklet entitled *Sabhyatar Sankat (Crisis in Civilization)*.

Our cup is full.
Give my life for China—Russia
Prayer to the spirit of India

If our proposals accepted no chaos—no disruption &c. Cripps—No Viceroy &c!
Only on refusal possibility of chaos.
If—Out of chaos—dancing stars of freedom.

Maulana
Acid test—Does our proposal help or injure cause War?—against aggression.

39

Effects of Jail Life[1]

16 April 1943

Darling Indu,

What shall I write to you, my dear? Of course I can write about a host of things. Reading your letter again I realize what a powerful effect jail has on our mental make-up. It makes us grow up mentally and gives us a different, and perhaps a truer, perspective on life and the world. Partly because we are thrown on our own mental resources much more than elsewhere, partly because of new experiences, new companions, so different from those we are used to. All of us are apart to live and move in our own little grooves, imagining that one's own particular rut is an epitome of the world. It is curious that jail life, which is a terrible narrowing of the world of experience and sensation, often gives us deeper experiences and sensations. It depends on the individual and his or her capacity to receive and profit by these new experiences and thus to grow in mind. Some do not and cannot profit by them and are even injured mentally and, of course, physically. Others develop a richer life, a deeper understanding, a more human outlook and a poise which gives a tone to their whole existence. For my part, I have no doubt that I have managed to profit by my visits to jail. The very lack of things in jail, the absence of normal family and social life, the long hours alone, the want of the most ordinary amenities we are so used to and take for granted, gives a value and significance to them and we enjoy them all the more when we have the chance. Prison is the true home of that dreadful thing ennui, and yet, oddly enough, it teaches us to triumph over it. And so we grow more vital, more aware of the manifold variety of life and even, in a sense, younger in mind. That is, in a sense, a contradiction for the mind grows older too in prison, or at least more mature. But then life is full of such contradictions. Immaturity is not really youth; it is more like childhood.

Being your father, my mind inevitably goes back to a similar period of my own growth. I took a mighty long time in growing—perhaps I am not quite grown-up yet! Or, more correctly, I am grown-up in part only; the rest of me

[1] To Indira Gandhi, Indira Gandhi Papers, NMML. Excerpts.

is still struggling to find out and understand. I was amazingly non-grown-up even in my middle twenties and even afterwards the process was slow. Possibly that is why I am still younger in mind and body than almost all my contemporaries. I imagine you are more grown-up now than I was when I was your age. That is easily understandable for you have lived through a far more turbulent period of history than I had done then. My life till then had been quiet and peaceful and almost uneventful—the events were piling up for later days.

It was about the time of your birth, or soon after, that these events started on their mad career. Almost you were a child of a turbulent world. I do not know what memories of these early days you carry about you. But whether you remember them or not, they must have influenced you and subconsciously they must cling to you. You wrote to me once about the old days in Anand Bhawan. But you have no real experience of those old days for the great change came in our lives when you were a babe in arms. It is difficult for the younger generation to picture to themselves that world which vanished, it seems now, so long ago. They have lived all their young lives transitionally, and we have all become travellers and wayfarers marching on and on, sometimes footsore and weary, but without resting place or haven. Yet, for those who can adapt themselves to this continuous journeying, there is no regret and they would not have it otherwise. A return to the dull and uneventful past is unthinkable.

I have few regrets. But one there is that in your childhood and early girlhood I saw so little of you.

Your inside is tough of course, I know that. I want that outside of yours also to grow tough. It is a nuisance otherwise. I am sure that you will succeed in strengthening your body. It requires will and intelligence.

My love to you darling one—

Your loving,
Papu

40

Cause and Effect[1]

4 September 1943

Darling Indu,

I have dipped into all manner of books on philosophy and science—from the Upanishads and Plato and Indian and Greek philosophy to many of the modern expositions and inquiries. It is a fascinating subject opening out innumerable avenues of thought, and yet it seems to lead nowhere. At any rate I do not think I am much wiser. Perhaps layer upon layer of their thoughts accumulate in the mind and give a certain depth. But my tendency is to turn away from metaphysical speculations. But no thoughtful person, however scientific he claims to be, can entirely turn away from some aspect of metaphysics, or let us call it the, for the present, unknown, if not unknowable. One simply must seek and inquire and delve deep—the Faustian attitude—whatever the consequences. (I am reading Faust again.) Recently I read Nietzsche. I remember reading him rather carelessly when I was in Cambridge. I dislike his fundamental thesis, but there is much that is attractive in what he says, or perhaps it is the manner of saying it that fixes the attention.

We come back after all to a certain pragmatic attitude. I think you are perfectly right in saying that our main trouble is a lack of organic connection with nature or life. We have gone off at a tangent from the circle of life, uprooted ourselves and thus lost the sense of fullness and coordination with nature. A peasant, at his very low level of living on the soil and for the soil, has that sense of organic connection. Hence, I suppose, his extraordinary tenacity and perseverance. But his level of existence is terrible low, and most of us had rather be uprooted than exist at that level. To live at a high level and yet to have that organic connection with life—that I suppose is the problem humanity is trying to solve now in its own crude, cruel and wasteful way.

Why does one do anything? Hardly because of reasoned thinking, though this may be behind the immediate urge to some extent. It is this urge, this impulse, overmastering and uncontrollable, that drives one on. Our moods depend even less on reason and the smallest things affect them, exalting them

[1] To Indira Gandhi. JN Papers, NMML. Excerpts.

or depressing them. Often one forgets or hardly remembers the cause for these exaltations or depressions, yet the mood prevails. I have felt sometimes extraordinarily exhilarated by the sight of a sunset sky, or the deep blue patch between the monsoon clouds, or even a flower which I had missed and have suddenly seen. For a moment I have felt at one with nature.

Why does one act? Impossible to answer unless one goes down deep into the depths of the unconscious self of man, a journey which is beyond our capacity. We may at best just glimpse into those depths and return mystified. Have you seen those lovely lines by Yeats on an Irish airman!

> Nor law, nor duty bade me fight,
> Nor public men, nor cheering crowds,
> A lonely impulse of delight
> Drove to this tumult in the clouds;
> I balanced all, brought all to mind,
> The years to come seemed waste of breath,
> A waste of breath the years behind
> In balance with this life, this death.

I have been reading Virginia Woolf (*To the Lighthouse*). The more I read her the more I like her. There is a magic about her writing, something ethereal, limpid like running water, and deep like a clear mountain lake. What is her book about? So very little that you can tell anyone; and yet so much that it fills your mind, covers it with a gossamer net, out of which you peer at the past, at yourself, at others. Did you ever meet her?

Love,
Papu

41

Bengal Famine[1]

21 September 1943

Reports from Bengal are staggering. We grow accustomed to anything, any depth of human misery and sorrow. And so we grow accustomed to starvation and death daily in Bengal. The first keen edge of horrified amazement is gone. But a dull horror remains and colours everything. More and more I feel that behind all the terrible mismanagement and bungling—Central government's & Provincial government's—there is something deeper. It is the collapse of the economic structure of Bengal—a social breakdown. If so, not all the relief works and remedial measures will end this trouble. It will grow and like a poisonous growth affect other parts of India. Indeed Orissa and parts of Madras are affected. . . .

The Pakistan business—often my thoughts have turned to it. How mad and foolish it is; how fantastic from any economic point of view. It means ruin industrially for the Pakistan area. The rest would not be greatly affected. And yet there it is: mad and foolish and fantastic and criminal and all that, and yet a huge barrier to all progress. What a lot Jinnah and his Muslim League have to answer for! They have lowered the whole tone of our public life, embittered it, increased mutual dislikes and hatreds, and made us contemptible before the outside world. I cannot help thinking that ultimately the Muslims in India will suffer most. . . .

But is it any good cursing others? They have misbehaved and betrayed the cause of our country and freedom? Agreed—what then? It is not good enough to analyse a situation in this way. Why did we permit them to do so? True, the British Govt. helped them and created the conditions under which they flourish. That too is not enough.

11 November

A few days ago I was reading Ashvaghosa's *Buddhacharita* and as I read Buddha's (or rather Siddhartha's, for he was not the Buddha then) answer to the

---

[1] Prison Diary with Letters, 1943. JN Papers, NMML. Excerpts.

THE ESSENTIAL WRITINGS OF JAWAHARLAL NEHRU

deputation that had come to beg him to return home, a thrill passed through me, almost an electric shock. 'I would enter a blazing fire, but I would not enter my home with my goal unattained'.

If that is my innermost feeling, am I strong enough to face the consequences, whatever they might be? I think so, though I cannot be sure—Am I prepared to give up all hope of gaining my objective during my lifetime, of remaining in the wilderness always, of reconciling myself to prison indefinitely, or many things that are far worse? I think I am ready for this, and if the conviction came upon me, that the future held nothing for me but this long fading away in prison, I would accept it. That would satisfy my inner urges, would be in keeping with what I have thought and said and done. And I would think wistfully that thus I was serving the cause of my own people and of the larger world.

I have no such convictions of course and I believe that I shall have to play, sometime or other, another kind of act on life's stage. I am pretty sure that big changes will come in India and I cannot escape from shouldering the burden of responsibility that these will bring.

That may happen or not. But in either event it would be a betrayal of myself and what I have always considered India's cause and the world's for me to humble and humiliate myself before British authority.

42

Philosophy and Life[1]

1 February 1944

Dear Indu,

Two of your letters, dated 19 and 23 January, came to me together soon
after I had sent you my last letter. They were full of the burden of sorrow and
an emotional upheaval at the suddenness of death and all the questionings that
this experience gives rise to. Out of this eternal questioning has arisen philosophy with all its problems, and throughout the ages innumerable people have
wondered over this mystery of life and death. Philosophy has come to you early
because not only of personal shock but also the larger tragedies that surround
us. It depends on each one of us how we face these questions, how we react to
them. Adequate answers we may not have but our imaginative self gives some
kind of an unconscious response which affects our individual lives. We weaken
under the stress and lose our sense of poise and equilibrium, or grow stronger
and more capable of riding the storm and yet being not too much affected by
it. Life is amazingly dynamic, and while it lasts, has an extraordinary capacity
to adapt itself and to express itself forcibly. We see this daily in the exuberance
of nature and we are parts of that nature and have, or should have, the same
exuberance and vitality. So we carry on along our appointed course, and,
though limited by circumstances, still endeavour to mould that circumstance
itself according to the urge that is within us.

Reason and agreement go some way to shape our minds and direct our
activities. Yet in the final analysis we act because of that inner urge within us,
which has been formed and conditioned by so many factors which have gone
to our making—our own experience chiefly, piling up one on top of the other
from birth and childhood onwards, the influence of others, our heredity and
our racial and cultural inheritance, our education, the sensations we have
known and experienced.

So our reactions to events vary. Some, and among them have been wise
men, think all this business of life a thing of sound and fury, signifying nothing.
Others have discovered or felt a meaning in it all. Yet others, uncertain whether

---

[1] To Indira Gandhi, JN Collection, NMML.

there is any meaning or not, still are compelled by some force within them to adopt objectives and codes of behaviour and follow them with all their might. Perhaps that itself signifies some deep intuitive faith in a meaning. However that may be, most of us, affirm life and it is right that we should do so positively, rather than just carry on negatively.

Twenty-five hundred years ago the Buddha addressing his followers said: '. . . while ye, O disciples, experienced this sorrow through long ages, more tears have flowed from you and have been shed by you, while ye strayed and wandered on this pilgrimage of life, and sorrowed and wept, because that was your portion which ye abhorred, and that which ye loved was not your portion, than all the waters which are in the four great oceans.'

A sad thought and though a true one, yet perhaps with an overemphasis on the pain and suffering of life. Buddha was frequently emphasizing this and many people therefore call Buddhism a religion of pessimism. Yet the face of Buddha in the statues that his faithful followers have made with loving care, and even more so in the image of him that I have in my mind, is so devoid of pain and sorrow, so full of peace and calm and compassion, that I cannot connect it with suffering. Or, does it represent the conquest over sorrow? I do not think of him as a man of sorrows.

And then going to the lands where Buddhism still flourishes, we do not find the people pessimistic at all. Where could there be more of the joy and affirmation of life than in the Chinese people? Is that a racial characteristic, I wonder which has overcome and transmuted the pessimistic tendencies of the faith, or is it something else? I do not know. But I do know that I am seldom depressed for long by events, however painful they might be for the moment, and a certain unreasoning faith in life rises up in me and keeps me going. I cannot argue about it, but it fills me, and therefore life is an affirmation to me and not a negation. Even if that subconscious faith were absent, I suppose, I would continue to function in much the same way, but that urge helps and gives me vitality. Experiencing this myself, I want others to share it with me.

What a letter I am writing! A vague and possibly unmeaning attempt at philosophy in its relation to life, or perhaps, just a glimpse of that restless and wandering creature, my mind. I have written as I have done because I want you to have such glimpses and to realize as I do the extraordinary fascination of life's adventure. That pilgrimage would be no adventure if it lay in the ruts of normal experience and cautious conduct, safety first in everything, like the slow moving river on an almost level plain. The body has its adventures and experiences, and many are worth having, but the real adventures are of the mind. Indeed all feelings and experiences are ultimately of the mind, and the mind itself is part of the body.

There is the adventure of the individual, the adventure of the race, and finally the world adventure—and all tend to get mixed up together—and we can be parties to all these adventures. If the individual's adventure has an ending, the others continue and carry us to an endless future. Our country, tragic as she may appear to us at the present moment, has been carrying on her story and her quest since the dawn of history many thousands of years ago. That quest will surely continue and merge itself in the conditions of the modern world, into the world-quest for life and freedom and adventures of the mind and spirit.

Papu

43

Children[1]

3 June 1944

Darling Indu,

Problem and such like children have, I suppose, always existed but undoubtedly they are peculiarly common in our present age, especially in Europe and America. They are the products of this age of transition where everything is changing so rapidly that it is difficult to have any standards of values to judge by. Also the small families which are so usual today—one child or two—result in problem children. A larger family, several children, has disadvantages but from the child's point of view it is usually better and he has a more normal life with companions growing up with him. To some extent, but not wholly (except perhaps in a socialist country like Russia), school and a communal life can take the place of family life.

A child has to be treated as an individual and given every opportunity to grow as an individual. But it is at least equally important to treat him as a social being who can live at peace and cooperation with others. That makes one think of the kind of society he will have to live in—difficult business today when society itself is changing. In any event the cooperative habits and traits have to be developed or else he will find it difficult to fit in anywhere. Usually single children, who have been looked after a great deal, have a hard time when they go out into the world and have to fend for themselves. Bertrand Russell says somewhere that parents are wholly unsuited to bring up their children; they are too intensely interested in them to take a dispassionate view or to treat them normally.

You say you want the child to be happy—of course. But then what is happiness? There is the solid content of a fairly prosperous peasant; there are higher grades of intellectual and emotional happiness. There is the happiness of the person who is drunk or who is under the influence of some drug. I suppose, if you analyse your mind, you will find that happiness is more often negative than positive—an absence of pain & suffering. And yet how is one to be happy if he knows and sees another in pain? A sensitive person will suffer continually on

[1] To Indira Gandhi. Indira Gandhi Papers, NMML. Excerpts.

behalf of others. An insensitive person may escape that but at the cost of much that is fine in life. Long ago (probably 140 years ago) Leopardi the Italian poet wrote to his sister on the occasion of her marriage: "Thou shall have children, either cowards or unhappy; choose thou the latter." That is perhaps an extreme view but there is some truth in it.

Ultimately we cannot be really happy till the whole world is happy and that is a large order. Mere avoidance of unhappiness, not easily possible, may itself result in isolation and boredom and a malaise which is worse than definite unhappiness. We are so organically connected with others and with the world that we cannot both live a full life and yet avoid the world's ills. Escapism does not pay in the long run, quite apart from its moral worth.

What then is one to do? That is a big question which has been asked almost since human beings began to think. It seems to me that the only thing to aim at is the power or capacity to extract happiness, or perhaps it is better to call it peace and calm, out of unhappiness itself. Not to escape from anything but to face it and yet be above it in a way; not to be overcome by it and to retain in spite of everything, a sense of life and its larger purposes, a feeling of life fulfilment. How to do that is a difficult enough job and each person has to learn for himself and it seems that only life, with all its waywardness and shock, can teach. The most we can do is to prepare the background for it.

Your loving,
Papu

44

The Moon[1]

It is more than twenty months since we were brought here, more than twenty months of my ninth term of imprisonment. The new moon, a shimmering crescent in the darkening sky, greeted us on our arrival here. The bright fortnight of the waxing moon had begun. Ever since then each coming of the new moon has been a reminder to me that another month of my imprisonment is over. So it was with my last term of imprisonment which began with the new moon, just after the *Deepavali*, the festival of light. The moon, ever a companion to me in prison, has grown more friendly with closer acquaintance, a reminder of the loveliness of this world, of the waxing and waning of life, of light following darkness, of death and resurrection following each other in interminable succession. Ever changing, yet ever the same, I have watched it in its different phases and its many moods in the evening, as the shadows lengthen, in the still hours of the night, and when the breath and whisper of dawn bring promise of the coming day. How helpful is the moon in counting the days and the months, for the size and shape of the moon, when it is visible, indicate the day of the month with a fair measure of exactitude. It is an easy calendar (though it must be adjusted from time to time), and for the peasant in the field the most convenient one to indicate the passage of the days and the gradual changing of the seasons.

[1] Ahmadnagar Fort, 13th April 1944. From the *Discovery of India*, p. 15.

45

Mental Perturbation[1]

5 August 1944, Saturday

Three weeks since I wrote last in this journal. Three weeks of growing perturbation and mental distress. I wrote then that I was not put out at all by various
developments and the two proposals Bapu had made, though I disagreed with
much that he had said and the manner of saying and doing. Well, I take all that
back. I am very much put out, angered and out of temper. The floods of statements, interviews, correspondence &c that have emanated from Bapu,[2] and the
very frequent utterances[3] of Rajagopalachari, have overwhelmed me and others
and I feel stifled and unable to breathe normally. For the first time in these two
years I have a sensation of blankness and sinking of heart. Today I have been
writing to Indu my usual Saturday letter. I found some difficulty in doing so
and could hardly finish my sentences.

Jinnah with his insolence has contributed to this,[4] and so the debate[5] in the
House of Commons and the general attitude of British press[6]—But after all
that is to be expected. It is Bapu's response to all this that bowls me over.

* * *

[1] Excerpts from Prison Diary. JN Collection, NMML.

[2] In response to the Viceroy's demand for a "definite and constructive policy", Mahatma
Gandhi declared in a letter on 27 July 1944 that he was prepared to advise the Working
Committee to renounce civil disobedience and to give full cooperation in the war effort if
independence was declared immediately and a national government responsible to Central
Legislature was formed, subject to the condition that during the war, military operation
might continue without the financial burden on India. He followed this with an appeal to
the British Prime Minister, "to trust and use me for the sake of your people and through them
those of the world."

[3] In his statements during July and August 1944, C. Rajagopalachari answered the critics
of his scheme for a communal settlement by emphasizing that the only alternative would be
the perpetuation of British rule.

[4] In his address to the Muslim League Council on 30 July 1944 and later in a press
conference, Jinnah denied that the Rajagopalachari formula had met his demand. He
described it "as offering only a maimed, mutilated and moth-eaten Pakistan and thus trying
to pass off as having met the Pakistan scheme and Muslim demand."

[5] In the debate on 26 July 1944, Amery said that the British Government would not
reopen formal negotiations with the Indian nationalists on the issue of independence, or on
the basis of Mahatma Gandhi's proposals.

[6] *The Times* wrote: "No agreement between Mr. Gandhi and Mr. Jinnah, however

My mind goes back: the conflicts in the Working Committee in 1936–37—that revealing incident after the Calcutta A.I.C.C. in 1937 (Oct.?) when Bapu completely lost control over himself over the Mysore resolution and cursed us as mischief-makers—the Rajkot incident when he fasted and then made a mess of everything—that 'inner voice' business—my attempts at resignation from the Congress presidentship and later the W.C.—Tripuri and after—the Calcutta A.I.C.C. again when I got out of the W.C.—September 1939 when the War began and I reverted to the W.C.—the War Sub-Committee of which I was chairman which never functioned!—the conflicts over nonviolence—the breaks with Bapu and subsequent reconciliations—Ramgarh Congress and after—Individual CD—Bardoli—December 1941—the Chiangs' visit and Bapu's reaction to them—Stafford Cripps—the Allahabad A.I.C.C. April-May 1942—another of Bapu's amazing series of articles in *Harijan*—the passion which seemed to envelop him—and so on to 8 August 1942.

And now? All these explanations without end and toning down of everything—this grovelling before the Viceroy & Jinnah—This may be the satyagraha technique. If so, I fear I do not fit in at all—it does not even possess the saving grace of dignity—Tall, talk and then excuses & explanations and humility.

What I may do outside after our release, I do not know. But I feel that I must break with this woolly thinking and undignified action—which really means breaking with Gandhi. I have at present no desire even to go to him on release and discuss matters with him—What do such discussions lead to? I suppose I shall see him anyhow. . . .

As for Rajagopalachari—is there a more dangerous person in all India?

* * *

Last night I created quite a disturbance by my shouting in my sleep—I woke up about half a dozen people—At last Kripalani came way down from his place to wake me and put me right.

---

satisfactory to their adherents, can materially advance political progress in India unless it takes into account the depressed classes. . . . the claims of the princes. . . ." The *Manchester Guardian* declared: "Indian nationalist leaders, whatever their declared policies might be, cannot be trusted with any share in the Government of India."

46

Beginning of Life[1]

12 August 1944

Darling Indu,

This is your last month and I suppose you will find it a little trying and your mind will be in a state of expectation.[2] It is curious how the most normal and ordinary processes of life are so full of mystery. So many things happen daily which we take for granted and which are yet very odd when we start thinking about them. Each individual is a mysterious person living in a private universe of his own, different from the world other people live in. Is it ever possible for one person ever truly to understand another? But few people ever worry themselves about such everyday matters and everyone thinks that his world is the only possible world and all others are deviations due to cussedness, knavery or just simple ignorance—And yet when we come face to face with the beginning of a life or the ending of one, suddenly we find ourselves peering into the dark unknown—How little we really know? Death too for all its effect passes and becomes a memory. But new life is an amazing, fascinating thing, full of the wonder of existence, of change and growth, and so always the process of giving birth to anything vital has been the most tremendous fact of existence in this world, for because of that the world continues in spite of the hateful instincts of man. The pain that sometimes accompanies it becomes trivial in comparison with the supreme satisfaction of creation.

Your loving,
Papu

---

[1] To Indira Gandhi. SWJN, Vol. 13, pp. 459–60. Extracts.
[2] Indira Gandhi's son Rajiv was born on 17 November 1944.

47

Philosophy of Life[1]

What was my philosophy of life? I did not know. Some years earlier I would not have been so hesitant. There was a definiteness about my thinking and objectives then which has faded away since. The events of the past few years in India, China, Europe, and all over the world have been confusing, upsetting and distressing, and the future has become vague and shadowy and has lost that clearness of outline which it once possessed in my mind.

This doubt and difficulty about fundamental matters did not come in my way in regard to immediate action, except that it blunted somewhat the sharp edge of that activity. No longer could I function, as I did in my younger days, as an arrow flying automatically to the target of my choice ignoring all else but that target. Yet I functioned, for the urge to action was there and a real or imagined coordination of that action with the ideals I held. But a growing distaste for politics as I saw them seized me and gradually my whole attitude to life seemed to undergo a transformation.

The ideals and objectives of yesterday were still the ideals of today, but they had lost some of their lustre and, even as one seemed to go towards them, they lost the shining beauty which had warmed the heart and vitalized the body. Evil triumphed often enough, but what was far worse was the coarsening and distortion of what had seemed so right. Was human nature so essentially bad that it would take ages of training, through suffering and misfortune, before it could behave reasonably and raise man above that creature of lust and violence and deceit that he now was? And, meanwhile, was every effort to change it radically in the present or the near future doomed to failure?

Ends and means: were they tied up inseparably, acting and reacting on each other, the wrong means distorting and sometimes even destroying the end in view? But the right means might well be beyond the capacity of infirm and selfish human nature.

What then was one to do? Not to act was a complete confession of failure and a submission to evil; to act meant often enough a compromise with some form of that evil, with all the untoward consequence that such compromises result in.

[1] From *The Discovery of India*, pp. 25–33.

My early approach to life's problems had been more or less scientific, with something of the easy optimism of the science of the nineteenth and early twentieth century. A secure and comfortable existence and the energy and self-confidence I possessed increased that feeling of optimism. A kind of vague humanism appealed to me.

Religion, as I saw it practised, and accepted even by thinking minds, whether it was Hinduism or Islam or Buddhism or Christianity, did not attract me. It seemed to be closely associated with superstitious practices and dogmatic beliefs, and behind it lay a method of approach to life's problems which was certainly not that of science. There was an element of magic about it, an uncritical credulousness, a reliance on the supernatural.

Yet it was obvious that religion had supplied some deeply felt inner need of human nature, and that the vast majority of people all over the world could not do without some form of religious belief. It had produced many fine types of men and women, as well as bigoted, narrow-minded, cruel tyrants. It had given a set of values to human life, and though some of these values had no application today, or were even harmful, others were still the foundation of morality and ethics.

In the wider sense of the word, religion dealt with the uncharted regions of human experience, uncharted, that is, by the scientific positive knowledge of the day. In a sense it might be considered an extension of the known and charted region, though the methods of science and religion were utterly unlike each other, and to a large extent they had to deal with different kinds of media. It was obvious that there was a vast unknown region all around us, and science, with its magnificent achievements, knew little enough about it, though it was making tentative approaches in that direction. Probably also, the normal methods of science, its dealings with the visible world and the process of life, were not wholly adapted to the physical, the artistic, the spiritual, and other elements of the invisible world. Life does not consist entirely of what we see and hear and feel, the visible world which is undergoing change in time and space; it is continually touching an invisible world of other, and possibly more stable or equally changeable elements, and no thinking person can ignore this invisible world.

Science does not tell us much, or for the matter of that anything about the purpose of life. It is now widening its boundaries and it may invade the so-called invisible world before long and help us to understand this purpose of life in its widest sense, or at least give us some glimpses which illumine the problem of human existence. The old controversy between science and religion takes a new form—the application of the scientific method to emotional and religious experiences.

Religion merges into mysticism and metaphysics and philosophy. There have been great mystics, attractive figures, who cannot easily be disposed of as self-deluded fools. Yet mysticism (in the narrow sense of the world) irritates me; it appears to be vague and soft and flabby, not a rigorous discipline of the mind but a surrender of mental faculties and a living in a sea of emotional experience. The experience may lead occasionally to some insight into inner and less obvious processes, but it is also likely to lead to self-delusion.

Metaphysics and philosophy, or a metaphysical philosophy, have a greater appeal to the mind. They require hard thinking and the application of logic and reasoning, though all this is necessarily based on some premises, which are presumed to be self-evident, and yet which may or may not be true. All thinking persons, to a greater or less degree, dabble in metaphysics and philosophy, for not to do so is to ignore many of the aspects of this universe of ours. Some may feel more attracted to them than others, and the emphasis on them may vary in different ages. In the ancient world, both in Asia and Europe, all the emphasis was laid on the supremacy of the inward life over things external, and this inevitably led to metaphysics and philosophy. The modern man is wrapped up much more in these things external, and yet even he, in moments of crisis and mental trouble often turns to philosophy and metaphysical speculations.

Some vague or more precise philosophy of life we all have, though most of us accept unthinkingly the general attitude which is characteristic of our generation and environment. Most of us accept also certain metaphysical conceptions as part of the faith in which we have grown up. I have not been attracted towards metaphysics; in fact, I have had a certain distaste for vague speculation. And yet I have sometimes found a certain intellectual fascination in trying to follow the rigid lines of metaphysical and philosophic thought of the ancients or the moderns. But I have never felt at ease there and have escaped from their spell with a feeling of relief.

Essentially, I am interested in this world, in this life, not in some other world or a future life. Whether there is such a thing as a soul, or whether there is a survival after death or not, I do not know; and, important as these questions are, they do not trouble me in the least. The environment in which I have grown up takes the soul (or rather the *atma*) and a future life, the Karma theory of cause and effect, and reincarnation for granted. I have been affected by this and so, in a sense, I am favourably disposed towards these assumptions. There might be a soul which survives the physical death of the body, and a theory of cause and effect governing life's actions seems reasonable, though it leads to obvious difficulties when one thinks of the ultimate cause. Presuming a soul, there appears to be some logic also in the theory of reincarnation.

But I do not believe in any of these or other theories and assumptions as a matter of religious faith. They are just intellectual speculations in an unknown region about which we know next to nothing. They do not affect my life, and whether they were provided right or wrong subsequently, they would make little difference to me.

Spiritualism with its seances and its so-called manifestations of spirits and the like has always seemed to me a rather absurd and impertinent way of investigating psychic phenomena and the mysteries of the after-life. Usually it is something worse, and is an exploitation of the emotions of some over-credulous people who seek relief or escape from mental trouble. I do not deny the possibility of some of these psychic phenomena having a basis of truth, but the approach appears to me to be all wrong and the conclusions drawn from scraps and odd bits of evidence to be unjustified.

Often, as I look at this world, I have a sense of mysteries, of unknown depths. The urge to understand it, in so far as I can, comes to me: to be in tune with it and to experience it in its fullness. But the way to that understanding seems to me essentially the way of science, the way of objective approach, though I realize that there can be no such thing as true objectiveness. If the subjective element is unavoidable and inevitable, it should be conditioned as far as possible by the scientific method.

What the mysterious is I do not know. I do not call it God because God has come to mean much that I do not believe in. I find myself incapable of thinking of a deity or of any unknown supreme power in anthropomorphic terms, and the fact that many people think so is continually a source of surprise to me. Any idea of a personal god seems very odd to me. Intellectually, I can appreciate to some extent the conception of monism, and I have been attracted towards the *Advaita* (non-dualist) philosophy of the Vedanta, though I do not presume to understand it in all its depth and intricacy, and I realize that merely an intellectual appreciation of such matters does not carry one far. At the same time the Vedanta, as well as other similar approaches, rather frighten me with their vague, formless incursions into infinity. The diversity and fullness of nature stir me and produce a harmony of the spirit, and I can imagine myself feeling at home in the old Indian or Greek pagan and pantheistic atmosphere, but minus the conception of God or Gods that was attached to it.

Some kind of ethical approach to life has a strong appeal for me, though it would be difficult for me to justify it logically. I have been attracted by Gandhiji's stress on right means and I think one of his greatest contributions to our public life has been this emphasis. The idea is by no means new, but this application of an ethical doctrine to large-scale public activity was certainly novel. It is full of difficulty, and perhaps ends and means are not really separable but form together one organic whole. In a world which thinks almost exclusively of ends and ignores means, this emphasis on means seems odd and remarkable. How far it has succeeded in India I cannot say. But there is no doubt that it has created a deep and abiding impression on the minds of large numbers of people.

A study of Marx and Lenin produced a powerful effect on my mind and helped me to see history and current affairs in a new light. The long chain of history and of social development appeared to have some meaning, some sequence, and the future lost some of its obscurity. The practical achievements of the Soviet Union were also tremendously impressive. Often I disliked or did not understand some development there and it seemed to me to be too closely concerned with the opportunism of the moment or the power politics of the day. But despite all these developments and possible distortions of the original passion for human betterment, I had no doubt that the Soviet Revolution had advanced human society by a great leap and had lit a bright flame which could not be smothered, and that it had laid the foundations for that new civilization towards which the world could advance. I am too much of an individualist and believer in personal freedom to like overmuch regimentation. Yet it seemed to me obvious that in a complex social structure individual freedom had to be limited, and perhaps the only way to read personal freedom was through some such limitation in the social sphere. The lesser liberties may often need limitation in the interest of the larger freedom.

Much in the Marxist philosophical outlook I could accept without difficulty: its monism and non-duality of mind and matter, and dynamics of matter and the dialectic of continuous change by evolution as well as leap, through action and interaction, cause and effect, thesis, antithesis and synthesis. It did not satisfy me completely, nor did it answer all the questions in my mind, and, almost unawares, a vague idealist approach would creep into my mind, something rather akin to the Vedanta approach. It was not a difference between mind and matter, but rather of something that lay beyond the mind. Also there was the background of ethics. I realized that the moral approach is a changing one and depends upon the growing mind and an advancing civilization; it is conditioned by the mental climate of the age. Yet there was something more to it than that, certain basic urges which had greater permanence. I did not like the frequent divorce in communist, as in other, practice between action and these basic urges or principles. So there was an odd mixture in my mind which I could not rationally explain or resolve. There was a general tendency not to think too much of those fundamental questions which appear to be beyond reach, but rather to concentrate on the problems of life—to understand in the narrower and more immediate sense what should be done and how. Whatever ultimate reality may be, and whether we can ever grasp it in whole or in part, there certainly appear to be vast possibilities of increasing human knowledge, even though this may be partly or largely subjective, and of applying this to the advancement and betterment of human living and social organization.

There has been in the past, and there is to a lesser extent even today among some people, an absorption in finding an answer to the riddle of the universe. This leads them away from the individual and social problems of the day, and when they are unable to solve that riddle they despair and turn to inaction and triviality, or find comfort in some dogmatic creed. Social evils, most of which

are certainly capable of removal, are attributed to original sin, to the unalterable-
ness of human nature, or the social structure, or (in India) to the inevitable
legacy of previous births. Thus one drifts away from even the attempt to think
rationally and scientifically and takes refuge in irrationalism, superstition, and
unreasonable and inequitable social prejudices and practices. It is true that even
rational and scientific thoughts does not always take us as far as we would like
to go. There is an infinite number of factors and relations all of which influence
and determine events in varying degrees. It is impossible to grasp all of them,
but we can try to pick out the dominating forces at work and by observing
external material reality, and by experiment and practice, trial and error, grope
our way to ever-widening knowledge and truth.

For this purpose, and within these limitations, the general Marxist
approach, fitting in as it more or less does with the present state of scientific
knowledge, seemed to me to offer considerable help. But even accepting that
approach, the consequences that flow from it and the interpretation on past and
present happenings were by no means always clear. Marx's general analysis of
social development seems to have been remarkably correct, and yet many developments took place later which did not fit in with his outlook for the immediate future. Lenin successfully adapted the Marxian thesis to some of these
subsequent developments, and again since then further remarkable changes
have taken place—the rise of fascism and Nazism and all that lay behind them.
The very rapid growth of technology and the practical application of vast
developments in scientific knowledge are now changing the world picture with
an amazing rapidity, leading to new problems.

And so while I accepted the fundamentals of the socialism theory, I did not
trouble myself about its numerous inner controversies. I had little patience with
leftist groups in India, spending much of their energy in mutual conflict and
recrimination over fine points of doctrine which did not interest me at all. Life
is too complicated and, as far as we can understand it in our present state of
knowledge, too illogical, for it to be confined within the four corners of a fixed
doctrine.

The real problems for me remain problems of individual and social life, of
harmonious living, of a proper balancing of an individual's inner and outer life,
of an adjustment of the relations between individuals and between groups, of
a continuous becoming something better and higher of social development, of
the ceaseless adventure of man. In the solution of these problems the way of
observation and precise knowledge and deliberate reasoning, according to the
method of science, must be followed. This method may not always be applicable in our quest of truth, for art and poetry and certain psychic experiences
seem to belong to a different order of things and to elude the objective methods
of science. Let us, therefore, not rule out intuition and other methods of sensing
truth and reality. They are necessary even for the purposes of science. But

always we must hold to our anchor of precise objective knowledge tested by reason, and even more so by experiment and practice, and always we must beware of losing ourselves in a sea of speculation unconnected with the day-to-day problems of life and the needs of men and women. A living philosophy must answer the problems of today.

It may be that we of this modern age, who so pride ourselves on the achievements of our times, are prisoners of our age, just as the ancients and the men and women of medieval times were prisoners of their respective ages. We may delude ourselves, as others have done before us, that our way of looking at things is the only right way, leading to truth. We cannot escape from that prison or get rid entirely of that illusion, if illusion it is.

Yet I am convinced the methods and approach of science have revolutionized human life more than anything else in the long course of history, and have opened doors and avenues of further and even more radical change, leading up to the very portals of what has long been considered the unknown. The technical achievements of science are obvious enough: its capacity to transform an economy of scarcity into one of abundance is evident, its invasion of many problems which have so far been the monopoly of philosophy is becoming more pronounced. Space-time and the quantum theory utterly changed the picture of the physical world. More recent researches into the nature of matter, the structure of the atom, the transmutation of the elements, and the transformation of electricity and light, either into the other, have carried human knowledge much further. Man no longer sees nature as something apart and distinct from himself. Human destiny appears to become a part of nature's rhythmic energy.

All this upheaval of thought, due to the advance of science, has led scientists into a new region, verging on the metaphysical. They draw different and often contradictory conclusions. Some see in it a new unity, the antithesis of chance. Others, like Bertrand Russell, say, 'Academic philosophers ever since the time of Parmenides have believed the world is unity. The most fundamental of my beliefs is that this is rubbish.' Or again, 'Man is the product of causes which had no prevision of the end they were achieving; his origin, his growth, his hopes and fears, his loves and beliefs are but the outcome of accidental collocations of atoms.' And yet the latest developments in physics have gone a long way to demonstrate a fundamental unity in nature. 'The belief that all things are made of a single substance is as old as thought itself; but ours is the generation which, first of all in history, is able to receive the unity of nature, not as a baseless dogma or a hopeless aspiration, but a principle of science based on proof as sharp and clear as anything which is known.'*

*Karl K. Darrow, *The Renaissance of Physics* (New York, 1936), p. 301.

Old as this belief is in Asia and Europe, it is interesting to compare some of the latest conclusions of science with the fundamental ideas underlying the Advaita Vedantic theory. These ideas were that the universe is made of one substance whose form is perpetually changing, and further that the sum-total of energies remains always the same. Also that 'the explanations of things are to be found within their own nature, and that no external beings or existence are required to explain what is going on in the universe', with its corollary of a self-evolving universe.

It does not very much matter to science what these vague speculations lead to, for meanwhile it forges ahead in a hundred directions, in its own precise experimental way of observation, widening the bounds of the charted region of knowledge, and changing human life in the process. Science may be on the verge of discovering vital mysteries, which yet may elude it. Still it will go on along its appointed path, for there is no end to its journeying. Ignoring for the moment the 'why?' of philosophy, science will go on asking 'how?', and as it finds this out it gives greater content and meaning to life, and perhaps takes us some way to answering the 'why?'

Or perhaps, we cannot cross that barrier, and the mysterious will continue to remain the mysterious, and life with all its changes will still remain a bundle of good and evil, a succession of conflicts, a curious combination of incompatible and mutually hostile urges.

Or again, perhaps, the very progress of science, unconnected with and isolated from moral discipline and ethical considerations, will lead to the concentration of power and the terrible instruments of destruction which it has made, in the hands of evil and selfish men, seeking the domination of others—and thus to the destruction of its own great achievements. Something of this kind we see happening now, and behind this war there lies this internal conflict of the spirit of man.

How amazing is this spirit of man! In spite of innumerable failings, man, throughout the ages, has sacrificed his life and all he held dear for an ideal, for truth, for faith, for country and honour. That ideal may change, but that capacity for self-sacrifice continues, and, because of that, much may be forgiven to man, and it is impossible to lose hope for him. In the midst of disaster, he has not lost his dignity or his faith in the values he cherished. Plaything of nature's mighty forces, less than a speck of dust in this vast universe, he has hurled defiance at the elemental powers, and with his mind, cradle of revolution, sought to master them. Whatever gods there be, there is something godlike in man, as there is also something of the devil in him.

The future is dark, uncertain. But we can see part of the way leading to it and can tread it with firm steps, remembering that nothing that can happen is likely to overcome the spirit of man which has survived so many perils;

remembering also that life, for all its ills, has joy and beauty, and that we can always wander; if we know how to, in the enchanted woods of nature.

> What else is wisdom? What of man's endeavour
> Or God's high grace, so lovely and great?
> To stand from fear set free, to breathe and wait;
> To hold a hand uplifted over Hate;
> And shall not Loveliness be loved for ever?**

**Chorus from *The Bacchae of Euripides*. Gilbert Murray's translation.

48

Memories and Fancies[1]

New Delhi, 3 July 1948

My dear Madame Chiang,

Your brief letter reached me sometime ago[2] and ever since then, and indeed before, I have been thinking of writing to you. I owe you a thousand apologies for this delay. But you know how the mind works when it has to face a continuous difficulty and worry. One does one's daily round of work because one must. But the things that one really wants to do remain undone for in order to do them one seeks a little leisure and peace of mind, a proper mood when one can empty the mind of its present troubles and seek repose and some content in memories and fancies. And so I did not write to you although I have been wanting to write ever so much.

I have been thinking of you so often for a variety of reasons, both personal and public. The memory of your visit to India, six long years ago,[3] remains fresh in my mind and I remember how I had then thought of visiting you in the not distant future. But that visit never came off and I do not know when it will come off, for we are all prisoners in prisons of our own making, and no prison is harder than that.

I have thought of you with all the enormous problems that you have to face from day to day and hour to hour, and curiously I have found some relief in that thought when my own problems and difficulties encompass me, and then, so often, I have compared China with India, both struggling hard to find a new life, both for the moment stopped and delayed by high barriers.

Six years ago and more since you came here for a brief while, what a lot has happened since then. I fear that I have grown much older than even these six

---

[1] To Madame Chiang Kai-shek. JN Collection, NMML. Excerpts.

[2] Madame Chiang Kai-shek had written on 13 May that the General and she would be seeing K.M. Panikkar the next day and would be glad to get first-hand information of Jawaharlal Nehru. "We think of you often and suffer with you the difficulties and trials attendant upon the setting up of a new government. For we in China, too, are faced with somewhat the same dilemma".

[3] Chiang Kai-shek and his wife visited India from 9 to 21 February 1942.

years of life, and feel worried and rather disillusioned. How much more time is spent on trivial activities which have little meaning. How full indeed is human life of triviality. We think and work for the high moments of life when the flame burns brightly for a brief while. But the high moments come rarely and when they come, they pass away too soon. And then again triviality and ever more of triviality and sometimes something even worse. But how have you fared during these long years? With your great courage and vitality you must have faced problems and difficulties with a smile. But however much we may smile, each experience leaves its mark somewhere on the screen of our minds. We grow wiser, they say, but I sometimes wonder if that kind of wisdom is so desirable after all.

Yours very sincerely,
Jawaharlal Nehru

49

Uncertainties[1]

New Delhi, 4 August 1948

Nan dear,

I have long got used to a state of complete uncertainty about my future. This affects me less than almost anyone I know. I carry on as if I was doing for eternity or worse and at the same time I have a feeling that the work I am doing may suddenly end. Something may happen which emphasizes one aspect of it or it may be my mood at the moment. Now it does not much matter and I really do not know how I shall function in the future. I may remain the Prime Minister for a considerable length of time or I may not. Here I am at present moving into this vast mansion as if I was going to stay here for years, Indu and Padmaja and others fitting it all up. It amused me to think that all this labour might not bear fruit.

I wrote to you because at that time that mood was dominant. It returns often enough. But I should not bother if I were you. When something happens we shall inevitably adjust ourselves to it.

One thing I want you to realize even if I have to leave the Prime Minister-ship, I do not want you to resign from such offices as you may be holding. This is for two reasons. First that it is not the right thing for a person to do so. Of course, if later difficulties of another nature arise then it is open to you to reconsider the matter. Secondly even if I resign I do not fade out of the picture and it may well be that after a little while I come back. I am too vital a person and too necessary to the scheme of things in India to retire to the mountains.

Your loving brother,
Jawahar

---

[1] To Vijayalakshmi Pandit. JN Collection, NMML. Excerpts.

50

Decisions and Responsibilities[1]

New Delhi, 29 August 1948

My dear Dickie,

You must be still in Canada, but I suppose by the time this letter reaches London you might be on your way back.

We have been having a very difficult time here and I have felt more than ever the weight of responsibility that has been cast upon me. Grave decisions have to be made by us and the alternatives between which we have to choose are equally undesirable. So, as often in life, we search frantically for the lesser evil. We try to look into the future and to provide for it, but that future is full of uncertainty. And so, we try to do what, in the context of things today, appears right.

What is right and what is wrong is a question that is never easy to answer except by those people who are happily in a position to see only a small part of the picture and who are full of a sense of their own rectitude.

In spite of your very generous praise of me on various occasions, I have myself no such sense of self-complacency or rectitude, and so, I grope rather blindly for the light. Fortunately, in spite of certain sensitiveness, I have grown essentially thick-skinned, and a certain element of vagabondage in my make-up saves me from too much oppression of the spirit.

Yours sincerely,
Jawaharlal

---

[1] To Lord Mountbatten. V.K. Krishna Menon Papers, NMML. Excerpts.

51

Life[1]

New Delhi, 4 September 1948

My dear Mr. Shaw,

Forty years ago, when I was 18 and an undergraduate at Cambridge, I heard you address a meeting there. I have not seen you again since then, nor have I ever written to you. But, like many of my generation, we have grown up in company with your writings and books. I suppose a part of myself, such as I am today, has been moulded by that reading. I do not know if that would do you any credit.

Because, in a sense, you have been near to me, or rather near to my thoughts, I have often wanted to come in closer touch with you and to meet you. But opportunities have been lacking and then I felt that the best way to meeting you was to read what you had written.

Devadas apparently asked you as to what we should do with Gandhi's assassin.[2] I suppose he will hang and certainly I shall not try to save him from the death penalty, although I have expressed myself in favour of the abolition of the death penalty in previous years. In the present case there is no alternative. But even now, in a normal case, I have grown rather doubtful if it is preferable to death to keep a man in prison for 15 or 20 years.

Life has become so cheap that it does not seem of very much consequence whether a few criminals are put to death or not. Sometimes one wonders whether a sentence to live is not the hardest punishment after all.

I must apologize to you for those of my countrymen who pester you for your views on India. Many of us have not outgrown our old habit of seeking testimonials from others. Perhaps that is due to a certain lack of faith in our-

---

[1] To George Bernard Shaw. *A Bunch of Old Letters*. pp. 500–1. SWJN. Vol. 7 (II series), pp. 716–17. Excerpts.

[2] Bernard Shaw wrote to Devadas Gandhi: "You and Nehru are in a delicate position as to the fate of the assassin. As the son of your father you must say "Pardon him". Nehru as Prime Minister must say "Hang him", whatever his private view of the death penalty may be. If he is not officially and judicially hanged he will probably be lynched. That is for Nehru to consider. . . . As for me, I am against all punishment as such, but no statesman can abrogate the right of civilized society to exterminate human as well as animal vermin."

selves. Events have shaken us rather badly and the future does not appear to be as bright as we imagined it would be.

There is a chance of my going to England for two or three weeks in October next. I would love to pay you a visit, but certainly not if this means any interference with your daily routine. I would not come to trouble you with any questions. There are too many questions which fill the mind and for which there appear to be no adequate answers, or if the answers are there, somehow they cannot be implemented because of the human beings that should implement them. If I have the privilege to meet you for a while, it will be to treasure a memory which will make me a little richer than I am.[3]

Yours sincerely,
Jawaharlal Nehru

[3] Bernard Shaw replied on 8 September: "I was greatly gratified to learn that you were acquainted with my political writings; and I need hardly add that I should be honoured by a visit from you, though I cannot pretend that it will be worth your while to spend an afternoon of your precious time making the journey to this remote village, where there is nothing left of Bernard Shaw but a doddering old skeleton who should have died years ago. . . . Though I know nothing about India except what is in the newspapers I can consider it objectively because I am not English but Irish, and have lived through the long struggle for liberation from English rule, and the partition of the country into Eire and Northern Ireland, the Western equivalent of Hindustan and Pakistan. I am as much a foreigner in England as you were in Cambridge". Because of crowded programmes in London, Nehru could not meet Shaw.

52

In Conversation with Norman Cousins[1]

Norman Cousins: . . . I wonder whether you would care to define for Americans the basis of Indian and American understanding and friendship today.

Jawaharlal Nehru: Well, I don't know that it is possible to define anything precisely in the modern world. The most one can do is to grope about and try to see a way toward any kind of objective that one aims at. Basically, I feel that it is of essential importance for India and the United States to understand and then possibly appreciate each other's outlook with a view to as large a measure of cooperation as possible. Having said that, I begin to think what our objectives are—possibly wider and more ultimate objectives involving a large part of Asia today and possibly the rest of the world. But for the moment I am speaking about India. We are—well, in search of our soul. That sounds rather metaphysical, but I am not, of course, discussing metaphysical matters. We are groping and trying some kind of adjustment—integration, if you like—of our national life, our international as well as individual lives.

Having passed through these periods of transition and very rapid change, we have to find some equilibrium. Well, normally this would have been difficult enough; but in the present state of affairs, after all that occurred since the War in India—the partition, independence, and so on—all this has shaken us up a good deal. And so we are trying to search to find out what our objectives are. Some of us may have some vague notions; others try to look at things objectively without any fixed ideas so far as possible. So when any—shall I say slogans or fixed concepts—are put, we use them in a measure, but we are rather suspicious, too, because slogans are apt to petrify a man's thinking.

NC: Mr. Prime Minister, exactly what slogans and fixed concepts do you have in mind?

JN: Every slogan, every word, almost, that is used by the socialist, the communist, the capitalist. People hardly think nowadays. They throw words

---

[1] Interviews with Norman Cousins, Editor, *The Saturday Review of Literature*, New York, was in two parts. JN Papers, NMML. Excerpts.

[2] The first part was published in *The Saturday Review of Literature* on 14 and 21 April, 1195, and later published as a book entitled *Talks with Nehru* (New York, 1951).

at each other. They talk about democracy, but when we sit down and think about democracy all kinds of aspects of it appear which do not necessarily come up in the average man's mind. An Englishman may think of democracy in terms of his system; an American in terms of his system. Russia talks about the people's democracy, which is completely different. They use the same word. People talk about equality. Equality has a certain meaning in people's minds—in Western Europe, in America—a certain meaning which is very largely political. And certainly something aiming at economic equality.

NC: For purpose of this discussion, Mr. Prime Minister, how would you define democracy in order to give it a universal meaning—something that people everywhere could understand and respond to?

JN: Now, I told you just now that definitions are very difficult, and I do not presume to define anything, because to define anything that is big is to limit it. Nevertheless, if I may vaguely suggest something, I would say that democracy is not only political, not only economic, but something of the mind, as everything is ultimately something of the mind. It involves equality of opportunity to all people, as far as possible, in the political and economic domain. It involves the freedom of the individual to grow and to make the best of his capacities and ability. It involves a certain tolerance of others and even of others' opinions when they differ from yours. It involves a certain contemplative tendency and a certain inquisitive search for truth—and for, let us say, the right thing. That is, it is a dynamic, not a static thing, and as it changes it may be that its domain will become wider and wider. Ultimately, it is a mental approach applied to our political and economic problems.

NC: In terms of the basic equalities inherent in democracy that you mention, Mr. Prime Minister . . . would you agree that political equality is the means through which people may achieve the other equalities? . . .

JN: Yes, Political freedom or political equality is the very basis on which you build up other equalities. At the same time political equality may cease to have meaning if there is gross economic inequality. Where, let us say, people are starving the vote does not count. They are thinking in terms of the next meal and not of the vote. But leaving that out for the moment, political equality is the basis for the other equalities.

NC: Would you say, Mr. Prime Minister, that it would then also follow that the state must submit itself regularly to the approval of the people? Because unless a people have the chance to pass upon the merits of a certain government political equality will be meaningless.

JN: I agree again. Although I accept that principle completely, in practice the people can be preyed upon so much by propaganda by rousing their passions in this or that direction that you may get some entirely wrong decisions

and wrong policies. But you must take this risk. It is far better to take this risk than the other risk.

NC: I suppose one thing that democracy, as you have defined it, does do is to protect the individual against dangerous error by government. What other hope is there that, despite the abuses and the confusions, the people can keep decisions in their own hands, which means that the individual must be protected in his right to change the state?

JN: The individual has to be protected. Also the social organism has to be protected against the predatory individual. You take steps against the gangster or the anti-social individual. So the process of protection is twofold. And it is just possible—in fact, not only possible but it has taken place innumerable times—that a group may gain power and may manage for sometime, at least, to preserve that power not merely by the physical means of guns but by deluding the public by propaganda or by other processes.

NC: In which case you might then also say that the people themselves have failed rather than democracy itself. Wouldn't you agree that democracy is actually a chance?

JN: There is an old saying, isn't there, that the people get the government they deserve? And the kind of democracy they deserve? Democracy requires obviously a higher standard among far more people than other forms of government. If they do not reach their standard it may be that their democratic apparatus may fail.

NC: . . . The individual, of course, does have obligations and responsibilities to society-at-large, but the state basically is created to advance the welfare of the individual?

JN: Undoubtedly. The individual is uppermost in my mind; but in a social organism an individual cannot be separated from the rest. The rights of the individual must be balanced by the obligations of the individual to the social organism. Without obligations there can be no real rights.

NC: . . . Suppose we begin by defining . . . what the principal obligations of the state are to the individual. After that suppose we go on to the obligations of the individual toward society as a whole.

JN: This business of definitions rather embarrasses me, because I am not a professor or a philosopher or even a very effective politician. I have dabbled in various things and given a great deal of thought to matters, because they interest me. A state's obligations to the individual or the individual's obligations to the state must necessarily have varied during different periods of history. The original state was a very, very simple state in which, practically speaking, all that the state had to do was to protect the individual from a foreign enemy or another tribe. Then, from that develops the concept of what might be called, without being offensive, a police state. A state preserves law and order, protects its citizens from foreign enemies, and takes taxes to carry on its business. For the rest, it was left to the individual or the group. The present idea of the state has grown far beyond that. A state is supposed to do much more. Every state— I am not talking about any particular brand of state—every state is trying to do ever so much more for the individual than has ever been attempted previously. So the state becomes more and more of a socially functioning organism—for the good of society or the individual, as you like. And the more it becomes that, the more benefits it confers on the individual, the more, in a sense, the individual has obligations to that state. So the two things, the rights and the obligations, march together. If the state and individual are properly integrated and organized there is no conflict. Otherwise, if one side goes ahead of the other, there is a lack of balance.

NC: Within that general framework what would you say an individual has the right to expect of a state—not only as a matter of protection against a foreign power but in his direct dealings with the state itself? How would you illustrate the "social functioning organism" you just mentioned?

JN: The state, apart from protecting the individual from foreign enemies or internal disorders, has the duty to undertake to provide him with opportunities of progress, of education, health, sanitation—generally, everything that would give him the opportunity to fit himself for such work as he is capable of doing. And, you see, the state, as everything else today, has grown more and more centralized. The deep problem of today, to put it in this way, is this: you cannot escape centralized authority, whether it is of the state, whether it is of the big corporation, whether it is of the trade union, or whether it is of any group. They all go on being centralized authorities. Now all centralization is a slight encroachment on the freedom of the individual. We want to preserve the freedom of the individual, and at the same time we cannot escape centralization in modern society. How to balance the two?

NC: . . . What is the answer to the conflict between centralization and individual freedom?

JN: Well, I should say that we cannot do without a large measure of centralization. But we should try to limit that as far as possible, keeping the minimum of centralization and as far as possible, decentralize the rest.

NC: Would you at this point, Mr. Prime Minister, care to discuss your own programme for India today, in the light of these objectives?

JN: I would hardly discuss that programme in any detail but the general idea is that we—the state, that is—try to function in a way, first of all, to provide for the primary needs of our people or, at any rate, to make such arrangements that people can get those primary needs. Then there are the important secondary needs. Now, the economic organization would have to be rather a flexible one so that we can vary by experience. It is inevitable that in India, where private resources are not great, any project must be a state project. Our river valley schemes must be state schemes. No one else can do them. And any other really big project can either be a state project or jointly owned by the state and private enterprise with a measure of state control, leaving a large field for private enterprise. Thus we get what I would call a public sector of our economy and a private sector and may be a sector where the two overlap, with part state control and largely a private sector managing under state control. So we have these three branches of our economy. There need not be any rigid lines between them, and we can see which functions better and more successfully and allow them to develop. Our approach is experimental and not dogmatic.

NC: . . . What is India doing today to safeguard and enlarge the rights of the people at a time when it is imperative for India to develop projects requiring centralization?

JN: So far as political rights are concerned I suppose that our Constitution has gone as far as any constitution can go toward safeguarding the political rights of the individual. So far as economic questions are concerned it is a question of a state interfering to protect, rather than keeping away, because in rather undeveloped economics there is a tendency in certain groups of vested interests to override the interests of the large groups by whatever methods they have. Now, we are, very largely speaking, an agricultural, agrarian country. And one of our first programmes is land reform; that is, to change the old big landlord system here—rather semi-feudal landlord system—in favour here and there of cooperative farms, which we wish to encourage. That removes one out-of-date system—the big landlord system—which came in the way of our growth. The changeover has been complicated because we have done it by constitutional means and by giving compensation, which is a heavy burden.

NC: . . . What are the people of Czechoslovakia, for example, to think about Russia? I suppose that few nations did more to make Soviet Russia feel acceptable than Czechoslovakia. How would you react to that statement?

JN: Well, I do not react well at all to that statement. I am greatly distressed at many things that have happened in Eastern Europe since the last War, most especially in Czechoslovakia. I do not wish to go into details but I do feel that this kind of development is bad for any particular country. But what troubles me more is that it is bad in the larger sense of the word, too. You see, as we are constituted today no government and no people can do without, let us say, armed force for defence, for protection, for security, and the rest of it. Nevertheless, I do believe fundamentally that armed force does not solve any problems. It is the spirit of man that triumphs—even over death.

I was in Czechoslovakia in 1938 at the time of the Sudeten crisis, and all my sympathies were with the Czech people. It was a great sorrow to me to see these brave, disciplined, democratic people thrown overboard at that time and falling into Hitler's hands; and it is a sorrow to me today, for these people today are still facing grave difficulties. Now I have no solution for these things, because there is no magic solution. One has to go deeper down and find the root causes. It is patent today that some of the great countries of the world are so full of fear of what might happen, of aggression, etc., that they prepare for it, with the result that others prepare for it, and so the preparation for war mounts up. Possibly even some of the aggression itself is caused rather by that fear that the other party might become dominant in that area. This does not lead to any peaceful solution; it merely leads you to the precipice of war where the slightest push might send you over.

NC: Coming back to Czechoslovakia: in 1945 and 1946 would you not agree that the world then was relatively free of fear? What steps do you think might have been taken at that time that might have been able to avert the overthrow of Czechoslovakia?

JN: I am afraid I cannot say and I would not say. It is too difficult a question, because since the last War so many things have happened, with one leading into another. The only basic step would have been to divert the world's attention toward less fear of aggression and less fear of prospective war and, of course, toward a continuous attempt to deal with these questions in the United Nations or in other powerful ways.

NC: Would you agree, Mr. Prime Minister, in connection with your last statement, that the world's last best hope of peace, then, is the United Nations—to revert to an earlier point in our discussion?

JN: When you talk about the United Nations a number of pictures come into my mind. One is the great ideal that inspired, that gave birth to the United Nations. Another is the Charter of the United Nations. Another is the structure of the United Nations, and so on. I do think that all these things are fundamentally not only worthwhile but essential. But that does not mean that I approve of everything that the United Nations does simply because it is the United Nations. That does not mean that the way the United Nations has sometimes functioned is always very desirable. In fact, it does not mean even that the present structure of the United Nations is ideal or is in line with what it was intended to be. So that if you want the United Nations really to be great— not only powerful in the material sense but a power affecting the minds and spirits of men—then it must function in a particular way to capture the minds and spirits of men. Now if the United Nations does not affect half of the world, well, it is not the United Nations and it cannot think of controlling a quarter of the world or half the world by military means.

Even if it succeeded in doing so the result would not be the democratic ideal but some military dictatorship all over the world. And yet, it is quite inevitable that something in the nature of the United Nations has to take charge of the world in the wider sense, not of compulsion so much. Compulsion can ultimately only be exercised over a small evil doer if society believes in a certain fundamental moral principle. If that principle itself is challenged by a great part of society then there is conflict. Ultimately the United Nations must not only be, of course, universal but must, shall I say, deprive to a certain degree other nations of some phases of their sovereignty. That is to say, it will have to develop the international order into an international government, in the largest sense of the term and without interfering with national autonomy.

The world today is a curious mixture of some degree of uniformity and a great variety—a great variety in the sense that there are differing historical backgrounds, cultural methods, ways of living, economic conditions. Some countries are very backward, some are underdeveloped, some are highly developed. Then there is this difference of cultural background. We do come nearer to each other because of rapid communications and transport, etc. But basic things such as racial backgrounds remain. How are we to deal with this variety? It is no good trying to make them uniform and regimented, and I do not think it would be a good thing to try to do this.

So it comes to this: giving as much freedom as possible for each way of life to develop along its own lines, helping it where possible without too much interference, understanding its ways and, of course, neither interfering with it nor allowing it to interfere with others. That is, in the world as it is we have to adopt the principle of live and let live but always with an evergrowing cooperation which gradually integrates the world more and more closely together. Any attempted forcible integration leads, can only lead, to some kind of military rule which would be bad from many points of view and most especially from the point of view of the development of the individual or the group. So one has to balance these factors all the time; one has to have more and more cooperation developing into a world order and at the same time more and more autonomy in respective regions for the people in those regions to function as they like.

NC: . . . Would India join other nations in proposing a re-examination of the United Nations with a view towards strengthening it?. . .

JN: I hope that I have some sense of moral value and standards. In fact, if I may say so, I do not think that life is worthwhile without some such standards—moral or spiritual in the widest sense. But I am terribly afraid of people who talk about morality or about crusading. The whole conception in India was built up, if you look at Indian history, on the principle of non-proselytization. Our religion is so based. We do not go out of our way to ask anybody to change his religion and belong to ours. He can believe in his own religion and in his own standards. If anything in us appeals to him, good, he can discuss it with us. It is a question for the individual to decide. Why should I impose my view of religion or spirituality or anything else on the other person or on the other nation, except insofar as out of discussion, consultation, cooperation we adopt each other's ways?

Therefore, my whole approach is somewhat different and not of this moral crusade, because it is not quite so easy to find out what is the right morality on a certain occasion. Oh yes, we use high words—high-sounding phrases and words—but behind those phrases may lie entirely different chains of thought, objectives, interests, and the like. Everybody talks in high terms now, especially in a democracy when we go to the election; but the fact remains that the person who talks like that may not necessarily act in that way. Therefore, I would personally prefer not so much talk about—well, shall I say high morality and the rest of it—and tackle the problem in a simpler way. May I mention another thing? More and more I am beginning to dislike slogans. Slogans, of course, came into the picture very much from Russia. The communist lives on slogans. Some of the slogans are not bad, but I dislike most slogans. They prevent the person from thinking. All slogans, I think, are rather confusing, although they may contain an element of the truth in them. So let us face this problem, certainly in a moral way, in a spiritual way, and, if I may say so, in a reverent way and, if I may also say so, with always the idea at the back of my mind that I may not be wholly right. There may be something else that might help me. There may be something else that has escaped me. If we approach it in that spirit, and then think of world cooperation, of building up a universal order— if possible through the UN, through the UN growing, becoming more universal, having more power to suppress any crime against humanity—we may do that; but we will do that only when in a large measure the organization itself begins to represent what might be called the will of the world community.

Part II[2]

Norman Cousins: Mr. Prime Minister, two years ago we had a discussion about, well, the state of the human race. To some extent it was what one might call a whither-are-we-drifting-and-why talk. Taking into account everything that has happened in those two years, throughout the rest of the world and here in India, how do you feel about the chances of the human species today for making a better world and better future? What, in short, are our chances for a world in which it is possible for a man to be an individual, to be free and yet to survive?

Jawaharlal Nehru: I should imagine that only the unwise give an opinion

[2] New Delhi, 3 September 1953. JN Collection, NMML. The second part of the interview was published in *The Saturday Review of Literature*, 12 December 1951

on such a subject. Like most things, the world picture today has its very good features and its very bad ones. Obviously we have arrived at a state which is highly dynamic, almost explosive. Either we find some new equilibrium or, well, we shatter ourselves into bits. The problem is to find that equilibrium somehow, for war has ceased to be any means of carrying out any policy. Defeat or victory have an importance, no doubt, but war is so bad that the original policy collapses anyway. Therefore, the point is whether, in avoiding war, one can maintain one's independence or general position and objectives. In war, one cannot.

It is a problem of human intelligence and human effort. It is a challenge that involves the art of cooperation and friendliness. Theoretically this is certainly possible. Practically whether it is going to happen or not is anybody's guess. On the whole I should imagine that the chances may be in favour of it.

NC: You indicated a moment ago, Mr. Prime Minister, that the important thing is to maintain one's values in the world today—without war if possible. For some things can only be preserved through colossal risk and effort. What would you say, looking towards the future, are these basic values?

JN: There is a certain vitality in the human race, a creative vitality, which leads to progress, leads to new things. You find in history a race sometimes being full of creative endeavour. It may be highly cultured in the sense of having achieved much. Then suddenly that race loses its vitality, becoming quiescent. You find that more especially, say, in Asia. You find two or three hundred years of just quiescence, a very cultured quiescence for a long time perhaps, but quiescence nonetheless. Yet at the same time you find that other races or peoples, which outwardly may have been more backward culturally, were actually more vital or dynamic. Then they proceeded to develop culture at a more rapid pace.

What, then, are the real values, apart from a certain appreciation and regard for fundamental truth and beauty and tolerance? When large numbers of people live together as they do in the world today, unless the nations respect the rights of each other, unless they develop a necessary toleration, there is trouble. I am afraid there is something of a tendency for less and less toleration now— less of even an attempt to understand. This, culturally speaking, is going backwards.

Now, when we talk about the world going to pieces, of course, one does not mean that every being will die. It really means that the cultural aspect of life will suffer an enormous setback. Even normal war brutalizes, as it has done in the past. Today's type of war is on an enormous scale and brings destruction and hunger and starvation. It is bound to degrade and dehumanize those who survive. That is the worst of it—not death; people die at the end of their days. Brutalization is the evil.

NC: What should the role of a government be—the role of an enlightened government—in helping to protect the people against brutalization—not only the brutalization brought about by war but the brutalization that sometimes exists within the nation itself?

JN: Partly, I suppose, it's an educational role, that is, if education is directed to that end. A person is influenced very greatly by his environment, not merely book environment or what he learns at school or at college, but what he reads in the newspapers, what he sees around him all the time, by his personal relationships. So, in a sense, if he is properly conditioned he lives in the type of society or social structure which encourages those positive values and discourages the wrong values, such as selfishness or pure acquisitiveness, instead of the quality of cooperative work and tolerance.

NC: Do world conditions today represent a threat to the maintenance and enlargement of those values? Isn't it possible that a powerful regime which finds the values of individualism repugnant could jeopardize progress on a world scale?

JN: Certainly. Today you see a very serious threat—also, to some extent, a response to that threat—that is, a determination to maintain those values. We have the constructive side and the destructive side—opposing forces at work in the world today. The particular things that are part of this destructive side, I should say, would include lack of toleration or a desire to force your will on the other person or the other nation. In other words, there is a certain narrowness of outlook in the individual or the group which thinks that it has the truth and that all the others are outside the pale and, so to speak, the real sinners. In fact, to some extent we are getting what corresponds to, well, a narrow religious outlook in politics. In religion there are at least certain countervailing features which tend to balance this narrowness, that is, in those religions in which narrowness may be said to exist. In politics, however, you get the narrowness alone. This idea of forcing your wishes, your ways, down the throats of others naturally leads to conflict. It may lead, of course, to the other party being compelled to assert himself. But even that is not very satisfactory in the end, because you do not produce any desirable type of human being if he does something only under compulsion.

NC: Mr. Prime Minister, when you used the word "you" just a moment ago I wondered whether you had a particular nation or person in mind?

JN: No, I was not thinking of any particular group or country.

NC: I asked that question because a certain totalitarian nation came to my mind as you spoke. I am aware, too, that some people would make an opposite assumption on the basis of what you had just said and point to the United

States. In fact, I have been disturbed in recent weeks by the tendency in a number of places I have visited on my way to India—a tendency to blame the United States for everything.

JN: No, of course, I was not thinking of America. This is common, to a more or less degree, all over the world today.

NC: What steps do you think, Mr. Prime Minister, can be taken by the nations acting as a group to create a stronger sense on the whole, to help create those conditions under which the individual or the group can maintain those values you spoke of a moment ago?

JN: I suppose the most important thing is, and perhaps the most difficult, is to try to get rid of the terrible prevalence of fear. Fear, in a way, is almost worse, I suppose, than any other reaction, because if you are afraid you are apt to act wrongly. You will feel hatred for the person you are afraid of. You will try to injure that person or group. And fear generates fear on the other side; fear is an expanding thing. So every step might well be judged according to whether it increases or decreases the element of fear in the world. If there is less fear then there is more reasoned thinking, more understanding. If there is more fear, well, one thinks poorly and only acts in an excited, and usually wrong way.

NC: Would you say that there is more or less fear in the world today—justified or unjustified fear—than when we spoke two years ago?

JN: Now I don't know. I should have thought on the whole that there might be a little less; but it is difficult to measure these things. Various good things have happened in recent months—the Korean War has ended, at least for the time being; there's certainly a relaxation in Europe, a very marked relaxation of that fear complex and expectation of disaster of which I spoke a moment ago and which, I think, prevailed much more two years ago. So, in that sense, I should say that conditions are somewhat better. Yet in a more basic sense, in the historical sense, they're much the same.

NC: Has the death of Stalin[3] had anything to do with the lessening of this tension? Do you believe that the passing of the Soviet dictator marks the beginning of a real change inside Russia?

JN: I do not know how far the death of Stalin has resulted in anything special; but certainly, since the death of Stalin, many things have happened inside Soviet Russia itself. Also there have been a few things done by the Soviet which may have relaxed tension somewhat in Europe. Now, it is quite immaterial what the motive behind that may be. The fact is some of the tensions have eased and therefore it is welcome.

[3] Josef V. Stalin died on 5 March 1953.

NC: What are some of the actual things that have been done by the Soviet that you feel have justified such an easing or relaxation of world tensions? Have the words been matched by deeds?

JN: I think the new Soviet leaders have done some things apart from saying them. There have been some changes for the better in Austria. Even in the Soviet-occupied territories in Eastern Europe, we have seen certain steps—not very big, to be sure, but certain steps—in the direction of a relaxation of tension. One has the impression that the new Soviet regime may be trying to concentrate on Russia's own economic development. Whatever the reason may be, there is little doubt in my mind that they are trying something of a new approach in their policy.

NC: Would you say, Mr Prime Minister, that there is any basic change in the long-range policy of the Soviet, apart from a possible present change in tactics?

JN: I don't quite know what you mean by "long-range", because nobody today can really talk in terms of, let us say, decades. But I think there has been a definite change in a particular direction and it is likely to endure for the next few years. Now, what happens after that nobody can say. Also, I think that the current feeling in the Soviet Union, or at any rate in their top-ranking people, is that by showing results in the economic field in their own country they can produce a more powerful impression on the rest of the world than though other means.

NC: There seems to be a feeling on the part of some nations, including the United States, that one contribution the Soviet could make to the building of a more stable world is by helping to develop the United Nations itself. You may recall that the last time we spoke you referred to the need for a "fresh start" inside the United Nations in order to give it such strength as would be required to guarantee the independence of the individual nations and to protect the world against aggression through workable world law. I believe you also called attention to the work of Mahatma Gandhi in this particular direction. Would you say that the events of the past two years have strengthened you in this belief?

JN: Yes, I do feel strengthened in that belief. It may be on account of events; it may be on account of my own thinking. As for the United Nations, it is facing a difficult time and unless some fresh adjustments are made the internal conflicts of the UN may increase. It is not particularly easy to suggest what the adjustments should be because these matters, after all, are not merely legal or constitutional. It is not the fault of the United Nations, which actually reflects conditions in the world. If the world doesn't pull together properly, the United Nations is affected. And so, while we may try to improve the United Nations, the real thing is to improve the environment of the United Nations or the things that are happening in the world. To repeat, we should try to lessen the world fear complex. If we do this it helps to create a proper atmosphere for the consideration of important problems. This helps in the possible reshaping or reorganization of the United Nations, so that it can protect the independence of nations and prevent the interference of one nation in the affairs of another and, at the same time, bring about a fuller cooperation of the nations as a whole.

NC: Do I take it from what you have just said that India will support such a fresh examination of the problem of the UN when the question of Charter revision comes up in 1955 on the agenda of the United Nations?

JN: Certainly. Exactly in what form it comes up, of course, I do not know, and much would depend upon that. When one talks about the independence of nations, remember that, in the mind of the average Indian or the average Asian, the fact springs up that there are many countries in Asia which are not independent. What about them? Many policies are being pursued in Asia and Africa which are the reverse of policies meant to preserve the independence or the national cultures or the way of life of any particular country. So that before we start thinking of putting the rest of the world right, the part of the world which is not right should be put right.

NC: Would these logically be some of the questions that should come up at a UN Review Conference in 1955?

JN: They ought to come up in some form or another certainly, because they are very vital questions. Almost all over Asia today you find that these are primary questions in the minds of people. Even in Africa today these questions are very much to the fore.

NC: Here in India I have been tremendously heartened by the evidence of progress since my previous visit. For example, I have gone out to places where there used to be refugee camps—I was looking for people I had met two years ago, and I was happy to learn that they had long since been resettled. And as I go around the countryside; as I see green fields where not long ago there were brown fields caused by the drought; as I see more food and clothes in the stores, I become heartened, as I say, by this evidence of progress. Would you care to review, from the desk of a Prime Minister, the principal steps that have been taken in the last two years to improve conditions in India?

JN: I think it is true that we have been making progress on many fronts—certainly in regard to the rehabilation of refugees. Also in developing a number of our industries. Most heartening of all, I think, is the improvement in our food situation. I can't say that we have solved the food problem, but we have gone much further than we thought we could go. In fact, we have done in a year or two a large part of what we had thought would take five years to accomplish. So that is all to the good. But at the same time an ever-increasing sense of urgency oppresses us. And it is good that this should be so, because nothing is more dangerous than a feeling of complacency. It is all too easy for governments to make this mistake. At the present moment the overall problem which is most in people's minds here is the problem of unemployment, chiefly urban, but really both urban and rural, and we are giving it hard thought.

NC: What are some of the problems in addition to unemployment?

JN: Unemployment surely covers so many problems that if we solve that problem we will have solved nearly all problems. You see, we start with the political problem. The internal political problem has been largely solved by independence. After the political problem comes the economic problem, which for us, an underdeveloped country, is a terrific one. It involves the economic health of all our people—providing opportunities of growth to all of them. Some of the particular economic problems you may have in America or western Europe are still too far off for us to consider since we have to deal with these primary problems. When we manage that we can think some more about the rest. Of course, we do think about these advanced problems too, but meanwhile there is the problem of finding food, housing, clothing, education and health for our people, who increase by four or five million every year. Obviously, the best way to achieve all this is through regular employment. Therefore, the problem of unemployment can better be expressed as the problem of employment, employment for all. Education, health, and other social services and activities, as I said, are directly connected with employment.

About two years back we announced a programme we hoped to complete in the ensuing five years. We presented an outline and invited criticism. After a year we finalized our programme but, in doing it, we made great changes and, I think, improved it. Now, after another year, we find that we should change it still more, that is, move faster, paying attention more especially to this problem of fuller employment. We are, at the present moment, trying to revise that programme with this in view.

NC: You spoke two years ago of your hopes that India might be able to develop village projects, local projects, that might preserve the cultural values of village life and yet provide the means for fuller employment and for improving the health and living conditions of the Indian people. Has anything specific taken shape along these lines?

JN: As far as I remember, when you came two years back there was not much said about community centres. Was there?

NC: No.

JN: That is a new thing entirely. Well, these community centres are not absolutely new but certainly represent for us a new approach to the old problem and, I think, a very hopeful one. We want to spread them out all over the country. In the first years we started fifty five such centres. Each centre comprises,

I think, some 300 villages, divided up into blocks of a hundred. We started in a fairly big way, and we have slowly increased the number of centres. And in the course of five years we should really cover about a third of India.

Right now we are going in a slightly different direction from before by instituting what is called a national extension service—rural, of course—which will cover much more rapidly the other areas, though not quite so intensively. We always have to decide, of course, whether to spread our activity or to concentrate in some areas. It is not a good idea to spread our activity so thin that it doesn't show at all.

NC: What about the condition of village life in general today?

JN: We are also thinking in terms of improving the living standards of the villages. We want as well to improve the agricultural standards and the cultural standards. We are attacking another problem: the drift to the towns. We have had, as you know, a considerable migration to the cities. But in many of the cities there is little additional work to be had. And so most newcomers join the ranks of the unemployed. Now, if we can build up the villages and offer jobs as well as a measure of some kind of cultural life, we stop this dangerous drift. So this whole idea of community centres has set us thinking along new lines.

In addition to those centres, we are having a national extension service which, in the course of the next three or four years, is meant to cover almost the whole of India, all 600,000 villages. It is a terrific job, and apart from the finances involved in it, the real difficulty is in training human beings. Therefore, we have training programmes in a large number of centres. That is, we are training them not as specialists as much as good village-level workers. We are now in the process of training some 80,000 village-level workers. That helps the employment programme, too.

NC: I should be very proud, Mr. Prime Minister, if the American people, through their programme of technical assistance or through the work of private foundations, have been helpful in the development of your community centres.

JN: Yes, they have been helpful, and they will probably be even more helpful in the future.

There is also another side to this general problem; that is, while we want technological development, we do not want technological development if it means technological unemployment. We don't want greater production at the expense of large numbers of human beings who would be thrown on the scrap heap, you might say. So we must balance the two.

NC: I had in mind not only American technologists but all the Americans who have come over to help. Today, for example, I met a group of American students from the University of California at Los Angeles. They told me of the schools in India they had helped to build with their bare hands. They told me of their work in the villages. I think these young people reflected something very deep in our country. It is the desire to have a human contact with the people of India and, indeed, with the people of the world. Wherever I have gone in the United States I have found this desire, and I am especially glad that I found it being fulfilled in India itself, where it could become apparent to the Indian people.

JN: Yes, I met this group of students and I have met a number of groups of students from the United States. I have been very much impressed by them—not only because of their general friendliness but because of their outlook, an eagerness to be cooperative, friendly, to learn and, if possible, to teach. And generally they behave in a manner which brings them very near to us. I think they have been very good ambassadors to India.

NC: To return to my opening question, Mr. Prime Minister, some time ago, before we set up these microphones, you were philosophizing about the future of the human race. May I ask you whether, in the light no only of the events of the past two years but in the light of your total experience in and out of government, whether you are optimistic or pessimistic about the future?

JN: As I said at the start, that is a question which, if you like, one can try to answer in a sentence or two or in a book, and still not answer it. Looking at the long perspective of history, however, one sees all kinds of terrible tragedies occurring and I have no doubt that during those periods this very same questions asked: namely, what is going to happen to the human race? Is it going to be submerged in barbarism? But, in spite of all those tragedies and disasters, the human race has survived, and I have no doubt today that man will survive—whatever lies ahead. He has an amazing endurance. Whether one can justify that by logic or reasoning or not, one has an inner feeling that it must happen.

NC: I am deeply grateful to you for this discussion today, Mr. Prime Minister. Once again, as I did the last time, I wonder whether there are any closing words you would like to say to the American people?

JN: I forget what I said the last time and I certainly don't wish to repeat myself; but it is obvious that in the world today the United States has an extraordinarily important task to fulfil and a tremendous responsibility. When a nation or a people are in that situation everything that they do big or small, produces an effect that is felt all over the world. I hope and believe that the United States, or rather the people of the United States, will utilize this great historic chance before them and that they will help the world to help itself, for ultimately everyone has to stand on his own feet. But certainly the United States can help the world to build and develop itself. And it can help to create that atmosphere of lack of fear and lack of hatred that can yet bring about a certain spirit of cooperative endeavour, of live and let live.

NC: Because of what you have just said, are you optimistic about good relations between India and America?

JN: I consider these good relations very important, naturally, because America, as I said, has such a great responsibility. What we do or do not do is powerfully affected by our relations with America. Therefore, I would like to work for continuing good relations and I am quite convinced that in doing so I am only doing the same thing that is being done by so many Americans themselves.

53

Kashmir and the Constituent Assembly[1]

Always, when I say something here or talk about Kashmir, the question that arises before me is, in what capacity I should speak and where I should lay more stress. Should I talk to you as a Kashmiri? Should I speak from my heart more or from my mind? Should I let emotions sway me or be influenced by the pressures of love and the storm emotions that threaten to overwhelm me? Or should I speak calmly, bearing in mind that by sheer chance I am in a position of great responsibility these days and speak from that high position? Shall I speak in the voice of the Government of India or in that of Jawaharlal? That does not mean that in this matter, there is much difference between the two voices. But still, difference does come in between what a responsible government says and what the heart speaks out of emotion. I want to make an effort, especially on this occasion, not to let my emotions sway me too much. I do not know how far I shall succeed because the pressure is great and I would like to speak calmly and in a responsible manner.

I am able to visit Kashmir off and on and whenever I come here, my heart is happy and draws fresh strength because I am weighed down by my responsibilities. A position in government is the most difficult, which has not only troubled me but in many people's view, changed me a little too. Only others can bear witness to this. It is obvious that man changes with responsibilities and new experiences and I too must have changed. But when I go to a few places in India and especially when I come to Kashmir, I realize that though I have certainly changed a little, a little of the old fire still burns in me, the old enthusiasm and the capacity to work at big tasks still remain. That is because though I have had varied experiences in life and in jail there is no bigger jail sentence than a position in government. There are enormous responsibilities and difficulties and especially when the question looms large as to whether one is fulfilling the dreams that one had, and finds thousands of obstacles in the way, then one is in a terrible dilemma. Is one to leave one's position and run away or give up the dreams and principles of a life-time? This is the dilemma. Anyhow a way does emerge somehow and if it does not, then the individual

[1] Speech at a session of the National Conference, Srinagar, 4 June 1951. AIR Tapes. NMML, Extracts.

enmeshed in the tangle becomes useless. I do not know what will happen to me. But I do realize that time has not yet come for me. When that time comes and I and the others begin to believe that I am no longer capable of doing good work, due to pressures of old age or any other reason, then perhaps I shall ask you to let me spend my last days in peace in some corner of these mountains. But perhaps that day will never come because for people who walk on the path that you and I and many of us have travelled on, there is no resting place where they can call a halt and relax. Their resting place is life's last moment and till then, their convictions pull them and force them to do the work that they have chosen, for as long as possible, because the tasks are never ending. The great tasks of a great nation go on forever and the most that an individual can do is to carry them forward with all his might and perhaps succeed in a small measure. And when he has done his duty till the end, to draw his last breath engaged in those tasks. There can be no greater satisfaction for a human being than this.

Anyhow, I am able to visit Kashmir sometimes and mostly for a day or two because I cannot get away for a longer duration. But even two days make a great deal of difference, firstly by seeing these mountains but more by meeting the people here and discussing their problems and by seeing how you and I are engaged together in the task of writing the history of Kashmir at the moment. It infuses a new strength just like the lives of the great infuse new strength in human beings. Please remember that man can rise only as high as his tasks will permit him to and small men engaged in big tasks gain in stature.

54

Sense of Jneffectiveness[1]

New Delhi, 9 June 1951

My dear Rajaji,

I have been so terribly busy for some weeks now that I have had no chance of a talk with you, although my mind has been greatly troubled. I hope that I shall have that chance before you go to Madras from Delhi. Meanwhile it is perhaps worthwhile for me to give you some indication of the working of my mind.

I have been feeling exceedingly exhausted, both physically and mentally. I do not remember ever having felt like this before. As a result of this my nerves have been on edge. I suppose I shall recover soon from it, now that the daily strain is a little less. . . .

I have an increasing feeling that such utility as I have had is lessening and I work more as an automaton in a routine way rather than as an active and living person. Throughout my public life, I have drawn my strength chiefly from my contacts with the people. Those contacts grow less and less and I find no recompense for them in my new environment. So I grow rootless and feel unhappy. The trend of events and what we ourselves do seems to take me away more and more from many things that I have valued in life and from such ideals as I have nourished. Functioning in such a way ceases to have much meaning.

Many of our policies, economic and other, leave a sense of grave uneasiness in me. I do not interfere partly because I am not wholly seized with the subject and partly because of myself being entangled in a web out of which it is difficult to emerge. We function more and more as the old British Government did, only with less efficiency. The only justification for less efficiency is a popular drive with popular enthusiasm. We have neither that enthusiasm of the people nor the efficiency. We rely more and more on official agencies which are generally fairly good, but which are completely different in outlook and execution from anything that draws popular enthusiasm to it. Complaints grow all round us and produce several others. Our economic approach is both conservative and unstable.

[1] To C. Rajagopalchari. JN Collection, NMML. Excerpts.

I feel that if I have to be of any real use in the future, I must find my roots again. I do not think I can do so by continuing for much longer in my present routine of life. I am prepared to continue for a while, but not too long. I do not think that my days of useful work have ended, but I feel sure that my utility will grow less and less in existing circumstances.

I hope that during the next month I shall have some leisure to think out some of the problems that confront us. I propose to remain in Delhi most of this time.

Yours,
Jawaharlal

55

Controlling Emotions[1]

My dear Krishna,

You complain of being harassed by petty and big things. Of course you are harassed and I am harassed and all of us are harassed. But I feel that a good part of the harassment is perhaps due to your own reactions which are sudden and sometimes strong.

You advise me on various matters and I consider your advice very valuable. But you seem to think that I function here as an autocrat and that you should also function there in London in a similar capacity. It is difficult, even if it was right, to function in that way. Certainly it is not possible for me with Parliament and all kinds of persons continually nagging at me and trying to find fault with me. If you read the Indian newspapers carefully, you will find the kind of things I have to put up with. Even then you would only get a very small part of the picture.

I have written to you about your telegrams to me, which are almost always "strictly personal."[2] Sometimes these telegrams are in answer to some enquiry from me. I am asked by my colleagues in the Cabinet what you have said in reply. Your reply is often such that I cannot place it before them and I am put in difficulty. Therefore, I have suggested that you should confine your personal telegrams to particular messages in addition to the main telegram. I cannot and should not take major decisions without reference to my colleagues. The impression gets abroad that you hold them and most people here in contempt or consider them as completely misguided and unable to understand a situation. That may or may not be so, but does not help at all. We have to work with such material as we have got, including the services.

You refer in one of your letters to my trust and confidence. Of course you have got that as well as my affection. But that does not necessarily mean that your judgement of what is happening in India or what can be done here is right.

---

[1] To V.K. Krishna Menon. V.K. Krishna Menon Papers, NMML. Excerpts.

[2] In his cable dated 22 July 1951, in which he had commented on the work of officers who had gone from India, Krishna Menon had requested Nehru to treat the cable as "strictly personal".

After all we have to carry people here and the mere rightness of an opinion is not enough. Sometimes your approach makes it difficult for me to carry people here, even when I agree with your views. I think that often you do injustice to yourself and needlessly add to your own difficulties and others' difficulties.

I have written to you repeatedly that you should take leave and cut yourself off from work completely for some months. I meant it even though I knew that this kind of physical rest may be extremely distasteful to you. I am glad that you are better as a result of your treatment. Nevertheless, I still hold to the opinion that it will be good for you to get away. I am gradually coming near a conclusion that I should do something of this kind. But about you, I am quite sure. I said in a letter to you that your staying on is neither fair to you nor to your work and you have asked me what I mean by this. I meant first of all that a person who is in ill health and often in a highly nervous condition cannot give his best to the work and his nervousness comes to others. It is true that even so your work is much more valuable than anyone else's can be. But if you do not give yourself a chance and it may lessen in value later. I also think that it is good for any set-up not to revolve completely round an individual. It must be capable of functioning for some time at least by itself without that individual. The bigger the organization, the more this applies. There is virtue in a one-man show, but there are grave disadvantages also. You do not like people telling you that you take too much upon yourself and do not allow others to assume responsibility. Yet that is a universal impression. Sometimes your letters and telegrams seem to indicate that you would like me to function in that way. I am sorry I can't, even physically, and I do not like doing so. Much therefore is done without reference to me or by subsequent reference. It may be it goes wrong. I take the risk. I am sure that it would be better for India House if you allowed others to function with responsibility and without reference to you within their particular fields. Of course you would be the boss and can call up any matter and generally keep an eye on everything. If things cannot function unless you yourself do practically everything, then the arrangement is wrong and things must get held up when you are away or unwell or even when you are well. You refer very often to the terrible hard work done by you as well as by many others in India House. I am sure this is so. But I often wonder how far this is due to the faulty organization and to a lack of spreading out responsibilities. There is no particular point in having senior officers if they do not have that responsibility. It must produce a sense of frustration in them and merely add to your burdens.

When I read some of your telegrams and letters, I sense high excitement, and I have a feeling that you are worked up to something. I can almost feel a temperature. That is not a good impression to give. That is undoubtedly due both to your ill health and overwork, as well as your extreme anxiety that something should be done. But somehow it has a slightly different effect and one begins to think less of the subject you refer to and more of you.

Everyone who comes back here from London brings reports of your ill health and nervous condition. Letters from various friends repeat this also. Whatever the truth may be, the fact of creating this impression is itself relevant. I have had reports of conversations of several British ministers. Each one is reported to have said that you were far too ill to work and should take rest and go away from work.

The world is a very complicated affair and not always amenable to our wishes and so repeatedly we suffer pain and disappointment. If we are sensitive, we suffer more. One has to get used to it and to react less to the good and the bad of it and to give that impression to others also. Otherwise we do not carry such conviction as we might do.

People tell me often that I am indispensable in India and all that. I recognize my worth and my importance in the context of things today. But nothing is more foolish, I think, than to consider oneself indispensable and, if one is really indispensable, then it is a bad lookout for the country. Things depend too much on that individual and the machine goes all wrong when he is not there. I am inclined to think that it would have been a very good thing for India if I had dropped out of the Prime Ministership some time ago. I could have come back probably with greater mental and physical vigour and at the same time people generally would have had a different kind of experience. There is a risk of course, but the risk has to be taken. As it is, I grow stale and the country slowly gets rather tired of me.

I have written to you frankly because I am myself facing much of the time, and more especially now, some kind of a crisis here. Because of this, I have been forced to think of all these matters.

Yours,
Jawaharlal

56

Touring in India[1]

Jaipur, 3 December 1951

My dear Edwina,

Forgive me for sending this type written letter to you. I am doing it to save time and time has somehow become very precious, or rather I am constantly trying to put in a day more work than it was meant for. One of my continuing troubles is how to cover the whole of India within a brief month or so. I rush about from north to the far south and from east to west and yet a vast area remains uncovered. Insistent demands come to me from all the states demanding my instant presence. What is more, they want to take me to out-of-the way places, covering a long stretch of road, not realizing that I have to visit scores of other towns and rural areas. . . .

The more I travel about in this way, the more a feeling of excitement seizes me. This is not, I think, due to elections and the like, bur rather to a fresh discovery of various parts of India and of the masses of human beings that inhabit them. Wherever I have been, vast multitudes gather at my meetings and I love to compare them, their faces, their dresses, their reactions to me and to what I say. Scenes from past history of that very part of India rise up before me and my mind becomes a picture gallery of past events. But, more than the past, the present fills my mind and I try to probe into the minds and hearts of these multitudes. Having long been imprisoned in the Secretariat of Delhi, I rather enjoy these fresh contacts with the Indian people. It all becomes an exciting adventure. I feel naturally physically tired by this constant movement and long speeches, but the tiredness passes off because of the feeling of adventure and excitement. Usually, when I return to Delhi, there is a reaction and I suddenly feel very tired.

I speak to these people and I try to tell them in some detail of how I feel and what I want them to do. I refer to the elections only casually because, I tell them, I have bigger things in my mind. The effort to explain in simple language our problems and our difficulties and to reach the minds of these simple folk is both exhausting and exhilarating.

[1] To Lady Mountbatten. JN Collection, NMML. Excerpts.

As I wander about, the past and the present merge into one another and this merger leads me to think of the future. Time becomes like a flowing river in continuous motion with events connected with one another.

Yours,
Jawaharlal

57

Mountains[1]

Burgenstock, 18 June 1953

My dear Lady Mountbatten,

Tonight, after dinner, we saw a film of the Swiss Everest Expedition of 1952. This has not been released yet and it was shown for the first time to us especially by the Swiss Alpine Society which organized this Expedition.

This film was one of the most exciting and moving of this type that I have ever seen. It was of course a good colour film. But it was something more than that and it brought out the tremendous conflict between human beings and Everest and, even though Everest was not reached by these people, it was a triumph of the human spirit.

Blizzards attacked these people and we could hear the hissing noise of the wind as it enveloped them. All of us who saw this picture were considerably affected. Tenzing played an important part in it together with the Swiss, Lambert.[2] These two reached within 800 feet of the summit and had then to come back. If you have the chance, see this film when it comes out.

As I saw this film, a feeling of sadness came over me that I would never be able to climb these mountains or reach these heights. Age and shortness of breath and feebleness of feet have become insurmountable barriers. I am greatly attracted to these wild regions of snow and blizzard, but my body, I suppose, is no longer capable of enduring them. I suppose that we must contend ourselves with trying to utilize such strength and energy as we have got in other types of human endeavour. There are many Everests in this world, perhaps more difficult of conquest than even the mountain of that name.

Yours sincerely,
Jawaharlal Nehru

[1] To Edwina Mountbatten. JN Collection, NMML. Excerpts.
[2] Raymond Lambert, a Swiss mountaineer and member of the Swiss Everest expedition as of May and October-November 1952.

58

Laying down Office[1]

11 October 1954

Dear Comrade,

You must have read in the newspapers about some statements I have made recently suggesting that I should unburden myself of the high office I hold. These statements have naturally led to much comment in the press and I have received a number of letters from friends and colleagues expressing some apprehension in regard to them.

I owe it to you and to other friends and colleagues to explain this matter a little more fully than I have so far done. I have occasionally referred to my feeling tired. That is correct, but it has no great significance. For many months past, the strain on me has been considerable and it is not surprising that I should feel somewhat tired. But that tiredness does not last and disappears with a little rest. I can assure you that I am in good health and as fit as any person at my age is expected to be.

Physical health is intimately connected with mental health. I think that both in body and mind I am healthy. I have a tendency to overdo things and sometimes overstrain myself, which of course is undesirable and should be avoided. But I am not careless of my health and I recover rapidly. That resilience itself, I suppose, is a good sign. Naturally, because of the heavy burdens I carry, I can hardly function in a carefree manner. That kind of existence is denied to me as it is to most other people. But I am convinced that hard work does not interfere with mental or bodily health, provided certain elementary precautions are taken. Indeed, on the whole, work is helpful even in maintaining flexibility of mind and body, which is an important element of health.

You will forgive me for discussing myself in this way. But, in view of some apprehension in the minds of people, I have ventured to do so. I can assure you that I am fit and that I propose to remain fit for many years to come. I do not believe in any kind of *valetudinarianism* and have a dislike of ill health. I feel that I have many tasks still to perform in our country and I am determined to keep myself fit for the purpose.

[1] Circular to Congressmen, AICC Papers, NMML. Excerpts.

Why then did I talk about tiredness and the like? Partly that represented my reactions at the time and my mood of the moment; partly it was something deeper. This was a feeling of staleness, which, I suppose, is almost inevitable, if one has to function like a machine. I can function effectively even as a machine, but it does come in the way of freshness of thought and outlook. I do not like this staleness and I feel it comes in the way of really effective work and creative thought which are so necessary for one who has to function in a highly responsible position. It was somehow to regain that freshness and creativeness that I wanted to leave the present routine that takes up all my time.

I have no intention of running away from work or from responsibility. I have absolutely no idea of going into the wilderness or retiring to the mountains. I feel that I have a function to perform and so long as a person feels that way, the urge to work and activity is there. I have that strong urge in me. It is only the functionless who bemoan their lot and are full of complaints and ailments.

We have passed through, during these last seven years or more of independence, a difficult time and we have faced heavy tasks. We may not have come up to the mark always, but I have no feeling of disappointment at the record of these years. Indeed, I have a sense of fulfilment not for myself only but for the nation. I think that we have progressively made good and are well on our way to more rapid advance. While fully conscious of our many problems and difficulties and even of our failings, I do not understand the habitual critic who sees little good in our country today. I think that reaction is misplaced and is often due to a kind of frustration resulting from a feeling of lack of function.

Indeed, it is because I think that our country has done well and that good and stout foundations for its progress have been made, that I think of some change in the nature of my activities. I want to work hard, but at the same time I want some leisure to read and think. One of the grave disadvantages from which those of us who are heavily engaged in government and like duties suffer is the lack of time to read and think and to confer with each other on basic matters.

Because of all this, the thought came to me that it would be better for me not to function as Prime Minister at least for some time.

Yours sincerely,
Jawaharlal Nehru

59

Human Relations[1]

Tibor Mende: An ever-increasing number of states realize that they have not the means to wage atomic war and they are unwilling to expose themselves to its ravages. So these states openly, or merely in sentiment, regard themselves as non-committed to the power motives of the great powers, which may contemplate modern war. Ultimately this spreading tendency to trust peaceful negotiation, rather than war, would leave only powers A and B, perhaps C as well, to arm to threaten and to entertain ambitions of settling issues by modern war; but A, B and C finding themselves without realiable allies and realizing that the risks of war are too great, may themselves, for that very reason, begin to talk to each other and try to reduce their armaments. This then ultimately may lead to a gradual dissolution of what we call today, blocs or military groupings. Is this crudely simplified version roughly correct?

Jawaharlal Nehru: I should think so. I do not know that it is up to anyone except professional philosophers to talk about the future. I am not a professional philosopher. I have no claims that way. I am interested in the problems of the day, certainly in the context of a certain future that one aims at. I am interested in the next step I have to take, I have to meet a problem, also always thinking of the context. Very often, every practical person, every politician has to choose between two courses, both of which he dislikes and he tries to choose the course which has the lesser evil. All these things, of course, happen but as things are, it seems to me that what you have said is a possible way of looking at the future. That is, to put it slightly differently, if people are absolutely convinced that war should be avoided, they will inevitably come to the other conviction, that we must accept things even if we dislike them and put up with them, provided those things do not interfere with us. In other words, we come back to something in the nature of those Five Principles, non-interference with each other, allowing each country to develop its own life, both because that is right, but also because doing anything else gets us into trouble, for both reasons. If we could bring about a more peaceful psychological background in the world, then I think it will be relatively easy to face the problems of the world. Naturally, we can never solve all the problems of the world because when we solve one, another takes its place, the more difficult one. In fact, it is the condition of life to have problems. As I said somewhere, only the dead have no problems.

[1] Interview with Tibor Mende, 8 January 1956. JN Papers, NMML.

TM: All these hopes, Mr. Prime Minister, if I may say so, reflect a strong ray of nineteenth century liberal ideals. Those ideals were based on three basic assumptions, belief in the inevitability of human progress, faith in the perfect ability of the individual, on belief that force can progressively be eliminated from human relations. But during this last half century we have had sharp setbacks and disillusionment and loss of faith in these ideals. We had in between two World Wars, Hitler, the gas chambers for millions and harnessing of all of mankind's wonderful inventions for the most destructive ends. In politics we have seen that the forces, which refused to believe in the possibility of the elimination of force from human relations had gained in strength both on the right and on the left. The reasonable middle course has been more and more on the defensive. Moreover, technological development is leading human society towards integrated blocs in which the decision is more and more in the hands of a few organisms and individuals. In the light of this, what can replace in the mind of a politician, who is also, as you are, Sir, a liberal humanist, the rationalist hope of self-propelling progress of humanity? What is this modified Utopia of this twentieth century humanist and what can be retained from his nineteenth century heritage?

JN: Well, first of all, I was born in the nineteenth century. So, perhaps, I have some bit of the nineteenth century in me, what you call nineteenth century liberalism, and it is true that faith in the inevitability of human progress has been largely shattered, I am certainly not sure of it myself, but that I can say without adducing any reason for it, that somewhere at the back of my mind I do believe that there is something in mankind, some strength which makes us survive. And it will survive, I think, in spite of all these difficulties and if it survives, it will survive on relatively higher planes at each step. But that is just an odd reaction and there is a possibility that it might not do so. What am I to do about it, whether it does or does not do so? It becomes rather an academic argument, except that one tries to work for ends which will avoid the greater dangers, not only of war but other dangers, hatred and bitterness and conflict which I think are really more dangerous than active war because they degrade human beings, they make them feel frustrated and narrow-minded and all that. I do basically believe that as in science every cause has its effect, so also in human relations, whether national or individual, every act that we do, every thought that we think, has an effect. It may be very small and therefore if the act or thought is an evil thought, it has a bad effect, whatever our motive may be. And unfortunately, war and the fear or war and the preparation of war make one think almost in a hundred per cent evil way, full of hatred and bitterness and anger and spirit of destruction which possibly harms the thinker and the actor more even than the opposite party. So we have to lessen this and then let the world go ahead as it chooses.

TM: Thank you very much.

60

Will and Testament[1]

I have received so much love and affection from the Indian people that nothing that I can do can repay even a small fraction of it, and indeed there can be no repayment of so precious a thing as affection. Many have been admired, some have been revered, but the affection of all classes of the Indian people has come to me in such abundant measure that I have been overwhelmed by it. I can only express the hope that in the remaining years I may live, I shall not be unworthy of my people and their affection.

To my innumerable comrades and colleagues, I owe an even deeper debt of gratitude. We have been joint partners in great undertakings and have shared the triumphs and sorrows which inevitably accompany them.

I wish to declare with all earnestness that I do not want any religious ceremonies performed for me after my death. I do not believe in any such ceremonies and to submit to them, even as a matter of form, would be hypocrisy and an attempt to delude ourselves and others.

When I die, I should like my body to be cremated. If I die in a foreign country, my body should be cremated there and my ashes sent to Allahabad. A small handful of these ashes should be thrown into the Ganga and the major portion of them disposed on in the manner indicated below. No part of these ashes should be retained or preserved.

My desire to have a handful of my ashes thrown into the Ganga at Allahabad has no religious significance, so far as I am concerned. I have no religious sentiment in the matter. I have been attached to the Ganga and the Jamuna rivers in Allahabad ever since my childhood and, as I have grown older, this attachment has also grown. I have watched their varying moods as the seasons changed, and have often thought of the history and myth and tradition and song and story that have become attached to them through the long ages and become part of their flowing waters. The Ganga, especially, is the river of India, beloved of her people, round which are intertwined her racial memories, her hopes and fears, her songs of triumph, her victories and her defeats. She has been a symbol of India's age-long culture and civilization, ever-changing, ever-

[1] 21 June 1954. JN Papers, NMML.

flowing, and yet ever the same Ganga. She reminds me of the snow-covered peaks and the deep valleys of the Himalaya, which I have loved so much, and of the rich and vast plains below, where my life and work have been cast. Smiling and dancing in the morning sunlight, and dark and gloomy and full of mystery as the evening shadows fall, a narrow, slow and graceful stream in winter, and a vast roaring thing during the monsoon, broad-bosomed almost as the sea, and with something of the sea's power to destroy, the Ganga has been to me a symbol and a memory of the past of India, running into the present and flowing on to the great ocean of the future. And though I have discarded much of past tradition and custom, and am anxious that India should rid herself of all shackles that bind and constrain her and divide her people, and suppress vast numbers of them and prevent the free development of the body and the spirit; though I seek all this, yet I do not wish to cut myself off from that past completely. I am proud of that great inheritance that has been, and is, ours, and I am conscious that I too, like all of us, am a link in that unbroken chain which goes back to the dawn of history in the immemorial past of India. That chain I would not break, for I treasure it and seek inspiration from it. And as witness of this desire of mine and as my last homage to India's cultural inheritance, I am making this request that a handful of my ashes be thrown into the Ganga at Allahabad to be carried to the great ocean that washes India's shore.

The major portion of my ashes should, however, be disposed of otherwise. I want these to be carried high up into the air in an aeroplane and scattered from that height over the fields where the peasants of India toil, so that they might mingle with the dust and soil of India and become an indistinguishable part of India.